STANDARD GUIDE TO

1950s

AMERICAN CARS

STUDEBAKER TRUCK

INTERNATIONAL TRUCKS

TAXI

CITY TAXI

D1402898

John Gunnell

©2004 Krause Publications

Published by

 **krause publications**
An imprint of F+W Publications, Inc.

700 East State Street • Iola, WI 54990-0001
715-445-2214 • 888-457-2873
www.krause.com

Our toll-free number to place an order or obtain
a free catalog is (800) 258-0929.

Library of Congress Catalog Number: 2004105228
ISBN: 0-87349-868-2

Designed by Gary Carlson

Edited by Tom Collins

Printed in United States of America

Dedication

To Joe, Will, and Kellen:
May you drive the road of life smoothly and safely – having
lots of fun as you cruise along.

Introduction

When my grandsons visit, a stop at the "car building" is usually in order. When the overhead door opens, four-year-old Joe darts to the red MG TD, anxious to slide into the driver's seat and take a "ride." Two-year-olds Will and Kellen just look on, eyes twinkling, waiting for the day they can "drive" the yellow MG TF that sits nearby.

Though it's been months, Joe remembers that the red roadster's cut-down door opens backwards and that the horn he likes to honk is on the dashboard, rather than on the steering wheel. Before long, he's twisting that wheel (it doesn't go far) and pushing the black button. "Beep! Beep!" goes the horn. Watching, I wonder what kind impact these infrequent sessions will have. Fifty years in the future, will Joe, Will, and "Kell" have the same passion for classic sports cars that I have for the '50s cars that surrounded me when I was their age?

Nov. 14, 1947 was a cold day in Staten Island, New York — the day I came into this world. I have no "re-car-lections" from that year, but by the time January 1950 rolled around they were stirring. When I was two or three years old, most cars had fat fenders, long hoods, and black paint. By the time I went off to kindergarten, automotive styling and color schemes were starting to change. My Laurel Green over Milano Ivory '53 Pontiac DeLuxe Catalina is more like the cars that stood out in my neighborhood back then.

By 1950, I had my first car — a gorgeous light gray "Torpedo" pedal car with red seats and red wheels. I have memories of that toy and of the tin gas station that served as my "car building" back then. (About 10 years ago, I bought the same toy gas station at an auction for $40. My dad said I was nuts, since he'd only paid $8 for it in 1950! He didn't know it's worth a few hundred bucks today!)

I also remember a heavy toy Bell Telephone truck with a pole-carrying trailer that attached to it. And I remember going to F W Woolworth's — or was it Kresge's — with my grandmother, to buy little tin cars with windshield wipers that moved back and forth as you rolled them along. You see, I've been a car nut for a long time. And I started at the right time . . . about 1950.

Our family car for much of that decade was a 1957 Ford Custom sedan. Later, we added a '58 Chrysler Saratoga four-door hardtop — the car I learned to drive on. The first car I owned was a 1955 Chevy 210 Del Ray coupe that my grandfather gave me. I

only had it a short time, but I want another one some day.

Later, in 1972, I bought a '54 Chevy 210 off a used-car lot in Linden, New Jersey. That car helped introduce me to the old-car hobby. My first hobby event was the New Hope Automobile Show in Pennsylvania. Back then, I didn't see much of a difference between my sedan and a '53 Buick Skylark at the show, but I got hooked on the whole idea of collecting cars, literature, and '50s nostalgia.

Since that day at New Hope in 1972, I have owned the following American-built 1950s automobiles: 1953 Pontiac Chieftain Deluxe sedan, 1956 Oldsmobile Super 88 Holiday sedan, 1954 Pontiac Chieftain Special two-door sedan, 1954 Chevrolet 150 Handyman Station Wagon, 1953 Chevrolet 210 four-door sedan, 1953 Pontiac Catalina Deluxe hardtop, and 1957 Buick Century four-door sedan.

The purpose of this introduction is not to brag up the cars I've owned (or show how few I've experienced, depending on your personal ownership history); it's to show you I have great memories of the era I grew up in. I remember things like sitting on the hood of a '55 Packard outside our apartment building and I remember hitting the side of a big, black '57 Cadillac with my Roadmaster bicycle.

I also remember the Good Humor man, the mosquito-spraying machine that we used to chase after and run in the smoke, seeing "Hoppy" sign autographs at the local grocery store, going to baseball games at the Polo Grounds and Ebbetts Field, bottle openers on the side of Coke machines, U.S. Navy blimps, grade school air raid drills, collecting Green Stamps, my first record ("Venus" by Frankie Avalon) and corny black-and-white television shows.

The *Standard Guide to 1950s American Cars* is a trip back to the postwar years through the medium of the automobile. Throughout the book I have tried to connect interesting facts about the "decade of dazzle" to the cars made by all of the major manufacturers in each of the 10 years from 1950 to 1959. Along with learning about the bore-and-stroke of a Studebaker, you will learn facts about the men, movies, music, and milestones that made the '50s what it was.

John Gunnell

Standard Guide to 1950s American Cars

Table of Contents

Buicks
of the Fifties

1950 *Buick*

The 1950 Buick Special sedan shows the famous front grille that is a 1950s icon.

"Two Spirited Tons of Supreme Satisfaction," may have been the most accurate summation of a '50 Buick ever used in a factory advertisement. Bigger meant better to the average American car buyer. The Dynaflow-driven Roadmaster sedan pictured in the ad was 17 feet, 4-8/10 inches long! It was the "...first of the fine cars in value."

Buick built three series of cars for 1950. The "small" Specials in the 40 series rode on a 121-1/2-inch wheelbase and measured *only* 204 inches from "buck-tooth" grille to rear bumper guard. Known as "three holers," based on the three chrome ventiports that decorated the rear sides of the massive lift-on-either-side hood, they had a bright metal Special signature that appeared behind the front wheel opening. Chrome around the windshield and backlight identified deluxe-trim versions.

Like other Buicks, the Specials had an overhead-valve (excuse me . . . "Fireball valve-in-head") straight eight in the engine bay. This was Buick's smallest version with 115 hp . . . 122 hp when you added the optional Dynaflow automatic transmission. A shiny Dynaflow script appeared on the sides of the rear fender in cars so equipped.

When you moved up the ladder to the Series 50 Super, you still got three ventiports on the hood sides, but a new F-263 engine was under it. The F-263 designation indicated "Fireball 263 cid." This engine provided 124 or 128 hp, depending on whether you ordered the standard three-speed manual gearbox or Dynaflow Drive. Supers had a 121-1/2-inch wheelbase and 205-inch overall length, unless you ordered the "Super-sized" Super four-door sedan, which had both measurements stretched an extra four inches.

Things were similar in the Series 70 Roadmaster line, where most body styles had a 126-1/4-inch stance with 208.8 inches of overall length. The 72R four-door was four inches longer in wheelbase and length. One ad called it the Roadmaster 130 and

explained the 130-1/2-inch wheelbase car's extra length was "...devoted to enlarging the rear-compartment area."

Some extra room was also needed to fit a fourth ventiport on the Roadmaster's hood and to stuff an even more powerful 152-hp in-line eight below it. That was the only power choice, as Dynaflow was standard equipment. Some of Buick's 1950 top-of-the-line models carried the Roadmaster name behind the front wheel opening. On Deluxe versions, the series name was embossed on a chrome strip that trimmed the window sills.

Buick boasted its 1950 bodies had "Taper-Through" styling and "Jet-Line" design. "A thing graceful of line, bold-fronted in husky chromed steel and marked along its tapering fenders with a rich and burnished sweep on metal," read an ad for the Roadmaster convertible.

Modern-looking one-piece windshields were seen on Supers and Roadmasters. The 1950 grille was what they call a "distinctive" design in the auto industry. "...it breaks the rules, but we're promoting it the best we can." The nine large "toothy" looking uprights were lined up like fence posts across the bumper and grille opening.

The bumper itself was big and the non-locking bumper guards looked like a pair of police-car sirens. They had the front parking lights built into them. One ad described this as a "Four-Way Forefront" and claimed the rugged front end set a style note, saved on repair costs (because the vertical bars were individually replaceable), avoided "locking horns," and made parking and garaging easier. Other Buick body features included push-button door locks, a self-locking trunk latch, back-up lights as standard equipment, and "double-bubble" taillights.

Buick said swayless, swerve-free, "ever-level" stability was provided by its sturdy ladder-frame chassis. The interiors of all models were said to offer increased roominess, despite a reduction in overall vehicle length. Ample headroom inside was a selling feature. Interior features included luxury upholstery, a new heating and ventilation system, faster window defrosting, recessed foot rests, and a "smart" instrument panel.

Buick's three "High-Pressure" Fireball straight eight engines for 1950 had some common attributes like stepped-up compression ratios and added horsepower. These, noted Buick, translated into better performance, increased acceleration, and improved gasoline mileage.

"Tap that treadle and hear the deep bass thrum of Fireball power that's eager for hill and highway," one Buick ad teased. Specials with Dynaflow and all other Buicks had hydraulic valve lifters.

Ride-softening coil springs were used at all four corners of the Buick body. A torque-tube drive system transmitted engine power to the rear end.

Safety-Ride wheel rims carried the low-pressure tires, which were size 7.60 x 15 on Specials and Supers and 8.00 x 15 on Roadmasters. All models had four-wheel hydraulic brakes.

Buick offered 21 models in 1950, of which seven were Specials, six were Supers, and eight were Roadmasters. While the family-oriented Special line was comprised of coupes, sedans and somewhat sexy "jet-back" sedanettes, both upper series offered the body styles collectors seem to favor most: a "Riviera" hardtop, a convertible and a "woodie" station wagon.

"A man has a right to excitement," was the catch phrase on an advertisement for the stunning model 76R Roadmaster Riviera hardtop. Priced at $2,764, this sleek pillarless coupe was often referred to as a "hardtop convertible"—the look of an open car, without the inconveniences of a fabric roof. It was actually the second most popular Roadmaster model, next to the four-door sedan. Another ad suggested the Roadmaster convertible was the car to buy if you wanted to "Give yourself a springtime lift."

"There'll come a time when you'll awake to find spring is here once more. The world is young again – and so are you – and you feel like flinging back the steel canopy of the family sedan and traveling free and open, one with the birds and fleeting clouds."

"Traveler's Aid," was the slogan used to pitch the Roadmaster Estate Wagon, which had wood trim on the doors, windows, and tailgate. "Outwardly fashioned to lend style on any occasion."

As Buick's most expensive car, the $3,407 Estate went to a mere 420 buyers, though 2,480 others opted for the smaller-but-just-as-handy $2,844 Super version. Both woodies were crafted by the Ionia Body Corporation, of Ionia, Michigan.

According to *Ward's Automotive Yearbook 1952*, Buick's 1950 model-year production started on June 30, 1949 for the Special series, with the Super and Roadmaster lines starting in December. The official production total was 588,439 cars, which includes 256,514 Specials, 253,352 Supers, and 78,573 Roadmasters.

1951 *Buick*

In 1951, the Buick Special sedan was powered by the famed "Fireball eight" engine.

A colorful ad promoted the 1951 Buick Special as "Room With Zoom." Buick's volume-production three-port-hole car-line got the bulk of attention this year. It even offered hardtop and convertible body styles. Sweep spear-style side trim gave the Special Deluxe models a more upscale look and the overall length of all Specials grew from 204 to 206.2 inches. Under their hoods was the bigger 263-cid Fireball straight eight with 120 hp.

"Sized for a Big Surprise" was just one of dozens of slogans used to highlight the Special's roomier new body. Even the two-door sedan — usually thought of as a car in the early '50s as a model that was fairly roomy in front, but cramped in the rear — had soft-cushioned rear seats with over 63 inches of hip room.

Said Buick, "All we know is that people come in, look it over, slip into its seats, take it out on the road, and say, 'Where do we sign?'"

The three-port-hole Super was now the same wheelbase as the Special and also had the F-263 engine, but with the same 124-hp rating advertised in 1950. All 1951 Supers — even stick-shift versions — had hydraulic valve lifters and a little more torque than the previous season.

Four-port-hole Roadmasters were on the same wheelbase, but had a few less inches of overall length due to bumper changes. The 320-cid 152-hp Fireball straight eight was again under the hood. Speaking of Buick's hood, it no longer had port holes. These decorations were moved to the upper, trailing portion of the front fenders. They were also round, instead of rectangular.

Buick cut its model count to 17, from 21. There were again three series, but the Special Sport Coupe and four-door sedan came in a new standard-trim sub-series that did not include sweep spear-style side moldings. This Sport Coupe was not a pillarless hardtop. Deluxe trim was used on Special two- and four-door sedans, two-door hardtops, and convertibles. Cars with Dynaflow Drive had an appropriate chrome script on the rear fender. The Special name appeared on the rear deck lid. Prices started at $2,046 for the Sport Coupe.

A fastback "sedanette" was offered only in two-door format in the Super series only. A pair of four-door sedans, a pillarless hardtop coupe, a convertible coupe, and an Estate were the other Super body styles.

Supers were priced from $2,248 for the Sedanette to $3,103 for the six-passenger station wagon, which still used real wood in its body. Supers were rarely seen in Buick advertisements this year. The Special was given the heaviest backing and the luxury Roadmaster was occasionally promoted. It was the Super that saw a popularity increase, accounting for 16.5 percent of total Buick output, compared to 13.7 percent the previous year.

Five models comprised the Roadmaster line up: Riviera hardtop, Deluxe Riviera hardtop, convertible coupe, Estate Wagon, and four-door sedan. One 1951 Buick advertisement said of these luxurious cars:

"The lordly levelness of its roadweight — riding on coil springs at all four wheels — and its touch of magnificence. The constant smoothness of Dynaflow Drive — the true ease of handling — the richness of custom interiors — all set a standard that's envied in the fine-car field. And there's the exultant power of this brilliant performer's mighty Fireball engine — matched by brakes new tailored for Roadmasters only — to give you the confident mastery of every mile you travel."

The $3,977 Roadmaster Estate Wagon was the most expensive Buick of the year. The Deluxe hardtop coupe (809 built) and the wagon (679 built) were the rarest.

A new "Push-Bar" front end greeted customers in Buick showrooms this year. The 25 smaller, stamped-steel grille bars did not cover the bumper and were designed to "give" with the massive wraparound bumper. Blade-style bumper guards added to the front-end protection. The red Buick emblem above the center of the grille, with its blue diagonal stripe, is a trademark every kid of the '50s remembers along with port holes and bombsight hood ornaments. Buick's look was now promoted as "Dreamline Styling" and featured tapered, car-length fenders that blended into the main body feature line.

On the inside was a new, aircraft-inspired "control panel" with "White-Glow" dials that brought night reading clarity without glare. A two-level heating system with a high-speed blower provided an abundance of heated air allowed drivers to "contol the weather" inside their cars. To maintain desired temperature settings, an automatic thermostat was used. Dynaflow Drive was once again standard in Roadmasters and optional in other models.

On Aug. 8, 1951, Buick built its one-millionth torque converter Dynaflow automatic transmission. This prompted Buick to run an advertisement headlined "Hand of the Free."

"More than a million people are now enjoying a freedom that was unknown four years ago. You can describe this freedom in several ways. It is freedom from the physical strain of pushing a clutch pedal hundreds of times a day. It is freedom from any thought of such things as low, second and high gears, and freedom from all the lag and limp of gear shifting. It is freedom from tension on a long day's drive – the tension of holding your throttle foot steadily in position. It's the freedom of Dynaflow Drive – which is now used in more than a million Buicks."

All Buicks continued to ride on rugged, X-braced chassis with a relatively low center of gravity. The company's salesman's guide, which outlined features and benefits of the 1951 models, stated: "The major source of Buick's swayless, swerve-free ever-level stability comes from its solid and sure-footed chassis, giving the car road poise and a solid 'seat' on the highway."

While the 1951 models did not mark another advance in automotive styling, two show cars Buick released that year made it clear the company was peering ahead. The LeSabre and the XP-300 replaced the sensational 1939 Y-Job as Buick's "cars-of-the-future." The supercharged LeSabre two-seater had a tail-finned body made of aluminum and magnesium and later gave its name to a production model. The XP-300 had a more conventional-looking frontal treatment.

Buick's 1951 model production started on Jan. 2, 1951 and the total number of cars built fell to 404,657, including 165,554 Specials, 172,235 Supers and 66,868 Roadmasters. The decline was partly due to the beginning of a so-called "Police Action" in Korea and production controls relating to it. They reflected the first return to full-scale production following World War II.

In 1946-1948, there had been a tremendous pent-up demand for cars, but factories couldn't build enough, due to parts shortages and labor unrest. When Detroit was able to build all the cars people wanted in 1950, buyers took up the slack. In 1951, things settled down to a more normal pace – even at Buick. But it was still the second best sales year in company history.

1952 *Buick*

The 1952 Buick Special Deluxe two-door hardtop was called the Riviera by Buick.

Buick started building its 1952 models on Jan. 2, 1952 and introduced them on Jan. 19, 1952. While demand for cars was strong, automakers like Buick were handicapped by government controls on raw materials, due to the fighting in Korea.

Through a system of quarterly percentage quotas for each corporation, the National Production Authority limited the industry to building 4,342,000 cars for the year. General Motors' quota called for it to make around 41 percent of all U.S. cars. GM exceeded its quota in each of the first three quarters and was forced to cut back in the final quarter. Quotas combined with a mid-year steel workers strike made a couple of 1952 Buick models rare vehicles.

The 1952 Buicks had 17 vertical grille bars, instead of the 25 used the previous year. Buick had long claimed that when better cars were built, Buick would build them and, in 1952, the company boasted "We did it again!"

The big push this year seemed to be on the Roadmaster, which had the mightiest engine in Buick history, the biggest brakes of any postwar Buick, the quietest ride of any Buick ever built, and – said one ad – "the greatest trunk space since spare tires moved off the front fenders." The Flint, Michigan automaker was careful to add:

"You'll find a host of notable features in Supers and Specials too – plenty to make them, as always, the standout buys in their fields – for ride, for comfort, for style, for room, and for power."

Perhaps because of its strong showing in 1951, the new Super was continued with the same wheelbase as 1951. The size of the Specials and Roadmasters also remained unchanged. The Special and Super again used the F-263 straight eight. Horsepower ratings were 120 for Specials with manual transmission, 124 for Supers with manual transmission and 128 for both with Dynaflow. The only Roadmaster engine was again the 320-cid Fireball Eight, but

now with a four-barrel "Automatic Airpower" carburetor and 170 hp at 3800 rpm, a gain of 18 horsepower.

An ad explained the principle behind the new four-barrel carburetor:

"Take one gallon of good gasoline – 8,350 gallons of ordinary air – mix well and feed in small doses to a Fireball engine – and what do you get? Well, mister… it's something like the mighty thrust of an airliner – swooshing down the runway for a take-off."

Buick said two barrels were designed to supply the right mixture for speeds from idle to 50 mph and the other two barrels gave the Roadmaster a "second wind."

The Buick Special came in the same body styles as in 1951 and two models had extremely low production. Only 317 standard four-door sedans were made and only 600 convertibles. Styling changes to Specials were modest, the most memorable being the small chrome tail fins tacked on top of the rear fenders of Deluxe-trim versions. The sweep spear moldings, also seen only on the Deluxe models, were restyled to serve as rear gravel guards as well. The fenders again carried three portholes. The rear fenders carried a "Special" script. Prices ranged from $2,115 for the standard Sport Coupe to $2,634 for the ragtop.

Super model offerings were again reduced, with only the two-door hardtop, convertible, wagon, and sedan remaining in the line up. A chrome "Super" script decorated the rear fenders. Lowest in popularity was the Super woodie wagon—of which 1,641 were made. It was followed by the convertible with its 6,904-unit production run. Super prices were in the $2,478-$3,296 bracket.

For the second year in a row, Buick's most popular car was the Model 52 Super Riviera sedan. It saw production of 71,387 units – enough to make the Super series the best-selling line again. Helping to clinch many of those sales was the new, $199-extra, power steering system, which was also available on Roadmasters.

One Buick advertisement promoted the "healthiness" of the Saginaw gear-type power steering, suggesting at least one doctor viewed it as a way to relieve heart strain. "It does your heart good…"

Another advertisement pictured a woman parking a huge Riviera four-door sedan in a tight space between two other Buicks.

"Buick's Power Steering supplies a helping hand at times like this – takes over four-fifths of the effort needed with conventional steering." Buick also claimed the Roadmaster had the shortest turning radius of any car of its length.

Roadmasters came in the same body styles as Supers at prices between $3,200 and $3,977. Four portholes and rear-fender model scripts identified the big Buicks. Only 359 Ionia-bodied Estate Wagons were made, while 2,402 convertibles left the factory. Buick ads spoke of the Roadmaster's "Million Dollar Ride," the "mighty power" of its F-320 engine.

Roadmaster interiors featured deep, soft seats with rich and luxurious upholstery materials. "Sombrero"-style full-wheel discs, which were very popular with car shoppers, were standard equipment on the top-of-the-line Buicks.

Larger luggage space was offered in the 1952 Buick. "There's room for roaming in the super-spacious trunk compartments" said the company's salesman's guide. There were claims you could load an entire family's suitcases in the "trip-sized trunk" and Buick was quick to point out the counter-balanced trunk lid "…practically raises itself."

Buick had always ranked close to the top of the chart, among all cars, in owner loyalty. In a 1952 new-car survey, 75.5 percent of Buick owners reported they would buy a Buick again. Model-year production totals included 120,898 Buick Specials, 136,404 Supers, and 46,443 Roadmasters.

On a calendar-year basis, 274,259 Buicks – 85 percent of all Buicks made – had Dynaflow Drive, a five percent increase for the year. Buick led the industry in the production of hardtop coupes and built 93,492 Riviera hardtops in 1953, an increase of 3,000 units.

1953 *Buick*

This 1953 Buick Super Riviera hardtop has an interesting two-tone color combination.

Buick was born of the times that spawned the motorcar in America and 1953 was the company's golden anniversary. David Dunbar Buick, of porcelain-surfaced bathtub fortune, founded his automobile company in 1903. By 1907, the company was America's number 1 automaker with a production of 30,000 cars. By 1908, the company became the cornerstone on which General Motors was established. Starting in 1931, Buick concentrated on building eight-cylinder autos. The big news in the company's 50th year was a new V-8 for Super and Roadmaster models.

That original 322-cid V-8 became the predecessor of "big" Buick V-8s for years to come. Design characteristics of this "nail-head" engine included pent-roof pistons and "Fireball" combustion chambers with the spark plugs at the top of the chamber and the valves at one side. Each exhaust valve had its own individual port and branch, creating a free-flowing exhaust system. Buick called this design "vertical valves."

Three versions of the 322 were offered. Installed in Supers with stick-shift was a version with an 8.0:1 compression ration, 164 hp at 4000 rpm and a Stromberg AAVB-26 two-barrel carburetor. A second variation with an 8.5:1 compression ratio (the highest in America according to one Buick ad) and 170 hp at 4000 rpm was used in Dynaflow-equipped Supers. The Roadmaster version was good for 188 hp at 4000 rpm as it had a Carter WCFB-996S four-barrel carburetor. The engine made the car 180 pounds lighter than straight-eight Buicks. Copywriters called it, "The most advanced V-8 engine ever placed in a standard-production American automobile."

With the Roadmaster 322, Buick buyers also got new Twin-Turbine Dynaflow Drive, which was optional at extra cost in other series. The engineers said the use of two turbines in the transmission enhanced its efficiency, increased the torque-multiplication factor and reduced the Dynaflow's distinctive noise.

"You can zoom from a standing start to a legal 25 mph before you can say and spell 'Jack Robinson,'" said one ad. "You travel in this swift silence with no break in your stride — in one perfect progression of infinite smoothness."

Buick installed Dynaflow Drive in more than 80 percent of its 1953 models and supplied 41,000 transmissions to Oldsmobile and Cadillac, after the Hydra-Matic transmission plant had a fire.

Three series of Buicks were offered again in 1953. The Special Series 40 soldiered on with the same 121-1/2-inch wheelbase and a 125-hp version of the in-line eight. Specials could be identified by a crease near the bottom of the rear fender, three portholes on the fenders and the lack of chrome trim around the side windows. There was no extension of their chrome sweep spear moldings onto the rear fenders.

Most Supers used the 121-1/2-inch wheelbase, but the Model 52 Riviera sedan still used a four-inch-longer wheelbase. Supers had a crease along the center of the rear fenders, a new chrome strip molding on the rear fenders, three front fender portholes, and chrome moldings around all windows. The Roadmasters shrunk down to Super size, which made them very "hot" with their more powerful four-barrel carbed V-8. They had a fourth porthole and a large extension of the sweep spear moldings onto the rear fenders.

Up front, the 1953 grille featured 25 vertical bars in a very handsome-looking arrangement below a "handlebar-mustache"-shaped grille bar carrying the B-U-I-C-K name.

Twin "spinner" bars decorated the front bumper. An oval in the center of the nose continued to carry the Buick shield emblem and atop the hood sat the traditional "bombsight" hood ornament. On the trunk was a jewel-like badge that read "Buick Eight," with a "V" in the middle of Supers and Roadmasters.

To celebrate its birthday, Buick issued an very exciting, factory-customized car called the Skylark Anniversary Convertible. Advertisements promoted it as "a six-passenger sports car" and a "stunning new luxury sports car."

Built on the Roadmaster chassis, it had its own fenders with open wheel housings painted red, white or black. A lowered convertible top and 40-spoke Kelsey-Hayes wire wheels made the car look exclusive. Practically every option was lavished on the Skylark as standard equipment, including the V-8 engine, Twin-Turbine Dynaflow Drive, power steering, power brakes, power windows, top and front-seat adjustment.

Wisconsin-born designer Ned Nickles had fallen in love with the MG TC, the MG TD and Siata sports cars but realized such cars weren't comfortable. He was convinced he could do better. He originally sketched his Skylark concept on May 3, 1951 and bought that year's Roadmaster convertible to customize.

The story goes Buick general manger, Ivan Wiles, saw the drawing by accident and decided to build a pilot model based on a 1952 Roadmaster. This car was shown to the automotive press in late 1952 and was road tested by former race car driver Wilbur Shaw for *Popular Science*. That year, Buick announced it intended to build and sell Skylarks on a one-to-a-dealer basis. A total of 1,690 of the $5,000 Skylarks were built.

Many 1953 Skylarks went looking for buyers. It was hard to sell a $5,000 model, when the next most expensive Buick cost $1,000 less — a real lot of money 50 years ago. Buick dealers used the cars to increase showroom traffic and in parades. Sometimes they just kept them.

Buick streamlined its series a bit more in 1953, with two- and four-door sedans, a hardtop and a convertible making up the Special line. They carried prices from $2,197 to $2,553 and the ragtop was the rarest model with 4,282 made. Three of the same body styles made up the four-model Super series, but an Ionia-bodied woodie wagon, at $3,430, was the most expensive Super and the rarest. Only 1,830 were made.

The Roadmaster series was comprised of the same body styles as the Super series, with the Skylark added as a fifth model. The wood-bodied station wagon, with a production run of 670 units, was even rarer than the Skylark.

In 1953, Buick Motor Division seemed to be "big" on the use of television advertising to promote its stunning new cars. In addition to sponsoring comedian Milton Berle's "Buick-Berle Show" on Tuesday evenings, there was the "Buick Circus Hour" every fourth Tuesday and the DuMont Network's "TV Football Game of the Week" on Saturday evenings. Buick's production leaped to 488,755 cars including 217,624 Specials, 191,894 Supers, and 79,237 Roadmasters.

1954 *Buick*

The highlights of 1954 at Buick Motor Division were all-new bodies and a new "factory hot rod" — called the Century. It featured the biggest Buick V-8 stuffed into the lightest Buick body. All models used V-8 engines. The Special and the Century shared a 122-inch stance and an overall length of 206.3 inches. Supers and Roadmasters rode on a 127-inch wheelbase and measured the same 216.8 inches end-to-end. The sporty Skylark was moved from the Roadmaster line into its own series. It was now based on the Century body and showcased a wild redesign.

The year's new "electric shaver" grille had more vertical blades, which were protected by redesigned bumpers and grille guards. A curved panoramic windshield wrapped fully around to each vent window.

"You can sweep your glance around a full 360-degree arc and find you see more and see it more easily, because all glass areas are greater," one advertisement claimed. "Every rear window is 3 to 4-1/2 inches wider…"

Super and Roadmaster four-door models had new built-in chrome windshield visors and rain covers over the side windows.

Thinner new body side moldings, still with a "sweep spear" design, decorated the sides of all models. At the rear were new twin-bullet taillight clusters. Inside, all Buicks featured a gimmicky Redliner horizontal speedometer on which the length of the red line increased in proportion to vehicle speed. Swing-out front doors, an X-braced frame, torque tube drive, coil spring cushioning, Safety-Ride wheel rims, an automatic choke, a Step-On parking brake, directional signals, a new front suspension, and a new parallel steering linkage were other '54 Buick selling features.

Specials and Centurys had a somewhat stubbier appearance than the big Buicks. The model names appeared in chrome on the sides of the rear fenders, with the first letter of the model name – "S" or "C" – within a chrome-outlined red circle. Both of these models had three portholes. A 264-cid V-8 was used in Specials.

Just 836 of the beautiful Buick Skylark convertibles were produced in 1954.

The stick-shift version had a 7.2:1 compression ratio and 143 hp at 4200 rpm. The Dynaflow version had an 8.0:1 compression ratio and 150 hp.

The Century–which carried a new 60 Series designation–used four-barrel versions of the 322-cid V-8. Cars with a stick shift had 8.0:1 compression ratio and 195 hp at 4100 rpm, while cars with Dynaflow had an 8.5:1 compression ratio and 200 hp at 4100 rpm.

Buick expanded the Special series to five body styles, two- and four-door sedans, two-door hardtop, convertible and new all-metal Estate Wagon. These were priced from $2,207 to $3,163. Collectible models included the $2,563 convertible with a run of 6,135 units and the station wagon, the most expensive and rarest body style, with 1,650 assemblies. The Century series did not have a two-door sedan and the four other body styles were priced between $2,520 and $3,470. The latter price applied to the metal Estate Wagon, of which only 1,563 were built. The $2,963 convertible saw 2,790 assemblies.

"Whenever the conversation gets around to horsepower, there's one name that men are sure to mention with respect, " said an ad. "That name is CENTURY – and the car which bears it is Buick's bid for supremacy in the performance field."

The copywriters pointed out the new model's "...fleet-lined look of a sports car," its 122-inch wheelbase, and its weight of "...3866 nimble pounds." Then came the punch line that promised buyers "...more power per dollar than you can get anywhere else in the American market."

Another Buick advertisement called the Century "...a brand-new thriller" and said it was "...deliberately built to deliver more horsepower per pound of weight and more horsepower per dollar than any other American automobile in its price class."

The 1954 Super, though sized to Roadmaster proportions, didn't get as many portholes (it had just three) or as much horsepower. Stick-shift versions used the 8.0:1 compression 322 with a two-barrel carburetor and advertised 177 hp at 4100 rpm. The Dynaflow version got an 8.5:1 compression ratio and developed 182 hp at 4100 rpm. Both versions had the same

Stromberg two-barrel carburetor. A four-door sedan, a two-door hardtop and a convertible (3,343 built) carried the Super name on their rear fenders. Price tags ranged from $2,626 to $2,964.

Four portholes on the front fenders made the Roadmaster stand by itself in the Buick pecking order. "Roadmaster *Custom Built* by Buick," was the slogan used in many ads to highlight the top-of-the-line model's "grace of greatness."

The only engine offered in this series was the 200-hp version and Twin-Turbine Dynaflow Drive was standard equipment as well. So was power steering, although power brakes, air conditioning, a four-way power-positioned front seat, and a power-operated radio aerial were extra-cost options.

In addition to the four-door sedan and the two-door hardtop, Buick made 3,305 copies of the Roadmaster convertible, which had a $3,521 price tag.

The one-of-a-kind 1954 Skylark convertible had a lot of the Buick Wildcat dream car in its dramatic new appearance. Starting with the Special-sized Century body, Buick modified the rear deck lid and fenders to slope towards the bumper, then bolted on a pair of show car-like chrome tail fins. Chassis modifications made the car ride lower than other Buicks.

"The car is less than five feet high, even when the top is up," said an AC Spark Plugs advertisement showing the Skylark.

The Skylark's front and rear wheel housings were enlarged and also tapered towards the rear. No portholes appeared on the front fenders of the sporty model. The 200-hp "nailhead" V-8 was under the hood.

Buick was able to bring the price of the sports convertible down to $4,355. The weight reduction over the Roadmaster-based 1953 version was in the range of 40 pounds. With more power, a nimbler size and less weight, the Skylark was a faster, better-handling car. In the end, only 836 of these cars were built.

During the 1954 model year, Buick became the first automaker to build a half million hardtop models. In fact, the 600,000th Buick hardtop was assembled on September 3. Model-year production totaled 444,609 and included 191,484 Specials, 81,983 Centurys, 119,375 Supers and 51,767 Roadmasters.

1955 *Buick*

The Buick Special convertible presents the handsome new styling for 1955.

Getting away from the "electric shaver" front end, Buick switched to a "wide screen," mesh-style radiator grille insert for model-year 1955. At the rear, the cars had the first hint of pointed tail fins (except for those bolted onto the '54 Skylark) and new jet-plane-inspired swept-back taillights. Other sales features included a 12-volt electrical system, dynamic-flow mufflers, a self-locking step-on parking brake, all-coil-spring ride, and the inclusion of directional signals on all Buicks as standard equipment.

A huge symbolic change was the use of four portholes on Centurys and Supers, as well as Roadmasters. This meant Buick was using four portholes to identify cars with the larger engine, rather than the longer wheelbase. Only the Special was left carrying three front fender decorations. Other new styling changes included chrome headlight brows and a new hood ornament (gold-finished on Roadmasters).

The Skylark sports convertible was gone, but Buick continued its hardtop manufacturing leadership (it called them *Rivieras*) by unveiling a four-door version for the Special/Century chassis on Dec. 20, 1954. It went into actual production in March of 1955. The Super and Roadmaster series would have to wait until 1956.

One advertisement showed a slick-looking Century four-door Riviera with a black body and red top. This "Hardtop with 4 doors" was credited with being a big reason for Buick's soaring 1955 sales.

"The new hit in hardtops that's taking the country by storm," said the copy. "The 'Convertible' look — but with separate doors for rear-seat passengers. Now in volume production to insure prompt deliveries."

Other literature pointed out that all four doors were front-hinged for greater safety and to make getting in and out of Riviera sedans easier.

A number of important driveline changes were among the 1955 Buicks' outstanding selling features including the use of full-skirted slotted pistons, newly-designed "hotter" camshafts, ported intake manifolds, and larger four-barrel carburetors with all models. The 322-cid V-8 engine used in Roadmaster, Super, and Century models equipped with Dynaflow now had a 9.0:1 compression ratio and 236 hp.

The 264-cid Special V-8 used with Dynaflow had an 8.4:1 compression ratio and developed 188 hp. Every 1955 Dynaflow transmission contained 20 variable-pitch stator blades that opened wide, when the accelerator was pushed to the floor, for quicker acceleration. The stator blades then returned to their normal, 1954-style position for cruising. They were said to aid fuel economy, too.

Road testers found the new Dynaflow transmission eliminated much of the sluggishness felt in earlier versions. The Century had a top speed of an honest 110 mph.

Specials continued to ride the 122-inch wheelbase and overall length was 206.6 inches. Other than the new four-door hardtop, the series included the same models as the previous year with prices that increased only in the $30 range. A chrome Special script was placed on the rear sides of the body just above where the sweep spear molding dipped down.

The Riviera pillarless sedan drew a strong 66,409 orders, convertible production climbed to 10,009 units, and even the rarest Special—the Estate Wagon—had an almost-doubled 2,952-unit production run.

Century models had scripts on the rear body sides, an added porthole on the front fenders, and, on four-doors sedans, the rear vent was part of the rear door.

In addition to gaining a four-door hardtop, the Century series was the basis for a unique new two-door sedan built exclusively for the California Highway Patrol. These cars used the Special body, but from the firewall forward they were Centurys with the 322-cid 236-hp V-8. Only 268 of these cars were built, half of them with three-speed manual transmission, which wasn't usually available with the 236-hp engine.

The Century Estate Wagon (4,243 built) and the Century convertible (5,588 built) were high-volume cars.

Supers shared Buick's longer 127-inch wheelbase with Roadmasters and stretched 215.9 inches from bumper-to-bumper. The same three models offered last year were carried over with prices about $200 higher on average. For identification, Supers had the model name script on the rear body sides. Four-door sedans had a built-in sun visor over the windshield and rear vent windows.

The series included Buick's rarest 1955 ragtop--only 3,527 Super convertibles were built. This was despite the fact an attractive advertisement depicted this model. The car illustrated in the ad had one of those flashy color schemes Buick was famous for in the '50s—yellow with a red interior, red tonneau cover, red wheels, and red wheel cover centers.

For some reason, 1955 Roadmaster prices increased less than those of Supers, with the hike being as little as $31 for the convertible. As usual, the ragtop was the rarest model and only 4,730 were made. The fanciest Buicks carried the Roadmaster name in gold script on the rear deck lid and grille and a Buick crest below the front vent window. Roadmaster sedans had the same windshield visor and rear vent windows as Supers.

Like most other American automakers, Buick Motor Division had a banner year in 1955. On a calendar-year basis, the Flint, Michigan manufacturer actually ascended to the third rank in industry production with 781,296 units for a 9.84 percent share of market.

Buick became the third automaker to build 700,000 cars in a model year and 750,000 in a calendar year, but that wasn't all. On March 16, Buick assembled its one-millionth V-8. Twenty days later, the eight-millionth Buick of all time was made. And on Aug. 3, 1955, the company rolled out its one-millionth hardtop. As we said, 1955 was a record breaker!

Dan Lyons

The 1956 Buick Special Riviera two-door hardtop looked great at the drive in.

1956 Buick

A new V-pattern grille, new bumpers, redesigned headlights, new ornamentation, and sporty full rear-wheel cutouts characterized the 1956 Buicks. The taillight cluster was again of the swept-back design, but with only a small circular red reflector in the veed center section. For the first time since prior to World War II, all Buicks had the same instrument panel. Under the hoods of the cars, the 322-cid V-8 was used in all models, although the Special had a slightly less powerful version.

The engine had a new combustion chamber design, higher compression ratios and more horsepower. Additional improvements were made to the Variable-Pitch Dynaflow transmission to improve fuel economy by two-tenths of a gallon per mile. Dynaflow was standard on Centurys, Supers and Roadmasters. All series now had four-door Riviera models. Prices rose an average of 2.5 percent, although Estate Wagon prices dropped.

As in 1955, four portholes appeared on Centurys, Supers, and Roadmasters, with three on Specials. The Super and Roadmaster were 213.6 inches long on a 127-inch wheelbase; the Special and Century were 205.1 inches long on a 122-inch wheelbase. The Special series offered the same body styles as 1955, with the four-door hardtop and lower-priced wagon gaining in popularity and all other models dropping in popularity from 1955 production.

The police-only Century two-door sedan did not return this season. The Super series gained a four-door hardtop which was, in fact, the most popular body style. The same thing happened in the Roadmaster lineup.

While advertised as "Best Buick Yet," the '56s were not the best selling, although the division managed to hold onto third place on the industry sales charts for one more year. The drop in sales had nothing to do with changing television sponsorships from the Buick-Berle show on alternate Tuesdays to the Jackie Gleason show every Saturday night. It related more to market saturation and a weakening of the economy as the year progressed.

Technically, Buick did a lot under the hood in 1956, boosting the two-barrel engine used in the Special to an 8.9:1 compression ratio and 220 hp, while the four-barrel version used in all other series had a 9.5:1 compression ratio and 255 hp. A built-in carburetor de-icer, Hi-Poised engine mountings, an extra-quiet ball-joint suspension system, and an automatic choke and idle control were advances Buick promoted.

Variable-Pitch Dynaflow drive was enhanced to provide quicker getaways while in "economy" pitch, faster action in "performance" pitch, better gas mileage in city driving and quieter operation at all speeds.

As usual, every Buick feature had a '50s-style name that sounds kind of corny today. There was the *Precision-Balanced* chassis, the *Power Peak V-8*, the *Deep-Oil-Cushioned Luxury Ride*, the *Sweep-Ahead* styling, the *Fashion Color Harmony* exterior and interior finishes, the *Smoother-Action* brakes, the *Stepped-Up Gas Mileage* driving economy, and the *Safety Power Steering* system.

On Specials, the model name appeared in its familiar place on the side of the car. It was on the rear door on four-door models on the rear fender on two-door models. Specials had all-chrome headlight bezels and on the four-door sedan, the rear ventipane was part of the rear door.

Standard equipment included directional signals, front and rear armrests, sliding sunshades, a cigarette lighter, a glove compartment light, a map light, dual horns, a step-on parking brake, a Redliner speedometer (new in the Special) and a trip mileage indicator. Prices ranged from $2,416 for the four-door sedan to $2,775 for the Estate Wagon.

Century models had Century scripts on the rear body sides and an added porthole on the front fenders. A stainless steel molding was placed above the side windows. Chrome headlight bezels were seen. In addition to the standard equipment used on the Specials, Centurys had foam seat cushions, a trunk light, an electric clock, and a rear license plate frame. With the convertible, you also received a power-operated top, power window lifts, and a horizon-

tal seat adjuster. The Century series no longer offered the CHP police special or a four-door sedan, but there was a new Deluxe four-door hardtop (Riviera sedan) designated Model 63D. Prices began at $2,963 for the two-door hardtop and went up to $3,306 for the convertible coupe. The ragtop was the rarest model, with only 4,721 built.

With the addition of a four-door hardtop, there were four Super body styles. Prices for the two-door hardtop started at $3,204; for the four-door sedan $3,250; for the four-door hardtop $3,340, and for the convertible $3,544. Only 2,489 of the ragtops left the assembly line. In addition to Super scripts on the rear body sides, these cars had all-chrome headlight bezels and narrow chrome trim along the rear edge of the fenders. Four-door sedans had a built-in sun cap over the windshield and a vent window behind the rear doors.

Roadmaster models were trimmed differently than the "lesser" Buicks. They had body-color headlight bezels with thin chrome trim around the lenses. Chrome "bombsight" ornaments decorated the front fenders above the headlights. The sides of the body had a clean look, but a chrome script spelling the Roadmaster name was placed below the front ventipanes. The rear deck lid carried the Roadmaster name in silver block letters. Suspender-like bands of chrome could be seen on the rear deck lid.

Prices for the four-door sedan started at $3,503; for the two-door hardtop $3,591; for the four-door hardtop $3,692, and for the convertible $3,704.

Buick's model-year production started on Oct. 19, 1955 and ended on Dec. 19, 1956. The new cars were officially introduced at showroom level on November 4. The Buick division managed to come in third one more time. Things would change in this regard in 1957, but 1956 was counted as another successful season. On November 7, the nine-millionth Buick was assembled.

1957 *Buick*

The 1957 Buick Century Caballero was a sporty four-door hardtop station wagon.

"**Y**ou're in for a barrel of thrills when you stand up close to the car pictured here," said the ad copy below the dramatic low-level photo of a 1957 Buick Century Riviera Coupe. "You'll find it's lower than you ever thought a full-size car could be — four feet, 10 inches from road to roof — the lowest

Buick yet. Inside, there's an even bigger surprise: You'll discover that while the 1957 Buick is up to 3.4 inches lower, the interior is roomy as ever."

As a '57 Century owner, the author of this book has to agree. The '57 Buick is a large car that looks ground-huggingly trim and sporty. I've spent hours viewing the handsome styling lines. The Century seems almost sports-car-like — until you slide inside and stretch out — Lazy-Boy-style — and realize there's oodles of interior roominess inside its streamlined body.

Buick's styling changes from 1956 models were vast. A new grille insert brought the look of an electric shaver back to the Buick front end. Across the hood was the B-U-I-C-K name in bold chrome letters. The grille looked much wider than before, with its massive "bumper bombs" spread to the outer edges. The headlights had neatly-visored chrome bezels like a custom car. The portholes were again allocated by horsepower, three to Specials and four to other models.

Parallel ridges were seen on the roofs of all hardtops and sedans, except on cars in the Super series. These sculptured creases added a crisp, aircraft fuselage look. New rear window treatments were seen, with rear window dividers in some Special, Century, and Roadmaster models. Roadmasters and Supers had wide, rear-slanting roof pillars.

A new design creation was the four-door Caballero station wagon, which had hardtop styling with no "B" roof pillars. Ten chrome bars decorated the ribs running down the Caballero's roof, from the top of the tailgate window to above the rear of the front seat. In midyear the Roadmaster 75 series was added with ultra-lavish versions of the Riviera coupe and sedan.

"No. 1 on the Zest-seller list," is how Buick introduced its best-selling series for 1957. The Special rode on the smaller 122-inch-wheelbase chassis and was a bit longer at 208.4 inches. Power came from a larger 364-cid two-barrel V-8 with a 9.5:1 compression ratio and 250 hp. Decorations included a sweep spear molding and a wide chrome trim panel between the rear wheel openings and the back bumper. The Special name appeared outside on the trunk lid only. In addition to the same body styles offered in 1956, a Caballero was offered. It was the priciest ($3,167) and rarest (6,817 built) model in this series.

"Take off in the dream car to drive!" was an advertising slogan that summed up the '57 Buick Century's market appeal. It looked lean and low and with the Roadmaster V-8 it could really go.

Although having the same 364 cubic inches, the Century added a four-barrel carburetor and a 10.0:1 compression ratio to get up to 300 hp. Buick said it had "the power-pack built right in at no extra cost."

The Century name was on the rear body sides (wagons said "Caballero"), above the sweep spear dip, and a chrome check mark below the Century script.

The trunk also displayed the Century name. A four-door sedan was reinstated in the Century series, while the deluxe four-door hardtop was dropped. The most expensive Century—the series' only wagon—was the $3,831 Caballero. The convertible, with 4,085 assemblies, had the lowest production of all Centurys.

"Two Nimble Tons of Fresh New Fashion," was Buick's description of the three-model Super lineup. Its selling point was good value: Roadmaster size — leg room, hip room, shoulder room, trunk room — with slightly less luxury and a lower price. The wheelbase was127-1/2 inches and overall length was 215.3 inches.

The engine was the same used in Centurys. Two-door hardtops and convertibles had three chevrons above the dips in the body side moldings. These were a direct "lift" from the 1956 Buick Centurion dream car. The Super name was spelled out in block letters on the trunk. Chrome plates between the rear wheel opening and bumper were also seen. The four-door hardtop (or "Riviera sedan") had the Super name in place of the chevrons. Only 2,056 Super ragtops left the factory in 1957, the rarest of 1957 Buicks.

Chevron-style side trim was used on all 1957 Roadmasters except for the Riviera sedan, which had the Roadmaster name and a Buick crest in the same position. Only a convertible and two- and four-door Rivieras were offered in this line. Two distinctive chrome ribs ran from the windshield post, along the length of the roof, down the rear window dividers, and along and down the trunk, and were optional on all Roadmaster Rivieras.

Some buyers didn't like the three-section back window treatment, so Buick offered a one-piece rear window substitution. The Roadmaster name was lettered across the trunk of all models. Chrome plates between the rear wheel opening and bumper were also seen on the top-series cars.

The midyear Roadmaster 75 series offered the Riviera coupe and Riviera sedan with cloth-and-leather trim and virtually every option that one vehicle could carry, other than air conditioning. The Roadmaster 75 Riviera coupe was a rare closed-bodied car — only 2,404 were ever built.

All 75 Series models had special "Roadmaster 75" nameplates on the rear doors or fenders and on the rear deck lid. Some people have referred to these cars as "75th Anniversary" models, but neither Buick or General Motors had a 75th anniversary in 1957. It was not David Dunbar Buick's 75th birthday. The "75" designation was simply the next number in Buick's coding.

Buick introduced its 1957 models rather late, on Nov. 5, 1956, but it was clear almost from the start that holding the number three position in industry sales was going to be a struggle. By Jan. 23, 1957, the division started a nationwide campaign of price advertising that was carried in 3,800 daily and weekly newspapers.

By the time the year ended, Buick made 24 percent fewer cars than it did in 1956, the greatest drop among all of the GM marques. As the brand slid into fourth place on the sales charts, its contract with the Kudner advertising agency was cancelled.

Model-year production of all Buicks totaled 405,086 cars, representing 6.4 percent of all U.S. car sales. This included some 220,700 Specials, 66,000 Centurys, 70,600 Supers, 33,000 Roadmasters and 15,000 Roadmaster 75s.

1958 *Buick*

Nothing announced your arrival in 1958 quite like the Buick Limited convertible.

Buick could have introduced a new top-series car called the "Chromemaster" in 1958. Tinsel was draped on all models, as if bright metal would brighten the company's sales-chart performance. Not counting the German Opel, which Buick dealers started selling, showroom visitors had chrome-laden Specials, Centurys, Supers, Roadmaster 75s, and Limiteds to select from.

Dimensionally the '58 Buicks were longer, lower and wider than the '57s, but the wheelbases and engines remained the same. The new overall lengths were 211.8 inches for Specials and Centurys, 219.1 inches for Supers and Roadmaster 75s, and a gigantic 227.1 inches for the Limited, which was the most glittery model of all.

In front, dual headlights sat above a "drawer-pull" grille with the fender tips "visoring" them. A big circular bull's-eye ornament with a "V" (for V-8) in the middle was placed in the center of the hood, above the chrome Buick name. Twin horizontal moldings ran from each side. The fenders were topped with smaller versions of the hood ornament and the trim piece on top of the hood also had a V-shape. The round parking/directional lights were housed in chrome "torpedoes" at either end of the grille. Below this gleaming ensemble was a massive front bumper bar.

In addition to sweep-spear-style body side moldings, the rear fenders and rear doors of four-door models carried bullet-shaped accent panels. Front fender portholes and rear window dividers were no longer seen. Chrome panels between the rear wheel opening and rear bumper were seen only on Limiteds, which also had 12 diagonal chevrons inside the rear fender accent panels, along with a "Limited" script and a crest medallion.

Centurys had a script nameplate inside the accent panels, Supers and Roadmaster 75s had an anodized panel. Other series had chrome bars on the lower rear quarters.

The rear styling featured pointed vertical tail fins with upright taillight clusters and wide chrome outline moldings that extended along the fender tips. The massive rear bumper incorporated a grille on the higher-trim-level models.

Limiteds also had four horizontal moldings segmenting the taillights and a crest medallion on the trunk lid with twin horizontal bright metal strips on each side. The larger Buicks had roof lines with backwards-slanting rear roof pillars, while Specials and Centurys had curved, forward-slanting rear window panels.

Buick dubbed these cars "the big, bold B-58 Buicks," as if they were gigantic U.S. Air Force "Stratofortress" bombers. They also had a B-12000 engine "with 12,000 pounds of thrust behind each piston stroke," according to ad copywriters. One full-page promotion said it was: "As advanced for land travel as the jet engines of the supersonic Delta wing bomber."

Other 1958 Buick selling features included Air-Cooled aluminum brakes with 45 radial fins that fanned in cooling air, Miracle Ride suspension, Rotoflow Torque-Tube stability, and Velvet Wall sound silencing.

An improved Flight-Pitch Dynaflow transmission was used in 98.5 percent of all 1958 Buicks. It had three turbines and the stator blades were adjustable to any performance need. A new option was the Air-Poise air-cushioned spring system, which turned out to be leak-prone and troublesome. Later, kits that converted the cars back to conventional coil springs were made available.

The 1958 Special series offered a seven-model selection, including two- and four-door sedans, two- and four-door Riviera hardtops, a convertible, a Riviera Estate wagon, and a non-Caballero station wagon, at prices between $2,700 and $3,265. The Riviera Estate wagon (called the Caballero in other series) was the rarest

Special with 3,420 assemblies. The conventional wagon had a slightly higher 3,663-unit run. The convertible found 5,502 buyers.

Five cars made up the Century line, which did not have a pillared two-door or a pillared station wagon. Prices began at $3,316 and ranged up to $3,831. Only 2,588 Century ragtops were made and only 4,456 Century Caballero wagons.

The two Supers were the Riviera coupe ($3,644) and the Riviera sedan ($3,789). Roadmaster 75 models shared the same body Supers had, but also offered a convertible. Prices for the three body styles ranged from $4,557 to $4,680 and even the Riviera sedan was relatively rare with only 10,505 leaving the factory. Only 2,368 Roadmaster 75 two-door hardtops were made and only 1,181 convertibles.

In the case of the huge Limiteds, they came in the same three body styles and were very hard to find even when new. Only 5,571 four-door hardtops, 1,026 two-door hardtops, and 839 convertibles left Buick assembly lines.

Buick remained big on television advertising in 1958 and was a sponsor of "The Patrice Munsel Show" on ABC on Friday

nights and the "Tales of Wells Fargo" on NBC on Monday nights. As a promotion for the latter program, Buick built a special Limited convertible for actor Dale Robertson, who starred in the TV Western.

This "Tales of Wells Fargo" Buick was owned for many years by Wally Rank, a well-known car collector and Buick dealer in Milwaukee, Wisconsin. The car featured wood-grained body side paneling and the interior was trimmed and outfitted in a western motif with saddle-tooled leather appointments and accessories.

After losing third place in sales in 1957, Buick switched to the McCann-Erickson advertising agency in 1958 and it was obvious the automaker was trying to change its "conservative-and-mature" image by appealing to the burgeoning youth market. In one series of black-and-white ads, Buicks were depicted on college campuses across the country.

Buick fell to fifth spot in calendar-year production in 1958. Ahead of it, in order, were Chevrolet, Ford, Plymouth and Oldsmobile. Model-year production came to only 241,892 cars for a 5.7 percent share of industry.

1959 *Buick*

Dramatic new styling was evident on the 1959 Buick LeSabre convertible.

The completely-redesigned and re-engineered 1959 Buicks drew rave reviews from all of the leading car magazines of the day as the new cars were inroduced to the public:
"*These 1959 Buicks are good, high-styled automobiles with excellent roadability and fine performance,*" said sage automotive writer Tom McCahill in his review in *Mechanix Illustrated*.

"*The '59 Buicks are beautifully styled and finished cars, well-built and powerful,*" reported *Car Life's* Jim Whipple.

In *Motor Trend*, William Carroll stated:

"*It appeared fast just sitting still with little evidence of great size, yet typically Buick in styling of wheel cutouts and block grille. Entry was no trouble, even for all my six feet two inches.*"

"*Probably not in all the latter-day history of the automobile has a car*

changed so radically in styling from one year to the next as has Buick for '59,*" opined Devon Francis in *Popular Science*.

Buicks were again lower, longer and wider. They featured new Vista-Panoramic windshields that curved back at the top, new Delta-Wing rear fenders, and a lean, clean trim treatment. All four-door hardtops except the most expensive one had new rear-overhang roofs, often called "flat-tops." To emphasize their fresh styling and the embodied in these dramatically different cars, technology, there were all-new series.

Sharing the same 123-inch wheelbase, but differing under the hood, were the base LeSabre and the one-step-up Invicta. Both were 217.4 inches long, 80 inches wide and about 55 inches high.

The LeSabre used a 364-cid V-8, while the Invicta had a 401-

cid Wildcat V-8. The bigger engine was also used in the larger Electra and Electra 225 models, which shared a 126.3-inch wheelbase, but had different overall lengths. The Electra was 220.6 inches long and closed Electra 225s had 225.4 inches between their bumpers. The Electra 225 ragtop was a "mere" 220.6 inches long.

Finding specs on the base version of the LeSabre engine, which was used in stick-shift cars, is difficult. It had an 8.5:1 compression ratio, but the horsepower rating was not widely promoted. The LeSabre V-8 was also available with Twin-Turbine Dynaflow, Twin-Turbine Dynaflow with Power Pack or Triple-Turbine Dynaflow, with different axle ratios used in each application. With Dynaflow, compression jumped up to 10.5:1 and the advertised horsepower rating was 250 at 4400 rpm. A Stromberg two-barrel carburetor was fitted.

The larger 401-cid Buick V-8 also had a 10.5:1 compression ratio, but it carried either a Carter AFB or Rochester 4GC four-barrel carburetor and advertised output was 325 hp. Twin-Turbine Dynaflow was standard with this engine (manual transmissions were not offered). Triple-Turbine Dynaflow was optional.

To carry its modern new bodies, Buick developed what it called an Equipoise Chassis. This was a box-sectional K-frame with full-coil-spring suspension. a new stabilizer bar and many other features designed to provide a "balanced" platform that combined a comfortable ride with effortless handling. The aluminum front brake drums featured cooling fins, while conventional cast-iron drums were used at the rear. The Air Ride rear suspension and posi-traction were optional in all models.

There were no series nameplates, no bright rocker panel moldings and no chrome edging around the wheel wells. Six body styles made up this line: two- and four-door sedans, two- and four-door hardtops, a convertible coupe, and a pillared station wagon. Prices started at $2,740 and went up to $3,320. Buick turned out 164,904 LeSabres in the model year.

Moving one peg up-market, the 1959 Invicta had model nameplates just forward of the front wheel openings. Why didn't the LeSabre have the same? Buick was smartly considering the buyer's psychology: no one wanted their neighbors to know they had the low-priced model, but once they moved up the pricing ladder, it was important to broadcast this fact.

Invictas also featured bright metal rocker panel moldings with "Buick" embossed in the front and metal edging around the front wheel openings only. The Invicta series did not have a two-door sedan in it, but it did have the other five Buick body styles. Invicta prices began at $3,357 and peaked at $3,841. Buick made just 5,231 Invicta wagons and 5,447 convertibles. Total series production was 52,851 vehicles.

Electra models had series nameplates just ahead of the front wheel openings, rocker panel moldings with the Buick name on front and trim around both the front and rear wheel openings. This series contained only the four-door sedan ($3,856), the four-door hardtop ($3,963), and the convertible ($3,818). Total output was 44,185 cars.

The same three body styles were offered in the Electra 225 series and the four-doors in this line had a five inch longer body. Since it did not pay to stretch the convertible body, the regular Electra ragtop was given richer trim and some additional standard equipment to make it an Electra 225.

These cars had Electra 225 nameplates just forward of the front wheels, bright metal rocker panel moldings that broadened out to double width on the front fenders (and from the rear wheel opening to the bumper on four-door models), an embossed emblem on the broad front section of the rocker sills (with a shorter wind split molding extending back), and a horizontally-ribbed beauty panel running across the back of the car just above the rear bumper.

Although the new Buicks were a hit, a steel industry strike had a devastating effect on calendar-year retail sales, which fell from 266,196 in 1958 to 242,500 in 1959. The strike closed Buick assembly plants for more than a month due to parts shortages and kept calendar-year production down even lower than in 1958.

Model-year production actually increased to 285,089 cars although that represented a smaller 5.1 percent of industry than Buick earned in 1958. The sales chart standings remained the same for the year.

A 1959 Buick served as the Official Pace Car at the Indianapolis 500-Mile Race. In its March 1959 issue, *Motor Trend* picked the 1959 Buick Invicta four-door hardtop as the "Best-Looking Car, Over-All" in America.

The 1959 Buick LeSabre two-door hardtop shouted "future" in its radical styling.

Cadillacs
of the Fifties

1950 *Cadillac*

Cadillac set a production record in 1950 with cars like the Series 62 convertible.

Cadillac was selling luxury in 1950 — and doing a good job of beating its rivals. So much so, in fact, that it taunted one of its competitors with an advertisement that asked, "At the height of the season, did you ever count the Cadillacs on Lincoln Road, in Miami Beach?"

Cadillac claimed its marketing professionals had statistically determined people "...whose means permit" made Cadillac their overwhelming choice in luxury cars and the claim rang true. The company would sell an all-time high of more than 100,000 cars this year and go on to dominate the segment, throughout the '50s, while Lincoln struggled and Packard faltered.

Described as "...gorgeously beautiful creations" that "...embodied all the good and wonderful things a motor car can currently provide," the 1950 models were completely restyled. They had a heavier look than the first all-new prewar models of 1948-1949. Turtle-shell roofs were adapted and one-piece windshields.

No longer available was the GM jet-back aerodynamic body, which was still used on Chevys, Pontiacs, Buicks, and Oldsmobiles. Cadillac traditions like the egg-crate grille and tail fin were maintained in slightly-modernized formats. Chrome Cadillac signatures decorated the front fenders, above the chrome body side moldings. The front and rear fenders now had one continuing feature line flowing from headlight to taillight. In front of the rear wheel openings were large, vertical air-intake moldings. Rear fender shields (skirts) were seen on all models.

All 1950 Cadillacs were 80-1/8 inches wide and four-door sedan heights ranged from 62 inches to 64-1/16 inches. It's interesting to note all Cadillacs, including the big Fleetwood, were lower than Chevrolets. Wheelbases and vehicle lengths varied by series. Fleetwoods used 8.20 x 15 tires and all other models used size 8.00 x 15. All Cadillacs had the same 331-cid 160-hp overhead valve V-8 with a Carter two-barrel carburetor. Hydra-Matic Drive was standard in the Series 62 and 60 Special models, while 61s and Fleetwoods had it as an option.

Cadillac's cleanest-looking cars were the Series 61 models. They had no rocker sill moldings or rear panel underscores. The 61 sedan lacked rear vent windows and featured a wraparound backlight. Only a Club Coupe ($2,761) and a four-door sedan ($2,866) were offered on the Series 61 chassis, which had a 122-inch-wheel-base. Both models had the GM "B" body, shared with Buick and Oldsmobile. Overall length, including bumpers and bumper guards, was 211-7/8 inches. The 61 was Cadillac's least-expensive line, but not its best-selling series. Production peaked at 26,772 units.

Next came the Series 62, featuring four models with a four-inch-longer wheelbase and overall length. It included Cadillac's two sporty models, the Coupe de Ville hardtop (4,507 built) and the convertible coupe (6,986 built). Prices in this series ranged from $3,150 to $3,654 and model-year output was 59,818 cars. 62s had the rocker sill moldings and rear panel underscores the 61s lacked.

Part of the reason 62 Series was Cadillac's sales-volume leader was this was the first full year of merchandising the popular Coupe de Ville. While the sedan was by far the favorite of buyers, the Coupe de Ville increased showroom traffic.

Larger than the 61s and 62s, the 1950 Cadillac 60 Special series rode a new 130-inch wheelbase, rather than the 133-inch wheelbase it held exclusive rights to between 1942 and 1949. Further identification came from eight vertical louvers on the bottom of the rear fenders, just ahead of the rear wheel openings. The only model in this car-line was a four-door sedan which sold for $3,797 and had a production run of 13,755 units.

Ultimate luxury was available from Cadillac Motor Division in the three Series 75 Fleetwood models, which included the sedan, Business sedan (just one was built), and seven-passenger Imperial Sedan. For the first time since 1941, the Fleetwood "limousine" body conformed to those of other Cadillacs, although it was built on a longer 146-3/4-inch wheelbase chassis and had a 236-5/8-inch overall length. Jump seats were provided in seven-passenger models. As many of these cars were owned by conservative buyers and driven by professional chauffeurs, Hydra-Matic Drive was *optional* equipment.

In 1950, Cadillac also built 2,052 Fleetwood 75 commercial chassis, which were used for ambulances, hearses, station buses, and other models built by aftermarket coach makers.

While the 1950 Cadillacs set the pace for a year of record sales, they were also viewed as America's ultimate high-performance machine in this era. No other domestic model came near the same horsepower rating. Sportsman Briggs Cunningham entered a pair of Cadillacs in the French Grand Prix at LeMans. One was a stock-bodied coupe and the other a special-bodied racing machine called "Le Monstre." Both had Cadillac V-8s tuned by Bill Frick. They finished 10th and 11th overall in the contest, a very respectable showing for an American competitor.

A 1950 Cadillac driven by Tom Deal, of El Paso, Texas, placed second in the 1950 Carrera-PanAmericana Mexico or Mexican Road Race. Deal started in 113th position, but his average speed of 77.362 mph for the race gave him second place by the time it was all over.

Cadillac produced 1,460 Series 75 cars (not counting commercial chassis) and 103,857 other Cadillacs in the model year. This was an all-time record, as well as the first six-figure-production year. Helping to sell many of these cars was a series of colorful advertisements that drove home Cadillac selling features from design leadership to endurance and dependability. Safety, comfort — even fuel economy, were stressed as Cadillac attributes.

The ads showed different Cadillac models along with other trappings of wealth that stood as "Standards of the World." A black convertible appeared below a photo of "Jewels by Cartier" and a red Cadillac Sixty-Special sedan was positioned beneath a woman wearing "Furs by Robert." Depicted in other ads were lesser-known jewelry makers' names such as Van Cleef & Arpels, Trabery & Hoeffer and Harry Winston.

Cadillacs, by association, were presented as standards of the automotive world. "When a man moves up to Cadillac, he does so expecting extraordinary things," stated one memorable line of copy.

1951 Cadillac

The epitome of comfort was the 1951 Cadillac Fleetwood 75 limousine.

If you liked the 1950 Cadillacs, chances are you also liked the 1951s. Only a few subtle styling changes were made. Miniature "ice-cube-tray" grilles were set into the outboard grille extension panels, below the headlights. Larger, bullet-shaped bumper guards were used and these rapidly became an automotive icon of the '50s.

These guards became known as Dagmars, the stage name of Ruth Egnor, a blonde '50s American entertainer. Between 1948 and 1951, the buxom Huntington, West Virginia, resident went from an office girl to being a $50,000-a-year TV star. She hosted "Dagmar's Canteen," usually in off-the-shoulder gowns and also appeared on NBC's late night "Broadway Open House" with comedians Jerry Lester and Morey Amsterdam. Cadillac's bumper guards, introduced in 1951, became associated with Dagmar's 39-inch bust. Her memory lives on among Cadillac collectors.

Cadillacs continued to be powered by the five-main-bearings 331-cid V-8, which had a 3-3/16 x 3-5/8-inch bore and stroke and a 7.5:1 compression ratio. Either a Carter WCD two-barrel or Rochester BB two-barrel carburetor was fitted. It produced 160 hp at 3800 rpm and 312 foot-pounds of torque at 1800 rpm.

Hydra-Matic Drive, still optional on the lowest and highest series, had what Cadillac described as a "major improvement." You could change from forward gear to reverse while the engine was racing to "rock" out of difficult situations like sand or snow. During calendar 1951, Cadillac installed 100,702 Hydra-Matic units and built its 448,229th Hydra-Matic of all time.

Series 61 Cadillacs had the same trim as 1950, with the exception of a medallion added to the rear roof pillar. The same 122-inch wheelbase was used. Due to the Dagmar bumper guards, the overall length crept up to 211-1/2 inches. Other measurements were unchanged. Standard equipment included a hand-brake warning lamp, a steering column cover, and an automatic choke.

The Series 61 Club Coupe sold for $2,810 and 2,400 were built. The sedan had a $2,917 price tag and 2,300 were made. With such sluggish demand, this was to be the price-leader Cadillac series' last year. It was dropped on May 1, 1951. In 1952, the 62 became the base series.

In 1951, the 62 continued to have a four-inch longer stance and four-inch longer length than the 61. It could be identified by the bright metal trim on its rocker panels and lower rear quarter panels. The 62 sedan had a conventional backlight and rear vent windows. A new Coupe de Ville chrome script was seen on the rear roof pillar of the hardtop and distinguished it from the plainer Club Coupe. Power windows were standard equipment in Coupe de Villes and convertibles. The four 62 body styles ranged in price from $3,436 to $3,987. Only 6,117 convertibles were built, while Coupe de Ville production shot up to over 10,000 units.

The Series 60 four-door sedan had a 130-inch wheelbase and a 224-1/2-inch overall length. It was face lifted along the lines of the other models and again had eight chrome hash marks on the rear fenders to identify it. Cadillac's new, non-Sombrero-style wheel covers were standard on 60 Specials. Despite a substantial price increase to $4,142, the 60 Special enjoyed a production increase to 18,631 units for the model year.

Part of the 60 Special's popularity rise in 1951 might have been due to a combination of social changes and a well-timed ad program. This was the start of the two-car-family era in America and many 1951 Cadillac ads were designed to sell cars to upsc homemakers.

"Highlight of the Day's Activities," read the banner on one such sales pitch. "Perhaps it's to be a visit to a friend's home . . . or perhaps she's meeting the man of the house in town . . . or, again, it may be only for a day's shopping. But whatever the trip — for the woman who enjoys possession of a Cadillac car, this is the highlight of the day's activities – *the journey behind the wheel of her Cadillac.*"

The same assortment Fleetwood 75 sedans returned in 1951. They had a 146-3/4-inch wheelbase and 236-1/4-inch overall length. The sedan was priced at $5,200 and 1,090 were made,

while the Imperial sedan listed for $5,405 and counted 1,085 assemblies. An additional 30 Business Sedans and 2,960 long-wheelbase chassis were sold for use by the professional-car trade. The Business Sedans became funeral cars, commercial limousines and, in rare cases, taxis. The chassis-only were used to build ambulances, funeral vehicles and station buses.

The powerful Cadillac engine wound up under the bonnet of hybrid models like the Cadillac-Allards, made by Englishman Sydney J. Allard. A trio of these cars made a 1-2-3 finish at Watkins Glen in 1951. Briggs Cunningham, who'd raced Cadillacs at LeMans in 1950, used the Cadillac engine in his limited-production C-2 Cunningham model.

Cadillac retained its position as America's No. 1 luxury car-maker in 1951. By the time that Dec. 31, 1951 rolled around, the company recorded its second-best year in history. Calendar-year production was 103,266, compared to 110,535 previously. However, Cadillac's market share rose from 1.66 percent in 1950 to 1.93 percent in 1951. Cadillac also built 3.9 percent of all convertibles made in the U.S. and four percent of all hardtops.

Things looked even better as the total included 2,205 Fleetwoods, 110,340 Cadillacs, and 2,960 Fleetwood 75 commercial chassis, all Cadillac records. On Nov. 27, 1951, the 300,000th Cadillac overhead-valve V-8 was produced.

In 1951, approximately 1,700 Cadillac dealers across the country sold 1.9 percent of all American cars and 4.6 percent of all General Motors cars. Had production restrictions not been in place due to the Korean War, Cadillac sales would have been even better.

At the end of 1951, with National Production Agency controls tightened up, Cadillac had a backlog of 88,000 unfilled new-car orders with substantial down payments on most of them.

The company did get some military orders to make up for lost car sales. It produced Walker Bulldog light tanks and spare parts for Cadillac-built World War II-era M-24 tanks still being used by the U.S. Army.

With civilian and military production humming, Cadillac reported the highest number of employees in company history. More than 12,000 people were on the company's payroll, including 900 in Detroit, Michigan and about 2,000 at the company's defense plant in Cleveland, Ohio.

1952 *Cadillac*

The Cadillac Automobile Company was formed in June, 1902, when Henry M. Leland met with backers of the floundering Detroit Automobile Company for the purpose of organizing a new firm. It was named for the French adventurer, Antoine de la Mothe Cadillac, who founded Detroit. The first Cadillac was put together on Oct. 17, 1902. Cadillac observed its 50th birthday in 1952 and the new cars introduced on Jan. 22, 1952 were called "Golden Anniversary" models.

Small styling changes, but bigger engineering improvements were the order of the day. The 331-cid overhead-valve V-8 got a four-barrel carburetor, a new free-flowing intake manifold, larger exhaust valves, and dual-exhaust manifolds. It now produced 190 hp at 4000 rpm. A new type of Hydra-Matic automatic transmission was standard in all models except Fleetwood 75s.

The transmission's two drive positions included one for oper-

ation on open roads and the other was for driving on congested city streets or in mountains. The first went through three gear ratios and the other went through four. Saginaw power steering was a new option. The hydraulic assist took over when three or more pounds of "pull" were exerted on the steering wheel. Ads said power steering eliminated up to 75 percent of normal steering effort. Also new was a 12-volt electrical system.

Cadillac promoted the 1952 model as a "Cadillac Among Cadillacs" and said the new lineup climaxed 50 years of progress.

"There can be little doubt that automotive history will record 1952 as a truly great Cadillac year," read one flowery claim. "For in this year a full half century of progress in engineering, in styling and in craftsmanship has climaxed in one magnificent motor car — the Golden Anniversary Cadillac."

The 1952 Cadillac Series 62 convertible has optional wire wheels and a continental kit.

A special Golden Anniversary model even turned up on the 1952 auto show circuit. This was the prototype for the limited-production 1953 Eldorado. The press release issued on Jan. 22, 1952, said:

"The motorist who shares the craftsman's pleasure in exquisite handicraft will instantly find kinship with Cadillac's fabulous ELDORADO. This exotic convertible dramatically blends two great fields of human endeavor. In an expression of the ageless arts, ELDORADO reveals a treatment of gold on a gleaming, ivory-like surface. A sports car in character, the long, low body of the ELDORADO is finished in a dazzling, white lacquer. Bright, East-Indian, Pepper Red leather heightens the enchanting effect of the artistic interior. The seatbacks are piped in modern horseshoe pattern with door inserts of the same theme. Crash pad and instrument board top are of an expanded Royalite skin, perfectly matching the leather. The steering wheel carries…its covering of hand sewn, East-Indian, Pepper Red leather which is baseball stitched on the back. The ELDORADO's instrument board inserts, door moldings and kick strips are of gold plated, ripple patterned material."

A second show car seen this year was the Cadillac Townsman, a gussied-up version of the 60 Special sedan that also had links to the 50-years celebration. The press release covering this car said:

"The Cadillac Townsman presents the luxurious 60 Special Sedan in appointments of regal splendor as a token of the Golden Anniversary. Lacquered a glistening Nubian black, the TOWNSMAN is crowned with a soft, gold-hued top…

In the world of automobiles the quest of interior artistry is ceaseless. Many attempts bring common results—a few are fine works. A masterpiece is achieved rarely—such is the TOWNSMAN. Those who view the interior gaze in hushed awe upon the jewel case-like interior of rich gold and soft, deep black. Here, indeed, the jewels do appear—for crested emblems of gold metallic thread have been woven into the cloth by Jacquard loomsmen. The cloth, on which the symbol of Cadillac has been reproduced, is a rich Deauville (golden beige) nylon. These gem-studded panels contrast elegantly with an edging of soft, black velour."

It took a good eye to spot design revisions made to the production-type Cadillacs for 1952. Instead of miniature egg-crate grilles below the headlights, there were now solid trim plates with small, gold, winged emblems in the same position. The V-for-V-8 emblem and Cadillac crest on the hood were wider. The trunk on the 62 sedan was made higher to increase its luggage capacity. At the rear, the directional lights and back-up lights were built into the taillights. That year, Cadillacs had four mufflers and tailpipes that exited through dual exhaust slits in the rear bumper.

The Cadillac 62 became the lowest-priced Cadillac line. It contained the same four body styles as in 1951 and prices ranged from $3,542 for the Club Coupe to $4,110 for the convertible, of which 6,400 were made. The 62s could be identified by the Cadillac crest over a broad "V" on the trunk lid. The Coupe de Ville again had a script nameplate on the rear roof pillar. They rode the same 126-inch wheelbase. Overall length was 215-1/2 inches for the sedan and 220-1/2 inches for the other models.

A "Sixty-Special" script on the trunk identified the 1952 model of the same name. It also had the trademark chrome louvers on the rear fenders, eight on either side of the car. Hydraulically-operated power window lifts were standard. The Sixty Special again used the 130-inch wheelbase and it had a 224-1/2-inch overall length. The price this year increased to $4,720 and production tapered off to 16,110 units.

Styling changes for the big Fleetwood 75 series conformed to the year's "Golden Anniversary" theme. Two models used the extra-long General Motors "D" body. The seven-passenger sedan and the limousine had jump seats and the limousine had a window separating the driver and passenger compartments. Cadillac built 1,400 of the $5,360 sedans and 1,800 of the $5,572 limousines.

Cadillac had a successful anniversary season, anchoring its hold on the top position in luxury-car sales. Its calendar-year output dropped six percent to 96,850 cars, but that had to be measured against an 8.5 percent drop for that segment of the market. In fact, Cadillac's 35.9 percent share of the luxury market was a half-percent gain. Model-year production included 2,200 Fleetwood 75 cars, 1,694 Fleetwood 75 commercial chassis and 90,715 other Cadillacs.

1953 Cadillac

Many options were standard on the 1953 Cadillac Eldorado convertible like wire wheels.

With the announcement of its 1953 models, Cadillac Motor Division was still leading the American automobile industry in engine power. Its 1953 V-8s developed 210 hp. The company's defense branch continued building T41E1 Walker Bulldog tanks and T41 Twin 40-mm gun motor carriages, largely for use in Korea. Cadillac's contracts for military production were valued at $700 million by the beginning of 1953.

"The year 1953 marks the beginning of Cadillac's *second* half-century of progress in the automotive world," said an advertisement for the 1953 Sixty Special. "Numerous changes in styling have made them unbelievably beautiful . . . and gorgeous new interiors, together with a wonderful new Cadillac Air Conditioner, offer unprecedented luxury and comfort."

Actually, most observers would probably consider the styling changes made in most 1953 Cadillacs to be quite modest. The front grille was redesigned and had a heavier integral bumper and bumper guards. The new "Dagmars" were gigantic. Smaller versions protected the rear bumper. The parking lights were mounted directly under the headlights, in ribbed panels that matched the wraparound grille extensions. The winged Golden Anniversary emblems were gone. New wheel covers appeared. They had a fuller outer edge and a dished center with the Cadillac medallion.

The limited-edition Eldorado convertible had additional styling updates including a lowered wraparound windshield, cut-down door sills and a flush-fitting tonneau cover. Laced wire wheels were standard equipment plus every option you could fit on one car, except air conditioning. No wonder it cost $7,750 and only 532 were built. The Cadillac Eldorado was a dream car brought to life.

As a publicity-getter, it pulled the curious into Cadillac showrooms where salesmen could sell them a more practical Cadillac. It was the "Let's-go-see-the-dream-car-down-the-street," approach to automotive marketing.

There was no special Eldorado V-8 in 1953. The enriched ragtop used the same improved 331-cid V-8 the other Cadillacs relied on. It did have a new 8.25:1b compression ratio that helped it crank up 210 hp at 4150 rpm. The four-barrel carburetor was a Carter WFCB or a Rochester 4GC model. An again-improved dual-range Hydra-Matic Drive was standard in 62s and 60 Specials.

On Apr. 16, 1953, Cadillac announced that Hydra-Matic Drive would be standard equipment on all models. The prices of the Fleetwood 75s were raised to include Hydra-Matic Drive. After the Hydra-Matic transmission plant in Livonia, Michigan, burned on Aug. 12, 1953, Cadillac stopped building cars and laid off about 80 percent of its workforce for three weeks. On September 8, all 10,000 Cadillac assembly line employees went back to work, building Cadillacs with Buick Dynaflow transmissions. Production of Dynaflow-equipped cars amounted to some 19,000 vehicles. Cadillac produced its 100,000th car of the year on Dec. 1, 1953.

Other standard equipment on 1953 Cadillacs included "Knee-Action" independent front suspension, a four-barrel carburetor, stannate pistons, an intake silencer, a hypoid rear axle, an oil bath air cleaner, and a mechanical fuel pump. Options included power steering, a heater, fog lamps, windshield washers, E-Z-Eye tinted glass, air conditioning (introduced in April), wire wheels, and white sidewall tires.

The Eldorado was added to the line as a sub-series of the four-car Series 62. The other body styles in this series were the sedan, the hardtop coupe, the Coupe de Ville hardtop coupe and the regular convertible. All remained on a 126-inch wheelbase with the sedan measuring 215-13/16 inches end-to-end and the two-doors being five inches longer. Non-Eldorado prices started at $3,571 and ranged to $4,144 for the convertible.

The Eldorado in the showroom did help sales, especially in the case of the convertible, which went to 8,367 buyers.. The 62s had a narrow body bumper strip on the front fender and door and the V-with-Cadillac-crest trunk lid treatment.

A decoration on the $4,305 Sixty Special was a wide rocker sill molding. The rear fender hash marks and the Fleetwood signature on the trunk lid were other identifiers. Narrow body bumper strips decorated the front fenders and doors of this 130-inch-wheelbase model, too. An even 20,000 examples rolled out the factory gates. The Fleetwood 75 series again offered a large limousine with a glass dividing partition and jump seats ($5,604) and a large sedan with jump seats only ($5,818). Both 146-3/4-inch-wheelbase models were now called 8-passenger, rather than 7-passenger, models. dan. Cadillac built 765 limousines and 1,435 of the big "stretch" sedans.

Cadillac introduced two dream cars at the General Motors Motorama on Jan.16, 1953. The first, called the Orléans previewed many 1954 to 1956 Cadillac styling features, such as the Panoramic windshield and four-door hardtop styling. The rear doors were hinged at the rear, like the 1957 and 1958 Eldorado Brougham. The Orléans looked like a closed-bodied Eldorado.

The other Motorama Cadillac was the Le Mans, a precursor of the 1957 and '58 Eldorado. This fiberglass-bodied two-seat convertible had 1954 Cadillac-style fenders, a low Panaromic windshield, open wheel housings and "turbine-fin" wheels. The Le Mans stood 5-1/2 inches lower than a regular convertible. It came with a rain switch and electrodes that detected rain drops. As the water shorted the electrodes, current was transmitted to a motor that automatically raised the convertible top. Cadillac built three slightly different Le Mans two-seaters.

On Dec. 10, 1953, Cadillac changed over to 1954 model production. But 1953 closed on a high note, despite Korean War production controls and the fact that only 4,812 cars were built during August, due to the transmission factory fire.

1954 Cadillac

The 1954 Cadillac got a longer, lower body and more, like this Coupe de Ville hardtop.

With the mid-'50s interest in General Motors' Motoramas — and with dream cars appearing at those and at other shows — Cadillac pitched its 1954 model as "The Dream Car of twenty-five million!" An advertisement showing one of the year's hardtop coupes pointed out: "...research among motorists indicates that literally tens of millions of people dream of owning this car."

The 1954 Cadillacs had the marque's first major restyling in four years. It featured the "million dollar grin" grille with a new "ice-cube-tray" textured insert and large round parking lights at either end of the grille cavity. The headlights no longer sat just on top of the grille, they were mounted higher with body-color sheet metal between them and the grille. The tops of the fenders wrapped over the round headlight lenses like soft-edged visors.

The Cadillac front bumper had an inverted "gull-wing" appearance. Its now-trademark "Dagmar" type bumper guards tapered to a point and a chromed, horizontal grille blade connected them. The ribbed extension panels wrapping around the front body corners no longer held any lights or decorations. The overall look of the front of the car was larger, but cleaner and more refined.

Cadillac often got new styling advances a year or two ahead of most other GM models and a new-for-1954 feature was the *Panoramic*, wraparound-style windshield. Below the windshield, there was a cowl-wide air intake with a screen-like texture. The flow-through front and rear fender feature lines were raised to windowsill height. Flatter roofs were seen on all models.

A fashion hit on two-door hardtop models was a new "Florentine" rear window pillar that curved backwards towards the bottom. On Coupe de Villes the model name was presented in a gold-colored script on the rear window sill. In some catalog artwork, the Coupe de Ville was shown incorrectly with body side moldings that extended about six inches further back on the doors than on the regular coupe. Both cars used the same molding running across the front fender and door and stopping about seven inches short of the rear door break line. Sedans had extending door reveal moldings and integral side-window sun visors.

Cadillac's new rear-end styling featured new vertical bumper extensions housing round dual-exhaust openings. The entire rear bumper was redesigned as well. Cars in the 62 Series had the familiar V-shaped trunk emblem with a Cadillac crest above it. The 60 Special four-door sedan substituted a V-emblem and a Fleetwood script on the trunk. This type of trunk trim was repeated on Fleetwood 75 eight-passenger sedans and limousines.

As Cadillac fought to maintain its edge in the luxury-car horsepower race, engineers pushed the envelope up to 230 hp still using the same 8.25:1 compression ratio. Four-barrel carburetors made by either Carter or Rochester were used in mixed production.

Hydra-Matic Drive was standard again and Cadillac added power steering and windshield washers to the no-extra-cost-equipment category.

All series were poised on three-inch longer wheelbases; 129 inches for 62s, 133 inches for 60 Specials and 149-3/4 inches for Series 75. In the Series 62 lineup, the sedan was 216-7/16 inches long, while the hardtop coupes and convertible had an additional seven inches between their bumpers.

The 60 Special was 227-7/16 inches long and the big Fleetwood 75s stretched nearly 10 inches more than that. The 75s rode on 8.20 x 15 tires and the other Cadillacs used 8.00 x 15s.

For all practical purposes, the 62 Series offered the same four body styles — coupe, Coupe de Ville, four-door sedan and convertible — at prices from $3,838 to $4,404, plus the Eldorado in its own sub-series. There was an "export" version of the four-door sedan—only a variation of the model for overseas buyers.

A single chassis-only was sold, a Sedan de Ville (four-door hardtop) was built as a one-off creation and an Eldorado coupe was made for the president of Reynolds Aluminum Company. Series 62 identification features were the same as in the past.

The Eldorado convertible returned, but it was more of a dressed-up Series 62 ragtop, than a real limited-production model. It featured special ribbed beauty panels on the lower rear quarters, a fiberglass tonneau cover, gold Cadillac crests on the door sills and rear fenders, a leather-trimmed interior, and chrome wire wheels. It was only available in Aztec Red, Azure Blue, Alpine White or Apollo Gold. With a $5,738 price tag, only 2,150 were sold.

The Fleetwood 60 Special had its famous eight louvers ahead of the front wheel opening. The Cadillac crest was positioned above the front "V," but the rear one had a Fleetwood script above it. A series of Cadillac advertisements that appeared this year pictured Cadillac 60 Special owners at balls, operas, grand hotels, and mansions. Headlines such as "The one car that fits the occasion!" or "Where a Man is at his Best" or "You Could Guess What Car They Came In," made it clear that the 60 Special was — as another ad stated — "Worth Its Price in Prestige."

In the '50s, Cadillac was very good at selling the "we've arrived" image of pulling up in a Cadillac. As popular song named "Lavender Cadillac" put it, "Gimme a car like Sugar Ray's, and I'll be loving you always." In addition to heavyweight champion Sugar Ray Robinson, other idols of the era, such as Marilyn Monroe and Frank Sinatra, were often seen driving Cadillacs — usually Eldorado convertibles.

The Fleetwood 75 Series limousine cracked the $6,000 price barrier by $90. Both it and the eight-passenger sedan, which now sold for $5,875, were larger cars this season. Unfortunately for Cadillac, this didn't help sales, which dropped to 869 for the lower-priced model and 611 for the fancier one. Also down — to 1,635 — was the number of chassis sold to builders of ambulances, funeral cars and station buses.

Cadillac presented three real dream cars at the 1954 GM Motorama. The El Camino coupe, the LaEspada roadster and the Park Avenue four-door luxury sedan all contributed many styling motifs and other design and engineering elements to future production models. [Actor Ronald Reagan, who later became President of the United States, enjoyed a "photo op" behind the wheel of the LaEspada at an auto show.]

Between the start of 1954 model assembly on January 4 and the changeover to 1955 models on October 4, Cadillac built 1,500 Fleetwood 75s, 1,635 Fleetwood 75 commercial chassis, and 96,680 other models. On September 7, the 1,500,000th Cadillac was made. Two weeks later, the U.S. Army awarded Cadillac a $35 million ordnance contract—a ton of money in 1954!

1955 *Cadillac*

A 1955 Cadillac Series 62 Coupe de Ville hardtop in the driveway always is special.

Cadillac—General Motors' representative in the fine-car field—was treated to a luxurious year in 1955. Weekly, monthly and quarterly sales and production records were snapped throughout the season. By the close of 1955, Cadillac "owned" 44.8 percent of all business in the high-priced market segment. Chrysler Imperial (20.9 percent) and Buick Limited (20.6 percent) were far behind; Lincoln (8.6 percent) and Packard (5.1 percent) were literally "out of the race."

The super-powered '55 Cadillacs (250 hp standard; 270 hp optional) were introduced on Nov. 18, 1954. They featured longer, lower bodies and power steering had become standard equipment. The redesigned radiator grille had the parking lights moved back into the ribbed panels directly below the headlights. Wider rectangular openings characterized the ice-cube-tray grille insert. The Dagmar-type bumper guards looked like bullets again.

On Cadillac 62s (including Eldorados) and 60 Specials, the body side moldings now extended a little further back on the body, meeting the vertical air-vent moldings on the cars' rear quarters at right angles. On most models, these vertical moldings no longer ran downwards, from the right angle where they intersected, to the body sills. However, the big Fleetwood 75s were still trimmed the "old-fashioned" way. It didn't pay to manufacture new moldings for such low-volume cars that were purchased by wealthy, conservative buyers who probably didn't care much for change anyway.

Cadillac continued to use the 331-cid overhead V-8, but it now had a 9.0:1 compression ratio and produced 250 hp at 4600 rpm. The same single Carter or Rochester four-barrel carburetors were used on the base engine. A version of this engine, with two Rochester 4GC four-barrel carburetors, was standard in the Eldorado. It made 270 hp at 4800 rpm. The Eldorado V-8 was available as an optional "Power Package" in other 1955 Cadillac models for $161 extra.

As usual, Cadillac had the same arrangement of body types in each line and only minor trim variations were made. There were only fractional changes in body measurements. On the fancier two-door hardtop in the 62 series, Coupe de Ville nameplates were again located under the rear side windows. The 62 four-door sedan (as well as the 60 Special version) now had the Florentine reverse-curve roof pillar styling. On all 62s the Cadillac name was seen in script on the front fender. Chrome beauty panels highlighted the body sills, fender skirts, and rear quarter panels of all models, except the distinctive Eldorado convertible.

While other Cadillacs retained the blunt, rounded P-38-style tail fins of the past, the 1955 Eldorado had new sharp-edged, "blade" type tail fins that came to a pointy angle at the rear, then dropped down to meet the dual round tail and back-up lights nestled in pods below each fin. The Eldorado's rear wheel openings were enlarged and only thin chrome moldings decorated them. There were no rocker panel moldings or rear quarter extensions on this ragtop.

The Eldorado's shelf-like rear bumper jutted out further than those of other models and had "jet pod" exhaust outlets on either end. Blade-style bumper guards surrounded the license plate recess on the trunk-latching panel, which was decorated with three vertical moldings on each side. No fender skirts were used on the fancy convertible, so viewers could see the special finned

Sabre wheels. On the trunk was a large chrome "V" and the Eldorado name in script. The Eldorado was available only in four colors. Power brakes were on the standard equipment list. A total of 3,950 Eldorados were assembled.

Cadillac must have made maximum profits on sales of 60 Specials, because this year it increased the number of chrome hash marks on the car's rear quarters. It now had 12 of the chrome ornaments to make it look even fancier. The advertising campaign showing 60 Special owners in upscale social and business climates (grand ballrooms and boardrooms) continued. "Styling the Whole World Admires" said one ad depicting a gold car; "Brings Out The Best In a Man!" was the pitch showing a pipe-smoking artist sculpting a bust of a VIP.

This year, Cadillac managed to build 18,300 of these "small" Fleetwoods. That was up over 2,000 units, so the ads may have helped sales a bit. Fleetwood 75 sales — both cars *and* commercial chassis —increased as well.

By the time the '55 model assembly lines ceased functioning in September, an unparalleled company total of 2,000 Fleetwood 75 eight-passenger sedans and limos, 1,975 Fleetwood 75 commercial chassis, and 140,778 Cadillac 62s and 60 Specials were counted up for the calendar year. Business was so strong that in July 1954, Cadillac announced it had purchased 6-1/2 acres of land to add to a 14-acre parcel it already owned across from its Detroit plant.

The total acreage was expected to provide space for future manufacturing expansion under Phase 2 of a Cadillac growth plan. Phase 1 of the plan, put into effect in 1954, had added 40 percent to Cadillac's production operations during normal working hours.

In March 1955, it was reported Cadillac would begin production, later in the year, of an ultra-plush 1956 model that would "...make people forget about the Rolls-Royce."

Initially expected to sell for about $8,500, annual output of 1,000 units was projected for this Eldorado Brougham hardtop sedan. Both targets were missed, as the price climbed and sales fell short of predictions.

With Ford Motor Company about to revive the Lincoln Continental, Cadillac also decided to revive the LaSalle name in 1955 — at least on a Motorama dream car. Two visionary versions were whipped up — a roadster and a four-door hardtop. Both were powered by an experimental V-6 and both had a fiberglass body and a 108-inch wheelbase.

The roadster looked like a '56 Corvette with front-end motifs pirated from the 1940s LaSalle. The four-door looked similar, but had smaller wheel openings and a longer rear end. Also seen on the show circuit was the Eldorado Brougham, which previewed the features of the 1956 limited-production model of the same name. A fascinating article in *Motor Trend* documented the creation of this prototype on a very short deadline.

1956 Cadillac

The colors of the 1956 Cadillac Coupe de Villes seem more for sherbets than cars!

More owners of competitive make cars switched to Cadillac during the '56 model year than ever before," said the *Ward's 1957 Automotive Yearbook*. "These buyers were largely responsible for the enormously successful '56 Cadillac automobile...."

The division turned out 154,631 cars, surpassing record-year 1955 by 10 percent. Used-car sales at Cadillac dealerships were up 22 percent and service and parts saw a 15 percent gain.

All of this was a very impressive performance in a year when the bulk of U.S. automakers experienced a "leveling-off" period from 1955's all-time industry highs. Cadillac advertising for 1956 was heavier than usual with a goal od attracting new customers.

"When a motorist makes the move to Cadillac, the odds are overwhelming that he has made his last move insofar as motor car preference is concerned," read one Cadillac sales pitch.

"There are many reasons why this should be so — Cadillac's inspiring beauty . . . its marvelous comfort . . . its magnificent performance . . .and, of course, the satisfaction of Cadillac ownership."

"Other ads suggested Cadillac division had "...welcomed a greater number of new owners to its motoring family than ever before in history" because of the cars' blend of beauty, luxury, performance and practicality.

"The lady of the house regards the family Cadillac from a very special vantage point," said an ad for the new 1956 Sedan de Ville four-door hardtop.

"For she knows and appreciates the car not only as a driver, but as a passenger as well. And it is here that Cadillac confers upon her some of its finest attributes." The selling points listed were roominess, quiet operation and *fashionable* upholstery touches.

Headlining the changes in 1956 Cadillacs were a 305-hp V-8, a brand-new Hydra-Matic transmission and the addition of two entirely new body styles. All models had a new aluminum grille (available in either gold- or satin-finished aluminum) with parking lights set into the bumper. On the driver's side of the grille was a Cadillac script.

Cars in the 62 Series were about two inches shorter than their 1955 counterparts. The 62s had narrow, horizontal moldings on the guide-missile-shaped "projectile" bulges on the rear quarter panels. Behind these moldings were nine short vertical moldings that curved over the sculptured projectiles.

The Coupe de Ville had a model nameplate and crest medallion on the front fenders, as did the new Sedan de Ville. Other models had the Cadillac crest only. Not counting export versions of the sedan and a handful of chassis-only, there were five models in the base 62 Series — four-door sedan, new Sedan de Ville (four-door hardtop), hardtop coupe, Coupe de Ville and convertible coupe — with prices from $4,146 to $4,711.

Two additional models were now in the Eldorado sub-series. The Eldorado Seville two-door hardtop and Eldorado Convertible Biarritz were both priced at $6,501 and Cadillac made 3,900 of the former and 2,150 of the latter. These cars had the elongated, blade-style tail fins. The special rear-end treatment introduced on the 1955 Eldorado was seen on the hardtop and the ragtop.

Both shared a new twin-fin hood ornament and a new ribbed chrome saddle molding that extended from the windshield to the rear window along the body belt line. The rear quarter panel moldings were thin and ran to the taillights instead of the bumper. Both Eldorados were fractionally longer than other 62s. Eldorados carried the Fleetwood name above the "V" emblem on the trunk.

The 133-inch-wheelbase Fleetwoods had "Sixty Special" name scripts on both front fenders and the Fleetwood name on the trunk. The chrome molding, with nine ribs behind it, used on the lower rear quarter panels was much heavier than that used on 62s. The Sixty Special was now priced at $4,992.

Like other 1956 models, the big Fleetwood 75s retained the same wheelbase and shrunk almost two inches in length due to bumper design changes.

The bore of the 1956 Cadillac V-8 was increased to 4.00 inches (from 3.81 inches) while the stroke remained at 3.63 inches. This brought displacement of the five-main-bearings engine up to 365 cubic inches. The compression ratio was also hiked to 9.75:1 making the stock output rating 285 at 4600 rpm with a single Carter four-barrel carburetor. The Eldorado came with a special version carrying two Carter four-barrel carburetors and producing 305 hp at 4700 rpm. This engine was an extra-cost option for other Cadillac and Fleetwood models.

Cadillac's new "Controlled Coupling" Hydra-Matic Drive was said to add new smoothness and durability to the GM-built automatic transmission. The efficiency and high-performance characteristics of previous versions were continued. GM claimed it spent

$35 million developing the larger transmission. Now we know where the army contract went!

In 1956, five more dream cars were exhibited in the GM Motorama. The Castilian was based on the standard Eldorado Seville and was an "Old Spain" theme. The Gala or Wedding Car — a silver Series 62 Sedan de Ville with pearlescent white leather trim — was the second mood car. The Maharani was a specially-appointed Sixty-Special with built-in kitchen sink and the Palomino was a Series 62 convertible with calfskin upholstery and Western-motif carpets. The Eldorado Brougham Town Car was a

fiberglass-bodied dream machine. The roof of its passenger compartment was covered with polished black landau leather and the rear compartment included gold-colored hardware. It featured a radio telephone for communicating with the chauffeur, air-conditioning, a vanity compartment, a cigar humidor and a thermos and glasses.

During 1956, Cadillac moved from 10th to ninth place in industry sales rankings based on calendar-year production of 140,873 new cars. Model-year production was counted as 146,840 units. This year's deliveries included the one-millionth Cadillac.

1957 Cadillac

A popular 1957 Cadillac was the Series 60 Special Fleetwood four-door hardtop.

In 1956, GM design chief Harley J. Earl — who once headed the Cadillac studio — made a statement suggesting the company's car designs were going to be less conservative.

"There was a time when we felt we had to hold back on some of our design ideas because the public wasn't ready for them yet," Earl reportedly said.

"When a new Cadillac car is imminent on the American motoring scene, it is usually expected that the car will be dramatically advanced in every way," boasted the division of its 1957 models. "But no one, not even Cadillac owners themselves, was fully prepared for the magnificent new Cadillac."

The ads again focused on beauty, luxury, rich interiors and performance. "Its new power, responsiveness and ease of handling are without counterpart even in Cadillac's glorious past," read one ad. "Car-of-the-future" styling updates made the '57 models stand out.

Changes started with a completely redesigned and lower body. The new front end look included rubber bumper guard tips and dual, circular parking lights set into a lower bumper section. Hooded headlights were lifted directly from the 1954 Park Avenue show car, as were the larger front wheel openings, the curved rooflines and the notched-back roof pillars. New twin-blade ornaments decorated the hood. There was new trim on the body sides and a new, Eldorado-inspired dual taillight grouping.

Underlying the '57 Cadillac's closer-to-the-ground appearance was a new tubular-center X-frame that gave the car greater torsional rigidity. There were 10 body styles with the center post elim-

inated on all models except the Series 75 seven-passenger sedan. The majority of '57s had broad, flat tail fins. The fins were canted towards the front of the car. The 1957 Eldorados had new "shark" fins. They were moved inboard of the rear body corners and blended into a custom-car-like "rolled" (rounded) rear end.

The 365-cid V-8 was retained in all models. It now had a 10.0:1 compression ratio. The Eldorado version again ran dual four-barrel carburetors, with horsepower upped to 325 at 4800 rpm. Standard in all other Cadillacs was the same engine with a single four-barrel carburetor and 300 hp at 4800 rpm. For all Cadillacs to offer over 300 hp was big news. Features of the new 300-hp engine included a redesigned carburetor and larger combustion chambers.

There were no model changes in the base 62 Series, where prices were in the $4,609 to $5,058 range. The regular 62s had a vertical body molding with seven horizontal wind splits just ahead of the rear wheel openings. This trim intersected the horizontal molding on the rear fender "projectile" bulges. The tail fins carried a Cadillac crest medallion. Coupe de Villes and Sedan de Villes had special front fender nameplates. The 62 wheelbase grew by one-half inch. Overall lengths were 215.9 inches for the sedan and Sedan de Ville and 220.9 inches for two-door models.

The Eldorado sub-series was $7,286 for the Seville two-door hardtop (2,100 built) and the Biarritz convertible (1,800 built). It was possible to order an Eldorado Sedan de Ville, but only four customers did. The Eldorado Seville and Biarritz shared the 62 wheelbase, but were 222.1 inches long with their larger rear bumper.

Up front, a special tri-section built-in front bumper was a unique touch. At the rear, the tail fins ran to a single round tail-light. In the center was a V-emblem with the Eldorado name above it. Below this was a chrome license plate recess surrounded by rolled-under body-color body panels. The chrome bumpers swept around each rear body corner and incorporated two pods on either side. One pod held the round back-up light lens and the other was an exit for the exhaust pipe on that side of the car. Eldorados also carried special decorations including wide chrome moldings around the rear wheel openings with chrome beauty panels below them.

The Fleetwood Sixty Special was now a long-deck four-door hardtop, rather than a sedan. It now said "Cadillac" in script on the front fenders, although the deck lid still carried the Fleetwood name above the V-emblem. A bright, ribbed beauty panel decorated a section of the rear doors and the entire lower rear body quarters. The rectangular back-up lights were built into the rear deck lid. With a $5,539 price tag, the Sixty Special saw production of a strong 24,000 units. The model continued the recent tradition of appearing in many of Cadillac's color advertisements.

The all-new Series 70 Eldorado Brougham was the "Rolls-Royce" of Cadillacs. It came out in March, by which time the price had climbed from the original $8,500 estimate to $13,074. This was the production version of the ultra-luxurious Park Avenue and Orleans Motorama show cars. It had a unique custom-car front end treatment with quad headlights, round parking lights below them and a disguised bumper. A sculptured body side cove ended just ahead of the ribbed lower rear quarter beauty panels. The roof was made of brushed stainless steel. Cadillac sold only 400 of these cars, missing its production target by 600 units.

For the first time, the big Fleetwood 75 sedans and limos were not the priciest Cadillacs. The seven-passenger sedan was $7,348 and the Imperial limousine was $7,586. Production of the two models was 1,010 and 890 units, respectively. Cadillac did construct 2,169 Fleetwood 75 chassis for ambulances and funeral cars.

There was no Motorama show in 1957 but Cadillac had Fleetwood craft a mood car named the Director from a Sixty-Special four-door hardtop. Designed to serve as an executive suite on wheels, it incorporated a front passenger seat that swiveled 180 degrees so a secretary could ride and take dictation at the same time. Other special features included a built-in desk, a Dictaphone, a telephone and filing space.

Cadillac's 1957 model year started Nov. 12, 1956, and saw the assembly of 146,840 cars. Calendar-year output of 153,236 was up nine percent from 1956 and only 98 cars short of the all-time record set in 1955.

1958 *Cadillac*

The 1958 Series 70 Cadillac Eldorado Brougham four-door hardtops were hand-built by Cadillac.

It was 1958. Despite the United States economy slowing down, retailers were selling stereo records, Barbie dolls and Hula-Hoops like crazy. NASA arrived and launched its first satellite — the Explorer I. The Yanks took the series 4-to-3, beating the Milwaukee Braves. Alvin the Chipmunk and the Purple People Eater inspired hit tunes. TV Westerns and films like "GiGi" and "Cat on a Hot Tin Roof" topped the charts. In New York City, the Guggenheim Museum represented a break with the past.

Cadillac continued its own break with the past by selling a car that "Outsteps its own great traditions."

Said the company in one ad, "This newest 'car of cars' represents a step beyond its own high standards of excellence."

The car pictured in front of the Del Monte Lodge at Pebble Beach — a Sedan de Ville — was the year's best-selling Cadillac with 23,989 deliveries. Despite the hyperbole, little changed from 1957.

Revisions in 1958 models included new front-end styling including a wider radiator grille with multiple round "cleats" at the intersection of horizontal and vertical members. The rubber-tipped bumper guards shrunk. Quad headlights were used on all models. The Motor Vehicle Manufacturers Association adopted this system, which General Electric had been developing since the 1930s, around 1956. It took two years for state laws to change.

The 1958 Cadillacs also had new fin-type front fender and hood ornaments. On the front fenders of all models, except the Eldorado Brougham, was a wind split ornament. A heavier chrome molding extended from the hooded headlights to the front doors. The rear body side moldings were redesigned and differed a bit on each car line. The tail fins on regular models had more of the Eldorado-type "shark" look.

They came to a point at the rear. Nestled side-by-side in oval-shaped chrome encasements below the tail fins were the circular back-up and taillight lenses. The rear bumper was a straight-across affair, concave in its center, with jet pods at either end. The exhaust exited through louvered vertical openings in each bumper end.

This year's version of the 365-cid V-8 had a 10.25:1 compression ratio and carried a 310-hp rating. Standard in the Eldorado Seville, Eldorado Biarritz and Eldorado Brougham was a 335-hp version with three Rochester two-barrel carburetors. Air suspension was heavily promoted as a 1958 technical advance, but the optional system was leak-prone. Many cars were converted to regular coil springs using a factory-issued, dealer-installed kit.

A new car in the 62 Series — the four-door sedan with extended deck lid — raised the U.S. model count to six. It was 8-1/2 inches longer than other models. Trim on the regular 62 models included Cadillac lettering on the tail fins, five horizontal wind split moldings ahead of the rear wheel openings and Cadillac crests on the front fenders.

A thin bright molding trimmed the rear projectile bulge of half the models, while the Coupe de Ville, Sedan de Ville and convertible had solid metal trim on the lower half of the bulge. On the rear deck lid, a Cadillac crest appeared above the V-shaped emblem. Wide rocker panel moldings were used on these cars.

Cars in the Eldorado 62 sub-series also included a single Special Eldorado Coupe made to customer order. These cars had a model identification script on the trunk and 10 vertical slashes of chrome ahead of the rear wheel openings. The rear quarter panels behind the wheel openings were sheathed in chrome. The distinctive tail fins and "rolled" rear end styling were the same as in 1957, except that the bumper design was changed. There were now "pods" at each side that looked like the nose of a racecar, complete with grilles covering the exhaust outlets. Up-curving pieces with vertical ribs flanked the chrome-framed license plate recess.

The Seville (855 built) and the Biarritz convertible (815 built) both sold for $7,500. The Fleetwood Eldorado Brougham, four-door hardtop, was in its own 70 series. It sold for $13,074 and only 304 were built. The hand-built Brougham — which was on its way out — looked like last year's, but had the upper door panels finished in leather instead of steel. There were new Brougham wheel covers and 44 interior trim combinations were available to coordinate with the 15 special monotone exterior finishes

All-dressed-up-with-places-to-go, the 1958 Fleetwood Sixty Special lived up to its name in looks. The rear body side projectiles wore the heavier chrome trim on their bottom halves and below that were broad, horizontally-ribbed chrome panels and fender skirts above wide rocker panel moldings and chrome underscores that ran entirely to the back of the car. Gold "Sixty Special" scripts appeared on the sides of the tail fins. The Fleetwood name script was on the truck. Power brakes, power steering, power windows and a power seat were standard.

Finishing up Cadillac's offerings were the stately 75 Series Fleetwoods, which were always rarities made for corporate executives and limousine services. Now listed as nine-passenger models, the $8,460 sedan and the $8,675 Imperial Sedan found 802 and 730 buyers, respectively. Another 1,915 Fleetwood 75 commercial chassis were sold.

A sick economy didn't help auto sales, but Cadillac did manage to increase its share of the market in 1958, when it built 2.6 percent of all America's cars (up from 2.4 percent in 1957). The 121,786 cars made in the model year included the two millionth Cadillac ever assembled.

1959 *Cadillac*

Big fins and just plain big were 1959 Cadillac hallmarks, like these Series 62 convertible.

The world was changing in 1959 and some of the revisions were radical. Fidel Castro took over in Cuba. A Russian Lunik III space probe took photos of the moon. Alaska and Hawaii changed the traditional 48-star flag, bringing the state count to 50.

Cadillac's new models were radical. "A new measurement of greatness" said the punch line in one ad, but it's unclear if the copywriter was suggesting measuring the length of the yellow Sedan de Ville or the height of the four-door hardtop's rocket ship-like tail fins. It's universally accepted the year's "Cad-doo" is the official icon of the '50s. Even the U.S. Postal Service honored the distinctive fin and bullet taillight on a postage stamp.

The '59s were longer and lower than '58 models, but the increase in length was not especially dramatic—about a half-inch for most body types. The Series 62 models, the Eldorados and the Sixty Specials shared a 130-inch wheelbase and 225-inch overall length. Heights were in the 54.8- to 56.2-inch range, which was more than a three-inch drop in many cases. Four-door hardtops were slightly higher than the two-door models, of course. The big Fleetwood 75s perched on the same 149.75-inch wheelbase used for years, but were about three inches lower than mid-'50s versions. A new body style was a four-door hardtop with a rear overhang.

Cadillac stroked the overhead-valve V-8 engine's displacement to 390 cubic inches and the compression ratio rose again, this time hitting 10.5:1. The Tri-Power Eldorado version was good for 345 hp and could be added to the other cars as an option. The single-four-barrel V-8 produced 325 hp and was standard in 62s, Sixty Specials and Fleetwood 75s.

A new jeweled-pattern grille greeted visitors to Cadillac showrooms in 1959. A wide horizontal chrome bar ran across the full width of the cars and continued around the front body corners, just below headlight level. Everywhere below this bar was grillework.

The high tail fins dominated the design. A projectile bulge ran horizontally down either side of the fins, with two pointy taillights emanating from the end of these "guided missiles." The chrome trim decorating the fins ran down to meet the bumper ends, which looked like jet engine outlets (with back-up lights in the center). The horizontal bumper was plain, but above it was a full-width beauty panel with the same jeweled texture as the front grille. On the deck lid was a V-shaped emblem and Cadillac crest or other model identification.

The Series 62 models included a straight, sweep spear-type side molding extending from the front wheel opening to the back of the car. A horizontal crest medallion was attached below this molding, on the front fenders. The Coupe de Ville and both Sedan de Villes (four- and six-window) had their model names in script on the rear fenders. These cars did not have the front-fender crest molding but did have a simpler rear grille. Prices for base Cadillacs started at $4,770. The de Villes were put in their own sub-series and priced from $5,252 to $5,498.

All 1959 Eldorado models had the model name on their rear deck lid trim strip. The convertible and two-door hardtop carried other distinctive trim. "Eldorado" was spelled out above the rocker panel moldings, just behind the front wheel openings. A broad, full-length bright metal rocker panel molding connected to a curved upper molding that extended forward from the back-up light pod to the front windshield pillar.

The Eldorado Brougham name was back, but this time it identified a distinctive model that was built by hand at Italian designer Pinin Farina's shop in Turin. This car had totally unique outer body panels that previewed the styling of the 1960 Cadillac, which was somewhat subdued, compared to the '59 version.

These cars featured a graceful-looking slim-pillared roof, a huge and flat non-wraparound windshield, a grille without the horizontal center bar and an overall cleaner look. Only 99 examples of the $13,074 four-door hardtop were created. Note that this Brougham was not a "Fleetwood." It had less standard equipment than earlier editions. Body trim consisted of a front fender crest medallion and a single, front-to-rear-bumper horizontal body side molding.

The Sixty Special came only as a four-door, six-window hardtop. The "Fleetwood" name appeared, in individual block letters, on the front fenders behind the wheel openings. It was also on a trim strip across the bottom of the rear deck lid. On the body sides, two bright metal moldings formed a projectile shape that enclosed a smaller, convex panel, with an air-scoop-type front trim piece, on the rear door and fenders. The Sixty Special also had the full-boat triple-tier rear grille arrangement.

The long-wheelbase Fleetwood 75s came in the same models and both got a little rarer. Production of the nine-passenger sedan peaked at just 710 and the Imperial sedan drew just 690 orders. However, the number of commercial chassis Cadillac sold rose a bit to 2,102.

Did the '59 Cadillacs sell when new? The answer is a qualified yes. Things would have been better, had it not been for a steel strike that forced the Cadillac factory to close. Model-year production was 142,272, an increase from 1958.

The brand's market penetration dropped 3/10ths of a percent. But company sales executives said they could have set an all-time divisional record if the strike had not occurred. By June, deliveries to U.S. customers had hit 77,134—the highest ever for any Cadillac model year.

Chevrolets
of the Fifties

1950 *Chevrolet*

In 1950, the Chevrolet Styleline Deluxe convertible sold more than 32,300 copies.

The "baseball-and-apple-pie" crowd tried to enjoy postwar prosperity in 1950, even though fighting between North and South Korea was threatening to explode into another global conflict. Average Americans watched the New York Yankees trounce the "Whiz Kids" Philadelphia Phillies 4-to-0 in the World Series. They viewed "Arthur Godfrey and Friends" on the 14 million black-and-white TV sets they bought that year.

And they flocked to their local Chevrolet dealerships in record numbers to see the exciting new Bel Air "hardtop convertible." There was certainly nothing akin to it in the low-priced market segment. Chevrolet's model-year production, which had been as low as 745,138 cars as recently as 1948, peaked at an all-time high of 1,387,828 units during 1950.

Chevrolet's advertising had an "educational" look in 1950, with illustrations of Chevrolet cars and their owners beside text explaining that the product was "first . . . and finest . . . at lowest cost." In some ads, the "first" was subjective, such as first in value or first in beauty; in others first was objective and referred to features like the new Powerglide automatic transmission (the sluggish, two-speed, cast-iron-case type). Likewise, the Chevy could be viewed as "finest by every measure of value" or "finest for powerful Valve-in-Head thrills."

When it came to price, Chevy's advantage was there, in black-and-white, for everyone to understand. The lowest-price Plymouth retailed for $1,371, the lowest-priced Ford cost $1,333, and the lowest-priced Chevrolet model listed for $1,329!

The '50 Chevys had the "envelope" body introduced in 1949. This terminology referred to the front fenders being flush with the outer door skins instead of bulging out like those on "fat-fendered" prewar-style models (which were, of course, carried over without major change until 1948). The rear fenders also stuck out less than those of "old-fashioned" cars, although they still looked like stuck-on pontoons. The lower part of the grille lost a few vertical elements and the new hood emblem had wings above it, instead of on

the side. Taller bumper guards gave better frontal protection.

There were two basic styles of 1950 Chevrolet bodies. The first was the "bustle back," which is usually referred to as a "notch back" today. The bustle back cars were called Styleline models. The convertible and the station wagon were also considered part of this line. Also available were two- and four-door "fastback" bodies. These were known as Fleetline models. The fastbacks were a bit sportier looking, but they had a prewar flavor to them, which soon caused them to lose favor in the forward-looking '50s. By the mid-'50s fastback styling would disappear for about 10 years.

In 1950, both the Styleline and Fleetline cars came with low-end "Special" trim or high-end "Deluxe" trim, although you could not get all models both ways. Some particular body styles, like the Styleline convertible, the Styleline Bel Air two-door hardtop and the Styleline station wagon, came only with Deluxe trim. The Deluxe trim "package" included fender skirts, chrome body side moldings, "Deluxe" script nameplates on the front fenders, windshield reveal moldings, chrome rear fender shields and richer interior trims and upholstery. Some models had gray striped broadcloth material with off-the-shoulder dark gray contrast panels, while others had vinyl or leather-trimmed seats.

Models available in the lower-priced Styleline Special series included two- and four-door sedans, a Sport Coupe, and a Business coupe. The latter had a single three-passenger bench seat up front and only a raised platform in the rear compartment. That was for salesmen to store their luggage and sample cases on. The business coupe was always a real "stripper" and always the lowest-priced model. Chevy made 20,984 business coupes in 1950, but you never see them at car shows.

The Fleetline Special line offered the same two- and four-door sedans available in the Fleetline Deluxe series. Even the most expensive Chevy — the four-door, eight-passenger station wagon — was priced below $2,000.

Chevy's tried-and-true 216.5-cid valve-in-head straight six was again under the hood. Essentially, this engine dated back 38 years. There had been refinements over that period, but not a heck of a lot of them mattered very much. The four-main-bearings, solid-lifter power plant put out 90 hp at 3300 rpm. When the new-for-1950 Powerglide option was ordered for $159 extra, a 235-cid in-line "truck" engine rated at 105 hp was used. This was the most powerful engine offered in a low-priced car in 1950.

It is also important to appreciate the fact that Plymouth and Ford did not offer optional automatic transmissions in 1950.

"Nowhere else in the entire field of low-priced cars, such a happy choice of driving methods and engine performance as this," boasted one Chevrolet ad. "You may have the finest no-shift driving at lowest cost by choosing a Chevrolet embodying the sensational Powerglide Automatic Transmission teamed with Chevrolet's 105-hp Valve-in-Head Engine."

All Chevrolets were built on a 115-inch wheelbase chassis. The sturdy box-girder frame was more ruggedly constructed than ever

before. The station wagon was 198.5 inches long and the other cars were an inch shorter. A torque tube connected the standard three-speed manual (or optional Powerglide) transmission to a semi-floating rear axle with hypoid drive. Standard equipment included 6.70 x 15 tires.

Every selling feature of the '50 Chevrolet seemed to have its own promotional name, and a couple even shared the same one. For example, one ad mentioned "Center-Point" steering and another referred to "Center-Point" seating. (Do you think someone made a mistake?) Other features included "Unitized Knee-Action Gliding Ride," "Proved Certi-Safe Hydraulic Brakes," "Panoramic Visibility," "Five-Foot" seats and "Silent Synchro-Mesh" transmission.

By the end of 1950, Chevrolet's calendar-year production was reported as 1,521,000 units, which meant that Chevrolet supplied 42.4 percent of all low-priced American cars and 22.78 percent of all domestic cars. The new 235-cid engine and Powerglide transmission were installed in 300,000 of those vehicles.

1951 *Chevrolet*

The 1951 Chevrolet Fleetline Deluxe two-door and sedan featured fastback styling.

The world seemed to be in an ongoing state of flux in 1951. In Korea, General Douglas MacArthur was relieved of his command. In Washington, D.C., Congress passed the 22nd Amendment, limiting a President to two terms. In New York City, CBS completed the first color-television broadcast. Yet, some things never change. The Yankees took the World Series from the "Jints" and Chevrolet was again America's best-selling automobile. "More people buy Chevrolet's than any other car!" was the truthful slogan seen in many of the carmaker's 1951 promotions.

A cleaner 1951 grille featured a lower section with no vertical bars that "looped" around the front parking lamps. The wings on

the hood emblem stuck straight out, while the Chevrolet emblem shrunk. Overall styling was the same as 1950, although Chevrolet hyped it as "New American Beauty Design" and claimed "brilliant new styling." That meant that the grille, parking lights, fender moldings and rear-end were revised to give the cars a "wider" appearance.

The Styleline Special had no chrome body strip, while the similar Styleline Deluxe had a chrome strip and Deluxe lettering. The fastback Fleetline two- and four-door sedans came in both trim levels. Again there were 14 models in the Chevrolet lineup for the 1951 model year.

Chevrolet adopted more powerful "Jumbo-Drum" brakes that had 15 percent more lining area and required 25 percent less pedal pressure. A curved "Safety-Sight" instrument panel had all instruments compactly grouped in two clusters and lighting that eliminated glare. Chevrolet's 1951 features included two-tone "Modern Mode" interiors, a new full-circle horn ring (in Deluxe models) Fisher Body construction, an overhead-valve in-line six-cylinder engine, improved "Center Point" steering, rivetless brake lining, "Knee-Action" front suspension, wide-base wheel rims, a standard Synchromesh transmission, hydraulic valve lifters (in the Powerglide engine), "Reflector-Guard" taillights, a large storage space area, torque-tube drive, a sealed exhaust system, a "Tip-Toe" clutch (with manual transmission), airplane-type shock absorbers, low-pressure tires, foam rubber seats, curved two-piece windshields and a counter-balanced crankshaft.

Model availability was the same as in 1950. Prices climbed a bit. The low-priced Styleline Special business coupe now listed for $1,460. All models in the base series sold worse than in 1950, except for the bustle-back four-door sedan. The popularity of the fastback Fleetline Special models took a huge dive: only 6,441 of the old-fashioned-looking two-doors and 3,364 of the similar four-doors were built. In 1950, the production totals had been 23,277 and 43,682, respectively!

Chevrolet's fancier Deluxe sedans sold better in 1951 and the sporty Bel Air saw a very nice production increase as well. On the other hand, convertible production fell from 32,810 in 1950 to 20,172 in '51 and the numbers of station wagons built dropped rather drastically (from 166,995 to 23,588). The fastbacks also lost popularity, with the four-door's production declining from 124,287 to 57,693 and the two-door's numbers declining to 131,910 from 189,509.

This year the 216.5-cid solid-lifter version of the "Stovebolt" six had a 6.6:1 compression ratio and 92 hp at 3400 rpm. The hydraulic-lifter 235.5-cid version used in Powerglide-equipped cars used a 6.7:1 compression ratio and delivered 105 hp at 3600 rpm. This combination was installed in 431,450 Chevrolets during calendar-year 1951. However, part of the reason this growth was somewhat modest was that the National Production Agency placed quotas on the number of automatics built to save aluminum and scarce steel alloys for the Korean War effort. In fact, the agency cut Chevrolet's installation rate on this option from 40 percent to 35 percent and held it there despite two appeals by General Motors.

Dealer introductions of the 1951 Chevrolet models were held on Dec. 8, 1950. The division's model-year production totaled 1,250,803 units. Calendar year sales were 1,118,096 cars, which represented 20.94 percent of the auto industry's total output. Although all of these numbers were decreased from 1950, Chevrolet remained America's number one automaker.

As its share of national defense work for the Korean Conflict, Chevrolet also tackled some huge military-production contracts. On July 20, the automaker announced that it was going to build $20,800,000 facilities in Tonawanda, New York, to supplement a government-owned plant there, to create additional capacity for the production of Wright R3350 aircraft engines. On October 2, Chevy disclosed plans to put up a $30 million aviation engine plant in Flint, Michigan. It was to double the manufacturing capacity for Wright R3350-26W and R3350-30W engines.

1952 *Chevrolet*

The 1952 Chevrolet Styleline Deluxe Bel Air two-door hardtop continued to be popular.

Comedy was big in 1952, as a war-weary America struggled to laugh its way past the failure of truce attempts in Korea. "Our Miss Brooks," the "Jackie Gleason Show," "I Love Lucy," "The Adventures of Ozzie and Harriet" and the "George Burns and Gracie Allen Show" were big hits on television. Dr. Jonas Salk's creation of the polio vaccine was a positive development and drug companies praised the use of chlorophyll in food and medicine as a scientific advance (although this would later be questioned). Chevrolet ads were selling the happy, positive points of Chevy ownership – "Pleasure? . . . Full measure! Price? . . . Pleasant surprise!"

Chevrolet's sales promotions were largely based on the concept that it offered the features of a high-priced car at the industry's lowest prices. To a degree this was true, as Chevy ownership gave you the same Fisher body quality found in a Cadillac and the option of ordering an automatic transmission — a high-priced car feature in those days.

Chevrolet's new-for-1952 grille had five vertical "teeth." They were spaced out across a horizontal center divider. The "floating" parking lamps were in the lower grille opening. The wider new nose emblem displayed the Chevrolet name and below it a "bow-tie" logo. Where Chevy fell down a bit, however, was in its lack of a V-8 engine. Ford had it beat in this regard and it would start to matter more and more in the next few years.

Chevrolet's calendar-year production did take a steep 21 percent drop in 1952, but it was handicapped more by wartime production controls than anything else. Like other automakers, Chevrolet had plenty of civilian orders — it just couldn't fill them all. It did lose 7/10ths of a point of market share, while Ford gained more than a whole point, but Chevy maintained the all-important number one sales position that it had held since 1935, for the seventh consecutive postwar season. Chevy's annual output included the one millionth car to get a Powerglide automatic transmission bolted into it.

The plainer Special Series no longer included Fleetline fastback models, which were being phased out of production. All Specials had bustle-back styling. They lacked chrome body side moldings and had rubber gravel deflectors and unshielded rear wheelhousings. Nine exterior colors and four two-tone combinations were provided for all sedans, Sport Coupes and business coupes, including Styleline Specials. Two-tone gray interiors were featured, with seat upholstery done in checkered pattern cloth. The four models ranged in price from $1,519 to $1,659 and only one — the Sport Coupe — had less than five-figure production. With 8,906 assemblies, it was the rarest 1952 Chevy, but the Business Coupe was right behind it, with 10,359 built.

Chevrolet's Styleline and Fleetline Deluxe models had body side moldings on the front fenders and doors, bright metal rear fender gravel guards with extensions, fender-skirts, and Deluxe script logos directly above the gravel guards on the rear fender pontoons. Bright metal windshield and window reveals were seen. A two-spoke steering wheel, with full blowing ring, replaced the three-spoke Special-type with horn button. Deluxes also had ivory plastic control knobs with bright metal inserts, dome lamps with automatic door switches, two inside sun visors and richer interior trims with foam rubber cushions. Upholstery combinations were reversed, with dark gray chevron pattern cloth and lighter toned upper contrast panels. As usual, convertibles, Bel Airs and station wagons had their own exclusive trim.

Bel Airs came only in the Deluxe line and could be ordered in one of four solid colors or 11 two-tone combinations. Convertibles came in 10 colors with five different top-color tops. Station wagons offered four finishes in combination with woodgrained trim panels. The Fleetline Deluxe coupe was the sole surviving fastback. Prices for the seven Deluxe models started off at $1,696 and the convertible ($2,113) and station wagon ($2,281) were the highest-priced Chevrolets. These models had production runs of 11,975 and 12,756 respectively.

Dealer introductions began Jan. 19, 1952. Model-year production reached 827,317 units, despite Korean War manufacturing limitations. Calendar-year production totaled 877,947 vehicles despite the effects of the war (whitewall tires were uncommon and an inferior chrome plating process was used). The 28-millionth U.S. or Canadian Chevrolet car or truck was built, amid some fanfare, in December 1952.

1953 *Chevrolet*

It seemed like the whole world was traveling in 1953. Baseball's Boston Braves relocated to Milwaukee, Wisconsin and the St. Louis Browns moved to Baltimore, Maryland to become the Orioles. Explorer Sir Edmund Hillary traveled to the summit of Mount Everest, while Americans traveled to movie theaters to watch films, like "Roman Holiday" and "I Love Paris" that featured faraway destinations they could travel to on vacation. In the hit tune "Doggie in the Window," singer Patti Page wondered how a certain doggie in the window of a pet store would cost, since she had to take a trip to California and needed a watchdog.

Chevrolet's advertising department must have been inspired by the travel trend. "Why is it, wherever people travel, you see more Chevrolets than any other car?" asked one '53 Bel Air advertisement.

All 1953 Chevrolets featured a new curved, one-piece windshield and more rounded "Fashion-First" body styling. They were grouped into three series. The Bel Air name was now used to identify all four body styles in the top-of-the-line series, rather than just the two-door hardtop. This car-line was added to the top of the model range, above the old Special and Deluxe categories. The total of 17 models in all series marketed in 1953 was the most ever offered by Chevrolet in one model year.

The low-rung Chevrolet Special 150 models were plain and had black rubber gravel shields on the front edge of the rear fenders. The sport coupe became the "club coupe" and there was a new "Handyman" station wagon. Inside, there was a standard steering wheel, a single sun visor and plain upholstery. The One-Fifty station wagon had Safety Sheet side door windows in place of Safety Plate glass. Prices ranged from $1,524 for the Business Coupe to $2,010 for the wagon.

The mid-range Deluxe 210 models had chrome body side moldings, chrome window moldings and bright metal gravel shields ahead of the rear wheel openings. The pillarless hardtop was not called a Bel Air. The six-passenger station wagon with

The 1953 Chevrolet Bel Air two-door hardtop featured a unique roofline.

folding second seat was called the "Handyman" (as was the same version with Special trim). The eight-passenger station wagon was called the "Townsman." The Townsman had three seats, the second and third units being stationary, but completely removable. It also had Safety Plate glass side windows. A 210 convertible was available, but only in the early part of the year. For a Chevy, this was a rare model, as only 5,617 were built. Seven models made up the 210 line at the start of the year. They were priced between $1,707 and $2,273.

Deluxe equipment also included a two-spoke steering wheel with horn ring, a cigarette lighter, an ashtray, dual sun visors and a 39-hour stem-wind clock. Heaters and radios were optional. When they were not ordered, blocker plates were used to cover dashboard holes The interior door handles had bright metal inserts in the black plastic knobs. Other interior appointments included foam rubber seat cushion pads in the front seats and in the rear seats of sedans and coupes, front armrests in all models, rear armrests in sedans and coupes, and bright metal moldings on the rear quarter panels of sedans and coupes.

Bel Airs had a double molding treatment on the rear fenders (rear door and fenders on four-door models) with a contrasting color band with a Bel Air script and Chevrolet crest. The rear wheel openings were shielded by fender skirts. Bel Airs also featured double windshield pillar moldings, extra wide window reveals on sedans, saddle moldings on sport coupes and convertibles, exposed bright metal roof bows and dashboard mounted rearview mirrors. The upholstery materials were a few notches up the luxury scale. Prices ranged from $1,620 for the Bel Air two-door sedan to $2,175 for the convertible.

Two new "Thrift-King" versions of Chevrolet's 235-cid "Blue-Flame" overhead valve in-line six offered 108 and 115 hp, respectively. The more powerful version was available, with Powerglide transmission only, in the 210 and Bel Air models. The Powerglide

engine now had a new full-pressure-lubrication system. New "Velvet-Pressure Jumbo-Drum" brakes were easier to operate and power steering was a new extra-cost option. Also new was ignition-key starting.

All of the redesigned Chevrolets rode on a 115-inch wheelbase. The overall length was 195-1/2 inches for passenger cars and 197-7/6 inches for station wagons. Chevrolet specified 7.10 x 15 tires for the convertible with Powerglide; 6.70 x 15 six-ply for the Townsman station wagon and 6.70 x 15 four-ply for all other models.

Dealer introductions of the 1953 models occurred in January 1953. A month later, with the signing of the Korean Armistice, the government dropped manufacturing restriction on automakers. Production almost immediately zoomed and Chevrolet and Ford were soon locked in a bitter, neck-to-neck car-sales race. Chevrolet had been America's best-selling nameplate since 1935, but Ford — which had the V-8, a new automatic transmission and the hot-selling Victoria hardtop — was threatening to steal that honor away. Things got downright nasty, with Chevy just about calling its rival an "also-ran."

Said one advertisement:

"This year the preference for Chevrolet is greater than ever. Latest available figures for 1953 show that over 200,000 more people have bought Chevrolets than the second-choice car!"

By the time the dust had cleared, Chevrolet was still ahead. Model-year production totaled 1,375,403 versus Ford's 1,240,000. Calendar-year production reached 1,477,299 Chevrolets against 1,184,187 Fords.

Chevrolet sold 24.08 percent of America's cars, while Ford had to be satisfied with 19.30 percent.

1954 *Chevrolet*

The first successful kidney transplant was carried out in 1954, which proved to be a year of spectacular achievements in many other fields as well. At the New York Stock

Exchange, prices reached their highest level since 1929. Also in the "Big Apple," the New York Giants won the World Series 4-zip over Cleveland (although the big baseball news was Cleveland's

The most popular 1954 Chevrolet was the Bel Air sedan shown here in twin form.

taking the American League title, after five straight years of New York Yankee league championships and Series victories). Out in California, Walt Disney Studios scored a major hit with its "Tales of Davy Crockett," a blockbuster television show that sent sales of "coonskin" caps soaring.

In the automotive world, Chevy was successful in hanging on to top position on the sales charts, although Ford put up a fight and some other manufacturers were doing their part to chip away at giant Chevrolet's hold on the market.

As *Ward's 1955 Automotive Yearbook* put it, "Although Chevy's hefty wallop rang the 1954 production bell loudest, several other manufacturers made more spectacular showings." Buick took over third place from the low-priced Plymouth, Oldsmobile went from seventh to fourth and Cadillac was up to ninth, a big gain from its old 13th spot. Buick, Olds, Cadillac and Ford actually boosted their output over 1953, which no other automakers managed to do. Each gain took away a little chip out of Chevy's market share. But, on the plus side, Chevy racked up its 18th consecutive first-place finish!

The 1954 Chevrolet was modestly changed, although the few alterations made in the cars seemed to greatly update their looks. A full-width grille made the bodies seem lower. The bumpers got new curved ends that made them look wider, too. The taillight housings were brighter and had a "tail fin" appearance. The line-up included 13 separate models. In addition to power steering (which cost less than in 1953), the '54 Chevrolets offered the low-priced line's first power brakes, but only on cars with Powerglide transmission. New electrically-operated Automatic Window and Seat Controls were available as an extra-cost option in Two-Ten and Bel Air models.

The plain-looking One-Fifty (or 150) Special had black window crank knobs and plainer interior appointments "smartly fashioned of durable materials." A black rubber windshield surround, rubber gravel guards and "bottle cap" hubcaps were among identifiers. The club coupe was gone and the business coupe was renamed the utility sedan, although it still had no back seat and a raised rear-compartment load floor instead. Powerglide automatic transmission was now available in One-Fiftys, which had Powerglide badges on their rear deck lids.

Two-Ten (or 210) Deluxe models had chrome moldings on the body sides, windshield, windows and rocker panels. Bright metal gravel guards protected the bulges at the fronts of the rear fenders. Genuine carpets covered the rear compartment floor. The cloth seats came in four colors and had vinyl contrast panels. The club coupe—called the "Del Ray"—featured all-vinyl, waffle-pattern upholstery and matching two-tone door panels. The Two-Ten "Handyman" wagon was upholstered in long-wearing vinyl with contrasting colors, including horizontally-ribbed door panels. The Two-Ten convertible and "Townsman" wagon were dropped.

Identifying all Bel Airs were full-length sweep spear moldings, double moldings on the rear fenders (enclosing a Bel Air script and Chevrolet crest), double windshield pillar moldings, window surround moldings, body belt moldings, rocker panel moldings, metal gravel guards and fender skirts. Newly-designed full-wheel discs, horizontally-ribbed vinyl door panels, an electric clock and full carpeting helped make the flagship models dressier.

The Bel Air two-door hardtop — called a "Sport Coupe" — had special "Fashion Fiesta" two-tone upholstery, rear pillar courtesy lights, chrome-plated inside roof garnish moldings, a chrome rear window frame and bright metal exposed roof bows. The convertible interior seemed even richer, with two-tone all-vinyl trims and a snap-on boot cover. The rearview mirror was no longer mounted atop the dashboard. There was a new Bel Air Townsman station wagon with Chevrolet's highest price tag ($2,263) and lowest production (8,156 units). The other closed cars cost $10 more than their 1953 counterparts

Chevrolet horsepower increases were part of the company's sales battle with Ford and the Dearborn-based manufacturer upped the ante this season by introducing an overhead-valve V-8 with 25 percent more horsepower than its old flathead V-8. Chevrolet's sturdy "Stovebolt" sixes could not match that, but they did stay competitive with Ford's base 223-cid 115-hp six. The stick-shift Chevy six went to a 7.5:1 compression ratio and was rated for 115 hp at 3700 rpm. The Powerglide version had the same compression ratio, but gained a new high-lift camshaft, full-pressure lubrication system and aluminum pistons with 125 hp at 4000 rpm.

Some sources say that Ford actually out-produced Chevrolet on a model-year basis this season and that Chevrolet dumped cars on dealers to increase factory shipments and capture first place on a calendar-year basis. The figures reported in industry trade journals do not support this contention.

They show Chevrolet with model-year production of 1,185,073 cars versus 1,165,942 for Ford and calendar-year production of 1,414,385 cars against 1,394,762 for Ford. However, the blue-oval brand did well enough to account for 25.31 percent of all car assemblies compared to 19.30 percent a year ear-

lier. Chevrolet's 25.67 percent was still tops, even though it represented a less than two percent jump.

Chevrolet produced its 8 millionth postwar car early in 1954. On June 23, the 31 millionth Chevrolet of all time was put togethar at the company's Tarrytown, New York assembly plant. On August 15th, the 2 millionth car with Powerglide transmission was produced.

1955 *Chevrolet*

Chevrolets, like the Bel Air hardtop, were new from end-to-end and V-8 powered.

"The 1955 Brooklyn Dodgers "stole the show" when they defeated the New York Yankees in a down-to-the-wire, 4-to-3 "subway series" baseball championship. Television's new "Gunsmoke" series, which had been a hit on radio for years, had Marshal Matt Dillon (James Arness) as its star, but saloon-keeper Kitty (Amanda Blake), Doc Adams (Milburn Stone), and sidekick/deputy Chester Goode (Dennis Weaver) often stole the spotlight. In Hollywood that year, it was actor Earnest Borgnine who "snuck" into stardom with his portrayal of a lonely, unmarried middle-aged man who's liberated by love.

In Detroit, Chevrolet advertisements claimed that the all-new '55 models were "Stealing the Show from the High-Priced Cars" and "Stealing the Thunder from the High-Priced Cars."

With Ford's constantly-growing market share, it was no longer prudent to sell Chevrolets based on the "America's-best-selling-car" theme.

Without admitting that there was a strong challenge to its sales supremacy, Chevrolet upgraded its image by promoting its products against higher-priced cars, rather than its low-priced rival.

With all of its new styling and technical features, the now-classic '55 Chevy was formidable competition for many makes. Its upgraded image pushed model-year output to 1,766,013 units versus 1,435,002 for Ford, despite the fact that the lowest-priced '55 Chevy cost $45 more than the lowest-priced Ford.

A Ferrari-inspired egg-crate grille, a flatter hood, visored headlights, new bumpers and parking lights, and a restyled hood orna-

ment made the front look different. Wraparound windshields and "Contour Cut" dips in the rear fenders or doors looked sportier. Other new styling elements included redesigned taillights and new Bel Air trim. A compact, overhead valve V-8 was available. Its "over-square" design meant less piston travel, less friction and less wear.

Also new were tubeless tires, a ball-joint front suspension, Anti-Dive braking, a 12-volt electrical system, Ball-Race steering, Touch-Down overdrive (for manual transmission cars), suspended brake and clutch pedals, high-level ventilation, push-button door handles and Hotchkiss drive in place of the old torque-tube drive system.

The One-Fifty series was Chevrolet's "grocery-getter" line and included all of the closed-bodied models you typically seen at the strip mall on Saturday morning when you went to shop at Sears or J.C. Penney. There were the two- and four-door sedans, as well as the "utility coupe" made for supermarket salesmen, along with the two-door station wagon (two less doors for a lower price).

While one might suppose that these bread-and-butter machines were made to please "most of the people most of the time," they were far from the best-selling models. Using the four-door sedan as an example, model-year production of this body style was 29,898 in the low-run series, 317,724 in the mid-range Two-Ten line and 345,372 in the Bel Air series. The real importance of these entry-level cars was Chevrolet could get folks into the showrooms, where salesmen could sell them a Two-Ten or a Bel Air.

The One-Fiftys were pretty plain, with rubber floor mats, S-spring (instead of foam rubber) seats and exterior trim limited to a Chevrolet script on front fender, chrome headlight rims and "bottle cap" hub caps. The six-cylinder-powered cars were priced from $1,593 to $2,030 and V-8s were about $100 more. The single-seat Utility Coupe was actually the year's second-rarest model with 11,196 built. Only the Bel Air Nomad station wagon had a lower production total. The funny thing is, you never see these Style No. 55-1211B ("B" for "business") coupes today. Do you think someone had an aftermarket business going putting rear seats in them for used-car dealers?

Moving one rung up the Chevrolet pricing ladder was the Two-Ten. It got a little racier by adding a Sport Coupe (two-door hardtop) of which only 11,675 were built. Other less dramatic added body styles were the Club Coupe and a four-door station wagon. Two-Ten trim added stainless steel windshield and backlight reveals, chrome front seat and sidewall moldings, a glove compartment light, ash trays, a cigarette lighter, armrests and assist straps. Additional exterior bright metal decoration included upper beltline and rear fender side and sash moldings. Two-Tens cost roughly $90 more than a comparable One-Fifty.

Buyers who wanted to spend about $100-$150 above Two-Ten prices could get a dressy-looking Bel Air — Chevrolet's "little Cadillac." Standard equipment on top-of-the-line models included carpets on closed body styles, a chrome ribbed headliner on the Sport Coupe, richer upholstery fabrics, horizontal chrome strips on sides of front fender and doors, narrow white-painted inserts on the rear fender horizontal side moldings, gold Bel Air scripts and Chevrolet crests behind slanting vertical sash moldings, ribbed vertical trim plates on the body sides (above the rear bumper ends), wide chrome window and door post reveal moldings and full-wheel discs.

Two fancy station wagons were available in the Bel Air line, the four-door Beauville and the Nomad two-door station wagon with special hardtop styling, which was introduced as a mid-year model. In addition to its pillarless roofline, the Nomad had enlarged rear wheel openings and special slat moldings on its roof and forward-slanting tailgate. It looked cleaner than other Bel Airs, as all rear fender trim was deleted. Only 6,103 Nomads were made.

In addition to the Nomad — which was inspired by a Corvette-based Motorama station wagon dream car — the Bel Air Sport Coupe and convertible have become hotly-collected models over the years. The Sport Coupe, which was priced at $2,067 as a six and $2,186 with a V-8, was promoted as having a "great profile" and the customers who bought 185,562 copies must have agreed. The convertible—$2,206 with the six and $2,305 with the base V-8—was featured in one of the most memorable car advertisements, which illustrated a Coral-and-Shadow Gray ragtop at the 1955 Pebble Beach Concours d' Elegance.

"Wherever cars are judged . . . for elegance, for comfort, for beauty of line and excellence of design . . . a surprising thing is happening," said the ad copy. "The spotlight is focusing on the new Chevrolets with Body by Fisher."

The base 235-cid Stovebolt six came in two versions. The 123-hp solid-valve-lifter version was used in stick-shift cars. A 136-hp edition with hydraulic valve lifters was standard with Powerglide, but optionally available in other Chevys. The all-new Turbo-Fire V-8 engine options started with the 265-cid, 162-hp two-barrel engine. Also offered was a "Power-Pack" version with a four-barrel carburetor and 180 hp.

In terms of sales and production, 1955 was a record season for Chevrolet with model-year deliveries peaking at 1,830,038 units. That represented a 26.5 percent increase over 1954 and kept Chevrolet at the top of the industry's chart. Chevrolet's overall share on the market was 23.04 percent, a figure that the company would die for today. With its great popularity, the 1955 Chevrolet Bel Air convertible was selected to serve as the Official Pace Car for the Indianapolis 500-Mile Race.

1956 Chevrolet

The heat was on in 1956. Bullets flew when Egypt seized the Suez Canal. In Cuba, Fidel Castro kicked off his seemingly hopeless revolution. In Hungary, the Soviet Union smashed an anti-communist movement with hot bullets. In baseball, the Yankees heated up again, beating the Brooklyn Dodges, in the World Series, four-games-to-three. In books, the hottest reading was Grace Metalious' Peyton Place. And at Chevrolet, things were more tepid than ever before. "The Hot One's Even Hotter," said the company's fiery ads.

The number of optional versions of the 265-cid overhead-valve "small-block" V-8 was expanded to four — and two of those were rated above 200 hp. Used as the base V-8 in stick-shift cars was the same 162-hp engine introduced in 1955. The base Powerglide engine was largely the same, but carried a higher 170-hp rating. The Power-Pack engine of 1955 became the "Turbo-Fire 205" V-8, which had a 9.25:1 compression ratio, a single four-barrel carburetor and dual exhausts. It developed 205 hp at 4600 rpm and 268 foot-pounds of torque at 3000 rpm. The most powerful option was a Corvette engine that cranked up 225 hp at 5200 rpm and 270 foot-pounds of torque at 3600 rpm.

The Chevrolet V-8s weighed less than the division's six-cylinder engines, which resulted in an outstanding power-to-weight ratio — one reason why the 1956 Chevrolet V-8s became known as the "Hot Ones." Jim Wangers — an advertising executive employed by Chevrolet's ad agency, Campbell Ewald — was an avid high-performance enthusiast. Wangers was instrumental in establishing Chevrolet's 1956 "The Hot One's Even Hotter!" advertising campaign. He promoted the idea of driving a '56 up Pikes Peak to set a new record.

Afterwards, Wangers used the Pike's Peak climb record in advertisements that he wrote:

"Nothing without wings climbs like a '56 Chevrolet! Aim this new Chevrolet up a steep grade–and you'll see why it's the Pikes Peak record breaker. Ever level off a mountain with your foot? Just point this new '56 Chevy uphill and ease down on the gas. In the merest fraction of a second you sense that big bore V-8 lengthening out its stride. And up you go with a silken rush of power that makes a mountain road seem as flat as a roadmap. For nothing without wings climbs like a '56 Chevrolet! This is the car, you know, that broke the Pikes Peak record. The car that proved its

The Bel Air Nomad station wagon continued to be the rarest Chevrolet in 1956.

fired-up performance, cat-sure cornering ability and nailed-down stability on the rugged, twisting Pikes Peak road. And all these qualities mean more driving safety and pleasure for you."

Chevrolet's sassy "Motoramic" styling for 1956 included a full-width grille, large rectangular front parking lamps, new front and rear bumpers and guards (except station wagons), inward angled dome-shaped taillights with back-up lights set into chrome-ribbed decorative housings and squarer headlight visors. The left-hand taillight housing now "hid" the fuel filler. New models included a Bel Air Sports Sedan (four-door hardtop) and nine-passenger 210 and Bel Air wagons. Chevy promoted "Glide-Ride" front suspension, Anti-Dive braking, tubeless tires, "Outrigger" rear springs, new Precision-Aimed headlights and a new Longer-Life battery.

One-Fifty models now had chrome moldings around the windshield and rear window and a horizontal body side moldings that ran from just behind the headlights to a point below the rear side window, where they were intersected by slanting sash moldings with windsplit-style indentations. Standard equipment included a two-spoke steering wheel with horn ring, one sun visor, a lockable glovebox, a dome light, cloth-and-vinyl upholstery (all-vinyl on station wagons), black rubber floor mats and small hubcaps. Prices rose about $140 for the same four models offered previously.

Chevrolet Two-Tens had chrome on the side window sills. On the body sides, a single horizontal molding swept from the front headlights to the rear bumper ends and a sash molding intersected it below the rear side window. All models had two sun visors, ashtrays, a cigarette lighter and upgraded interior trims. The Del Ray coupe featured deep-pile carpets and all-vinyl upholstery, while other Two-Tens had vinyl-coated rubber floor mats and vinyl-and-cloth upholstery. A Sport Sedan was added to the line. Prices were a modest $80-$90 higher than One-Fifty prices. The Two-Ten's role in the Chevy lineup was more important this year. In 1955, the division had made 786,307 Two-Tens and 770,955 Bel Airs. In 1956, the totals were 737,371 Two-Tens and just 669,053 Bel Airs.

Bel Airs had model nameplates and emblems on their rear fenders. On these models, the slanting sash molding blended into a horizontal chrome belt that ran forward to the headlight crease, then doubled back and swept down towards the rear bumper. Full wheel covers were standard. There was an extra chrome treatment around and between all window groups.

Three-spoke steering wheels and deep-pile carpets graced all models except the Beauville nine-passenger station wagon, which had vinyl-coated-rubber floor mats. The convertible (41,268 built) and Nomad (7,886 built) were found only in this series. Bel Airs had electric clocks and lighted, lockable glove compartments.

All Chevys shared a 115-inch wheelbase. Station wagons were 200.8 inches long and other models were 197.5 inches long. The tread width was 58 inches up front and 58.9 inches in the rear. The tires used were 6.70 x 15 six-ply on nine-passenger models and 6.70 x 15 four-ply otherwise, but 7.10 x 15 four-ply tires were optional.

Generally speaking, 1956 was a year in which sales and production of American cars both declined. Logically, this might have been anticipated after a record-busting 1955 — but Detroit isn't logical and most manufacturers had projected increases. Not that 1956 was a bad year at all.

As *Ward's 1957 Automotive Yearbook* noted, "Their sorrow was not entirely justified, however, for actually, the only measure by which 1956 appeared logy was in comparison to 1955, the most productive period in industry history." In numerical terms, total vehicle sales dropped 18.3 percent to $11.8 billion. Production of 5,816,109 passenger cars was actually the third highest ever, surpassed only by 1955's total of 7,920,186 and 1950's total of 6,116,948.

Chevrolet's model-year production was 1,574,740 units. Calendar-year production hit 1,621,005. With Ford counting 1,373,542 assemblies for the calendar-year, Chevrolet was once again crowned America's number one automaker.

1957 *Chevrolet*

The 1957 Chevrolet Bel Air convertible stands out in the natural surroundings.

The youth movement was in motion and American was getting "hipper" in 1957. "Wake Up Little Susie," "That'll Be the Day," and "Jailhouse Rock" were among the year's be-bopping Top Ten hits. "American Bandstand" brought a jitter-bugging generation dancing into millions of homes every afternoon. The term "Beatnik" was coined to identify counter-culture non-conformers. Brigitte Bardot starred in "And God Created Woman" — a film banned by some and backed by others. In literature, Jack Kerouac took America *On the Road*.

Chevrolet's new-for-1957 models were in tune with their times. They had a hipper, more youthful, tail-finned look that was "radical" for America's bread-and-butter "family" car. "'57 Chevrolet! Sweet, smooth and sassy," said one advertisement.

"Chevy goes 'em all one better for '57 with a daring new departure in design (looks longer and lower, and it is!), exclusive new Triple-Turbine Powerglide automatic drive, a new V8 and a bumper crop of new ideas including fuel injection!" Revolutionary and sexy, the '57 Chevy was "really built for the road" claimed one advertising copywriter. Ads showed it on the road, passing the Santa Fe Railroad's famous Super Chief and climbing a snow-covered mountain highway.

The '57 Chevrolet seemed more modern and sportier. Its oval-shaped front bumper grille featured "bomb-type" bumper guards. A horizontal bar "floating" across the delicately cross-hatched grille insert had a Chevy emblem at its center and round parking lamps at each end. Wind split bulges with bombsight ornaments ran up both sides of the flat hood panel. The headlights had grilles around them. The rear fenders were shaped into broad, flat tail fins. This year the gas filler was incorporated into the chrome molding at the rear edge of the left-hand fin.

Special 150 models were trimmed much the same as in 1956 while Deluxe 210 models featured double side moldings on the rear quarters with a painted contrast panel. Bel Airs had an even richer look with gold radiator and headlight grilles, gold front fender chevrons and silver anodized inserts between the twin body side moldings.

All V-8 models, except those with the standard three-speed manual transmission, carried a new 283-cid V-8, which offered up to 283 hp in "super" fuel-injected format. A new Turboglide automatic transmission promised "Triple-Turbine Take-Off." In Chevy lingo, this meant an unbroken flow of power from standstill to cruising speed. Turboglide transmission was a running production change, so some early cars may have had 265-cid V-8s with Powerglide transmission. A new Grade Retarder feature provided extra braking power going down steep hills.

Triple-Locking door latches and High-Volume ventilation were listed as new selling features. All Chevrolets with V-8 power had large, V-shaped hood and deck lid ornaments, which were bright metal on 150s and 210s and gold on Bel Airs.

Body styles offered in the low-rung, grocery-getter series included two- and four-door six-passenger sedans, a three-passenger Utility Sedan and the "Handyman" two-door station wagon. Prices began as low as $1,885 for the "business coupe" with the base 235-cid 140-hp six-cylinder engine. The V-8-powered wagon, at $2,407, was the highest-priced model in the 150 series.

This year's Two-Ten followed the "sassier-for-'57" theme by looking more Bel Air-like, especially with optional two-tone paint. Three two-tone interior schemes, with cloth-and-vinyl trim combinations, were available at standard prices. Rather than a cheap one-seat coupe, this series offered the regular two-door sedan, plus the dressier-inside Del Ray version. The four-door sedan was a must, but hardtops were also included, both two- and four-door versions. There was a Handyman wagon, plus two-versions of the four-door Townsman wagon, one with nine-passenger seating. The lowest-priced 210 cost $2,122 and the highest was the three-seat Townsman at $2,663.

Extra rich in all ways, the Bel Airs carried rocker sill, roof, window and tail fin outline moldings. Chevrolet scripts decorated the hood and trunk and gold Bel Air scripts and Chevrolet bow tie crests were on the rear fenders. Distinctive two-tone interiors were seen. The Nomad wagon with its hardtop styling, ribbed roof and tailgate slats returned. In addition to the Nomad and two- and four-door sedans and hardtops, the Bel Air line offered a convertible and a fancy Beauville four-door wagon. Prices started at $2,238 and climbed to $2,857 for a V-8-powered Nomad.

In addition to the "Blue Flame" six, seven V-8 options were possible, although some were quite rare. The base V-8 was the Turbo-Fire 265, a 162-hp version of the 265-cid small block used only in stick-shift cars. With Powerglide, the base V-8 was a 283-cid small block with a two-barrel carburetor that put out 185 hp. A four-barrel carburetor and dual exhausts gave the Turbo-Fire 220 (220-hp) version of the 283-cid V-8 more muscles to flex.

Dual four-barrel carbs were featured on the Turbo-Fire 245 V-8. Fitted with a Rochester mechanical fuel-injection setup, the Ramjet 250 version of the 283-cid engine was another choice. Next in horsepower was the Super Turbo-Fire 270 V-8 which combined dual Quadrajet carbs with a higher 9.5:1 compression ratio. Chevy's legendary Super Ramjet 283 V-8 was the top option combining the Rochester F.I. system with a 10.5:1 compression ratio. Don't tell a Chrysler 300 or DeSoto Adventurer fan the awesome engine was a "milestone." Chevrolet promoted this solid-lifter fuel-injection V-8 as the first American production-car engine to provide one horsepower per cubic inch of displacement.

Actually, Chevy was a bit conservative when it came to hyp-

ing horsepower this season, and with good reason. On April 10, a New Hampshire state senator made national news with his charges that the auto industry was "engaged in a ridiculous and dangerous horsepower race." By June 6, the Board of Directors of the Automobile Manufacturers Association recommended to member companies that they take no part in auto racing or other competitive events involving tests of speed and that they refrain from suggesting speed in passenger car advertising or publicity.

In most ads, Chevy mentioned "V-8s up to 245 hp" and then footnoted information about the 270-hp high-performance engine and 283-hp Ramjet fuel-injection engine in small print.

Dealer introductions for 1957 Chevrolets were held October 1956. Model-year production peaked at 1,515,177 cars. Calendar-year sales were counted at 1,522,536 units, the third best number in Chevrolet's long history. Chevrolet outsold Ford by only 136 cars on a calendar-year basis, but Ford actually built more 1957 models than Chevrolet. It was a neck-and-neck battle between the two firms this season.

In 1957, Chevrolet produced its 38 millionth car of all time, while the five millionth car with a Powerglide automatic transmission was made that November.

Chevy also said it had made more cars between 1946 and 1957 than it turned out in its entire prewar history.

1958 *Chevrolet*

Chevrolet started a distinctive rear-end taillight treatment with its 1958 Impala models.

Perhaps it was due to an economic slowdown that caused a sharp rise in unemployment, but whatever the reason, Americans, in 1958, seemed more interested in leisure activities than ever before. They watched (often on television) as Arnold Palmer won his first Masters golf tournament and New York Yankees beat Milwaukee, 4-3, in the World Series. At night, they went out dancing the "Cha Cha" or tuned in "The Tonight Show" starring Jack Parr.

Ads pictured 1958 Chevrolet owners yachting, antiquing and going to the movies. The copywriters pitched economy and safety, rather than "quicksilver" performance. "The happiest traveling on the highway" was promised in one promotion. "The beautiful way

to be thrifty," said another ad aimed at penny-pinchers (of which there were more of that year). There were occasional mentions of the new 250-hp Turbo-Thrust V-8, but phrases like "Easier Handling . . . Safer Going" got the biggest headlines.

An all-new, one-year-only car, the '58 Chevy had an all-new Safety Girder chassis. Body revisions included lower, wider, longer sheet metal, sculptured body styling, a new front end with dual headlights and a dream car look, gull-wing rear fenders and revamped side trim treatments. The base series was now called Del Ray after the former interior package, the mid-range Biscayne models were named for a Motorama show car and the top-of-the-line Bel Air got a new one-step-up Impala sub-series. A new 348-

cid Turbo-Thrust V-8 was available and was Chevy's first "big-block" V-8. Popular 1958 Chevrolet selling features included Glide-Ride front suspension, Ball-Race steering, Outrigger rear springs, High-Volume ventilation, Fisher Body work, Triple-Locking door latches and Precision-Aimed headlights.

The plainest Chevys still carried chrome body side moldings. Del Ray nameplates marked the rear fender coves of four body styles priced from $2,013 to $2,574. These cars had single belt-line moldings and lacked bright metal side window trim. Del Ray interior appointments had standard steering wheels, rubber floor mats and fewer bright highlights. A sedan delivery truck was a new model. There were two "Yeoman" station wagons, one with two doors and one with four.

Biscaynes and Brookwood station wagons had dual moldings on the front fenders and doors. Like the Del Ray models, Biscaynes came standard with small hubcaps, no sill moldings, no chevrons and no fender ornaments, but they did feature slightly up-market interior trims. They were priced from $2,236 to $2,785.

Bel Airs had series scripts and Chevrolet crests at the rear of the coves. The upper edge of the cove was outlined with a single-level molding that intersected a spear-shaped horizontal molding with indented concave contrast band towards the rear and a horizontally grooved, missile-shaped "spear tip" at the front. Bel Airs also carried four front fender chevrons, four short vertical strips on the rear fenders, front fender top ornaments, chrome side window moldings, roof pillar beauty plates and full wheel discs. Interior appointments were rich and fancy. Four Bel Airs were offered — two- and four-door sedans and hardtops — and there was also a Bel-Air-like four-door Nomad station wagon. The top-priced Bel Air was the V-8 Sport Coupe at $2,554. The V-8 Nomad carried a $2,835 price tag.

Impala trim features included a model script, insignia and crossed-flag emblem at the front of the cove, ribbed body sills, air scoops ahead of the rear wheel, a competition style steering wheel with Impala medallion, an Impala dashboard script, a rear radio speaker grille (with Impala script and medallion) and triple tail-lights (replacing two taillights on other cars and one on all wagons). The Impala Sport Coupe had a chrome-edged, rear-facing

dummy air scoop and curved contour crease molded into the back of the roof. With a base V-8 below the hood, the Impala Sport Coupe listed for $2,693 and the Sport Convertible was $2,841.

Engine selections started with the 235-cid in-line six, which gained five horsepower. The base 283-cid two-barrel V-8 was good for 185 hp. Next came the Super Turbo-Fire 230 V-8, which had a four-barrel carburetor and dual exhausts. The Super Turbo-Thrust 250 V-8 was a big-block version of the four-barrel, dual-exhaust choice. Offering the same 250 hp was a Ramjet injected 283-cid hydraulic-lifter small-block.

Cracking 280 hp was the Super Turbo-Thrust tri-power version of the 348-cid big-block V-8. A special solid-lifter Ramjet fuel-injected 283 with an 11.5:1 compression ratio could be ordered by anyone needing 290 hp. Ten more horses were available in the Super Turbo-Thrust 300 version of the 348-cid four-barrel V-8 that ran an 11.0:1 compression ratio. The Super Turbo-Thrust 348 also came in an all-out 315-hp version with three two-barrel carburetors.

All 1958 Chevys were on a considerably longer 117.5-inch wheelbase and had a larger 209.1 inch overall length. They were 77.7 inches wide and heights of various models ranged from 56.4 inches to 57.4 inches. Convertibles and station wagons had 8.00 x 14 tires and other models had 7.50 x 14 tires. The new Chevy chassis featured full-coil-spring suspension, anti-dive braking and built-in leveling. A foot-operated parking brake was used this year. The fuel tank held 20 gallons of gas and 12-volt electrics were used again.

Dealer introductions of 1958 Chevrolets took place on Halloween in 1957, which lent itself to interesting promotional activities. Model-year total was 1,283,584 cars for a 30.1 percent share of industry. That included some 9,000 Corvettes. Calendar-year production was 1,255,935 cars. While Chevrolet followed the entire industry down this year, it did recapture the number one spot on the sales charts, after being outsold by Ford in 1957. Chevrolet new-car registrations totaled 1,233,477 cars, which was 205,317 ahead of its biggest rival. At the end of 1958, Chevrolet claimed that one in every four vehicles in use on American roads were Chevrolets.

1959 *Chevrolet*

The 666-mph Boeing 707 brought the jet age to American travelers in 1959. "Jet Setters" could now hop around the world in a few hours. Chevrolet had a new car that looked like a jet plane ready to take to the skies with its air-slot front end and gull-wing tail fins. It was the company's third all-new product line in three years. "Nothing's New Like Chevy's New!" said an ad of the year promoting the Bel Air sedan and Impala Sport Coupe. "One look tells you '59 Chevrolet has a whole new slant on driving, from the overhead curve of its windshield to the sheen of its Magic-Mirror finish."

An interesting twist in Chevrolet's 1959 advertising program was the many ads showing less-expensive Biscayne models. "Maybe you can't please everybody, but this car comes might close," was the sales slogan for the plain-Jane sedan. This initiative was probably based on the fact that the ads were planned in 1958, when the economy was in a tizzy. By 1959, the economy was getting back on track.

The "Slimline Design" 1959 Chevrolets were lower, wider and longer than ever before. Innovations included a new radiator grille, a "Spread Wing" rear treatment, increased glass area and flat-top roof styling on Sport Sedans. The "cat's-eye" taillights were very distinctive. All Chevrolets had more glass.

Inside were wider seats with "lounge like comfort" according to Chevrolet. New Safety-Master brakes featured air-cooled drums and 27 percent more bonded lining area. Also featured were a full-coil-spring suspension and acrylic lacquer exterior body finish. Another new feature was easy-ratio steering. New on the 1959 optional equipment list was Level Air suspension. Engine options were greatly expanded, offering 13 choices (including 12 "vim-packed" V-8s) with up to 350 hp.

Biscaynes had only front fender side moldings. Standard equipment on the low-line models included rear foam cushions, electric windshield wipers and an oil bath air cleaner for cars with V-8s. The passenger-car line consisted of the two-door Utility Sedan,

The 1959 Chevrolet Impala four-door hardtop shows off dramatically new styling.

the two- and four-door sedans and two- and four-door Brookwood station wagons. Prices were reduced from 1958 and fell into the $2,160 to $2,756 range.

This year's station wagons were actually treated as if they were in a separate station wagon series, rather than Biscaynes, Bel Airs and Impalas. And many magazine ads featured the wagons, as Chevy continued its sales battle with Ford—the car industry's traditional "wagonmaster." The push was strong, too.

"Chevy holds everybody and his brother — beautifully!" said an ad showing Mom and her four kids with a Brookwood. "Handiest helper a family ever had" was the sales pitch on a Nomad being used by a smaller clan with a passion for gardening. "If the Joneses haven't got one, it's their turn to catch up!" teased the tag line on a Kingswood (Bel Air) wagon announcement.

Bel Airs were mid-priced cars now. Model script nameplates and crests decorated the front fenders. While Biscayne side moldings ran from the headlights to the center of the front doors, Bel Air moldings ran full length and had painted inserts. Another enrichment was front fender top ornaments. Kingswood and Parkwood station wagons had Bel Air trim, but their own model name script on the front fenders.

Standard equipment was the same as for Biscaynes, plus Deluxe features, front foam seat cushions, Deluxe steering wheel and a power tailgate on Kingswood wagons. In this series, the Utility sedan was replaced by a Sport Sedan or four-door hardtop and there were two station wagons. The six-passenger wagon was the Parkwood and the nine-passenger style was the Kingswood. Bel Air prices were in the $2,386 to $2,970 bracket.

Impalas had model nameplates and crossed-racing-flags emblems inside the painted insert area of the full-length side trim moldings. The front fender ornaments also had rear extension strips. The deck lid indentation and taillight lenses had chrome trim. Closed cars had simulated roof scoops. Nomad wagons had Impala trim with different I.D. script. Impala equipment included an electric clock, dual sliding sun visors and aluminum trim. The line consisted of the four-door sedan, two- and four-door hardtops and convertible and the Nomad wagon was somewhat comparable to an Impala, as well. The low-priced model was the

six-cylinder sedan, which wore a $2,592 window sticker. You had to add $417 to that to afford a V-8 Nomad wagon.

Listing all the 1959 Chevy engines could be a book in itself and we'll refer you to *The Standard Catalog of V-8 Engines 1906-2002* for specifics on all of them, except the base 235-cid 135-hp "Hi-Thrift" six. This engine had less horsepower, but was said to deliver 10 percent more miles per gallon. The base V-8 was again a 283-cid Turbo-Fire small-block with a two-barrel carburetor and 185 hp at 4600 rpm.

Next came a 230-hp version with a four-barrel. There were also 250-hp and 290-hp Ramjet fuel-injected versions of the 283. The 348-cid big-block offered 250-hp (four-barrel), 280-hp (Tri-Power), 300-hp and 305-hp (high-compression four-barrel), 315-hp (high-compression Tri-Power), 320-hp (11.25:1 compression four-barrel), 335-hp (11.25:1 compression Tri-Power) and 350-hp (11.25:1 compression Tri-Power) options.

A longer 119-inch wheelbase carried the 210.9-inch long '50 bodies. They were 79.9 inches wide and had heights between 54 inches and 56.3 inches. Convertibles and station wagons had 8.00 x 14 tires and other models had 7.50 x 14 tires. The fuel tank again held 20 gallons of petrol.

Dealer introductions were held October 1958. Calendar-year sales were 1,528,592 units versus 1,352,112 for Ford. Model-year production totaled 1,481,071 Chevys against 1,394,684 Fords. In unit terms, Chevy had a nice increase from '58, but the company's share of total industry fell over three percent to 26.6 percent.

As you can see, Ford and Chevy ran neck-and-neck again, although Chevy actually turned out more cars built to 1959 specifications. It is interesting to note, however, that 7,100 dealerships across America were selling Chevrolets in 1959, compared to 6,834 selling Fords. With that many more "stores," Chevy's numbers really should have been higher.

Before bowing out of the decade of dazzle, Chevrolet introduced the 1960 Corvair on Oct. 2, 1959. This all-new compact gave a hint of things to come, as Chevy would continue launching new nameplates like the Chevy II/Nova, Chevelle, and Camaro as the fabulous '50s turned into the sensational '60s.

Chryslers & Imperials
of the Fifties

1950 *Chrysler and Imperial*

The stately 1950 Chrysler Royal Town & Country wood-trimmed station wagon.

As the calendar turned to a new decade in 1950, "Guys and Dolls" premiered on Broadway and the strands of "Good Night Irene" crackled over millions of radios across America. TV hero Hopalong Cassidy was at the peak of his popularity and "Hoppy," with his tall, black cowboy hat, would have been very comfortable sitting in a new Chrysler or Imperial that year. Chrysler president K.T. Keller was famous for wearing a Fedora and for favoring "box-on-box" styling.

Such styling was first seen on the 1949 models, but it was still new enough to be promoted as the latest and greatest a year later. "To Chrysler's reputation for mechanical excellence, superb performance, and dependability, have been added distinctive styling and enduring beauty," said the year's product guide.

Chrysler advertisements of the era described the 1950 models as "Today's New Style Classic" and pointed out the cars had a lower, longer, and lovelier look. Actual size differences were really quite small. The six-cylinder Royal and Windsor models shared the same 125.5-inch wheelbase used in 1949, except for the big sedans and limousines, which had a 14-inch-longer stance. Saratogas, New Yorkers, the Town & Country hardtop, and regular Imperials all had a 131.5-inch wheelbase.

The 8-passenger Crown Imperials also had 14 extra inches between their hubcaps (a big 139.5-inch wheelbase). Vehicle lengths increased by about two inches.

To give Chrysler products a lower look, the grille was redesigned along a more horizontal theme. The main grille bar protruded in and out, but ran across the entire front end and wrapped around each body corner, just below the headlights. There was a bowed bar above it and another in-and-out bar running across the front end between the large, almost-square, parking lights. These were set into grooved trim panels that curved around the body corners. Below them was a full-width bar, similar to the main one, that didn't run quite as far back on the body sides. The lower-rung models had a winged emblem above the grille, while upper-range models carried the Chrysler name in script. The hood ornament was large and ran back, nearly halfway down the center of the hood.

Other than being smaller than other Chrysler products, Royal and Windsor models could be identified by the model names on

their front fenders. Both used an in-line 250.6-cid flathead six that generated 116 hp. The big, long-wheelbase Royals and Windsors must have crawled along with this "high-compression" six in their two-ton chassis, but it was a durable and reliable engine that served many Chrysler owners well. The company's reputation for top-notch engineering was well-deserved.

The Royal series, which was in its final season, contained a Club Coupe, a four-door sedan, a rare Town & Country wagon (only 99 were built) and a "regular" station wagon, which was a "woodie" and cost more than the all-steel T & C, as well as a long-wheelbase eight-passenger sedan.

Prices began at $2,113 and the big sedan was the most expensive model at $2,855. Optional at $120.90 was a Prestomatic "semi-automatic" transmission.

Windsors were a bit fancier than Royals and this line included several additional—and more interesting—body styles. First, there was the Traveler, a four-door sedan in which the rear seat could be folded to create a luggage area that extended from just behind the front seat to the rear of the car. A roof-top luggage carrier with wooden slats was standard. Only 900 of these rare cars were made. Second, was the Newport, Chrysler's catch-up-to-GM hardtop that had a very attractive, three-piece, wraparound rear window.

A convertible was also part of the series, but only 2,201 were built. In the long-wheelbase sub-series, there was a Windsor limousine joining the eight-passenger sedan. Windsors cost about $200 more than comparable Royals. The Traveler was $2,560, the Newport was $2,637, the convertible was $2,741, and the limousine was $3,176.

The "Saratoga" name on the front fender indicated a larger car with Chrysler's 323.5-cid in-line eight under its hood. This 135-hp flathead engine was also used in New Yorkers, Imperials, and Crown Imperials. There were only two Saratogas, the Club Coupe for $2,616 and the four-door sedan for $2,642.

The only real difference in the Windsor and New Yorker models was that the New Yorkers had richer interior appointments and some additional body styles. The added New Yorker models included the Newport hardtop for $3,133, the convertible for $3,238, and the Town & Country hardtop, a wood-bodied Newport that listed for $4,003. All were low-production models with 2,800 Newports, 899 ragtops, and 698 Newport Town & Countrys being built.

With prices just above $3,000, the Imperial line offered a four-door sedan and a Deluxe four-door sedan. These cars were actually customized versions of the New Yorker sedan with a very unique "hardtop-style" roofline. The rear window was of a three-piece, wraparound design like that on Newport two-door hardtops. Only 10,650 of these were made in both standard and Deluxe format.

The larger Crown Imperials came in eight-passenger sedan ($5,229) and eight-passenger limousine ($5,334) variations.

Special custom-coach-built bodies by Derham Body Company, of Rosemont, Pennsylvania, were offered on the large Crown Imperial chassis. An interesting fact about the Crown Imperials of this era is that they used self-energizing disc brakes. Also introduced by Chrysler this year were electric window lifts.

Chrysler model-year production was 176,000 cars. Calendar-year production was 168,278 for a 2.52 percent share of the industry. This included 127,000 sixes and 41,000 eights. The number was artificially low, due to a three-month-long strike, although it was an all-time high for the Chrysler nameplate.

1951 and 1952 Chrysler and Imperial

The 1951 Chrysler Windsor Deluxe convertible wears its red paint job well.

It might be a bit of an exaggeration to put the first Hemi engine up there with world-shaking events, but the new V-8 from Chrysler Corporation was a revolutionary advance in the world of automobiles. Until 1950, Cadillac had held the horse-power crown thanks to a 331-cid V-8 with 160 hp. The best Chrysler could do, with its almost-as-large 323.5-cid straight eight, was 135 hp. Then along came the Hemi.

Featuring the same displacement as Cadillac's renowned high-compression overhead-valve V-8, the first-generation "Firepower" Hemi churned up 20 additional "horses." This was viewed as an earth-changing feat. Even Oldsmobile's legendary "Rocket 88" engine was maxed out at 135 hp! And Lincoln could manage just 152 hp. Chrysler shook up Detroit with this power plant.

"You must drive it to believe it!" said a full-page Chrysler advertisement showing only a head-on illustration of the new V-8.

"It's the most revolutionary new car motor in 27 years! Months of testing prove it will run smoother and more carbon-free, last longer, cost less to maintain than any other engine you can own. Its matchless power in reserve gives you, with ease, better acceleration, responsiveness and mile-eating stamina than you have ever felt. With all this goes great economy, and design that will use regular gasoline."

The only Chryslers not to use the Hemi were the Windsor and Windsor Deluxe models. For 1951, these lines had the same models as the previous Royal and Windsor series, plus an ambulance created by slightly modifying the all-steel Town & Country station wagon. Only 153 of these were made before the model was discontinued. Chrysler considered the 1951 and 1952 models to be a

continuing series and counted their production together, although some body styles were offered only one year. In 1952 the Windsor Deluxe Club Coupe and Traveler sedan were discontinued.

Windsor four-door sedans adopted the wraparound rear window introduced on smaller Imperials in 1950. Other body trim included bright rocker panel moldings that met large chrome gravel shields and a second horizontal molding on the rear fenders. The rear bumper had a new, horizontally-ribbed license plate recess. The Windsor Deluxe interior had richer appointments. Prices were about $250 higher than for comparable 1950 models.

By simply changing grille and body molding treatments, Chrysler claimed "brilliant new beauty" for its 1951 cars, but they were basically face-lifted 1950 models. The Chrysler grille had moldings running fully across the top and bottom of the radiator opening. Both wrapped around the front body corners, the lower one extending to the wheel opening and the upper one running completely down the fender onto the door. In the center was a vertical member with grooved side plates.

There were also grooved side plates extending around each body corner to the front wheel opening. Square parking lamps were set into these plates directly under the headlights. Sixes said "Chrysler" on the front center of the hood. All models (except Imperials) had the series name spelled out on the front fender, a few inches behind the headlights.

The Hemi was installed in all eight-cylinder series, starting with the Saratoga line, which now used the same chassis and bodies as six-cylinder Windsor/Windsor Deluxe models. This line was expanded with the addition of a Town & Country station wagon on the 125.5-inch wheelbase and a jump-seat sedan and division-window limousine on the 139.5-inch wheelbase. The Saratoga limo was dropped in 1952. A Club Coupe and a four-door sedan were also built on the smaller Saratoga wheelbase. Prices ranged from $2,989 to $4,240.

When you moved up to a New Yorker in 1951 or 1952, you got the 131.5-inch wheelbase chassis and a suitably lengthened body (though not as long as the eight-passenger jobs in the lower-priced series). On paper, the New Yorker model offerings were unchanged from 1950, but the car now called a New Yorker Town & Country was an all-steel station wagon, rather than a Newport hardtop with wood panels on the doors and trunk.

The Town & Country was still a rare car (251 made) and it was offered only in 1951. In 1952, it was dropped, along with the New Yorker Club Coupe. New Yorkers were around $350 pricier that comparable Saratogas.

An entirely different grille identified the front of Imperial models. A chrome hood lip molding, which had 11 vertical scores in it, bowed up to create an opening above the upper grille bar. There was also a matching lower grille bar and a double-deck bumper with a horizontal air slot in its center and two massive vertical bumper guards. The parking lights and grooved beauty panels that held them were smaller than those on Chryslers. Imperials had no front fender molding.

The Imperial (or Crown Imperial) name was mounted lower on the front fender, behind the wheel opening. The rocker panel molding ended in a smaller, thin, scalloped gravel shield. The rear fenders were skirted and had a horizontal molding running across the shirts onto the fender on each side

The 131.5-inch wheelbase Imperials were the Club Coupe, sedan, Newport (3,450 built) and convertible (650 built) for 1951, with the ragtop being discontinued for 1952. In both years, the 145.5-inch Crown Imperial chassis was available with a choice of eight-passenger sedan or limousine models.

Chrysler's new V-8 generated enough sales excitement to push it from third place to second place on the charts in 1951, when it put out 156,000 cars in the model year. Due almost entirely to government controls on manufacturing during the Korean War, materials shortage, and a steel workers strike, model-year production dropped to 91,253 cars in 1952. Calendar-year production for 1951 was 164,936 cars or 3.09 percent of industry.

The corresponding numbers for 1952 were 120,678 cars and 2.78 percent of industry.

Several handsome Chrysler show cars were seen in 1952. The Chrysler Special featured an Italian-built body on a 180-hp Saratoga chassis. Also built by Ghia in Italy, the K-310 was a sleek coupe with a spare tire impression embossed on its rear deck lid. Another Saratoga-based Ghia creation was the C-200 convertible. Three dual-cowl parade phaetons were also constructed on the Crown Imperial chassis and gifted to the cities of Detroit, New York, and Los Angeles. These cars, which were later updated 1955 sheet metal, still exist today.

1953 *Chrysler and Imperial*

The well-mannered Chrysler Windsor Deluxe convertible with optional wire wheels.

The fighting ended in Korea in 1953 and President Eisenhower ended all wage, salary, and price controls imposed during the conflict. The goal was to give Americans the potential to earn more money and to keep the peacetime economy rolling. No wonder "Rags to Riches" was a Top 10 tune late that year, hitting number one early in December.

"Everyday is richer when you own a car like this!" advertised Chrysler, which billed itself "America's First Family of Fine Cars: Windsor, New Yorker, Imperial." The company contended: "…even a millionaire can't have what you have in your next new car . . . unless he, too, drives a Chrysler!"

As always, early promotions described the new models as "The Most Beautiful Chryslers Ever Designed." That's a subjective evaluation, but at least they weren't essentially the same as the previous year. Many changes took place between the 1952 models and the 1953s. They started with a new body featuring a one-piece windshield. The flathead "Spitfire" in-line six was standard under the hood of Windsors. The 'Fire-Power' V-8 was used in New Yorkers, Custom Imperials, and Crown Imperials.

On Windsors and New Yorkers, a much more delicate grille featured two or three horizontal moldings that ran across the front of the cars and rounded the front body corners. In the center of the grille was a vertical member that carried a red medallion in its center. A massive bumper was seen. Both lines had horizontal moldings on the front and rear fenders, rocker panel moldings and bright metal gravel guards. Most ads showed four "wind splits" on the gravel guards, but some showed smooth gravel guards. We're not sure if this was a production variation or just an artist's overactive airbrush.

The standard Windsor line offered a Club Coupe, four-door sedan, and all-steel Town & Country wagon on the 125.5-inch wheelbase and an eight-passenger sedan on the 139.5-inch wheelbase. Windsor Deluxes came as a four-door sedan, a Newport two-door hardtop, and a convertible all on the 125.5-inch wheelbase. These cars said "Windsor" or "Windsor Deluxe" on the front fenders and "Chrysler" on the front of the hood and the rear deck lid. Windsors had only two horizontal grille moldings. The top one extended down the body sides to the front door. The bottom molding extended back only to the wheel opening. There was no molding between the oblong parking lights positioned on the body corners between the two grille bars. Prices began at $2,442 and the long-wheelbase sedan was the most expensive offering at $3,403.

Five New Yorker and New Yorker Deluxe models shared the 125.5-inch wheelbase. The lower series included a four-door sedan, Club Coupe, Newport two-door hardtop, and all-steel Town & Country station wagon at $3,121 to $3,898. Three of these body styles also came with Deluxe trim, but a Deluxe convertible (950 built) replaced the T & C wagon. Prices were $3,264 to $3,945. An eight-passenger New Yorker (non-Deluxe) sedan was also offered on the 139.5-inch wheelbase with only 100 being built.

All New Yorkers had a grille with three horizontal moldings. The top one extended to the doors, the added center molding ran between the oblong parking lights, and the bottom molding culminated at the front wheel opening. A winged-V emblem was on the center of the hood and the Chrysler name was on the left-hand side. The front fenders said "New Yorker" or "New Yorker Deluxe." There was a V-shaped molding on the center of the rear deck lid and the Chrysler name was on the passenger side, just below the lid.

Two versions of the Imperial were offered again and they again had distinctive body trim. Both also had their own distinctive wheelbase. Two Custom Imperial models — a four-door sedan ($4,225) and a new Town Limousine ($4,762) — were on a 133.5-inch wheelbase. There was also a Custom Imperial Newport hard-

top ($4,525) on a 131.5-inch wheelbase. The Crown Imperial models — an eight-passenger sedan ($6,872) and a partitioned limousine ($6,994) — were on a 145.5-inch wheelbase.

The Imperial grille and front end trim were very similar to that described in the 1951-'52 Chrysler and Imperial section, except the grooved beauty panels holding the parking lights were a bit longer where they wrapped around the body corner. There was no "Imperial" name or molding on the front fender and rear fender skirts were no longer standard.

The rear gravel guards were curved and smooth and the horizontal rear fender molding ran from the gravel guard to the extreme rear of the fender. The Imperial hood mascot was a gleaming eagle with pointed swept-back wings. Chrysler ads claimed that the Imperial was, "Virtually custom-built" and "surpassingly beautiful in line and décor."

Both Chrysler engines retained the same horsepower ratings — 119 for the six and 180 for the Hemi. Other selling features included Oriflow shock absorbers, an automatic choke, an Oilite fuel filter in the gas tank, resistor-type spark plugs, ignition-key starting, directional signals, back-up lights, a weather-proof ignition system, electric windshield wipers, safety-rim wheels, and a dash panel safety pad. Fluid-Matic drive was standard in Windsor Deluxes and New Yorkers and $130 extra in Windsors. All Imperials included Fluid-Torque Drive, power brakes, and electric window lifts. Full-time power steering and disc brakes were standard in Crown Imperials and optional in Custom Imperials.

The Thomas Special — named for C.B. Thomas, vice president of export — was constructed this year. It featured another Italian-built body on a 180-hp Saratoga chassis. It was similar to the earlier Chrysler Special, but had a different grille, air intakes, door latches, and trunk. The car, which still survives in the famous Bortz Dream Car Collection, has two-tone green finish, green leather upholstery, and chrome wire wheels. The similar GS-1 coupe was built in 1953 for exhibition at 1954 auto shows.

Chrysler had a rather rocky year in 1953. By the time it was all in and done, model-year production totaled 162,187, up more than 70,000 units from 1952. Calendar-year output came in at 160,410 cars or 2.61 percent of the industry total.

1954 Chrysler and Imperial

A 1954 Chrysler New Yorker Deluxe Newport two-door hardtop with many options.

In government, the year 1953 saw the Supreme Court lead the way toward sweeping social changes with its ruling that race-based segregation in schools was unconstitutional. In medi-

cine, Dr. Jonas Salk championed a healthier America by beginning to inoculate children with his polio vaccine. In the world of religion, Billy Graham shepherded a tide of increasing interest in

Christian revival meetings. In the automotive industry, Chrysler claimed, "The power of leadership is yours in a beautiful Chrysler."

It was Chrysler's 30th anniversary that season. Over those three decades, the Highland Park (Michigan) automaker had paved the way to many pioneering advances. In its first year, 1924, the company introduced high-compression, high-speed engines, and hydraulically-activated four-wheel-brakes. Other Chrysler "firsts" included enclosed rubber engine mountings in 1925, rust-proofed bodies in 1931, the helical-geared transmission in 1933, Safety-Rim wheels in 1940, self-energizing disc brakes in 1949, and the Hemi V-8 in 1951.

Said *Ward's 1954 Automotive Yearbook* in a commemorative survey of Chrysler's history, "When [the] industry eyes focus on [the 19]55 models, Chrysler Division cars will be leading the parade that the Chrysler Six 70 started 30 years ago."

Product changes from 1953 included new grilles, new convex-type bumpers, redesigned taillight clusters, and newly-designed stone shields. The horsepower of the FirePower V-8 was increased from 180 to 235 (a new industry high), thanks to a new four-barrel carburetor, while the L-head six remained at 119 hp. A new, fully-automatic PowerFlite automatic transmission provided clutch-free, no-shift driving. The PowerFlite's advantages included smooth, lurch-free acceleration and deceleration.

There were now five lines: Windsor Deluxe six, New Yorker V-8, New Yorker Deluxe V-8, Custom Imperial V-8, and Crown Imperial V-8. The Windsor Deluxe series offered a Club Coupe, sedan, Newport, convertible, and T & C wagon on the 125.5-inch wheelbase and eight-passenger sedan on the 139.5-inch wheelbase. New Yorker, New Yorker Deluxe, Custom Imperial, and Crown Imperial model offerings were identical to 1953.

Windsor Deluxe models said "Chrysler" on the front of the hood and below the rear deck. "Windsor Deluxe" appeared on the rear fenders. There were three gold triangles on the chrome grille medallion. The combination headlights and directional signals had chrome visors. Prices started as low as $2,511 and ran as high as $3,462 for the long-wheelbase eight-passenger jump-seat sedan. A three-speed manual transmission was standard and PowerFlite was a $189 option. The smaller Windsors used 7.60 x 15 tires, but the "stretch" sedan required 8.20 x 15.

New Yorkers had V-shaped emblems on the front of the hood and the rear deck lid (with a "C" medallion on Deluxe versions). "New Yorker" nameplates appeared on the rear fenders, with "Deluxe" added on Deluxe models. "Chrysler" was seen on the chrome grille medallion. New Yorker Deluxe models had an extra curved, chromed member integrated into the center horizontal grille bar. The New Yorker Club Coupe for $3,167 was the series' lowest-priced model and the $4,333 "stretch" sedan was the priciest. Prices for New Yorker Deluxe models ran from $3,371 for the Club Coupe to $3,903 for the ragtop. The big sedan had 8.20 x 15 tires and the other models used 8.20 x 15.

Imperial identifiers included a beautiful mascot and a winged "V" emblem with a gold crown on the front of the hood. "Imperial" scripts with gold crowns above them decorated both front fenders. The distinctive grille used only on Imperials had five vertical dividers on top of the center horizontal grille bar and round parking lights at either end of that bar.

Imperial advertisements listed the American leaders who drove Imperials, including Douglas Aircraft Company president Donald Douglas, Mississippi Governor Hugh White, Detroit Baseball Company president Walter O. Briggs, Jr., and Charles J. Hardy, Jr., the president of American Car & Foundry Corporation. Custom Imperial prices ran from $4,225 to $4,762, while Crown Imperials climbed to as high as $6,994.

Chrysler opened its new Chelsea Proving Grounds in 1954, showing off a gas-turbine-engined car at the ribbon-cutting ceremony. Chrysler test drivers teamed with Indianapolis champion Tony Bettenhausen to complete a 24-hour endurance run of 2,836 miles, driving a 235-hp Chrysler at an average 118.184 miles per hour!

Automobile production volume in the United States in 1954 slipped 10.2 percent, prompting mergers between independent manufacturers including Studebaker and Packard, Nash and Hudson, and Kaiser and Willys. There was intense competition for whatever sales did exist and General Motors and Ford were the winners. While considered part of the Big 3, Chrysler Corporation was far smaller than the two powerhouses.

It had fewer dealers and a smaller budget for advertising and promotions. By the end of the year, Plymouth would fall from third to fifth on the sales charts, with Buick and Oldsmobile passing it. Further down the ladder, Cadillac raced in to take ninth spot and Chrysler came in 10th.

The 1954 Chryslers didn't sell. The company began the year with the factory doing double shifts, but by mid-June, there were five short workweeks in a row. Model-year production slipped to 97,933 cars — a drop of over 64,000. Calendar-year output of 101,743 cars was 58,667 short of the previous season. Chrysler's share of total industry production fell to a dismal 1.85 percent.

1955 Chrysler and Imperial

Although one of the greatest future thinkers — Albert Einstein — passed away in 1955, other visionaries were stepping up to pursue fame or success through the act of looking towards tomorrow. Dr. Martin Luther King, Jr. stood at the forefront of the first major U.S. civil rights activity, a bus boycott in Montgomery, Alabama.

Chrysler did forward thinking of its own to bring revolutionary "*Forward Look*" styling to the automotive world in 1955. The results paid off in sales success for Chrysler Corporation and fame for its chief designer Virgil Exner, who crafted the new body styling. This cosmetic initiative transformed the box-on-box

Chrysler image to one of a fighter jet on wheels. Rakish, front-slanting rooflines and tail fins imparted a sensation of speed.

A Chrysler advertisement explained, "Yes — America is falling in love with THE FORWARD LOOK…discovering the most contemporary styling…with a sense of motion even when the car is standing still! "

At Chrysler Division, "THE FORWARD LOOK" was so tuned into its times, that sales picked up almost immediately when these cars were launched on November 17. As *Ward's 1955 Automotive Yearbook* put it: "The 36.6 percent output decline suffered in 1954 was followed by prospects of a 'golden harvest' for 1955."

The memorable profile of the 1955 Chrysler New Yorker Newport hardtop.

By December, Chrysler factories were reporting heavy overtime to keep up with orders. By the end of the year, Chrysler reported an all-time high of 164,500 sales at the retail level.

The completely new bodies and styling weren't the only changes for 1955. Chrysler also introduced the limited-edition Chrysler 300 on February 10 and the first transistorized car radio on April 27.

On June 12, two special trim packages named Blue Heron and Green Falcon were advertised in The New York Times Magazine. Both packages featured color-coordinated nylon and white leather cloth trim and matching two-tone exterior finish with custom moldings and badges. They were available for Windsor Deluxe four-door sedans and Windsor Deluxe Newport two-door hardtops. Also historically significant was the division's 1955 decision to market Chryslers and Imperials as two separate cars.

The entry level Chrysler was the Windsor Deluxe series, which included a four-door sedan, a "budget" two-door Nassau hardtop, a fancier two-door Newport hardtop, a convertible, and (after Jan. 5, 1955) a Town & Country station wagon. All were on a 126-inch wheelbase and 218.6 inches long. Power was supplied by a 301-cid 188-hp Spitfire V-8, which was of "polyspherical" rather than "Hemi" design. Prices in the Windsor Deluxe series ranged from $2,605 to $3,277 and PowerFlite automatic transmission was a $189 extra.

For identification purposes, "Windsor Deluxe" scripts appeared on the front fenders and rear deck lid. A medallion showing a castle-and-block design was placed between the grille wings and on the rear deck lid. On most Windsors, a straight sweep spear molding extended from just behind the headlights to a "V" medallion on the rear fender.

All Newports—and sedans with the Blue Heron or Green Falcon options—had dual-sweep side moldings that coordinated with various two-tone color treatments. Nassau and Newport hardtops also had model nameplates on their rear window pillars.

Models available in the New Yorker Deluxe series included the four-door sedan, the Newport two-door hardtop, the upscale St. Regis two-door hardtop, and the convertible, with a Town & Country wagon added in early January. Prices began at $3,439 and rose as high as $4,154.

These cars used the 331-cid Hemi Firepower V-8. They were the same size as Windsors, but had 250 hp to move them along more rapidly. The Powerflite automatic transmission was standard

equipment. Power steering was $113 additional, and Chrysler AirTemp air conditioning could be added for $567.

A "New Yorker Deluxe" rear fender script was one identifier of these models. On the grille and rear deck lid was an emblem with a lion holding a shield. New Yorkers had oval-shaped parking lights enclosed in the grille.

The Newport hardtop had dual sweep side moldings like other New Yorkers. The St. Regis had a full-length sweep spear molding and a curved molding that started at the rear window pillar and swooped forward to a point just behind the headlight.

The Chrysler C-300 was the brainchild of Bob Rodgers, a Chrysler engineer, who watched earlier Chryslers struggle through the Mexican Road Races. Rodgers convinced management a car was needed to compete with the Corvette and Thunderbird.

The C-300 was given an Imperial grille, leather upholstery, and a version of the Hemi V-8 fitted with dual four-barrel carburetors. The body was stripped of extraneous chrome trim for a cleaner appearance. Nicknamed "The Beautiful Beast," the C-300 took the NASCAR Grand National Stock Car and the AAA Stock Car Racing Championships. Only 1,725 Chrysler C-300s were made, but they brought many people into the showrooms.

The 1955 (no-longer-Chrysler) Imperial was advertised as "The Flagship of the FORWARD LOOK." Imperial (130-inch wheelbase) and Crown Imperial (149.5-inch wheelbase) series were marketed. Both used the 250-hp Hemi engine and had entirely new bodies and styling, with a massive divide grille, a "New Horizon" wraparound windshield, "gun sight" taillights mounted on top of the rear fenders and a built-in "sun cap" visor.

The Imperial series consisted of a four-door six-passenger sedan ($4,428) and a Newport two-door hardtop ($4,665). The Crown Imperials were an eight-passenger sedan ($6,888) and an eight-passenger limousine ($7,010). Common identification features included "Imperial" scripts on the front fenders and rear deck lid, an Imperial crown medallion on the hood, and a sculptured eagle medallion between the grille sections and on the rear deck lid. Only 172 Crown Imperials were built with just 45 of those as limousines.

Chrysler increased model-year output to 159,037. Calendar-year output was 176,039 for a 2.22 percent industry share.

1956 Chrysler and Imperial

The 1956 Chrysler Windsor Newport hardtop shows that year's mild facelift.

In 1956, it looked like Americans could expect great things in the years ahead. Congress approved the National Highway and Transportation Act that allowed future construction of the Interstate Highway System. The first transatlantic telephone cable went into operation. In many ways, it seemed like a better tomorrow was just around the corner, but one automaker from Highland Park, Michigan believed it had already arrived.

"Push this button and all other cars seem outdated," promised one Chrysler advertisement promoting one futuristic feature — Pushbutton PowerFlite automatic transmission. A pod to the left of the driver had four buttons marked "N" (neutral), "D" (drive), "L" (low), and "R" (reverse).

"Push that 'D' button and step on the gas. You're off like a Navy jet catapulted from a flight deck," said the copy. Other ads called the new Chrysler the YEAR-AHEAD CAR.

Both New Yorker and Windsor models had new grilles, new "Flight Sweep" rear fender styling, redesigned taillight assemblies, and new chrome and color treatments. Other changes included new hooded headlights on New Yorkers, new wheel covers, and redesigned bumpers. While both series continued to ride a 126-inch wheelbase, the cars were longer. Windsors were either 219.5, 220.4, or 223.4 inches long, depending on body style. New Yorkers were 220.3, 221.2, or 224.2 inches long, again depending on body style. For Imperials the wheelbase was 133 inches and overall length was 229.6 inches. Crown Imperials had a 149.5-inch stance and measured 242.5 inches end to end.

Chrysler brought out a four-door hardtop body this year and this "Newport Sedan" was the only new body style in both Chrysler series and the 133-inch Imperial series. The name used for both the two- and four-door Imperial hardtops was "Southampton."

Windsor prices rose roughly $200 and New Yorker prices rose $300. Imperial prices were roughly $300 higher on the smaller versions and $650 higher for the eight-passenger jobs. The high-performance Chrysler 300 B coupe returned, giving this series the well-known "Chrysler Letter Car" tag. It used the Imperial-type grille but adopted the new "Flight Sweep" rear fenders. The badge between the grille halves was a distinctive "300" emblem. It was priced at $4,242 and only 1,102 were made.

On Windsors, the model name appeared in script below the rear deck lid on the right side of the car. "Chrysler" scripts were seen on the front fenders, below the chrome-sweep spear molding. A castle-and-block emblem was placed above the grille, which had three large horizontal chrome dividers. There was also a "V" medallion on the rear fenders below the sweep spear molding. A special two-tone color treatment using an extra curved molding on the rear fender to create a contrast panel was optional on some Windsor models.

In the upper Chrysler series the "New Yorker" model name appeared in script on the front fenders, above a small medallion. Eight vertical louvers were placed on the rear fenders, above the sweep spear molding. The grille had multiple horizontal louvers with a lion-and-shield medallion in the center.

"Chrysler" was spelled out in block letters above the grille and on the rear deck lid just above the triangular medallion. The New Yorker Deluxe St. Regis hardtop had a special three-tone color treatment. The same special two-tone color treatment, with an extra curved molding on the rear fender to create a contrast panel.

The 1956 Imperials had the new "Flight Sweep" rear fender styling, new headlight hoods, and a new, flared side molding. It started behind the headlights and ran the full length of the car, enclosing the back-up lights at the rear. There was a new bumper and bumper guards, a narrower chrome molding along the bottom of the rear fenders, and redesigned wheel openings. A unique, divided grille characterized the front end of all Imperials. "Gunsight" type taillights were mounted on the rear fenders.

Both Chrysler V-8s were enlarged and had boosted horsepower ratings. The "Spitfire" engine, with its polyspherical combustion chambers, was bored to 331 cid, the same as last year's Hemi. Two versions, both with an 8.5:1 compression ratio, were offered. The first, with a two-barrel carburetor, generated 225 hp at 4400 rpm. A four-barrel version — available only with PowerFlite automatic transmission — put out 250 hp at 4600 rpm.

The Hemi-head "Firepower" V-8 was bored out to 354 cid. A 280-hp Hemi with a 9.0:1 compression ratio and a single four-barrel carburetor was used in New Yorkers and Imperials. In the Chrysler 300 B, a 340-hp Hemi with 9.0:1 compression and two four-barrel carburetors was standard. A version of this engine with a 10.0:1 compression ratio was optional. It produced 355 hp at 5200 rpm, better than one horsepower per cubic inch. This was prior to Chevrolet's 283-hp, 283-cid fuel-injected V-8 of 1957! The availability of the Chrysler engine was limited mainly to stock car racers or special buyers.

Chrysler didn't really advertise its horsepower ratings as the Automobile Manufacturers Association was trying to downplay the horsepower race at this time. The company did make it clear it had some of the most powerful cars on the American highway.

The '56s were promoted as "PowerStyle Chryslers" and the Hemi engine was often referred to in advertisements as "the airplane-type V-8."

Chryslers of this era had many features not found on other American cars — Instant Heating System, Highway Hi-Fi (under-dash record player), concealed exhaust outlets, and safety door locks — as well as many other standard items.

While Chrysler Division followed the industry's downturn in 1956, a bright spot was the Imperial, which was making gains in the high-priced market niche. Calendar year production was listed as 95,356 Chryslers and 12,130 Imperials.

1957 *Chrysler and Imperial*

The Saratoga series, like this 1957 hardtop, was a mid-level Chrysler model.

The year 1957 was a "mighty" interesting season. The "Eisenhower Doctrine" pledged the might of the United States to defend Middle Eastern nations against Communism. In the World Series, the mighty bats of the Milwaukee Braves won it, 4-games-to-3, over the New York Yankees. In Russia, mighty rocket engines launched Sputnik I, the world's first artificial satellite, into orbit.

In the automotive world, the mighty Chrysler took The Forward Look one step further with its towering tail fins and Flight Sweep styling.

The 1957 Chryslers and Imperials looked totally different from the 1956 models and nothing like each other. A third series, which revived the old Saratoga name, was added to the Chrysler lineup between the Windsor and New Yorker. In addition to the fins mentioned above, there was a new massive bumper grille with wide, horizontal parking lights under wraparound bumper wings. Dual headlights were options, but only were allowed in a few states. All Chryslers looked longer, lower, and wider, although the wheelbase was unchanged and overall lengths were slightly reduced.

"Torsion-Aire Ride" was Chrysler's name for a new front suspension system employing torsion bars instead of springs. It was said to do a better job of absorbing road shocks and provide more level stops, starts, and turns. Chrysler claimed improved handling. A new Torque-Flite automatic transmission was also available in all series.

The entry-level Windsors carried a model name script on the rear fenders. Body side moldings were not standard, but all Windsors were available with a bullet-shaped molding treatment on the rear fenders and buyers had the option of a two-tone paint treatment in which the area between the moldings was painted a contrasting color. The same contrasting color was available on the roof. Windsor body styles included two- and four-door hardtops, a sedan, and a Town & Country wagon at prices between $3,033 and $3,520. Torque-Flite was $220 extra.

A new 285-hp version of the Spitfire V-8 was used in Windsors. As in 1956, this two-barrel engine had the same displacement as the previous year's Hemi — 354 cubic inches.

"Saratoga" was written in script on the front fenders in Chrysler's new line. A single, full-length body side molding sweeping gently from the center of the headlights to the bottom of the taillights was standard. An upper rear molding positioned parallel to the top of the fin was a trim option. Being the era of two-toning, when this molding was added, the area between the two chrome strips was often done in a contrasting color and the same contrasting color was available for the roof. The Saratoga line had the same body styles as the Windsor line, except for the wagon. Prices were $3,658 to $3,772. The Saratoga used a 295-hp version of the 354-cid Spitfire V-8 with a four-barrel carburetor.

On Chrysler's upper series the "New Yorker" name, in script, was carried on the front fenders. There were seven vertical louvers on the rear fenders and dual-sweep spear moldings were standard side trim. The New Yorker had a bored and stroked Hemi with 392 cubic inches that put out 325 hp.

The third-edition Chrysler 300—called the 300-C—had a unique trapezoid-shaped grille and a chrome molding on the rear quarters that "speared" a circular medallion carrying a red-white-and-blue 300 badge. Functional brake-cooling vents were incorporated below the headlights.

New this year was the Chrysler 300 convertible. The Hemi V-8 used in the 300 had a high-lift camshaft, extra-stiff valve springs and two four-barrel carburetors. It delivered 375 hp at 520 rpm. A special 390-hp version with solid valve lifters was made available, on a limited basis, for racing. It had a 10.0:1 compression ratio and four-bolt cast-iron exhaust headers with a 2-1/2-inch, low-back-pressure exhaust system. A Dodge three-speed manual transmission was used in cars fitted with this engine.

The '57 Imperial was called the "Finest expression of The Forward Look." It was completely restyled with a new lower, wider body carrying a new aluminum grille and massive, wraparound front bumpers. The new upswept rear fenders had a distinctive "fluid look" and carried taillights that seemed like the Statue of Liberty's torch laid on its side. Two- and four-door hardtops had a new landau style roof treatment. Swept-back wheel openings and optional dual headlights, where permitted, were other features.

There were three Imperial series, all constructed on a 129-inch wheelbase. A four-door sedan and two- and four-door Southampton hardtops were offered in all, except the new top-of-the line Imperial LeBaron series, which had only the four-door models. An Imperial name script was on the front fenders. Crown Imperials had a crown emblem above it, eagle medallions at the base of the windshield, and gold crowns on the front fenders just above the headlights. LeBarons also had special "LeBaron" name-plates on the front fenders. Prices ranged from $4,661 to $5,668.

Chrysler also produced 36 custom-built Ghia Crown Imperials with custom body work by the Italian coachbuilder on a 149.5-inch wheelbase chassis. These cars had 244.7-inch long 8-passenger limousine bodies and black leather roof trim. Purchasers of the cars included the White House, King Saud of Saudia Arabia, the rulers of Kuwait and Qatar, New York Governor Nelson Rockefeller, and David Sarnoff of NBC. Prices started at $12,000.

On a calendar-year basis, Chrysler enjoyed a 45.8 percent increase in production to 156,679 cars (including 118,733 Chryslers and 37,946 Imperials). Model-year production included 115,858 Chryslers and 35,734 Imperials.

1958 Chrysler and Imperial

The 1958 Chrysler Saratoga four-door hardtop was one of the "Mighty Chryslers."

Power plays were in the news when 1958 arrived. Nikita Khrushchev came into power in Russia and Charles de Gaulle regained power in France. In football, the Baltimore Colts powered to a 23-17 victory over the New York Giants to capture the NFL championship.

Chrysler was selling power in the engine bay of "The Mighty Chrysler," which promised to make: "...driving exciting all over again." One advertisement suggested car shoppers should: "Let Chrysler prove its power. Touch the accelerator and surge ahead."

TorqueFlite automatic transmission was standard equipment in all 1958 Chryslers and Imperials. A 354-cid Spitfire V-8 was used in the Windsors and Saratogas. The Windsor version delivered 290 hp with just a two-barrel carburetor. The Saratoga's four-barrel carburetor upped this to 310 hp. New Yorkers used a 392-cid Hemi V-8 with a four-barrel carburetor, a combination that produced a whopping 345 hp.

The low-production, high-performance 300 D featured a hopped-up 380-hp Hemi with dual four-barrel carbs and 380 hp.

A rare fuel-injected version with 390 hp was released, then recalled. Only a few cars were not converted back to 380-hp specs.

This author learned to drive on a 1958 Chrysler Saratoga four-door hardtop and will testify even this mid-range machine was a powerhouse. This car always seemed long, low, wide, airy and full of get-up-and-go. The car had a rocket-ship-like character.

The '58 models had new front end styling with a rectangular grid facing above the center horizontal grille bar and a full-width air scoop below. Dual headlights were standard on all Chryslers this season. There were mid-season sales upgrades to the exterior bright work packages, such as the Windsor Dartline model.

The Dartline trim added an extra "branch" of sweep spear molding at the front and the space between it and the regular straight molding was filled in with an anodized panel and three gold crown emblems.

Early-season ads spoke of Chrysler's "clean and lustrous" lines, which really were very attractive. Since 1958 was a recession year, car sales plummeted. It was felt that hanging some more "tinsel" on the lower-rung Chryslers might make them look more expensive and seem a better value.

With window stickers as low as $3,074 for a Windsor four-door sedan, Chrysler pushed its cheaper models with slogans like: "It's all Chrysler and you'll like the price!"

Windsors were the price-leaders with their name in script on the rear fenders and the standard trim was a single molding running from behind the front wheel well to the rear of the car.

In addition to the sedan, this line contained two- and four-door hardtops and six- and nine-passenger Town & Country station wagons. Production totals also show two convertibles were made. All were on the 122-inch "Dodge" wheelbase, also used for Plymouth wagons and DeSoto Firesweeps.

The one-step-up Chrysler had a "Saratoga" script on the front fenders. The molding treatment started at the front-door break line. A smaller upper molding angled away from the main molding on the rear of the car and had a shield medallion towards the rear. The space between the moldings was often done in a contrasting color that matched the roof color. This line offered the sedan and two hardtop models in the $3,818 to $3,956 range. The Saratogas used a larger 126-inch wheelbase.

New Yorkers had their model name on the front fender. The side molding started just behind it and there were dual parallel moldings towards the rear. A large, gold "C" appeared on the upper molding below the rear side molding and an ornament with seven vertical chevrons was seen on the rear fenders. All body types including the convertible (666 built) were offered on the 126-inch wheelbase New Yorker chassis priced from $4,230 to $5,018.

The Chrysler 300-D "letter car" had a cleaner look with a trapezoid grille and only a straight rear fender molding that intersected a large, round red-white-and-blue "300-D" badge. This series offered a two-door hardtop for $5,173 and a convertible for $5,603. Chrysler built just 618 sport coupes and 191 ragtops.

A new radiator grille with multiple flat, extremely elongated blades arranged in a rectangular pattern characterized 1958 Imperials. Dual headlights were standard on all models and new, round parking lights were set into the front bumper. Imperial, Imperial Crown, and Imperial LeBaron models were offered. The Imperials had a model-name script on the front fenders and came in four-door sedan and two- and four-door Southampton hardtop models, with prices between $4,763 and $4,870.

The Crown Imperial line offered the same styles, plus a convertible in the $5,313 to $5,684 range. The flagship models were the LeBaron sedan or four-door Southhampton, both priced at $5,894. All Imperials shared the 345-hp Hemi and a 129-inch wheelbase. Chrysler also built 31 Crown Imperial limousines on a 149-1/2-inch wheelbase with a base price of $15,000.

In addition to a V-8 and TorqueFlite, all 1958 Chryslers came with power steering. The Torsion-Aire Ride front suspension was standard equipment for all models.

Chrysler put great emphasis on promoting Imperials as a separate car line. Total Chrysler Imperial production for calendar-year 1958 was 63,186 cars, of which 21.6 percent were Imperials. Model-year production came to 60,873 Chryslers and 16,102 Imperials.

1959 Chrysler and Imperial

Only 31 Crown Imperial limousines were built in 1959, priced at $15,000 each.

"Big" was an important word in 1959. In the movies Ben-Hur was the big-screen epic of the year and won big by racking up 11 Oscars. Westerns were big with Americans, who made "Maverick" and "Rawhide" the biggest TV hits. Chrysler had its own "space race" going in 1959—a race to squeeze more room for people inside each car. Highland Park claimed roomy new interiors made "…all other cars seem cramped."

One advertisement invited buyers to: "Stretch out in new dimensions of leg-room, head-room, and hip-room." Another ad pointed out wider, taller doors for 1959, a raised roof, and rear seat "pushed" rearward to let riders stretch out. Seat cushions were raised for comfort and the seats were "snugged" closer to the doors.

Another clever 1959 ad showing a Nocturne Blue and Ivory White Windsor two-door hardtop was headlined "Space Travel… it's pushbutton driving ease with room to spare!" Chrysler played off two meanings of the word "space," talking about the car's interior space as well as its "space-age" instrument panel.

Major styling updates for 1959 Chryslers included a new cellular grille with parking lights centered under the dual headlights. There was a dramatic new roof treatment with bright metal trim around the center section and (usually) two-tone finish. New side trim treatments were seen on all series.

Windsor models had a chrome "lightning bolt" down the sides and chrome rocker panel moldings that ran a few inches along the rear wheel openings. The Chrysler name appeared in a chrome rear-fender script. On the front doors was an emblem depicting a golden "leaping lion" as related to the use of new "Golden Lion" 383- and 413-cid V-8 engines. The Hemi was dropped this season.

These so-called B-Series *intermediate* V-8 engines had "wedge-head" combustion chambers and a new 10.10:1 compression ratio. The 383 was used with a two-barrel carburetor in Windsors and with a four-barrel carburetor in Saratogas. The convertible was a regular Windsor model this year (961 were made) and other models were the same as 1958. Prices dropped roughly $100-$200, depending on body style

Saratogas came in the same three body styles as 1958, also at lower (by about $150) prices. With a four-barrel carburetor, these cars cranked out 20 additional horsepower — 325 hp to be exact. A Saratoga nameplate adorned the rear fenders and fancier side trim moldings curved downwards, from just behind the headlights to the rear bumper, gradually flaring out as they swept across the rear fenders. The center of the molding was sometimes done in a contrasting color, usually matching a second color used on the roof. Golden lion emblems also adorned the front fenders..

On New Yorkers the series name and golden lion medallions appeared on the front fenders. The same six body styles were priced from $4,020 to $4,753. Only 286 New Yorker convertibles were made, along with just 444 six-passenger wagons and 564 nine-passenger wagons.

As usual, the Chrysler 300 Letter Car continued with is trapezoid grille and very simple body side trim, although the letter on the large circular medallion changed into an "E." The most significant change was the dropping of the Hemi. The Chrysler 300-E used the larger 413-cid "wedge" V-8, although it was fitted with twin four-barrel carburetors and put out 380 hp compared to the New Yorker's 350 hp. The $5,319 hardtop had a production run of only 550 units and the $5,749 convertible, just 140 assemblies.

Moving upscale to the Imperial lineup, the basics were little changed except for the switch to the 413-cid engine . . . the same version used in New Yorkers.

A new brushed stainless steel "Silvercrest Landau" roof with simulated leather trim was optional. One major alteration was the use of a new, stronger frame. This allowed a lower floor and greater leg room, particularly in the rear compartment.

Imperial Crown models could be picked out by small crown medallions above the V-shaped medallions on the headlight "eyebrows" and on the bright metal trim strips at the rear of the projectile-shaped taillight housings. LeBarons had nameplates on their front fenders and coat-of-arms medallions on the wide, bright-metal sections at the rear of the side trim moldings.

A new option was swiveling front seats with a lever on the front seat frame that allowed the seats to be rotated towards the door openings. Also new was a rear air suspension system.

In 1959, Chrysler Division car production for the calendar-year totaled 90,374 units, a 43 percent improvement over 1958. Twenty-three percent of those cars were Imperials. Model-year output was 62,244 Chryslers and 17,262 Imperials.

The California sun has been kind to this 1952 Chrysler Windsor Deluxe convertible.

Corvettes
of the Fifties

1953 *Corvette*

An original, the 1953 Corvette was one of only 300 copies made that year.

"Don't Let The Stars Get In Your Eyes" was a Number 1 song in 1953, but Chevrolet Motor Division was perfectly content to put stars in car buyers' eyes when it brought a dream car to life as the 1953 Corvette. In fact, film stars like John Wayne were provided with early examples in hopes that their fame would generate publicity for the new "All-American Sports Car." Dave Garroway, a TV celebrity of the era who was known as a sports-car buff, praised the new model in a sales promotion film called "Halls of Wonder."

A prototype Corvette was shown at the 1953 GM Motorama in New York City, then the sleek roadster was rushed to the assembly line. The first production Corvette was built on June 30, 1953, in Chevrolet's Flint, Michigan, assembly plant. In fact, all '53s were constructed there, in an area at the rear of the customer delivery garage on Van Dyke Ave.

It would not be until 1954 that manufacturing of the new sports car shifted to a factory in St. Louis, Missouri. Chevy expected to make 1,000 Corvettes per month in St. Louis and predicted 10,000 per year could be sold by its dealers. It took more than a few years to prove that and the first Corvette to achieve five-figure production numbers was the 1960 model.

Chevrolet's original plan was to build 300 fiberglass-bodied Corvettes and then switch to a steel body. But the new technology captured public attention "Corvette Shows The Way For Plastic Cars" read the headline of a *Life* magazine article. It showed photos of the 54 plastic parts that went into the body and of a workman lifting the 35-pound hood and fender section by himself. In addition, fiberglass bodies were cheaper to build. According to one estimate, GM paid $400,000 to make 300 Corvette bodies that would have cost $4.5 million to make from steel!

The Corvette had a chrome-framed grille with 13 heavy vertical chrome bars and recessed headlights that were protected by chromed wire-screen headlights. Like most true sports car of the era, it was a genuine "roadster" — an open car with no side windows. In fact, it did not even have outside door handles. One of the earliest wraparound windshields was used. At the rear were protruding, fender-integrated taillights.

The Corvette's interior featured a Powerglide two-speed automatic transmission, which was a rather radical departure from standard sports-car practice. However, gear shifting was still accomplished via the traditional floor-mounted lever. Oil pressure, battery, water temperature, and fuel gauges were fitted in the dashboard, along with a tachometer and a clock.

Each 1953 model was virtually hand-built and a lot of minor changes were made during the production run. All of the first-year Corvettes were Polo White with Sportsman Red interiors. According to an article published in *Life* magazine: "…white is the plastic's normal color and a demand for other colors has not materialized." The magazine reported Chevrolet's claim that Corvettes would be easy to repair. "If the tough plastic is punctured in an accident it can usually be patched like new with a blowtorch for a couple of dollars."

All had black canvas convertible tops that manually folded into a storage space behind the seats. Other 1953-only features included special valve covers, a one-piece carburetor linkage and a small trunk mat. Short exhaust extensions were used on all '53s (and early '54s), since the cars were prone to drawing exhaust fumes inside through the vent windows. A black oilcloth window storage bag was provided to protect the 1953 Corvette's removable plastic side windows when they were stowed in the trunk.

The Corvette's $3,498 list price included a "hopped-up" version of Chevrolet's 235.5-cid in-line six-cylinder engine. This cast-iron-block, overhead-valve power plant was well known by its "Stovebolt Six" nickname. It combined a 3.56 x 3.96-inch bore and stroke, an 8.0:1 compression ratio and three Carter Type YH one-barrel carburetors to generate 150 hp at 4200 rpm. A single breaker-point ignition system was used.

Tipping the scales at 2,705 pounds, the Corvette rode a 102-inch wheelbase and measured 167.3 inches end-to-end. It had a 57-inch front tread and a 58.8-inch rear tread. The 6.70 x 15 tires were mounted on steel disk wheels. Front suspending was by coil springs, with tubular shock absorbers and a stabilizer bar. Leaf springs were fitted at the rear, in combination with tubular shocks and a solid rear axle. Drum brakes were found at all four corners. A

3.55:1 rear axle ratio was standard. A six-volt electrical system was supplied.

In addition to being the first Corvette made, the 1953 model is also the rarest ever made — that is, if you don't count the one 1983 pilot model Chevy built or some of the rare option packages. Model-year production for '53 peaked at 300 units. About 200 of the 300 Corvettes made in 1953 are known to still exist today. Calendar-year sales were also 300 cars.

Zora Arkus-Duntov joined Chevrolet Motor Division on May 1, 1953. Duntov believed a combination of passion and practicality sold cars. He felt sporty cars like the Corvette lacked practicality and had to have extra emotional appeal to garner sufficient sales. He thought higher performance could create such appeal. Duntov would soon become chief engineer of the Corvette. By making it a V-8-powered model and adding other upgrades, he came to play a major role in shaping its destiny and success.

1954 *Corvette*

The 1954 Corvette was one of an estimated 80 percent that were painted white.

As the year 1954 arrived, a song named "Ebb Tide" was at the top of *Your Hit Parade*. Corvette sales were also caught in an ebb tide. After delivery of the first 300 cars in 1953, buyers stopped coming in. It is said about half of the nearly-unchanged 1954 models just sat in dealerships, watching as traditional Chevrolet customers stocked up on 150s, 210s and Bel Airs. It would not be until 1955, when Zora Arkus-Duntov stuffed a V-8 under the hood and went racing, that the Corvette found its true niche as Chevrolet's "new-image" car. As *Road & Track* magazine stated it in 1954: "The Corvette heralds a new approach, offers new hope, for the individualist."

Production of the six-cylinder-powered 1954 Corvettes began Dec. 23, 1953 in the St. Louis assembly plant. For all practical purposes, the 1953 and 1954 models were the same car. The price was dropped to $2,774 as Chevrolet did what it could to help its anxious dealers move some additional units. It didn't help much. The 1954 Corvette did not achieve its sales target of 10,000 cars. In fact, a total of just 3,640 Corvettes were delivered and over 1,100 remained unsold when the year ended.

Minor running production changes were made to the window storage bag, the air cleaners, the starter, and the locations of the fuel and brake lines. A new style of valve cover was used. It was held on by four bolts through the outside lip instead of two center studs. The valve cover decals were different and had larger lettering.

The optional AM radio had Conelrad National Defense System icons on its face. Early in 1954, the original two-handles hood latch was changed to a single-handle design. Corvettes after the car with serial number E54S003906 had integrated dual-pot air cleaners. A clip to hold the ventipanes closed was added in late 1954. Dimensions and chassis specifications remained the same as in 1953.

Unlike the previous year's all-Polo White model, 1954 Corvettes were also available in Pennant Blue, and Sportsman Red and Black. Approximately 80 percent of 1954 Corvettes were painted white. About 15 percent had a Pennant Blue exterior with Shoreline Beige interior. About three percent were red with a red interior and some black cars with red interiors were built. In addition, Metallic Green and Metallic Brown cars are thought to have been built. The soft convertible top was now offered in beige.

The Corvette engine was initially unchanged, but later in the model year a new camshaft upped horsepower to 155. With the early-year engine, a 1954 Corvette could go from 0 to 60 mph in 11 seconds and from 0 to 100 mph in 41 seconds.

It has been suggested the release of the Ford Thunderbird, on Sept. 23, 1954, actually saved the Corvette. With dismal sales up to that point, Chevrolet was giving serious consideration to the possibility of dropping their sports car.

"There was talk of the Corvette being discontinued," Zora Duntov once told me. "But when the Thunderbird arrived, GM was suddenly reluctant to drop the Corvette. I believe the T-Bird got Ed Cole's competitive spirit going."

Cole was Chevrolet's chief engineer. And another Corvette booster was Harley Earl, who had conceived the original Motorama roadster. So, while the Corvette had some detractors in 1954 — it also had some powerful backers.

The Corvette returned to the 1954 GM Motorama in three new "dream car" variations that, unfortunately, did not make it to the production line in show-car form. The first was a thin-pillared coupe with a lift-off hardtop, the second was the Nomad station wagon, which became the inspiration for the Bel Air of the same name (as well as the Pontiac Custom Safari), and the third was a fastback coupe called the Corvair, which later gave its name to Chevrolet's first compact.

1955 *Corvette*

Jerry Heasley

This 1955 Corvette in the new Gypsy Red shade was one of 700 made that year.

The hit tunes of 1955 reflected America's mid-century fascination with color and excitement. There was "Cherry Pink and Apple Blossom White," "The Yellow Rose of Texas," "The Naughty Lady of Shady Lane" and "Whatever Lola Wants." This was also a year in which Chevrolet's Corvette sports car added dazzling new exterior and interior colors and the excitement of a powerful V-8 engine.

Flashy new Corvette colors for 1955 included Metallic Copper with a beige interior and Harvest Gold (an eye-catching shade of yellow) with green-and-yellow trim and a dark green top. The latter was a bright and popular two-tone combination. Bright Gypsy Red exteriors replaced Sportsman Red and red Corvettes now featured a light beige interior to make them look "lighter and lovelier."

Even the new interior material had an exciting '50s-style trade name — Elascofab. Soft convertible tops were offered in canvas and vinyl. New top colors included white and dark green. It was obvious that Chevrolet was using a new spectrum of colors to brighten the Corvette's appearance and showroom appeal.

While six Corvettes were reportedly turned out with the carryover six-cylinder engine, the new overhead-valve V-8 was an instant and overpowering hit. Chevrolet soon realized the six was dead and started plugging the six-cylinder engine-mounting holes in the frame. The "small-block" V-8 engine was cast-iron and along with the cylinder heads. It had some simple, but effec-

tive design characteristics like independent rocker arms. With a 3.75 x 3.00-inch bore and stroke it offered 265 cubic inches of displacement.

A special camshaft, an 8.0:1 compression ratio, solid valve lifters, and a single Carter WCFB four-barrel carburetor helped the "Corvette" V-8 produce 195 at 5000 rpm and 260 foot-pounds of torque at 3000 rpm (a bit more than the version used in Chevy passenger cars).

Very late in the model year, a three-speed manual transmission became standard in Corvettes. A single dry-plate clutch was used with this gearbox. The two-speed Powerglide automatic transmission that was the sole transmission available up until that point, was then added to the options list.

The 1955 Corvette frame had to be modified to allow room for the fuel pump used with the V-8 engine. Since the V-8 retained less heat than the six-cylinder power plant, it required a smaller radiator. The V-8 also weighed 30 to 40 pounds less than the six, which added to the car's performance numbers. The Corvette V-8 could zoom from 0 to 60 mph in 8.7 seconds and 0-to-100 mph took only 24.7 seconds.

Production of 1955 Corvettes began Oct. 28, 1954. The car's basic styling remained the same as that of last year's model, although there were improvements in the quality of the fiberglass body, which was thinner and smoother. The V-8-powered cars had an enlarged gold "V" within the word Chevrolet on the front fenders. They also featured a 12-volt electrical system, while cars with the six-cylinder engine retained a six-volt electrical system. Electric windshield wipers replaced the old vacuum type.

The 1955 Corvette retained the same dimensions, the same front and rear suspension setups, and even the same 3.55:1 rear axle ratio as the 1953 and 1954 models. Optional equipment consisted of only about eight items including directional signals for $16.75, a heater for $91.40, a signal-seeking AM radio for $145.15,

a parking brake alarm for $5.65, Powerglide automatic transmission for $178.35, and 6.70 x 15 white sidewall tires for $26.90 above the cost of standard "blackwalls."

With the six-cylinder engine, the '55 Corvette listed for $2,779 and weighed 2,705 pounds. Only a half dozen sixes were built. With the new V-8 engine, the Corvette had a $2,934 window sticker and gained 175 pounds. Total production of both six-cylinder and V-8 models combined was 700.

1956 Corvette

New styling marked the introduction of the 1956 Corvettes.

In 1956, the world's problems seemed to flare up, mainly in faraway places like the Sinai Peninsula and Hungary. Here in America, things seemed nearly perfect. The nation's beloved "Ike" was re-elected President, handily defeating Adlai Stevenson for the second time. American Grace Kelly made the perfect transaction from Hollywood actress to Princess Grace of Monaco. New York Yankee hurler Don Larsen pitched a perfect World Series game against the Brooklyn Dodgers.

In the automotive world, Chevrolet's Corvette began to define itself as "the" true American sports car. "A lot of people would have been *perfectly* content if Chevrolet had frozen Corvette styling with the 1956 model," automotive historian Charles Webb once noted.

Production of 1956 Corvettes began Nov. 4, 1955. The same basic grille styling was kept intact, but the "teeth" in the grille looked a bit slimmer. Chevrolet styling studio chief Clare MacKichan directed the 1956 redesign. He was somewhat inspired by the thrusting headlamps and twin-bulge hood of the Mercedes-Benz 300SL gull-wing coupe.

There were many changes, including new front fenders housing chrome-rimmed headlights, glass windows, external door handles, chrome-outlined concave side body coves and sloping, taillight-integrated rear fenders. The dashboard layout was themed the

same as in 1953-1955 models. A new rearview mirror, located at the center of the top of the dash, was adjusted by using a thumbscrew. Carrying a $3,149 price tag, the 1956 Corvette roadster weighed 2,730 pounds. The model regained a little popularity and 3,467 were made – five times the amount sold in 1955.

Better-fitting convertible tops were standard equipment in 1956. A power top was optional, as was a removable fiberglass hardtop. Upholstery colors were limited to beige or red, but seven nitro-cellulose lacquer body colors were available. They were Onyx Black with a silver panel (black or white soft top); Polo White with a silver panel (black or white soft top); Venetian Red with a beige panel (beige or white soft top); Cascade Green with a beige panel (beige or white soft top; Aztec Copper with a beige panel (beige or white soft top); Arctic Blue with a silver panel (beige or white soft top) and Inca Silver with a Imperial Ivory panel (black or white soft top).

The base engine for 1956 was basically the same small-block V-8 introduced in 1955, but the compression ratio was upped to 9.25:1. This helped generate 210 hp at 5200 rpm and 270 foot-pounds of torque at 3200 rpm. It now had hydraulic valve lifters. This was the first year the Corvette was offered with optional V-8s and there were two available. Both were performance variations on the same 265-cid block. The Turbo-Fire 225 option featured solid valve lifters, twin Carter four-barrel carburetors and a dual-exhaust system. It was good for 225 hp at 5200 rpm and 270 foot-pounds of torque at 3600 rpm. The Turbo-Fire 240 option added a high-lift camshaft to get to 240 hp.

A close-ratio three-speed manual all-synchromesh transmission with floor-mounted gear shifter was standard Corvette. The two-speed Powerglide automatic transmission was again optional at $175 extra.

Retaining a 102-inch wheelbase, the new Corvette measured 168 inches long. It stood 51.9 inches tall and was 70.5 inches wide. Tread widths were 57 inches up front and 59 inches at the rear. Ground clearance was just six inches. Chevrolet again used 6.70 x 15 tires.

The fiberglass body rode on a welded-steel box-section, X-braced frame. The front suspension consisted of independent, unequal-length A-arms up front with coil springs and tube shocks. The rear suspension incorporated a live axle on semi-elliptic leaf springs, an anti-roll bar and tubular shock absorbers. Steering was Saginaw worm-and-ball with a 16:1 ratio and a 37-foot turning circle. A hypoid semi-floating rear axle was fitted. Four-wheel hydraulic, internal-expanding brakes with 11-inch diameter drums provided 157 square inches of effective lining area (121 square inches with optional sintered metallic linings). The standard rear axle ratio with the three-speed manual gearbox was 3.70:1; with Powerglide: 3.55:1. Optional axle ratios included 3.27:1, 4.11:1 and 4.56:1.

The 1956 options list included a heater for $115, a signal-seeking AM radio for $185, a parking brake signal for $5, courtesy lights for $8, a windshield washer for $11, white sidewall tires for $30 extra, the auxiliary hardtop for $200, and a hydraulic folding top mechanism for $100. Electric power windows were offered for the first time at $60 and only 547 buyers ordered them. The special high-lift camshaft was a $175 package and the dual four-barrel carburetor equipment cost $160.

Chevrolet general manager Ed Cole and Corvette chief engineer Zora Arkus-Duntov decided it was time for the Corvette to go racing in 1956. Duntov drove one car to a two-way average of 150.583 mph at Daytona's Flying Mile. John Fitch also set a record of 90.932 mph for the standing-start mile at Daytona and 145.543 mph in the production sports car class.

In the spring of 1956, at Pebble Beach, Calif., dentist Dr. Dick Thompson finished second overall and first in class in a sports car road race. Thompson went on to take the Sports Car Club of America (SCCA) 1956 championship with his Corvette. A 225-hp 1956 Corvette could go from 0-to-60 mph in 7.3 seconds; from 0-to-100 mph in 20.7 seconds.

1957 *Corvette*

A rare few of the '57 Corvettes had fuel injection. Most of them, like this one, did not.

Rock-and-Roll was catching on throughout America in 1957, with songs like "All Shook Up," "Party Doll," "Jailhouse Rock," and "Little Darlin'" zooming to the top of the charts. Chevrolet's Corvette was starting to zoom, too, both on racetracks and in sales. With support from his high-placed friends at GM, Zora Arkus-Duntov was turning the "'Vette" into something more than a boulevard cruiser. His efforts were rocking things up and sending Chevy's fiberglass sports car off on a winning roll. Business picked up a bit this season and 6,339 Corvettes were assembled by year's end.

Production of 1957 Corvettes began Oct. 19, 1956. The 1957 model looked the same as the 1956 model, although major changes started taking place under the hood. In five short years, the Corvette had gone from offering a single six-cylinder engine to offering a selection of six powerful V-8s. More importantly, Chevrolet began to prove Duntov's thinking that the Corvette image could help sell other Chevrolets. One advertisement of the year pictured a Seafoam Green Corvette parked outside a garage it was sharing with a red Bel Air Sports Coupe. "Chevy puts the purr in performance," the sales slogan said.

The Corvette's price was now at $3,176. It weighed 2,730 pounds. Standard included dual exhausts, all-vinyl bucket seats, a three-spoke competition-style steering wheel, full carpeting, an outside rearview mirror, an electric clock, and a tachometer. The thumb-screw-adjusted rear view mirror of 1956 was replaced with a lock-nut type that required a wrench to adjust it.

Corvettes were now available in seven colors: Onyx Black (black, white, or beige top); Polo White (black, white, or beige top); Aztec Copper (white or beige top); Arctic Blue (black, white or beige top); Cascade Green (black, white, or beige top); Venetian Red (black, white or beige top) and silver (black or white top). White, silver, and beige were optional color choices for the elliptical side cove.

The big news of the year was the availability of a 283-cid 283-hp fuel-injected V-8, which took the fuel-injected '57 Corvette into the then-considered-magical one-horsepower-per-cubic-inch high-performance bracket.

The Corvette's continuous-flow fuel-injection system was a joint effort of Zora Arkus-Duntov, John Dolza, and General Motor's Rochester Division. Only 1,040 of the 1957 Corvettes were fuel-injected. A 283-hp fuel-injection 1957 Corvette could go from 0-to-60 mph in 5.7 seconds and from 0-to-100 mph in 16.8 seconds. It had a top speed of 132 mph. While only 1,040 Corvettes were equipped with the fuel-injection system, but its availability surely symbolized the Corvette's transition into a high-performance car.

The base Corvette engine had new 3.875 x 3.00-inch bore and stroke measurements and displaced 283 cubic inches. It ran an 8.5:1 compression ratio in conjunction with hydraulic valve lifters and a two-barrel carburetor. This Turbo-Fire 283 was available only with Powerglide transmission. It was rated for 185 hp at 4600 rpm and 275 foot-pounds of torque at 2400 rpm. Next came a version with 9.5:1 compression, dual exhausts and a four-barrel carburetor that produced 220 hp at 4800 rpm and 300 foot-pounds of rotational power at 3000 rpm.

Adding dual Carter WCFB four-barrels produced the next power option, which upped horsepower to 245 at 5000 rpm and produced the same 300 foot-pounds of torque at higher (3800) revs. A second dual-carb "Super-Turbo-Fire" V-8 with a special camshaft generated 270 hp at 6000 rpm and 285 foot-pounds of torque at 4200 rpm.

Two "Ram-Jet" fuel-injected versions of the 283 were on Chevy's "plate" for the '57 Corvette. Both used the same Rochester mechanical fuel-injection setup. The first, with a 9.5:1 compression ratio, generated 250 hp at 5000 rpm and 305 foot-pounds of torque at 3800 rpm. The second had a 10.5:1 compression ratio and cranked out one horsepower per cubic inch at 6200 rpm. Rated torque was 290 at 4400.

A close-ratio three-speed manual all-synchromesh transmission with floor-mounted gear shifter was standard equipment. A two-speed Powerglide automatic transmission was optional. A close-ratio four-speed manual all-synchromesh transmission with floor-mounted gear shifter was added to the options list after May.

Dimensionally, the 1957 Corvette was a match for the 1956 model and the chassis specifications were mostly the same. The standard rear axle ratio with the three-speed manual gearbox was 3.70:1. A 3.55:1 was again fitted to cars with the Powerglide transmission, unless optional ratios were ordered. Available options included 3.27:1, 4.11:1 and 4.56:1.

Another important option was the competition suspension package RPO 684 which included heavy-duty springs, shocks, and roll bars, 16.3:1 quick-ratio steering, a Positraction differential, special brake cooling equipment, and Cerametallic brake linings.

Dick Thompson and Gaston Audrey won the 12-hour Sebring race in Corvettes and Thompson took the SCCA B-production championship for the second year in a row.

1958 *Corvette*

The 1958 Corvettes received quad headlights and a new front-end treatment.

When the first Thunderbirds came out, nearly all Ford advertisements pictured the sporty two-seater with coupes, sedans, or station wagons. It took Chevrolet awhile to realize a limited-production sports model attracted many car buyers to the showroom. By 1958, the message got through.

"Nothing goes with springtime like a bright new Chevy!" said one full-page promotion. "Here are cars to rejoice in . . . sports-minded, fun-hearted and beautiful as all outdoors." The cars shown were a Salmon-colored Impala Sport Coupe and a black-and-silver Corvette roadster. The Impala was described as "gull-wing glamour" and the Corvette was: "...America's only authentic sports car."

A second, similar advertisement featured a red Bel Air four-door sedan and a snappy-looking yellow Corvette. "The beautiful way to be sporty! New 1958 Corvette with new style, new power and new sparkle, strictly for those who speak the Corvette's special language," said the wording. "Get the feel in the new '58 Corvette cockpit. Sample any one of its four ultra-compact V-8s (including the 290-h.p. Fuel-Injection version); and its three transmissions. You'll be driving the absolutely best road car in America."

Despite such claims by Chevrolet copywriters, some sports car purists felt that Corvette styling was a little too jazzed up for 1958. There were now four chrome-rimmed headlights with fender length chrome strips running between each pair of lights. As if that weren't enough glitter, fake louvers were placed on the hood. The grille was similar to the previous year, but had four fewer vertical bars. Three horizontal chrome strips were added to the new cove. A couple of vertical chrome bars decorated the trunk (and detracted from an otherwise graceful rear-end treatment). The wrap-around front and rear bumpers were also larger—and heavier.

The 1958 Corvette's interior changed dramatically. The gauges were clustered together in front of the driver, rather than spread across the dash as before. A center console and passenger assist (sissy) bar were added. Seat belts were made standard equipment, after being a dealer-installed option in 1956 and 1957.

There were six exterior body colors offered: Charcoal (black or white soft top), Silver Blue (white or beige soft top), Regal Turquoise (black or white soft top), Signet Red (black or white soft top), Panama Yellow (black or white soft top) and Snowcrest White (black, white, or beige soft top).

The 1958 Corvette sold for $3,591 and weighed in at 2,781 pounds. Standard under the hood in 1958 was a 283-cid 230-hp V-8 with 9.5:1 compression, hydraulic lifters, a four-barrel carbure-tor, and dual exhausts. This 283 was also available with dual four-barrel carburetors and 245 hp. A fuel-injected version produced 250 hp. Switching to solid lifters upped the rating of the dual-quad V-8 to 270 hp. The top option was a fuel-injected solid-lifter V-8 with an 11.5:1 compression ratio and 290 hp at 6200 rpm.

Transmission choices were the same as in 1957, as were dimensions, chassis specifications, and axle ratios. Factory options included a heater for $96.85, a signal-seeking AM radio for $144.45, a parking brake alarm for $5.40, courtesy lights for $6.50, windshield washers for $16.15, white sidewall tires for $31.55 extra, an auxiliary hardtop for $215.20, electric power windows for $59.20, an optional cove color for $16.15, and a power-operated folding top mechanism for $139.90.

The Powerglide automatic transmission cost $188.30. Racing enthusiasts could get a four-speed manual transmission for $215.20 additional. Those interested in higher performance could get the 245-hp engine for $150.65, the 270-hp engine for $182.95, the 250-hp fuel-injection engine for $484.20. A Positraction axle with 3.70:1 or 4.11:1 ratios was $48.45 (with a 4.56:1 ratio $45). A heavy-duty racing suspension could be ordered for $780.10 and five wider 15 x 5.5-inch wheels were a no-cost option.

Production of 1958 Corvettes began Oct. 31, 1957. A 1958 Corvette with the standard 230-hp V-8 and 4.11:1 rear axle could go from 0-to-60 mph in 9.2 seconds. It could do the quarter mile in 17.4 seconds at 83 mph and had a top speed of 103 mph. A 1958 Corvette with the optional 250-hp fuel-injected V-8 and 3.70:1 rear axle could go from 0-to-60 mph in 7.6 seconds and from 0-to-100 mph in 21.4 seconds.

It could do the quarter mile in 15.7 seconds at 90 mph and had a top speed of 120 mph. A 1959 Corvette with the 290 hp fuel-injected engine took only 6.9 seconds to go from 0-to-60 mph. Almost 11 percent of the 9,168 Corvettes made this year were powered by the 283-cid 290-hp fuel-injected V-8.

1959 *Corvette*

By 1959, Corvettes were an American institution and star of the TV series "Route 66."

"Everything's Coming Up Roses" — a Top 10 tune in 1959 — could have been the Corvette's theme song for the last year of the decade. With the exterior cleaned up from 1958, but not much changed mechanically, Chevrolet's sports car started getting great reviews in the automotive press. Ray Brock of *Hot Rod* had only good things to say when he road tested the Corvette roadster and *Road & Track* described the '59 as "a pretty package with all the speed you need and then some."

Motor Trend tested the Corvette against a Porsche 356 convertible in its April 1959 edition and the only thing the Porsche could boast about afterwards was that it had the best fuel economy of the two. All other kudos went to the Corvette, which accelerated better and handled better. People in the know were starting to recognize the fact the Corvette, even if not the most exotic car around, was becoming a "world-class" sports car with a price tag much lower than the competition in that category.

At its core, the '59 Corvette was little more than a cleaned-up version of the 1958 model. The unnecessary tinsel found on the '58 — fake hood louvers and vertical chrome strips on the trunk — were gone. Interior changes included redesigned bucket seats and door panels, a fiberglass package tray under the "sissy" bar, and concave gauge lenses. Listing for $3,563 — about $100 less than in 1958 — the Corvette had a production run of 9,670 units for the model year.

A tachometer, an outside rearview mirror, seat belts for the driver and passenger, dual exhausts, and an electric clock were among the standard features found in all Corvettes. Interior sun visors became optional equipment. New concave instrument lenses reduced reflections. The optional four-speed manual transmission had a T-shaped reverse-lockout shifter with a white plastic shifter knob. There were plenty of performance options, but Ray Brock said, "There is absolutely no need for any of the heavy-duty racing extras unless the car is intended for sports car racing."

There were seven exterior body colors offered for 1959 Corvettes: Tuxedo Black (available with a black or white soft top), Classic Cream (black or white soft top), Frost Blue (white or blue soft top), Crown Sapphire (white or turquoise soft top), Roman Red (black or white soft top), Snowcrest White (black, white, tan, or blue soft top), and Inca Silver (black or white soft top). Blue, red, turquoise and (for the first time) black interiors were listed. The armrests and door handles were in a different position in the 1959 model. Its seats had a new shape and a shelf was added.

Under-hood options were the same as in 1958. All power options were based on the 283-cid "small-block" Chevy V-8, which came in five versions. A 230-hp rating was standard and options included 245-, 250-, 270- and 290-hp engines. The respective torque ratings were 300, 300, 305, 285, and 290 foot-pounds. A 3.70:1 rear axle ratio was standard with 4.11:1 and 4.56:1 options.

The 290-hp fuel-injection engine with the 4.11:1 rear axle was the hot setup in '59. A car so equipped could do 0-to-60-mph in 6.8 seconds and had a top speed around 128 mph. It could do the standing start quarter mile in 14.9 seconds with a trap speed of 96 mph. By comparison, a car with the mid-range 250-hp engine took a second longer to reach 60 mph. It could do the quarter mile in 15.7 seconds at 90 mph and its flat-out top speed was around 120 mph.

The Corvette again rode on a 102-inch wheelbase with a 177.2-inch overall length. The front tread was 57 inches and the rear was 59 inches. The fiberglass body was 72.8 inches wide and height to the top of the windshield was 51.6 inches. A new Saginaw recirculating ball steering system had a 17:1 ratio, 3.7 turns lock-to-lock and a 38.5-foot turning circle. At 2,842 pounds the '59 weighed about 60 pounds more than a '58 model.

A tachometer, dual exhausts, and electric clock all were standard on 1959 Corvettes.

De Sotos
of the Fifties

1950 De Soto

Many roomy DeSotos were used for taxis. This 1950 Custom was a family sedan.

Decisions, decisions, decisions! The year 1950, was one for making hard choices. President Harry Truman declared a state of emergency after Communist China became involved in the Korean conflict. Throughout the country, 14 million consumers decided to buy televisions.

In its 1950 advertising campaign, De Soto urged car buyers to "Drive a De Soto before you decide!" One ad pointed out that more people had purchased De Sotos in 1949 than ever before.

The 1950 De Soto was a car characterized as: "…built for owner satisfaction." It rode better, steered better and stopped better than previous models. A Floating Power engine mounting system made the car smooth running. Its Balanced Weight Distribution, Synchronized Springing, airplane-type shock absorbers and Super-Cushion tires enhanced its riding qualities. Safe-Guard brakes with Cyclebonded linings gave the 1950 model smooth, controlled stops. Safety enhancements included an all-steel body with increased rigidity.

De Soto's salesman's guide noted the boxy 1950 models were "…easy to get in and out of…" and said: "…people can sit in the seats in a comfortable chair-high position with full visibility." Removable fenders were highlighted as a good feature to have if the car was involved in a fender-bender type accident. They could be repaired or replaced at a reasonable cost. De Soto also noted its flat windshield could be replaced at a "minimum of expense."

De Luxe (spelled as two words, like the De Soto name) and Custom lines were offered in 1950 and both series included short- and long-wheelbase models. The smaller cars had a 125-1/2-inch stance and the larger ones added a substantial 14 extra inches between their wheel centers. In the lower-priced De Luxe line was a Club Coupe, a four-door sedan and a versatile model called the Carry-All sedan.

Aimed at salesmen and other businessmen, this model had a rear seat that folded flat with the luggage compartment floor to allow carrying large loads. The seatback and the luggage floor were trimmed with chrome rub rails that protected the vinyl upholstery and made it easy to slide heavy cargo intro position. Only an eight-passenger four-door sedan was offered in De Luxe trim on the longer chassis. Prices ranged from $1,976 to $2,676.

The short-wheelbase Custom models were the Club Coupe, four-door sedan, convertible, Sportsman hardtop, wood-bodied station wagon, and steel-bodied station wagon. Customs offered with the longer wheelbase included an eight-passenger four-door sedan and a nine-passenger Suburban sedan. In addition to extra passenger roominess, the latter model came standard with a roof-mounted luggage rack. Only 623 of these cars were built. The overall price range for Custom models was $2,156 to $3,179.

De Luxe models could be identified by the lack of nomenclature on the front doors, which were plain, except on the Carry-All sedan. This model had a "Carry-All" nameplate. The fancier De Sotos said "Custom" on the front doors, except in the case of the Suburban, which had its name spelled out there, and the Sportsman, which had its own name on the front fenders.

All De Sotos were powered by the same 236.7-cid L-head six with a 3.438 x 4.25-inch bore and stroke. A new "high" compression ratio of 7.0 to 1 gave the De Soto more drive than ever. The carburetor—called a 4-in-1 design—was said to provide: "…exactly the right fuel mixture for economical operation at any speed."

Different versions of the Ball & Ball E7L carburetor were used on stick-shift cars or cars with Tip-Toe shift. That was the name of the fluid-drive unit that was standard in Customs and optional in De Luxes.

"There is new responsiveness and new surging power awaiting the command of the driver's foot," said De Soto literature.

In 1950, one of De Soto's claims to fame was it held the all-time record for most sales in the first year of a new nameplate. The company had been organized by Chrysler in 1928 and sold 81,065 cars in 1929, its first year of vehicle production. The De Soto plant used in 1950, located on Wyoming Avenue in Detroit, was purchased in 1934 and started turning out De Sotos the following year. In 1950, about 85 percent of all De Soto final assembly operations took place in this 842,450-square-foot facility. Also that year, a new 1,100,000-square-foot body plant was opened on Warren Avenue in Detroit.

De Soto marked its second consecutive calendar-year production of over 100,000 cars with 127,557 assemblies in 1950.. A big part of De Soto's output came from its taxicab output. These delivery vehicles were known for their excellent engineering and dependable, high-mileage service. The commercial taxicabs were built on the long-wheelbase chassis. The many De Soto cabs seen on the streets of New York and other cities were good for sales.

Except for a handful of sporty models built from 1955 up, postwar De Sotos are rarely thought of as "exciting." The author's family owned a 1949 De Soto Custom—similar to the 1950 model, except for its center grille trim—from 1953 until well into the '60s.

I can remember the day we went to H & L Oldsmobile, on Hylan Boulevard, in Staten Island, New York, to pick this car out. It was gray on the outside, with a very plush interior. I was about six- years-old and remember being absolutely stunned by the wood-grained dashboard and window surrounded with medallions picturing the Spanish explorer Hernando De Soto, the car's namesake. I was too young at the time to have known the difference between a six and an eight, but I do know the stately-looking De Soto Custom sedan was a very exciting machine to me.

Today's collectors will want to look for the two-door hardtops and ragtops that seem to be most desirable – and in this case rare. De Soto made only 4,600 Sportsman hardtops in 1950, along with a mere 2,900 convertibles. Even rarer are the two station wagons, which had production runs of 600 units for the woodie and 100 units for the steel station wagon.

1951 and 1952 De Soto

The 1951 DeSoto Sportsman Custom two-door hardtop was an upper echelon model.

Things you can ride in were found in the titles of three leading films of 1951 — can you name them? They were "The African Queen," "Strangers on a Train" and "A Streetcar Named Desire."

Another thing that you could ride in back in 1951 (and 1952 as well) was a De Soto. In fact, the Chrysler branch claimed of its product, "No other car rides like a De Soto." Whether this was an accurate statement or not, it became the new DeSotos marketing theme..

"Easy, shock-free Center-line steering is found in the 1951 De Soto," said the year's guide for salesmen. "The steering wheel is placed at the most comfortable angle for the driver and anti-friction roller bearings contribute to turning and parking ease."

Six-cylinder De Sotos of both model years were considered to be part of the S-15 series. This line of cars, in De Luxe or Custom trim, initially entered production in January 1951. After Nov. 28, 1951, De Luxe sixes in the S-15 line were considered 1952 models. Cars in the Custom six line weren't considered 1952 models until after Dec. 28, 1951.

On Valentine's Day 1952, a new S-17 series with a powerful Fire Dome V-8 engine was introduced. This new line was sold only in late 1952 and all-new S-16 and S-18 six- and eight-cylinder series were introduced for the 1953 model-year. .

Well-known automotive historian Don Butler described De Soto's 1951-1952 styling as "more than a minor change, but not quite a major revamp."

The hood line was lower and less rounded and had a raised center panel. The front fender feature lines were re-contoured. A new radiator grille featured a more horizontal theme, seen especially in the parking light housings that wrapped around the front body corners. Nine "twisted" teeth ran across the grille. On the front in 1951 was a wingless shield-shaped badge and a hood mascot featuring the helmeted head of Hernando de Soto. A chrome De Soto script was placed right above the center of the grille.

In 1952, the front badge used on sixes was thinner and higher, the De Soto name above the grille was spelled out in block letters and—on some cars, probably late in the year—the "Hernando"-style hood mascot was replaced with the same "air vent" type used on eight-cylinder cars. In addition, the 1952 taillights had an outline that tapered towards the top and included integral back-up lights.

Late-1952 Fire Dome eights had a third style of hood trim, which seems to have been used on sixes as well. This included a front badge that looked more like the 1951 type, but was lower and wider. It also had the air vent hood mascot and the De Soto name in block letters. The air-vent hood mascot was a large chrome sculpture that looked like a backwards fin riding on the wings of a jet aircraft. The air-vent hood design enhanced the appearance of the car, while providing a greater intake of fresh, cool air delivered directly to the carburetor to increase the engine's power output. it.

The models in the two six-cylinder sub-series were the same in 1951, except for the "woodie," which was gone. Prices for Deluxe sixes ranged from $2,319 to $3,142. Customs were about $220 higher. The V-8-powered De Sotos were in a single series, but had all the same trappings and body styles as the Custom Six series.

A four-door sedan was offered on both wheelbases. Other models came only on the shorter 125-1/2-inch wheelbase. Prices for the V-8 model ranged from a low of $2,718 for the Club Coupe to $3,547 for the eight-passenger long-wheelbase sedan.

On Nov. 23, 1951, De Soto unveiled a new "push-button" V-8 engine plant. This 328,229-square-foot factory was built in a location adjoining the body shop in the Warren Avenue plant in Detroit. It featured completely new "Transfermatic" engine-building machinery capable of producing 60 V-8 engines an hour.

On Feb. 10, 1952, De Soto's new Fire Dome 8 engine was introduced. It was an impressive power plant derived from the Chrysler "Firepower" V-8. The five-main-bearings Hemi had a 3-5/8 x 3-11/32 bore and stroke for 276.1 cid. Using a Carter two-barrel carburetor, the engine delivered 160 hp at 4400 rpm.

Six-cylinder De Sotos of both years continued using the "old-tech" flathead engine—now called a Powermaster Six—with a couple of revisions. It had a larger 4.5-inch stroke and as a result displaced 250.6 cubic inches. With the added piston displacement, as well as a new carburetor, horsepower was increased to 116 at 3600 rpm.

Tip-Toe Shift (optional on De Luxe models in 1951) was De Soto's attempt to compete with other automakers who were selling more and more automatic transmissions. This "semi-automatic" Fluid Drive transmission relied on the accelerator to control shifts once the car was in gear and moving. A kick-down passing gear supplied an extra surge of power when needed. In 1952, a new Fluid Torque Drive system featuring a torque converter became optional. Other new-for-'52 selling points included 12-inch brake drums, electric windshield wipers, a heavy-duty generator, tapered-leaf rear springs, a tank-mounted fuel filter, straddle-mounted steering gear, and (on V-8s only) a fixed-shunt oil filter.

Model-year production figures totaled a respectable 105,000 cars (in round numbers) for 1951. The decline was attributable to two factors that De Soto could not control: government controls on production due to the Korean War and a mid-year steel workers strike. In 1952, production dropped another 19 percent to 87,000 units.

1953 De Soto

The V-8-powered DeSoto Firedome sedan was the most popular 1953 model.

"Lady of Spain," "April in Portugal" and "Vaya Con Dios" were hit songs of 1953 that reflected a American fascination with things Latin. The Chrysler Corporation car named after a Spanish explorer proved to be a hit in its 25th anniversary year as well. With new styling, a brighter appearance and more power options than ever before, the "Distinguished De Soto" enjoyed a bounce back in model-year production from an estimated 87,000 units in '52 to 129,000 in 1953, the best in the company's history.

Part of the reason for the big increase was the end of fight-ing in Korea and the relaxation of production controls imposed by the National Production Agency. No one was complaining, especially De Soto employees. After the all-new 1953 De Sotos were introduced on Nov. 13, 1952, it became obvious it was going to be a good year.

By January, the automaker added a second assembly shift at the Detroit factory. By the end of the first three months of the year, despite manpower and steel shortages, 34,059 cars had been put together. Car building was dominated by the V-8 model, which accounted for 67.3 percent of calendar-year production. In fact, De Soto relocated its six-cylinder engine manufacturing to a factory in Trenton, Michigan, to add more V-8 production capacity at the Warren Avenue plant in Detroit.

The '53 De Soto featured a longer, lower body with swept-back front fenders that extended through the body sides and blended in with the pontoon-style rear fenders. There was a lowered hood line with a chrome-plated air-vent air intake at the front, a larger one-piece curved windshield, a "sweep-around" rear window (except on certain body styles) and a lower roof line.

Eleven "teeth" now ran across the radiator grille, instead of nine. The oval-shaped front parking lights sat outboard of the grille and no longer had chrome extensions curving around the front body corners.

The fuel tank filler cap was newly positioned below the rear deck lid on the left-hand side and the trunk had 44 percent more room inside. There was a new push-button trunk lock and new combination tail, stop and back-up lights. While retaining a 125-1/2-inch standard wheelbase, the shorter De Sotos now measured 213-3/8 inches end to end (station wagons were around an inch shorter). On bigger cars, mainly for taxicab use, the wheelbase was 139-1/2 inches and overall length was 224-3/8 inches. These long-wheelbase De Sotos actually continued to use the 1952-style body shell, but with the 1953 grille and the new one-piece curved windshield. The large De Sotos did not feature the new "sweep-around" rear window treatment.

Early in the 1953 model year, De Soto reported 61 percent of its V-8 models were leaving the assembly plant with power steering. That compared to 55 percent in 1952.

Overall, counting both sixes and eights, power steering was ordered for 37 percent of all cars made in the calendar year, a total of 48,000 installations. De Soto's 1953 V-8 models had unchanged or lowered prices, while prices were increased for six-cylinder cars at the beginning of the model year. On March 25, 1953, across-the-board price cuts were made.

In addition, the prices on 11 of 18 options were reduced at the same time. Models offered in the Powermaster Six series were a Club Coupe, a four-door sedan, the Sportsman two-door hardtop, the all-steel station wagon and the eight-passenger long-wheelbase sedan. Prices for these cars ranged from $2,334 to $3,251. The Fire Dome V-8 series had the same models, plus a convertible on the standard wheelbase, priced from $2,622 to $3,529. De Sotos, as a rule, appealed to family buyers and 75 percent of all cars made were four-door sedans.

Cars in the S-18 — or Powermaster Six — series had a plainer look with no chrome sash on their front fenders. The Powermaster name appeared on the front fender sides, about halfway up, near the door break line. There was no V-shaped ornament below the badge on the front of the hood or on the rear deck lid. S-16 — or Fire Dome Eight — models with the Hemi V-8 engine.

They had the Fire Dome name on the front fenders along with a V-8 emblem, the word "Eight" on the right-hand side of the body below the rear deck lid, V-shaped hood and rear deck lid decorations to signify the V-8 engine and a chrome sash on the front fenders of all models except the station wagon and the long-wheelbase sedan.

Both the in-line six and the V-8 were carried over from 1952. Either engine could be hooked to a choice of transmissions: a standard three-speed synchromesh transmission, a standard three-speed synchromesh transmission with overdrive or Tip-Toe Shift with fluid drive.

In addition, V-8-powered De Sotos could be ordered with Tip-Toe Shift with Fluid-Torque Drive, which featured a new torque converter. Available extra-cost options now included air conditioning.

While celebrating its anniversary in 1953, De Soto played it low key. There were no special anniversary models, no commemorative option packages and, in fact, no mention of the milestone in most advertisements. Something that did get constant "play" among the ad copywriters was De Soto's sponsorships of Groucho Marx in "You Bet Your Life" on both NBC radio and television.

Keeping pace with an industry trend, on Nov. 8, 1953, De Soto introduced a factory "dream car" called the Adventurer. This experimental four-passenger sports coupe was built on a 111-inch wheelbase. It was 185 inches long and only 53 inches high. Unlike GM's Corvette of the same year, the Adventurer did not make it to the production line, although the name was later used for a production model introduced in February 1956. This Adventurer (or "Golden Adventurer") was a limited-production Fireflite two-door hardtop with gold trim and a 320-hp Hemi V-8 that was essentially a De Soto version of the Chrysler 300 letter car.

De Soto sales promotions for 1953 continued to focus on the practical, or as one advertisement very simply stated it: "A steering wheel you never wrestle . . . A brake you never jam on . . . An engine you never nurse . . . Gears you don't shift!"

Unfortunately, this brand of practicality appealed to only 2.12 percent of America's new-car buyers in 1953. As the nation's 12th best-selling car, the De Soto was far from the leader in the middle-price class.

1954 De Soto

The popular 1954 DeSoto Firedome sedan in the first year for automatic transmission.

"Hernando's Hideaway," went to number one on the top tunes charts in August of 1953. And another was the caricature of Hernando de Soto's helmeted head that had last been seen in some early 1953 De Soto advertisements.

Once De Soto started using photography in its ads, rather than artists' illustrations (around mid-1953), it was time to hide the Spanish explorer's picture and look for new symbols that represented a more modern image.

Production totals seem to indicate this corporate awakening came a little too late to help De Soto's bottom line in 1954. The company's model-year car output fell an amazing 46.3 percent to 69,844 units. That was De Soto's lowest peacetime volume since 1938 and it came despite some significant technical updates that should have helped both production and sales.

PowerFlite—De Soto's first fully-automatic transmission—stood out as an important advance on the new models when they were introduced on Nov. 5, 1953. Priced at $175, this option was $45 less than the semi-automatic transmission it replaced. Before long, De Soto would announce that 97.6 percent of the cars it was building had the new automatic transmission installed. De Soto's automatic transmission had the highest starting ratio of any automatic transmission. Ads said: "It takes you from a dead stop to highway speed fast — without the slightest lag or hesitation."

Another technical improvement in the 1954 De Soto was a coaxial power steering system that had the entire hydraulic operating mechanism on the same axis as the center of the steering column. Its compact, cylindrical design resulted in fewer parts, lighter weight and less maintenance. The new power steering system was 100 percent hydraulic. It had no springs in it. The company claimed full-time power steering did 80 percent of the work of turning or holding a steady course over rough spots.

For identification, the 1954 models had a new grille with nine redesigned "teeth." The combination parking lights and directional lights were circular and sat deeply within a "floating" horizontal grille bar. The front and rear bumpers were less "guard rail"-like.

"Tree branch" front fender moldings (now used on both the Powermaster Six and Fire Dome V-8 models) looked similar to those used on 1953 Pontiacs, with the model name showing between the two "branches" on the front fender sides. The chrome molding continued along 80 percent of the front door. A straight chrome molding, at the same height, decorated the rear fenders, which also had chrome gravel shields. Chrome rocker panel moldings also were standard. These were pretty bright cars!

The De Soto name was spelled out in chrome block letters across the lip of the hood and the red and gold De Soto shield was still located above it. Powermaster models had that name on the front fender, a Powermaster crest on the front of the hood and a horizontal chrome handle on the trunk lid. Firedomes had the model name on the front fenders and a V-8 emblem below the shield emblem on the hood, as well as on the tips of the rear fenders and the rear deck lid. The air-vent type hood was continued on all De Sotos and the vent ornament was again brightly plated.

Individual model offerings were about the same as those offered in 1953, except for a new Special Club Coupe on the six-cylinder chassis. We haven't found a reference that describes the "special" features of this car.

Prices for the series S-20 Powermaster Six models were roughly $70-$100 lower than 1953 prices, indicating De Soto was struggling to find buyers in a rough year for the industry as a whole and and for De Soto in particular. The Firedome series, now designated the S-19 line, contained the same five standard-wheelbase models as well as the long-wheelbase sedan. Prices were between $2,652 and $3,559.

There were many rare models this year. They included the Powermaster Special Club Coupe (250 built), the Powermaster station wagon (225 built), the Powermaster eight-passenger sedan (263 built), the Firedome eight-passenger sedan (165 built) and the Firedome all-steel station wagon (946 built). The Firedome convertible, with 1,025 assemblies, was relatively "plentiful"—at least by De Soto standards—especially for an open car.

A midyear model called the Coronado bowed at the Detroit Auto Show and was released in the spring. This high-fashion four-door sedan carried a special trim package designed to spur a few extra sales. Most competitors used hardtops or convertibles as custom models, but De Soto's choice was its popular sedan. It had a Coronado rear fender script and medallions on the rear roof pillars.

With the horsepower race getting into full swing, the flathead six under the hood of Powermaster models was so far out of the running De Soto left it unchanged at 116 hp. On the other hand, the 276-cid Fire Dome V-8 was given a higher 7.5:1 compression ratio and other upgrades to boost output to 170 hp at 4400 rpm. In addition, larger-diameter valves were used in some V-8s made late in the model year.

With the drastic fall off in demand for new De Sotos, factory cutbacks were part of the company's history in 1954. Early in January, car building speeds were reduced by 10 vehicles per hour. Even this wasn't enough of a reaction to the weak market. By February, shortened work weeks were instituted. By mid-June, De Soto reported monthly output at the lowest level since 1952 .

De Soto again held firmly to its position as America's 12th largest automaker in 1954. It did a fairly good job of getting the most profit from each sale by marketing cars with lots of extra-cost options. Power steering was added to 39,469 cars or more than half of the total built. A total of 37,627 were fitted with power brakes.

A full 98.9 percent of all 1954 De Sotos – 66,966 cars – featured the new fully-automatic PowerFlite transmission. "From the moment you turn the key in a De Soto Automatic, you do less and the car does more!" said one catchy sales theme.

1955 *De Soto*

The veteran 1955 DeSoto Fireflite Sportsman hardtop was a top model when it was new.

How smart were Americans? That was a question asked frequently in 1955. On television, contestants smart enough to answer "The $64,000 Question" could, perhaps, win a fortune on the first of the big quiz shows. At the same time, Rudolph Flesch published *Why Johnny Can't Read* that severely criticized the U.S. education system. The intelligence of Dr. Jonas Salk was beyond question – his polio vaccine was saving lives. And everyone was hoping that some smart decisions would come out of the 1955 Summit Conference in Geneva, Switzerland.

In Detroit circles, the 1955 De Soto was advertised as "Smartest of the smart cars." Buyers were urged to drive a De Soto before they decided which car to purchase.

"It's hard to say which will give you the biggest thrill," one ad explained. "The freshness of the new De Soto body styling, the pulse-quickening excitement of De Soto performance, or the miracle of a car that does almost everything for you except decide where to drive."

Like other 1955 Chrysler products, the new De Sotos exhibited the corporate "Forward Look," a totally modernized appearance featuring many aircraft motifs and credited to stylist Virgil Exner. It was a dramatic change from the box-on-box theme of the past, giving all cars a lower, longer and wider visage.

And it was all-new from the chassis up, rather than just a revision of sheet metal surfaces. In addition to the completely changed silhouette, there was a wraparound windshield, a redesigned grille and broad, flat, upright "tail fins" at the rear. These slanted forward at the top, perhaps inspiring the trade name for the new design.

The grille kept the trademark "teeth" in front to let people know they were viewing a De Soto. It was hard to say if there were seven or nine teeth, as the bumper guards played a dual role—they protected the redesigned bumper and served as larger, outer "teeth." Since the opening was lower than ever, it was shaped to rise up at each end, above the two bumper guards.

The De Soto name was again seen above the grille in block letters. The front hood ornament also served as the now-traditional De Soto air vent on the extreme front edge of the hood. The hood mascot resembled a jet. The headlights were single circular units. On Fireflite models these had chrome fins at top center that extended back down the fender top. Body side decorations also varied by series.

Exclusively V-8 powered for the first time, the '55 De Sotos placed more emphasis on hardtop models than before. At the same time, one station wagon, all Club Coupes and the taxicab-targeted eight-passenger sedans went by the wayside. Body colors were much brighter and two-tone paint treatments were "in."

The entire lineup of cars was offered in 13 solid colors and 42 two-tone combinations, with 39 separate interior trim combinations offered. To be a better competitor in the now-speeding horsepower derby, De Soto made a "power pack" with a four-barrel carburetor available as optional equipment.

Several months after the 1955 models came out, a dual exhaust system was added to the options list. It featured separate, straight-line exhaust scavenging for each bank of the V-8 engines. Dual exhausts could be added to both the 180- and the 200-hp V-8s.

The base Hemi V-8 engine had new 3.72 x 3.34 bore and stroke dimensions, which upped its displacement to 291 cubic inches. With a 7.5:1 compression ratio and a Carter two-barrel carburetor, the output of this Fire Dome V-8 was 185 hp at 4400 rpm and 245 foot-pounds of torque at 2800 rpm.

When the Carter WCFB four-barrel carburetor was substituted, it became the FireFlite V-8 with 200 hp at 4400 rpm and 274 lbs.-ft. of torque. A column-mounted three-speed manual gearbox was standard, overdrive was available and PowerFlite automatic transmission (with a new "Flight Control" selector lever jutting out of the dashboard) was $189 extra.

The base Firedome series consisted of the Coupe Special (a price-leader hardtop), the four-door sedan, the Sportsman two-door hardtop, the convertible, and the six-passenger station wagon. Prices ranged from $2,453 to $3,125. There were just three Fireflite models: four-door sedan, Sportsman two-door hardtop, and convertible priced between $2,682 and $3,106. In the springtime De Soto announced the newest version of the specially-trimmed Coronado sedan, which boasted a three-tone color treatment, exclusive new interior fabrics and some special exterior nameplates. One advertisement described the Coronado as a "rare jewel." It added: "No detail has been spared to bring you a car that is a distinction to own . . . a car to turn heads wherever you drive."

Once again, it seemed odd for De Soto to pick the sedan for a special trim treatment, until it is realized that the company sold predominantly sedans — at least up until this point.

The 1955 Firedome De Sotos had the model name in script on the front fenders. A constant-width chrome molding ran along the sides of the body. There were no chrome ornaments along the tops of the fenders and no rocker panel moldings. The Sportsman hardtop in this series carried "Sportsman" nameplates and round medallions on the rear window pillars. Fireflite models had that model name on the front fenders and the chrome headlight fins, plus rocker panel moldings.

The four-door had a single flared molding, while the convertible and the Sportsman hardtop had contrasting "color Sweep" panels as a standard feature. These could be ordered as optional extra-cost equipment on other De Soto models.

In the mid-'50s, the car industry was changing its timetable for model-year introductions, which had traditionally taken place each January. Slowly but surely, the dates on which the cars appeared in dealerships were becoming fall dates. While GM, Ford and Studebaker were releasing cars as early as October, Chrysler picked November to debut most of its products and De Sotos bowed on the 17th of that month.

From that day on, it was fairly obvious that the new Foward Look cars were a giant hit with the buying public. In fact, 9,066 De Sotos were registered to new owners in December 1954 alone and 25.7 percent were from the more expensive Fireflite series. It was also reported that 30 percent of all De Sotos being built were hardtops.

Both of these statistics were signs De Soto was enjoying success in changing the image of its products and rebalancing its market thrust. In 1956, car buyers were getting younger and the mid-priced automakers like De Soto were struggling to keep up with the new trend.

1956 De Soto

When new, some 1956 DeSoto Adventurer hardtops raced at Pike's Peak and Daytona.

In 1956, the U.S. Congress authorized construction of the Interstate highway system. The national ribbons of interconnected highways expanded the growth of a new suburban lifestyle in America and contributed to the decline of the traditional inner-city environment.

De Soto suddenly appeared to be more in touch with this trend and advertised its substantially face-lifted 1956 products as cars made "...for the super-highway age!"

For the first time in many years, the De Soto was toothless, at least in terms of its grille design. Though the opening was shaped the same as in 1955, a screen-like insert with a gold V-shaped emblem in its center filled the hole. The bumper guards that integrated with the grille were retained. The flat tail fins of 1955 were modified with fin-shaped overlaps that came to a sharp point at the rear. The redesigned taillight clusters featured three tiers of turret-like lights. Decorating the rear deck lid were the De Soto name in block letters and a V-shaped adornment. New upswept color effects were available on many 1956 models.

Other innovations for the new model year included cradle-type front engine mountings, floating Center Plane brakes with 25 percent more braking surface, sealed beam headlights (an industry first on late 1955 models), an instantaneous heater, a 15-jewel steering wheel watch, dual rear radio antennae and a Triad horn arrangement.

The base Hemi V-8 engine was again enlarged and powered up. It had new 3.72 x 3.80 bore and stroke dimensions, which upped its displacement to 330.4 cubic inches. Compression was hiked to 8.5:1. The two-barrel Fire Dome power plant was now good for 230 hp at 4400 rpm and 305 foot-pounds of torque at 2800 rpm Then came the four-barrel Fire Flite V-8, also with 330.4 cubic inches and 8.5:1 compression. It was good for 25 additional horses and 20 additional units of torque at a higher 3200 rpm, but the engine possibilities no longer stopped here.

In addition to these choices, a new limited-edition De Soto Adventurer model featured a larger 341-cid Hemi with a 9.25:1 compression ratio and dual four-barrel carburetors. It churned up 345 hp at 5200 rpm and 356 foot-pounds of torque at 4000 rpm.

The Firedome Coupe Special was renamed the Seville two-door hardtop in 1956. The fancier Sportsman two-door hardtop was available again, too. In addition, four-door Seville and Sportsman hardtops were added as a brand new body style. There were also four-door sedan, convertible and station wagon models in the Firedome line. The station wagon body shell was a bit unusual in that it used the 1955 style rear end without the same new pointed tail fins seen on other De Sotos. Fire Dome prices started as low as $2,633 and went as high as $3,326.

In addition to Firedome front fender nameplates, the lower-priced De Sotos had all-chrome headlight hoods and no chrome ornaments on top of the front fenders. The standard side molding was a single horizontal strip. One arrangement of color sweep moldings and contrast panels was optional on hardtops and four-door sedans. These were not the same as those found on Fireflite models because the upper branch of the molding was the same width all along its length and stopped a few inches short of the taillight molding on the rear fenders. The station wagon was available with its own special color sweep treatment with a scalloped shape at the rear.

The Fireflite model lineup consisted of four-door sedan, two- and four-door Sportsman hardtops and the convertible. A special Pacesetter version of the ragtop was released on January 11, 1956. It was a replica of the white and gold Fireflite convertible that was selected to pace the years Indianapolis 500-Mile Race and came only in those colors. It has been estimated by automotive historians that only a few hundred of these cars were made. In May of 1956, De Soto's president L. I. "Irv" Woolson drove the actual pace car at the "Brickyard," hitting over 100 mph in the process. Fireflite prices ranged from $3,074 to $3,570.

Naturally, Fireflites had appropriate front fender nameplates. On these cars, the headlight hoods were painted, but chrome fender ornaments extended down the tops of the front fenders, behind the headlights. Decorating the body sides of hardtops and convertibles was a color sweep treatment with the upper branch of the molding extending in an unbroken line from behind the headlights to the extreme rear of the car. This double molding widened at the front edge of the front door and flared to its widest point on the rear fender. It could be ordered for some other De Soto models at extra cost.

With the 300 letter car generating lots of publicity for Chrysler's Chrysler Division, De Soto decided that it should have its own performance car and added the Adventurer hardtop to the model lineup on February 18, 1956.

In addition to more cubic inches, a higher compression ratio and two big carburetors, the Adventurer's Hemi included a higher-performance cam grind, stiffer valve springs, modified pistons, heavy-duty rods, heavy-duty crank pins, and a beefier crankshaft.

At Daytona Beach, Florida, prior to Speed Weeks, an Adventurer was driven on the beach race course to 137.293 mph. Later, the same car circled the Chrysler Proving Ground, in Chelsea, Michigan, at 144 mph. Adventurers came in white and gold, black and gold or all gold and were often referred to as Golden Adventurers. With a $3,683 price tag, only 996 were made. Originally, De Soto scheduled the production of 500 units. These sold out in six weeks and the target was raised to 1,000 cars. Most sources say that 996 were actually built.

De Soto experienced a 15 percent dip in registrations in 1956. Production totaled 104,090 cars, 1.79 percent of industry output.

1957 De Soto

A unique color scheme was used on this 1957 DeSoto FireFlite Sportsman convertible.

Rock and roll was sweeping the nation with songs like "Peggy Sue," "Jailhouse Rock," and "Wake Up, Little Susie" climbing high on the industry's Top 10 charts. De Soto had a long ways to go before becoming "the car" of the rock-and-roll set, but the '57 models were a stylishly big and successful step in the right direction. Model-year production climbed to 117,326 cars and market share increased 1.9 percent.

"This baby can flick its tail at anything on the road!" said an advertisement showing off De Soto's new towering tail fins from a dramatic rear three-quarter view angle. De Sotos were lower, wider, and longer than ever before. A massive new combination of chrome and bright metal served as bumper and grille in front.

Just below the lip of the hood was a flat, oval-shaped opening with wedge-shaped parking lamps tucked in each end. Below it was a scoop-shaped opening filled with a grid of thin vertical and horizontal bars. Some models had dual headlights in states where this new feature was legal. (By late-1956, not every state legislature had agreed to law changes permitting dual headlights.)

Vertical chrome tail fin inserts held three turret-shaped taillight lenses stacked on top of each other above a flat-oval bumper-tip exhaust outlet. The center turret included a round white lens that lit when the car was backing up. The bumper bar was in the shape of a wide "U." At the center of the rear deck was a recess that housed the license plate and the De Soto name was spelled out in chrome letters. Dual, tail fin-mounted radio antennas were available.

The new Firesweep line (based on the 122-inch wheelbase Dodge platform) included a four-door sedan, two- and four-door Sportsman hardtops and a pair of station wagons (six- and nine-seaters) priced from $2,732 to $3,265. In the Firedome series a convertible was substituted for the wagons and prices ran from $2,907 to $3,311. The regular Fireflite series contained all body styles with prices from $3,432 to $4,069. Two months after its regular model-year introductions, the special Fireflite Adventurer series was released. It contained a two-door hardtop for $3,942 and a $4,217 convertible.

Firedome and Fireflite models shared a 126-inch wheelbase. The new Firesweeps were 215.8 inches long, while the larger series were 218 inches long. Station wagons in both lines were 1.5 inches longer than other models. Other measurements were in proportion and smaller 8.00 x 14 tires were used on cars in the new series, while the carryover lines used size 8.50 x 14. All three types of De Sotos were powered by V-8 engines with 10.0:1 compression. A new 325-cid V-8 was used in Firedome models. It had an 8.5:1 compression ratio and Stromberg two-barrel carburetor giving 245 hp at 4400 rpm (260 hp with an optional four-barrel carburetor).

The 341.1-cid Hemi V-8 was used in Firedome and regular Fireflite models, both with 9.25:1 compression, but different carburetors. The Firedome version utilized a Carter two-barrel and was rated for 270 hp at 4600 rpm and 270 foot-pounds of torque at 2400 rpm. The Fireflite's engine had a Carter WCFB four-barrel which boosted its output to 295 hp at 4600 rpm and 375 foot-pounds at 2800 rpm.

To make the Adventurer special, De Soto bored the Hemi slightly to get to 344.8 cubic inches. With a single four-barrel carburetor, it generated 345 hp at 5200 rpm and 356 foot-pounds at 4000 rpm. This made the 1957 De Soto Adventurer V-8 the first base engine to provide on horsepower per cubic inch of displacement. (The '57 Chrysler 300 and the '57 Chevrolets were available with optional 1-hp-per-cubic-inch V-8s).

Cars in De Soto's luxury line carried the Fireflite name on their rear fenders. Round medallions were added to the upper molding on the front fenders. Wind split moldings were standard on the top of the fenders. The headlights were separate from the grille and sat in notches on each side of the hood. Color sweep style trim in a contrasting color was standard on hardtops and convertibles and optional on other models. Hardtops had "Sportsman" front fender scripts and station wagons had "Shopper" or "Explorer" front fender scripts, depending on their seating capacity.

Adventurers had nameplates on special triangular-shaped aluminum inserts on the rear fenders and special bright metal strips on the rear deck lid. A host of optional features were standard.

As model-year 1957 progressed, an economic recession took hold in America and many medium-priced cars went looking for buyers. De Soto's Firesweep accounted for 35 percent of the company's output.

1958 De Soto

The 1958 DeSoto Firesweep sedan was the entry level model with a Dodge chassis.

> *Sha na na na, sha na na na na,*
> *Sha na na na, sha na na na na,*
> *Sha na na na, sha na na na na,*
> *Sha na na na, sha na na na na,*
> *Yip yip yip yip yip yip yip yip*
> *Mum mum mum mum mum mum*
> *Get a job Sha na na na, sha na na na na*

So went the lead-in lyrics of the hit song "Get a Job," sung by a group called the Silhouettes. It was on the Top 10 charts during the first quarter of 1958 and underlined the fact the nation's economic recession was deepening.

Things were even worse at the dying Chrysler branch now run by J. B. Wagstaff. De Soto's Model-year production peaked at 51,552 cars, a 66 percent decline from 1957. Calendar-year production was just 36,556 cars.

Though little changed overall, the '58 De Soto had a new honeycomb grille texture and round parking lights at the outer ends of a smaller opening under the center, horizontal grille member. Dual headlights became standard equipment on all models. The rear end looked the same as in 1957.

The body sides of De Sotos were decorated with chrome moldings in an arrangement shaped somewhat like a long jet plane in profile view. The moldings met just above the front wheel opening, with the top molding protruding just a bit further towards the front on cars in the Fireflite series. The area between the moldings could be finished in a contrasting hue. This "color-sweep" treatment was standard on Fireflite hardtops and convertibles and optional on other De Sotos.

Only one change was made in the body styles offered in 1958. That was the addition of a new convertible in the "Dodge-sized" Firesweep series. The "Chrysler-sized" Firedome and Fireflite models came in the same body styles. Prices were raised modestly from 1957–mostly in the $40-$50 higher range. As in 1957, there was a top-of-the-line Fireflite Adventurer sub-series offering hopped-up versions of the two-door hardtop and convertible. All of the 1958

DeSoto convertibles were rare: 700 Firesweep, 519 Firedome, 474 Fireflite, and 82 Fireflite Adventurer ragtops were built.

All De Sotos had the series name on the rear fenders and some body styles carried special model names like "Sportsman," "Shopper," and "Explorer" on their front fenders. Firesweeps had the big band of chrome between and over the headlights and no front fender top ornaments..

A handful of 1958 Fireflite Adventurers were sold with an optional Bendix electronic fuel-injection system and carried special "fuel-injection" nameplates above their front fender medallions. These cars produced 355 hp at 5000 rpm and only a handful were made. Not very long after its introduction, this $637 option was retracted and cars fitted with the fuel-injection hardware were recalled to have it removed. They were converted to the "standard" Adventurer setup with dual four-barrel carburetors. At least one fuel-injected car is being shown today.

For 1958, De Soto introduced a new "Turboflash" V-8. This "deep-skirt" engine was described as "the most advanced engine design on the road today!" Standard in Firesweeps was a 350-cid version of this engine that was not used in any other De Soto carline. It had a two-barrel carburetor, five main bearings, hydraulic valve lifters and a 10.0:1 compression ratio. Output was 280 hp at 4600 rpm and 380 foot-pounds of torque at 2400 rpm.

A 361-cid V-8 was used in all other models, but four different versions were available. All had five main bearings, hydraulic valve lifters and used a 10.0:1 compression ratio. The first engine, which was standard in Firedomes and optional in Firesweeps, had a two-barrel carburetor and produced 295 hp at 4600 rpm and 390 foot-pounds of torque at 2400 rpm. The Fireflite base V-8 added a four-barrel carburetor and was rated for 305 hp at 4600 rpm and 400 foot-pounds of torque at 2800 rpm. With dual four-barrel carbs, the Adventurer engine developed 345 hp at 5000 rpm and 400 foot-pounds of torque at 3600 rpm. The final option was the short-lived 355-hp Bendix-fuel-injected engine.

Powerflite automatic transmission was optional in Firesweeps. Torque-Flite automatic transmission was standard in Fireflites and optional in other models. Torque-Flite was said to provide, "…liveliness without lurch and a whisper-silent flow of power in every driving range."

With the 1958 recession driving employment down, the buying power of American shoppers was drastically reduced and some automakers like De Soto were hit particularly hard. This

turned out to be the final season that De Sotos were produced in their own "De Soto" factory. After 22 years of manufacturing in the Warren and Wyoming Avenue locations on Detroit's east side, De Soto moved its main car assembly facilities across town. The new location was Chrysler's Jefferson assembly plant and De Soto occupied it jointly with the Chrysler Division.

Despite the sales decline, De Soto celebrated its 30th anniversary on Aug. 4, 1958. Early in the year, the division announced that one million De Sotos were in use on U.S. roads and, by the end of the year, it was announced the company was nearing its two-millionth assembly of all time.

Unfortunately, it would be soon that De Soto workers would be in the job market and no longer laughing when "Get a Job" came on the radio.

1959 De Soto

In 1959, the Fireflite sedan was one of the top choices among De Soto buyers.

Twelve-years-old is a wonderful age and the songs of 1959 bring memories of that time flowing back . . . family memories; memories of laughing to "The Chipmunk Song," "Purple People Eater," and "Charlie Brown" with other members of the family. It was a time when a family-oriented tune like "The Children's Marching Song" could make the charts . . . when three kids riding in the back of a tail-finned Mopar could sing about "The Battle of New Orleans," but not worry about any real-life battles in distant places like Afghanistan or the Middle East. De Soto's advertising people decided to highlight family values.

"The only rattle you'll ever hear in a '59 De Soto," said a promotion showing a mother holding her baby in the rear seat of a Fireflite two-door hard-top. Only a small picture of the car itself appeared.

The year's optional new swiveling front seat was promoted as "a car seat that lets your wife get in and out like a lady." Another ad ended with the advice, "See the very newest at your De Soto dealer today. And take your wife along."

It was as if, after four years of trying to build a more youthful, performance-car image, De Soto was throwing in the towel and swinging toward family cars. And it probably made sense to those

in charge. Only 45,406 cars left the factories iin 1959 (Firesweeps were built at a Dodge plant, other De Sotos at a Chrysler plant) and well over half of them–or 26,531 to be exact—were four-door sedans! De Soto made only 15,997 hardtops (9,126 with two doors). They also reported assemblies of a mere 871 convertibles, and just 1,907 station wagons.

De Soto built the perfect family car, at least in design terms. Even the entry-level Firesweep had a family-sized 122-inch wheelbase and 217.1-inch overall length (an inch less for wagons). The cars on the 126-inch wheelbase were three-inches bigger.

The only real problem was in how the cars were marketed. If your family wanted a car like the lower-end Firesweep model, getting a Dodge was a better choice; it was essentially the same car with a lower price tag. Conversely, if your family was doing well and you wanted a car that reflected this, why get a De Soto? You might as well get the Chrysler for a little more money.

Although De Soto was struggling, it refused to give up the ghost in 1959, coming to market with the same full slate of models it offered in 1958. And prices were actually cut about $100 per model, which was good news for the family budget.

In addition to the Sports Swivel seat, other new-for'59 features included a new Adventurer V-8 with twin four-barrel carburetors and a high-lift camshaft that was optional for all models, and new Level-Cruise Ride (read air springs or "automatic load leveling").

Styling changes for model-year 1959 included a massive, integrated tri-level bumper-grille ensemble. On the bottom was the bumper, a rather ornate affair that wrapped around each body corner. It had built-in circular guards flanking the license plate support and an air slot just above it. The second level consisted of oval-shaped air slot on each side of center separated by a wide, slanted indentation holding a gold V-shaped emblem. The air slots were filled with the grille texture, which also filled the third level. This texture consisted of horizontal and wide-spaced vertical bars that intersected each other. The dual side-by-side headlights sat at the outer ends of this third tier.

As usual the side trim treatments (described below) were changed. Firesweep models had no series nameplates. This side trim looked like an elongated check mark running from just behind the headlights and curving downwards to a point behind the rear wheel opening, before curving back up towards the tail fin.

The Firedome and Fireflite models had the same basic exterior trim, but could be distinguished from each other by series nameplates on the front fenders and by a large, round medallion above the dip in the side trim molding on the rear fenders of Fireflites. The silver color sweep treatment was optional on both models and sedans had bright metal side window trim.

Flagship models in the De Soto lineup had "Adventurer" scripts on their front fenders, gold color sweeps on the sides of the body and a gold grille. A narrow, vertical medallion appeared above the point where the "check mark" dipped down behind the rear wheel opening. Wide chrome moldings accented the rocker panels and arched along the edge of the rear wheel openings.

This year the 361-cid "Turboflash" V-8 was standard in Firesweeps. It had a two-barrel carburetor, five main bearings, hydraulic valve lifters and a 10.0:1 compression ratio. Output was 290 hp at 4600 rpm and 390 foot-pounds of torque at 2400 rpm.

The first engine, which was standard in Firedomes, had a two-barrel carburetor and produced 305 hp at 4600 rpm and 410 foot-pounds of torque at 2400 rpm. The Fireflite base V-8 added a four-barrel carburetor and was rated for 325 hp at 4600 rpm and 425 foot-pounds of torque at 2800 rpm. With dual four-barrel carbs, the Adventurer engine developed 350 hp at 5000 rpm and 425 foot-pounds of torque at 3600 rpm. With calendar-year production of 41,423 cars, De Soto recorded a 13.3 percent increase.

When rumors began to fly that Chrysler was going to stop building De Sotos, the company announced it was planning to spend $25 million designing new models, of which $7 million was earmarked for 1960 and the rest of 1961 to 1963 models. As late as Nov. 20, 1959, Chrysler was denying any plans to discontinue the De Soto, but a year and 10 days later, the end came.

The 1959 DeSoto Adventurer convertible shows its tall tailfins and twin radio antennas.

Tom Collins

Dodges
of the Fifties

1950 *Dodge*

The entry level 1950 Dodge Wayfarer models included this three-passenger roadster.

In 1950, 14 million Americans bought TV sets to watch programs such as "SHOWTIME . . . U.S.A.," which billed itself as the "greatest show on television." It appeared on the ABC network and it was sponsored by the Dodge division of Chrysler Corp.

The Dodge name was part of the auto industry since 1901, when brothers John and Horace started making automotive parts. By 1914, the Dodge Brothers were manufacturing a four-cylinder, 35-hp touring car. The one-millionth Dodge was on the road by 1923 and a year later bankers Dillon and Read bought the firm. It became a part of Chrysler on June 1, 1918. The company operated a huge 5,480,312 sq.-ft. factory known as Dodge Main in Hamtramck, Michigan, and built 90 percent of its vehicles there in 1950.

Dodge products had prices starting a little higher than its sister Plymouth division and an enviable reputation for value and reliability. For 1950, Dodge was America's eighth largest automaker in terms of calendar-year production behind Chevrolet, Ford, Plymouth, Buick, Pontiac, Oldsmobile and Mercury in descending order. The company was valuable to Chrysler because it also made trucks which were sold in the U.S. under the Dodge name and in other countries under the Fargo and De Soto names.

"Yes, you could pay $1,000 more for a car and still not get all the extra room . . . ease of handling . . . famous dependability of today's big Dodge," said one 1950 Dodge advertisement. A "hat-high" roof line, doors that opened wide, interior roominess, husky brakes, a "Super-Size" luggage compartment, and Gyro-Matic semi-automatic transmission were highlighted by copywriters as some of the outstanding features of a Dodge.

The flathead six-cylinder engine under the hood was described as, a "Big get-away engine – power-packed with plenty of zoom! Amazingly economical . . . a miser on gasoline. Rugged and dependable, too . . . engineered for long life, low cost of upkeep."

Some of the selling points Dodge promoted in 1950 were also hedges to increased sales, since the public's taste in automobiles was changing towards sportier styling, the convenience of fully-automatic transmissions, and the use of the more powerful V-8 engines. However, 1950 Dodges were solidly-built cars that still had vast appeal to America's more conservative car buyers interested in practicality. They were traditionally handsome, richly appointed, and with few moving parts. The flathead six lasted longer and cost less to operate than many other power plants.

In several advertisements, Dodge used endorsements from long-time owners like Walter Boyd of Los Angeles, California, John J. Tunmore of Garden City, New York, and James Patrick O'Shea of Chicago, Illinois. Not surprisingly, all three were mature, white-shirt-and-tie types who symbolized the "typical" Dodge owner of that era.

Dodge stressed it had the cars "...built around people." People riding in a Dodge, getting in or out of one or loading luggage in the trunk were always illustrated in ads. The company invited potential buyers to "Take the Dodge 'Magic-Mile' Ride." The ads promised this would convince car shoppers: "Dodge is the biggest dollar value on the market today."

The 1950 Dodges were split into Wayfarer, Meadowbrook, and Coronet series. All had a facelift from 1949. The grille was now made up of three heavy horizontal bars, with the upper one curving down at the ends. The second and third bars formed an oblong opening with the parking lights placed at either end. In the center was a large chrome plaque bearing the Dodge crest. The new taillights were set flush into the high-crowned fender. The front fenders were trimmed with a sweep spear molding that extended onto the doors. The rear fenders also had a horizontal molding and bright metal moldings decorated the rocker sills.

The Wayfarer line was most unusual as it featured three distinctive-looking models on a short 115-inch wheelbase. The coupe and the Sportabout (Dodge's new name for this model) had a short greenhouse and long rear deck, which made them stand out at a glance. While the open-bodied Wayfarer had previously been a true roadster with removable windows, it was converted to wind-up windows and renamed the Wayfarer Sportabout in mid-year 1949. The Wayfarer two-door sedan was a fastback model. Wayfarer prices ranged from $1,611 to $1,738.

A "Wayfarer" series nameplate decorated the front fenders. Wayfarers were about six inches shorter than most other Dodges in overall length and used smaller (size 6.70 x 15) tires. Production of the Wayfarer Sportabout and coupe was relatively low at 2,903 and 7,500 units, respectively. However, 65,000 of the two-door sedans left the factory.

The "big" Dodges were the Meadowbrooks and Coronets that, in most cases, shared a 123-1/2-inch wheelbase and 202-7/8-inch overall length (the station wagon was 211-1/2 inches long and the eight-passenger Coronet sedan on a 137-1/2-inch wheelbase was 221-3/4-inches long). Series nameplates appeared again on the front fenders. The Meadowbrook series consisted only of a four-door sedan. It was the same size as its Coronet counterpart, but had less bright work and a lower $1,848 price tag. Chrome rear fender gravel shields weren't seen on this model.

Eight Coronets were offered, including the $2,617 eight-passenger sedan. The other models were the Club Coupe, the four-door sedan, the Town Sedan, the Diplomat two-door hardtop (a sporty new body style for Dodge), the convertible, the "woodie" station wagon, and the Sierra all-metal station wagon, which were

priced from $1,914 to $2,865. The Town Sedan was a four-door version with richer interior appointments and fancier upholstery. The woodie wagon was more expensive to build and cost $250 more than even the stretched-wheelbase sedan.

The all-steel wagon was the "wave of the future," although the Sierra version lasted just one year and only 100 of these cars were made (along with 600 woodies). The convertible (1,800 built) and the Diplomat two-door hardtop (3,600 built) were also lower-production models of interest to collectors today. The Diplomat featured a three-piece wraparound rear window. Only 1,300 of the eight-passenger sedans were made.

Standard features of 1950 Dodges included an oil-bath air cleaner, improved 4-in-1 carburetion, a fast-flow intake manifold, Safety-Rim wheels, airplane-type shock absorbers, independent front wheel suspension, Safe-Guard brakes, cyclebond brake linings, an Oilite oil filter, resistor-type spark plugs, an independent parking brake, a generator-type oil pump, full-pressure lubrication, exhaust valve seat inserts, an automatic choke, armored ignition cables, a compensated voltage regulator and an inside hood lock. Options included Gyro-Matic Drive with a "Sprint-Away" passing gear, an All-Weather Comfort system, chrome wheel trim rings, MoPar radios, back-up lights and a deluxe steering wheel.

Dodge's estimated model-year production for 1950 was 350,000 cars.

1951 and 1952 Dodge

The 1951 Dodge Meadowbrook was once again a sedan-only model.

"Drive the very new, very beautiful '52 Dodge," suggested one of the Hamtramck, Michigan automaker's ads that year. The truth is the cars were basically the same as 1951 models, since Chrysler Corporation built the same series through two model years. The reason was Chrysler Corporation — and Dodge in particular — were busy turning out military vehicles for use in Korea. There was little time to spend to completely redesign the civilian cars.

The Wayfarer series, previously designated the D33 line, became the D41 line in 1951 and was continued in 1952. The

Meadowbrook/Coronet line, which was previously called the D34 series, was redesignated the D42 series.

New-for-1951 styling changes started at the front of the cars, where a new grille appeared. A large chrome bar "looped" across the entire width of the front end at the bottom. On its upper portion were five scores that created four segments at the center. Round parking lights and directionals were nestled in either end on the loop.

On the bottom the chrome bar rose up to meet with the bumper guards. Above the loop was a vent-like molding with six open segments. Above the grille, the Dodge name was spelled out in chrome block letters below a shield carrying the Dodge emblem of the day. A ram's-horn hood mascot appeared on the nose, with a chrome molding extending from it back down the center of the hood. The headlights were round with chrome trim rings and the front bumper was of wraparound design with twin bumper guards.

Body side bright-metal trim was similar to that seen in 1950, with a horizontal molding running down the front fender and extending onto the door, a horizontal rear fender molding and bright rocker sill moldings. A split-style, flat-glass windshield was used. Series nameplates decorated the front fender, below the horizontal molding.

Some advertisements depicted Dodges with white sidewall tires, but many showed them with black sidewall tires. Many cars were being delivered without whitewalls, since continued fighting in Korea was limiting the availability of these tires.

Dodge continued to stress the value of its cars in advertisements, many of which were still printed in black-and-white. "Cars costing up to $1,000 more can't match this combination," said a 1951 announcement that promoted the performance of the "Get-Away" six, operating economy, the comfort of knee-level seats, the ease of optional Gyro-Matic Drive or standard Fluid Drive, the "years-ahead" styling and D-E-P-E-N-D-A-B-I-L-I-T-Y ("Dodge put the word in the dictionary" it boasted.) The sales theme was essentially unchanged in 1952, although the price differential between the Dodge and its higher-priced competitors was adjusted downward.

"It's new! It's true for '52! " said one ad. "You could pay hundreds of dollars more and not get all this new '52 Dodge gives you."

In 1951, the Wayfarer series contained the same cars, but prices went up to the range of $1,795 to $1,936. The wheelbase was again 115 inches. Overall length increased to 199-7/8 inches. For 1952, prices increased by a little over $100 on the closed cars, while the Sportabout's price was unchanged.

For some reason, the 1952 Wayfarers were an inch shorter in specifications. Dodge built only 11,002 Wayfarer Sportabouts and dropped this model before the 1952 model-year started. Over the two-year span, 6,702 Wayfarer coupes and 70,700 fastback sedans were also made.

The 1951-1952 Meadowbrook and the Coronet models were again constructed on the 123-1/2-inch wheelbase and had 206-7/8 inches of overall length. The Town sedan and the woodie station wagon were dropped by the beginning of the 1951 model year and the eight-passenger sedan disappeared not long afterwards. Prices for the other body styles ranged from $2,132 to $2,768 in 1951 and from $2,240 to $2,908 in 1952. Over the two years, 5,550 Coronet convertibles were built and production of Diplomat hardtops increased quite a bit to 21,600. Dodge also kept producing the Sierra all-steel station wagon, building 4,000 of these during the two years.

All Dodge models made between 1946 and 1952 were powered by the same in-line L-head six-cylinder engine. It had a 3-1/4 x 4-5/8-inch bore and stroke and 230.2 cubic inches of displacement. The four-main-bearings engine had a 6.70:1 compression ratio and a single Stromberg 1-1/2-inch single-barrel downdraft carburetor. From 1950-1952, output was rated at 103 hp at 3600 rpm and 184 foot-pounds of torque at 1200 rpm. Despite Dodge's "Get-Away" name for this motor, it's real-life strengths were durability and reliability, not power and speed.

From a production standpoint, the 325,694 cars built by Dodge in calendar-year 1951 was the second highest total in company history, after 1950's record of 332,782 assemblies. Even though production "ceilings" were instituted by the National Production Agency, Dodge was able to increase its share of total industry output that year from 4.99 percent to 6.10 percent.

Dodge passed by Oldsmobile and Mercury to become America's sixth largest automaker. Dodge held onto sixth position in 1952, when calendar-year output was 259,519 units and Dodge made 5.98 percent of America's cars.

Car collectors are more interested in model-year production totals, which tell you how many cars of each design were built. Even though the 1951 and 1952 designs were, for all practical purposes, identical, their production was quite different. A total of 292,000 of the 1951 Dodges were made, while the number of 1952 Dodges built was just 206,000. Dodge changed the month in which the model year began during this period. Production of 1951 Dodges started that January, while production of 1952 Dodges began in November of 1951.

One might think the longer 1952 model year would have increased sales, but the opposite happened. This had a lot to do with the lack of a V-8 engine. Chrysler was aware of the problem and started to do a major revamp of Dodge Main, during 1951, to prepare for assemblies of V-8s for the 1953 models.

Six-cylinder engine building facilities were phased out and parts inventories were built up to tide over production work while various departments were relocated. The changeover was not completed by the end of the year, but Dodge cleared enough space to install the giant new "transfermatic" machines used to build V-8s.

1953 Dodge

The "Action car for active Americans" was the 1953 Dodge. According to ads of that year, it was: "…brand new, all new, distinctively new . . . a thrill to drive and a joy to own!"

Part of the Dodge's appeal was the "…sensational New 140 Horsepower Red Ram V-8 engine." A six-cylinder engine was still available. Dodge's new styling also won awards from the Art Students League of New York, the Chicago Academy of Fine Arts, and the Chouinard Art Institute in Los Angeles.

Though still retaining a front-end similarity to the previous models, the new Dodge body was smaller. A 114-inch wheelbase was used for Club Coupes and four-door sedans, while other body styles had a 119-inch wheelbase. The overall lengths were 201-3/8 inches for Club Coupes and sedans, 191-1/4 inches for convertibles and Diplomat hardtops and 189-5/8 inches for Suburbans and Sierras. Dodges were now totally slab-sided and no longer had protruding rear fenders. The total glass area was said to be increased by 244.8 sq. in., which enhanced the driver's visibility.

The front end had two horizontal grille bars that included the round parking lights. The two horizontal bars were separated by five vertical bars. New decorative treatments appeared on the nose

A 1953 addition to the Dodge Meadowbrook lineup was the two-door station wagon.

of the cars, though these varied by series and engine type. A new ram's-horn mascot was seen and new oval taillights were placed in the rear fenders. The fuel filler pipe, formerly on the rear fender, was relocated below the deck lid on the left-hand side. A new one-piece windshield was employed.

Standard features included Oriflow shock absorbers, a front sway bar, angle-mounted leaf-type rear springs, a Center-Balance steering system, Safety-Rim wheels, Safeguard hydraulic brakes with cyclebond linings, electric windshield wipers, an automatic choke, ignition-key starting, an oil-bath air cleaner, and — on all models except Meadowbrook Specials — a water-proof ignition system. Among approved options were a heater, a radio, whitewall tires, a windshield washer system, directional signals, back-up lights, Solex tinted glass and full wheel discs.

Dodge's entry-level series grew a bit and had a new name. This line was now known as the Meadowbrook Special series. All Meadowbrook models had only a Dodge crest on the front of the hood. A Club Coupe ($1,958) and a four-door sedan ($2,000) were included. Both were on the standard 119-inch wheelbase and both came only with the flathead six-cylinder engine. These cars had no standard body side trim, except for front fender series nameplates.

The moldings around the windshield and back window were black rubber and the side windows had no moldings. These cars were intended largely for sales fleet use and were Spartan in all regards. In April of 1953, the Meadowbrook Special series was discontinued, so these cars, though quite plain, are somewhat rare to see.

For about $120 more, both of the above body styles came in Meadowbrook trim on the 119-inch wheelbase. There was also a Meadowbrook Suburban (six-passenger two-door station wagon) on the 114-inch wheelbase. These cars had the same hood trim as Meadowbrook Specials, but they carried body side trim moldings. A horizontal molding started at a point very low on the front fender and ran back across the doors before kicking up over the rear wheel opening. The molding continued, at that level, to the back of the car. Passenger cars in this line did not have bright metal gravel shields, but Suburbans did. Prices began at $2,077 and the Suburban, though shorter, was still the priciest model at $2,176. Meadowbrooks came only with the six-cylinder engine.

Coronet models added an air-scoop decoration on the front of the hood. This was promoted as the "Jet Air-Flow" hood. A V was placed across the opening on cars with the V-8 engine and the words "Dodge Eight" appeared below the ornament. At first, all 1953 Coronets had the V-8 engine, but a Coronet Six series was introduced in April 1953, when the Meadowbrook Special disappeared.

Coronets had side trim like the Meadowbrooks, with chrome gravel shields on the Sierra six-passenger station wagon. Coronet models on the 119-inch wheelbase were offered in both six-cylinder and V-8 series. The sixes were $2,198 for the Club Coupe and $2,220 for the four-door sedan. The V-8s cost $109 and $114 extra, respectively. The $2,361 Diplomat two-door hardtop, the $2,494 convertible, and the $2,503 Sierra two-door station wagon came only with a V-8 under their hoods. The two-door models used the shorter 114-inch wheelbase.

The six-cylinder engine was basically the same 230.2-cid 103-hp one used on other postwar Dodges. The new Hemi V-8 was promoted as the "Red Ram" engine, thanks to its red-painted valve covers with "Red Ram Dodge" lettering in white and the small icon of a ram. This small Hemi had a 3.44 x 3.25-in. bore and stroke. It displaced 241.3 cubic inches and had two rocker shafts per cylinder head. The engine used a 7.1:1 compression ratio and a Stromberg WW-3 two-barrel carburetor. It was rated for 140 hp at 4400 rpm and 220 pounds-feet of torque at 2000 rpm.

According to Dodge advertising, the Red Ram V-8 was "...the only engine designed to bring you the triple power advantages of hemispherical combustion chambers . . . short stroke design . . . and high-lift lateral valves."

The Dodge topped all other American eights in the famous 1,206-mile Mobilgas Economy Run between Bakersfield, California and Los Angeles in 1953. NASCAR drivers also liked the powerful Dodge V-8s and drove them to six checkered flags in 1953. These were the first stock-car-racing victories that Dodge had ever taken. On May 6, 1953, a Dodge V-8 was clocked at 102.6 mph by the American Automobile Association (AAA).

Dodge offered four different types of transmissions in 1953. The standard drive gave smooth, manual shifting. Automatic overdrive provided a fourth economical cruising gear. No-shift Gyro-Matic Drive gave two driving ranges for different road conditions. Gyro-Torque Drive, used only with the Red Ram V-8, offered high-performance no-shift driving.

Thanks to the V-8, Dodge's model-year production saw an increase to an estimated 304,000 units, second best in company history. Calendar-year production climbed to 293,714, but Dodge's market share decreased to 4.79 percent. That dropped the company back to eighth rank as Mercury and Oldsmobile, in that order, passed it by again. Part of the reason was Dodge still lacked a fully automatic transmission. Chrysler rectifiedy this problem in 1954.

In April 1953, Dodge began selling cars optionally equipped with Chrysler's Air-Temp air conditioning system. And on November 12, a dream car called the Dodge FireArrow appeared at auto shows. This was a sporty 115-inch wheelbase roadster designed to get car buyers excited about what might come in the future. While it was an exciting car for the 1950s, it would be decades before Dodge offered anything remotely similar in its V-10-powered Viper.

1954 *Dodge*

This 1954 Dodge Royal V-8 sedan wears an interesting color combination to the bank.

"All dressed up — and a million places to go!" was one of the sales slogans Dodge used to promote its new cars in 1954. With bright new exterior colors and seats upholstered in rich-textured patterns of exquisite Jacquard fabrics (previously used only in a few of the more costly cars), it was easy to tell Dodge was putting more luxury into its Meadowbrook, Coronet, and all-new Royal models. All in all, it was clear why the '54 Dodges were described as "Elegance in Action" since they were fancier and faster than ever before.

Dodge did have a million places to go and millions of potential customers to reach with its mass-media marketing messages. A record-setting radio and television promotion was launched in January 1954. Radio listeners who tuned in the popular Roy Rogers Show heard about the Dodge features.

On the relatively new medium of television, Dodge sponsored the "Danny Thomas Show" and Bert Parks' program. In another type of promotion, a bright yellow Dodge Royal convertible with a continental spare tire and wire wheels became the first Dodge ever to pace the Indianapolis 500-Mile Race on May 31, 1954. Dodge built a special edition of 701 cars to honor this historic event.

Unfortunately, a bumpy economy held car sales down industrywide. Despite launching a February 7 advertising contest to celebrate its 40th year as a car maker, Dodge managed to make just 151,766 cars in the calendar year, chalking up its poorest performance since 1938. Despite a 48 percent decline from 1953, the com-

pany did cling to eighth rank in total U.S. auto making. Model-year production was estimated at 150,930 units, a 52 percent fall from the prior year. Even worse, Dodge's market share dropped from 4.79 percent to 2.75 percent as GM products, especially Buicks and Oldsmobiles, went on a tear.

Styling changes for 1954 were modest. A new grille ensemble was housed within a loop of chrome that rose up below the hood. The chrome molding on the hood lip was wider than the '53 style. A large chrome upright in the center of the grille replaced the five vertical dividers used previously. The bumper guards were now of a "bullet" design (they looked almost like the '53 guards turned upside down).

On V-8-powered Dodges, the Jet Air-Flow hood ornament had the "8" within the V and no wording underneath. Six-cylinder cars had a non-vented hood decorated with a red-and-white striped shield that had the Dodge name lettered vertically, against a blue stripe, down the center.

The mascot on the nose of the car was a more stylized version of the Dodge ram with the animal's head being a smoothly sculptured piece of chrome with just a hint of the once-prominent curved horns. This "ram" projected out further to the front then before, although it was smaller overall. Cartoon versions of the ram were suddenly absent in 1954 promotions.

It was obvious that Dodge was trying to create a more modern image by phasing out such links to its past. How ironic that the traditional ram is a major part of the company's advertising and promotions today.

Chrome gravel shields protected the rear fenders of all 1954 Dodges — not just station wagons.

Meadowbrook models had the series name in script on the rear fender. On this car line, body side trim was limited to just a short chrome sweep spear running across the front fender and part of the front door. This year the Meadowbrook Club Coupe and four-door sedan were available with either the six or the lower-horsepower version of the Red Ram V-8. The sixes had prices almost $100 lower than 1953 models, while the V-8s were about $50 higher than the same 1953 six-cylinder models.

The Coronet name on the rear fenders indicated Dodge's one-step-up line. These cars had the full body side trim treatment, but did not have rear fender-top moldings. The Club Coupe, the four-door sedan and two all-new four-door Sierra station wagons (six- and nine-passenger) were built on the same 119-inch wheelbase as Meadowbrook models, while the two-door hardtop (a.k.a. Sport Coupe), the convertible, and the two-door Suburban wagon on a five-inch-shorter wheelbase.

All Coronets, except the V-8-only Sport Coupe and convertible, were offered with a choice of a six or a V-8. Prices ranged from $2,084 for the six-cylinder Club Coupe up to $3,006 for the V-8-powered Sierra eight-passenger wagon.

All-new for 1954, the Royal V-8 was now the Dodge division's flagship series. It could be distinguished by the "Royal V-8" script on the rear fender, its rear fender-top moldings (serving as small chrome tail fins) and the use of bright rocker sill moldings. Club Coupe and four-door sedan models were offered on the 119-inch wheelbase along with Sport Coupe and convertible models on the 114-inch wheelbase. Prices started at $2,324 and rose to $2,607 for the ragtop.

This year's edition of the 230.2-cid flathead six had a higher 7.25:1 compression ratio and a different Carter one-barrel carburetor. This helped it churn out 110 hp at 3600 rpm. The Meadowbrook V-8 was the same 140-hp version used the previous season. The Coronet, Sierra, and Royal V-8s used a new version of the same block with 7.25:1 compression, but it used the same Stromberg two-barrel carburetor. The compression boost raised horsepower to 150 at 4400 rpm and torque went up to 222 foot-pounds at 2400 rpm versus 220 at 2200 rpm. This engine was promoted as the "New Red Ram 150 V-8."

Also new at Dodge in 1954 was the division's first fully-automatic transmission. PowerFlite Drive was a no-shift transmission that combined a torque converter with a simple, two-speed planetary gearbox for exceptional accelerating ability and constant smoothness, regardless of speed.

The run of 1954 Dodge models ended on Aug. 25, 1954 and no cars were built from then until the last few days of September, as the company started changing over its production facilities to build the completely revised 1955 models.

1955 *Dodge*

An interesting model was the 1955 Dodge La Femme, French for "woman."

In the events and social changes of 1955, one could see the future being shaped. While no one realized it at the time, the increasing popularity of blue jeans, rock & roll, and comic books would shape future American society.

The year 1955 set trends for tomorrow and the same happened at the Dodge division. "The future is at your fingertips from the moment you take your place behind the wheel. Expect the unexpected in Dodge for '55!" said one ad.

It was the year of Virgil Exner's "Forward-Look" at Chrysler Corporation and the Dodge branch expressed this move into modernity with the slogan "New Dodge Flashes Ahead in '55."

The 1955 Dodges were completely redesigned with a new chassis, a longer and lower silhouette, new chrome treatments, and that snazzy "wrap-around" windshield. The new model lineup emphasized hardtop styling with three Sport Coupes. All five Club Coupes were dropped, but station wagon offerings were expanded to eight, with lower prices to spur sales.. A Coronet six two-door sedan was added, while all Meadowbrook models were dropped. A new Custom Royal V-8 series was introduced at the top of the model lineup. New "Flair-Fashion" three-tone paint schemes were a big hit, too. Optional V-8 engine offering increased to three and they all had more horsepower than ever before. Sixes got a new two-barrel carburetor.

All Dodges were now on a 120-inch wheelbase. Overall length was 212.1 inches for cars and 214.9 inches for station wagons. Coronet sixes used 6.70 x 15 tires and V-8 models had 7.10 x 15 tires. Overall width was 74.5 inches and a loaded four-door sedan stood 60.6 inches high.

Dodges now had a grille opening on either side of a "veed," body-colored center divider. A horizontal chrome bar housing the parking lights ran across each grille opening and wrapped around the front body corners. These bars were each decorated with three windsplit moldings. The Dodge name in chrome script was placed above the left-hand grille opening. At the center was a Dodge emblem and, on V-8-powered cars, a V-shaped emblem.

Running completely across the lower front end and wrapping around the body corners was a bumper with two massive grille guards. The single, round headlights had chrome rims, sometimes with visors on top. The hood panel was open at the front like a large air scoop and had a wide, chrome decoration with chrome moldings extending back to the belt line. New side trim varied by series. Twin, stacked round taillights were housed in a body extension at the rear, above the wraparound bumper.

Coronets had the series name in script (but no V-8 emblems) on the rear fender. The tops of the rear fenders were plain. The headlight surrounds were not visored. The roof drip moldings were painted. Side trim consisted of a straight molding running from behind the headlights to the rear of the front door. Coronet V-8s had a "V" emblem above the center of the grille.

Five Coronet sixes were offered: two- and four-door sedans, a two-door Suburban wagon and two- and three-seat Sierra four-door wagons. In addition to these styles, the Coronet V-8 series added a Club Sedan and a Lancer two-door hardtop. The Lancer hardtop had curved side trim like a Custom Royal, but no chrome fins on the rear fenders. Coronet prices went from $1,988 to $2,643.

The V-8-powered Royals had Royal rear fender scripts and V-8 nose emblems. Side moldings looked like longer versions of the Coronet moldings and extended back to the series script on the rear fender. The Royal lineup included a four-door sedan, a Lancer two-door hardtop and two- and three-seat versions of the four-door Sierra wagon. The Royal Lancer hardtop, also had curved side trim like a Custom Royal, as well as the chrome rear fender fins. Royal models were priced from $2,285 to $2,736. The Royals shared their V-8s with the Coronets.

The Custom Royal series offered a four-door sedan, a four-door Lancer sedan, a Lancer two-door hardtop, and a Lancer convertible. Prices ranged from $2,448 to $2,723. The four-door sedan had a Royal name script and special front fender badge. The curved sweep spear moldings on the sides merged with the headlight bezels and extended to the medallion on the rear fender.

The Custom Royal Lancer hardtop and convertible had special curved belt moldings on the sides, chrome fins on the rear

fenders, rocker sill moldings, front fender series scripts, and gold emblems on the rear quarters where the side trim dipped. They were pretty jazzy cars.

Coronets and Royals used the base Red Ram V-8, which had a new 3.63 x 3.26-inch bore and stroke and 270.2-cid displacement figure. With a new 7.6:1 compression ratio and a Stromberg two-barrel carburetor it was good for 175 hp at 4400 rpm and 246 foot-pounds of torque at 2400 rpm.

A Super Red Ram version of this same engine was used in Custom Royals. It generated 183 hp at 4400 rpm and 245 foot-pounds of torque at 2400 rpm. Also available was a Super Red Ram V-8 with a "Power Pac" (four-barrel carburetor and dual exhausts) that put out 193 hp at 4400 rpm and 254 foot-pounds of torque at 2800 rpm.

From the time they were introduced on Nov. 17, 1954, the 1955 Dodge models were a hit with buyers. Model-year production zoomed to 273,286 units. Calendar-year production was 313,038 or 3.94 percent of industry. That put Dodge in eighth place again.

1956 *Dodge*

The 1956 Dodges began to show tail fins, like this Coronet Lancer two-door hardtop.

"Hound Dog," "Love Me Tender," and "Sixteen Tons" were some of the BIG hit tunes of 1956. In the automobile world, Dodge claimed it had "a truly fine BIG CAR that is actually larger and more luxurious than cars costing up to a thousand dollars more!" "Something BIG happened in the low price field!" read the headline in an advertisement showing a black, yellow, and white Coronet Lancer hardtop. "New '56 DODGE!"

The Dodges themselves were about the same size as the '55 models, although a revised, "Jet-Fin" rear-end treatment with towering tail fins made them look a bit longer. The modestly restyled grille had a new crest medallion on the vertical center post. Three windsplit moldings on each of the main grille bars were replaced with small fins, except on Coronet models. The front and rear bumper guards were also of a new, somewhat more compact design. A new hood molding appeared, along with new "Saddle-Sweep" side trim moldings on certain models. The taillight clusters were redesigned, as were the rear wheel openings, which had more of a scalloped look. A new body style offered this year was a four-door Lancer hardtop.

The Coronet six-cylinder Sierra wagons were dropped. Eight Coronet V-8s were listed: the two-door Club Sedan, the four-door sedan, two- and four-door Lancers, the convertible, the Suburban wagon, and two- and three-seat Sierra wagons. On these cars the rear fenders carried a Coronet script, but no V-8 emblem. The headlight bezels were chrome and the roof drip moldings were painted. The Coronets had no strip of lower body color along the rear edge of the rear fenders and no grooves in the back-up light and taillight housings. Even the lowest-priced Coronet six was $2,159 this year.

The Royal series included a four-door sedan, a Lancer two-door hardtop, a Lancer four-door hardtop, and Custom versions of the Suburban and both Sierras. Custom station wagons had chrome fins on top of their rear fenders, three fins on each main grille bar and painted headlight bezels. The eight-cylinder Sierra three-seat wagon, at $2,787 was the priciest model.

Custom Royal models were Dodge's fanciest offering in 1956. This series included a four-door sedan, a Lancer two-door hardtop,

a Lancer four-door hardtop and a convertible at prices between $2,588 and $2,877. These had "Custom Royal" name scripts and V-8 emblems on their rear fenders. The headlight bezels were painted and visored. The grille bars had chrome fins. The back-up light and taillight housings were grooved. The roof drip moldings were bright metal.

The Saddle-Sweep side trim started on the top of the front end, slashed down to the sides of the body along the cowl and swept gradually down from that point to one near the rear bumper. A strip of the lower body color extended up the end of the rear fenders around the taillights. Custom Royal models also had small, bright-metal gravel shields.

All of the V-8-powered Dodges (including station wagons) were also available with a special D-500 engine, which added roughly $230 to the total price. The D-500 series was available after March 12, 1956, on cars marketed as Coronet 500s, Royal 500s, Custom Royal 500s, Suburban 500s, Sierra 500s, and Custom Suburban or Custom Sierra 500s. The most richly-appointed of these cars were the ultimate Dodges available this year. The D-500s were decorated with special nameplates calling out their high-performance engine.

With its new two-barrel carburetor, the flathead six managed to deliver 131 hp at 3600 rpm. Then came the five V-8s. Coronets continued to use the 270.2-cid Red Ram Hemi with compression boosted to 8.0:1. This combination added up to 189 hp at 4400 rpm and 266 foot-pounds of torque at 2400 rpm. Standard in Royal and Custom Royal models was a new 315-cid (3.63 x 3.80-inch bore and stroke) Super Red Ram Hemi with 8.0:1 compression and a two-barrel Stromberg carburetor. It delivered 218 hp at 4400 rpm and 309 foot-pounds of torque at 2400 rpm.

A Power-Pac version of this engine was good for 230 hp at 4400 rpm and 316 foot-pounds of torque at 2400 rpm. The D-500 mill was a solid-lifter version of the 315-cid Hemi which moved up to two rocker shafts per cylinder head , 9.25:1 compression and a single four-barrel Carter carb. It generated 260 hp at 4800 rpm and 330 foot-pounds of torque at 3000 rpm. This V-8 could also be ordered with twin four-barrel carburetors which gave it 295 hp at

4400 rpm. The D-500 Dodges terrorized Fords and Chevys at the drag strip.

This year, the dashboard-mounted control for the PowerFlite automatic transmission was dropped in favor of "Magic-Touch" push-button gear selection. The push-buttons were located in a pod to the left of the steering wheel on the instrument panel. There were four buttons: "N" for neutral, "D" for drive, "L" for low and "R" for reverse.

The two-spoke steering wheel allowed the driver a good view of the fully-instrumented dashboard.

Automakers experienced another bad year in 1956 and Dodge was no exception. The division's model-year output dropped to 233,686 cars, or 1.7 percent of the total industry. On a calendar-year basis, 205,727 cars were made—a 3.55 percent share. Dodge retained its grip on the Number 8 sales position on the charts.

1957 Dodge

The Dodge Custom Royal convertible was one of the good-looking choices available in 1957.

It was 1957 — and the world was fascinated by jet aircraft and the beginning of the Space Age. Despite the fact that 70 people died in six aircraft accidents during the year, there was no stopping America's "up, up and away" attitude.

No wonder the '57 Dodge had everyone buzzing about its "Swept-Wing" styling and "air-craft-type" engine. Even the hood mascot was a representation of two jet planes — or were they rocket ships?

One advertisement depicted a red-and-white '57 Dodge Royal Lancer Sport Coupe parked near an Air Force jet and two fighter pilots discussing its "autodynamics."

While such hyperbole was probably never uttered, there's little reason to doubt proud Dodge owners did brag up their '57s, since they were exciting-looking cars with lots of "juice" under the hood. The completely new Swept-Wing design resulted in long, low-slung bodies featuring upswept rear fender fins, new side trim, a new "floating" gull-wing grille and hooded "Twin Set" front lights. These were not dual headlights.

Some 1957 cars were sold with dual headlights (called "four-headlight systems" at the time), but only in states that permitted their use. Dodge's Twin Set lights were different. The larger outer lamp was a headlight and the inboard lamp was a kind of running light. Many states prohibited more than two headlights at this time because it was very difficult to correctly aim separate low-beam lamps. During 1956, the Automobile Manufacturer's Association,

the Lighting Manufacturers, and the American Association of Motor Vehicle Administrators jointly promoted four-headlight systems. A new mechanical aiming device corrected the aiming problem. Tests conducted in 1956 provided evidence of the superiority of properly-aimed four-headlight systems. That evidence was needed to get the laws in all 48 states changed by Jan. 1, 1958.

Other new features of '57 Dodges included a torsion-bar front suspension called Torsion-Aire Ride, smaller 14-inch wheels and tires, a three-speed Torque-Flite automatic transmission, a Swept-Back Broad-Horizon windshield, safety-recessed door handles, total-contact Center-Plane brakes and "Super-Enamel" body paint.

All Dodge models had a new 122-inch wheelbase and 212.2-inch overall length They were 77.9 inches wide and the Coronet hardtop was actually a tad over 4-1/2 feet tall at 54.1 inches. Royals, Custom Royals, all station wagons, and the Coronet convertible used 8.00 x 14 tires, while all other Coronets wore size 7.50 x 14. Larger 8.50 x 14 tires were an option.

Coronets had front fender series nameplates and painted headlight trim. The lower grille bar was plain. The six-cylinder line included only a two-door Club Sedan for $2,335 and a four-door sedan for $2,416. The 230-cid six now had a 9.25:1 compression ratio and produced 138 hp at 4000 rpm. Two- and four-door Lancer hardtops and a convertible were additional body styles available in the Coronet V-8 range. Models in this car-line were priced between $2,443 and $2,807. Base engine was a new 325-cid Red Ram V-8 with 8.5:1 compression and a two-barrel carburetor that put out 245 hp at 4400 rpm and 320 foot-pounds of torque at 2400 rpm.

Dodge Royals included a four-door sedan and two-and four-door Lancers in the $2,677 to $2,783 price bracket, all using the same standard V-8 as Coronets. Royals could be spotted by their chrome-trimmed headlight hoods, the V-shaped emblems on rear deck lid and the Royal front fender nameplates.

Custom Royals had a few distinguishing trim items, such as the three "fins" on top of the lower grille bar at each side of the car, gold-colored Dodge emblems on the hood and trunk, and "Custom Royal series nameplates on the front fenders. There were four body styles to choose from: four-door sedan at $2,846, two-door Lancer hardtop at $2,885, four-door Lancer hardtop at $2,956, and Lancer convertible at $3,111. A four-barrel carburetor, which upped horsepower to 260, was standard.

Dodge station wagons this year were lined up in two separate series. The lower-priced D70 line included the two-door Suburban and both four-door Sierra versions.. Also new was a rear-facing third seat in the nine-passenger wagon that was called a "Spectator Seat. The pricier D71 Custom Sierras were around

$200 more expensive. They had the fancier grille with three chrome fins at either end of the lower bar. On wagons, the front fender scripts said "Suburban," "Sierra" or "Custom Sierra." The D70s were trimmed similar to Royals and the D71s looked like Custom Royals.

In addition to the 245- and 260-hp V-8s, there was a 285-hp D-500 (double rocker shaft) version with a single four-barrel carburetor and a Super D-500 version with dual four-barrel carburetors. At midyear, an even more powerful D501 option became available. It was a larger 354-cid Hemi with 10.0:1 compression and dual four-barrel carburetors that was virtually identical to the 1956 Chrysler 300B engine.

The '57 Dodge models – especially the dressy Custom Royals - were truly icons of the '50s with their abundant bright metal accents, their four-bladed "spinner" wheel covers, their optional dual radio antennas mounted on the rear deck and, of course, their wonderful two-tone paint treatments.

Dodge sales zipped upwards like a jet, too. Model-year production hit 281,359, making Dodge the source of 4.5 percent of all of America's new cars. The calendar-year number was 292,386 for a 4.78 percent share of market. That allowed Dodge to take seventh position in January to December production. It was a good year!

1958 *Dodge*

A new Dodge Royal Lancer four-door hardtop is pictured at the Dodge factory.

In 1958, Arnold Palmer putted to the first of his Masters golf tournament wins. The "Cat on a Hot Tin Roof" was drawing folks to movie theaters. Perry Como was trying to "Catch a Falling Star," and Danny and the Juniors were "At the Hop." Westerns ruled on TV with "Wagon Train," "The Rifleman" and "Have Gun Will Travel" at the top of the charts.

While most adult Americans of this era had lived through the Great Depression, the latest economic downturn was something new. Financial analysts labeled it a recession. Automakers, like Dodge, felt the pinch. The company's model-year output of 133,953 cars was less than half of what it had been in 1957. Calendar-year production of 114,026 cars dropped Dodge back to eighth place and a meager 2.69 percent share of the market. Even

the company's popular TV pitchman, Lawrence Welk, couldn't sell as many "Dotches" this year.

New-for-1958 front-end styling featured a cellular grille with massive bumper bombs on the outer edges. The grille insert had intersecting vertical and horizontal bars. Below the headlights, were bars that swept around the body corners. At the inner end of these bars were tubular "bumper bombs." Below the grille insert was a massive wraparound bumper that rose up over the center license plate recess. The Custom Royal models had three "fins" on each end of the lower bumper bar. Dual headlights were now legal in all states and were found on all Dodges.

Due to sluggish sales, several fancier models were added to the lineup in mid-1958. Cars with a new Spring Swept-Wing package added a grille center medallion. These cars had a grooved panel (called a "sculptured crown of gleaming chrome") in the area behind the tail fins and above the upper taillight. A massive chrome escutcheon was placed around the rear license plate.

In 1958, one model was added to the low-priced Coronet six series and the new Custom Royal Regal Lancer two-door hardtop was introduced at the top of the heap.

Modest price hikes increased most models by less than $100. The new six-cylinder Coronet Lancer sold for $2,537, while the fancy Custom Royal Regal Lancer cost $3,200. Station wagon offerings were the same as 1957. All 1958 Dodges could be purchased as D-500s. The cost for this engine option was $122 on all Coronet V-8s except the convertible ($92). It was $100 on Royals, $36 on Custom Royals and Custom Sierras and $59 on Suburban station wagons. New options for the year included swiveling front seats and a Sure-Grip differential.

Coronets were the plainest-looking Dodges and many were used as police cars. Dodge was spelled out on block letters across the hood lip. A chrome band ran over the edge of the headlight hoods and across the lip of the engine hood. Body side moldings on these cars ran only from behind the headlights to a point just above the rear of the rear wheel opening. The "Coronet" name was on the rear fender behind this molding.

Dodge Royals had the same basic lower body side moldings as Coronets. A horizontal "D" front fender emblem was located behind the wheel opening, below the body side molding, on four-door sedans. This emblem was also seen on the non-Custom Sierra four-door station wagons. The Royal, Suburban or Sierra name appeared on the rear fenders, angling up to the top of the fin.

This was not true on Suburban wagons. When the Custom Royal name appeared on the rear fender the cars (and Custom Sierra wagons) also had the "flared" upper body side molding. Knight's head medallions were seen on the front fenders of four-door sedans and Custom Sierra wagons. The Dodge lettering on the hood and trunk of Custom Royals was gold-finished. All Custom Royals had four rectangular insets across the bottom of the inside front door trim and a special tail fin medallion showed a knight's jousting lance.

Introduced in February 1958, the new Regal Lancer two-door hardtop was a special Custom Royal with different body side moldings, a unique paint scheme, and a special interior.

Custom Royals with the Spring Swept-Wing treatment were fancier than regular Custom Royals. They had special color-keyed interiors and wider body side moldings that went from headlight to taillight. One advertisement described a: "...broad new sweep of chrome from front to rear."

While Dodge's six-cylinder engine was virtually unchanged, there were significant revisions to V-8 choices for the upper series and station wagons in 1958. Coronets, Custom Coronets and Royals used the single-rocker-shaft 325-cid Red Ram Hemi with a higher compression ratio. The two-barrel version produced 252 hp, while the optional four-barrel edition was good for 265 hp. Four new "wedge-head" V-8s rounded out the engine options.

The base engine was a 350-cid Ram Fire V-8 with 10.0:1 compression and a single four-barrel carb that produced 295 hp. Two D-500 engines were now based on a 361-cid V-8, also with 10.0:1 compression. The single four-barrel version generated 305 hp and the dual four-barrel Super D-500 was good for 320 hp. For a short time, a version of the 361 was offered with Bendix electronic fuel injection. After being installed on a handful of Dodges (in the De Soto factory) the EFI system was recalled and retro-fitted with dual four-barrel carburetors.

1959 Dodge

John Gunnell

This 1959 Dodge Coronet Lancer hardtop appeared at the 2000 Iola Old Car Show.

It was a year for great escapes . . . 1959. In Cuba, President Fulgencio Battista fled the country on New Year's Day, allowing Fidel Castro to take over the following month. In Tibet, the Dalai Lama fled the Red Chinese and took refuge in India.

A 1959 Dodge advertisement showed some well-dressed ladies and gents fleeing the city in their Dodge Custom Royal Lancer four-door hardtop. "The Newest of Everything Great – the Greatest of Everything New" is what the company promised consumers this year.

In November 1958, more than 3,500 Dodge dealers and 10,000 Dodge salesmen gathered together, in 71 major cities across the country, to witness a "Compar-A-Rama" pitting Dodge products and prices against the competition. When it was over, they were pumped-up to sell new Dodges, but the '59s were in short supply. An 18-day-long strike in December 1958 shut the factory and drastically reduced initial inventories of 1959 models.

Late-1950s Dodges were aimed at American families that wanted more in the low-priced field. They fit a unique rung in the automotive marketing ladder, above the entry-level Chevrolet-Ford-Plymouth offerings.

Though still sporting the Swept-Wing body design, the '59s reflected some restyling. They retained the 122-inch wheelbase, but grew to an overall length of 217.4 inches (an inch shorter for station wagons). The grille and hooded headlights treatment was a refined version of the '58 look. The tail fins were higher and pointier and the twin stacked with tapered "Jet-Trail" taillights. .

The Coronets had series nameplates on their front fenders. The lower side trim molding on these cars started at the front wheel opening. It was narrower than on other series. A rear quarter panel chevron ornament was optional on all series, as was a score, bright-metal fin cap molding covering the "notch" between the top of the fin and the upper taillight bezel. You could get a Coronet for as little as $2,283 or as much as $2,816.

Six-cylinder models included the Club Sedan, four-door sedan and Lancer two-door hardtop. The V-8 series also offered a Lancer four-door hardtop and a convertible. A special Silver Challenger e Club Sedan was released on June 1, 1959 for $2,297 with the six or $2,408 with a V-8.

On Dodge Royals, the lower trim molding started on the headlight brow, wrapped around the side of the car, outlined the front wheel opening and extended the full length of the car. The long, straight section from the front wheel opening to the rear of the car was wider than on Coronets and had horizontal scoring. A Royal nameplate was located on the molding at the front of the tail fin. These cars had a lance-and-shield medal-lion ahead of the front wheel opening. The series included the sedan and both Lancers at prices in the $2,672 to $2,797 range. Custom Royals were similar to Royals on the outside, except for the Custom Royal nameplates on the fin caps. Interior appointments were richer and the optional swivel seats were popular with female buyers. The Custom Royal sedan listed for $2,868, the Lancer two-door hardtop had a $2,993 sticker and the convertible prices started at $3,125.

Dodge dropped the two-door Suburban station wagon for 1959, leaving the four-door Sierra and Sierra Custom wagons with a choice of two or three seats. The rear-facing third seat could be folded down to create a flat rear cargo platform.

Dodge cut back to five V-8s in 1959. None were Hemis. A 326-cid 255-hp engine was standard in Coronets. It had a new 9.2:1 compression ratio and a two-barrel Stromberg carburetor. The 361-cid Ram-Fire V-8 was standard in Royals and Sierras. It had a 10.10:1 compression ratio and a Carter two-barrel carb. The output was 295 hp. A four-barrel version of this V-8 was standard in Custom Royal models. It had 305 hp. A new 383-cid D-500 V-8 with 10.10:1 compression and a single four-barrel carburetor was available at extra cost in all series. It cranked up 320 hp at 4600 rpm and 420 foot-pounds of torque at 2800 rpm.

For those who wanted even more acceleration, there was a Super D-500 version ($502 in Coronets, $304 in Royals and Sierras and $414 in Custom Royals and Custom Sierras) that delivered 345 hp at 5000 rpm and 420 foot-pounds at 3600 rpm.

Calendar-year 1959 Dodge production totaled 192,798 units for a 68.8 percent gain over the 114,206 turned out in 1958, but nearly 43.5 percent of the cars produced in 1959 were 1960 models.

Dodge's model-year showing of 151,851 cars produced was just 13.4 percent better than the total of 133,953 models built to 1958 specifications.

A 1959 Dodge Coronet Lancer hardtop was seen on the street at a 1999 car show.

Tom Collins

Edsels
of the Fifties

1958 *Edsel*

The 1958 Edsel Pacer Citation convertible shows off its new horse-collar grille.

We live in a world today where "branding" is considered an important marketing tool. Many modern brands were created in the '50s. The year 1958 marked the birth of the consumer credit industry when American Express launched its charge card and The Bank of America introduced what became the VISA card. In Wichita, Frank Carney read about the teenage "pizza fad" and borrowed $600 from his mom to open Pizza Hut.

One new brand introduced in 1958 wasn't successful. The Edsel name was created by Ford Motor Co., but lasted only three model years: 1958, 1959, and 1960.

The Edsel was designed to fill a gap between Mercury and Lincoln where Ford owned just a 14.3 percent share of market. The car was officially named as early as November 1956, but didn't debut until the 1958 model year.

As early as Aug. 7, 1956, Ford established five regional sales offices for its Special Products Division to form the nucleus of a nationwide sales organization. That October, District Sales Managers were appointed to sell the new car in 24 cities.

As "Uncle" Tom McCahill wrote in *Mechanix Illustrated*, "When I went to Michigan to test this new offering it was like Alumni Day at the Reform School, as I met old friends and acquaintances at every water cooler and desk. In fact, the new Edsel Division was stacked from top to bottom with the cream of former Lincoln, Ford, and Mercury engineers."

By January 1957, Ford was talking up its "distinctive-from-any-angle" looks and predicting 200,000 first-year sales. Five plants were committed to Edsel production and 1,200 to 1,400 dealers were expected to carry the brand.

"More than a new make of car . . . THE EDSEL is a billion dollar measure of a company's faith in the American economy" said a full-page ad signed by chairman of the board Ernie Breech and Ford president Henry Ford II.

Ford was so sure of the new car's success it went to market with a full line of 18 models in four different series. From lowest-to highest-priced they were named Ranger, Pacer, Corsair, and Citation. Body style offering included sedans, hardtops, and station wagons in both two- and four-door models, plus convertible coupes. The lower-priced Edsel Rangers and Pacers were based on the 118-inch wheelbase Ford Fairlane and 116-inch wheelbase Ford station wagon bodies. Higher-end Corsair and Citation models, shared part of the Mercury body shell and had a 124-inch wheelbase.

The base series Ranger was $2,300 to $2,446, the only Edsel to come in a two-door sedan model. The Ranger nameplate was on the front fender. They had no bright metal front fender or door moldings or roof rails. Four-door hardtops had triangular rear window pillars with round medallions, while two-door hardtops and all sedans had narrow roof pillars without medallions. Two-door wagons were called Roundup models, while the Ranger-like four-door, six- and nine-passenger wagons were called the Villager. Prices for these 116-inch wheelbase wagons were $2,630 to $2,736.

The one-step-up series was the $2,499 to $2,771 Pacer, identified by Pacer front fender nameplates, bright metal moldings across the front fender and door and bright metal roof trim. Four-door hardtops and sedans were of the same basic design as Rangers, but a convertible replaced the two-door sedan. There was no Pacer two-door wagon and the four-door wagon was the Bermuda, which also came in six- and nine-passenger versions. Prices for these wagons were $2,922 and $2,975.

The junior Edsels were powered by an E-400 362-cid V-8 with a 303-hp (at 4600 rpm) rating. It was part of the FE series of Ford engines introduced in 1958. This solid-lifter motor carried a Holley four-barrel carburetor and had a 10.5:1 compression ratio. It produced 400 foot pounds of torque at 2800 rpm.

Corsairs represented the lower rung of the senior Edsels. The two-door hardtop listed for $3,066 and the four-door hardtop was $3,139. They could be identified by Corsair front fender nameplates. They had no silver aluminum trim inside the accent panels on the sides of the rear fenders. The top-rung Citations were $177 pricier than Corsairs and also offered a $3,489 convertible, the most expensive Edsel. The flagship models could be identified by their Citation front fender nameplates, bullet-shaped silver anodized trim inside the rear accent panels and the use of broad rectangular rear window pillars with medallions (except on the convertible.)

Under the hood of Corsairs and Citations was the E-475 410-cid V-8 that cranked up 345 hp at 4600 rpm and 475 foot pounds of torque at 2900 rpm.

Tom McCahill tested a senior Edsel. "With only myself in the big Corsair with its 410-inch engine, it was impossible on any type of road surface, including ribbed concrete, to give it a full jump start. On ribbed concrete, every time I shot the throttle to the floor quickly, the wheels spun like a gone-wild Waring Blender. This car has enough torque to yank the Empire State Building off its foundations."

Edsel selling features included the Teletouch push-button shift for automatic transmission. Its buttons were mounted in the hub of the steering wheel, where the horn button usually appeared.

This required some special engineering, since the buttons had to stay fixed in position when the wheel was turned. An ingenious gearing system permitted the outside of the wheel to turn while the center hub, with its buttons and wires, remained stationary. With this system, after the transmission was put in park, it was locked and couldn't be taken out of park until the ignition was turned on.

The Edsel bowed to the public on Sept. 4, 1957 and it was quickly obvious the sales goal of 200,000 units wouldn't be hit. Buyers seemed to have problems understanding where the car fit. Its "Alfa Romeo" type grille and richer trim didn't hide its obvious link to contemporary Fords and Mercurys. There were so many models and such a wide range of prices, it was difficult for the average buyer to form a clear image of the Edsel.

Only 60,000 cars were sold. Model-year production of 63,110 cars was only 1.5 percent of total industry output. The number for calendar-year 1958 was only 26,563 cars for a .62 percent market share. The Edsel survived a bit longer, though the handwriting was on the wall for the Ford Motor Company.

1959 *Edsel*

The 1959 Edsel Villager was an attractive six-passenger station wagon.

Xerox manufactured the first plain-paper copying machine, its Xerox 914, in 1959. The Edsel that Ford manufactured that year wasn't a carbon copy of the original 1958 version, but it certainly copied its poor performance in the marketplace. Model-year production dropped off to 44,891 units or just 0.8 percent of total industry. Calendar-year production actually rose slightly to 29,677 but the share-of-market that this number represented dropped from .62 percent to .53 percent. And the calendar-year total included all 1960 Edsels, which were built in the fall of 1959 only.

Edsel launched its 1959 program with a "new kind of car" that stressed greater operating economy. The model lineup was cut back to eight passenger cars in two series and two wagons in a single series. Production was limited to Ford's Louisville, Kentucky, assembly plant. Only the Ranger and Corsair series remained in the Edsel lineup and both were on a new 120-inch wheelbase. Overall length was 210.8 inches. Station wagons were reduced to a pair of Villagers on a 118-inch wheelbase.

Edsel's new front end styling had the dual headlights enclosed in the grille. The "horse collar" grille motif was retained in the form of an upright center section with horizontal ribs and a green triangular badge in its center. This stood out from a horizontal grille surrounded by a heavy chrome molding. The horizontal grille had three horizontal bars and three trim segments on each side of the horse collar. The bumper, which dipped down below the horse collar, had the parking lights embedded in each corner, where they were prone to being damaged. The roof was flatter.

The Ranger lineup encompassed the two- and four-door sedans and two- and four-door hardtops at prices between $2,398 and $2,515. Rangers could be identified by the Ranger nameplates on the lower rear fenders. These models looked a bit fancier than they had in 1958, since they carried full-length body side moldings.

Sometimes the area between the upper and lower moldings was done in a contrasting color. The lower side trim moldings dipped to a sharp point below the front vent windows. The Edsel name appeared on the front body sides and door and above the upright horse collar grille. Ads described the Ranger as being, "High in distinction — but low in price!" and "Luxury without going overboard."

The Villager station wagons had Ranger-style trim. Wagons were offered in six- and nine-passenger versions priced at $2,715 and $2,792 respectively. The rear of the station wagon did not have the gull-wing look. Instead there were small tail fins that canted slightly outwards. The round taillights were mounted, side-by-side, below the fins in chrome housings. Running across the entire rear end was a large concave panel with the Edsel name spelled out across it and large round lights at each end. The Villager name was carried in a black indentation at the center of the upper molding.

The Corsair was now the sole up-market Edsel model. It came in a four-door sedan, two- and four-door hardtop and convertible models at prices between $2,567 and $2,807. Corsairs could be identified by the Corsair nameplates on their lower rear fenders. They also had dual side trim moldings that flared out on the rear doors and/or quarter panel to enclose a silver anodized aluminum panel with a round medallion near its forward end. The Edsel name appeared in the same places as on the lower series.

Standard power for the Ranger series was now the 292-cid Y-block V-8, which had been available in Ford models since 1955. This solid-lifter engine had 8.8:1 compression and a single two-barrel carburetor. It generated 200 hp at 4400 rpm and 285 foot pounds of torque at 2200 rpm. Standard in Villager station wagons and the Corsair series was FoMoCo's 332-cid V-8, which was also a Ford engine. It had slightly higher 8.9:1 compression and hydraulic valve lifters to go with its two-barrel carburetor. Ratings on this engine were 225 hp at 4400 rpm and 325 foot pounds of torque at 2200 rpm. An extra-cost option was the 361-cid V-8 carried over from 1958. Ford's 223-cid in-line six-cylinder engine was a delete option in Rangers.

A three-speed manual transmission with column-mounted gear shift was standard equipment with the 233-, 292- and 332-cid engines. A two-speed Mile-O-Matic automatic transmission was optional in all models with any engine, but was rarely used with the big 361-cid V-8. Three-speed Dual-Drive automatic transmission was optional only with that big V-8. Though not officially offered, at least three Edsels were made with over-

drive. New carburetors, designed to give extra fuel economy, were adopted this year. Also new was an aluminized exhaust system and 18-mm spark plugs said to give greater efficiency.

On Oct. 15, 1959, the 1960 Edsels were put on sale. These cars, although not 1950s models, were built only during the '50s. They were little more than face-lifted versions of the redesigned 1960 Fords. Styling was all new, with a Pontiac-like divided grille.

Only the Ranger line was marketed. All models had the Edsel name on their rear fenders and in a concave panel between the taillights. Sedans, hardtops and the convertible had the Ranger name in script on the front fenders. Station wagons had the Villager name there and on the tailgate. The 223-cid six was the basis of a separate six-cylinder series this year. Both lines had all of the closed body styles, but the convertible came only as a V-8. Prices ranged from $2,334 for the cheapest six-cylinder two-door sedan to $2,810 for the nine-passenger Villager wagon with the V-8.

Model-year production came to just 2,846 cars with 889 made in September 1959, 1,767 built in October and 190 in November. That was it. On Nov. 19, 1959, Ford announced the end of the Edsel, after making just 110,847 of them.

Fords
of the Fifties

1950 *Ford*

The Custom Deluxe Club Coupe was a popular choice among 1950 Ford buyers.

In 1950, there were 149 million Americans earning a median salary of $2,992 and paying 14 cents for a loaf of bread and about $1,400 for a "shoe box" Ford. On Jan. 17, 1950, a band of masked men emerged from a financial institution in Boston with $1,218,211.29 in cash and $1,557,183.83 in securities. If they listened to earlier thieves like John Dillinger and Clyde Barrow, the perpetrators of the "The Brink's Job" would have driven a V-8-powered 1950 Ford when they pulled off their "crime of the century."

At first glance, the 1950 Ford seemed identical to the 1949 model, but it was said to include "50 improvements for '50." Obvious changes were very modest. Once again a heavy chrome molding curved from the top of the "Air Foil" grille down to the gravel deflector. Instead of the Ford name, a shield-shaped badge now sat above the center of the grille. The horizontal center bar again extended the full width of the opening. In the center was a large spinner with either a "6" or "8" designation. The center grille bar now wrapped around the body corners. Horizontally-ribbed plates, which housed the rectangular parking lights, were now seen between that bar and the bumper. Door handles were push button rather than older style pull down.

A chrome strip extended from behind the front wheel openings to just above and behind the rear wheel opening. On fancier models, this molding had a spear-tip-shaped nameplate on the front fender. The gas filler cap was now hidden behind a lift-up door on the upper left-hand rear fender. A new finned "knight's helmet" hood ornament was seen. Other changes included a three-bladed cooling fan and push-button handles on exterior doors. When a fancy steering wheel was fitted, it included a flat-topped horn ring.

Dimensionally, the 1950 Fords were similar to 1949 models. All body styles rode on a 114-inch wheelbase. The overall length was 196.6 inches, except in the case of station wagons, which were 206 inches long. The overall width of all models was 72.8 inches. Size 6.00 x 16 tires were standard, but those who wanted a low-to-the-ground '50s look could opt for 6.70 x 15 on most models. Station wagons, however, required larger 7.10 x 15 tires to support the heavier weight of their wood body. The "Country Squire" station wagons included a stowaway center seat, a flat-deck loading plat-

form and a rear seat that was easily removable without the use of tools. With the "Level-Loading" tailgate lowered, there was 38.8 square feet of flat deck to handle half a ton of freight with ease.

Important selling features for 1950 Fords included an Equa-Flo cooling system, full-pressure engine lubrication, "Deep-Breath" intake manifolding, "Power-Dome combustion chambers, the use of four-ring pistons, Equa-Poise engine mountings, a Loadomatic ignition system, a Soft-Action clutch and Black-Light dashboard dials. Dual downdraft carburetion was featured on V-8 models. Ford also promoted Mid-Ship Ride, Lifeguard body construction, Hydra-Coil springs, Magic-Action brakes and Fender-Guard bumpers.

Inside, Fords offered more hip room and more shoulder room than any other car in their price class. The "Jewel Box" interior featured non-sagging front seat springs and special foam rubber seat cushions that claimed to be more comfortable than ever before. The seats themselves were described as being "Sofa-Wide." Interior fabrics came in a choice of broadcloth or mohair.

"You travel first class without extra fare in the Big Ford," said an advertisement promoting the Custom Deluxe Tudor sedan. Another ad described this particular model as "A 'personal' car with all Ford quality features! Mid Ship Ride! Lifeguard Body! 35% easier-acting King-Size Brakes! And a Deep Deck Locker that holds all the bags and baggage!"

The Deluxe series was the base trim level for 1950 Fords and cars in this line had a black rubber windshield gasket, black rubber window moldings, a horn button instead of horn ring, one sun visor and an armrest on the driver's door only. There was no chrome trim around the side windows or windshield. A single chrome body strip without nameplate decorated the body sides.

The Deluxe model lineup consisted of the Business Coupe and two- and four-door sedans. (Ford actually described the latter models as the "Tudor" and "Fordor" sedans). A choice of an in-line six-cylinder or flathead V-8 engine was offered. Prices began at $1,333 for six-cylinder-powered Fords. The priciest V-8 was the Fordor sedan, which listed for $1,545.

The Custom Deluxe series was Ford's top trim level and the cars in this line included chrome window moldings, a chrome horn ring, twin sun visors, armrests on all doors and passenger assist straps on the interior "B" pillars (for easier rear seat egress). The word "Custom" was spelled out in capital letters on the spear-tip-shaped nameplates on the front fenders.

Four body styles were offered in the Custom Deluxe six-cylinder lineup. These were the Club Coupe and Tudor Sedan (both priced at $1,511), the Fordor sedan ($1,558) and the wood-bodied station wagon ($2,028). It cost about $79 to add a V-8 engine to these models.

Also available only with the V-8 engine was the $1,711 Crestliner two-door hardtop and the $1,948 convertible. With just 8,703 assemblies, the 1950 Crestliner was rare for a Ford.

Said one Ford advertisement, "When the moon looks cool as sherbet, it doesn't take a share of Fort Knox to enjoy it . . . it merely takes a Ford convertible. For no car, yes, no car, has a happier way with your heartstrings for so little money."

Ford's 226-cid L-head six had a 6.8:1 compression ratio and a Holley one-barrel carburetor. It made 95 hp at 3300 rpm. The 239-cid L-head V-8 had the same compression, but combined it with a two-barrel Holley carburetor to generate 100 hp at 3600 rpm. Both engines came only hooked to the standard Ford transmission, which was a three-speed manual type with a semi-centrifugal-type clutch and a three-speed helical gearset with synchronizers on second and third. A three-speed manual gearbox with automatic overdrive was optional.

The 1950 Fords were introduced in November of 1949 and had an estimated model-year production of 1,209,548 cars. Of these, 897,463 were V-8s and 289,659 were sixes. Calendar-year output was 1,187,120 units, representing 17.79 percent of total industry production. For the second year in a row, the Ford was named "Fashion Car of the Year" by New York's famed Fashion Academy.

1951 Ford

The 1951 Ford Custom Deluxe station wagon was called the Country Squire.

According to the March 26, 1951 issue of *Quick* magazine, "The productive genius of the Ford Motor Co. solved a year-old dilemma." The problem was how to keep children from "liberating" the red-white-and-blue golden lion crests from the hoods of 1950 Fords. The kids liked to put these on beanies, belts and bikes. Ford's solution was to tell kids they could write to Ford to get a free miniature crest.

Considering the Ford emblems' popularity among potential future customers, it's no wonder the crest remained on the hood in 1951. Other styling changes were again minor. The new grille featured dual "spinners" that were positioned at the outer edges of the center grille bar. The new front parking lights were round. The hood ornament looked like an abstract bird.

At the rear of the car, Ford's "Tell Tale" rear lamps were decorated with jet-style chrome spears that tapered towards the front as they ran down the slab-sided body. The simple chrome moldings decorating the lower body sides of Custom Deluxe models now ran to the extreme rear of the body. Series or model names appeared on a front fender trim that looked like a fin.

The Deluxe or Custom names appeared on this plate on most '51 Fords, but the plate on the all-new hardtop model said Victoria.

"The car that gives you the smart styling of a convertible with the snugness of a sedan," is how ad copywriters described this model. The wood paneled wagons did not have room for moldings, but carried the Country Squire name in script on the upper front corner of the front doors. The woodie was promoted as a "Double Duty Dandy." Cars with V-8 engines under the hood also had a V-8 emblem on the front fender.

Ford offered the coupe, Tudor sedan and Fordor sedan in the Deluxe Six series at prices between $1,324 and $1,465. These body styles also came as Deluxe eights. For some reason, the coupe cost $87 more with a V-8, while the two- and four-door sedans cost only $75 more with a V-8.

Chances are, the Deluxe six coupe was used as a "loss leader" to feature in print ads to get buyers into the showroom. This might explain the larger discount for a six-cylinder version. The "Mileage Maker" in-line six was the same 226-cid 96-hp job used in 1950. Ditto for the 239-cid 100-hp "Strato-Star" flathead V-8.

Ford offered the Club Coupe, Tudor Sedan, Fordor Sedan and Country Squire station wagon in the Custom Deluxe Six series at prices between $1,505 and $2,029. These body styles also came as Custom Deluxe eights, along with the Crestliner Tudor Sedan, the convertible and the Victoria hardtop, which were V-8-only cars.

The Crestliner, first introduced in 1950, was a special two-door sedan with a vinyl top, extra chrome, a special steering wheel, special two-tone paint and full wheel covers. The Victoria was Ford's first pillarless hardtop and was aptly described as "the Belle of the Boulevard!" It featured "Luxury Lounge" interiors that were color-keyed to the finish of the car, which was usually two-toned. Prices for the fanciest Fords ranged from $1,590 to $2,110.

Ford engines featured a waterproof ignition system, Loadomatic distributors, an Equa-Flow cooling system with a Silent-Spin fan, Forced-Feed lubrication, a "Full-Flo" fuel pump, Power-Dome combustion and "Rota-Quiet" valves. A three-speed manual gearbox was standard and overdrive was optional. Ford described its popular overdrive as an automatic fourth gear that reduced engine wear and cut fuel costs up to 15 percent.

A fully-automatic transmission was offered for the very first time in 1951, but only in cars with V-8 engines. Ford advertised that the new Fordomatic transmission provided "the magic of liquid-smooth, effortless automatic drive." This unit consisted of a torque converter with a three-speed automatic planetary gear.

The five-position Semaphone Drive Selector with an illuminated dial was positioned on the steering column.

"The Fordomatic Ford brings you automatic driving at its finest and flexible best," said Ford. "You get flashing getaway . . . instant acceleration . . . plenty of zip for passing and hill climbing . . . and all with real economy."

Automatic Ride Control was the name of a new, heavily-advertised Ford feature for 1951. It was as a "three-way partnership" between the Hydra-Coil front springs, the variable-rate rear leaf springs and the viscous-control telescopic shock absorbers. Designed to maintain a level ride and eliminate pitch, jounce and roll, it was advertised as "...a new and unique springing system which automatically adjusts spring reaction to road conditions."

Ford interiors were highlighted by a new Safety-Glow control panel with knobs and dials that were easy to reach and easy to read. Ignition-key starting was new this year.

"Just turn the ignition key to the right — your engine starts. No reaching for a button — no stretching for a starter pedal," Ford explained. The "Chanalited" instrument cluster had all of the gauges located within the speedometer scale for easy readability. The speed indicator incorporated a ring at its end that circled the traveling speed in red and glowed at night. All controls had "Glow-Cup" lighting for night-driving convenience.

"Automatic Posture Control" was Ford's trade name for a design in which the entire seat was angled for maximum comfort. Cushioning was by foam rubber over non-sag springs. The seats featured long-wearing Fordcraft fabrics and new harmonized appointments, while "Colorblend" carpeting covered the floor. A "Magic-Air" weather-control system was optional.

Although the image of the "shoe box" Ford didn't change much in 1951, Ford general manager L. D. Crusoe was focused on the goal of making Ford the top-selling car brand in America.

In addition to offering free replicas of the company's crest to youngsters who might buy Fords tomorrow, he was carefully plotting the course to better future sales with the introduction of modern features like automatic transmissions and hardtop styling.

Unfortunately, the United States government threw up roadblocks in 1951 by instituting production controls due to the Korean crisis. They held Ford's output to 24 percent below the 1950 figure.

Model-year production was 1,013,391 vehicles, which included 753,265 cars with V-8 engines and 147,495 sixes. Calendar-year output was 900,770, giving Ford second place on the sales charts, but only 16.87 percent market share, down from 17.79 the previous year.

This year, the sales were lost to Chrysler, which gained market share for all of its divisions. The only GM branch to gain market share in the calendar year was Cadillac. This was a sure sign that the big overhead valve V-8s offered by MoPar and Cadillac had sales appeal. Certainly, Ford was watching this trend as its sights were set in the direction of introducing a new V-8 in the not-too-distant future.

1952 *Ford*

The Federal-Aid Highway Act of 1952 authorized $25 million for the interstate highway system on a 50-50 matching basis. These were the first funds authorized specifically for interstate road construction and Ford Motor Company ran a series of "American Road" advertisements to support the initiative. The ads touched on the history of American roads from single-file Indian paths, to "Good Roads" movements to modern cloverleaf highways.

"We need more of those superb new turnpikes, expressways and superhighways with their overpasses and underpasses, and glittering silver-steel bridges that soar across rivers of the land," one ad suggested. It also pointed out that Ford had put 35 million cars on those roads over the years.

The new Fords introduced to the public on Feb. 1, 1952 were better-suited for highway travel than any others. They were wider, longer, roomier, stronger and more powerful than ever before. Highlighting new-model introductions was the first totally new body for Ford since 1949. The cars were arranged in three different, renamed product lines with each series — Mainline, Customline and Crestline — offering different combinations of body styles, trim and engines. Some body types and all Crestlines were available only with the V-8 engine.

Styling-wise, the 1952 Fords featured a new Curva-Lite Safety-View one-piece curved windshield with no center bar, a 48 percent larger full-width rear window, Search-Mount headlights with protruding round parking lights directly below behind "triple spinner" bars, a round three-bladed spinner in the center of the grille bar, a simulated air scoop on the rear quarter panels, a redesigned instrument panel and "Power-Pivot" suspended clutch and brake pedals. This year, the gas filler pipe and neck were concealed behind a hinged rear license plate.

The Mainline series was the base trim level for 1952. Cars in this line had rubber window moldings, a horn button instead of horn ring, one sun visor and an armrest only on the driver's door. There were four body types in this range: Business Coupe, Tudor Sedan, Fordor Sedan and new all-steel two-door Ranch Wagon.

The 1952 Ford Crestline series included this Victoria two-door hardtop.

All were available with both engines. The six-cylinder engine was now an overhead-valve type, while the V-8 remained an L-head or "flathead" motor. The six-cylinder-powered Business Coupe sold for just $1,389. On the other end of the spectrum, the six-passenger Ranch Wagon cost $1,902 with a V-8 under its hood.

The Customline series was the intermediate trim level for 1952 and included chrome window moldings, a chrome horn ring, two sun visors, armrests on all doors, passenger assist straps on the interior "B" pillars (for easier rear seat egress), a horizontal chrome strip on the front fenders and a chrome opening on the rear quarter panel scoop. Three sixes were offered in Customline trim: the Club Coupe, the Tudor and the Fordor. These were priced between $1,570 and $1,615. These were available with a V-8 for $70 more. A four-door Country Sedan station wagon was also offered in the Customline V-8 series for $2,076.

Crestline was the name of the top-trim-level series for 1952. Crestline models included the Victoria hardtop, the Sunliner convertible and the Country Squire. The latter was a four-door all-metal station wagon that came with wood grain side trim appliqués. All three "name" cars were offered only with V-8 engines. This series included all features of the Customline models, plus full wheel covers and additional chrome trim along the bottom of the side windows.

Prices were $1,925 for the "Vicky," $2,027 for the Sunliner (which included a push-button-operated power soft top) and $2,186 for the eight-passenger Country Squire. This top-of-the-line station wagon had a production run of only 5,426 units, making it the year's rarest Ford product.

The new overhead-valve Mileage Maker Six had a 3.56 x 3.60-inch bore and stroke and 215 cubic inches of displacement. With a 7.0:1 compression ratio and single-barrel Holley carburetor, it was good for 101 hp at 3500 rpm. Some said this six performed better than the old 239-cid Strato-Star V-8, which was boosted to 110-hp. The flathead engine ran a 7.2:1 compression ratio and used a two-barrel carburetor.

Of course, any V-8-powered Ford could be "improved" with aftermarket goodies, while there was not nearly as much "hop-up" equipment available for the in-line six. Automatic Power Pilot was the name given to Ford's completely integrated carburetion-ignition-combustion system. It featured a downdraft carburetor that automatically switched to economy jets for idling and a Loadomatic ignition distributor that automatically controlled spark advance.

Ford's standard transmission was a three-speed manual-type of the usual design. Three-speed manual with automatic overdrive was a $102 option. Fordomatic transmission was a $170 option. Fordomatic featured a torque converter transmission with automatic planetary gear train, a single stage three-element hydraulic torque converter, hydraulic-mechanical automatic controls (with no electrical or vacuum connections), forced-air cooling and power flow through the fluid member at all times. Cars with the automatic transmission had a Fordomatic nameplate on the trunk lid. Others said "Overdrive" in the same spot.

All three Ford series shared a 115-inch wheelbase. The overall length of all models was 197.8 inches. The cars were 73.2 inches wide. Rear axle gear ratios varied by transmission application: 3.90:1 with stick shift, 4.10:1 with overdrive (3.15:1 optional) and 3.31:1 with Fordomatic (3.54:1 optional). The standard tire size was 6.00 x 16, but larger 6.70 x 15 tires were optional and recommended for heavier models like ragtops and wagons.

A new line of custom accessories was brought out by Ford to match 1952 styling. Interesting additions on the list were a speed governor, turn indicators, illuminated vanity mirror, engine compartment light, five-tube Deluxe radio, seven-tube Custom radio, spring wound clock, electric clock, color-keyed rubber floor mats, wheel discs, wheel trim rings, rear fender skirts, rocker panel trim strips, hand brake signal lamp and Magic Air heater and defroster.

L.D. Crusoe managed to grow Ford Division in 1952, opening nine new parts depots nationwide and starting work on three more new facilities in the East and Midwest.

Government restrictions, along with a steel strike and other disputes, held model-year production to 671,725 units. For the calendar-year, Ford built 777,531 cars or 17.93 percent of the industry total. A significant 32 percent of cars built this year had Fordomatic gear shifting and more than 20 percent of the cars built with manual transmissions had the overdrive option. Ford also led the industry in station wagon production with 32 percent of total industry output for this body style.

1953 Ford

Two versions of the 1953 Ford Crestline Victoria two-door hardtops are shown.

On Jan. 20, 1953, Dwight D. Eisenhower took the oath of office as President of the United States. By his side was Richard M. Nixon, who was sworn in as "Ike's" Vice President. The inaugural address was broadcast on live, coast-to-coast television for the first time in history. Ford, of course, had already made effective use of the new broadcasting medium, sponsoring early car collector (and opera singer) James Melton's "Ford Festival" program on NBC-TV in 1951-1952.

Ford held dealer introductions for its 1953 "Golden Jubilee" models on December 12, 1952. The new cars utilized 1952 bodies with moderate trim updating. However, they were said to offer "41 Worth More Features." Selling features for the year included double-seal Magic-Action brakes, push-button door handles, a self-lifting deck lid, "Hull-Tight" body construction, Silent-Doorman two-stage front door checks, Center-Fill fueling, a flight-style control panel, a K-bar frame, high alloy exhaust valves, aluminum pistons and a Safety-Sequence drive selector in cars with Fordomatic transmission.

The 1953 grille incorporated a larger horizontal bar with three vertical stripes on either side of a large spinner. The length of this bar was increased and it now wrapped around the front edges of the fenders. The parking lights were horizontal rectangles instead of circles. The Ford crest appeared in the center of the steering wheel hub and contained the words, "50th Anniversary 1903-1953."

Ford's Mainline series was the base trim level for 1953 and cars in this line included rubber windshield and rear window moldings, fixed rear vent windows, a horn button instead of a horn ring, one sun visor and an armrest on the driver's-side only. Mainline models had no chrome sweep spears on the front and rear fenders. Partial chrome gravel deflectors accented the bulges on the rear quarter panels, just ahead of the rear wheel openings. The Mainline name appeared on the front fenders. The two-door Ranch Wagon, which was part of this series, had no wood-look exterior panels. Body style offerings were identical to those offered in 1952. Prices on the Mainline Sixes ran from $1,497 to $1,846. The same four body styles came with V-8 power for $70 additional.

The Customline series was the intermediate trim level for 1953 and included chrome windshield and rear window moldings, a chrome horn half-ring, two sun visors, armrests on all doors and passenger assist straps on interior "B" pillars for easier rear seat egress. A horizontal chrome strip decorated the front fenders just above the wheel opening. Chrome gravel deflectors capped the entire front height of the rear quarter panel scoops. There was another horizontal chrome strip running from the scoop opening, above the rear wheel opening, to the back of the body.

The Customline name was on a spear tip at the leading edge of the front fender molding. If a V-8 was installed, an appropriate emblem was placed behind the spear tip. The Country Sedan wagon in this line had four doors, but no exterior wood grained paneling. Body style offering were the same as in 1952 with prices of $1,582 to $1,628 for the three Customline Sixes and $1,653 to $2,076 for the four Customline V-8s.

The Crestline series was the top trim level for 1953 and was again offered only with V-8 engines. This series included all trim in the Customline series plus wheel covers and additional chrome trim along the bottom of the side widows. The Victoria hardtop listed for $1,941, the Sunliner convertible listed for $2,043 and the Country Squire wood-trimmed wagon listed for $2,203.

Engine choices in 1953 looked identical to those of the previous season. Three-speed manual transmission was again standard. Overdrive was a $108 option. The automatic overdrive function cut in at 27 mph and cut out at 21 mph. Fordomatic automatic transmission was a $184 option. Other 1953 Ford options included Master Guide power steering (introduced June 16) at $125, power brakes at $35, a six-tube Deluxe radio at $88, an eight-tube

Custom radio at $100, a recirculation-type heater at $44, a Deluxe MagicAire heater at $71, an electric clock at $15, directional signals at $15, windshield washers for $10, I-Rest tinted glass for $23 and white sidewall tires at $27.

Ford's Automatic Ride Control suspension design was improved for 1953. The new "balanced" system integrated a rubber-cushioned front suspension with variable-rate rear leaf springs and diagonally-mounted telescopic shock absorbers to minimize side sway on turns. The front tread width was two inches wider than the rear tread width to give better "footing" for easier handling.

Business wise, 1953 had a "split personality" at Ford Division. During the first part of the year, auto production was hampered by government limitations, strikes and disputes with parts suppliers. The production schedules changed to six-day weeks as Ford's output exploded to a level 52 percent ahead of 1952. By the time the dust cleared, model-year production stood at 1,240,000 cars, of which 876,300 were estimated to be V-8s. Six-cylinder model production nearly doubled to 307,887.

Calendar-year production climbed steeply to 1,184,187 units or 19.30 percent of industry, although Chevrolet gained nearly four full points of market share compared to just over one point for Ford.

Fordomatic transmission grew so popular in 1953 that production schedules had to be expanded.

However, due to a 10-week supplier strike at Borg-Warner, which made the Ford automatic, 85 percent of the cars made in June were equipped with stick shift. Nevertheless, 346,939 cars got the automatic. The power steering option released in June was popular enough to go into eight percent of all 1953 Fords made by the end of the year. Ford also upped its production of station wagons to 38 percent of total industry output and made more convertibles (39,945 in the calendar year) than any other automaker.

The anniversary year brought several milestones. In May, a specially-trimmed 1953 Ford Sunliner convertible paced the Indianapolis 500-Mile Race. Ford also opened a new Technical Service Laboratory, at Livonia, Michigan, during the year.

1954 Ford

The 1954 Ford Crestline Skyliner was available with a tinted-glass roof window.

In 1954 the average American made just under $4,000 a year and lived in a house that cost $22,000. He or she paid 92 cents for a gallon of milk, 22 cents for a gallon of gas, 17 cents for a loaf of bread and three cents for a postage stamp. *The Old Man and the Sea* was popular reading and its author, Ernest Hemingway, took a Nobel Prize for his "mastery of the art of narrative" and for "the influence that he exerted on contemporary style."

Contemporary style was also reflected in the '54 Ford's appearance. "Ford brings you tomorrow's clean uncluttered look today," said an advertisement. In truth, this was an easy accomplishment, since barely any changes were made from the cars' 1952-1953 styling.

The same basic body was used. The modestly-updated grille incorporated a large horizontal bar with large slots on either side of a centrally located spinner. Round parking lights were located in smaller spinners at either end of the horizontal bar. Making news was the availability of a new V-8 engine (promoted as the Ford "Y-8") with overhead valves. It was now optional in all models.

This new engine was rated at 130 hp or nearly 25 percent more than the 1953 flathead.

Ford added many new convenience items to its optional equipment list in 1954. Among them were power windows, four-way power seats and power brakes. Ball joints replaced king pins in the front suspension. The biggest Ford news of all was the Feb. 20, 1954 announcement of an all-new personal luxury car called the Thunderbird. It was scheduled to be introduced in the 1955 model year.

Mainline, Customline and Crestline car-lines were offered again and all body styles in all three trim levels were available with either engine. This added up to 14 body style and trim combinations, times two engines, for a total of 28 basic Ford models.

All Fords continued to ride a 115-1/2-inch wheelbase. Cars were 198.3 inches long and station wagons were 198.1 inches long. Selling features promoted by Ford salesmen of the day were primarily the same ones offered in 1953 and included center-fill fueling, hull-tight body, two-stage door checks, non-sag seats, a K-bar frame, variable-rate rear leaf springs, full-displacement tubular shock absorbers, tailored-to-weight coil front springs, a semi-floating rear axle and hypoid gears.

The Mainline series was the base trim level for 1954 and included a Business Coupe, a Tudor Sedan, a Fordor Sedan and a two-door Ranch Wagon with six-passenger seating. These cars had rubber window moldings, a horn button instead of horn ring, a single sun visor and an armrest on the driver's door only.

The Mainline name appeared in chrome script on the front fender of the passenger cars, just ahead of the door break line. Station wagons had a Ranch Wagon script plate instead. Small gravel shields were seen on the rear fender "pontoons," just ahead of the rear wheel openings. Naturally, V-8-powered cars had "Y-8" badges just ahead of the front wheel openings. Prices were $1,471 to $1,846 for Mainline sixes and $71 additional for V-8-powered models.

The Customline series was the intermediate trim level for 1954. The Customline Six series offered a Club Coupe, a Tudor Sedan, a Fordor Sedan, a two-door Ranch Wagon with six-passenger seating and a four-door Country Sedan eight-passenger wagon. These cars had chrome window moldings, a chrome half-horn ring, two sun visors, armrests on all doors and passenger assist straps on the interior "B" pillars. On the passenger cars, the Customline name appeared in chrome script on the upper front "corner" of the rear fender pontoon. Two-door Customline wagons had a Ranch Wagon script in the same location and their four-door counterparts had a Country Sedan script there.

A sweep spear molding ran from the front to the rear of the car at just-below-headlight level. This trim dipped down in a scalloped V-shape around the upper front corner of the rear fender pontoon. The same small gravel shields used on Mainlines were placed just ahead of the rear wheel openings. Prices were $1,582 to $2,006 for the Mainline sixes and the same $71 additional for V-8s.

The Crestline series was the top trim level for 1954. This car line included the exciting new Skyliner hardtop that had a tinted, transparent roof panel above the driver's seat. There was also a Fordor sedan, a Victoria two-door hardtop, a Sunliner convertible and the four-door Country Squire eight-passenger wagon with simulated wood-grained trim. The Crestline models were offered with a six-cylinder engine for the first time since the series began in 1950. This series included all of the Customline trim features, plus three chrome hash marks behind the gravel shields, chrome "A" pillar moldings, additional chrome trim along the bottom of the side windows and full wheel covers.

The Crestline name appeared on the rear fender pontoon of all models except the wagon, which had Country Squire scripted on the front door instead. On the Victoria, Skyliner and Sunliner models, the model name was engraved in the chrome windowsills along with multiple hash marks. All hardtops had special rear roof pillar trim plates (gold-colored on Skyliners) with medallions. Pricing for Crestline sixes ran from $1,726 to $2,133 and the V-8 was a $71 option.

The overhead-valve in-line six was bored out to 223 cid. It also had a new 7.2:1 compression ratio and a two-barrel carburetor, upping output to 115 hp at 3900 rpm. The new overhead-valve V-8 (or "Y-8") retained the old 239-cubic-inch displacement figure. It also had a 7.2:1 compression ratio and a two-barrel carburetor. The V-8 was rated for 130 hp at 4200 rpm. Transmission options were as in the past.

Public presentation of the 1954 Ford line was made on Jan. 6, 1954. Of the total 1,165,942 Fords built in the 1954 model year, industry sources estimate that 863,096 had V-8 engines installed. Calendar-year production was 1,394,762 cars representing 25.31 percent of the total industry figure. This was a huge gain for Ford, which came very close to knocking Chevrolet out of its number 1 ranking on the sales charts. Both companies actually "force fed" cars to dealers as they competed hotly for the "best-selling-car" title. The 1,000,000th Ford of the 1954 production run was turned out Aug. 24, 1954 and in December, Ford announced it had recorded its best year since 1925.

1955 *Ford*

That wonderful year 1955 brought us 12 months filled with changes. In Great Britain, Sir Anthony Eden took over as Prime Minister after Sir Winston Churchill stepped down. Nikolai Bulganin replaced Georgi Malenkov as premier of the Soviet Union. In Argentina, dictator Juan Peron got the boot after 10 years as "El Presidente" (although he'd return in the '70s).

Ford's 1952-1954 styling also got the boot in '55, but the really big change in Dearborn was the all-new Thunderbird "sports-personal" car.

The new Fords were longer, lower and wider. Actual dimensions included a 115.5-inch wheelbase, 198.5-inch overall length (197.6 inches for station wagons) and a 75.9-inch body width. (The two-seat Thunderbird had a 102-inch wheelbase, 175.3-inch length and 70.3 inch width.) Fords had a new concave cellular grille, new side trim treatments, a wraparound windshield, T-Bird-like rear fenders and a Fairlane series that replaced the Crestline. Station wagons were now grouped in a separate series.

Mainline remained the base trim level and included rubber window moldings, a horn button instead of chrome horn ring, one sun visor and an armrest only on the driver's side. These cars had a Ford crest on the hood, no series nameplates, no side trim moldings and untrimmed body-color headlight "doors." A Business Sedan with just a front seat ($1,606), a Tudor sedan ($1,707) and a Fordor Sedan ($1,753) comprised the Mainline Six offerings. All three models could be had with a V-8 for an extra $100. In this case, "Y-8" emblems were placed just ahead of the front wheel openings.

The Customline was the intermediate trim level for 1955 and the cars in it included chrome window moldings, a chrome horn half-ring, two sun visors and armrests on all doors. A horizontal chrome strip ran the length of the body from below the headlights to the center of the taillights. A Customline script decorated the front fenders. Only Tudor ($1,801) and Fordor ($1,845) Sedans remained in the Customline Six series. Both came with a V-8 (and "Y-8" emblems) for $100 more.

The Fairlane series was the top trim level for 1955 and included chrome window and "A" pillar moldings (hardtops and Sunliner), chrome eyebrows on the headlights and a chrome side sweep molding that dipped on the front doors. The Fairlane name appeared on the hood, below the Ford crest. There were six

The 1955 Ford Fairlane Crown Victoria was available with and without a glass roof.

Fairlane Six models: two-door Club Sedan ($1,914), four-door Town Sedan ($1,960), Victoria two-door hardtop ($2,095), Crown Victoria two-door hardtop (a $2,202 car with a tiara-style roof band), Crown Victoria Skyliner ($2,272) with a transparent forward roof section and Sunliner convertible ($2,224). All could be had with the V-8 for an extra C-Note. The Town Sedan and Club Sedan had rear fender tip scripts. The others had the model name on the door, just behind the dip in the chrome molding.

The two-door Ranch Wagon was the base station wagon for six passengers. The Custom Ranch Wagon carried Customline body side moldings. Both of these cars had "Ranch Wagon" scripts on the front fenders. Six- and eight-passenger Country Sedans were offered. The six-passenger had Customline trim with "Country Sedan" on the front fenders, while the eight-passenger had dipping Fairlane sedan trim with "Country Sedan" on the rear fenders. The Country Squire was the top station wagon. It was trimmed on the outside with mahogany-grain panels and blonde fiberglass moldings. The model name was seen on the rear fenders. All five wagons were available with the six-cylinder engine at prices between $2,043 and $2,991. Here again, it was $100 to get a V-8.

The original Ford Thunderbird had many outstanding selling features. Its styling was less radical than other American sports cars. L.D. Crusoe insisted the new car be based on a full-sized Ford for "family" identity and to ensure major parts would be interchangeable with other 1955 Fords. Parts sharing cut development time, too.

The T-Bird's dimensions were based on those of the Corvette and the Jaguar XK-120. Designer Alden "Gib" Giberson, a native of the Southwest, suggested the name "Thunderbird." Although the car-buying public had a few peeks at the T-Bird early in 1954, it wasn't until October 22 that the production version was officially unveiled. Its introductory retail price was $2,695. Later, the price was increased when a fiberglass hardtop became standard equipment.

Looking very much like a scaled-down Ford, the Thunderbird was trim, though not sub-compact. The standard telescoping steering wheel allowed large T-Bird drivers to get comfortable inside the car. The styling of the car was quite pleasing. Its "frenched" headlamps gave it a forward-thrusting look at the front, while the crisp

tail fins seemed to send a little message to every slower car passed on the highway. A firm ride made the first Thunderbird feel like a sports car. It hung in the corners well enough to take them at 10 to 15 mph faster than most contemporary, full-size American cars.

Thunderbird features included dual exhausts, a 6-volt electrical system, a three-speed manual transmission, a ball-joint front suspension, an Astra-Dial control panel with illuminated control knobs, a 150-mph Astra-Dial speedometer, a tachometer and electric clock, a full-width seat with foam rubber padding, an adjustable steering wheel, floor carpet, a half-circle steering wheel horn ring and (as a running addition) the fibreglass hardtop.

At the beginning of the 1955 model-year, Ford Motor Company projected that it would sell 10,000 Thunderbirds, which proved to be a conservative estimate. Dealers reportedly took 4,000 orders on Oct. 22, 1954, the first day it was available. The *1956 Ward's Automotive Yearbook* listed Sept. 7, 1954 as the day Thunderbird production began, but the Classic Thunderbird Club International reports the earliest production unit had serial number P5FH100005 and was made on Sept. 9, 1954.

The 223-cid in-line six used in big Fords was boosted to 120 hp in 1955, thanks to a new 7.5:1 compression ratio. The new Y-8 used in regular passenger cars and wagons had a 3.62 x 3.30-inch bore and stroke for 272 cid. With a 7.6:1 compression ratio and two-barrel carburetor, it registered 162 hp at 4400 rpm. This rose to 182 hp at 4400 rpm with a "Power Pack" option. The larger 292-cid Thunderbird Special four-barrel V-8 had 8.1:1 compression (8.5:1 with Fordomatic) and developed 193 hp at 4400 rpm (198 hp at 4400 rpm with Fordomatic).

Production of 1955 Fords began on Oct. 25, 1954 and ended Aug. 30, 1955. The 1955 Ford was introduced to the public on Nov. 12, 1954. Production of 1955 Thunderbirds ended Sept. 16, 1955.

The model year produced 1,435,002 cars including an estimated 1,546,762 V-8s and 217,762 sixes. Of the V-8-powered cars, 16,156 were Thunderbirds. Calendar-year production was 1,764,524 (22.22 percent of industry) compared to 1,830,038 (23.04 percent) for rival Chevrolet. The 1955 run was the second best in Ford Motor Company's history, trailing only 1923, when Ford Model Ts dominated the entire industry.

1956 *Ford*

A continental kit in back was typical of the 1956 Ford Thunderbird roadster.

A brand new NBC Television program called "The Ford Show" bowed to the public on Oct. 4, 1956. Many people think the Ford Motor Company-sponsored show was named for its star — Tennessee Ernie Ford. The entertainer had been a big hit in 1955 and 1956 in his own "Tennessee Ernie Ford Show" that aired during daytime hours.

The new prime-time evening show increased Ernie's popularity immensely, while selling lots of Fords and Thunderbirds at the same time. Eventually, "The Ford Show" would become the top half-hour variety program in the United States. Ford's trademark closing number was almost always a hymn, gospel or spiritual song. The advertising gurus had flinched when this was proposed, but it turned out to be the winning touch that made the show a big success.

In 1956, Ford reused its 1955-style body shell. Wheelbase, length, width and height (60.4 inches for a sedan) were unchanged. There were several new models including a Customline Victoria two-door hardtop, a four-door Fairlane Victoria hardtop and a Fairlane-trimmed Parklane two-door sport wagon. A 12-volt electrical system was adapted for the first time.

A wider grille had oblong parking lights at its outer ends. All body side decorations were revamped and the Mainline models finally got body side moldings. Newly-designed taillights featured large, round red lenses with protruding ribbed-chrome center rings. The hood ornament looked like a chrome rocket in a soft tortilla shell. Safety was a popular theme in 1956 and the new Fords featured a completely redesigned instrument panel.

A "Lifeguard Safety Package" with dashboard padding, padded sun visors and other ingredients was optional. The steering wheel featured a 2-1/2-inch recessed hub designed to lessen injury to the driver in the event of an accident. Seat belts were also offered for the first time.

The Mainline series was the base trim level for 1956. Mainline models built early in the year had rubber window moldings, a horn button instead of horn ring, one sun visor and an armrest on the driver's door only. Later models had bright metal windshield and window molding and a unique molding treatment along the body side. This consisted of two parallel moldings running forward from the taillights, with the longer upper molding curving downwards,

to a spear tip plate, below the rear side window. The lower molding stopped about a foot back and an upward-curving molding connected it with the upper molding near the spear tip. The area between the moldings could be finished in a contrasting color, sometimes matching the roof color. The trunk carried a Ford crest with horizontal chrome bars jutting from either side. Mainline Six models were the same as in 1955 and priced from $1,744 to $1,891. A V-8 was $100 more.

The Customline series was the intermediate trim level and included chrome window moldings, a horn ring, two sun visors, armrests on all doors and passenger assist straps on two-door interior "B" pillars. A constant-width body side molding started on the sides of the front fenders, just behind the headlight hoods, and curved slightly downward, extending past the "Customline" nameplates on the rear doors (or rear quarter panels of four-door models).

The rear sections ran from the nameplate to a point just above the taillights. Where the two moldings met there was a "tree branch" effect. Trunk lid identification again consisted of a Ford crest with horizontal chrome bars on either side of the crest. The Tudor ($1,936), the Fordor ($1,982) and the new Victoria Tudor ($2,089) formed the Customline Six series. The $100-more-expensive V-8 models came in the same body styles.

The Fairlane series was the top trim level for 1956 and included chrome window moldings and chrome "A" pillar moldings on Sunliner convertibles. Fairlane nameplates and crests appeared on the hood and the rear deck lid. Body style nameplates were placed on the front doors. A wide, flared body side molding started on top of the headlight hoods, curved down to dips on the front doors and extended to the rear taillights. Sections to the rear of the "dips" had triple horizontal scoring with eight vertical intersects near the rear. This gave the side trim on the body an "external exhaust pipe" look. The trunk emblem was a black trapezoid with a V-shaped molding on V-8-powered cars. There were seven Fairlane models with the new four-door Victoria hardtop added to the 1955 carryover offerings. Prices for six-cylinder cars ranged from $2,043 to $2,403. You had to add $100 to get a V-8 engine.

Station wagons continued as their own series for 1956. The Ranch Wagon was the base trim level two-door station wagon.

Country Sedans were the intermediate trim level and Country Squires were the top trim level with simulated wood grain exterior paneling. The level of equipment paralleled the Mainline, Customline and Fairlane series of passenger cars. You could get a six-cylinder Ranch Wagon for as little as $2,185 or cough up as much as $2,633 for the V-8 powered "woodie." The all new Parklane two-door Sport Wagon was not a hardtop like some other non-Ford '56 wagons, but it was decorated with Fairlane side moldings and large chrome trim plates around the front door windows to give it a snazzy, competitive look.

Although the 1956 Thunderbird shared the same body as the 1955, there were a few significant changes that made the 1956 model unique. Probably the most visible change was the outside location of the spare tire, which gave much more room in the trunk. Also, the 1956 Thunderbird included wind wings on the windshield, cowl vents on each fender and a different rear bumpe configuration with the simplified dual exhaust routed out the ends of the bumper. The two-passenger convertible was now priced at $3,151.

Ford offered a total of eight engines throughout the model lineup this year. The 223-cid overhead-valve six had another compression ratio boost to 8.0:1, which gave it 137 hp at 4200 rpm. A Holley one-barrel carburetor was fitted.

When it came to V-8s, big Fords with manual transmissions started with a 272-cid, 173-hp job that had 8.4:1 compression and a two-barrel carburetor. With Fordomatic, the rating went up to 176 hp at 4400 rpm. A 292-cid 200-hp V-8 with a Holley four-barrel was optional. The base Thunderbird V-8 was another dual-exhaust version of the 292 that developed 202 hp at 4600 rpm.

Performance buffs could order a 312-cid 215-hp Thunderbird Special V-8 with manual transmission or overdrive. By bumping compression up to 9.0:1, Ford got the Thunderbird Special V-8 with Fordomatic transmission attachment up to 225 at 4600 rpm. With two Holley four-barrels and 9.5:1 compression, the Thunderbird Special V-8 produced 260 hp.

Production of 1956 Fords started on Sept. 6, 1955 and the 1956 Thunderbird began production on Oct. 17, 1955. Model-year production peaked at 1,468,733 units, which was an all-time record for the company. Calendar-year production hit 1,375,343 vehicles. Both of these figures include Thunderbird production, which dropped off slightly to 15,631 cars for the model year.

1957 *Ford*

A new design greeted buyers of the 1957 Thunderbird, all decked out in white.

"The Ford Show" remained popular in 1957 and most likely the television program contributed a lot to Ford Division's achievement of its long-time goal of out-producing Chevrolet that year. It was the first time in decades Dearborn built more cars than Flint did. For the model year, Ford produced 1,655,068 cars or 26.6 percent of the industry's total. Chevrolet, in contrast, built 1,552,471 cars for a 25.5 percent share of industry. Chevrolet was still calendar-year king, but by just 130 units or 1,522,536 of the Chevys versus 1,522,406 of the Fords. That gave Chevrolet 24.90 percent to Ford's 24.89 percent in "sales."

Tennessee Ernie Ford's televised pitches for T-Birds and Fairlanes hit home with his fans, and sold lots of cars for Ford that year. In April 1957, his show became the Number 1 30-minute variety show on TV, a status it maintained through 1961.

Ford—both the entertainer and the car company—"ruled" Thursday night programming for four solid years. All that changed in June 1961, when the man who had helped FoMoCo make automotive history in 1957 surprised everyone by retiring on a high note and becoming a part of television history.

The 1957 Fords were completely restyled and had several new series designations. They bore only a slight resemblance to 1956 models.

Fairlanes were five inches lower than before. They had a two-and-one-half-inch longer wheelbase and were nine inches longer in terms of overall length. Custom models were three inches longer overall and had a one-half-inch longer wheelbase. All Ford models had 14-inch wheels for the first time. The smaller-diameter wheels also contributed to their low-slung lines.

Other design changes included a rear-opening hood, streamlined wheel openings and a wraparound windshield with posts that sloped rearward at the bottom. All Fords also sported tail fins, which the automaker described as "high-canted fenders." The big news was the Skyliner model. This car was the world's only true hardtop convertible—or retractable hardtop, depending on how you look at it. A push-button automatic folding mechanism retracted the car's roof into the trunk.

Fords in the base Custom car-line had no series nameplates on their fenders. The body side moldings extended from the center side window pillar to the taillights, with a pointed dip on the rear door or fender. Body style offerings consisted of three sedans called the Business Tudor ($1,854), the Tudor ($1,965) and the Fordor ($2,017). V-8 versions of each style were $100 additional.

The Custom 300 was a new, upper trim level in the short-wheelbase Custom series. Two body styles were available, the Tudor ($2,080) and the Fordor ($2,132). They had added bright work such as chrome window moldings and a chrome horn ring. Inside there were two sun visors and armrests on all doors. The word F-O-R-D was spelled out in block letters above the grille and a small Ford crest appeared on the trunk lid. There were no series nameplates on the sides of the body.

A full-length side molding came with an optional gold aluminum insert that made the smaller, less-expensive Custom 300 look somewhat like a Fairlane 500. The difference was on the Custom 300 series, the rear portion of the molding behind the door dip ran straight to the taillights instead of accenting the tops of the tail fins. This trim lured the author's father into buying a Custom 300 instead of a Fairlane 500, since he felt there wasn't enough difference in the two to justify the Fairlane's higher price. Ford's trim upgrade obviously appealed to buyers of the less-expensive cars. For $100 extra, you could turn your Custom 300 Six into an Eight. (Dad did at least get the V-8!)

Fairlane was the base trim level for the longer wheelbase Ford series. There were four body styles in this car-line and each was available as a six, at the base price, or as a V-8 for $100 additional. Base prices were $2,210 for the two-door Club Sedan, $2,261 for the four-door Town Sedan, $2,268 for the Club Victoria (two-door hardtop) and $2,332 for the Town Victoria (four-door hardtop). These cars had bright Fairlane nameplates on their rear fenders, extra chrome around the roof "C" pillar and bullet-shaped accent panels on the rear fenders (and rear doors of four-door models). The Fairlane name appeared in script on the side of the fenders, above the grille and on the trunk lid.

A large, V-shaped Fairlane crest appeared on the trunk lid whenever V-8 engines were added.

Fairlane 500 was the top trim level in the Fairlane series and included all the trim used on the Fairlane models plus slightly more chrome on the "C" pillars and different side trim. The side trim was a modified version of the Fairlane sweep, which included a gold anodized insert between two chrome strips. It began on the sides of the front fenders, dipping near the back of the front doors, merging into a strip and following the crest of the fins to the rear of the body.

Five Fairlane 500s could be had with a six-cylinder engine: Club Sedan ($2,256), Town Sedan ($2,308), Club Victoria ($2,314), Town Victoria ($2,379) and Sunliner convertible ($2,480). All of these were available with V-8 power for $100 more, but a sixth V-8 model was also offered. This was the Skyliner convertible (retractable hardtop) priced at $2,917.

The Ranch Wagon was the base trim level 1957 Ford two-door station wagon. Country Sedans were the intermediate level with four-door styling. Country Squires were the top trim level, also with four-door styling. The level of equipment paralleled Custom, Custom 300 and Fairlane 500 models of passenger cars. Wagon prices ran from $2,301 to $3,693.

The 1957 Thunderbird was the two-passenger sporty car's first major change. A longer rear section provided improved storage space. Riding and handling qualities were greatly enhanced by relocating the spare tire in the trunk. Tail fins and large round taillights characterized the rear end. The new instrument panel came from the full-size 1956 Ford with an engine-turned insert added. The T-Bird was available with a soft top or a hardtop and the fiberglass roof could be had with or without port hole windows. This year prices started at $3,408.

This year's version of the 223- six produced 144 hp. The base Ford V-8 was a 272-cid 190-hp two-barrel version, while the T-Bird got a 292-cid 212-hp job. The Thunderbird Special V-8 was the 312 cubic incher available in a 245-hp single four-barrel version, a 270-hp dual four-barrel version, a 285-hp racing version and a 300-hp version (340-hp in NASCAR tune) with a McCulloch/Paxton centrifugal supercharger. The supercharged "F-Birds" are rare and valuable.

Introduction of 1957 Fords and Thunderbirds took place in October 1956. The Fairlane 500 Skyliner with retractable hardtop was introduced as a midyear addition to the line. Overdrive or FordOMatic could now be ordered for any car with any engine.

1958 *Ford*

Travel was a big business in 1958. Vice President Richard Nixon traveled to Latin America and South America on a goodwill tour that didn't go so well. (He was roughed up by Peruvian protesters and his limousine was rocked in Venezuela.) Making underwater travel history, the nuclear submarine Nautilus cruised under the polar ice cap. In America, National Airlines started the first domestic jet passenger service between New York and Miami. For international travelers, round-trip London-to-New York flights cost $453.

Ford Motor Company went traveling, too. The automaker sponsored a "Nothing Newer in the World" sales promotion in which a pair of Fairlane 500 Town Victoria four-door hardtops were driven around the world to test their ruggedness. Most advertisements and TV commercials running that year were keyed to the theme "58 Ford: proved and approved around the world."

Photos showed one blue-and-white Ford kicking up dust near Turkish hillside dwellings and blasting up a winding mountain path in Afghanistan. The "famous Round-the-World 58 Ford" rolled into Paris, France, and twisted its way through hairpin turns in the Alps and Himalayas. The second car, a red-and-white edition of the same body style, traveled over the Khyber Pass and the jungle roads of Vietnam.

Looking showroom new is a 1958 Ford Country Sedan station wagon at the lake.

Even companies like Avis Rent-A-Car supported the program. "A local call to Avis reserves you a car anywhere in the world," said an ad showing a very 50-ish red telephone and another blue-and-white '58 Fairlane 500 Town Sedan. (This one had colors applied in a different manner.)

The 1958 models used the same basic body with many new styling ideas. A simulated air scoop hood and honeycomb grille were borrowed from the Thunderbird. Dual headlights and a sculptured rear deck lid created a more futuristic image. Cruise-O-Matic three-speed automatic transmission was offered for the first time, along with 332-cid and 352-cid V-8s. Also new was the one-year-only Ford-Aire air-suspension system for Fairlanes.

Custom 300s included chrome window moldings, a horn button instead of a horn ring, one sun visor, an armrest on the driver's door only and a single chrome strip on the body side. This molding began on the side of the front fender, continued horizontally to the back of the front door, then turned down and joined a horizontal chrome strip that continued to the back of the body. A top-of-the-line Styletone trim option duplicated this side trim, except it was a double strip with a gold anodized insert.

A mid-level Special trim option was also available with a small horizontal chrome strip that turned upward just behind the door. Model offerings were the same as 1957 with prices up $70 to $90. This year adding a V-8 cost $137.

The Fairlane model was the entry-level long-wheelbase Ford. It included chrome window moldings (with slightly less chrome around the "C" pillar than Fairlane 500 models) and different side stripe treatments. The initial version had two strips. The lower molding began at the rear of the front wheel opening, then went straight to the back of the front door. From there it began to gradually curve upward. The upper strip began at the front of the fender and went straight back, to the back of the front door. It then began to curve gradually downward, merging with the lower strip directly over the rear wheel opening.

A Fairlane script appeared on the rear fenders and directly above the grille opening. Starting at midyear an additional sweep spear of anodized aluminum trim was centered in the panel between the moldings and three "port hole" style trim pieces were added at the rear. The same body styles were carried over at prices between $2,196 and $2,394 ($137 more for V-8s).

The Fairlane 500 models had the top trim level in the Fairlane series. They included all the trim used in the Fairlane models plus

slightly more chrome on the "C" pillars and different side trim. The side trim was a double runner chrome strip with a gold anodized insert. The top chrome strip began on the side of the front fender, sloped slightly, and terminated at the top of the rear bumper.

The lower molding split from the upper strip where the front door began, dropped in a modified Fairlane sweep and merged with the upper strip at the rear bumper. Fairlane script appeared above the grille and on the trunk lid while the Fairlane 500 script appeared on the rear fenders, above the chrome side trim. This series also had the same styles as last year with similar price differentials.

The Ranch Wagon was the base trim level two-door and four-door station wagons for 1958. A new two-door Del Rio wagon was introduced. Country Sedans were intermediate level station wagons and Country Squires were the top trim level. You could buy a cheap six-cylinder Ford wagon for as little as $2,372 or move up a full 12 notches to the V-8-powered Country Squire with its $2,876 list price. Ford sure packed a lot of station wagon models into a $500 price range.

The first four-passenger "Square Bird"—the all-new Thunderbird Tudor—was introduced later than other Fords on Jan. 13, 1958. A convertible version was delayed until June. These cars grew 16 inches and gained 1,000 pounds. The Tudor had an extended top with a squared-off "C" pillar. It had chrome trim along the base of the top and a small Thunderbird crest directly above the trim. A massive, one-piece bumper surrounded a honeycomb grille. The honeycomb pattern was duplicated around the four circular taillights. A Thunderbird script appeared on the front fenders and five heavy, cast stripes appeared on the door. Inside, bucket seats and a vinyl-covered console were used for the first time. Ford built 35,758 of the new Tudor and 2,134 ragtops.

This year, the 223-six gained one horsepower. The base Ford V-8 was the 272 with 205 hp and a Holley two-barrel. A new 332-cid Interceptor V-8 was good for 240 hp with a two-barrel carburetor and 265 hp with a four-barrel. There was also a 300-hp Interceptor Special V-8 with a single four-barrel carburetor and 10.2:1 compression ratio.

Dealer introductions for 1958 Fords were held Nov. 7, 1957, but the new 1958 Thunderbirds bowed on February 13. Production at three factories — Memphis, Buffalo and Somerville — was phased out this season. In June 1958, a new plant, having capacity equal to all three aforementioned factories, was opened at Loraine, Ohio. Model-year production of Fords and Thunderbirds totaled 967,945 cars. Calendar-year sales peaked at 1,038,560 units.

On a model year basis, 74.4 percent of all Fords built in the 1958 run had a V-8 and 68-percent had automatic transmission.

Thunderbird and Rambler were the only U.S. marques to see sales increases for 1958. Due to an economic recession, smaller cars made in other countries— including some nations that the traveling '58 Fords had stopped in—stole sales away from the big Detroit (and Dearborn) "iron" this year.

1959 *Ford*

Ford won awards for its 1959 design, like these Galaxie Sunliner convertibles.

The 1958 Brussels World's Fair drew 42 million visitors to Hetsel Park, in Brussels, Belgium, to celebrate the theme, "For a more human world." The six-month-long extravaganza involved 4,645 expositors from 51 different nations. Ford Motor Company used the fair to launch its redesigned 1959 models. The "Altogether New" '59 Fords were awarded a Gold Medal by the Comite' Francais de L'Elegance, honoring their distinctive style and beautiful proportions.

Even now, many Ford enthusiasts and collectors consider the 1959 Fords to be the most beautifully styled Fords ever built. Elegant and understated, the cars showed remarkably good taste. When other automakers were designing cars that looked capable of interstellar travel, Ford exercised great restraint.

A new full-width front grille featured an insert with a pattern of "floating" stylized stars. The parking lights were recessed into the bumper. The flat-top front fenders had hooded dual headlights. They had a sculptured effect along the sides of the front fender and doors and rolled over the side trim. An exceptionally flat hood characterized these long, low cars with bright new colors.

The Custom 300 series was the base trim level for 1959. These cars wore no series nameplates, but had a Ford crest medallion on the rear deck lid. "Tee Ball" front fender ornaments were optional, as were four "Flying Dart" rear quarter panel ornaments. The side trim consisted of a single molding running back along the front fender/door feature line, then curving upwards the top of the tail fin which it trimmed straight back to the rear of the car. The Business Tudor ($1,934), Tudor ($2,015) and Fordor ($2,065) were offered as Custom 300 Sixes. All three were available as Custom 300 V-8 models for $110 additional.

The 1959 Fairlane was the intermediate trim level and included features that weren't standard on Custom 300s: chrome window moldings, a chrome horn ring, two sun visors and armrests on all doors. The Fairlane name appeared on the rear fenders. There was a second molding on the front fender and door that flared slightly outwards as it ran rearwards. It ran farther back than the upper molding and a curved piece joined the two. This piece created a bullet-shaped pattern at the front of the rear fender "tube."

Painted finish within the two front fender/door moldings was standard and an aluminum insert was optional. The rear deck lid had a bright metal "V" with a gold aluminum insert in the area below the Fairlane name only. The Fairlane Tudor Special sedan was $2,143 ($2,253 with the base V-8) and the Special Fordor was $2,193 ($2,303 with a V-8.)

Early in the 1959 model year, Ford's top-of-the-line car was the Fairlane 500. It included all Fairlane trim as well as the aluminum insert between the front moldings. The "Fairlane 500" name appeared at the extreme rear end of the rear fender tubes. A large, finely-ribbed aluminum panel surrounded the rear wheel opening and ran to the rear bumper. Optional stainless steel fender skirts offered an even larger expanse of bright metal trim. The rear deck lid was trimmed with a huge chrome V molding that had the Fairlane 500 name above the center of the "vee." Five Fairlane 500 Sixes were available: the Tudor Special Sedan ($2,255), the Fordor Special Sedan ($2,305), the Tudor Victoria hardtop ($2,311), the Fordor Victoria hardtop ($2,371) and the Sunliner convertible ($2,591). The V-8 series offered all of these models for $110 more and the Skyliner retractable hardtop was priced at $3,063.

Shortly after Ford made its new model introductions on Oct.

17, 1958, the Galaxie was introduced, a Fairlane 500 sub-series. It carried the Fairlane 500 name on the deck lid, but the Galaxie name on the rear fender tubes. The Galaxie series had five six-cylinder cars and six V-8s including the Skyliner. The two-door sedan was called the Tudor Club Sedan. The four-door sedan was called the Fordor Town Sedan. The hardtop coupe was called the Club Victoria and the four-door hardtop was called the Town Victoria. The Sunliner and Skyliner names were retained.

The difference between the Galaxie and the Fairlane 500 was its roof styling. Galaxies used the standard top with a Thunderbird style "C" pillar, one of the best looking cars ever to come out of Dearborn. Galaxies were priced $48 higher than comparable Fairlane 500s.

The 1959 Ranch Wagons were base trim level two-door and four-door station wagons. The Del Rio Ranch Wagon was essentially the two-door Ranch wagon with Country Sedan trim. Country Sedans were the intermediate trim level, comparable to Fairlanes. Country Squires were the top trim level. The level of equipment paralleled Fairlane 500 and Galaxie. The 12 wagons were sold in a narrow $500 price range between the $2,339 six-cylinder two-door Ranch Wagon and the Country Squire V-8.

The big Fords were available with a choice of four engines, starting with the 145-hp Mileage Maker Six with an 8.4:1 compression ratio. The 292-cid 200-hp Thunderbird V-8 had 8.8:1 compression and two-barrel carburetor. Next came the 332-cid 225-hp Thunderbird Special V-8, also with a two-barrel carb, but having a higher 8.9:1 compression ratio. The top option was the 352-cid 300-hp Thunderbird Special with a four-barrel Holley carburetor and 9.6:1 compression.

Selling features for '59 included Ford's rugged "Lifeguard"

design with a husky frame that spread out a full foot wider around the passenger compartment for greater side-impact protection.

Automatic Ride Control teamed a new front suspension with Tyrex tires and the variable-rate rear suspension for a smoother, better-controlled ride. A lighter, simplified version of Fordomatic Drive promised satin-smooth shifting and greater durability.

The 1959 Thunderbird featured a new horizontal-louver pattern in its air scoop grille, with the same pattern repeated in the recessed taillight panels. Broad, bright metal trim outlined the front of the guide-missile-shaped projectile moldings. The Thunderbird nameplate moved from the front fender to the lower door, where it was placed on the projectile molding. The round Thunderbird medallion seen on the rear window pillar of the '58 model was replaced by a sculptured Thunderbird medallion. The $3,696 Tudor hardtop found 57,195 buyers, while the ragtop, in its first year, increased to 10,261 sales.

The 352 Thunderbird Special V-8 was standard equipment below the hood, while a Lincoln-like 430-cid Thunderbird Special V-8 with a four-barrel, 10.0:1 compression and 350 hp was optional. This engine came with Cruise-O-Matic transmission only.

The Thunderbirds offered an Angle-Poised ball-joint front suspension, individually-contoured seats, 20 cubic feet of trunk space, a Lifeguard Design steering wheel and single unit-body construction with the floor pan, frame, body side panels, front and rear fenders, roof panel and cross braces all welded together into one durable unit of double-walled sculptured steel.

In March 1958, Ford reported it had reduced the cost of making an automobile by $94 per unit between 1954 and 1958. On a model year basis, 78.1 percent of all 1959 Fords had V-8 power and 71.7 percent featured automatic transmission.

The 1959 Ford Galaxie Club Victoria two-door hardtop also was a good looking car.

Hudsons
of the Fifties

1950 *Hudson*

The Hudson Custom Commodore 6 sedan was the highest trim level for 1950 models.

On Oct. 2, 1950, a new comic strip called "Peanuts" appeared. Charles "Sparky" Schulz, a 28-year-old Minnesotan, had been trying to sell his strip—originally known as "L'il Folks"—for quite awhile. Like Schulz, the Hudson Motor Car Company of Detroit, Michigan, struggled to sell its products in postwar America.

With a long, rich history, Hudson once had been among America's largest auto-manufacturing firms, but the postwar decade would leave it struggling to survive. The struggle culminated in its 1954 merger with Nash, to form American Motors. The Hudson badge would cling to existence through 1957.

A shorter Pacemaker 500 model was Hudson's new "baby" in 1950. It had the season's new look, which included a grille with four horizontal blades that widened as they neared the bumper and twin struts forming a triangle with a company medallion at the top.

Pacemaker 500 features, including lighted grille and hood medallions, twin taillights and a new streamlined hood ornament. Deluxe Pacemakers (about $15-$20 extra) had a bit of extra trim and slightly richer appointments. The Pacemaker 500 Six lineup included a four-door sedan, a two-door Brougham, a Club Coupe, a Coupe and the Convertible Brougham at prices from $1,807 to $2,444. All models except the low-priced coupe were available with the Deluxe trim package. Series production was 39,455 Pacemaker 500s and 22,297 Pacemaker Deluxes with no breakouts. About 1,865 Pacemaker 500 convertibles and 660 Pacemaker Deluxe convertibles were built.

Hudson Supers retained their 1949 styling, but added the 1950 grille appearance. A small spear tip ornament at the front of the body contour line, just above the wheel opening, identified these cars, which also had a broad body sill panel molding.

Supers all had basic Pacemaker items, plus striped Bedford cloth upholstery, a two-tone woodgrain dash, a clock and other interior upgrades. They shared items like ribbed carpet-like front mats, rear

carpets, seat armrests, rear ventipanes, bright metal window and windshield reveal moldings, fender skirts, twin air horns, seat ashtrays and envelope-style seatback pockets with Custom Commodores. Super sixes came in four body styles—sedan, Brougham, Club Coupe and Convertible Brougham at prices between $2,105 and $2,629. Super eights were $84 more. Strangely, the Convertible Brougham came only as a six and only 464 of those were built.

Custom Commodores had rich interiors, four bumpers guards, front fendertop ornaments, broad body sill panels and a strip of molding that followed the body contour line, several inches below it, with model nameplates at the front. At the rear, the molding widened and curved into the sill panel behind the fender skirts.

The equipment list included all basic features, the additional items shared with Supers, plus items like nylon Bedford Cord upholstery (in tan with brown stripes or blue-gray with blue stripes), foam rubber seat cushions, bright metal seatback hand grips, a leather grained dashboard and window garnish moldings and a three-spoke steering wheel. Basic items were slightly upgraded, such as an extra-large, deluxe rearview mirror.

There were three Custom Commodore models and each available with an in-line six or an in-line eight. Six-cylinder model prices were $2,257 for the Club Coupe, $2,282 for the four-door sedan and $2,809 for the Convertible Brougham. An eight under the hood was $84 additional. The Convertible Brougham came with hydraulic windows and leather trim. Convertible top colors were tan, black or maroon. A Fold-Away rear window was optional with all convertibles. Approximately 700 Custom Commodore Six convertibles and 426 Custom Commodore Eight convertibles were built.

The 119-inch Pacemaker 500s were powered by a 232-cid in-line six with four main bearings. With a 6.7:1 compression ratio and Carter one-barrel carburetor it made 112 hp at 4000 rpm. A larger bored-out version with a Carter two-barrel carburetor and 123 hp powered the larger 124-inch-wheelbase Super and Commodore sixes. All Hudson eights used a 254-cid straight eight with the same two-jet carb that made 128 hp at 4200 rpm.

A high-chrome-alloy engine block was used in all applications and the engines included features like a floating-type oil intake, a compensated crankshaft, a special alloy flywheel, aluminum alloy pistons and a high-compression intake manifold. Hudson-designed spark plugs were fitted to the cars when they left the factory. Three-speed stick shift was standard and transmission options included overdrive and two semi-automatics called DriveMaster and Supermatic. Manually-shifted cars featured a fluid-cushioned clutch.

Hudsons of this era were most famous for their Step-Down Ride. A step-down zone between the wide frame members permitted a lower center of gravity for greater safety, improved roadability, smoother ride and more seat and head room. The

Hudson's all-welded, all-steel Monobilt Body-and-Frame structure surrounded the passenger compartment with a "steel girder" that enhanced driver and passenger safety. True Center-Point steering kept the cars on course with a minimum of effort and Triple-Safe hydraulic brakes helped stop them.

All Hudsons included front and rear jacking pads, Super Cushion tires, front and rear stabilizers, an extra-wide windshield, Teleflash turn signals, recessed door panels, a "master size" baggage compartment and a parcel locker in the dashboard.

The 1950 Hudsons were introduced on Nov. 18, 1949. By year's end, the company slid to 13th rank in the American industry, with model-year sales of 121,408 cars and calendar year output of 143,586 units. Hudson reported a $12 million profit on sales of $267 million. Canadian production, which had been suspended during World War II, was resumed at the Hudson factory in Tilbury, Ontario, in April 1950.

1951 *Hudson*

The 1951 Hudson Super Custom Six sedan shows off that year's new center grille guard.

Awesome power was in the news in 1951. That May, the United States set off a hydrogen bomb on a Pacific atoll that was many times more powerful than the conventional atomic bombs that helped bring World War II to a close. The same year, the Atomic Energy Commission announced that a Department of Energy laboratory in Idaho had used a "breeder" reactor to produce electricity from atomic energy.

The 1951 Hudsons did not use atomic energy — instead they advertised "Miracle H-Power" (now, where do you think they got the idea for that name?).

"Sensational new H-145 engine in the fabulous New Hudson Hornet" said one announcement. Another boasted: "Miracle H-Power is here! It's the world's most thrilling high-compression performance!"

The ad claimed this in-line, L-head six produced "...blazing getaway" and "...new command of the road at any speed." It sure was colorful as depicted on the magazine's pages — blue block and head, yellow intake, fuel pump, carburetor and fan belt, red air cleaner and fan.

To back the new engine's high-performance image (which really did help sell many cars), the Hudson factory supported Hornet stock car racing efforts by providing special "export" and "severe usage" parts. The hopped-up Hudsons were able to win 12 of the 41 NASCAR Grand National contests in 1951. Top Hudson Hornet drivers included Marshall Teague, Herb Thomas, Tim Flock and Dick Rathmann.

A special dual carburetion package helped Thomas take a checkered flag in the second Southern 500, at Darlington, S.C.

His average speed was 86.21 mph. *Motor Trend* and *Mechanix Illustrated* determined the top speed of the stock 1951 Hudson Hornet to be 97 mph. Thomas even captured Top Driver honors on the NASCAR circuit.

The Hudson grille was changed again this year. It now had three horizontal blades. The top two were bowed to meet the bottom bar. A twin-strut triangle was seen near the center. Rectangular parking lights were housed outboard of the main grille bars on either side. The lamp housings were slightly rounded where they wrapped around the Pacemaker body corners, but looked squarer on other models.

Pacemaker Custom models had spear-tip body side ornaments (without spears) and broad lower sill panels running from behind the front wheel opening to the extreme rear of the car. Inside was gray special-weave cord upholstery with red and brown stripes and Dura-fab plastic trim. The wheelbase remained at 119 inches. Overall length was 201-1/2 inches. This series used the same 112-hp six as the previous version. Body style offerings were also unrevised. Prices climbed about $160, on average, for the year. Priciest was the Convertible Brougham and only some 425 of these were made.

Super Sixes were carried over, but not Super Eights. The five models — Club Coupe, Brougham, four-door sedan, Convertible Brougham and Hollywood hardtop — were given the new frontal treatment. They had the same basic side trim used on 1950 Commodores, but without the outer grille guards. Small hubcaps were seen. Rear ashtrays housed in recessed panels on the doors and inner rear quarter panels (instead of front seatback) were standard in cars of this series, as were wing-type ventipanes for sedan rear quarter windows. Upholstery was in tan Bedford cloth with brown and maroon stripes.

The new Hollywood model, with two-door pillarless hardtop styling, was introduced in September of 1951 as a late-year addition to the line. A new, rounded corner trapezoid-shaped front center grille guard was seen on all big Hudsons, including the Supers. Prices for the cars in this series ranged from $2,238 to $2,827. All models used the 123-hp straight six. They rode a 124-inch wheelbase and measured 208-3/32 inches end-to-end. Approximately 1,100 Hollywood two-door hardtops and 282 convertibles were built in this series.

Commodores continued to offer a choice of engines: the 123-hp Super Six or the 128-hp straight eight. They had larger front fender nameplates, outer grille guards, front and rear metal hand grips on front seatbacks, rear window reveal moldings and three-dimensional weave upholstery with stripes and Antique Crush Dura-fab

trim. The Commodore convertible came in nine standard or four extra cost colors with dark red or blue genuine top grain leather upholstery and harmonizing leather grain trim.

The ragtop included hydraulic window lifts and a hydraulic roof with tan, black or maroon top material. A large, plastic rear window was optional. Six-cylinder prices were $2,455 for the Club Coupe, $2,480 for the four-door sedan, $2,780 for the Hollywood hardtop and $3,011 for the Convertible Brougham. Eights were $88 additional. Six-cylinder production included 819 six-cylinder Hollywoods and 211 convertibles, while 669 Hollywoods and 181 convertibles were built with the eight under their hoods.

The first of the famed Hudson Hornets was really a Commodore with a special high-performance six-cylinder engine. It also had a few distinctive identification and appointment details like a gold-and-chrome-plated "Skyliner Styling" hood mascot, roof pillar assist straps in coupes and sedans. Deluxe robe hanger hand grips and tailored pockets were on back of the lounge-wide front seat.

There were also Hornet H-145 medallions in each front door valance panel, a polished-chrome dash housing on a leather grained panel (with non-glare Dura-fab top) and gleaming, rocketship-shaped "Badges of Power" in front of the body side rub moldings and on the trunk.

These badges showed a rocket piercing two vertically angled bars, with Hornet lettering turning them into a letter "H." Upholstery was of the Commodore type and came in tan-brown with gold stripes or blue-gray with blue stripes. Antique Crush-type leather grained Dura-fab trim combinations were used. The high-compression, aluminum "Power-Dome" cylinder head was standard on the Hornet engine, but the regular iron alloy head was a no-cost option.

This series offered a Club Coupe for $2,543, a four-door sedan for $2,568, a Hollywood hardtop for $2,869 and that Convertible Brougham for $3,099. Series production was 43,666 Hornets including approximately 2,101 Hollywood two-door hardtops and 551 convertibles.

The new line was introduced in September 1950 and continued in production through January 1952. Hollywood hardtops were a late edition to the 1951 line. Hudson wasn't as much of a force in the sales department as it was in the horsepower race. Model-year deliveries hit 131,915 units of which only 14,243 were eights. Calendar-year production dropped to 93,327 cars.

Hudson was ranked 15th in the American industry. A loss of $1,125,210 was reported on sales of $186,050,832. Labor unrest and delays in getting government authorization to raise prices during the Korean conflict were behind the poor business climate.

1952 *Hudson*

On May 2, 1952, British Overseas Airways Corporation started the world's first scheduled passenger jet service using a De Havilland Comet. Passengers found it hard to believe that they could travel through the air at a speed of almost 500 mph.

In America, some of the automakers offering cars with overhead-valve V-8s found it hard to believe that the Hudson Hornet — with is big "flathead" six — was blowing their doors off. Hornet stock cars won 27 of 34 NASCAR races in 1952. Hudson drivers included Herb Thomas and Tim Flock. Marshall Teague began

driving Hudsons in AAA competition, after taking the 1952 NASCAR Daytona stock car race in a Hornet. His car was torn down after the race and proved to be 100 percent stock. In AAA racing, Teague took 14 checkered flags for Hudson, while other drivers captured a total of five. For the year, the Hornets had captured 40 wins in 48 major stock car races. It was quite a feat.

The Pacemaker was again the low-priced Hudson and had an even plainer look for 1952. The twin-strut grille arrangement was deleted and fender skirts were optional. The "spear tip" body side trim had a staggered look. A boomerang-shaped fin became the

The 1952 Hudson Hornet sedan shows new taillights and a larger rear window.

hood mascot. The rear end was Spartan, having small oval taillight lenses and only outer bumper guards. Gray special-weave cord upholstery with red and brown stripes was standard. The same models were merchandised with prices raised about $165 above 1951. The 112-hp six was used.

The new Wasp Six was built off the 119-inch-wheelbase. It was a bit longer — 202-15/32 inches versus 201-1/2. The engine used was a 262-cid flathead, in-line six with 6.7:1 compression and a Carter one-barrel carburetor. It produced 127 hp at 4000 rpm.

In terms of price, the Wasp replaced the Super. In terms of character, it was to the Pacemaker what the Hornet was to the Commodore Eight: a slightly fancier and more powerful version of the same car. Standard features included tan special-weave cord upholstery with red and brown stripes, rear compartment carpeting, a dark brown leather grained dash, door courtesy lamps and a three-spoke steering wheel with half-circle horn ring.

The series included a Club Coupe, two-door Brougham, four-door sedan, Convertible Brougham and Hollywood hardtop priced between $2,413 and $3,048. Approximately 1,320 Hollywood two-door hardtops and 220 convertibles were built in the Wasp series.

The 1952 Commodore line featured new Hudson Aire identification and appointment items. Hudson used the term "Hudson-Aire Hardtop Styling" in its advertising, although the cars were not pillarless hardtops. The Commodores included double rub rail moldings that ran along the body contour line, from the front fenders to the rear fenders, with a downward sweep towards the back bumper, a twin-strut grille arrangement, front and rear center bumper guards, front fender nameplates, rocker sill beauty panels, large deluxe hubcaps and taillights styled to form a continuous horizontal trim line.

Four sixes were offered — Club Coupe, sedan, Convertible Brougham and Hollywood — and priced from $2,646 to $3,248. Commodore sixes used the same engine as Wasp models.

The Commodore Eight had differences from the Commodore Six including nylon three-dimensional weave upholstery in tan-brown with gold stripes or blue-gray with blue stripes, foam rubber seat cushions, front and rear carpets, a deluxe steering wheel, an electric clock, crank-type front ventipanes and a printed jute trunk mat. The front fender spear tips on sixes were decorated with a number 6, and on eights with a number 8.

Front parking lenses for all Commodores were of the wraparound style seen on Wasps, but not on Pacemakers. The Commodore eight line offered the same body styles for $95 additional. Approximately 100 Hollywood two-door hardtops and 20 convertibles were built in the Commodore Six series, but more of both styles (about 190 Hollywood hardtops and 30 convertibles) were built with the 128-hp straight eight.

The Hornet for 1952 was based on the Commodore Eight. Special features seen on the Hornet included dark blue or brown leather grained window garnish moldings, Hornet "Flying-H" identification on the side of front fenders and rear deck gold and chrome hood mascot, Hornet medallions on front door valance panels and the high-compression H-145 six-cylinder engine. All other specifications matched those of the Commodore Eight. On a model-for-model basis, the two series were priced the same, with Commodores weighing 30 pounds more than Hornets.

The Hornet six had a 3-13/16 x 4-1/2-inch bore and stroke for 308 big cubic inches of displacement. It ran a 7.2:1 compression ratio in combination with a two-barrel Carter carburetor. Output was 145 hp at 3800 rpm. Like the other Hudson engines, the big Hornet Six had all component parts matched and balanced, at the factory, prior to assembly. All engines also featured a waterproof ignition system, compensated crankshaft, Power-Dome cylinder head, aluminum alloy pistons and a floating oil intake.

Hudson's standard transmission was a conventional three-speed manual gearbox. Overdrive was optional for all stick-shifted models. Hydra-Matic Drive, sourced from General Motors, was an extra-cost option. A dual-carburetor setup known as Twin-H Power, was optional on Hornets, Wasps and Commodore Sixes.

The 1952 Hudson line was introduced during January 1952. With model-year sales of 70,000 cars and calendar year deliveries of 79,117 units, the company's sales rank moved up one notch to 14th position. In May 1952, Hudson announced that it was starting to tool-up for production of a new line of 1953 compact-sized Hudson Jets. Like the De Havilland Comet, these neat little cars were trend setters that proved unsuccessful in the long haul.

1953 *Hudson*

The 1953 Hudson Hornet was powered by a 308-cid 145-hp six-cylinder engine.

Francis Crick and James Watson announced the discovery of the "double-helix" structure of DNA at Cambridge University on April 25, 1953. Their findings stemmed partly from the work of Rosalind Franklin, another Cambridge researcher, whose colleague Maurice Wilkins leaked her research to Crick and Watson. As we all know today, DNA — which stands for Deoxyribose Nucleic Acid — has come to play an important role in the understanding of human genetics and in solving many criminal cases.

The 1953 Hudson line of cars was made up of 15 six-cylinder models arranged in five series: Jet, Super Jet, Wasp, Super Wasp and Hornet. The line was introduced in November 1952 and there was a strand of Hudson "DNA" in the new compact-sized Hudson Jet that took flight that season.

"In all the world, no other car like this!" boasted a Hudson advertisement promoting the new model. Also new at Hudson for the year was a Super Wasp model and the discontinuation of the straight eight..

Though related to the Wasp and Hornet in a basic mechanical sense, the all-new Jet did not look like its fastback brethren, although it did share the floor-recessed-within-the-frame construction of other Step-Down design cars. The Jet's styling was marked by a slab-sided appearance and a conventional notch back body design. The grille had a flat oval appearance and a fake air scoop decorated the hood. Fender skirts were optional.

Only a four-door Jet sedan priced at $1,858 was offered in the base series. Riding a 105-inch wheelbase, all Jet models had a 180-11/16 inch overall length.

A "Super Jet" script appeared on the fenders of cars in the more highly trimmed car-line, which also had an air scoop ornament, oversize tires, wing-type rear ventipanes, automatic dome lamps and two-tone blue or green woven wool upholstery with Dura-fab leather grained trim. The Super Jet sedan was $1,954 and there was also a Super Jet coupe for $1,933.

Both Jet lines used a 202-cid in-line L-head six with four main bearings and solid valve lifters. It utilized a 7.5:1 compression ratio and a one-barrel Carter carburetor to help produce 104 hp at 4000 rpm. Hudson Twin H-Power carburetion system was optional in Jets and Super Jets, as was Dual-Range Hydra-Matic Drive.

Hudson said its small new car was "Exquisite as a jewel case . . . quick and powerful as a panther." Tartan-plaid lettering was used in advertisements to emphasize the Jet was "...economical as a Scot."

The Wasp now became a mid-size Hudson offering with traditional Step-Down styling on a 119-inch wheelbase. Appearance changes included deletion of the twin-strut grille guard and the addition of an air scoop hood. Upholstery was in tan weave cord with red and brown stripes and Dura-fab trim. Power came from the former Pacemaker Six. A standard steering wheel, plain-top fenders and small hubcaps were identification features.

A new Super Wasp car-line was comprised of models that were comparable to the 1952 Hudson Wasp. They were upholstered in new nylon combinations with special check weave and Dura-fab trim.

Standard equipment on Super Wasps also included a special 127-hp six-cylinder engine, large hubcaps, front fendertop ornaments, combination fuel and vacuum pump, foam rubber front seat cushions, and Deluxe steering wheel.

There were three Wasp Six models, the Club Coupe ($2,311), the two-door sedan ($2,264) and the four-door sedan ($2,311). For about $150 extra, these styles were available as Super Wasps, along with the Hollywood hardtop ($2,812) and the Convertible Brougham ($3,048). Hudson built 17,792 of all these cars including just 590 Hollywood two-door hardtops and 50 Convertible Broughams.

The base Wasp six engine was similar to the Jet engine in being a four-main-bearing in-line power plant with solid lifters, but it was larger and more powerful. It displaced 232 cubic inches. Using a 6.7:1 compression ratio, it churned out 112 at 4000 rpm. A Carter one-barrel carburetor was used. The Super Wasp engine was even larger, having 262 cubic inches and generating 127 hp at 4000 rpm. All Wasp models were 201-1/2 inches long (202-1/2 inches for Super Wasps) and used 7.10 x 15 tires.

The 1953 Hudson Hornet was similar to the previous, except the strut bar look was eliminated from the grille and the air scoop hood look replaced it. The rocketship-shaped Hornet front fender and trunk ornaments were seen again.

There were four Hornets—Club Coupe, four-door sedan, Hollywood hardtop and Convertible Brougham, priced between $2,769 and $3,342. The convertible rode on 7.60 x 15 tires and other models used size 7.10 x 15. Below the hood was

the H-145 L-head engine with a "Power Dome" aluminum cylinder head. This huge 308-cid in-line six had 7.2:1 compression ratio and two-barrel Carter WGD carburetor. It made 145 hp at 3800 rpm. Twin-H Power was available for slight extra cost.

A special Hornet 7-X engine package was released for "severe usage," such as stock car racing. A power rating of 200 hp was estimated for cars with this option. Hudsons captured 22 (out of 37) major NASCAR races, with driver Herb Thomas winning championship honors for the season.

Model-year sales were 66,143 units. Calendar-year production peaked at 67,089 cars. Hudson was the 15th ranked American car producers.

1954 Hudson

(Jerry Heasley)

The 1954 Hudson Hornet Club Coupe shows its modified body style that year.

"That wonderful year 1954" was a year of starts and beginnings. Things got started right on New Year's Day when color broadcasts of the Rose Parade originated from Pasadena, California. That year, television's famous "Tonight Show" also began. Another milestone was the creation of American Motors Corporation.

AMC began its formation on Jan. 14, 1954, when Hudson Motor Company's directors approved a merger with Nash-Kelvinator. On March 24, stockholders OK'd the merger. On May 1, 1954, Hudson was part of American Motors Corporation.

Hudson's 1954 models changed very little. The grille used on the 1954 Jet had four ribs on each side of the main blade and a center embossment. At first, there were two models. The two-door Utility Sedan had a $1,837 list price and weighed 2,715 pounds. The four-door sedan cost $21 more, but weighed 40 pounds less.

On April 12, a new Family Club Sedan was added to the line as a stripped economy model. Priced $216 under the base sedan, this two-door Jet had a plain grille, a black rubber windshield surround and more Spartan interior..

The Jetliner was a new top-level offering characterized by Jetliner fender block lettering, rear wheel covers (fender skirts), Custom wheel discs, rear fender horizontal rub moldings, body sill highlights, bright rear gravel shields, and chrome rear taillight trim.

Both of the higher series offered a Club Coupe and a four-door sedan. The two-door cost $1,933 as a Super Jet and $2,046 as a Jetliner. The four-door prices were $1,954 and $2,057, respectively. The engine was the same one used in 1953. This year Hudson made a total of 14,224 cars in the Jet, Super Jet and Jetliner series.

The big cars were restyled to look more like the Jet. The grille had a heavy, bowed molding tracing the upper radiator opening. There was a full-width, flat horizontal loop surrounding the wedge-shaped parking lights at each end. The main bar was ribbed towards the middle and held a triangular Hudson medallion in a finned housing. Behind this was an angled plate with four, wide-spaced ribs. Block letters spelled out "Hudson" on the hood.

The mid-sized Wasp or Super Wasp signature scripts were placed on the front fender tips above a full-length horizontal rub molding. Two-door hardtops had a Hollywood script at the upper rear edge of each front fender. A panoramic one-piece windshield and protruding tip taillights were new.

Super Wasp prices were lowered about $60 from 1953 and they continued to use a 232-cid 126-hp flathead six.

Super Wasps had the same features plus large hubcaps, front foam seat cushions, Custom steering wheel, passenger assist handles, crank-type front ventipanes on Hollywoods and convertibles, courtesy door lights, combination fuel and vacuum pump, and two-tone blue or green check pattern tweed cloth upholstery with worsted bolster material and Plasti-hide trim. In Super Wasp convertibles blue, maroon or green leather cushions with standard Plasti-hide side trim were the standard interior upholstery.

The Super Wasp Hollywood hardtop had brown, blue or green nylon cord seats with snowflake design cloth upholstery and harmonizing Plasti-hide bolsters. The Super Wasp Club Coupe, Club Sedan and four-door sedan were about $210 more expensive than Wasp versions, while the Hollywood hardtop was $2,704 and the Convertible Brougham was $3,004. Hudson made about 11,603 of both Wasps and calendar-year output included 2,654 Hollywoods and 222 convertibles. A 262-cid straight six powered the Super Wasps and output rose to 140 hp at 4000 rpm.

Hornets continued to ride a longer 124-inch wheelbase. The change to Jet-like styling brought an end to the front fender rocketship ornaments. Hudson signature script was seen on the fenders, but only the trunk lid had a special badge.

Two-door hardtops also had Hollywood script at the high trailing edge of front fenders, above the full-length horizontal body rub moldings. Hornets had most Super Wasp equipment plus crank-type front ventipanes on all models, cast aluminum "high-compression" head, electric clock, foam rubber rear seat cushions, Custom wheel discs, hydraulic window lifts (in convertibles) and special trims.

The Hornet sedan ($2,769) and Club Coupe ($2,742) were upholstered in 15 percent nylon worsted Bedford cloth with broadcloth bolsters and Plasti-hide trim in different shades of the same colors of brown, blue or green. The Hornet Hollywood hardtop ($2,988) had similarly toned, snowflake design nylon cord

seats with Plasti-hide bolsters. The Hornet Convertible Brougham was done in blue, maroon or green genuine leather with Plasti-hide side trim. Convertible tops were available in maroon, black or tan.

Specific combinations of top colors with car finishes were recommended. The Hollywood hardtop was available with tri-colored seat and headlining combinations of antique white Plasti-hide and red, blue and green bolsters, at no extra cost.

The last models introduced by Hudson, in Detroit, were the Hornet Specials on March 19, 1954. They had Hornet Special front fender scripts, a Hornet engine and a subdued level of exterior brightwork, but Super Wasp interior trims. Series production included 24,833 Hornet Specials and Hornets.

Twenty-six Hudson Italia coupes were built in 1954 on the Jet platform. The Italia body was crafted by Carrozzeria Touring, Milan, Italy, based on sketches by Hudson's Frank Spring.

This sporty, $4,800 GT coupe had aluminum coachwork, functional front fender scoops with brake cooling ducts, wraparound windshield, contoured leather bucket seats, Borrani wire spoke wheels, white sidewall tires, and back-up lights and turn signals stacked in Jet-tube pipes tunneled into rear fenders. Italias used the 202-cid Jet engine with a 7.5:1 compression ratio rated at 114 hp. Twin-H Power with dual manifolding was standard.

The Italia was announced as a production model, on Jan. 14, 1954. The 26 cars were actually designed and custom built as four-passenger Grand Touring "image" cars. Twenty-five were production models, while a coupe prototype and four-door X-161 pilot model also created. Twenty-one of these cars are known to still exist.

After Hudson became part of American Motors Corp. on May 1, 1954, Hudson dealers sold four-cylinder Metropolitans with replacement grille center inserts having an "H." The cars were otherwise identical to Nash Metropolitans.

Model-year production totaled 51,314 cars. Calendar-year production peaked at 32,287 cars, including 4,239 Ramblers. On Oct. 30, 1954, the 1954 Hudson model run ended in Detroit. Eleven days later the first Hornet/Rambler was built in Kenosha, Wisconsin and an era in Hudson history came to an end.

1955 *Hudson*

The 1955 Hudson Rambler Cross Country station wagon was a rebadged Nash Rambler.

Anew "Disneyland" television program debuted on Oct. 27, 1954, five days after the new-for-1955 "AMC Rambler" line bowed in Nash and Hudson dealerships across the country. The TV show quickly became the first ABC series to rank in the top 10. The tie-in with the popular program helped the new company sell a lot of extra cars for several years.

The cars in Hudson's Rambler series looked almost like Nash Ramblers, except for the use of a Hudson medallion in the center of the grille. Product offerings started with a pair of Fleet Special models—stripped, three-passenger cars with painted headlight rims, rubber windshield surrounds and Spartan appointments. This rare line included a two-door Deluxe Business Sedan for $1,457 and a two-door Utility wagon for $1,570.

These models had assemblies of 21 and 34 units, respectively. Under the hood of all Hudson Ramblers was the 195.6-cid 90-hp Rambler "Flying Scot" in-line six.

The next step up was the Deluxe series. These cars had plated headlight rims, Deluxe front fender scripts, an untrimmed air scoop, no hood ornament and slightly up-market interior trim. There were three models called the two-door Club Sedan, four-door sedan and two-door Suburban.

A hood ornament and air scoop trim band were seen on the Hudson Rambler Super series, priced in the next higher bracket. This car-line offered the same body styles at prices about $98 higher, plus a four-door Country Club station wagon for $1,975.

At the top of the heap was a Custom series, with Custom front fender scripts, a standard continental spare tire, enriched interior trimmings and all other Super features. The sedan, five-passenger Country Club or a six-pasenger Country Club station wagon were priced between $1,989 and $2,098.

The 1955 Hudson Wasps and Hornets were introduced at the Chicago Auto Show on February 23.

Styling and engineering changes, though based on the unitbody Nash platform, were planned to give Hudsons a distinct character. For example, the former Jet engine was under the hood of Wasps, while Hornets got the famed racing Championship 6.

Hudson's "dual braking" system was also retained. Gone, however, was Hudson's traditional, wider-in-the-front "crab tread" stance. The 114.5-inch wheelbase Wasp now had a front tread that was 3/16-inch narrower than its rear tread.

As far as sheet metal similarities went, the only interchangeable body panel between Nash and Hudson models was the rear deck lid. A massive egg-crate grille filled the area below and between the single headlights, with an inverted steer-horn-shaped bar bordering the top.

This upper border bar had a Hudson badge set into a housing at its center. Hudson block letters decorated the hood with its full-width cowl vent near the base of the windshield. Horizontal moldings stretched across the front fenders and doors. A higher molding swept rearwards from the wraparound windshield post towards the upper back fender region. A stand-up hood ornament and Wasp front fender nameplates were seen on Super models, which also had Super script on the sides of the cowl.

Custom Wasps had a flatter hood ornament and Custom cowl side script. They included a continental spare tire as standard equipment. Wrapover rear roof pillars were seen on all models.

The 1955 Hudson Hornet had the same styling as the Wasps on a seven-inch-longer wheelbase. Hornet nameplates were seen on the front fenders. Hardtops had Hollywood cowlside script as well. The Super Six four-door sedan listed for $2,565. A V-8 version was $260 additional. Hornet engine choices included the standard (160-hp) or Twin-H (170-hp) versions of the big 308-cid six or a new V-8 built and supplied by Packard.

Packard's overhead-valve V-8 had a 3-13/16 x 3-1/2 inch bore and stroke. It displaced 320 cubic inches. The modern five-main-bearings motor with non-adjustable hydraulic valve lifters ran a 7.8:1 compression ratio. With a Carter two-barrel carburetor it made 208 hp at 4200 rpm. Packard's new Twin Ultramatic transmission was both standard and mandatory in V-8 Hudsons.

Higher-quality interiors and a continental spare tire carrier distinguished Custom Hornets. The Hornet Custom Six line included a four-door sedan for $2,760 and a two-door Hollywood Hardtop for $2,880. The V-8 versions cost $255 to $265 more.

Heavily-promoted selling features of the true 1955 Hudsons included tubeless tires, the wraparound windshield, Triple-Safe brakes (with a mechanical reserve system that stopped the car if hydraulic pressure failed), Depp-Coil Ride, airplane-type double-acting shock absorbers and Twin Ultramatic transmission on V-8 models. Available options included Twin-H power (Standard on Hornet custom Sic models), power steering, power brakes, power-lift windows, and reclining "Twin Bed" seats.

The Nash-Hudson air conditioning system was said to provide "year-round springtime." It heated, cooled and filtered the air from a single control and did not require a separate heater.

Model-year production included 25,214 Ramblers, 7,191 Wasps, 6,911 Hornet Sixes and 6,219 Hornet V-8s for a total of 45,535 Hudsons.

A national contest offering new Hudsons and trips to Disneyland was open to the public. Hudson's headquarters was still in Detroit but 1955 models were made in Kenosha, Wisconsin.

1956 *Hudson*

The 1956 Nash-bodied Hollywood attempted to preserve Hudson's rich heritage.

It was 1956. The annual income of the average American wage earner, after taxes, was $1,700. That might not sound like much, but it was up $63 from a year earlier. The typical worker — the guy with a wife and two kids that you saw in all those goofy car ads — took home $74.04 every other Friday. The nation's gross national product was $408 billion, but a dollar bought only as much food in 1956 as 41¢ bought in 1939. There were 39,628 motor vehicle related deaths in 1956, but AMC was so sure its single-unit construction cars were safe that it offered $25,000 of personal automobiler accident insurance against fatal injury to Hudson and Nash buyers.

The plan worked like this: Husband and wife (if members of the same household at time of car purchase) each got insurance providing for payment of $12,500 to beneficiary or estate of either — if either or both should be fatally injured while driving or riding (separately or together) in their new private passenger American Motors car, anywhere in the world, during the first year of ownership, if a fatality occured within 100 days after the accident. Such a deal!

Production of the Hudson Jet had been discontinued by 1956, but Hudson dealers still had compact cars to sell under the AMC "family plan." The small Hudson Ramblers were totally badge-engineered cars. They were, in fact, identical to 1956 Nash Ramblers, except for having hubcaps with an "H" in the center and "H" logo circular grille inserts.

A sedan was the only model in the cheap Deluxe line. The next-step-up Super series offered the same four-door family car for $110 more, plus a four-door wagon ($2,290) and four-door hardtop wagon ($2,491). Custom versions of all three cost $110-$120 additional. Only 20,496 Hudson Ramblers were put together this season.

Moving up to the middle-sized Wasp models, a completely redesigned V-shaped grille with a Hudson medallion set into another V-shaped dip in the center was seen for 1956. Other changes included a new hood ornament and new rectangular front parking lamps set into wedge-shaped chrome moldings that accented the V-shape of the grille. There were air scoop fender-top ornaments and new body side rub rail moldings, which also had a

V-shaped dip on the rear doors or fenders. In addition, the taillights were redesigned.

Wasp models could be identified by their Wasp nameplates inside the V-shaped dip in the rub rail molding. They could also be spotted by the chrome-enclosed panel on the rear fender sides, which was finished in lower body color.

Popular features included Deep-Coil ride, Triple-Safe hydraulic brakes (with a reserve mechanical system), positive action hand brake, Double-Safe single-unit construction, tubeless tires, Select-O-Lift starter, drawer-type glove compartment, wraparound windshield and rear window and double-acting airplane-type shock absorbers. The only model available in the 1956 Wasp lineup was the Super four-door sedan priced at $2,416. Only 2,519 of these were made. Twin-H power was optional.

The 1956 Hornet had the same general styling changes as the new Wasp, but rode on a seven-inch longer wheelbase. It came with richer interior appointments and more standard equipment. All Hornets had identification nameplates in the V-shaped dip in the side rub rail moldings. Custom Hornets had a continental style spare tire and a chrome enclosed, gold-finished panel just to the rear of the V-shaped dip in the side molding.

However, Super Hornets didn't have these features. Instead, the crome-enclosed rear fender panel was painted lower body color. The Packard engine was used in Hornet V-8s. Ultramatic transmission was again a mandatory with the V-8. Hornet Sixes came with the famous 308-cid Hudson Championship Six and could be had with three-speed manual transmission, overdrive, or Hydra-Matic Drive.

The Hornet Super Six series offered only the four-door sedan, which listed for $2,777. The Custom Six was available in the same style for $3,019 or as a Hollywood hardtop for $117 more. This latter model was rarest, with only 358 built. The V-8-powered sedan listed for $3,286 and had a 1,962-unit production run, while the V-8-powered Hollywood was $3,429 and 1,053 were built.

On March 5, 1956, the Hornet Special returned. It was a different type of car than the 1954 Hornet Special, which was a cheaper version of the standard-wheelbase Hornet. The 1956 Hornet Special had a lower price, but was actually something of a high-performance car. It came with a new AMC-built 250-cid overhead-valve V-8 in the 114-1/4-inch wheelbase Wasp-type chassis. Exterior trim and interior appointments were comparable to those of Super Hornets.

Three-speed manual transmission was standard and both overdrive or Hydra-Matic Drive were available at extra cost. Hudson built just 1,528 of the $2,626 Hornet Special four-door sedans and only 229 of the $2,741 Hornet Special Hollywood two-door hardtops.

Introduction date for the 1956 Hudson Wasp, Hornet Six and Hornet V-8 was Nov. 30, 1955. The 1956 Hudson Ramblers were then introduced on Dec. 15, 1955. It wasn't until March 5, 1956, that the Hornet Special V-8 appeared. Calendar-year output amounted to 10,671 units. Model-year production hit its peak at 22,588 assemblies, excluding Hudson Ramblers.

1957 *Hudson*

Tom Collins

The 1957 American Motors-produced Hudson included the Hornet V-8 Super sedan.

Historians typically focus on "firsts" as highlights of past years. In 1957, there were plenty of firsts, such as Tang breakfast drink, frozen pizza, Velcro and the "AA" size alkaline battery. It was also a year of famous "lasts." Trolley cars made their last appearance on New York City streets. Jackie Robinson played in his last baseball game. Brooklyn's beloved Dodgers (a.k.a the "Brooklyn Bums") played their last game at Ebbets Field, before departing for the "Left Coast."

Detroiters experienced somewhat similar emotions when the last Hudson motor cars were built on Oct. 25, 1957. Everyone it was the final chapter in a great automotive legend.

As the end approached in the fall of 1956, Hudson trimmed its car-lines by an amazing 11 models and its roof lines by an equally amazing two inches. The Hudson Rambler, Wasp and Hornet Special series were all dropped. If you wanted a 1957 Hudson, you wanted the larger 121-1/4-inch-wheelbase Hornet.

New-for-1957 features included 14-inch wheels, a new "Flashaway" Hydra-Matic transmission with a parking gear, a standard 327-cid V-8 with dual exhaust, a ball-joint front suspension, restyled and modernized interior appointments and a standard padded dashboard in all cars. Hudsons were available in a choice of 32 eye-catching color combinations.

The annual styling changes included a new "V"medallion in the center of the radiator grille, new dual-fin front fender ornaments, rear tail fin-style fenders with vertical taillights and a new side trim treatment with front fender and door accent panels.

On Supers, the accent panel was painted. There were Hornet and Hollywood nameplates inside the accent panel on the hardtops, as well as front fender medallions. The Super Sedan had Hornet front door nameplates and no "H" medallions.

Only two models comprised the entire Super Hornet V-8 lineup. The four-door sedan, which listed for $2,821 weighed 3,631 pounds. Even though it was the year's second-most popular Hudson model, only 1,103 examples were built. The Super Hollywood two-door hardtop was much rarer. Hudson built only 266 of these $2,911 cars. They tipped the scale at 3,655 pounds.

Hornet Customs could be identified by the textured aluminum insert panels used on the front fenders, between the trim moldings. Nameplate and medallion placements on Customs were the same as on comparable Super styles. The same two body styles were offered in the Custom V-8 series. The window sticker for the four-door sedan read $3,011 and 1,256 left the assembly line.

The two-door hardtop was at $3,101 and rarer, with just 483 assemblies. The coupe weighed 3,693 pounds. Total Hornet series production, including exports, was 4,108 units. An additional 72 Hudson Sixes were shipped overseas in "knocked down" form.

Other than the cars sent overseas, Hudsons used the 327-cid AMC V-8. This overhead-valve V-8 incorporated five main bearings and hydraulic valve lifters. It had a 4.00 x 3.25 inch bore and stroke, a 9.0:1 compression ratio and a four-barrel carburetor that helped it produce 255 hp at 4700 rpm.

All of the '57 Hudsons were perched on a 121.25-inch wheelbase and strtetched 209.25 inches overall. They had a 59-1/16-inches front tread width. The rear tread was 60-1/2 inches.

Equally mysterious was the fact Hudson was "slim outside for easy maneuvering" and "wider inside than any other car." Standard tires were size 8.00 x 14 blackwalls.

Outstanding selling features this year included single-unit body construction, a 12-volt electrical system, Torque-Tube drive, 14-inch wheels, duo-servo brakes and the famous Nash Weather-Eye heating and ventilating system. Power brakes were standard on Custom models. Power assists like Hydra-Matic Drive and a heater were optional, as were the popular Airliner reclining seats.

Three-speed manual transmission was standard and overdrive was $110 extra. Hydra-Matic automatic transmission cost $232. Available rear axle gear ratios were 3.15:1 and 4.10:1.

Kaisers and Frazers
of the Fifties

1950 *Kaiser and Frazer*

The 1950 Kaiser DeLuxe Virginian sedan had a vinyl roof that made it look like a convertible.

A fictitious homemaker created nearly 30 years earlier by The Washburn Crosby Company of Minneapolis, Minnesota, became a big hit in 1950. "Betty Crocker" was the persona devised in 1921 to answer questions about baking. Bill Crocker was a retired Washburn Crosby executive. "Betty" was just a friendly-sounding name. Although Betty never actually existed, her *Picture Cook Book* became a best seller. Its popularity reflected the postwar movement to elevate the status of the kitchen.

The "cooking room"—once reserved for wood-burning ovens, iceboxes, and even claw-foot bathtubs, was now being furnished with "fridges," ranges, dishwashers, and mangles. Cooking seemed less of a chore and more of an art and Betty helped the modern housewife. Another trend that evolved after the war was the movement towards colorful, richly-upholstered automobiles and a new company named Kaiser Frazer was a leader in this regard.

After World War II ended, industrialist Henry J. Kaiser teamed with Joseph W. Frazer, a former Graham-Paige motor car executive, to create new postwar cars with slab-sided bodies and novel styling gimmicks. Kaiser was chairman of the board. Frazer was vice-chairman of the board. The two men did not always get along.

More than 70,000 sales were achieved by their 1947 models, but the cars were pricey and sales declined in 1949. A massive loan from the postwar Reconstruction Finance Corp. allowed Kaiser to survive for a time, although the Frazer nameplate passed from the scene in 1951.

Kaiser Frazer Corporation couldn't make some planned major revisions for 1950. On Nov. 3, 1949, company dealers were advised they would get new serial number plates for their leftover 1949 models. Salesmen were specifically told not to represent them as being updated.

Technically speaking, the 1950 model year lasted only from then until March 15, 1950, when all-new 1951 models arrived.

In the 1950 Kaiser models, K-F promoted All-Direction roominess, a sway-eliminator bar, coil front springs, Super-Cushion tires,

double channel frame construction, ball-type midship bearings, a two-piece propeller shaft, floating shoe brakes, Centrifuse brake drums, three-point engine mounting, a vibration damper, direct-acting shock absorbers, spring leaf lifters, rubber-cored spring shackles, a hypoid rear axle, a Clear-Vision steering wheel, an external oil filter, a ball bearing water pump, and an automatic choke.

The lower-priced Kaiser Specials could be identified by the use of narrow chrome rocker panel strips below the doors and the lack of front fender insignias. The pricier Deluxe models utilized a 112-hp power plant with a dual intake manifold and two-barrel carburetor as standard equipment. The Special series offered a four-door sedan ($1,995), the hatch-back Traveler four-door utility sedan ($2,088) and a taxicab, of which only 2,641 were built. The Deluxe four-door sedan ($2,195) was distinguished by wider chrome rocker panels below its doors.

A fancy version of the utility sedan was called the Vagabond ($2,288). The Virginian ($2,995) was a four-door sedan with a Nylon roof that made it look like a convertible. The Deluxe four-door convertible ($3,195) was the priciest Kaiser. Some models carried identifying front fender nameplates or unusual chrome script plates calling out the main body color.

Frazers for 1950 were also identical to '49s in virtually every respect. Standard models had narrow chrome strips below the doors. All models had "Frazer" across the front radiator grille. Company literature highlighted welded steel body construction and features the same as or very similar to those found on Kaisers. The only model in the standard series was a $2,395 four-door sedan.

The costlier Frazer Manhattan series continued with two four-door models, the sedan ($2,595) and the convertible ($3,295). They could be identified by the wide "double-level" chrome strip below the doors and the Manhattan script plate attached to the trailing edge of the upper front fender sides. Fender skirts, with double-level moldings on their lower edges, were standard on the convertible sedan. Full chrome wheel discs, chrome wheel trim rings, concealed floor lamps, front seat assist handles, chrome instrument panel moldings and non-glare rearview mirrors were standard equipment features.

Total 1949-1950 Frazer production was 24,923 cars, of which about 14,700 were standard sedans and 10,020 were Manhattan models.

The engine used in standard Kaisers was a 226.2-cid in-line L-head six with four main bearings and solid valve lifters. It had a 7.3:1 compression ratio and a single-barrel downdraft carburetor. Output was 100 hp at 3600 rpm. Deluxe models and all Frazers used the dual-manifold version with a two-barrel carburetor. This engine was also offered in Kaiser Special taxicabs.

Both Kaisers and Frazers rode on a 123-1/2-inch-wheelbase chassis and had an overall length of 203 inches. Tread widths were 58 inches up front and 60 inches in the rear. Size 7.10 x 15 tires were used.

These cars became well known for their colorful exterior treatments and 15 different hues were available for exterior body finishing on Deluxe 1950 models (the Kaiser Special offered nine body colors). Kaiser Deluxe interiors could be ordered in five different fabrics that came in 16 different "coordinated" colors. There were also three vinyl-trim options for Deluxe models.

The exact model year production of 1949-1950 Kaisers was 95,175 units and Kaiser output in the same period came to 24,923 units. Kaiser-Frazer was America's 12th ranked automaker in 1950.

1951 *Kaiser and Frazer*

The 1951 Traveler sedan exhibits "Dutch Darrin" styling, including the "Darrin Dip" roof brow.

After receiving a much-needed loan from the Reconstruction Finance Corp., Kaiser-Frazer finally had enough money to redesign its products. This permitted the company to survive for a time, although the Frazer would soon pass from the scene.

To revitalize the remaining cars, master craftsman Howard "Dutch" Darrin was employed to restyle the line. Heavy emphasis was placed on upgraded interior appointments, with major responsibility in this area falling to designer Carlton Spencer, who accomplished an outstanding job.

The '51 Kaiser was less boxy, with more glass area. Gone was the bull-nosed front end. A horizontal-bars grille was used. A K-and-buffalo badge and a dart-like mascot sat on the hood. The roof had a dip (called the "Darrin Dip") above the center of the windshield.

Big news for the year was an all-new compact two-door sedan Henry J. With a 100-inch wheelbase and 174-1/2-inch overall

length, the Henry J had the choice of two Willys-built engines, a 68-hp four-cylinder or an 80-hp six. A separate marque (though everyone knew who built it) the standard four-banger was $1,363 and the Deluxe "six shooter" listed for $1,499.

The first Henry J was advertised as "the most efficient car in America" because it moved a greater payload with less dead weight. There were also owner reports that it could travel 30 miles on a gallon of gas. The new, small "Kaiser" had full-sized doors and a 58-inch wide seat. It didn't have a trunk lid. Kaiser-Frazer's early compact did fairly well, with model-year production of 88,959 units. Eventually, Sears, Roebuck & Company would sell a badge-engineered version of the Henry J, with a trunk, in the South and Southwest as the Allstate.

Kaiser's "Anatomic Design" fit the anatomy of a human body. It provided more head and leg room. Kaisers had the largest windshield in the industry, rear door safety locks, scientific weight distribution, Direct-View instruments, a Tuck-Away spare tire well, rubber body mountings, steel-covered rear springs, wraparound bumpers, an insulated body, a large-diameter driveshaft, Hotchkiss drive, an air-cooled clutch, a 115-hp high-compression six with mushroom tappets, a vibration damper, full-length water jacketing, a balanced crankshaft, and an external oil filter.

Two car-lines bowed in February 1950 and remained unchanged through the winter 1951. Early Specials lacked chrome trim. Five styles were offered — Business Coupe, two- and four-door sedan and two-and four-door Traveler — at prices from $1,992 to $2,317. Specials built later in the year had narrow chrome side strips. The three-quarter length strips, mounted low on the body, ran from behind the front wheelhousings to above the rear bumper.

The Kaiser Deluxe models had the same new styling as Specials, but could be identified by the wide strip of chrome around the bottom of the body, the foam rubber seat cushions, the Deluxe dashboard treatment and the rear-seat ash trays. Also included were bumper end wing guards, stainless steel belt moldings, bright window reveals, a cotton headliner with wool facing, front compartment carpeting, a padded vinyl dashboard, and a Tenite plastic Deluxe steering wheel with a horn-blowing ring. Deluxe interior combinations included Stockholm, Beaumont or Normandie cloths, genuine leather options and pleated, patterned vinyl in Travelers.

A two-door Club Coupe with six-passenger seating replaced the business coupe in the Deluxe line. Otherwise the high-trim body styles were a match for those in the Special series. Prices ranged from $2,275 to $2,380. In November 1950, the famous Kaiser Dragon option appeared. Named for K-F's heavy seat-facing material — which was jokingly compared to the skin of a dragon — Kaisers with this option seem to have come with Hydra-Matic transmission, white sidewall tires and interior/exterior enrichments.

First series Dragons were sold through Feb. 6, 1951. They came in a choice of nine color combinations, each of which complemented a seven specific "Dragon vinyl" trim combinations. On early Dragons the roof was painted while second series Dragons had padded tops. The cars offered three exterior color choices. Golden Dragons came with Arena Yellow paint and black "dinosaur" vinyl trim. Silver Dragons came in Mariner Gray with scarlet dinosaur vinyl trim. Emerald Dragons were Cape Verde Green (Metallic) with matching dinosaur vinyl fabrics.

The third series cars, offered after April 27, 1951, also had padded tops. They came only as Tropical green "Jade Dragons" with straw-colored interiors. Dragon features, such as a removable armrest in second series editions and padded "Sport Topping" roof treatments, later became options for other

Kaisers. The GM-made Hydra-Matic four-speed automatic transmission was also available as an individual option for the first time in 1951.

The Frazer was heavily facelifted for its last year. The new body was based on Darrin's ideas as executed by Herb Weissinger. It was now bigger than the Kaiser, with a 123-1/2-inch wheelbase and 211-3/8-inch overall length. Like its "cousin," it featured crisp, highly-defined body lines with rakish windstream curves and unbroken fender contours.

Large taillights were set into the high-crowned rear fenders. There were sculptured crease lines on the sides of the fenders and around the rear wheel opening. A heavy chrome "wind-tunnel" grille was used.

The standard Frazer series offered two body styles: four-door sedan for $2,359 and four-door Vagabond hatchback for $40 more. The latter combined conventional sedan features with station wagon flexibility. Frazer used a unique dual rear hatch design. One panel folded down to form a tailgate, while the upper hatch opened upward to give nearly floor-to-ceiling access to the interior. The rear seat folded forward to give a station-wagon-like flat cargo floor. "Frazer" appeared on the rear door of standard sedans and "Frazer Vagabond" was on the utility model.

The 1951 Frazer Manhattan line consisted of two four-door cars, a "hardtop" sedan similar to the 1950 Kaiser Virginian and a convertible sedan. Both combined convertible lines with steel-roof convenience, but were not true pillarless hardtops.

Manhattan identification features included the model name in script on the rear door and distinct body styles. The standard Deluxe equipment included a carpeted luggage compartment, an automatic trunk light, door armrests, a chrome trimmed steering wheel, and bright metal interior moldings and trim. A Manhattan sedan was announced, but apparently was not produced.

To finish the task of remaking Kaisers and Frazers, a powerful six from Continental Engines Co. — a Kaiser Industries subsidiary firm — was improved with new manifolding to produce more "get-up-and-go." The 115 hp produced by this 226.2-cid "Supersonic Six" was a fine engine. It used a 7.3:1 compression ratio.

The 1951 Kaiser line was publicly introduced on Feb. 16, 1950. The 1951 Henry J, was introduced in October 1950. Model-year production was 145,031 units. Calendar-year registrations peaked at 52,286 cars. The 1951 Standard Frazer line went on sale during March 1950. Frazer Manhattan models were introduced in August 1950. Model-year sales totaled 10,214 units. Calendar-year sales of all Kaiser-Frazer products was 99,343 cars. The company was America's 14th-ranked automaker this season.

1952 *Kaiser*

On March 8, 1952, surgeon John Heynsham Gibbon used a heart-and-lung machine that he had started developing during the 1930s to keep a 41-year-old patient alive. Dubbed the *artificial heart*, Gibbon's creation paved the way for future advances in pulmonary medicine.

Before its introduction to medicine in 1952, heart surgery was impossible because there was no way to keep a patient alive during

the procedure. Unfortunately, this wonderful device did not work on automakers like Kaiser Frazer, that needed help "staying alive."

By the end of 1951, Kaiser's car sales were down to 32,000 units per year. The company had fallen far short of selling all the '51 models it produced. To clear out excess inventory, the leftover cars were "redecorated," renumbered, and reintroduced as 1952 models. A truly new car would not appear until the "remainders" were

Tom Collins

Kaiser's Henry J Corsair Deluxe was new for 1952 and was powered by a new 161-cid engine.

gone, so Kaiser's new-model introductions did not follow the normal model-year dating used by larger carmakers.

The 1952 Kaiser Virginians were redecorated cars. They were 1951 Kaisers, all carrying the name of what had previously been a special "four-door hardtop" model. A Virginian script appeared on the front fenders, but there were no other essential changes. When they hit the market on Dec. 15, 1951, even the prices were unchanged. A continental tire kit was a factory option. Kaiser was simply trying to stay competitive, without spending a lot of money.

There were two lines of 1952 Virginians. The Special series included the Business Coupe, two- and four-door sedans and two- and four-door Traveler Utility Sedans at prices between $1,992 and $2,265.

The models were the same as in the Special series, except that a Club Coupe replaced the Business Coupe. Prices ranged from $2,275 up to $2,433 for the four-door version of the Traveler hatchback. A total of just 5,578 of these 1952 Virginians were built between December 1951 and March of 1952.

On March 14, 1952, Kaiser brought out "true" 1952 models with new styling elements and higher prices. The grille had one large full-width bar that ran horizontally across the front of the car. Below it was a more massive "bridge" type grille guard that housed the license plate.

A curved, one-piece windshield was new, as was the lance-like hood ornament. A key-operated starter switch replaced the old button type. Larger taillamps were seen, along with a more massive bumper with chrome pods at each end.

The Deluxe series was now the base trim level and could be identified by the words Kaiser Deluxe on the sides of the front fenders. Kaiser Manhattan was now the name of the top series. Manhattans carried "Kaiser Manhattan" nameplates on the sides of front fenders. They also featured wide chrome trim around the bottom of the body. Styling features were the same as the 1952 Kaiser Deluxes. There was also a wide dart-shaped belt line molding with an embossed treatment, a Deluxe instrument panel with padded crash pad, and a chrome horn-blowing ring.

Full carpeting and lavish upholstery trims were standard equipment and many options were available. The Club Coupe,

two- and four-door sedans and two-and four-door Travelers were listed as available models — at prices between $2,622 and $2,757.

Both first-series Virginians and second-series Kaiser Deluxe and Manhattan models continued using the 226-cid 115-hp Supersonic Six. All specificatioins for the first-series cars were unchanged from 1951 models.

Like the big Kaisers, the compact Henry J came in an early Vagabond series that was the same as 1951. It could be distinguished by the outside mounting of a Continental wheel and tire at the rear. A Vagabond nameplate dressed up the front fenders. The four-cylinder Vagabond two-door sedan had a base price of $1,407.

The 134-cid Willys-built four generated 68 hp at 4000 rpm. Overdrive and Hydra-Matic Drive were optional. The six-cylinder Vagabond Deluxe cost $145 more for a Willys in-line six that made 80 hp at 3800 rpm. Vagabonds were built between Dec. 15, 1951 and the start of Corsair production early in the 1952 calendar year.

The new Henry J Corsair was introduced on Feb. 26, 1952. It had the model name on the front fenders. An entirely new grille was seen.

The Corsair engine was the same used in the Vagabond four, but the Corsair had special features to justify its $110 higher price. It featured woven plastic upholstery that could be washed over and over again. There were new improvements to the spring suspension and shock absorbers.

The 1952 Kaiser Deluxe and Manhattan lines were introduced on March 14, 1952. The 1952 Allstate and 1952 Henry J were both introduced on Dec. 20, 1951. Model-year production (beginning February 1952) peaked at 32,131 units.

On Sept. 26, 1952, Kaiser Corporation announced its intention to market a plastic-bodied sports car designed by Howard "Dutch" Darrin. The 700,000th Kaiser-Frazer automobile was built on Oct. 6, 1952.

Although the Frazer car disappeared, Joe Frazer remained vice-chairman of the company. Henry J. Kaiser continued as chairman of the board and Edgar F. Kaiser was president.

During calendar year 1952, Kaiser fitted 12,320 cars (excluding Henry Js) with overdrive transmissions, while 26,362 additional units featured Hydra-Matic Drive.

1953 *Kaiser*

The 1953 Kaiser Manhattan two-door sedan shows cosmetic changes like a new hood ornament.

A box-office blockbuster of 1953 was "The Robe," a religious epic, set in Roman times, starring Richard Burton, Jean Simmons and Victor Mature. Lloyd C. Douglas wrote the novel and 20th Century Fox studios shot the film version using a radical new process called *CinemaScope*. For back-up, "The Robe" was also filmed simultaneously in standard *Academy* format, but *CinemaScope* proved so popular the standard version of the movie was never shown in a theatre.

Unfortunately, not every radical new product that evolved in postwar America proved as popular as *CinemaScope*. The unique Kaisers of this era are a good example. They departed from the norm and went largely unappreciated. By 1953, Kaiser's automotive venture was "on the ropes." Model-year production between September 1952 and December 1953 would total just 31,272 Kaisers and 17,505 Henry Js.

Kaiser instituted economy measures that reduced the number of available 1953 body styles. Some refreshing design changes were seen that season. Most were detail refinements that could be made at minimal cost. A chrome strip was added to the rear fender tops to create miniature tail fins. Concealed hinges on the rear deck looked more modern. Wider chrome caps, patterned after the aftermarket chrome "eyebrows" in vogue at this time, were added to the headlights. A new bird-in-flight hood mascot was adopted. With some slight tweaking, Kaiser got the horsepower rating of the base version of the 226-cid "Supersonic Six" up to 118 at 3650 rpm.

The Deluxe series cars could be identified by their Kaiser Deluxe front fender scripts, the lack of bumper end caps, the use of small hubcaps, unskirted rear fenders, untrimmed window sills, and side trim consisting of a narrow chrome spear running from behind the front wheel housing to the rear of the car on the lower body.

Features being promoted included over-sized, self-centering brakes, Safety-First lighting, wraparound bumpers, and bin-type glove compartments. There were three Deluxe models. The

four-door sedan listed for $2,513 and weighed 3200 pounds. A total of 5,069 were built. The two-door sedan, priced at $2,459 weighed about 50 pounds less and 1,227 were made. The last — and rarest — model was the four-door Traveler. Only 946 of these $2,619 hatchbacks were produced. They weighed 3,315 pounds.

Kaiser Manhattans were one step up the totem pole. They featured the same styling refinements as Kaiser Deluxes and, officially came in the same three body styles. It's likely no Manhattan Travelers were ever built. Identifying features of the higher trim level cars included dart-shaped window sill moldings, a wide chrome side spear running from front to rear fender, bumper wing caps, fender skirts with wide chrome moldings, full wheel discs, and a series nameplate high on the trailing edge of the front fender sides. The four-door sedan ($2,650) and the two-door Club Sedan ($2,597) had production runs of 18,603 and 2,342 units, respectively. Manhattans weighed about 70 pounds more than comparable Kaiser Deluxe models.

A new Kaiser Dragon was introduced, as an addition to the line, on Oct. 31, 1952 — Halloween day. This $3,924 model was a treat, but some buyers may have been tricked into thinking that it was a Packard or Cadillac. Standard equipment included all features normally listed as part of Kaiser's Group 100 options package, which carried a retail value of $1,273.98. The extras included Hydra-Matic transmission, E-Z-Eye tinted glass, a radio with antenna and rear speaker, white sidewall tires, Deluxe wheel covers, windshield washers, a heater and defroster, air conditioning, a shaded backlight, gold-plated hood and fender nameplates, door lock shields, a personalized owner's glovebox nameplate and a "Bambu" vinyl-padded top. This later material was also used for most of the interior appointments.

As with previous Dragons, three different series were released for the 1953 run, each having specific interior and exterior paint, fabric and trim combinations. Some Kaiser

Deluxe models have even been found with Dragon features. Dragons weren't true pillarless hardtops, but sedans with the padded top applied in a manner resembling the style of hardtops (a border showing body color was left around the window openings). Survivors among the 1,277 built are collectors' items today.

The Kaiser Carolina four-door sedan ($2,373) and two-door Club Sedan ($2,313) were a running addition to the line on March 20, 1953. They represented a stripped economy offering with less chrome, plainer upholstery, and fewer standard equipment features. There were no sweep spears on the side of the Carolina bodies, no pads atop the dashboards and no chrome horn ring. Inexpensive vinyl upholstery was fitted. These "cheap" Kaisers did not sell well and the company built only 1,136 four-door sedans and 308 Club Sedans.

With a new hood ornament, a new padded dashboard, and a longer curved wrap-around rear bumper, the Henry J entered

1953 with two series. Standard Corsairs could be spotted by their rubber windshield molding and the Corsair name on the front fenders. Under the hood was the same 68-hp four-cylinder engine. The Corsair Deluxe had the 80-hp "Supersonic Six," Corsair Deluxe fender nameplates, chrome wheel discs and a chrome windshield molding. Prices were down about $130.

A prototype Darrin sports car was exhibited by Kaiser on Feb. 22, 1953. Kaiser reported a net operating loss of $10,796,754 in the first half of the year. On April 28, 1953, Kaiser Motors formally purchased Willys-Overland. Kaiser-Frazer Corporation got a name change to Kaiser Motors Corporation. The acquisition of Willys created Willys Motors, Inc. and Kaiser Motors became part of Willys. Kaiser-Willys Sales Corp. marketed Kaiser vehicles. Joe Frazer's name no longer appeared on the list of Kaiser executives and company headquarters moved from Willow Run, Michigan, to Toledo, Ohio.

1954 *Kaiser*

New for 1954 was the Kaiser Darrin, a fiberglass-bodied roadster with unique sliding doors.

Cracker Barrel cheese, M & Ms candies, Butterball turkeys and Trix cereal were some of the famous products first introduced in 1954. Another new product that set automotive history was the Kaiser-Darrin, a unique sports car with a fiberglass body and doors that slid completely into the front fenders. The Darrin was an instant collector's item, because of its novel features and because it proved to be an extremely rare automobile.

For 1954, there was again two different series of Kaisers. The first series consisted of 1953 leftovers that carried body number plates from the Willow Run, Michigan, factory and serial number plates from the Willys plant, in Ohio. All cars in

the later series were constructed at Willys' Toledo facility.

General styling changes for 1954 were inspired by Buick's famous XP-300 show car. There was a new "jet airscoop" grille with a bowed oval shape and multiple vertical louvers. A matching "air intake" chrome vent decorated the front of the simulated hood scoop. Massive, hooded headlights enclosed the front parking lamps. The new front bumper had a vertical crease at its center and twin, vertical guards replaced the single unit "bridge" type arrangement. The taillight clusters were redesigned to be visible from the side as well as rear.

Some 3,500 cars left over in 1953 were turned into 1954 Specials by adding new grilles, taillights, trim, and data plates.

These cars had one-piece, non-wraparound rear windows, wide three-quarter-length lower body moldings, 1953-style interior, and chassis features and Kaiser-Frazer (Willow Run) firewall code plates. A Kaiser script was on the left edge of the hood with Kaiser Special signatures on the front fenders.

When all of the leftovers were sold out, a second series of Specials appeared. These later cars had much thinner, three-quarter-length lower body side moldings and somewhat less chrome on the roof gutters and around the windows. They also featured the trimmer new crash panel dashboard and a three-piece wraparound rear window like the 1954 Manhattans.

Specials included wheel covers, bumper guards, a chrome exhaust deflector, a Deluxe steering wheel, electric windshield wipers, an electric clock, an oil bath air cleaner, directional signals, a rear cigarette lighter (except two-door Special sedans) and a tilt-type rearview mirror.

This was actually a case of "clearing options off the shelf," rather than offering more fully equipped cars. Prices were increased accordingly. List prices were the same for first- and second-series cars: $2,192 for the four-door sedan and $2,141 for the two-door Club Sedan. In addition to the 3,500 cars converted into 1954 models, and estimated 749 sedans and 180 Club Sedans were made to second-series specifications.

Kaiser Manhattans had the same general styling changes outlined for Specials, plus the three-section wraparound rear window (also used on second-series 1954 Kaiser Specials). This window treatment featured curved glass, chrome division bars and curved outer glass panels that swept around the rear quarter region of the roof. The Manhattan interior was also redone with an aircraft-inspired treatment.

Kaiser lettering appeared, in script, on the left-hand tip of the hood and Kaiser Manhattan chrome signatures decorated the upper front fender sides.

The big news was under the hood where a McCulloch centrifugal supercharger was standard equipment. The Manhattan four-door sedan was priced at $2,454 and about 4,107 were built. The Club Coupe, which had a $2,404 list price, was much rarer with an estimated 218 assemblies.

The 1954 Henry J could only be easily distinguished from the 1953 model by checking its serial number prefix, which was "54." The four-cylinder Corsair was down to $1,286 this year, while the six-cylinder Corsair Deluxe listed for $1,437 or $124 less than its 1953 counterpart. Features of these compact Kaiser products included a Penny-Minder carburetor (30 mpg was claimed), a Safety-Mounted windshield that pushed out on impact, a Safety-Padded dashboard, Triple-Tooth steering and a Zero-Start battery.

A new Kaiser-Darrin sports car was first offered to the public on Jan. 6, 1954. Some sources indicate actual car deliveries began the same day. The fiberglass-bodied vehicle incorporated a number of radical ideas, including doors that slid forward into the front fenders. Other features included a three-position convertible top. The 100-inch-wheelbase roadster carried a factory price of $3,655 and weighed 2,175. Only 435 were built in 1954.

A variety of engines were found below the hoods of 1954 Kaiser models. Specials continued to use the 226-cid 118-hp six with a 7.3:1 compression ratio and Carter two-barrel carburetor. The 140-hp "Super-Power" version was used in all Manhattans.

This engine used the McCulloch aeronautical-type supercharger to provide a secondary torque source. The fuel-air mixture was delivered to the carburetor and combustion chambers under pressure, instantly providing a highly volatile charge that helped produce more power.

The 1954 Kaiser Manhattan was introduced on Feb. 3, 1954, along with the first-series Kaiser Special. The second-series Kaiser Special was introduced on March 23, 1954. Production of cars built to 1954 specifications was halted on June 30, 1954. On July 19, some 400 workers were put on furlough and the car-building assembly lines were then utilized for manufacturing Willys commercial vehicles and Jeeps.

Tom Collins

Buick's XP-300 show car influenced the 1954 Kaiser Manhattan's styling.

1955 *Kaiser*

The 1955 Manhattan was the final Kaiser offered in North America.

The 1955 Kaiser Manhattan was the only model marketed by Willys Motors, Inc., (a subsidiary of Kaiser Motors Corporation) for 1955. The Manhattan retained the basic 1954 styling, but the height of the center fin decorating the simulated hood scoop was increased. Also, two smaller side fins were added. This gave a total of five decorative fins surrounding the scoop.

Model year output was exactly 1,231 cars. Of these, 409 were built in May and 612 were built in June to fill an order from Argentina. These 1,021 vehicles were the only cars made in the calendar-year 1955. Apparently, the remaining 210 cars were built late in calendar-year 1954 and sold in the United States, along with another 270 leftover 1954 units that were re-titled as 1955 models. A total of 959 Kaisers were registered in the United States as new cars during calendar-year 1955.

A four-door sedan and a two-door Club Sedan were offered in both the 1954 carryover series and the 1955 domestic series. They were priced at $2,670 and $2,617, respectively. The Club Sedan weighed 3,335 pounds and the four-door model weighed 40 additional pounds. Automotive historians have estimated that 226 sedans and just 44 Club Sedans were put together.

During 1955, Kaiser dealers also continued to sell remainders from the run of approximately 435 fiberglass-bodied Darrin sports cars that had been built during 1954 at the Kaiser-Frazer plant in Jackson, Michigan. This factory previously built Kaiser and Frazer four-door convertibles. The Darrins, at $3,400, had been difficult to sell the first year because they cost as much as a Cadillac or Lincoln. And the number of Kaiser dealers was dwindling. As a result, there were plenty of Darrins still available in 1955.

The Kaiser-Darrin was actually a fairly good sports car with a tachometer mounted right in front of the driver and a top speed of 100 mph, as recorded by *Auto Age* in October 1953. It was only six miles per hour slower than the six-cylinder-powered 1953 Corvette.

When Kaiser production ended in mid-1955, several unfinished Darrins were still sitting on the assembly line. Dutch Darrin bought these cars and finished building them at his studio in Santa Monica, Calif., installing Cadillac V-8s into a few.

The Kaiser-Darrin is probably the most collectible Kaiser automobile ever made. The company built a grand total of 442 of the cars — if you count seven pre-production prototypes — and it is believed that about 400 of them still survive.

Willys Motors, Inc., ceased passenger car operations after shipping the final cars off to Argentina. The name Kaiser and the design didn't completely disappear. The tooling was sold to IKA, in Argentina, where the Kaiser Carabella was built from 1958 through 1962.

All 1955 Manhattans were powered by the supercharged 140-hp Kaiser 226. In addition to its aeronautical-type supercharger, the engine included positive exhaust valve rotators for increased valve life and efficiency, silicon-chromium intake valves for better heat and corrosion resistance, and a new piston ring combination with a heavy, chrome-plated top ring.

The 1955 Kaiser line was introduced on Jan. 6, 1955, but a half a year later it was over. The last Kaisers built in the United States were shipped to Argentina that June. Kaiser Motors was renamed Kaiser Industries, Inc. and became a platform for the creation of publicly-held Kaiser business operations.

Willys Motors, Inc. continued commercial vehicle manufacturing operations as a subsidiary of Kaiser Industries Corp. Leftover Kaiser-Darrin sports cars were marketed by some Kaiser dealers during the 1955 model year.

Lincolns
of the Fifties

1950 *Lincoln*

The 1950 Lincoln Cosmopolitan models had heavy chrome brows over the wheel wells..

Harry S. Truman was elected Vice President in 1944 and became the nation's 33rd president 82 days after he was inaugurated, following Franklin D. Roosevelt's unexpected death in April 1945. Truman was president when World War II ended. He approved dropping the atomic bomb on Japan and contributed to the founding of both the UN and the birth of Israel. His Truman Doctrine offered military aid to help countries resist communism and NATO was formed to militarily challenge Soviet influence in Europe. Truman's presidency had a major effect on the history of the early '50s.

While he personally liked Chrysler products, one of the official cars that Truman rode in was a specially-built 1950 Lincoln Cosmopolitan 7-passenger Presidential limousine.

Like most automakers, Lincoln entered the postwar period selling warmed-over 1942 models. With a gorgeous automobile like the Lincoln Continental, that wasn't all bad. It was one of those rare cars that became an instant classic. The Continental was highly regarded for its styling. Its sales were not that good, but the classic-looking Continental did help Lincoln's image.

When the first postwar Lincolns debuted in early 1948 (as 1949 models), the company had nothing to compare with the Continental. The top-of-the-line Cosmopolitan looked much like the standard Lincoln series. The standard Lincoln resembled a Mercury. This was logical, since the two FoMoCo models shared the same bodies.

A new full-width horizontal-bar grille with multiple vertical elements enhanced the appearance of the standard Lincoln for 1950. The grille styling was simpler than in 1949 and gave the 1950 models a lower, wider look. A Lincoln nameplate was in the same front fender location as last year, but it was larger. Inside Lincoln used fiberglass padding on the floors and ceiling for noise control. The streamlined body styling was said to be quieter as well. Both the body and engine were rubber-mounted and exceptionally quiet.

The two-door Club Coupe was the least expensive Lincoln at $2,529. It weighed 4,090 pounds. In mid-model year, the Lido Coupe was added to the line. It featured a vinyl top and custom interior. This car was advertised as being: "...gay in spirit, young in heart."

A full-length molding ran from headlight to taillight on each side of the car and bright underscores trimmed the rocker panels.

The Lido was essentially a dressed-up version of the Club Coupe that listed for $2,721. It weighed about 55 pounds more. Lincoln counted production of the two models together as 5,748 units. In the middle, price-wise, was the Sports Sedan that listed for $2,574. Lincoln made 11,714 of this 4,115-pound four-door car.

The Cosmopolitan received a new grille and dash for 1950. Its name now was written in chrome on the lower front fenders, behind the wheel opening, on most models. A horizontal gob of chrome decorated the sides of the front fenders above the wheel opening. Bright rocker panel moldings and rear fender skirts were seen. Power windows (optional in Lincolns) were standard with "Cosmos." Four models were offered. "Nothing could be finer," claimed one advertisement showing a burgundy-colored 1950 Cosmopolitan Sport Sedan.

The Club Coupe listed for $3,187 and weighed 4,375. Lincoln built 1,315 of them. The Cosmopolitan Capri ($3,406) — another variation of the Club Coupe model — had a padded leather roof and custom interior. It also had an additional horizontal chrome "brow" on the rear quarter panels parallel to the ones on the front fenders. On this model, the Cosmopolitan name was placed directly behind the front fender molding, instead of on the lower front fender.

The Capri was introduced to make up for Continental's lack of a two-door hardtop. It weighed 10 pounds more than the Club Coupe and 509 were made. Lincoln said the Capri brought "new meaning to luxury." The Cosmopolitan series also had a Sports Sedan ($3,240, 4,410 pounds and 8,332 built) and a convertible. At $3,950 the ragtop was the priciest Lincoln model. It was also the heaviest at 4,640 pounds. Unfortunately, only 536 of these beautiful cars were built.

All of the 1950 Lincolns used the same huge L-head V-8. With a 3.50 x 4.37-inch bore and stroke it displaced 336.7 cubic inches. A 7.0:1 compression ratio and Holley two-barrel carburetor contributed to its hefty, for the time, output of 152 hp at 3600 rpm. The Lincoln V-8 featured full-flow cooling, a counter-balanced crankshaft, a concentric-float carburetor and alloy-steel exhaust valves.

The Merc-bodied Lincoln had a 121-inch wheelbase and 213.8 inches between its bumpers. Despite the Cosmopolitan's longer 125-inch stance, it was over an inch and a half shorter than the Lincoln. Both models had a 58.5-inch front tread and 60-inch rear tread. The Lincoln used 8.00 x 15 rubber and the Cosmopolitan 8.20 x 15. A three-speed manual transmission was standard. A three-speed manual transmission with overdrive and an automatic transmission were extra-cost options.

Lincoln featured two distinctive looks in this era. Both its headlights and taillights were recessed. Also, Lincoln sedans, like Mercury, retained "suicide" rear doors at a time when most American sedans featured conventional four-doors that hinged at the front and latched at the rear.

Important selling features stressed to Lincoln salesmen in 1950 included "Salon" interiors, foam rubber seats, a folding rear-seat armrest, "Sea-Leg" rear shock absorbers, Hotchkiss drive, a large luggage compartment, passenger-assist loops, fool-proof locks, a map light, a two-way ignition system, a short turning radius, "Picture Window" visibility, cable-operated emergency brakes, concealed running boards, and automatic entrance lights.

Lincolns won two of the 19 NASCAR Grand National races held in 1950.

1951 *Lincoln*

The 1951 Lincoln Cosmopolitan had a forward-pointing chrome trim spear and continued using recessed headlights.

In 1951, Remington Rand Corporation introduced the first commercial digital computer to the world. The "UNIVAC" (Universal Automatic Computer) was a refined version of the experimental "ENIAC" computer of 1945. The U.S. Census Bureau bought the first of these monstrous machines. Lincoln Motor Car Division didn't have a UNIVAC, but the 1951 Lincolns did have the "InVincible V-8" under their hoods. This big flathead engine gave the Lincolns power to go with their luxury-market appeal.

Seven separate cars in two distinct series made up the 1951 Lincoln offerings. Cars were built that season in factories in Detroit and Los Angeles. The company wound up with model-year production of 32,574 cars. On a calendar-year basis, it made 12,556 Lincolns and 11,945 Cosmopolitans. One-half percent of all cars registered in the United States in 1951 were Lincolns. The brand was most popular in Colorado, Florida, and Nevada.

The front of the 1951 Lincoln looked like a 1950 model that entered a fist-fight — and lost. The 1951 Lincoln grille design was simpler and was protected by more massive bumper guards that now dropped to the bottom of the bumper. The horizontal bar was not as wide. It now ran from behind one bumper guard to behind the other one and had only five "fins" along its top. The bumper was heavier. It protruded at the top and extended a bit further around the body corners to give full wrap-around protection. New parking lights were mounted at either end of the grille opening and had a simpler, more enhancing appearance.

The smaller Lincoln models had a horizontal chrome strip running from the front fenders to the rear fenders along the middle of the body side. A chrome script spelling out the Lincoln name was placed below the molding, in back of the front wheel opening. New wheel covers with concentric circular ribs were used. A short, ribbed chrome molding appeared above the rear bumper ends.

While Lincoln kept its recessed headlights, new vertical taillights enhanced the rear view of the car.

The same three models were offered. Both prices and weights were down slightly. The Club Coupe was again the least expensive Lincoln. The 4,065-pound two-door listed for $2,505. The Lido Coupe was back at $2,702. It now weighed only 35 pounds extra. Lincoln counted production of the two models together as 4,482. The 1951 four-door Sports Sedan listed for $2,553. Lincoln made 12,279 copies of this 4,130-pound model.

Using the sales slogan "Nothing could be finer," Lincoln emphasized the luxury features of its 1951 models in its advertising and promotional materials. Inside, the cars were equipped with new interior fabrics, new smartly-styled hardware, a re-designed steering wheel, and new instrument control knobs. Fiberglass soundproofing materials were again used to shut out annoying road and wind noises. The Lincolns were described as "Studio-Quiet Riding" cars. Lincoln promised "…relaxing quietness at any speed, over any road surface."

The Lincolns and Cosmopolitans included countless convenience features like dash-control ventilation, directional signals, illuminated ash trays and cigar lighter pockets, a map light, door-operated entrance lights, and more.

Lincoln advertising stressed durability, dependability, stamina, and performance, as well as economy of operation. As proof of the latter, a 1951 Lincoln with optional overdrive outperformed all other cars in the 1951 Mobilgas Economy Run and won the Grand Prize Sweepstakes Award.

Except for an upright chrome "fin" at the front of the body side molding and chrome rocker panel moldings, the new Cosmopolitan looked pretty much like the standard Lincoln. The distinctive brow of chrome on the front fenders of the previous two years was mercifully removed.

Also, the Cosmopolitan name was placed on the upper front fenders, behind the chrome fin. Next to the convertible, the snazziest model was the Capri coupe. It featured a canvas or vinyl roof, Deluxe upholstery and (like all Cosmopolitans) standard fender skirts.

The Cosmopolitan Club Coupe listed for $3,129 and weighed 4,340 pounds. Lincoln built 1,476 of them. The Cosmopolitan Capri ($3,350) now weighed 20 pounds more than the Club Coupe and grew a bit more popular in its second season; 1,251 were made. Also available was the Cosmopolitan Sports Sedan, which sold for $3,182 and tipped the scales at 4,415. Lincoln also sold more—12,229—of these cars in 1951. Even the $3,891 Cosmopolitan convertible, though rare, was up in popularity with 857 assemblies. And it lost 25 pounds for 1951.

The 336.7-cid V-8 was again the Lincoln power plant in all models. Although all basic specs were the same, it gained two horsepower at the same 3600 rpm. The 1951 V-8 featured improved oil drainage, hydraulic valve lifters, better spark control, a two-way ignition system, a gear-type oil pump, aluminum-alloy pistons, one-piece valve guides, and a high-capacity generator. A three-speed manual transmission was standard. Overdrive and Hydra-Matic Drive were extra-cost options.

The Merc-bodied Lincoln had a 121-inch wheelbase and gained an inch in overall length (214.8). The Cosmopolitans rode a 125-inch wheelbase and measured 222.5 inches bumper guard to bumper guard.

Important selling features stressed to Lincoln salesmen in 1951 included directional-flow cooling tubes, Finger Tip controls, duo-servo brakes, Picture Windows (large glass areas), girder-type frame construction, stone deflector shield, and new taillights. Options available included a Comfort-Flo heater and white side-wall tires.

Benson Ford was the general manager of the Lincoln-Mercury Division this year. Dealer introductions were staged for Nov. 15, 1950. Production of models built to 1951 specifications was quartered at Detroit, Michigan and Los Angeles, California, assembly plants, although a new factory in Wayne County, Michigan, was nearly completed this season and went into operation for production of 1952 Lincolns. In November 1951, the 125-inch wheelbase series was discontinued.

1952 *Lincoln*

In 1952 and 1953, Lincolns finished first through fourth in the Carrera Panamericana (Mexican Road Race) stock car division. Lincoln driver Chuck Stevenson won both times, with Clay Smith as his co-driver. The racing victories and surrounding publicity helped to highlight some big changes made to Lincoln products in this era.

Lincoln was locked in another competition – a sales race with Cadillac. At that time, both luxury makes were viewed as high-performance cars and the Lincoln racing wins certainly helped move cars out of the showroom. In fact, Lincoln was one of just two automakers to produce more cars in 1952 than in 1951. Its output of 31,993 units for the calendar year represented a 26 percent increase over the 25,386 cars turned out in 1951.

For model-year 1952, Lincoln dramatically changed its appearance. The cars bore no resemblance to the previous year's models, but shared the corporate look all Ford Motor Co. cars had that year. Although Lincolns had participated in previous Pan American Road Races, this was the first year the make dominated the event.

With their new styling, the 1952 Lincolns had a lean, racy look. The bumper and grille were integrated instead of being recessed. The headlights seemed to stick out slightly from the fenders. A wraparound windshield and rear window added a modern touch to the car's styling. Lincoln advertisements compared the bright, airy interiors to "…living in the glass-walled home" and noted that the cars offered up to 3,721 square inches of glass area. "The world is all around you," one ad pointed out. "The fenders and the road can be seen with ease." The large vertical taillights were vaguely similar to the vertical, Mercury-style versions used in 1951. They gave

a distinctive look to the tail of the car.

Body refinements for 1952 included wide, easy-entrance doors and a sloping hood that gave the driver a better view of the road ahead. Cushion body mounts helped isolate the body from chassis vibrations and plenty of insulation was used to keep out noise. A counter-balanced deck lid covered a roomy luggage area in the rear of the car. Salesmen were told that the '52 Lincoln provided "the finest in contemporary coach craft."

A completely redesigned chassis introduced some basic engineering advances like a new ball-joint suspension. This clearly improved the Lincoln's handling and ride. Lincoln claimed it brought "…an entirely new feeling to the fine-car field." A double-braced frame provided a feeling of solid, road-hugging stability. All models rode on a 123-inch wheelbase and had an overall length of 214 inches. Tread widths were 58.5 inches up front and in the rear. Size 8.00 x 15 tires were worn.

Lincoln offered a lineup of just five cars arranged in two series. The lower-priced Cosmopolitan series included a Sport Coupe and a four-door sedan. The high-priced Capri series offered a two-door hardtop coupe, a four-door sedan and a convertible coupe. Both used a completely new overhead-valve V-8 engine.

With a 3.80 x 3.50 inch bore and stroke, the new cast-iron-block, five-main-bearings V-8 displaced 317.5 cid. Lincoln combined, hydraulic valve lifters, a 7.5:1 compression ratio and a Holley two-barrel carburetor to create 160 hp at 3900 rpm and 284 foot-pounds of torque at 1800 rpm. Engine features included free-flow manifolding, "Hi-Swirl" combustion chambers, perfected engine balancing, slipper-type pistons, chrome top rings, rotating valves, and automatic spark control.

The 1952 Lincolns received all new styling including large taillights like this Capri convertible.

Cosmopolitan models had the series name on their rear fenders. There was no chrome curb-buffer strip along the bottom of the body. Side trim consisted of a nearly full-length spear that ran down the middle of the body sides from behind the front wheel opening to the taillights. On the rear door or rear quarter panel this moldings divided a wide, ribbed, forward slanted molding that trimmed the forward edge of the rear fender bulge. The Cosmopolitan Sport Coupe had a $3,293 list price and weighed 4,155 pounds. The four-door sedan listed for $3,198 and weighed 30 pounds less.

The Capri was now Lincoln's top-of-the-line model. The Capri sedan featured fabric and leather upholstery. Like the Cosmopolitan it resembled, its gas tank filler was hidden behind the rear license plate.

The Cosmopolitan was a fairly well-dressed car, yet the Capri added bright rocker panel models (Lincoln called then "curb buffers"), and the Capri name replaced the Cosmopolitan name on the rear fenders. There was a bit more bright trim around the Capri's windows and some added interior richness. The two-door hardtop was priced at $3,518 and weighed 4,235 pounds. The

sedan listed for $3,331 and tipped the scale at 4,140 pounds. The convertible had a base price of $3,665 and was the heaviest Lincoln at 4,350 pounds. It was also the rarest model, with only 1,191 produced.

A power front seat (a.k.a. "automatic" front seat adjustment) and power windows were standard in the convertible and optional in other models.. Other extra-cost options included a "Comfort Control" heater and defroster, white sidewall tires, a radio, and "Sea Tint" glass. Hydra-Matic automatic transmission was standard. A "maximum duty kit" was available for owners who wanted to race their Lincolns.

For the 1952 model year, Lincoln built 27,270 cars, which was the highest total in the company's history. In October of that year, the company discontinued making cars at its Detroit factory—the original Lincoln factory built by company founder Henry Leland. Nearly half a million Lincoln automobiles were made there.

Lincoln's main assembly lines were then moved to a new plant in Wayne County, Michigan. The company also built smaller numbers of vehicles in factories located at Los Angeles, California, St. Louis, Missouri and in Metuchen, New Jersey.

1953 *Lincoln*

On June 15, 1953, nearly 60 million people across America watched as Mary Martin spoofed women's fashions and Ethel Merman performed a song and dance routine during Ford's "50th Anniversary TV Show." It was billed as the greatest TV show in the history of that era, with the largest audience ever under a single sponsorship.

Lincoln advertisements in 1953 characterized Ford's luxury brand as the "Crowning achievement of Ford Motor Company's 50th Anniversary." The '53 Lincoln was billed as: "The one fine car designed for modern living — completely powered for modern driving."

Power plant improvements were a big part of the Lincoln news that season. Big engines and big horsepower ratings were associated with luxury cars in this era and Lincoln was in a heated contest with Cadillac to be biggest.

In 1952 Cadillac had offered a 190-hp V-8 versus Lincoln's 160 hp. Both makers upped the ante in 1953. When the dust cleared, Lincoln had a big gain in horsepower, though not quite enough.

With an unchanged bore and stroke, the overhead-valve V-8 remained at 317.5 cid, but the engine's compression ratio was boosted up to 8.0:1. Combined with the use of a new Holley 2140 four-barrel carburetor, this pushed brake horsepower to 205 at 4200 rpm and torque to 305 foot-pounds at 2300 rpm. The corresponding numbers for the '53 Cadillac were 210 hp at 4150 rpm and 330 foot-pounds at 2700 rpm.

Though Cadillac was biggest again, Lincoln did have other things. "True, Lincolns won the first four places among stock cars in the Mexican Pan-American Road Race, plus first among fine cars in the Mobilgas Economy Run," one ad pointed out. "But today's Lincoln is far more than a superbly powered car. It has a new kind of beauty that comes from the spirit of modern living. Its lines are clean — not pompous. Its interiors are striking without being ostentatious."

Outwardly, the 1953 Lincolns had styling that was basically the same as the previous year's model. A new chrome "V" insignia appeared on the upper section of the grille and the word Lincoln

The word "Lincoln" was spelled out on the hood of the 1953 models like this Capri convertible.

was printed in block letters across the face of the hood. The model lineup was unchanged, with a two-door pillarless coupe and a four-door sedan in the Cosmopolitan series. All these models plus a convertible were in the Capri line.

For some reason, the two-door Cosmopolitan was called a Sport Coupe and the Capri version was called a Hardtop Coupe. Lincoln introduced power steering and power brakes as extra-cost options in 1953.

Cosmopolitan models had a "V" insignia and the word "Cosmopolitan" on the rear door or quarter panel and untrimmed rocker panel moldings. Prices for the two body styles were the same as in 1952. The Sport Coupe even weighed the same, while the '53 version of the sedan gained 10 pounds. Lincoln reported building 6,562 examples of the two-door model and 7,560 of the sedans.

The flagship of the Lincoln line continued to be the Capri. Except for the chrome moldings on the rocker panels and the Capri signatures on the rear fenders, it was difficult to tell the fancier cars from their Cosmo counterparts. In this series, the two-door models had carryover prices, while the sedan cost $3,453 — or $93 more than the '52 version. Production totals reported for this series were 12,916 hardtops, 11,352 four-door sedans and 2,372 convertibles.

In the production race, Lincoln took the green flag quickly and was on pace for a record year until disaster struck. Between January

1953 and August of that season, Lincoln sales were running 67 percent ahead of comparable 1952 volume. But on August 12, a fire at General Motors' Hydra-Matic factory in Livonia, Michigan, stopped production of the Hydra-Matic-equipped Lincolns for 55 days. This reportedly caused Lincoln to lose 7,000 sales.

By the end of the year, sales were only 31 percent ahead of 1952. Calendar-year production wound up at 41,962 cars compared to 31,992 the previous year, but Lincoln's share of total industry output for the calendar year dropped to .69 percent (compared to .74 percent in 1952). Lincoln's model-year production topped out at 40,762 cars.

A noteworthy Lincoln event of 1953 took place on April 26, when Lincoln-Mercury Division staged an eight-day showing of its custom-built models. This "Detroit Style Preview of Tomorrow" production featured ornately-furnished production cars and an experimental "car of the future" named the XL-500. This show culminated in a big increase in sales — to a record 5,009 units — in May. In fact, despite the transmission factory fire, Lincoln set an all-time record of 39,169 dealer level sales and missed hitting an all-time production high by just 1,726 cars.

When the manufacturing of cars resumed after the fire, it was already November 11 and dealer's stocks were dangerously low. As a result, Lincoln switched over immediately to making 1954 models and the dealers had little problem cleaning out their inventory.

1954 *Lincoln*

The year 1954 was one in which Americans were very interested in modern ideas and modern new inventions. Baseball's World Series was broadcast in color for the first time and the New York Giants made the Cleveland Indians blue with a four game sweep. IBM ("Big Blue") told the world that it had created the first "electronic brain" for use in business applications. Elvis Presley made his first recordings (included were "Blue

Suede Shoes" and "Blue Moon of Kentucky") and General Electric introduced a new idea for modern living: pastel-colored home appliances.

Being "modern" was the key to success in 1954 and the '54 Lincoln was said to be, "Designed For Modern Living—Powered For Modern Driving." Advertising copywriters wrote: "If you like your living modern, if you want to drive the way you live, there is

A new bumper treatment and "check-mark" style stone guard were among 1954 Lincoln changes.

only one thing to do. Accept your Lincoln dealer's invitation to try a Lincoln or the Lincoln Capri. We believe you will never go back to old-fashioned driving!"

The overall look of the '54 model that bowed on Dec. 3, 1953 was similar to the previous Lincoln, but the details were cleaned up. The bumper-grille had a straighter, wider look and the rear fenders were more slab-sided than ever before. The cars were fractionally longer and wider, but the small increases in dimensions did make a true visual difference. Under the hood, Lincoln stuck with the 205-hp engine one more time. However, the engine had several refinements including a larger, more flexible distributor control, a carburetor with venting action, redesigned hydraulic tappets, and a novel filter element in the fuel pump.

The new combination bumper-grille with three vertical dividers between the bumper guards characterized the front-end design. A new "V" medallion appeared on the front of the hood. The moldings running down the sides of the cars started at a higher level a few inches above the front wheel opening. They started about a foot or so behind the chrome headlight ring and ran back to the taillights.

Ahead of the skirted rear fenders was a chrome trim plate from which a second molding extended rearwards toward the bumper. A ribbed triangular shield with a gold knight's head emblem decorated the trim plates. The rear bumper was of a new wraparound design and also new were the vertical taillight clusters, which were ribbed at the bottom of the red lenses.

Lincoln was particularly proud of its range of modern interior trim options. "You've never seen such dramatic colors and fabrics on wheels before," said one announcement that year. "Nylons, gabardines, broadcloths, genuine leathers (available in Capri sedans as well as in convertibles and coupes) – with shades ranging from pale Ivory to glowing Reds and deepest Blacks."

The base Cosmopolitan models had the Lincoln name on the front fenders and no series designations on the body sides. There was no chrome trim around the roof on the four-door

sedan and the Custom Coupe. Lincolns grew an inch in length 9214.8 inches) and width (77.4 inches) this year. The Cosmopolitan series again included just two models, a two-door hardtop coupe ($3,625, 4,155 pounds and 2,994 made) and a four-door sedan ($3,522, 4,135 pounds and 4,447 made).

Cars in the upper series had the Capri name in script above the triangular emblem on the rear doors or fenders and bright rocker panel moldings. The four-door sedan and Custom Coupe had chrome trim around the entire roof, in addition to chrome trim at the top of the side windows. There were again three cars in the lineup. The two-door hardtop (Custom Coupe) listed for $3,869, weighed 4,250 pounds and had a production run of 14,003. Lincoln built nearly as many (13,596) examples of the four-door sedan, which had a base retail price of $3,711 and weighed five pounds less than the hardtop. The $4,031 convertible weighed in at 4,310 pounds and had a run of 1,951 units.

Selling features of the 1954 Lincolns included two-stop doors, a center-fill gas tank, a full-flow oil filter, full-length water jackets, a fuel tank filter, a semi-floating rear axle with hypoid ring and pinion, a 63-plate battery, a four-barrel carburetor, an automatic choke, vented contact points, longitudinal semi-elliptic rear springs that required no lubrication, rotating valves with self-adjusting hydraulic lifters, two compression rings, and one expander-type oil ring for precision oil control. The brake drums were increased to 12 inches in diameter to provide 8.7 percent more gripping area.

Lincolns took first and second place at the 1954 Pan American Road Race. The race was won by Ray Crawford in a privately-entered Lincoln that had been prepared by Bill Stroppe. Walt Faulkner came in second in a factory-sponsored car. The other team cars were forced out of the contest through a combination of accidents and mechanical problems.

Lincoln's model-year saw 36,993 vehicles leaving the factory. Calendar-year output was 35,733 for a .65 percent share of industry. That made Lincoln America's 14th largest automaker.

1955 *Lincoln*

A longer Lincoln was offered in 1955 along with a new front bumper and revised tail section.

The year 1955 was one of classic innovations, changes and events that would have a long-lasting affect on American culture. On January 19, the board game Scrabble was introduced, challenging many future generations of spellers.

In the automotive world, the 1955 Lincoln was a classic case of a good car made even better. A new combination bumper-grille with multiple horizontal bars set into recessed grille openings gave the front end of all Lincolns a cleaner look. The new hooded headlight treatment seemed very Ford-like. The Lincoln name was lettered across the lip of the hood in bright block letters. Above it was a gold-outlined shield-like emblem. The hood ornament resembled a golden knight's head wearing a chrome helmet that extended over the nose of the car.

The taillight clusters were redesigned and slanted into the new tail fins. The all-new quarter panels had sleeker side blisters. Although the full-length side chrome spear remained, the rear fender stone shield was changed. It now curved down and rearwards from the point of the fender blister to the front edge of the rear fender skirt. On lower-priced Lincolns, the stone shield met a shorter chrome spear that ran back to the bumper, across the fender skirt. On Capris, the area below this molding was decorated with a wide band of chrome. All Lincolns retained the 123-inch wheelbase, but overall length increased to 215.6 inches.

The lower-priced series was now simply called "Lincoln" or "Custom" and had the Lincoln name, in a chrome script, on the front fenders just behind the headlights. There was no medallion or series nameplate on the rear fender blister and the simpler stone shield treatment was used. As usual, this series offered a Sport Coupe (two-door hardtop) and a four-door sedan.

Of the three Capri models, the $3,910 Sport Coupe was the most popular and 11,462 of these 4,305-pound cars were put together. The 4,245-pound sedan, despite its greater practicality and lower $3,752 list price, saw a lower 10,724 assemblies. As always, the 4,415-pound convertible remained the rarest Capri with its 1,487-unit production run. It was the first standard-production postwar Lincoln to break the $4,000 barrier (by $72).

The 1955 Lincoln's used a bigger, more powerful V-8. The new engine had a 3.93 x 3.50-inch bore and stroke. It developed 225 horsepower at 4400 rpm and 342 foot-pounds of torque at 2500 rpm. The engine had a new 8.5:1 compression ratio and retained a four-barrel Holley carburetor. Dual exhausts were standard with this motor.

Lincoln also introduced a new, Lincoln-built automatic transmission on all models in 1955. Promoted as "Turbo-Drive," this gearbox had a unique kickdown feature that allowed selection of different gear ranges with "the tip of a toe." The kickdown gear could be used to get instant acceleration or getaway or an intermediate gear could provide extra passing power.

Other hot 1955 Lincoln selling features included the ball-joint front suspension (which Lincoln had used for several years, but many other cars of the era still lacked), tubeless tires (new in 1955), two-position door checks, 8-leaf variable-rate rear springs, stamped-steel wheels, hydraulic valve lifters, a full-flow oil filter, an "automatic" four-barrel carburetor, foam rubber seats, a 50-ampere generator, double-panel doors, rotating-type overhead valves, full-vacuum spark control, pressure cooling, and baked enamel finish.

A novel new feature (which actually harkened back to the 1930s) was the Multi-Luber, a powered lubrication system. This device automatically lubricated all 11 chassis-lubrication points at the touch of a button.

Unfortunately, the classy 1955 Lincolns did not enjoy the classic high-production boost that most American automakers experienced in 1955. The best that could be said was that the year turned out to be the third most productive in the company's 33-year history. Calendar-year production was up slightly at 39,995 units, but that represented a significantly smaller .5 percent share of total industry output. Model-year production was 27,222 cars, the lowest since 1948.

On April 18, 1955, Lincoln became a separate division of the Ford Motor Company.

1956 *Lincoln*

The Lincoln Continental Mark II featured tasteful lines, a short deck, and long hood treatment.

The portable black-and-white television was an exciting new product in 1956. The year's redesigned Lincoln was also one exciting package. It came in black or white, too, but it looked far more enticing in pastel colors like salmon pink, lemon yellow, turquoise, and bright red. On Oct. 21, 1955, the brand new $9,500 Continental Mark II had its public introduction. This modern interpretation of the Edsel-Ford-designed Euro-styled original (of 1940) was an even more exciting product from Ford's new Lincoln Division. Even by that early date, more than 600 Lincoln dealers had signed up to sell the new, sophisticated, high-dollar, super-luxury model.

Even the regular Lincolns were attractively restyled for 1956. Their new look was based on the XL-500 and XM-800 concept cars and shared the show car's hooded headlights. The year's new radiator grille incorporated three full-width horizontal louvers above and below a massive horizontal center member that housed individual parking and directional lights at each side.

The rear fenders were now sculptured and culminated in pointed tail fins. There were taller new taillights with bumper ports beneath them that served as exhaust exits. A full-length tire-level side molding was incorporated onto the standard fender skirts. A new scored chrome trim band ran across the back of the car below the rear deck lid.

The new Lincolns were more than seven inches longer, 2-1/2 inches lower and two inches wider than the 1955 models. Under the hood was a new 368-cid V-8 with a 4.00 x 3.65-inch bore and stroke. This five-main-bearings motor used hydraulic valve lifters, a higher 9.0:1 compression ratio, and a Lincoln four-barrel carburetor. Other new features included bigger exhaust manifolds. As usual, Lincoln was aiming to top the 250-hp and 270-hp Cadillac V-8s of 1955, so it gave the new engine 285 hp at 4600 rpm (and 402 foot-pounds of torque at 3000 rpm). Unfortunately, the 1956 Cadillac V-8 came out with the same 285-hp rating.

The Sport Coupe and sedan in the Capri series had the Capri name in script, plus a "V" medallion, on each rear fender. All Lincolns had base prices above $4,000, though a bargain compared to the Continental's window sticker. The Lincoln Sport Coupe was $4,119 and the sedan was $4,212. The two cars weighed about the same (4,305 pounds for the coupe and 10 pounds more for the sedan) and had nearly the same production numbers, 4,355 for the two-door and 4,436 for the sedan.

It was easy to see why the new Lincoln Premiere won an award of excellence from the Industrial Designers Institute. It had all the good looks of the new Capri with tastefully bejeweled rear fenders sporting a gold star emblem and fancier wheel covers. Like all 1956 Ford products, the Premiere had a lot of safety-design features including improved door latches, a deep-dish steering wheel, and heavily padded seatbacks and door panels. Power windows and four-way power front seat were standard.

Like the former top-of-the-line series, the Premiere line offered buyers three models. Numbers for the Sport Coupe were $4,601, 4,357 pounds and 19,619 built. The four-door sedan had the same window sticker, weighed 10 pounds less and saw a nearly equal 19,465 assemblies. The sportiest Lincoln was the $4,747 convertible, which weighed 4,452 pounds and had a production run of 2,447 units.

The Lincoln-Continental name returned this year with the introduction of the Mark II. It made its world debut on Oct. 6, 1955, at the Paris Automobile Show. A long hood, short deck, restrained use of chrome and near perfect proportions helped the Mark II show the world just how beautiful a production American automobile could be.

Like its predecessors, it was an instant classic. Yet it was not an imitation of the original. The Mark II was unmistakably modern in design. Its $9,507 price accentuated how special this car was. It tipped the scales at 4,825 pounds and only 2,550 copies were made.

The Mark II V-8 used in the Continental was the Lincoln engine with a 10.0:1 compression ratio and a Carter four-barrel carburetor. This gave the Continental 300 hp at 4800 rpm and 415 foot-pounds of torque at 3000 rpm. In case you're wondering, that was less than the 1956 Cadillac Eldorado's 305 horses.

The Mark II engines were said to be "triple tested." Lincoln claimed every Continental V-8 was tested on a dynamometer alone, with its transmission attached and in the car.

Like the Lincoln, the Continental Mark II was built on a 126-inch-wheelbase chassis. It was 4-1/2 inches shorter at 218.5 inches. It was 77-1/2 inches long compared to the "big" Lincoln's 79.9-inch width.

Calendar-year production for 1956 was a record-breaking 47,670 Lincolns and 1,325 Continentals amounting to a .84 percent market share for both marques combined.

1957 *Lincoln*

The '57 Lincoln Premiere convertible appears to be at home in this sunny California setting.

"The bigger the better" was the thinking of most Americans in 1957. In California, the San Francisco and Los Angeles stock exchanges merged to form a larger entity. Nationally, the Gaither report suggested the United States could win the cold war with larger stocks of guided missiles and more fall-out shelters.

In one of the year's top films, moviegoers marveled as British POWs built a bigger-and-better bamboo bridge over the River Kwai for their Japanese captors. In Michigan, American engineers were stretching miles of cable and tons of concrete to make a five-mile-long bridge over the Straights of Mackinaw. At the time, The Mackinac Bridge boasted the world's longest suspension span between cable anchorages.

Automotively, the 1957 Lincolns expressed the bigger-is-better philosophy to the max. While all models retained a 126-inch wheelbase, the overall length of Capris and Premieres grew nearly two inches to 224.6 inches.

"No other car is so Lincoln long . . . Lincoln low . . . and Lincoln lovely!" said one advertisement. It wasn't only a few extra inches that made the cars look larger than life-size, they also had a pair of towering, canted, pointy tail fins that added to their immense image.

The unchanged Continental Mark II remained a smaller, more sophisticated-looking car, but only 587 were made as 1957 models. Apparently, a national economic downturn kept buyers out of Lincoln showrooms.

The Capri and Premiere models received a facelift that was unpopular with new-car buyers of the day, although today's collectors love its "fabulous '50s" flamboyance. Styling changes included a new Quadra-Lite grille, massive new front and rear bumpers, new rear deck lid trim and new series nameplate.

The Lincoln name, in block letters, was still spelled out across the front of the car. Wider parking and signal lights were seen. A full-length mid-body side molding blended with a piece of chrome below the rear windows that curved up to trim an air vent at the front of the canted tail fins. All 1957 Lincolns wore bright rocker panel moldings.

At the rear of the car, above the wraparound bumper ends, the body side moldings dipped down to accommodate V-shaped emblems. Continuation moldings outlined a ribbed beauty panel that ran across the rear end of the car. For the first time in years, the Lincoln's rear fenders were unskirted. A new stand-up hood ornament was used.

The Capri models, which were rarely shown in advertisements, had the model name in chrome script behind the headlights. A $4,734 four-door hardtop, called a Landau Hardtop Sedan, was a new body style. This was the heaviest Capri at 4,600 pounds. Only 1,451 of these cars were constructed. The pillared four-door sedan carried the same base price. It weighed 4,540 pounds and had a production run of just 1,476 units. The $4,589 two-door hardtop weighed in at 4,373 pounds and was the most popular Capri with 2,973 assemblies.

Except for the "Premiere" block lettering and star medallion on the front fenders, exterior differences between the Premiere and the Capri were very minor. Power seats, power steering, electric windows, and power brakes were standard equipment on the four-car upper series. The Premiere line also gained a four-door Landau Hardtop Sedan priced at $5,233 and weighing 4,538 pounds. It was bought by 11,223 customers.

The $5,088 two-door hardtop was even more popular. This 4,451-pound Sport Coupe saw 15,185 assemblies. The four-door sedan, priced the same as the four-door hardtop, had a 4,527-pound weigh-in and 5,139 were produced. The rarest big Lincoln continued to be the convertible. In 1957, it sold for $5,321, weighed 4,676 pounds and only 3,676 examples were turned out.

This was the second and last year for the beautiful Mark II. Outside of a slightly lighter frame, it was identical to the previous year's model. Two convertibles were specially built. Power steering, power brakes, carpeting, radio, heater, power seats, power windows and white sidewall tires were standard. The price was increased to $9,891. It tipped the scales at 4,800 pounds. As mentioned earlier, model-year production was 587 units.

Lincoln retained the 368-cid engine for all of its 1957 models, but the output was boosted to Mark II V-8 specs (300 hp at 4800 rpm and 415 foot-pounds of torque at 3000 rpm). This matched the power of the base Cadillac V-8, but the 325-hp Eldorado with twin four-barrel carburetors was still more powerful, as was the Hemi-powered 345-hp Chrysler Imperial. Still, there was no doubt the Lincolns and Continentals had plenty of "juice" for highway cruising.

Although it was bigger in size, bigger in power and bigger in luxury, the 1957 Lincoln had a much smaller production total than its predecessor. Model-year production came to 41,123 Lincolns and 587 Continentals. Calendar-year output declined from 47,670 in 1956 to 37,426 in 1957.

1958 *Lincoln*

Lincoln introduced dramatically new styling in 1958, like this Continental Mark III Landau.

The '50s was an era that worshipped the "latest and the greatest" and 1958 was a year full of new trivia and trends. On the dance floor, the "Cha-Cha-Cha" was all the rage. New in the home entertainment world was the stereo record.

All 1958 Lincoln models shared a completely new body design, as well as a new engine.

Four different "Lincoln Continental" models were available and hold the distinction of being the largest regular-production cars in America's postwar automotive history. In certain parts of the country, owners were legally obligated to place red reflectors on the rear of their new Lincolns and amber clearance lights on the front. All models had a 131-inch wheelbase and a 229-inch overall length.

Interestingly, the 1958 Continental was called the Mark III and was originally perceived as the third in the line of "classic" Continentals. That line included the 1940 to 1948 series and the high-priced 1956 to 1957 specialty model. The very similar 1959 model would then be dubbed the Mark IV, with the Mark V — also similar — arriving in 1960.

These cars weren't well received in their day—but are collectible today. Lincoln's cleaner design in 1961, showed even some corporate backlash against the over-stylized giants.

Later in its history, the company would "disavow" the 1958-1960 cars were true Continentals by reviving the Continental Mark III designation in 1970. That car was followed by the 1972 Mark IV and the 1977 Mark V.

The 1958 to 1960 models must be viewed in the context of their times and other designs like the 1958 Oldsmobile and 1959 Cadillac to be truly "understood" and appreciated. The Capri and Premiere were completely changed automobiles with lines shared by the 1958 Continental. Lincoln switched to unitized body construction in 1958, eliminating the chassis. The suspension, driveline and engine units were fastened to the body structure.

A new horizontally-louvered grille with five wide-spaced vertical members graced the front end. The Lincoln name was spelled, in gold script, on the left-hand side of the grille. One of the standout design characteristics of the cars was their canted dual headlights and upper front fenders. The lower front fender sides were heavily sculptured to create a "cove" around the front wheel opening. Sculptured fender panels accented the rear wheel openings. New, lower tail fins were also canted outwards and had chrome-trimmed rear points.

At the rear was a new oval-shaped bright metal grille that ran across the back end and housed three taillights on either side. A unique roof design, stylized front and rear bumpers and wraparound front and rear windows were other traits. The side chrome spears were lower and not as long as those used on the previous year's model.

In addition to a low, pointed sweep spear molding on the doors and rear fender, Capris had their model name in script on the rear fenders. Both the four-door sedan and the Landau (four-door hardtop) were priced at $4,951. The former weighed 4,799 pounds and had 1,184 assemblies; the latter weighed 11 pounds more and 3,084 were built. The last model was the two-door hardtop that listed for $4,803, weighed 4,735 pounds and had a 2,591-unit production run.

A chrome rocker panel, a star at the forward tip of the side chrome spear and its distinct nameplate were the easiest ways to tell cars in the Premiere series. Lincoln Premiere buyers could get either leather-and-fabric or all-fabric upholstery. This car-line included the same three body styles. The price was $5,505 for the four-door cars and $5,259 for the two-door hardtop. They weighed within a few pounds of their Capri counterparts and garnered more sales. Lincoln built 1,660 sedans, 5,572 Landau Hardtops and 3,043 Sport Coupes.

The 1956 and '57 Mark II featured a criss-cross pattern aluminum grille. A full-length lower-body molding and a grid pattern rear panel were exclusive to the new Mark III. A retractable rear window meant with a flick of the switch on the driver's armrest, the rear window slid from sight to provide open-car ventilation.

The Continental convertible featured a glass back window that slid out of sight at the touch of a button. There was an exclusive two-tone top with the same "roof line" as other Continental models. The top folded out of sight, beneath a hinged, all-steel, flat-topped rear deck panel.

The Premiere four-door sedan and Landau Hardtop both sold for $6,012 and each weighed just under 4,900 pounds. Lincoln made 1,283 of the first and 5,891 of the second. The Sport Coupe sold for $5,765, weighed 4,802 pounds and had a run of 2,328 production units. The $6,223 convertible tipped the scale at 4,927 pounds and found a surprising 3,048 customers.

Lincoln's new V-8 had a 4.29 x 3.70-inch bore and stroke and 430 cubic inches. A 10.5:1 compression ration and Holley four-barrel carburetor contributed to a 375 hp at 4800 rpm rating. The combustion chambers of this engine were fully machined right into the engine block, instead of into the cylinder head. This simplified design was said to "squeeze more power out of every drop of gas." The engine was hooked to a Twin Range Turbo-

Drive automatic transmission which was redesigned and enlarged to transmit increased torque output and provide faster, smoother response.

Two percent of Lincolns wasn't a very large number in 1958. The company's model-year production fell to 29,684 cars against 41,710 the previous season. That 28 percent decline can be contributed to a disapproval of styling changes and more.

Lincoln had picked the recession year to change its marketing program to emphasize sales of the higher-priced Premieres and Continentals. Things might have been a bit better if the Capri had been featured in more advertisements. Today, 1958 Lincolns of any series are hard-to-find, pricey discoveries.

1959 *Lincoln*

The most popular Lincoln Continental Mark IV model in 1959 was the four-door hardtop.

William C. Scott, president of Outboard Marine Corporation; Gen. Carlos P. Romulo, a Philippine soldier, statesman and diplomat; venerable actress Helen Hayes; Donald Douglas, chairman of Douglas Aircraft Company of Los Angeles. All of these 1959 personalities drove Lincolns or Lincoln Continentals and each appeared in a Lincoln Motor Car Company advertisement that year.

"Design is the vital thing—and Lincoln proves it beautifully," noted Donald Douglas, who drove a powder blue Premiere version of the same body style to his home in Rolling Hills. Using such endorsements, Lincoln was trying to make its controversial styling more powerful to America's elite, who bought luxury automobiles. The plan didn't work very well as model-year production took another tumble to 26,906 Lincolns and Lincoln Continentals. On a calendar-year basis, the number of cars built was a bit higher at 30,375, but that included 12,000 or so 1960 models.

Major 1959 styling changes included a U-shaped grille with the integrated headlights. The front parking lights were set into "delta wing" nacelles at the outer ends of the bumper. New bright brushed aluminum trim underscored the rear quarter panel. A redesigned rear grille contained a scored decorative insert, oval-shaped taillights and rectangular back-up lights.

All 1959 Lincolns were equipped with Turbo-Drive dual-range automatic transmission, power brakes, power steering, dual exhaust, back-up lights, an electric clock, foam rubber cushions, a padded instrument panel and sun visors, wheel covers, a non-glare inside rearview mirror and a remote-control outside mirror.

The Capri became the basic Lincoln in 1959. It was nearly two inches shorter than the previous year's model, but with its 227 inches of overall length nobody confused it with a Rambler American. The body side chrome trim was a bit gaudier. The brushed-aluminum trim covered the lower quarter panel and was connected to a chrome spear (at a level above the rear tires) that continued almost to the front fender. The sedan sold for $5,090, weighed 5,030 pounds and had a run of 1,312 units; the Landau Hardtop sold for $5,090, weighed 5,000 pounds and had a run of 4,417 units and the Hardtop Coupe sold for $4,902, weighed 4,925 pounds and had a run of 2,200 units.

The best way to identify a Premiere was to look for its name-plate. On the outside, these cars looked the same as those in the lowest-priced Lincoln series. Premieres came with power windows, a rear license plate frame and a Four-Way power front seat.

The Premiere sedan sold for $5,594, weighed 5,030 pounds and had a run of 1,282 units; the Landau Hardtop sold for $5,594, weighed 5,015 pounds and had a run of 4,606 units and the Hardtop Coupe sold for $5,347, weighed 4,920 pounds and had a run of 1,963 units.

The Continental Mark IV featured a criss-cross pattern grille, a full-length lower body molding, four taillights and a reverse slant-rear window that could be lowered. The back window of the convertible was made of glass and was retractable.

Mark IV equipment included Turbo-Drive dual-range automatic transmission, power brakes, power steering, a non-glare inside rearview mirror, a remote-control outside mirror, Six-Way power seats, power-operated vent, side and back windows, tinted glass, a Travel-Tuner radio with dual speakers and white sidewall tires. They were available in exclusive metallic paints.

The sedan sold for $6,845, weighed 5,155 pounds and had a run of 955 units. The Landau Hardtop sold for $6,845, weighed 5,155 pounds and had a run of 1,703. There were three other body styles in this series. The convertible sold for $7,056, weighed 5,175 pounds and had a run of 2,195 units. A Formal Sedan sold for $9,208, weighed 5,450 pounds and had a run of 78 units. The Executive Limousine sold for $10,230, weighed 5,450 pounds and had a run of just 78 units.

In 1959, the Lincoln 430-cid V-8 was slightly de-tuned. The compression ratio dropped down to 10.0:1. This reduced the horsepower rating to 350 at 4400 rpm, while torque declined to 490 foot-pounds at 2800 rpm (from 490 at 3100 rpm). To make the cars look lower, Lincoln changed to new 9.50 x 14 tires.

Mercurys
of the Fifties

1950 Mercury

An unmodified 1950 Mercury convertible shows how the originals appeared.

Throughout this book, we have tried to relate some of the events that took place in the 1950s with the cars built in those years, but in the case of the 1949 to 1951 Mercurys, the cultural tie-in is the film "Rebel Without a Cause," released in 1955. Starring James Dean, director Nicholas Ray's film took one of the first realistic looks at teen life in postwar America.

Dean played the troubled teen anti-hero who tried to take on the world. His co-stars in this classic included Natalie Wood, Sal Mineo, Dennis Hopper and a customized 1949 Mercury coupe. The car still survives in the collection of the National Automobile Museum in Reno, Nevada. Today the 1949 to 1951 models are affectionately known as the "James Dean Mercs."

For 1950, the basic Mercury styling was similar to the famed movie-mobile. As in 1949, the M-E-R-C-U-R-Y name appeared on the front of the hood, but it was embossed into a bar-shaped chrome emblem. Instead of being separate as in 1949, the parking and signal lights were set into rectangular chrome housings at the ends of the grille. The trunk chrome design was altered, as was the tip on the chrome body side spear. The biggest change was inside the car where a new and completely restyled "Safe-T-Vue" instrument panel appeared.

Technical improvements were also made. A new "Econ-O-Mizer" carburetor was designed to prevent vapor lock and stalling, while giving greater economy of operation. In its salesman's guide, Mercury claimed owners had reported between 17 to 19 mpg from their '49 models and promised better performance with the 1950 cars.

Mercury said a new straight-pull parking brake was: "...50% more efficient." A new "Stedi-Line" steering system included a redesigned steering wheel and a higher steering ratio. In addition, the use of new narrow-tread tires also made steering easier.

Other top selling features of the 1950 Mercurys included a trunk lid lock, "Super-Safety" brakes, a short turning radius, a front suspension stabilizer bar, foam rubber seat cushions, "Mid-Section" seating, a rear seat foot rest, "Cushion Coil" springs, three-point engine mountings, a counter-balanced crankshaft, precision timing, low-pressure tires, a hood safety catch, concealed running boards, dual air-electric horns, directional turn indicators, safety-type inside door handles, an inside hood latch and courtesy lights.

There was just one series of cars with seven models. The least expensive was the six-passenger coupe for $1,875. It also was the lightest Mercury, tipping the scale at 3,345 pounds. The priciest body style was the convertible, which retailed at $3,412 and up. Only 8,341 ragtops were built. The heaviest Mercury—due to its wood-trimmed body—was the station wagon. It weighed in at 3,755 pounds. With a production run of 1,746, it was the rarest Mercury made that year.

To compete with General Motors' and Chrysler's two-door hardtops, Mercury introduced the Monterey coupe with a $2,146 list price. It featured a padded canvas or vinyl top and a custom leather interior. A total of 151,489 Mercury coupes were made in 1950, but there were no separate breakouts.

Even though other automakers of the early '50s were moving to overhead-valve V-8 engines, Mercury stuck to a flathead V-8 with a 3.19 x 4.00-inch bore and stroke. The 255.4-cid engine had three main bearings, solid valve lifters, a 6.80:1 compression ratio and a Holley two-barrel carburetor. It was rated for 110 hp at 3600 rpm and 200 foot-pounds of torque at 2000 rpm. These Mercurys rode on a chassis with a 118-inch wheelbase and all models except the "woody" wagon were 206.8 inches long. The station wagon was 213.5 inches long. Tread widths were 58.5 inches in front and 60 inches in the rear. Size 7.10 x 15 tires were standard equipment.

The one-millionth Mercury was built during 1950. It was a basic four-door sedan. Mercurys won two NASCAR Grand National races this year and a Mercury convertible served as the official pace car for the 1950 Indianapolis 500.

Production of the 1950 Mercury models began in November 1949. Output for the model year peaked at 293,658, which was slightly down from 1949 when the all-new postwar styling first appeared. Calendar-year production was 238,854 cars, representing a 4.47 percent share of the total market. Mercury was America's eighth largest automobile manufacturer in 1950.

1951 Mercury

This 1951 Mercury convertible sports fender skirts, a popular option in the 1950s.

The year 1951 was a year of some notable births. Actress Jane Seymour was born on February 15th. The famed clothing designer Tommy Hilfiger arrived on March 24 and stock car legend Dale Earnhardt made his appearance on April 29. Another new arrival was conceived when the Mercury Division of Ford Motor Company mated with Borg-Warner Corporation to create Merc-O-Matic Drive — the automaker's first automatic transmission.

This transmission included a pair of automatic forward gear ranges — Intermediate and High — as well as Emergency Low (for rocking out of mud and snow) and Reverse. After the car got going, it would automatically change to High gear range between 17 mph and 62 mph. If the car slowed to less than six miles per hour, the transmission gears automatically switched back into the Intermediate range. "Merc-O-Matic is smoother, more efficient and thriftier, too!" said one advertisement.

With the addition of the new fully-automatic transmission, Mercury gave buyers what it promoted as a "3-way choice" of transmissions. The standard three-speed manual gear box with the gearshifter on the steering column was the basic setup. Touch-O-Matic overdrive was the next choice and the top option was Merc-O-Matic.

Things were pretty much the same with Mercurys as they'd been the previous season. The same bodies were used again, although the front end carried a new grille that was integrated with the directional signals. Vertical taillights replaced the horizontal type found on the 1949 and 1950 Mercurys. New, fluted lower rear quarter panel trim, behind the rear wheel openings, made the wraparound bumper appear to extend even further around the sides of the cars than before. The rear window now featured one-piece glass that gave the driver a wider view out the rear of the car. Chrome gravel shields and rocker panels, a vinyl or canvas roof, and a custom interior were standard on the Monterey coupe.

Mercury offered buyers the same seven body styles in 1951 at prices between $1,745 and $2,530. There were two coupes, a cloth-topped Monterey (formerly called the Monterey Business Coupe), a "leather" topped Monterey (formerly called the Monterey Custom Coupe), a four-door Sport Sedan, a convertible, and the station wagon. Production-wise, all coupes (even Montereys) were counted together and 142,166 were built. Mercury also put together 157,648 Sport Sedans, 6,759 convertibles and 3,812 "woody" wagons.

Mercury stuck with its 255.4-cid "Hi-Power Compression" flathead V-8 for under-hood chores using the same 6.8:1 compression ratio and same Holley two-barrel carburetor. However, the power output went up by two horsepower to 112 at 3600 rpm. Torque also increased very slightly to 206 foot-pounds at 2000 rpm. The Mercury engine included exhaust valve inserts, a gear-type oil pump, a counter-balanced crankshaft, and three-point engine mounting system, which were all promoted as selling features.

Other heavily-promoted Mercury features and benefits included plastic parking lights and taillights, a medallion steering wheel, foam seat cushions, low-pressure tires, a cable-type parking brake, a "Safe-T-Vue" instrument panel, an inside hood latch, courtesy lights, a trunk lid lock, fiberglass insulation, "Cushion-Coil" springing, a short turning radius, all-steel body construction, big quick-acting brakes, and "Econ-O-Mizer" carburetion. Mercury placed first in its class in the Mobilgas Economy Run for the second year in a row.

The 1951 Mercurys were advertised as "Restful Riding" cars built from the ground up with passenger comfort in mind. They rode on a 118-inch wheelbase chassis and had the same overall lengths as in 1950. The four-door Sport Sedan was 76-20/32 wide and 63 inches high. It had a shipping weight of 3,470 pounds. Size 7.10 x 15 black sidewall tires were standard equipment.

In terms of model-year production, it was a good year for Mercury with a record 310,387 cars leaving the assembly lines in Detroit and Wayne County, Michigan, Los Angeles, California, St. Louis, Missouri, and in Metuchen, New Jersey. This brought the company's all-time output since 1939 up to 1,390,000 cars of which 81 percent had been built since World War II ended. Calendar-year production reflected a drop to 238,854 cars from 334,081 in 1950.

This decline had little to do with product popularity and more to do with the worsening intensity of the Korean Conflict. The calendar-year figures included late-summer and fall production of 1952 models and the numbers were capped by government restrictions on output enacted as a wartime conservation measure. The reality was, as *Ward's Automotive Yearbook 1952* put it: "...sales consistently prodded production." In other words, the Mercurys were so well accepted the company was able to sell more cars than the National Production Agency would allow it to build.

1952 Mercury

The 1952 Mercury Monterey convertible features a popular '50s option, the continental kit.

In 1952, television, like today's Internet, was a frontier of new and interesting ideas. Some new shows that premiered this year would become landmarks in American television history. On Jan. 14, 1952, NBC viewers saw the first "Today Show" with anchor Dave Garroway. In Philadelphia, teens watched the premier of "American Bandstand," later an ABC network staple. And CBS viewers saw the first live link between East and West coasts on Edward R. Murrow's "See It Now."

Mercury's TV and print advertising was aimed at those who wanted to see proof to be convinced of a new car's practicality. And FoMoCo gave the economy of its all-new '52 models the hard sell.

"It's hot — Mercury. 'America's No. 1 Economy Car!" said one pitch line. "Why buy a 'back-number' — when you can get this years-ahead economy champion?" asked another. "No 1. in Ecomomy Run," another ad pointed out, to stress that the '52 Merc had again run off with top honors in the nation's most famous test of on-the-road economy . . . the Mobilgas Economy Run. "Take a look at Mercury's record," the company urged car shoppers. "3 wins in its class in 3 years. That's economy you can count on – the kind of economy you want in your car."

Like all Ford Motor Company cars, the Mercurys were completely restyled for 1952. They featured a one-piece curved windshield, a wraparound rear window, a fake hood scoop, a massive integrated bumper-grille and vertical taillights and back-up lights encased in chrome in a manner that made them look like extensions of the rear bumper. The fender-level hood line helped give all 1952 Mercurys an aggressive look.

"Nothing warmed over here," said one advertisement. "Mercury's new all over—from the Interceptor panel with pilot-type controls to the six more inches of hip room in the rear seat, from the Jet-scoop hood to the swift, tapered lines of the graceful rear deck. Walk around, step inside, compare. Then you'll see how really new a car can be."

A new Custom series was the base car-line, while the Monterey name was now used on the cars in a new and fancier series. Although it was Mercury's entry-level car, the Custom came in a full lineup of five body styles that included a two-door Sport Coupe, a two-door sedan, a four-door sedan and six- and eight-passenger station wagons. Prices ranged from $1,987 to $2,570. The total production of all 1952 Custom and Monterey four-door sedans was 63,475. The total production of all station wagons was 2,487. The company also produced 30,599 Custom Sport Coupes and 25,812 Custom two-door sedans. Suspended pedals were new and the rear doors of Mercury sedans now opened in the conventional manner, swinging forward.

Except for the addition of chrome rocker panel moldings and fancier wheel covers, the exterior styling of the Monterey models resembled that of the cars in the lower-priced Custom series. Standard Monterey features included a two-tone paint job and a leather-and-vinyl interior. This series included Mercury's first two-door hardtop (24,453 built), the four-door sedan and a convertible (5,261 built).

This year, Mercury boosted compression of the 255.4-cid flathead V-8 up to 7.2:1. Otherwise, things were pretty much the same, but the higher compression ratio upped advertised horse-power by 12 percent to 125 at 3700 rpm. Developed torque also climbed the same 12 percent to 211 foot-pounds at 2000 rpm. Underhood improvements included a new "Centri-Flo" carbure-tor, an automatic choke, a waterproof ignition system, and improved vacuum spark control. A three-speed manual transmis-sion was standard. Overdrive and Merc-O-Matic automatic trans-mission were optional.

Drastically changed on the outside, the 1952 Mercurys also fea-tured some important new internal features including a new box-type frame with five supporting cross members that cradled the rid-ers between the axles in a "comfort zone."

Both series continued to use a 118-inch wheelbase. The overall length was down a bit more than four inches at 202.2. Tread widths were 58 inches up front and 56 inches rear. Most models used 7.10 x 15 tires, but convertibles and station wagons came with 7.60 x 15 tires.

Selling features included integral rear fenders, a "Mono-Pane" windshield, a "Finger-Lift" hood, airscoop trim, Hotchkiss drive, dual-duct ventilation, "Stedi-Line" steering, a "Feather-Lift" trunk lid and "Auto Action" brakes. Almost half of all 1952 Mercurys came with automatic transmission and about 33 percent of the manual shift cars were equipped with a three-speed with overdrive.

While the new Mercurys were modern-looking automobiles with good economy and performance, it turned out to be a bad year for business as a steelworkers strike, wartime government restrictions, and parts shortages teamed up to hold model-year out-put more than 18 percent below 1951 levels at 172,087 units.

Calendar-year production came in at 195,261 cars. While below the 1951 record, this number represented 4.5 percent of all United States auto sales compared to a 4.47 percent share the previous year.

1953 Mercury

Aftermarket "spinner" wheel covers have been added to this '53 Mercury Monterey convertible.

In 1953, the Korean War ended with an armistice and "Ike" (President Eisenhower) ended all wage, salary and price con-trols. People sat in theaters wearing cardboard eyeglasses with one green lens and one red lens to watch the first 3-D movie called "Bwana Devil." Airplane buffs marveled when Jacqueline Cochran became the first woman to go faster than the speed of sound in her F-86 Sabrejet. Ads invited automobile buffs to visit their Mercury dealer to "…test the best-performing Mercury in his-tory."

While that might have been true overall, it did not reflect any changes under the hood, where a 125-hp flathead V-8 resided for one last year. An enlarged tailpipe and new, straight-through muf-fler greatly reduced back pressure and may have added a little more on-the-road go power.

The 1953 Mercurys that entered production on Dec. 9, 1952, again came in two series. The Mercury Custom line was cut back to three body styles, the Sport Coupe, the two-door sedan and the four-door sedan. The Monterey Special Custom line now contained four body types — the coupe, the four-door sedan, the convertible, and the station wagon. This reduced the model count

from eight to seven. All models again had a 118-inch stance and 202.2-inch overall length. Maximum body width was 74 inches. The four-door sedan was 64-7/64 inches high.

A major styling change for 1953 was made to the Mercury grille. It was still integrated with the bumper, but the bumper guards were now bullet-shaped. Side chrome trim consisted of a full-length mid-body spear and rear fender molding. The "Two-Stop" doors could stay in position either halfway or fully opened. This was promoted as: "…a great convenience in the garage, drive-way or other narrow places." The trunk featured a new medallion.

Cars in the Mercury Custom series had the word "Mercury" on the rear fenders, while the front fenders carried no nomenclature. The two- and four-door sedans had narrow chrome rear quarter trim with three diagonal scores, but didn't have chrome around the side windows. The two-door sedan came without rear wheel "pants" (fender skirts). The Sport Coupe had horizontally-scored rear quarter chrome, but the chrome trim did not completely sur-round the side windows.

The Mercury Custom two-door sedan retailed for just $2,004 and weighed 3,405 pounds. Mercury built 50,183 of these value-leader cars. The four-door sedan could be bought for as little as $2,057 and thanks to those extra doors and door mechanisms, it weighed an additional 45 pounds. With 59,794 assemblies, the four-door sedan was the most popular Custom. Chances are it's still the most available model today. Prices for the Sport Coupe started at $2,117. It weighed 3,465 pounds and 39,547 were assembled.

Two-tone paint, fender skirts and chrome rocker panels were standard on Mercury's top-of-the-line Monterey Special Custom series. In addition to the Mercury name on the rear fenders, the Monterey name was placed on the upper front fenders (except on those built early in the model year). Montereys also had chrome rocker panel moldings and chrome trim around the side windows. The four-door sedan had wide multi-scored chrome trim on the rear quarters of the body. The Special Custom Coupe had horizontally-scored chrome rear quarters and chrome trim that completely surrounded the side windows. The rear side windows of the station wagon featured sliding glass.

The four models in the series ranged in price from $2,133 for the 3,425-pound four-door sedan to $2,591 for the 3,765-pound wood-trimmed station wagon. The convertible carried a $2,390 list price and tipped the scale at 3,585 pounds. The 3,465-pound two-door hardtop had prices that started at $2,244. The hardtop was

the most popular Monterey with 76,119 assemblies and the station wagon was rarest with 7,719 built. Production of the other models was 64,038 for the four-door sedan and 8,463 for the ragtop.

Technically, the 1953 models were about the same as in 1952. Power brakes were first offered in April of 1953. Fifteen percent of Mercurys were eventually equipped with them. A month later, power steering was introduced. Only eight percent of 1953 Mercurys were sold with this option. Other rare-to-find extras included an electric seat adjuster and electric window regulators.

With government restrictions relaxed, Mercury was able to sell the new cars to its potential and realized a nearly 64 percent gain in production in 1953. Model-year output zoomed to 305,863 cars, the second best in history. For the calendar year, the total was a record-smashing 320,369 units. Even better, this represented a much larger share of overall industry totals at 5.22 percent. Mercury announced that the year's output raised its all-time production total to 1,900,000 vehicles.

One of the 1953 cars — a Monterey convertible — turned out to be the 40-millionth vehicle built by Ford Motor Company since its start, 50 years earlier, in 1903. In December 1953, Mercury introduced its first overhead-valve V-8 for use in 1954 models. For the company, 1953 truly turned out to be "that wonderful year."

1954 Mercury

Tom Collins

New for 1954 was the Sun Valley that featured tinted Plexiglas in the front portion of the roof.

In 1954, prices on the New York Stock Exchange skyrocketed to their highest levels since 1929, the year of the crash and beginning of the Great Depression. Americans' worries about nuclear fallout inspired them to start building backyard bomb shelters. On the plus side of the ledger, the first successful kidney transplant promised a healthier future for those whom radioactivity didn't get. When they weren't worrying about nuclear waste disposal, Americans were flocking to the movies to see flicks like "On the Waterfront," "Rear Window" and "The Seven Samurai."

Like the stock market, Mercury's postwar sales were skyrocketing. According to one 1954 advertisement, there had been a 480 percent increase in the number of Mercurys on the road since 1946. According to the copywriters, this translated into more car sales per dealer and lower overhead expenses per car. It suggested Mercury dealers: "...can afford to give you a better deal."

Mercury also promoted "years-ahead styling," although the cars looked basically the same as 1953 models. Wraparound vertical taillights were the most noticeable change made in 1954. The grille was modestly restyled, but was still integrated with the front bumper. The model name was written in chrome on the rear fenders, above the full-length mid-body-side spear. Also redesigned were the bright metal stone shields and the chrome-plated wind split moldings on the leading edges of the rear fenders. A new overhead-valve V-8 was under the hood and a new ball-joint front suspension improved handling and ride qualities.

Cars in the Mercury Custom series had the Mercury name, in chrome script, on the rear fenders. There were three models starting with the two-door sedan for $2,194, continuing with the four-door sedan for $2,251 and ending with the two-door hardtop for $2,315. Weights ranged from 3,435 pounds to 3,480 pounds.

The four-door model had no chrome trim above the side windows and standard chrome trim around the windshield. In addition to 15,234 hardtops, Mercury put together 37,146 two-door and 32,687 four-door sedans. All of these models shared an unchanged 118-inch wheelbase and measured 206.2 inches overall.

Cars in the Monterey line featured name in chrome script above the side trim on the rear fender. Round medallions were placed near the tip of the chrome side spear on the front fenders and on the rear quarter posts. Chrome rocker panel moldings and rear fender skirts were standard on all models except the station wagon. All models had special wide chrome trim on the windshield posts and chrome trim above the side windows.

The most unique Monterey model was the Sun Valley two-door hardtop. The front half of its roof was made of a green-tinted, transparent Plexiglas panel. As in previous years, the station wagon had simulated wood trim.

There were five Montereys with prices ranging from $2,333 for the four-door sedan to $2,776 for the wagon. Weights of the five cars were in the 3,515- to 3,735-pound range. The station wagon, of which 11,656 copies were built, was priciest and heaviest '54 Merc. The $2,610 convertible was rarest with 7,293 assembles.

The Sun Valley hardtop was built only 9,761 times. In contrast, the regular two-door hardtop was the most popular model of the year with 79,533 put together. The sedan with 65,995 assemblies was a rather distant second.

With a 3.62 x 3.10-inch bore and stroke, the new V-8 brought Mercury into the valve-in-head era. It had almost the same displacement — 256 cid versus 255.4 — as the previous flathead. It was rated 36 hp higher than the old engine.

Like Ford's new V-8, it was promoted as a "Y" block because the 90-degree cylinder banks appeared to form the upper arms of the letter "Y," while the deep skirt extending below the crankshaft centerline formed the vertical leg of a "Y." The five-main-bearings power plant used a 7.5:1 compression ratio and a Holley four-barrel carburetor. It delivered 161 hp at 4400 rpm and 238 lbs.-ft. of torque at 2500 rpm. A three-speed manual transmission was standard. Overdrive and Merc-O-Matic automatic transmission were optional.

Although Mercury set a new-car sales record for the first quarter of 1954 and gained 20 percent over 1953 by the end of the first half, its model-year output was 259,306 vehicles. That was the fifth best production run in company history.

This was largely due to an eight-week strike over work standards in the St. Louis plant beginning July 19. The strike was said to have cost workers $1.2 million in wages and Mercury 14,000 car assemblies. Calendar-year output peaked at 256,729 for a lower-than-1953 market share of 4.66 percent. That made Mercury America's seventh largest-selling car, a notch down from the sixth rank it had gained in 1953.

1955 *Mercury*

It didn't get much better in 1955 than the Montclair convertible.

Wherever you looked, memorable things were taking place in 1955. Dr. Martin Luther King Jr. was in the news with the bus boycott in Montgomery, Alabama— the first big civil rights demonstration. "Ike" was struck with a heart attack.

The nation watched television shows like "Truth or Consequences," "Name That Tune," and "You'll Never Get Rich." It was also a good year for future Hollywood buffs, as Kirstie Alley, Kevin Costner and Debra Winger, all born that year.

A restyled '55 Mercury entered the world, too. The year's 11 models were arranged in three series called Mercury Custom, Mercury Monterey and — new at the top — Mercury Montclair. The cars were longer (119-inch wheelbase; 206.3 inches overall), lower (60.5-63.1 inches), and wider (76.4 inches).

Wagons had a one-inch shorter wheelbase and were slightly shorter overall. Although modernized, they continued to bear a definite resemblance to the 1954 models. The redesigned bumper-integrated grille had three heavy vertical bars between the upper and lower bumper. "Mercury" was spelled out in block letters on the center horizontal member.

A new "Big M" medallion decorated the front of the hood. The hooded, forward-canted headlights looked very distinctive. A "Full-Scope" one-piece wraparound windshield was another update. As usual, side trim treatments were revised and varied according to series and model. New bumper guards were seen. The tall, vertical taillights had a "chubby cheeks" look.

The Custom had slightly different side chrome than the other series. Sedans and hardtops in this series had a "Mercury" script on their front fenders, but no round medallions. The sweep spear molding on the rear fender was mounted higher than on the Montclair and Monterey models and the large metal molding at its forward end was shorter, with a more horizontal design that used on other series. The Mercury Custom station wagon had no fake wood trim.

Four Customs were priced from $2,218 to $2,686. Production totals were 7,040 for the two-door hardtop, 13,134 for the all-steel six-passenger station wagon, 21,219 for the four-door sedan and 31,295 for the popularity-leading two-door sedan.

On the mid-range Montereys, the model name appeared in script on the front fenders of passenger cars, along with a round medallion. On Monterey station wagons, simulated wood-grained exterior panels were standard and dictated moving the chrome name script and medallion to the rear door.

Rear fender trim on the cars was lower than the Custom, running at a level just above the rear fender skirts. Chrome rocker panel moldings and bright chrome moldings underneath the windows were standard. There were three Montereys, the $2,400 four-door sedan (70,392 built), the $2,465 two-door hardtop (69,093

built), and the $2,844 four-door station wagon (11,968 built). At 3,510 to 3,770 pounds, the Montereys were about 100 pounds heavier than Customs.

The new four-model Montclair series was now the flagship of the line. The strong seller in the series was the regular all-steel-topped two-door hardtop, which listed for $2,631 and realized 71,588 assemblies. In contrast, the four-door sedan, priced $54 higher, found only 20,624 buyers. The $2,712 Sun Valley hardtop moved to this series and its production was just 1,787 units. Even the ragtop, with the same price, had a higher 10,668-unit run.

In addition to round medallions and the model name scripts on the front fenders, Montclairs also had a narrow band of chrome under the side windows, which outlined a small panel that was often painted in a contrasting color. The Montclairs stood lower than other Mercurys and this design feature was heavily promoted in ads. As in 1954, the unique Sun Valley hardtop had a tinted Plexiglas section over the front half of its roof.

This year, all Mercurys used a larger overhead-valve V-8, but the cars in the Custom and Monterey lines got a less-powerful version than the Montclairs. The new 292-cid engine had a 3.75 x 3.30-inch bore and stroke. With a 7.6:1 compression ratio and a four-barrel carburetor, the output was 188 hp at 4400 rpm and 274 foot-pounds of torque at 2500 rpm. The more powerful engine was standard in Montclairs and optional in other models with automatic transmission. It had an 8.50:1 compression ratio and produced 10 more horses and 12 additional units of torque.

Model-year 1955 was a wonderful season for American automakers and Mercury was no exception. Its model-year production zoomed to an all-time high of 329,808 units. For the calendar-year, the number was an unheard of 434,911 cars. That equated to a 5.48 percent market share for Mercury, another record breaker.

Sales for the year climbed to 394,948 units, 50 percent better than 1954 and 25 percent better than the previous record of 320,355 in 1950. Mercury was still seventh in the overall industry rankings. The marque shared honors with Chevrolet as *Motor Trend* magazine's "Car of the Year." Part of the credit for this belonged to the Merc's improved, ball-and-socket joint front suspension.

1956 *Mercury*

Election-year 1956 sent American voters flocking to the polls to pick incumbent President Dwight D. Eisenhower over Adlai Stevenson for the second time in a row. It was a year of entertainment epics with "My Fair Lady" packing them in on the "Great White Way," while blockbuster films like "The Ten Commandments" and "Around the World in 80 Days" filled motion picture houses coast to coast. A tune about a "Heartbreak Hotel" introduced a hip-swiveling former Memphis, Tennessee, truck driver to fans of the new rock-and-roll craze. Wacky comedian Jerry Lewis did his last show with his 10-year partner Dean Martin at the Copa in New York City. After that, Mr. "M" went on to join Frank Sinatra's Las Vegas "Rat Pack."

To prove it hadn't run out of "M" names for its cars, Mercury named its low-priced cars the Medalist series. A two-door sedan with frugal use of side chrome was introduced in September 1955.

Three additional models — with more elaborate trim — were added to the Medalist lineup when it achieved full series status at midyear.

Medalist models lacked the front bumper guards found on more expensive Mercurys, but still wore a big "M" medallion on the front of the hood. The word "Mercury" was spelled out in block letters on the center horizontal grille bar. Mercury built 20,582 of the initial Medalist model, then produced 11,892 two-door hardtops, 6,685 four-door hardtops and 6,653 four-door sedans. These cars ranged in price from $2,254 to $2,458 and weighed in at roughly 3,400 to 3,500 pounds.

Chrome window trim was the main styling difference between the Custom and the Medalist. The Custom four-door sedan also had a thin strip of the roof color extending down the rear pillar to the body belt line and a section of the front door between the

The bright two-tone paint scheme accentuates this '56 Mercury Monterey two-door hardtop.

windshield pillar and the vent window was painted, rather than finished in chrome. The station wagon had the same round medallions as Montereys, but other models did not.

The Custom name appeared in script on the front fenders. This series had all the same models, plus a convertible and six- and eight-passenger station wagons. The latter was the priciest and heaviest (3,860 pounds) Custom. Suggested retail prices on all seven models ran from $2,351 to $2,819. As far as production, the totals were 12,187 four-door hardtops, 20,857 two-door hardtops, 16,343 two-door sedans, 15,860 four-door sedans, 2,311 convertibles, and 17,770 station wagons (of which 9,292 were three-seat models).

The 1956 Monterey looked a lot like the previous year's model. The hooded headlights, vertical "chubby cheek" taillights, and bumper-integrated grille were little changed. Montereys featured heavy chrome trim around the side windows and chrome rocker panels. The side body molding made a sort of lightning bolt pattern. "Monterey" was written in chrome on the front fenders. The four-door hardtop sold for $2,700, weighed 3,800 pounds, and had a production run of 10,726 units. Its two-door counterpart sold for $2,630, weighed 3,590 pounds, and had a much higher production run of 42,863 units. The $2,652 four-door Sport Sedan tipped the scales at 3,550 pounds and 11,765 were built. Other models included the $2,555 four-door sedan of which 26,735 were made and the four-door station wagon which sold for $2,977. The wagon weighed 3,885 pounds and Mercury made 13,280 of them.

Top-of-the-line Mercury Montclairs had a narrow color panel surrounded by chrome trim below the side windows and chrome

rocker panels. A round medallion was placed near the tip of the front fender side trim. "Montclair" was written, in chrome, on the front fenders. Early in the model year, the four-door Sport Sedan was replaced by a four-door hardtop model that Mercury called a "Phaeton." These cars were priced from $2,765 to $2,900 and weighed between 3,610 and 3,725 pounds. Mercury built 23,493 four-door hardtops (Phaetons), 9,617 four-door Sport Sedans, 50,562 two-door hardtops, and 7,762 convertibles.

This year's V-8 was bored and stroked (3.80 x 3.44 inches) to bring it up to 312 cubic inches. The base version with 8.00:1 compression was used as standard equipment in Medalist, Custom, Monterey, and Montclair models with stick shift. It generated 210 hp at 4600 rpm and 312 foot-pounds of torque at 2600 rpm. A version of this power plant used with Merc-O-Matic transmission had an 8.40:1 compression ratio. This bumped the output up to 220 hp at 4600 rpm while torque went to 320 foot-pounds at 2600 rpm. At midyear, a new camshaft raised the output in the standard and 225-hp V-8s by 10. Also a high-performance M-260 package (two four-barrel carburetors, 260 hp) was offered in all series late in the year.

The 1956 Mercurys were introduced on Sept. 29, 1955. Model-year production was 327,943. Although slightly down from 1955, this was excellent compared to the majority of United States automakers in 1956. Mercury's share of the total industry output for the model year went from 4.6 percent in 1955 to 5.2 percent in 1956. The calendar-year picture was quite different, with the total dropping to 246,629 units or 4.25 percent of industry. Mercurys proved to be a hot ticket in motor sports this year and the company won five NASCAR Grand National races.

1957 Mercury

A year of memorable events in 1957 included the first electric watch, America's first underground nuclear test and 13-year-old U.S. chess whiz Bobby Fischer, who took the world championship. At Mercury, it was the year of "Dream-Car Design For '57." Highlights included a jazzy new Turnpike Cruiser one of which was used as the year's Indy 500 Official Pace Car.

While Mercury advertisements described Dream-Car Design as: "…a clean break with the plump, bulging lines of many of today's cars" and "…a sleek, clean-cut, dynamic look," the overall appearance was not what we would think of as a "clean" car design today.

It had plenty of the gold-finished and chrome-finished bright work we love on the cars of this era, as well as a few styling gim-

Long fender skirts and continental kit were Mercury options on this '57 Montclair convertible.

micks designed to make it stand out in the crowd. The basic lines were very straight and square. They followed the longer, lower, wider theme that characterized almost all cars of this era.

The front bumper jutted out and looked like the front of a jet with big air intakes on either side of the center. The full-width grille, no longer integrated with the bumper, featured multiple concave vertical louvers. The hood was hinged at the front and lifted from the rear. The cowl had vent intakes. Dual headlights were standard on the Turnpike Cruisers and optional on other models.

Concave, guided-missile-shaped spears were seen on the rear fenders (and rear doors of four-door models). The sculptured rear deck had a depressed center section. The rear bumper resembled the front dummy jet-plane-like "exhaust pods." Other decorative touches included unique V-shaped taillights and a chrome "M" placed between the grille and the bumper.

There were five car-lines for 1957: the Monterey, the Montclair, the Turnpike Cruiser, station wagons and the one-model Convertible Cruiser series.

Monterey offerings included two- and four-door sedans, two- and four-door Phaetons (hardtops), and the Phaeton Convertible. These were priced between $2,352 and $2,752. The Montclair line offered all of the same models except the two-door sedan at prices from $2,922 to $3,147. The Turnpike Cruiser line included two- and four-door hardtops at $3,452 and $3,537, respectively. Trim-wise, the station wagons roughly corresponded to each series.

The Monterey-like Commuter wagon offered two- and four-door models with two seats and a four-door three-seat version as well. The Montclair-like Voyager wagons came in two-door six-passenger and four-door nine-passenger editions. The Colony Park was Mercury's wood-grained nine-passenger four-door wagon. Station wagon retails ranged from $2,657 to $3,377. The Convertible Cruiser listed for $3,773.

Cars in the bottom series had the Monterey name in script on their front fenders. The headlight "cylinders" on these cars were painted (often in a contrasting color on two-tone cars). The bright metal panels inside the rear bumper pods had a horizontally-textured finish. The body side molding was the same width from headlight to rear of the car. There was no package shelf ornament.

Production in this series came to 157,498 cars and the rarest was the convertible, of which 5,003 were built.

Chrome headlight cylinders, nameplates on the upper front fenders, an ornament on the rear shelf of sedans and hardtops and a rectangular grid design in the rear bumper pods were some of the differences between Montclairs and Montereys. Convertibles in both series had a Plexiglas wraparound rear window. The front section of the body side molding was wider than the section on the rear doors and fenders. Total production of the four Montclair models was 75,351, including just 4,248 ragtops.

The Turnpike Cruiser was one of the most gadget-laden cars ever built. Mercury said that it was based on the XM-Turnpike Cruiser, although the opposite was the case. All power items were standard. Other special features included an overhanging roof with a retractable rear window, streamlined air ducts mounted on top of the windshield (with fake aerials sticking out from them), a power seat with a memory dial, rubber instrument bezels, a special starter button, a clock and odometer, sliding door locks, a rear deck lid "hood ornament," a special interior with a perforated vinyl head-liner, and a gold anodized insert in the upper rear fender concave section that led to the taillights.

The Convertible Cruiser was, technically, in a separate series. These collectible cars had a production run of 7,291 two-door hardtops, 8,305 four-door hardtops, and only 1,265 convertibles.

Station wagons also were a separate series this year. The top-of-the-line model was the Colony Park. It featured four-door hardtop styling and fake wood trim. The mid-priced wagon was the Voyager. It had a rear vent window like the Colony Park, but did not have wood trim. The lowest priced wagon, the Commuter, looked about the same as the Voyager but lacked a rear vent window. With six models to sell, Mercury still built only 35,792 station wagons. The rarest (2,283 made) was the two-door Voyager.

Base engine in the Monterey, Montclair and Voyager models was a single four-barrel-carburetor version of the 312-cid V-8 with a 9.70:1 compression ratio and 255 hp at 4600 rpm. This was promoted as the "Safety-Surge" V-8. The Turnpike Cruiser and Colony Park models came standard with a larger V-8 that was optional in other models. This was a bored and stroked version with 368 cubic inches. It had a 9.75:1 compression ratio and a Carter or Holley four-barrel carburetor. It put out 290 hp at 4600 rpm and 405 foot-pounds of torque at 2600 rpm. An M-335 power package with two four-barrel carburetors (368-cid/335-hp) was optional for Montereys.

The '57 Mercurys had a 122-inch wheelbase and measured 211.1 inches end-to-end. Overall height was in the 56.5-inch range (it varied slightly by body style) and all models had a maximum width of 79.1 inches. The majority of Mercurys used 8.00 x 14 tires, but convertibles and station wagons came with wider 8.50 x 15s to support their heavier weights. On Turnpike Cruiser and Station Wagon models, a new feature was Air Cushion suspension.

With this setup, air-filled cushions at vital chassis points absorbed road shock and provided smoother handling and a softer ride.

Model-year 1957 was not a great selling season for Mercury, although the calendar year saw an improvement. The model-year production total was 286,163 units (4.6 percent market share). For the calendar year, output peaked at 274,820 vehicles.

With the exception of the Turnpike Cruiser, the 1957 Mercurys with two headlights had model names at the front of the front fenders, above the side trim. The models with four headlights had their model names on the front fenders behind the wheel wells and below the side trim. About one-third (32.6 percent) of 1957 Mercurys came with four headlights.

1958 Mercury

The 1958 Mercury Montclair convertible wears the Turnpike Cruiser option package.

People in the United States had been paying three cents to mail a letter since 1932. That changed in 1958, when stamp prices rose a penny. Although the increase was only one "red cent," the timing was bad for about 5.5 million people who were out of work that year. America was suffering its worst recession since World War II. As the economy worsened, Mercury brought back a Medalist-type model and simply called the production version Mercury. It was a "stripper" model aimed at giving the low-price cars some added competition.

Strangely, the sinking economy may have also explained the thinking behind another new 1958 Mercury, the huge and pricey car Park Lane model. Just think of it this way: There were 4,065 drive-in theaters in operation — the highest number in history — in 1958 and they offered cheap entertainment. The perfect Big "M" (Mercury) to take to the "open-air movies" was the 220.2-inch-long Park Lane. Theater operators sometimes charged admission per carload and you could fit the whole family (plus a couple of neighbors and their pets) in your Park Lane!

There were six 1958 Mercury series in all. Five of them — Medalist, Monterey, Montclair, Montclair (with Turnpike Cruiser) and station wagon — rode a carryover 122-inch wheelbase. Passenger cars in all these lines were 213.2 inches long, while station wagons stretched an additional inch. The Park Lanes, of

course, had a longer 125-inch wheelbase to go with their extended body length. These majestic Mercs were also a tad higher (56.8 inches) and wider (81.1 inches) than other models.

Styling of all models was characterized by a new combination bumper-grille with multiple concave vertical dividers, plus a parking light, in each massive "Jet-Flow" bumper pod. The radiator grille was divided into two sections enclosed in the massive bumpers. A chrome "M'" was placed in the center of the grille. The hood was a bit more upright in front and the front fenders were a bit flatter on top. Dual headlights were now standard equipment. Body side trim was revised and varied per model. New rear deck styling was seen and V-angle taillights were used on all models. Torch-shaped taillight housings were seen at the base of the guided-missile shaped rear fender coves.

Only prototypes carried the Medalist name. Actual production cars in the economy series were simply called Mercurys. The side window trim was painted on the models in this series. There were only two body styles: two- and four-door sedan. The two-door was $2,547 and the four-door was $2,617. Production was 7,750 and 10,982, respectively, so the cheap Mercs were not a big success story.

Monterey models had a single body side molding running from below the headlights to the top of the rear bumper pods. At a point behind the front seat, a second molding rose to a wave-like peak, then continued to the front of the car before curving around the body corner to the top of the headlights. The area between the moldings was often finished in a contrasting color which, in some cases, matched the roof color.

The rear bumper pods contained concave dividers. The Monterey name, in chrome script, was placed on the front fenders between the moldings. This series included two- and four-door sedans and Phaetons (hardtops), as well as a convertible. Prices began at $2,652 and ran to $3,081. Mercury built 62,312 Montereys and collectors focus on the convertible, of which only 2,292 were built.

Distinguishing features of the Montclair were "Montclair" front fender nameplates, dual full-length side chrome strips with optional contrasting trim between them and chrome headlight rims. The base Montclair series consisted of the four-door sedan, two- and four-door Phaeton hardtops, and the convertible priced from $2,966 to $3,086. Series production for all four body styles came to only 14,266 units, all fairly low-production cars. Production totals included 4,801 sedans, 5,012 two-door Phaetons, 3,609 four-door Phaetons, and just 844 convertibles.

The Turnpike Cruiser was now part of the Montclair series. The Turnpike Cruiser models included two-door and four-door Phaeton hardtops, but not a convertible. Both body styles featured an overhanging rear roof, a retractable rear window and twin air intakes on the roof above both sides of the windshield. The two-door carried a $3,498 window sticker and weighed 4,150 pounds. The four-door was priced from $3,597 and weighed an additional 80 pounds. Production totals included 2,864 two-doors and 3,543 four-doors.

The 1958 Mercury Commuter station wagons were based on the Monterey, while the Voyager and Colony Park wagons were based on the Montclair. The Colony Park had simulated wood trim. Like the Voyager and Commuter models, it featured a pillar-less hardtop look. Body style offerings were unchanged from 1957. Prices ranged from $3,035 to $3,775. A total of 22,302 wagons were assembled including just 568 two-door Voyagers and 1,912 two-door Commuters.

The new Park Lane was introduced to compete with Buick's Roadmaster. Front fender ornaments, rear roof panel nameplates, chrome headlight rims, and a rectangular trim pattern in the rear bumper pods were styling features of the Park Lane. Like the Montclair, the Park Lane convertible had a wraparound rear window. This series offered three models. The two-door Phaeton listed for $3,867 and 3,158 were made; the four-door Phaeton listed for $3,944 and 5,241 were built, and the $4,118 convertible had a run of just 853 units.

Each series of '58 Mercs had its own engine, except the Montclair Turnpike Cruisers and Park Lanes, which shared the big 430-cid "Lincoln" V-8. This 10.5:1 compression motor used a Holley four-barrel and put out 360 hp at 4600 rpm. Base Mercurys (Medalists) used a 312-cid 235-hp V-8 as standard equipment. Montereys and Commuter wagons came with a 383-cid V-8 with 10.5:1 compression and 312 hp at 4600 rpm. In Montclairs, Voyagers, and Colony Parks, this engine was rated for 330 hp at 4600 rpm.

The bad 1958 economy definitely had its impact on production and sales of Mercury products. In fact, the company slugged its way through its worst calendar year since 1947. Its total of 128,428 cars built between January 1958 and January 1959 was a 55 percent decline from 1957! Model-year production was counted at 133,271 cars or 3.1 percent of industry. These drops came despite countless television pitches for the Big "M" by popular variety show host Ed Sullivan. Mr. Sullivan even appeared in print advertisements.

1959 Mercury

Gary and Lynne Rosenkild

This 1959 Mercury Park Lane two-door hardtop looks like it just came from the dealer.

Early in 1959, The United States and Canada celebrated the opening of the St. Lawrence Seaway, a waterway that made it possible to sail from the Atlantic Ocean to the Great Lakes. In New York, patrons of the arts celebrated as the doors to the modern-looking Guggenheim Museum swung open. In the fall, the new Los Angeles Dodgers baseball team celebrated a four-to-two games victory over Chicago in the World Series. Meanwhile, in Detroit, Ford celebrated the second decade of its Mercury nameplate. "20th Anniversary '59 Mercury: Built to Lead — Built to Last," boasted the company's advertisements.

Mercurys once again shared a strong family resemblance with Fords, at least from the front. Last year's bumper-integrated grille was replaced by a new, two-piece die-cast cellular grille. A massive, plain, wraparound front bumper now housed the signal lights. The concave "guided missiles" on the body sides now extended almost to the front fenders. A larger wraparound windshield that curved upwards gave fuller vision of the road ahead.

The "Safety-Sweep" tandem windshield wipers were also designed to give a "clear 5-foot span of the world's largest windshield." They cleared off the "middle area" that the wipers on many other brands of cars did not reach.

Mercury's back window was larger, too. Two- and four-door hardtop models had forward-slanting rear window pillars and a backlight that curved upwards. Two- and four-door sedans had a unique roof line and a large, wraparound rear window. Canted, V-shaped taillights were seen again. The rear end panel had different decorative treatments on different car-lines. Mercury advertised the Super Enamel finish on its 1959 models would stay new looking longer because it resisted the effects of sun, rain, snow, and salt.

Rather large increases in wheelbase turned the '59 Mercurys into truly large cars. Montclairs, Montereys and station wagons shared a 126-inch wheelbase. The passenger cars in these series were 217.8 inches long and the wagons were an inch longer. Park Lane models had a 128-inch wheelbase and stretched 222.8 inches end-to-end. The engines were moved further ahead in the chassis, permitting a 45 percent decrease in the size of the transmission "tunnel."

Combined with a new instrument panel design, it provided a huge increase in the amount of front passenger space. There were an additional nine inches of front knee room and the doors were up to six inches wider than those on other cars in Mercury's class. Mercury ads also pointed out the '59 model's bigger trunk had a "six-foot span."

In addition to distinct front fender nameplates, Montereys had three chrome bands on the upper rear fenders, in front of the taillights, and a horizontally-ribbed rear end panel. The same five models were offered in this series at prices between $2,654 and $3,150. Production totals were 12,694 two-door sedans, 43,570 four-door sedans, 17,232 two-door hardtops, 11,355 four-door hardtops, and 4,426 convertibles.

Mercury Montclairs had four chrome bands on the upper rear fender, full-length lower body moldings, bright metal "cubed" grid pattern appliques on the rear end panel and special nameplates under the chrome spears on the front fenders. A fabric-and-vinyl interior, padded dash, windshield washer, electric clock, parking brake, warning light and foam rubber cushions were standard equipment.

Model offerings were cut-back to the four-door sedan ($3,308), two-door hardtop ($3,357) and four-door hardtop ($3,437). Production, in the same order, was 9,514 sedans, 7,375 hardtop coupes, and 6,713 four-door hardtops.

Styling distinctions of the Park Lane included chrome-plated projectiles on the rear fender coves, full-length lower body moldings, large aluminum gravel guards on the lower rear quarter panels, bright roof moldings, and front fender (instead of hood) ornaments. The rear end panel trim was the same as that used on the Montclair. Once again the Park Lane convertible (like the Monterey) had a wraparound rear window. Park Lanes came equipped with the same items as Montclairs, plus power steering, self-adjusting power brakes, dual exhausts, back-up lights, a rear center armrest, and a rear cigarette lighter. The two-door hardtop had a $3,955 sticker price and 4,060 assemblies compared to $4,031 and 7,206 assemblies for the four-door version. The ragtop sold for $4,206 and 1,257 were made.

The Commuter station wagons shared trim styling with Montereys. Voyager and Colony Park station wagon trim was like that used on Montclairs, except the Colony Park had simulated wood panels. The model count was reduced to the two- and four-door Commuters, the four-door Voyager, and the Colony Park. Prices ranged from $3,035 to $3,932 and 24,628 wagons in all were made. Only 1,051 had two doors.

Reacting to an up-tick in imported-car sales in 1958, many American automakers made efforts to promote special economy engines in 1959. Mercury's slightly de-tuned Monterey base V-8 was a 312-cid version with 210 hp at 4400 rpm. It had a lower 8.75:1 compression ratio and a smaller two-barrel Holley carburetor. Base V-8 in Commuter wagon (optional in Montereys) was the 383-cid job with 10.0:1 compression and a two-barrel for 280 hp at 4400 rpm.

Montclairs, Voyagers and Colony Parks came standard with a 322-hp four-barrel version of the same 383. The Park Lane V-8 (optional in other models) was the 430-cid job with 10.5:1 compression and a Carter AFB four-barrel carburetor. It generated 345 hp, 4400 rpm, and 480 foot-pounds of torque. A 430-cid/400-hp V-8 with three two-barrel carburetors was optional on all series.

A three-speed manual gearbox was standard on Montereys and Commuter station wagons.

Merc-O-Matic automatic transmission was standard on Montclair models as well as Colony Park and Voyager station wagons. Power steering and power brakes were standard on Park Lanes. A power rear window was standard on Voyager and Colony Park station wagons. All other power assists, a radio, a heater, air conditioning, a memory-type power seat, and a Safety-Speed Monitor (that buzzed when certain pre-set speeds were hit) were optional on all models.

Mercury struggled through the close of the '50s much like it had during the past two years. Its share of industry output dropped to its lowest point (2.7 percent) since 1942. Model-year production did see a modest increase to 150,000 cars (almost 17,000 more than the previous season). For the calendar year, assemblies at Mercury factories totaled 156,765 cars.

Nashs
of the Fifties

1950 *Nash*

While its style was new, Nash remained a practical and economical choice for 1950s drivers.

With models like the Statesman and the Ambassador in its product lineup, the Nash Motor Company probably could have pulled off a promotional coup by supplying courtesy cars for the opening of the United Nations building in New York City in 1950. And speaking of the "Big Apple," that's where the first credit card was launched in 1950. Ralph Schneider's Diner's Club Card could only be used in 27 restaurants in New York City, but it was the beginning of something big.

The car formerly known as the Nash 600 was renamed Statesman for 1950. The old "600" designation indicated how far a Nash could go on a full tank of fuel. That might have decreased slightly in 1950 since the L-head six-cylinder engine had a one-quarter inch larger stroke. It grew from 172.6 cid to 184 cubic inches and horsepower went from 82 to 85. Despite the larger engine displacements, company advertisements pointed out that many Nash owners were getting 25-30 mpg in normal operation.

The one-piece windshield, introduced on 1949 Nash models, was carried over for 1950. A significant styling change made in this year was a much larger rear window. This was helpful to the drivers trying to see out the rear window of the fastback bodies. The bumper guards also grew slightly thicker and the cars had a Statesman script on their front fenders. Seat belts — the first for an American car — were available as an option.

In addition to a low-priced ($1,633) "line leader" Deluxe Business Coupe, Statesman models came in Super and Custom trim levels. Custom models had rear seat armrests, carpets, courtesy lights, a Custom steering wheel and full wheel discs. Both car lines included a two-door Brougham, a two-door sedan, and a four-door sedan. Supers were priced from $1,713 to $1,738 and Customs were in the $1,872 to $1,897 range. Car collectors will note that the Broughams were quite rare, with only 1,489 Super versions and 132 Customs built.

The 1950 Nash Ambassador had a longer hood than the 1949 model, as well as the enlarged back window. Otherwise, there were not many significant changes. An Ambassador script appeared on the fenders for identification. The year's major innovation was the introduction of a GM-built Hydra-Matic transmission, which was available only on the 1950 Nash Ambassador. A new cylinder head design was also introduced for the 234.8-cid overhead-valve Ambassador six. It raised the output to 115 hp. Custom models differed from the Supers by featuring a rear seat with a folding center armrest, front floor carpeting, courtesy lights, a Custom steering wheel, and large wheel discs.

Body styles were the same as in the Statesman series. Super prices ran from $2,039 to $2,064 and Customs from $2,198 to $2,223. The Brougham was also rare in this series, with 824 being built, of which only 108 were Customs.

Perhaps the most notable 1950 Nash was the compact Rambler, which was introduced in March 1950. In 1958, the "Little Nash Rambler" became an official icon of the '50s when it was memorialized in the tune "Beep, Beep" recorded by a group known as The Playmates. This platter made the top 40 Billboard charts on June 9, 1958. It stayed there for 12 weeks and rose as high as number 4. The song made "Rambler" a household word in America. The first cars built by Nash's predecessor firm, the Thomas B. Jeffery Co. of Kenosha, Wisconsin, had also used the Rambler name.

The first Rambler model introduced was the two-door Convertible Landau. A two-door station wagon was introduced two months later on June 23. Both models came loaded with options such as radio and antenna, a Custom steering wheel, turn signals, full wheel discs, an electric clock, courtesy lights, Custom upholstery, and foam seat cushions. On the Convertible Landau only, a sliding top (in black or tan fabric) could be raised over "bridge beam" side rails above the doors.

The Rambler used the 82-hp six from the Nash 600 and had Hotchkiss drive, unlike the torque-tube drive of other Nashes. Both 1950 Rambler models had a base retail price of $1,808. The convertible weighed 2,430 pounds and the station wagon was 85 pounds heavier.

The Rambler was built on a 100-inch wheelbase and was 176 inches long. The Statesman had a foot longer wheelbase and was more than two feet longer (201 inches) overall. Ambassadors rode a 121-inch wheelbase and measured 210 inches bumper to bumper. The Ramblers had diminutive 5.90 x 15 tires, while other Nashes used more normal automotive sizes (6.40 x 15 on Statesman models and 7.10 x 15 on Ambassadors).

The Nash unitized body was promoted as "Airflyte Construction" and was unusual in 1950, although unit-body cars are the norm today.

"This unique type body construction utilizes revolutionary engineering principles," Nash told its dealer sales force. "Body and frame are built together in one solid, welded unit." Nash Motor Company's "Airflyte Design" styling was based on streamlining principles. The cars had fastback roof lines and a novel rounded front end with enclosed front wheels.

Inside, the cars also had unusual interior features with operating instruments grouped in a "Uniscope" positioned just below the driver's line of vision. Another famous Nash feature was the Weather Eye Conditioned Air System, first introduced in 1938. Operating on fresh air, the system distributed conditioned air to all parts of the interior and was said to virtually eliminate glass fogging.

Production of 1950 Nash products began in September 1949. A total of 145,782 Statesman and Ambassador models, along with 26,000 Ramblers, were produced for the model year. Calendar-year output was 189,543 units, representing a 2.84 percent market share. Sales were counted at 191,665 cars, putting Nash 10th in the auto sales race. This broke the all-time record for Nash production. The compact Rambler line was an immediate success. In fact, the two Rambler body styles helped Nash achieve the assembly of 71 percent of all convertibles and 3.6 percent of all station wagons built in the United States in calendar-year 1950.

Several Nash models competed successfully in stock car races during 1950. Although they were not as fast as other cars, such as V-8-powered Oldsmobiles, the greater fuel economy of the Nashes required them to make fewer pit stops.

1951 Nash

In 1951, the Nash received a new grille plus restyled rear fender treatment.

That wonderful year 1951 brought us "Dennis the Menace" in the funny papers and "Flying Leathernecks" (starring John Wayne) in the movies. Early in the year, Congress passed the 22nd Amendment limiting United States Presidents to a maximum of two terms. Towards the end of the year, in November, the first coast-to-coast dial-it-yourself phone service was initiated.

In Kenosha, Wisconsin, the year brought car buyers a couple of new Rambler models, while Nash Motor Company got a government contract to build Pratt & Whitney aircraft engines for the Korean War effort. On the downside, the military "action" in Korea meant materials shortages and there were vendor and shipper labor strikes. Nash would wind up building fewer cars, while earning a greater share of total industry output.

The 1951 Nash Statesman featured a new electric shaver-type grille and side marker lights, along with new rear fenders and

fender lights. A "Statesman" script was on the front fender for identification. Super models had basic features. Customs also had foam seat cushions, front floor carpets, courtesy lights, a rear seat center armrest, a Custom steering wheel and full wheel discs. Hydra-Matic automatic transmission made its debut in the 1951 Statesman models.

Model offerings were unchanged from 1950 and prices for the seven models ranged from $1,710 to $1,815. Nash built only 52 of the cheap Deluxe Business Coupes and 190 Broughams, of which only 38 were Custom-trimmed cars.

The 1951 Nash Ambassador received the same revised front grille and side marker lights and new rear fenders as the 1951 Statesman. The major difference from the Statesman was the Ambassador's nine-inch longer front end. Super models had basic features and Customs had the normal upgrades in decorations, equipment and trim. Prices for the three Supers and three Customs together were in the $2,137 to $2,321 range. Only 40 Super Broughams and 37 Custom Broughams were made.

A major change for the 1951 version of Nash Motor's hot-selling Rambler compact was a new body style called the Country Club hardtop. It was the first compact-sized two-door hardtop to be introduced in the United States. This body style had been popularized by the introduction of two-door hardtops in several GM and Chrysler car-lines. Rambler prices ranged from $1,673 for the two-door Deliveryman Utility Wagon to $1,936 for the Country Club Hardtop. The Landau Convertible was $1,837.

The new Deliveryman was a station wagon-type vehicle, with only one seat. It was intended strictly for commercial package carrying work. In most reference sources it was listed as a truck and described as a utility wagon. Thanks to continued strong sales of Ramblers during 1951, Nash wound up making 6.9 percent of all convertibles, 3.9 percent of all hardtops and 15.2 percent of all station wagons produced in the United States.

All Nash models used in-line six-cylinder engines. L-head motors were used in Statesman and Rambler models, while Ambassadors used an overhead-valve six. The Rambler six had a 3-1/8 x 3-3/4-inch bore and stroke for 172.6 cid. With a one-barrel Carter carburetor and 7.25:1 compression ratio, it was rated

for 82 hp at 3800 rpm. The Statesman six had the same bore, but a longer 4-inch stroke, giving it 184 cid. It had a 7.0:1 compression ratio and produced 85 hp at 3800 rpm. A 3-3/8 x 4-3/8-inch bore and stroke gave the Ambassador six 234.8 cid. This motor had a 7.3:1 compression ratio and developed 115 hp at 3400 rpm.

Annual model introductions were held on Sept. 22, 1950. The Nash Rambler Country Club hardtop was introduced, as an addition to the line, on June 28, 1951. Korean War allocations prevented introduction of a Rambler four-door sedan. In November 1951, the company received permission from the Economic Stability Agency to increase prices. The subsequent jump was $64 in Rambler, $48-$55 in Statesman, and $61-$66 in Ambassador.

Model-year production counted 125,203 standard-size models and 80,000 compact Ramblers, with the production run beginning in September 1950. Calendar-year production hit 161,209 units or 30.2 percent of total American industry output. Over 82,731 Nash products were assembled with optional overdrive transmission, while another 64,775 cars had the optional, GM-built Hydra-Matic automatic transmission. During the calendar year, 25,962 automatic transmission attachments were sold, while 82,731 cars had the optional Warner Gear overdrive.

1952 Nash

A rare 1952 Nash Rambler Super two-door wagon, one of just over 2,900 made.

What a year — 1952. Puerto Rico became part of the United States and "Ike" became U.S. President for the second time. Within weeks of the election, he was in Korea, trying to find out how to stop the fighting. It was a year that brought us the first televised atomic bomb explosion and the first sex-change operation. Curley Howard, of Three Stooges fame, passed away.

In Kenosha, Wisconsin, the Nash Motors Division of Nash-Kelvinator Corporation marked the 50th birthday of its automotive "family." The original Thomas B. Jeffery Company had built its first automobile in 1902. Nashes were redesigned, a fancy Rambler wagon was created and an all-new Nash-Healey sports car saw limited production.

Nash used its golden anniversary to introduce a totally redesigned line of big cars called Nash Golden Airflytes. "Take Command . . . It's Your Golden Airflyte," read the headline in one advertisement that urged car buyers: "If you dare to let your dreams come true — drive the Golden Airflyte. Here is America's first car styled by Pinin Farina, world's foremost custom car designer. Here are comfort and luxury features so advanced that other new cars seem outdated in comparison! Here's the supreme thrill of new Super Jetfire performance – with new horizontal Direct Draft carburetion! (Plus, of course, traditional Nash economy). Here is the widest, most comfortable seating to be found in any car . . . the best eye-level vision, front and rear . . . the deepest windshield (and new Road-Guide fenders to rest your driving eyes.)"

These cars were actually partly styled by Italian designer Pinin Farina and had more conventional lines than the 1949 to 1951 models. The Statesman and the Ambassador again shared sheet metal from the cowl back. The 1952 Statesman had its wheelbase increased to 114-1/4 inches and the engine was stroked one-quarter inch to 195.6 cid. This increase in displacement boosted the Statesman engine's output to 88 hp at 3800 rpm.

Model offerings were cut back a little for 1952 and the Deluxe Business Coupe was deleted entirely. Two- and four-door sedans were offered in the Super series and these two styles plus the Country Club hardtop came with Custom trim. Prices for the five Nash cars ranged from $2,144 to $2,433. All models weighed between 3,000 and 3,100 pounds. Total series production was a strong 50,500 cars, but only 869 Country Club Hardtops were built.

The 1952 Nash Ambassador shared the same styling and design changes as the 1952 Nash Statesman, the major difference being the seven-inch longer front end. The 1952 Nash Ambassador came in two series: Super and Custom.

Supers had basic features and Customs added foam seat cushions, two-tone upholstery, an electric clock, directional signals, chrome wheel discs and front and rear courtesy lights. For 1952, the Ambassador engine was bored one-eighth of an inch, yielding 252.6 cid. The same five models in this series sold at prices from $2,521 to $2,829. Series production was 40,700 units.

The 1952 Nash Rambler line received no major changes from 1951. Custom models came with the Nash "Weather-Eye" conditioned air system and a radio as standard equipment. The Greenbrier station wagon was an upgraded model with two-tone paint and richer trim. Prices started at $1,842 for the Utility Wagon and ran to $2,119 for both the Convertible Landau and the Greenbrier Station Wagon. In all, 53,000 Ramblers were made.

The all-new Nash-Healey sports car had a special two-passenger open body made of aluminum, an adjustable steering wheel, and leather upholstery. The first Nash-Healey sold for $4,063 and used a 234.8-cid 125-hp Nash six with 8.0:1 compression. It is sometimes called the "951" model. The second version, priced at $5,909, switched to a 252.6-cid 140-hp "LeMans" engine with dual carburetion.

The English-built sports car's styling included a grille of outward-curved vertical chrome bars entirely circled by a heavy chrome molding. There were model designations on the front fender and in back of the wheel opening. The full hood had a unique hatch cover (air scoop) with a vertical grille opening.

These cars were built at Warwick, England, and sold by Nash dealers. Styling by Pinin Farina was seen on 1952 models and late in the year, the more powerful LeMans engine was released. According to *Ward's Automotive Yearbook 1953* the official introduction date of the Nash-Healey, in the United States, was February 16, 1951. A total of 254 Nash-Healeys were made this year, of which 150 had the LeMans six.

The 1952 Nash Ambassador and Statesman models were introduced March 14, 1952. The updated Rambler appeared on Apr. 1, 1952. The Nash-Healey (sometimes considered a 1951 model) made its American debut as a 1952 Nash offering. Production hit a peak of 152,141 units or 3.51 percent of American auto sales. Model-year production included 99,086 Statesman/Ambassador models and 55,055 Ramblers. Over 20 percent of all Nash products, or 28,950 cars, had Hydra-Matic Drive this year. The optional Warner Gear overdrive was installed in 74,535 units.

The new Nash-Healey took first place in its class in the French Grand Prix, at LeMans, plus a third place overall. These racing models used the LeMans "Dual-Jetfire" Ambassador engine, later released as a production car power plant.

1953 Nash

Tom Collins

The Nash-Healey was available in roadster form, as well as a coupe, in 1953.

It was January 1953. A new president was about to take office, fighting continued to rage in Korea, and the United States had its first hydrogen bomb. The really big news was that Lucy was going to have a baby. Sixty-eight percent of America's televsion viewers tuned in for the big event on January 19. A month later, Lucy and her then-better-half Desi Arnaz inked an $8,000,000 deal to continue their "I Love Lucy" series for three more years. Nash Motors Division would make even bigger money — $14.8

million on sales of $478.7 million. That was up from $12.6 and $358.4 million, respectively, in 1952, so it was a strong selling season.

The Golden Anniversary styling introduced on the 1952 Statesman and Ambassador models was carried over with very modest changes in 1953. Some vertical chrome strips were added to the fresh air intake below the windshield. Rambler models, however, were completely restyled. They had a lower hood, a single horizontal bar in the front radiator grille and enclosed front and rear fenders.

"Statesman" in script on the front fenders identified cars in the lower-priced Nash series. Supers again had basic equipment and Custom models added foam seat cushions, two-tone upholstery, an electric clock, directional signals, chrome full wheel discs, and front and rear courtesy lights. The model lineup was again to Supers (two- and four-door sedans) and three Customs (the same sedans, plus the Country Club Hardtop). Prices began at $2,144 and topped out at $2,433. Series production was 56,250 cars with the Super four-door sedan being the most popular (28,445 built) and the Custom two-door sedan being rarest at 1,305 built.

The 1953 Nash Ambassador had the same minor alterations as the Statesman models. Super and Custom models were offered again. Customs included the same extras listed for the Statesman line. In addition, a new dual carburetor LeMans Dual-Jetfire engine (similar to the engine used in the Nash-Healeys raced at LeMans and thusly named) was made optional on 1953 Ambassadors. This engine produced 140 hp at 4000 rpm. In one advertisement, Nash hinted that this engine might appeal "To the boy who wanted a Stutz Bearcat."

Prices for Ambassadors started at $2,521 and climbed as high as $2,829 for the Custom Country Club Hardtop. "Today we invite you to be young again — to thrill to the wonder and romance of travel again," the ad copywriters said. "Come take command of the proudest car ever styled by Pinin Farina of Europe—this new Ambassador Country Club." Such ads seemed to have wide appeal, and 32,850 Ambassadors left the assembly lines.

The 1953 Nash Rambler was completely restyled. The new styling was again credited to Pinin Farina. Custom models came with the Nash "Weather-Eye" conditioned air system and a radio as standard equipment. Custom convertible and Country Club hardtop models included a continental spare tire. Dual-Range

Hydra-Matic became an option available for the first time on the 1953 Nash Rambler and the Hydra-Matic-equipped cars were rated at five more advertised horsepower. Nine Deliveryman trucks were made using the station wagon body, but the Country Club Hardtop was far better selling with 15,255 assemblies. Nash also built 1,114 standard wagons, almost 10,600 fancier wagons (3,536 with Greenbrier trim and 7,035 with wood-grained DiNoc trim), and 10,598 Convertible Landaus.

All Nash products continued to feature in-line six-cylinder engines with solid valve lifters. The Rambler used a 184.1-cid 85-hp engine (90-hp with Hydra-Matic) with 7.25:1 compression and a one-barrel carburetor. The Statesman used a new 195.6-cid 100-hp "Powerflyte" six with 7.45:1 compression and a two-barrel carburetor. The Ambassador used a 252.6-cid 120-hp engine with 7.30:1 compression and a "double-barreled" carburetor. The optional Ambassador "Dual-Jetfire LeMans Six" used the 252.6-cid block with 8.00:1 compression head and multiple carburetors that gave 140 hp at 4000 rpm.

Lifting (with a twist) the "He Drives a Duesenberg" promotional phrase once used by the classic automaker, Nash pictured the wife of actor Jimmy Stewart in one of its 1953 Rambler ads and headlined it "She drives a Rambler!" The ad described Mrs. Stewart's blue-and-white Country Club hardtop as "a woman's dream-of-a-car come true!" It also offered ladies a one-hour test drive. "Try a new Nash Rambler for one wonderful hour—with Dual-Range Hydra-Matic Drive if you like. Then you'll know why —among two-car families—four out of five prefer to drive their Rambler."

Vital statistics for the Rambler included a 100-inch wheelbase and 176-inch length with 5.90 x 15 tires. When the continental spare tire was added, the length grew to 185-3/8 inches. Statesman models rode a 114-1/4-inch wheelbase and measured 202-1/4 inches end-to-end. For Ambassadors, the wheelbase grew to 121-1/4 inches and length was 209-1/4 inches. Statesman tires were 6.70 x 15; Ambassador tires were 7.10 x 15.

Model-year production for 1953 amounted to 89,100 Nash models and 31,788 Ramblers. In calendar-year 1953, Nash built 135,394 cars including 3,501 convertibles, 13,533 station wagons and 34,356 hardtops. Its share of the total market for American cars dropped by more than a full percentage point to 2.21 percent in 1953, compared to 3.51 percent the previous calendar year.

1954 *Nash*

Tory was made in many ways in 1954. The first issue of *Sports Illustrated* magazine was published and the last episode of "The Lone Ranger" was heard on radio. (The popular Western had been a mainstay for 21 years. It continued on television with actors Clayton Moore and Jay Silverheels.)

Patty Hearst, Oprah Winfrey, John Travolta, and Ron Howard were born, while the famed French Impressionist painter Henri Matisse died. In a faraway Asian country named Viet Nam, guerilla fighters were whipping the French Army. At the time, no one guessed that Americans would be dying in the same Southeast Asian jungles in less than a decade. Automotive history was also made in May of 1954, when Nash-Kelvinator Corporation merged with the Hudson Motor Car Company to form the American Motors Corporation.

Styling changes for 1954 Nash automobiles included new concave grilles and new chrome-ring headlight bezels on Ambassador and Statesman models. Continental rear tire mounts became standard equipment on all Custom models. All models had new interiors and the Nash Ambassador and Nash Statesman shared a redesigned instrument panel. In Rambler models, new chrome sectors were added to the Weather-Eye air intake and a new body styles became available.

A brand new sub-compact car called the Metropolitan also became available at Nash/Hudson/AMC dealerships in 1954. The "Metro" or "Met" evolved from a prewar Nash idea for a small, but full-featured, high-quality automobile. Based on a prototype vehicle called the NXI (Nash Experimental International), the car became a reality when a Nash executive bumped into a British

John Gunnell

The Nash Rambler Custom convertible is a rare car. Just 221 were made in 1954.

automaker during a cruise. The A40 Austin drive train was employed. Metropolitan bodies were built by Fisher & Ludlow in Birmingham, England, and shipped to the Austin factory in Longbridge, England for final assembly. They were then sent to Nash (and later Hudson) dealers in the United States.

Following the May merger, Metropolitans — as well as Ramblers — were sold as both Nashes and Hudsons. The cars were virtually identical, except for wearing different badges and trim. At the same time, Nash dealers sold the Statesman and Ambassador lines, while Hudson dealers handled Hornets, Wasps and Jets. A few franchises sold both brands of cars in the same dealership, but this was rare. Most continued to operate as independent Nash or Hudson dealers through 1956.

The 1954 Statesman models again came in two series and three different body styles. The Super series offered a 3,025-pound two-door sedan for $2,130 and a 3,045-pound four-door sedan for $2,178. The four-door was much more popular, having a 11,401-unit production run versus only 1,855 two-doors. Custom versions of these models were about $190 more expensive and 25-50 pounds heavier. Only 24 Custom two-doors left the assembly line, along with 4,219 four-doors. There was also a Country Club Hardtop in this series. It listed for $2,468, weighed 3,120 pounds and had a production run of 2,726 units.

The 1954 Nash Ambassador had a seven-inch longer wheelbase than the Nash Statesman, but shared the same product changes. The body style offerings were the same, except that no two-door sedan was available in the Custom level. Nash made only 283 of the $2,360 Ambassador Super two-door sedans, along with 7,433 of the Super four-doors, which listed for $2,412. In the Custom line, the $2,595 four-door sedan had a run of 10,131 units, while the two-door hardtop, listing for $2,730, was built just 3,581 times.

The Nash Rambler received no major appearance changes for 1954. Several models were added to the lineup. New body styles included a four-door sedan and a four-door station wagon on a new, longer 108-inch wheelbase. Also added were Deluxe and Super two-door sedans on the 100-inch wheelbase. These were low-line price leaders. To cut costs, radios and heaters were made optional equipment. In all, there were 11 Rambler models priced from $1,444 to $2,200 and 36,231 Nash Ramblers were produced. The 56 Utility Wagons made are rare and only 221 convertibles were built.

Although the engines used in 1954 Nashes were basically the same, some models got a small horsepower boost. Ramblers feature the 184.1-cid 85-hp six (195.6-cid 90-hp six with Hydra-Matic). The Statesman used a new 110-hp version of the 195.6-cid "Powerflyte" six. The 252.6-cid Ambassador six now put out 130 hp at 3700 rpm. The "LeMans Dual-Jetfire Six" remained at 140 hp. This motor was advertised as an engine "that has won many Grand Prix d'Endurance awards."

The new Metropolitan became part of the Nash model lineup in March 1954. It was built on an 85-inch wheelbase, with a 149.5-inch overall length. Styling was by Pininfarina and resembled that of the company's other cars. In fact, *Motor Trend* described the Metropolitan as "a scaled-down version of everything good in a Nash."

A two-seater only, the Metropolitan came in coupe and convertible models. A low, one-piece, rear-hinged hood held a decorative air scoop. A single horizontal bar formed the grille insert. There was a circular Nash medallion at the center. The fenders stood taller than the hood, but the fender line dipped down on the doors. Both the front and rear wheels were partly enclosed. Standard equipment included dual Lucas horns, twin sun visors, an ash tray, a cigarette lighter, a 17-inch steering wheel, a glove box, a map light, a rear view mirror, chrome window frames, a 12-volt electric system and a continental spare tire with a cover. A single instrument cluster in front of the driver held the speedometer, fuel gauge and telltale monitor lights. There was no trunk, but the seatbacks swung forward to give access to a stowage area.

A small, occasional rear seat officially made the Met a 2-3-passenger car. The two-door Hardtop Coupe had an East Coast Port-of-Entry price of $1,445. The Convertible was $24 additional. The two models weighed 1,825 and 1,785 pounds, in the same order. A total of 13,085 Metropolitans were produced during 1954. The Metropolitan had a top speed of 70 mph and got 30-32 miles per gallon in city driving and 37-40 mpg on the highway. In fuel economy tests prior to the car's debut, a Metropolitan achieved 41.57 mpg, at an average speed of 34.83 mph, going 24 hours non-stop.

Nash Motors' calendar-year production included 37,779 Ramblers and 29,371 Nashes. The total of 67,150 cars made Nash America's 13th largest automaker. Model-year production was 62,911 units.

1955 *Nash*

The 1955 Nash Ambassador Super sedan was a popular large Nash offering.

The year was 1955 and plenty of news was being made here in the United States and throughout the world. Dr. Martin Luther King, Jr. led a history-making bus boycott in Montgomery, Alabama. "Sugar" Ray Robinson won boxing's world championship and President Eisenhower suffered a heart attack and was in the hospital for the better part of a month.

According to American Motors Corporation, the automotive news of the year was Nash topped most U.S. cars in resale value.

"Official!" said the announcement. "Nash Ambassador returns a higher percentage of original cost than 14 of all 17 other — tops every one of the four largest-selling "Big 3" cars — according to the latest (June) N.A.D.A. *Official Used Car Guide*."

For Ambassador and Statesman models, changes included a new "Scena-Ramic" wrap-around windshield. Another new feature was a long character molding that ran from the front to the rear fender. The headlights were enclosed in a redesigned oval grille. The new concave grille had multiple vertical chrome dividers. Custom models had a continental spare tire mount.

The Statesman was built on a 114-1/2-inch wheelbase and measured 202-1/4 inches long (212-1/4 inches with a continental kit). Size 6.70 x 15 tires were used. Model offerings included the Super four-door sedan for $2,215, the Custom four-door sedan for $2,385, and the Custom two-door hardtop for $2,495. Series production was 12,877 four-door models and 1,395 hardtops. Base engine in Statesman models was a 195.6-cid 100-hp in-line six with a 7.45:1 compression ratio and a Carter one-barrel carburetor. A 110-hp version with an 8.0:1 compression ratio and twin one-barrel carburetors was optional.

The 1955 Nash Ambassador received the same type of appearance changes as the 1955 Nash Statesman including a new wrap-around windshield, new long character moldings from front to rear fenders, and headlights enclosed in a redesigned oval-concave grille. The Ambassador rode a 121-1/4-inch wheelbase and stretched 209-1/4 inches long (or 10 inches longer when wearing a continental tire). Size 7.10 x 15 tires were used. Model offerings in the six-cylinder series included the Super four-door sedan for $2,480, the Custom four-door sedan for $2,795 and the Custom two-door hardtop for $2,675. The Ambassador's 252.6-cid over-

head-valve six used a 7.6:1 compression ratio and a one-barrel carburetor. It produced 130 hp at 3700 rpm. Series production was 13,809 four-door models and 1,395 hardtops.

The year 1955 marked the introduction of an overhead valve V-8 engine in the Ambassador line. The new power plant was purchased from Packard. It was only available with Twin Ultramatic transmission. The 1955 Nash Ambassador V-8 was distinguished by V-8 emblems on its rear fenders and Ambassador (Custom or Super) V-8 emblems on front fenders. Styling was otherwise the same as on the Ambassador six. The V-8 models were about $300 pricier than the sixes.

The Ambassador's overhead-valve V-8 had 3-13/16 x 3-1/2 inch bore and stroke for 320 cid. It used a 7.8:1 compression ratio and a Carter WGD two-barrel carburetor. Brake horsepower was 208 at 4200 rpm. This Packard-built engine had non-adjustable hydraulic valve lifters and five main bearings. Series production included 8,805 four-doors and 1,775 two-door hardtops.

The 1955 Nash Rambler received a minor face lift over 1954. New features included the addition of a new cellular grille and full wheel cutouts in the front fenders. Both Nash and Hudson marketed versions of the Rambler in 1955. Both had the Rambler name on the front fenders, but they carried different medallions in the center of the grille. Nash offered five body styles in four series.

The cheapest Nash Rambler was the rarest model. This two-door Utility Wagon was built just 14 times. The Deluxe line included a three-passenger Business Sedan, a two-door Club sedan, and a four-door sedan at prices from $1,328 to $1,695. The Super Series offered a two-door Club Sedan, a two-door Suburban, a four-door sedan, and a Cross-Country four-door hardtop for prices between $1,683 and $1,869. Custom models included the two-door Country Club hardtop, the four-door sedan, and a four-door station wagon priced from $1,985 to $2,098.

Two-door Rambler models had a 100-inch wheelbase and measured 178-1/4 inches long without a continental kit. Four-door models had a eight inch longer wheelbase and eight additional inches of length. Cars with continental kits were 7.125 inches longer. The in-line 195.6-cid six-cylinder engine produced 90 hp at 3800 rpm.

Nash dealers also continued to sell the 85-inch wheelbase Metropolitan and the Nash-Healey sports car. Both were captive imports, produced in England, but sold by American Nash dealers (and Hudson dealers in the case of the Metro). The sub-compact came as a $1,445 hardtop or a $1,469 convertible. It was still powered by the 73-cid 42-hp Austin A-40 four-cylinder engine. A total of 6,096 Metropolitans were produced in calendar-year 1955. The Nash-Healeys sold in 1955 were leftover 1954 models, as the last Nash-Healey produced was put together in August 1954. The Nash-Healey had the 252.6-cid 140-hp "Dual-Jetfire" six.

Nash got off to a slow start in 1955, but, once started, moved along at a warm pace. The company wound up the model year with sales of 109,102 units. Calendar-year output was 83,852 Ramblers and 51,315 Nashes for 10th place in the industry. Dealer contests and sales promotions were instrumental in stimulating deliveries. An added feather in Rambler's cap was its consistent holding of number one spot in used car value, as reflected in NADA reports. Model-year production began October 1954 and included 40,133 Statesman/Ambassadors and 56,023 Ramblers.

1956 *Nash*

Sitting by itself at a car show was this 1956 Nash Rambler Custom sedan.

The Atomic Age was underway in 1956 as the Atomic Energy Commission approved the creation of nuclear power plants and Americans began to dream about everything from atomic energy for heating homes to atomic-powered cars.

The 1956 Nash didn't have atomic power, but it could advertise "Blazing V-8 Power with Traditional Nash Economy." The 220-hp AMC-built "Jetfire" V-8 had turned in an impressive 20.7 miles per gallon fuel economy rating in the 1956 Mobilgas Economy Run.

Statesman models received a new six-cylinder engine and a major facelift. The front and rear fenders were restyled with larger, more visible front running lights and new taillights. A revised hood ornament and a one-piece rear window were seen. Chrome side stripping revisions included a shallow "Z" shape on the side of the car and outline moldings on the hood and rear fender sides.

The only Statesman model available for 1956 was the four-door Super sedan with a base retail price of $2,385 and weighing 3,199 pounds. A total of 7,438 were built. Its 195.6-cid engine was redesigned to an overhead valve configuration. With a 7.47:1 compression ratio and a Carter or Stromberg two-barrel carburetor, it produced 130 hp at 4500 rpm. A 12-volt electrical system was used for the first time.

The 1956 Nash Ambassador six was available in only, the four-door Super sedan. It shared all the styling changes of 1956 Statesman models on the seven inch longer wheelbase of the Ambassador platform. An Ambassador Super script appeared on front fenders. Base-priced at $2,689, the 3,555-pound sedan had a

run of 5,999 units. The Ambassador eight shared the same styling changes, but offered a Custom Sedan ($3,195) and a Country Club two-door hardtop ($3,338) as well as the Super sedan ($2,956). The Super V-8 sedan was equipped and trimmed similar to the Super Six sedan. Customs had the name "Ambassador Custom" on the front fenders and "Ambassador Country Club" on the hardtops. On later production models, vertical chrome moldings were added to the Customs' front fenders.

The V-8, again a Packard-built engine, used a larger 352-cid displacement block and produced 220 hp at 4600 rpm This engine was only available with Packard's Ultramatic transmission attached. Series production included 3,885 four-doors and just 796 two-doors.

The Nash Ambassador Special V-8 was introduced as a midyear 1956 model and came out in April with a 250-cid 190-hp V-8 engine of AMC's own design and manufacture. The Ambassador Special was available as a Super or Custom four-door sedan and a two-door hardtop coupe at prices between $2,365 and $2,541. Supers had single side rub-rail moldings and chrome moldings across the front of the hood and fenders. Power brakes, an "Airliner" reclining seat and continental tire mounting were standard on Custom models. They also had double chrome side rub-rail moldings enclosing a separate color area and a chrome band across the front of the hood and fenders. Later production models added vertical chrome moldings to the front fenders of Customs. A total of 4,145 sedans were made in both series, as well as 706 Custom two-door hardtops.

The 1956 Nash Rambler received a major redesign of the long-wheelbase four-door sedan and station wagon. The short-wheelbase cars were dropped. (They would reappear, with a few minor changes, as the 1958 American.) The 1956 models had a new oval-shaped grille housing the headlights located inside the grille. Running lights (front parking lights that stayed on even when the headlights were turned on) were set high in each front fender. They complemented the new rear fenders and revisions to the rear deck. Chrome trim and three-tone color treatments were available. A wraparound rear window appeared and the first four-door hardtop station wagon.

The Rambler offerings included one Deluxe sedan for $1,829. There were two Supers, the sedan for $1,939 and the station wagon for $2,233. The four Custom models were the four-door Country Club station wagon, the four-door Custom sedan, the four-door Custom Cross Country station wagon, and the Custom four-door hardtop. These ranged from $2,056 to $2,491. Total model-year production in this series was 46,077 cars. The 195.6-cid Rambler six put out 120 hp.

The original 42-hp Metropolitan remained available at many Nash dealerships that had failed to sell the cars in 1954 and 1955. The true 1956 Metropolitans were second-generation cars with a new "1500" Austin A-50 engine. The new 1489-cc overhead-valve four put out 52 hp at 4500 rpm and 77 foot-pounds of torque at 2500 rpm. It used a Zenith one-barrel downdraft carburetor. Nash claimed a top speed of 78 mph with 40 mpg fuel economy.

The 1956 Metropolitans had a new oval-shaped grille opening with a cellular insert. The air scoop was eliminated from the hood and a new body side molding treatment was seen. A horizontal molding started at the headlight and ran to a point just behind the first door break line. It then slanted down and back, to mid-body level, before continuing horizontally to the rear. This molding served as a separation line for two-tone paint schemes. Standard upper body colors of Caribbean Green, Sunburst Yellow, Coral Red, or black were used on the upper part of the body. The roof and lower body were done in Snowberry White. The more powerful hardtop carried an East Coast Port of Entry price of $1,527 and the convertible cost an additional $44. Production came to 9,068 cars in both body styles.

Dealer introductions of 1956 models took place on Nov. 22, 1955. Cars were sold by both Hudson and Nash dealers and the Series 10 models were known as American Motors Ramblers. The Hudson and Nash products were comparable, except for hood medallions and their "N" or "H" wheel cover insignias. The company's automotive division sustained a sizable loss while its appliance division enjoyed its most profitable year since 1950. The corporation sold idle plants and equipment (El Segundo, Calif., and the Hudson-Gratiot plant in Detroit) for $5.3 million.

Calendar-year 1956 saw production by American Motors of 104,190 cars (79,166 Ramblers, 17,842 Nashes, 7,182 Hudsons). American Motors Corp. produced its 2,000,000th single-unit construction car on March 27.

Genuine leather trims were available in Ambassador Six and Ambassador V-8 sedans, Ambassador Country Club hardtops, Rambler sedans, Rambler four-door hardtops and Rambler Country Club station wagons.

1957 Nash

The final year for the large Nash was 1957 with models like this Ambassador Custom sedan.

Americans were traveling in 1957. Federal troops traveled to Little Rock, Arkansas to integrate the public schools. Beat writer Jack Kerouac traveled across the country in a Hudson to "research" his best-selling book *On the Road*. Colonel John Glenn, of the United States Marines, flew from California to New York in less than 3-1/2 hours, setting a new transcontinental speed record in the process.

As far as new cars went, the 1957 Nash was advertised as "The World's Newest and Finest Travel Car!" while AMC claimed that its Rambler 6 Cross-Country, with overdrive, could travel "coast-to-coast (at) 1-cent a mile for gas." (This claim was based on a Rambler wagon getting 32.09 mpg on a NASCAR economy run.)

Promoting the cars to travelers had a lot to do with the

famous (or infamous) Airliner reclining seats and Twin Travel Beds featured in the Nashes. Other outstanding features of the '57s included their double-coat baked enamel finish, 12-volt electrical system, torque-tube drive, big 11-inch diameter brakes and the optional Weather-Eye heating and ventilating system. Power brakes were standard on Custom models.

The Ambassador for 1957 was available only with a 327-cid AMC V-8 engine in two-door hardtops and four-door sedans. Super and Custom trim levels were provided. The Nash Ambassador six and Statesman six were discontinued. The new Ambassador received a major facelift incorporating the first four-beam headlight system used on any American car. Also seen was completely new front end styling, including a new cellular grille, front parking lights on top of the front fenders, and new "lightning streak" side trim.

The Ambassador Super had its name on the front fenders in script, small hubcaps and single lightning streak side trim with no upper beltline molding. Ambassador Customs had script with that name on the fenders, dual molding lightning streak trim, and full wheel covers. This was the last year for Nash production.

The Nash Ambassador 8 four-door Super sedan listed for $2,821. It tipped the scale at 3,639 pounds and 3,098 were built. The Nash Ambassador 8 four-door Custom sedan listed for $190 additional. It weighed 3,701 pounds and had a run of 5,627 units. Prices for the Super two-door hardtop started at $2,910. Only 608 of these 3,655-pound cars were made. The priciest model in the Nash lineup was the Custom two-door hardtop. With a $3,101 suggested retail price, the 3,722-pound Nash found just 997 buyers.

The Rambler six for 1957 continued the 108-inch wheelbase with a few minor changes. Included were new vertical front running lights with horizontal bright metal dividers that were positioned below the headlights. A new wing-shaped ornament was positioned on top of the rectangular grille section. The side color accent trim running over the roof was discontinued. Three series were again available. Deluxe models had the lowest level of trim and equipment and were essentially built for fleet customers. Deluxe models came with no series name or side moldings.

The Deluxe four-door sedan listed for $1,961 and weighed 2,911 pounds. The Deluxe four-door wagon was more expensive and heavier at $2,292 and 3,034 pounds. Series production included 9,402 sedans and 75 wagons. Super series models carried a single, full-length side molding with the word "Super," in script, on the rear fenders. This car-line offered the same body styles as the Deluxe series, as well as a four-door hardtop. The sedan sold for $2,123, weighed 2,914 pounds, and had a 16,300-unit run. The wagon sold for $2,410, weighed

3,042 pounds, and had a 14,083-unit run. The four-door hardtop sold for $2,208, weighed 2,936 pounds, and only 612 were built.

The Custom series models came with Rambler Custom script on the front fenders and dual side moldings, with a round medallion at the forward end. The $2,213 sedan was a 2,938-pound vehicles, of which 10,520 were made. The $2,500, 3,076-pound wagon was more popular. With a 17,745-vehicle run.

The Rambler, for 1957, was also available with a 250-cid V-8. The same four-door station wagon and sedan styles were offered with this brand new Rambler power plant. Super and Custom trim levels were provided. Super series models carried a single, full-length side molding with the word Super, in script, on the rear fenders. Deluxe models came with no series name or side moldings.

The Custom series models came with Rambler Custom script on the front fenders and dual side moldings, with a round medallion at the forward end. Prices ranged from $2,253 to $2,715. Production totals included 3,555 Super sedans, 2,461 Super wagons, 3,199 Custom sedans, 485 Custom four-door hardtops, 4,560 Custom station wagons, and 182 Custom hardtop station wagons.

The 1957 Rambler Rebel used the Ambassador 327-cid engine in a Rambler V-8 body. This limited-production car was available exclusively in light silver-gray metallic finish. It had black nylon and silver-gray vinyl upholstery. However, many of the cars were later repainted by dealers, due to excessive fading of the silver-gray paint. The 1957 Rebel featured a side molding of bronze/gold anodized aluminum, which ran the full length of the car. The four-door hardtop body style was the only one available and the Rebel version sold for $2,786.

The 3,353-pound Rebel was the first attempt by American Motors to build a high-performance car. In fact, this was the first time a large engine had been placed in a true intermediate-size chassis (an idea Pontiac would find great success with in the GTO) by any automaker. In an April 1957 *Motor Trend* test, it was found that the only car capable of a faster 0-to-60 mph time than the Rebel was the fuel-injected Corvette. Fuel-injection had actually been planned for the 1957 Rebel with 288-hp possible. However, problems with the electric control unit prevented its production. A mildly re-worked 327-cid Ambassador engine was used. Only 1,500 of these cars were built.

Dealer introductions for the 1957 models were held Oct. 25, 1956. Calendar-year production of 3,561 Nash automobiles gave the marque a .06 percent market share. The Rambler nameplate did somewhat better with calendar year production of 109,178 cars for a 1.78 percent slice of the pie. Model-year production included 10,330 Nashes and 84,699 Ramblers.

1958 *Rambler*

It was a year for shockers in 1958 as Elvis Presley was drafted and sent off to serve with the U.S. Army in Germany. Sharon Stone, Alec Baldwin, Tim Robbins, and Drew Carey were born, but Liz Taylor's husband Michael Todd died in a plane crash.

A shocker to some automotive enthusiasts in 1958 was the disappearance of the Nash nameplate. American Motors Corporation cars were now called Ramblers, Ambassadors, and Metropolitans.

The disappearance of the Nash and Hudson names from the

The 1958 Rambler Rebel now was a mid-level model in the restyled series.

Ambassador was a last minute decision made by AMC chief executive officer George Romney and his upper management. A number of pre-production cars were built with Nash and Hudson emblems ahead of the Ambassador nameplates on the sides of the front fenders. Factory photos show Nash Ambassador nameplates and early factory literature has noticeable emblems airbrushed out of the catalogs.

Although the 1958 Ambassador was promoted separately from the Rambler, it was now built off of the 108-inch Rambler chassis. A nine-inch longer front-end sheet metal section turned the Rambler into the Ambassador. The 1958 Ambassador had model identification just above the grille, on the front fenders, and on the rear deck lid. Side trim featured "dual jet-stream" side moldings, which were painted a contrasting color.

The tone used for the insert harmonized with body colors used on Super models. Silver aluminum side trim was used inside the moldings on Custom models, which also featured model nameplates on the rear deck lid or tailgate. There were three bright-metal wind splits on the rear window pillars of hardtops and sedans and on the wide pillars of station wagons. Super nameplates were on rear fenders.

The Ambassador line offered two Super models — a four-door sedan and a four-door station wagon — at $2,587 and $2,881, respectively. There were four Custom models — four-door sedan, four-door hardtop, four-door station wagon and four-door hardtop station wagon — priced from $2,732 to $3,116. Series production included 3,825 Supers and 10,745 Customs. The hardtop wagon was especially rare, with only 294 assemblies. These cars were built on a 117-inch wheelbase and measured 200.14 inches long (207.898 inches with a continental kit). They used the 327-cid AMC V-8 with 9.7:1 compression and a Holley four-barrel carburetor. This produced 270 hp at 4700 rpm.

The 1958 AMC American revived the former Nash Rambler and joined the lineup in January. A two-door sedan was the only model available. It came in Deluxe Business Coupe ($1,775), Deluxe two-door sedan ($1,789), and Super two-door sedan ($1,874) models. The Super version featured bright metal windshield and belt line moldings to distinguish it from the Deluxe versions. The 195.6-cid L-head six was used with its water pump moved to the front. Engine specs included an 8.0:1 compression ratio, a Carter one-barrel carburetor, and a rating of 90 hp at 3800 rpm. Series production included 184 Deluxe Business Coupes, 15,765 Deluxe two-door sedans, and 14,691 Super two-door sedans.

The Rambler Six received new front and rear fenders. It represented a major restyling of the 108-inch wheelbase 1957 Rambler body. The new front fenders featured quad headlights on all but Deluxe models, which had single headlights as standard equipment and dual headlights optional.

The 1958 Rambler rear fenders featured small, restrained tailfins. This was a move towards conforming with current styling trends. The Rambler line was one of the last to add tailfins to its cars and one of the first to drop them. Custom and Super models also featured new side trim moldings. The engine used was the overhead-valve version of the 195.6-cid in-line six with an 8.7:1 compression ratio and a one-barrel Carter carburetor. It was good for 127 hp at 4200 rpm.

There were two Deluxe models — four-door sedan and four-door Cross-Country station wagon — priced at $2,047 and $2,376, respectively. Supers came in three models — four-door sedan, four-door Country Club, hardtop and four-door Cross-Country station wagon — priced from $2,212 to $2,506. The Custom series offered a four-door sedan for $2,327 and a Cross-Country wagon for $2,621. Total output of Rambler sixes was 106,916 cars

The V-8-powered Rebel shared the styling of the Rambler six, with the biggest difference being the power train. Rebel Customs earned V-8 front fender emblems. New was a deep-dip rust-proofing process. A wide side trim panel with a 'half-spear-tip' front shape was used. It had a contrasting beauty insert. Split-fin hood ornaments were used and Custom models had the fancier side trim treatment. The Fleet Deluxe sedan sold for $2,177 and only 22 of these 3,287-pound cars were built. The Super line offered two models, the four-door sedan for $2,342 and the four-door Cross-Country station wagon for $2,636.

There were three Customs — four-door sedan, four-door Cross-Country wagon, and four-door Country Club hardtop — priced between $2,457 and $2,751. A total of 10,057 Rebels were built including just 410 Country Club hardtops. All used the AMC 250-cid V-8 with 8.7:1 compression and a single Holley four-barrel. Output was 215 hp at 4900 rpm.

After the Nash and Hudson names faded away at the end of the 1957 model year, Metropolitans were marketed as American Motors models sold by Rambler dealers.

The price on the hardtop coupe increased to $1,626 and the convertible now listed for $1,650.. Metropolitans cost $52.65 extra when delivered to West Coast ports. The 1500

engine was used again with the horsepower rating raised to 55 at 4600 rpm (from 52 at 4500 rpm).

The AMC American appeared in dealer showrooms in January. Model-year production peaked at 162,182 units. Calendar-year sales of 199,236 cars were recorded.

The company made a $26 million profit after two straight years of losses. A business expansion program was initiated by year's end.

1959 *Rambler*

The 1959 Rambler Rebel V-8 Custom Country Club hardtop was an upscale version of the popular car.

The American nation grew larger in 1959. On January 3, the frozen tundra of Alaska became the 49th state in the Union and the Aloha State became a reality on August 21. That put the 50th star on Old Glory.

The AMC American didn't grow in 1959. It soldiered on as a compact car in a sea of land yachts. Its newfound popularity, inspired by an economic recession, was amazing, since its styling dated to 1954. Front fender name scripts now said "American" instead of "Rambler American." No body side moldings were seen. The grille had a rectangular shape and surrounded by a chrome housing with rounded corners. A grid-type insert was used and a round medallion was housed in the center of the grille.

AMC built three each of two rare Panel Delivery commerical versions, with both side windows and solid steel panels. Passenger versions came in Deluxe and Super trim. Deluxes had black rubber windshield and rear window trim and lacked belt moldings.

A Business Sedan, two-door sedan, and station wagon were offered at prices between $1,821 and $2,060. The two-door sedan and wagon also came as Supers for about $90 more. Super models had bright metal trim around the windshield and rear window. The Super two-door sedan was rated for one more pas-

senger than other noncommercial models..

Rambler had a new grille, body side trim and re-contoured rear tailfins. The new fender treatment blended the fins into the upper beltline in a smooth, down-curving line. A horizontal gap ran above the upper grille bar and between the dual headlights. Stand-up chrome letters, spelling the word Rambler, appeared in the gap. The manufacturer's name also decorated the deck lid or tailgate. A four-door sedan and four-door Cross-Country station wagon were offered in Deluxe, Super, and Custom series. Buyers could also get a four-door Super hardtop, a rare car. Only 2,683 were built.

Prices of Rambler sixes ran from $2,098 to $2,677. Deluxe models had no series nameplates or side trim and dual headlights were optional. Super models had nameplates within the tip of the missile-shaped side trim. The straight front molding stopped just beyond the middle of the front door, without hitting the rear trim. Custom models had nameplates at the front of the rear missile-shaped body side molding. A narrower, straight molding extended along the upper body side from just behind the headlights to the missile-shaped molding. The Rambler six contributed 242,581 cars to the model-year production count.

The V-8-powered Rebel shared the same body styling features as the Rambler six. The major external difference was Custom models had Rebel V-8 emblems on the front fenders, ahead of the wheel openings. The scripts placed within the missile-shaped rear molding panel earned the name of the trim line, except on the plain-looking Deluxes, which had no script. The four-door sedan was in all three series. The Cross-Country wagon was also in the Super and Custom series.

The rare four-door hardtop came only with Custom trim when a V-8 was under the hood. A total of 691 were made. It was the rarest body style in the overall Rambler product line. The total output of Rambler Rebel V-8s was 16,399 cars.

The 1959 Ambassador retained the basic 1958 styling, with changes comparable to those on Ramblers and Rebels. The wide gap above the upper grille bar had Ambassador spelled out in stand-up block letters. Custom models had silver aluminum trim inside the dual side moldings.

The front of the side trim spear had "Ambassador" lettering at its tip. The body side trim, although similar to the Rambler type had more of a lightning bolt shape than a missile shape. The upper molding zigged upwards just below the rear side window, but the lower molding did not zag. The Ambassador grille was distinctive in that it had a full-width horizontal central bar, instead of a cellular grid-type insert. The bar had a V-shaped dip at its center.

A Deluxe four-door sedan was offered, but only 155 were built. This model and the Cross-Country four-door station wagon also came with Super trim. Four Custom models were offered: four-door sedan, four-door Country Club hardtop, four-door Country Club hardtop wagon, and four-door Cross-Country wagon. The four-door hardtop had "Custom Country Club" written on the rear fender tips. Other cars, depending on trim line, read "Deluxe," "Custom" or "Super" in the same spot. Prices ranged from $2,369 to $3,116. AMC made 23,749 Ambassadors.

After Oct. 8, 1958, Metropolitans still at dealerships were registered as 1959 models. Prices were lowered to $1,398 for the hardtop and $1,421 for the convertible. Starting Feb. 18, 1959, the true 1959 models with an opening trunk lid became available. These started with VIN E59048 and Engine No. IH14004. At this point the prices increased slightly to $1,441 for the hardtop and $1,464 for the ragtop. These are Port of Entry prices and do not include Ocean Transport Costs which were $107.90 to East Coast ports and $160.55 to West Coast ports in 1959.

A real trunk seemed to give the Metropolitan more initial appeal and production increased to 22,309 cars. A total of 94,986 Meropolitans were produced between 1954 and 1962.

The American used the old 195.6-cid 90-hp L-head six which had an 8.0:1 compression ratio and single-barrel carburetor. The Rambler six got an overhead-valve version of the same motor with 8.7:1 compression. The 250-cid 215-hp V-8 under the Rebel's hood had an 8.7:1 compression ratio and a Holley four-barrel carburetor. The Ambassador used the bigger 327-cid V-8 and managed 270 hp with a 9.7:1 compression ratio and a four-barrel.

Size-wise, the '59 models lined up as the Metropolitan with an 85-inch wheelbase and 149.5-inch overall length, the American with a 100-inch wheelbase and 178.32-inch overall length, the Rambler with a 108-inch wheelbase and 191.15-inch overall length and the Ambassador with a 117-inch wheelbase and 200.15-inch overall length.

All AMC models were introduced (or updated in the case of the Metropolitan) on Oct. 8, 1958. Model-year production peaked at 374,240 units.

A record profit of $60,341,823 was earned by AMC and the Rambler slipped into fourth spot in American car sales for the first time. Resale value was high, a fact Rambler salesmen often stressed.

A popular choice in 1959 was the Rambler Six Custom sedan, like this well-preserved model.

Oldsmobiles
of the Fifties

1950 *Oldsmobile*

This 1950 Olds 88 Holiday two-door hardtop includes the "Futuramic" label in chrome.

It was a year for setting records — 1950. And it started just 17 days into the year when 11 hold-up men got away with $2 million from an armored car in Boston, Massachusetts. The "Great Brink's Job" was just the beginning of the record-setting year, too.

In May, a ship named St. Roch put in at Halifax, Nova Scotia, after becoming the first vessel to circumnavigate the North American continent. In England, in August, Florrie Chadwick swam the English Channel in just under 13-1/2 hours. And during the same year, Oldsmobiles set many motor sports records. The "Rocket 88s" took 10 of 19 big NASCAR races.

Olds pilot Bill Rexford was declared the championship stock car driver of the year. South of the border, Hershell McGriff and Ray Elliott took the checkered flag in the 1950 Mexican Road Race with their No. 52 Olds coupe. Car owner Roy Sundstrom got 150,000 pesos ($17,341.04) for their victory. McGriff, a 32-year-old lumber truck driver at the time, won by a one-minute-and-19-second margin. (McGriff raced until 2002, when he retired, at age 74, in the middle of a race). McGriff's Oldsmobile was one of 13 that competed in that first La Carrera Panamericana.

It was the final year for the six-cylinder Olds 76. The company's next six-cylinder engine —released in the '60s — would be built by Buick. Standard equipment on 1950 sixes included bumper guards, dual horns, parking lamps, a dome light, rubber front floor mats and aluminum sill plates. Deluxe equipment added foam rubber seat cushions, robe rails, stainless steel gravel shields and extra chrome moldings.

A new Holiday Coupe (two-door hardtop) was introduced and this was the last year for an Oldsmobile station wagon until 1957. The 76 Series lineup included five two-door models, the sedan, the Club Sedan, the Club Coupe, the Holiday Coupe and the convertible, as well as a four-door sedan and a station wagon. Prices ranged from $1,615 to $2,360. Series production came to 33,257 for the model year, including just 538 Holiday Coupes, only 973 convertibles and a mere 368 station wagons.

In its second year on the market, the Olds 88 continued to be one of the hottest-performing (and hottest-selling) cars available off the showroom floor. The 88 could be readily identified by the "88" insignia with a rocket placed on the rear deck lid. It was the focus of most Oldsmobile advertising in 1950. "Make a date with a 'Rocket 8,'" urged one announcement that described the tidy-sized V-8 model's "high-compression power" and "velvet-action Hydra-Matic Drive."

The copywriter noted the Rocket 88 was: "A sensation for a Demonstration!" Another called it: "The big number with the new low price."

The Olds 88's body and chassis were quite similar to those of cars in the 76 series. A one-piece curved windshield was a midyear upgrade for 88s. Standard and Deluxe equipment packages were available. Upholstery choices included broadcloth, striped cloth, nylon and a variety of colored leathers. Standard tire size was 7.60 x 15 inches.

The same body styles were offered in the "Olds 88" series as in the 76 series. They were priced between $1,725 and $2,585. The 88 series was successful in catching the public's fancy and ultimately contributed 268,412 cars to Oldsmobile's model-year production total.

Like Cadillac, the Oldsmobile branch of General Motors used its senior cars to preview the styling that would be seen on lower-priced cars the following year. The 1950 Olds 98 showed buyers what the 1951 Olds 88 would look like. It was the first slab-sided Oldsmobile and the first sedan with wraparound rear windows.

On all 98s, the word "Oldsmobile" was seen at the extreme bottom edge of the hood, spaced out to the full width of the hood. The grille had one curved bar and one straight bar instead of two curved bars like the smaller models.

A four-door fastback body style was re-admitted to the Olds 98 line. Standard equipment included all items from the 88, plus foam rubber seat cushions, chrome interior trim, a lined luggage compartment and a counter-balanced trunk lid.

The Deluxe equipment package added a rear seat center arm rest, a deluxe electric clock, a deluxe steering wheel and horn button, special door trim and stainless steel wheel trim rings. Upholstery came in nylon fabric, striped broadcloth or leather. The standard tire size was 7.60 x 15. Three two-door models (Club Sedan, Holiday Coupe and convertible) joined the four-door sedan and four-door Town Sedan and prices for the five cars ranged from $2,095 to $2,615.

The 231.5-cid straight six used in the 76 was a flathead engine with solid valve lifters and a 6.5:1 compression ratio. A one-barrel Carter downdraft carburetor was mounted and it had an automatic choke. Olds advertised 105 hp at 3400 rpm. The 303.7-cid V-8 used in 88 and 98 models was quite different in nature. It had overhead valves with hydraulic valve lifters and ran a 7.25:1 compression ratio. Its output was 135 hp at 3600 rpm. That didn't match the 160 hp of a '50 Cadillac or the 152 hp of a contemporary Lincoln, but it was enough to make the Olds 88 a road rocket.

The small Oldsmobiles shared a 119-1/2-inch wheelbase, while the 98 had a 122-inch stance. Overall length was 202 inches for all of the short-wheelbase models, except the station wagon, which was 205 inches long. The 98 was 209 inches.

Options for 1950 Oldsmobiles included a standard Condition-Air heater and defroster for $45 (deluxe $60), a standard radio for $85 (deluxe $110), a Futuramic electric clock for $15, a deluxe steering wheel with horn ring for $20, stainless steel wheel trim rings for $10, deluxe wheel covers for $17, turn signals for $15 and an under hood light for $2. Even an outside rear view mirror was $3 extra. The standard transmission was a column-shifted manual three-speed. Hydra-Matic Drive was available on any 1950 Olds. Heavy-duty oil-bath air cleaners were available on both the six and V-8. A full-flow oil filter was an option for V-8s only.

The 1950 Oldsmobiles were introduced in December 1949. Model-year output amounted to 407,889 cars. Calendar-year output was 396,757. Oldsmobile's industry ranking this year was sixth. At the Olds factory in Lansing, Mich., S.E. Skinner occupied the general manager's desk. His designers turned out the "Palm Beach" dream car. Based on the Holiday hardtop, the Palm Beach featured alligator hide and basket weave wicker trim.

1951 *Oldsmobile*

War in Korea meant cars like the 1951 Oldsmobile 88 sedan went without whitewalls.

> *"You may have heard of jalopies*
> *You heard the noise they make*
> *Let me introduce you to my Rocket 88*
> *Yes, it's great, just won't wait*
> *Everybody likes my Rocket 88"*

When the author of this book wants to zone out a little, in the middle of the day at work, he just plops on the headphones, slips Rhino Record's "Hot Rods & Custom Classics Cruisin' Songs & Highway Hits" into the CD player and settles in for a mid-afternoon trip "back to the future."

One of the ditties on that CD is the 1951 rhythm-and-blues number "Rocket 88," by Jackie Brenston and his Delta Cats, that some (including Sun Records pioneer Sam Phillips) credit as the *first* rock-and-roll record. The interesting thing is "Rocket 88" was written by Ike Turner and recorded by his Kings of Rhythm band, in which Brenston wailed on sax.

The record's lyrics touch on a major motivation for car collecting—a cool car's romantic appeal to the opposite sex. There is no

"correct" answer to what was the first rock-and-roll tune and "Rocket 88" never made it to the top 10. It was one of the year's top R & B hits and it clearly reflected the contemporary American view of the Olds Rocket 88 as a hot showroom item.

This factory hot rod also went racing again and captured 20 of 41 checkered flags in stock-car competitions. "Ride the Rocket and Rule the Road!" Oldsmobile advertised in 1951. The company even promoted the 98 as a "Rocket 98" to try to boost its sales and a pricier new Super 88 lineup was released as a way to increase profits from Rocket 88 sales.

The original Rocket 88 was coded as the 88-A series and the cars in it were almost identical to 1950 models. A chrome running board strip along the bottom of the body identified the 88. Two body styles were offered. Standard features included bumper guards, a dome light, rubber floor mats, stainless steel body side moldings and a lined trunk. Deluxe 88s had foam seat cushions, rear ashtrays and stainless steel gravel shields. Upholstery choices were nylon or nylon cord. Standard tire size was 7.60 x 15 inches.

Near the end of the model year, 88-A production was dropped altogether and the car disappeared from later editions of the 1951 catalog. The two-door sedan was the "race car" model with its low $1,815 price and light 3,585-pound weight. Olds built 11,792 of these. There was also a four-door sedan that cost $56 more and weighed 25 pounds extra. It accounted for 22,848 assemblies during the model year.

The new, mid-price-range Super 88 series was restyled and completely different than the 88 series. In fact, the tables were turned this year with the restyled 88 predicting some of the 1952 Ninety-Eight's styling cues. With five body styles, the Super 88 series offered buyers more selection than the other 1951 Oldsmobiles. A Deluxe package was offered on this series. It included items from both the standard and deluxe 88 packages, plus low-pressure tires, special interior chrome door trim, exposed chrome roof bows and dual rear quarter courtesy lights. Upholstery choices were colored leathers, nylon cloth or nylon cord. The standard tire size was 7.60 x 15 inches.

Super 88 models could be identified by a chrome slash on the rear fenders and the "88" insignia just ahead of the slash. As if to prove that the Super 88 line was the sportiest series, four models were two-door styles: sedan, Club Coupe, Holiday Hardtop and convertible. There was also a four-door sedan. Prices started at $1,928 and peaked at $2,333. Olds built 34,963 two-door sedans, 7,328 Club Coupes, 14,180 Holidays, 3,854 ragtops and 90,131 four-doors. The closed cars weighed 3,600 pounds and change. The open car was around 240 pounds heavier. A hydraulically-operated seat and windows were standard in the convertible.

The 98 topped the Oldsmobile line again for 1951. Three body styles were available. The four-door sedan and convertible came only with deluxe equipment, while the Holiday hardtop was available with either deluxe or standard trim. Standard equipment included all items from the lower series, plus an illuminated ashtray, foam rubber seat cushions and extra chrome moldings.

Deluxe equipment included a special rear door ornament, a rear seat center armrest, a deluxe electric clock, a deluxe steering wheel with horn ring and special chrome trim. Upholstery choices were nylon cord, nylon cloth and leather. Prices ran from $2,267 to $2,644 and production numbers included 17,929 hardtops, 78,122 sedans and 4,468 ragtops.

The hydraulic-lifter Rocket 8 again had a 3-3/4 x 3-7/16-inch bore and stroke and displaced 303 cubic inches. It developed the same 135 at 3600 rpm and 263 foot-pounds of torque at 1800 rpm. The 1951 Rocket engine did have a couple of notable improvements like a shielded electrical system, new durability and higher efficiency for better fuel economy. An improved Hydra-Matic transmission permitted the car to be "rocked" when stuck on mud or ice. It was a $159 option.

The '51 Oldsmobile had a brand new chassis that featured a six-point suspension ride. The rear springs were extra-large, tapered semi-elliptic leaves. They were 58 inches long, 2-1/2 inches wide and angle-mounted to give smoother riding characteristics. Direct-acting airplane-type shock absorbers assured greater road-hugging stability.

The 1951 Oldsmobiles debuted in showrooms in January 1951. Model-year production was 285,615 units, while the calendar-year production total included only 19 additional cars. Oldsmobile ranked seventh on the industry sales charts this year. Jack Wolfram became the new general manager of Oldsmobile Division—the 13th man to hold that position.

1952 Oldsmobile

The rarest Oldsmobile 98 model was the 1952 convertible with just over 3,500 sold.

Big things were happening in the world in 1952. In the United States, Senator Richard Nixon, running for vice president on the Republican ticket, was accused of using money from supporters for personal use. He defended himself in a famous nationally-televised speech named for his dog Checkers. (In part of the speech, Nixon stated, "I own a 1950 Oldsmobile

car.") The big news in England was their development of an atomic bomb. In Helsinki, Finland, the Olympics made big headlines. In Puerto Rico, the big change was the island becoming a U.S. Commonwealth. In Denmark, there was big interest in Christine Jorgensen, the first person to undergo a successful sex-change operation.

In the automotive world, the Oldsmobile was a big car. "Every inch a classic!" said one advertisement for the Olds 98. And they noted it's 213-inch length. Copywriters described the two-tone blue Holiday Coupe in the illustration as "Long on looks — nearly eighteen feet of modern styling."

It was, indeed, an era in which the size of a car made a statement about its desirability and performance. Small cars were for taking on errands and "land yachts" were for driving. The Olds 98 may have seemed like a "boat" to some people, but it was definitely a luxury liner that sailed down the highway smartly and as smooth as silk. New options introduced in 1952 included the autronic eye automatic headlight dimmer and power steering.

Oldsmobile maintained its simple three-car format in 1952. Starting things off was a two-model series known as the Deluxe 88 line. It shared a 120-inch wheelbase, chassis features and most body features with the Super 88. A little less chrome was used and a slightly lower-powered version of the Rocket V-8 was fitted.

Standard equipment included bumper guards, gray rubber floor mats front and rear, an electric clock, dual horns, aluminum door sill plates and rubber gravel shields. There was a "Rocket 88" nameplate on the rear deck lid and black rubber gravel shields protected the rear fenders. Upholstery was a gray basket-weave corded cloth. Standard tire size was 7.60 x 15 inches. The $2,050 two-door sedan weighed 3,565 pounds and 6,402 were made. The four-door sedan was priced $60 higher and weighed an additional 43 pounds. With twice as many doors, it was nearly twice as popular, too, and 12,215 were assembled.

Similar to the Deluxe 88, the five-model Super 88 lineup was the most popular Oldsmobile series. "Ride the Rocket and Save!" suggested an ad for the Super 88 two-door sedan. "Master of the miles and miser with your money — that's Oldsmobile's all-new Super '88'! Thrilling action plus exceptional economy are yours in this newest 'Rocket' Engine car!"

The economy-of-operation claims were based on the reputation of the "revolutionary new" Carter Quadri-Jet carburetor, which was considered a high-tech four-barrel in its day.

The Super 88 outsold the 88 by a six-to-one margin. Part of the reason it sold well was the Super 88 shared a new, more powerful Rocket V-8 with the 98. Other standard equipment included all Deluxe 88 items, plus foam rubber seat cushions, a rear fender chrome slash, and stainless steel gravel shields. There was a Rocket 88 emblem on the trunk. Upholstery choices were broadcloth, nylon sharkskin, nylon Bedford cord or leather.

There were five body styles priced from $2,126 to $2,595. Four

—a sedan, Club Coupe, Holiday Coupe and convertible—had just two doors and a four-door sedan rounded out the lineup. Series production was 118,558 cars, including just 2,050 Club Coupes and 5,162 ragtops.

The 98 models remained as the top-of-the-line Oldsmobiles. There were just three body styles. Standard features included Super 88 items plus front and rear carpeting, an electric clock, stainless steel wheel trim rings, a windshield washer, a deluxe steering wheel with horn ring and back-up lights low in the rear fenders.

The big Oldsmobiles had "Ninety-Eight" spelled out in chrome script between the gravel guards and the chrome trim slashes. These cars also had hooded parking lights and a one-piece, wrap-around rear window. Upholstery selection was broadcloth or six colors of leather. Standard tire size was 8.00 x 15. Pricing started at $2,532 for the four-door sedan (58,550 built) and ranged to $2,940 for the convertible (3,544 built). The $2,750 Holiday Coupe was a two-door hardtop with a 14,150-car production run.

Both Olds engines were modern 303-cid overhead-valve V-8s with a cast iron block and hydraulic valve lifters. The version used in Deluxe 88s had a 7.5:1 compression ratio and a two-barrel carburetor. It put out 145 hp at 3600 rpm and 280 foot-pounds of torque at 1800 rpm. The Super 88 and 98 engines added a four-barrel carburetor to reach 160 hp at 3600 rpm and 284 foot-pounds of torque at 1800 rpm.

High-lift valve action, a short stroke and automatic spark control were features of the Rocket V-8. Oldsmobile's optional Hydra-Matic Super Drive transmission had dual power ranges for all highway and traffic conditions from mud to mountains.

Other Oldsmobile selling features included a stabilized chassis, a noise-proof drive line, Dual Center Control steering, super hydraulic brakes and Fisher Unisteel bodies.

During 1952, Oldsmobile was the top-selling car in America with automatic transmission and the fourth best selling car on industry sales charts (a new high for the company). The one-millionth Rocket V-8 was built. Model-year production came to 213,420 cars. Calendar-year production was 228,452. That was a 20 percent drop from 1951, but the decline was due mainly to government production restrictions because of the Korean War. Market share and share of verall GM business was down only slightly.

The Southern 500 stock car race at Darlington, S.C., on Labor Day 1952, was the biggest of three NASCAR events Oldsmobiles won in 1952.

1953 *Oldsmobile*

On Oct. 14, 1947, Chuck Yeager became the first person to break the sound barrier in his X-1 rocket plane. It wasn't until Nov. 20, 1953 that the next milestone in rocket-plane history was set when Scott Crossfield became the first pilot to hit mach 2.01 in a Navy D-558-II. By December 12, Yaeger regained his "world's fastest man" title by hitting mach 2.5 in a Bell X-IA. As we all know, Yaeger later served as a spokesperson for the Corvette sports car, but one has to wonder if he drove an Oldsmobile "For a Rocketing Good Time" in 1953.

That's how ads of the year described Olds ownership, again urging potential buyers to "Make a date with a 'Rocket 8.'" Also called

the "Big 'Feature' Car of the Year," the '53 Olds was the first to offer power brakes and power steering. The front of the car was completely restyled and the Oldsmobile name appeared, stamped in block letters, on the center bumper bar.

The chrome slash used on the rear fender of some models now had a slimmer look and more of an "S" shape to it. The bright gravel guards — now used on all models — were also thinner and curvier. The ornaments below the headlights, which housed the front parking and directional lights, were more rounded in appearance. The rocket hood ornament became a triple-engine type with jet pods at the tip of each outspread wing.

The limited-production '53 Fiesta convertible was a midyear introduction by Oldsmobile.

Oldsmobile continued to offer a relatively modest Deluxe 88 entry-level series with just two body styles. The two-door sedan was priced at $2,065 and the four-door version cost $2,126. Production was 12,400 and 20,400, respectively. Both models had straight sweep spears on all fenders, front spears that stopped short of the headlights, chrome gravel guards (but no rear fender slash moldings) and no chrome trim around the side windows.

A 303-cid 150-hp two-barrel Rocket V-8 with 8.0:1 compression was exclusive to this series. Standard equipment included bumper guards, an electric clock, a lined trunk, dual horns, a cigarette lighter, chrome moldings and twin interior sun visors. A total of 17 colors were available with 15 two-tone combinations on the order form. Two-tone pattern cloth upholstery was used. Standard tire size was 7.60 x 15 inches.

Again Oldsmobile's Super 88 series offered the most body styles and had the highest sales. The model count was down to four: two-door sedan ($2,253) with 36,824 assemblies, Holiday Coupe ($2,448) with 34,500 assemblies, convertible ($2,615) with 8,310 assemblies and four-door sedan ($2,252) with 119,317 assemblies.

The Super 88's body and chassis were similar to the Deluxe 88, but it shared a higher horsepower Rocket V-8 with the Olds 98. This made the Super 88 sort of a factory-built hot rod. This series carried the same standard equipment as the Deluxe 88, plus rear seat robe rails, special rear stainless steel trim and chrome window ventipanes. Upholstery selections included nylon cloth or leather. The rear door or fender had "88" logos, which the Deluxe 88 models did not use. Super 88s also had rear fender slash moldings, but no side window moldings. The front fender and door moldings did not hit the headlight rims.

The Super 88/98 V-8 had the same 3-3/4 x 3-7/16-inch bore and stroke and 303 cubic inches of displacement. Like the base engine, it had an 8.0:1 compression ratio. Advertised output was 165 hp at 3600 rpm and 284 foot-pounds of torque at 1800 rpm. A four-barrel Rochester 4GC or Carter WCFB carburetor was mounted.

The regular 1953 Olds 98 models had all items from the lower series cars as standard equipment, plus a padded dashboard, windshield washers and a deluxe steering wheel with horn ring. Model offerings included a Holiday Coupe that listed for $2,771, a convertible with a $2,963 price tag and a $2,552 four-door sedan. Production totals were 27,920, 7,521 and 64,431 in the same order. The 98s could be identified by the words "Ninety-Eight," in script, on the rear door or fender and by their front fender moldings that blended into the headlight rings. There were also chrome slash moldings on the rear fenders and chrome trim moldings around the side windows. Upholstery selections were broadcloth, gabardine or leather. Standard tire size was 8.00 x 15.

The normally plush 98 series got an even richer, limited-production model late in the year. Only 458 of these rare Fiesta convertibles were built. They predicted 1954 styling features such as the "panoramic" wraparound windshield. Fiestas also came with virtually every Olds option offered, except factory air conditioning. They listed for a steep $5.715 and weighed 4,459 pounds. Under the hood was a special version of the 303-cid Rocket 8 with an 8.3:1 compression ratio. It generated 170 hp at 4000 rpm.

The 1953 Oldsmobiles were introduced on Jan. 9, 1953, and the limited-production Fiesta convertible was introduced at midyear. A total of 334,462 Oldsmobiles were built to 1953 specifications. A calendar-year run of 319,414 units put Olds in seventh place in the industry.

The fiberglass-bodied Starfire toured this year's auto shows. During the year, a fire destroyed the General Motors Hydra-Matic plant and a number of Oldsmobiles were then built with the Buick Dyna-Flow automatic transmission.

The Oldsmobile factory in Lansing, Michigan released a number of heavy-duty factory parts that helped make '53 Oldsmobiles more competitive in NASCAR racing. As a result, Oldsmobiles captured checkered flags in nine events, including Buck Baker's win at the Southern 500. Bob Pronger set a new mark of 113.38 mph in the Flying-Mile at Daytona driving an Olds 88 two-door sedan. Later, he rolled the car on the beach race course during the 160-mile Daytona stock car race, which Bill Blair won in another Olds.

1954 *Oldsmobile*

It was 1954, the year of smooth-sounding songs like "Hernando's Hideaway," "Mister Sandman" and "Young at Heart." The youth culture was getting in gear and the new generation had a smoothly-styled '54 Oldsmobile to go cruising in.

Sedans were a goner from the automaker's advertising program. In most cases, Holiday hardtops were depicted, but a Yellow and Bronze Super 88 "Convertible Coupe" showed up in at least one ad. Another showed the even sportier Starfire in

The top-of-the-line 1954 Oldsmobile was the beautiful 98 Starfire convertible.

Turquoise Blue with White trim. Oldsmobile was definitely "the ride" for the young and young-at-heart in the post-Korean War years.

The '54 models featured a new grille with a "floating" horizontal center member and air-scoop type bumper guards. The Oldsmobile name was spelled out across the hood lip in chrome letters. Round parking/directional lights sat below the headlights but were no longer connected to them. A new panoramic windshield wrapped around the sides of the body and a car-wide cowl ventilator let fresh air in. The tops of the rear doors or fenders featured new "contour-cut" dips and 98s had new Sweep-Cut wheel openings (in front only on the four-door sedan).

All Oldsmobiles had a two-inch-longer wheelbase, 122 inches for 88s and 126 inches for 98s. The 88 and Super 88 models grew a little over an inch in overall length to 205.26 inches, but the nine-inch-longer 98 was a fraction of an inch smaller than the 215-inch 1953 version.

Series names and model offerings were revised a bit, along with engines. The entry-level Olds series was now simply the 88. A Holiday Hardtop was added to this car-line. Oldsmobile built 18,013 of the $2,066 two-door sedan, 25,820 of the $2,230 Holiday Hardtop Coupe and 29,028 of the $2,126 four-door sedan. Weights on the these cars were around 3,700 pounds.

The 88 upholstery was either gray, green or blue pattern cloth. Standard tire size was 7.60 x 15 inches. Trim consisted of a straight body side molding on the front fenders and doors. On the rear was a saddle molding that swept down from the dips in the fender line to the middle of the body side, then ran straight back to the back-up lights. An "88" emblem appeared below the rear fender molding and no rocker panel moldings were used.

A larger Rocket 8 was introduced. As before, the overhead-valve V-8 had a cast iron block and non-adjustable hydraulic valve lifters. It used a 3-7/8 x 3-7/16-inch bore and stroke and displaced 324.3 cubic inches. With an 8.25:1 compression ratio and a Carter WGD dual-downdraft carburetor, the engine produced 170 hp at 4000 rpm and 295 foot pounds of torque at 2000 rpm. The engine featured Auto-Thermic pistons, full-pressure lubrication and an automatic choke.

The Super 88 continued to be Oldsmobile's bread-and-butter series. Super 88s had the same trim as 88s, but the "88" emblems were in a circular medallion above the rear fender moldings and the rocker panels were trimmed with chrome moldings. Sedans had a belt molding. There was also a newly-styled "Rocket 88" hood emblem.

Standard equipment on cars in this series included all items from the 88 series, plus a deck lid ornament and foam rubber seat cushions. Upholstery selections featured a nylon-and-orlon cloth combination or a variety of colored leathers. Standard tire size was 7.60 x 15 inches. Body styles were the same as those offered in 1953 at prices between $2,189 and $2,615. Oldsmobile built 27,882 Super 88 two-door sedans, 42,155 Holiday Coupes, 6,452 convertibles and 111,326 four-door sedans.

The engine used in the Super 88 and 98 models was essentially the same as the 88 V-8 with a Carter WCFB carburetor. This was an improved, more efficient Quadri-Jet carb and raised advertised horsepower to 185 at 4000 rpm. Torque increased to 300 foot pounds at 2000 rpm. On some cars, a Rochester 4GC four-barrel carburetor was used, rather than the Carter model. The Starfire convertible was now a regular part of the 98 series.

With three models, the 98 series was again atop the Olds line. A slightly higher horsepower Rocket V-8 was shared with Super 88 models. The 98 four-door sedan had the "Ninety-Eight" model name spelled out in script on the rear door. A short chrome sweep spear molding ran forward from the taillights. There was chrome trim around the side windows and Sweep-Cut style front wheel openings on this model.

The Starfire convertible was named after the previous year's dream car. It and the Holiday Coupe had nameplates on the front fenders, short sweep spears running forward from the back-up lights, Sweep-Cut wheel openings front and rear and a diagonal chrome molding that blended with the main curved side molding to form a sharp, pointed "V" on the rear fenders.

The 98 sedan sold for $2,552, weighed 3,863 pounds and 47,972 were made. Next in price was the Holiday Coupe at $2,570. This two-door hardtop weighed 3,840 pounds and had a production run of 38,563 units. Most expensive at $2,963 and rarest at 6,800 assemblies was the Starfire convertible.

Most 1954 Oldsmobiles were introduced on Jan. 20, 1954, but Deluxe 88 and Classic 98 Deluxe Holiday hardtops and the Starfire convertible were added later. Model-year production was 354,001 units. Olds took fourth place in industry output with cal-endar-year production of 433,810 units. The 1954s were the fastest Olds ever.

They could do 0-to-60 mph in 12.4 seconds and cover the quarter-mile in 18 seconds. Oldsmobiles took 11 NASCAR victories, but the banning of heavy-duty factory parts kits later in the year hurt the performance of the Oldsmobile stock cars. An Oldsmobile dream car called the Cutlass F-88 toured the show circuit in 1954.

During 1954, Oldsmobile began using photography, instead of artist illustrations, in its advertising. In one interesting series of General Motors corporate ads, Oldsmobile Holiday Coupes were shown along with fashionably-dressed female models in fancy, upscale settings. One depicted a Super 88 Holiday Coupe by a stately building in Westchester, N.Y., and the model was wearing a Givenchy sports tweed outfit. The theme of the ad was to emphasize the car's Fisher Body styling.

1955 *Oldsmobile*

The 1955 Oldsmobile 98 Holiday two-door hardtop has a typical 1950s color scheme.

For some Americans, "1955" began on Friday, Dec. 31, 1954, when the New Year's holiday was observed by the federal government. There were 11 national holidays and 16 local holidays ranging from National Freedom Day on Tuesday February 1 to Bill of Rights Day on December 15, a Thursday.

Oldsmobile was also loaded with Holidays in 1955, as the automaker continued to use the word "Holiday" as a synonym for "hardtop" and applied it to its all-new Super 88 and 98 four-door hardtops. These cars were promoted as Holiday Sedans, while the popular two-door hardtops remained "Holiday Coupes." It was clear to see that the four-door hardtop had been developed as an alternative body style for the young family man who wanted a sporty car, but needed the convenience of a four-door model. With the "youth market" niche growing among the car-buying public, Olds was a brand that aimed at upscale younger buyers. And 1955 was the year the GM brought them a pillarless four-door car in the middle rungs of its pricing ladder.

Buick offered such a car — called a "Riviera Sedan" — only in its smaller Special and Century lines. Oldsmobile, on the other hand, offered Holiday Sedans in the smaller Super 88 line and the larger 98 line. (Apparently, it was felt the 88 series didn't need one.) Other GM makes would follow suit in 1956 when the Cadillac Sedan DeVille, Chevrolet Sport Sedan (210 and Bel Air only) and Pontiac Catalina Sedan (in all car-lines) arrived. Still, in 1955, it was a big plus for Oldsmobile to have this new body style available on both the 122- and 126-inch wheelbase. It certainly helped push sales to a new record high.

Design changes from 1954 models included a restyled grille with the word "Oldsmobile" spelled out in three-dimensional letters set atop the center horizontal grille bar. The vertical dividers were removed from the two large "bumper-bomb" openings. Other changes included Sweep-Cut wheel openings on all models, redesigned body side moldings, new recessed headlights with chrome-lined caps, a redesigned "world" emblem on the hood and rear deck lid, a new rocket hood ornament and new taillights. The Rocket V-8 remained unchanged in displacement, but gained in horsepower again.

Again the entry-level Olds series was the 88 with its three body styles. These cars had chrome "88" insignias on their front fenders and the four-door sedan did not have side window moldings. There was a two-door sedan, Holiday Coupe, four-door sedan and Holiday Sedan at prices from $2,297 to $2,546. All weighed in the 3,700-pound bracket (just under or just over). Two-door production included 37,507 sedans and 85,767 hardtops, while the four-door figures were 57,778 sedans and 41,310 hardtops.

Exclusive to this series was a 185-hp Rocket V-8 with 8.5:1 compression and a Rochester 2GC two-barrel carburetor. The Super 88/98 engine was now a $35 option. Upholstery choices were gray, green or blue pattern cloth or morocceen and pattern cloth. Standard tire size was 7.60 x 15 inches.

This year a new 202-hp "98" V-8 series engine was slipped into the 88 body to make the Super 88. These cars had "Super 88" in a circular emblem on the front fenders, stainless steel body belt moldings and rocker panel moldings. Prices ranged from $2,436 to $2,894. Weights were about 50-100 pounds heavier than a base 88. Olds built 11,950 Super 88 two-door sedans, 62,534 Holiday Coupes, 9,007 convertibles, 111,316 four-door sedans and 47,385 Holiday.

Standard Super 88 equipment included all 88 series items plus foam rubber seat cushions, stainless steel rocker panel moldings, a front seatback robe cord, spun-glass hood insulation and rear window vent panes.

The 98 again had a longer wheelbase and overall length than other Oldsmobiles. It shared a standard-equipment 202-hp V-8 with the Super 88.

All 98 models had a "Ninety-Eight" script in the rear deck lid. The four-door sedan had stainless steel side window trim, plus another "Ninety-Eight" nameplate on the front fenders. The two- and four-door hardtops had a "Holiday" nameplate on the front fenders and the convertible had a "Starfire" nameplate.

The factory introduction of the 1955 Oldsmobiles was Nov. 5, 1954. Dealer introductions were held exactly two weeks later. Public announcement of the 1955 Holiday four-door hardtop was made Jan. 6, 1955, two days after Buick announced its own Riviera four-door hardtop. It turned out to be the best-ever model year for the company with production of 583,179 units. The calendar-year output was 643,549 cars, good for fifth in the industry.

The 1955 Super 88 sedan did 0-to-60 mph in 10.6 seconds and covered the quarter-mile in 17.6 seconds. Stock-car drivers Dick Rathman and Jim Pascal raced Oldsmobiles for the Wood Racing Team. This year's factory show car was the Delta, with cast aluminum wheels and a tachometer and console.

1956 *Oldsmobile*

The 1956 Oldsmobile 88 two-door sedan was among several popular hits that year.

In 1956, life in these United States was changing. In February, the King of Rock and Roll, swivel-hips Elvis Presley, got on the Top 10 charts for the first time with "Heartbreak Hotel." In July, President Eisenhower signed joint resolution making "In God We Trust" the national motto. Late in the year, International Business Machines announced the development of a new items called a "hard disk" that could store five millibytes of information.

Oldsmobile ads of that year depicted young Americans building new homes and retirees at a modernistic golf club. The message was that Americans, young or old, were enjoying a new modern lifestyle the 1956 Oldsmobiles fit right into.

Styling changes from 1955 models included a new dual front bumper design encircling grille with six horizontal louvers divided by a massive vertical center post. The styling face lift introduced a "swept flank" look that departed from the somewhat boxier appearance of the 1954 and 1955 models. Also seen were redesigned headlight hoods, rear bumpers and taillight trim. New body side molding arrangements and two-tone treatments highlighted the updated styling.

The 88 and Super 88 models shared the 122-inch wheelbase and 98s had a four-inch-longer stance. The Super 88 and 98 shared a more powerful Rocket 8 with a four-barrel carburetor.

The 88 was again the entry level series. On these cars, a body side molding extended from the front wheel cut out to the back-up light housing in a straight, unbroken line. Free-standing chrome "88" numbers appeared on the front fenders, behind the wheel opening and below the body side molding (except on four-door hardtops). No body belt moldings were used on the bottom series cars. On four-door hardtops, the "88" on the front fenders was replaced with chrome letters spelling out H-O-L-I-D-A-Y above the body side molding.

The base 88 series had the same four body styles — two- and four-door sedan and two- and four-door Holiday hardtops. Prices ran from $2,166 to $2,397. Oldsmobile built 216,019 cars in this line and all body styles sold fairly well.

In 1956, the 88 line was probably a very important one for Oldsmobile Motor Division, since the strong American economy was beginning to tighten a bit, anticipating the recession that hit in 1957. The 88 didn't look that much different than other Oldsmobiles, but its cost was low enough to be advertised as "budget-priced." The coupe was advertised as a "Holiday on a budget!"

The production of 88s outpaced Super 88 output by 37,000 units, while the number of 98s assembled did not reach 100,000. So the 88 was the big contributor to the bottom line that season.

With its five body styles (a convertible was added) the Super 88 contributed 179,000 units to the 1956 model-year total. On all models except the Holiday Sedan, the "88" front fender emblem was placed inside a circular medallion. There was also a rocket emblem and "88" numbers on the left corner of the trunk lid. Two- and four-door sedans had stainless steel body belt moldings. The Super 88 Holiday Sedan had the same H-O-L-I-D-A-Y lettering on the front fenders, in place of the round "88" medallion. However, it carried the rocket and "88" decorations on the trunk.

Prices for Super 88s ranged from $2,301 to $2,726. Two body styles had production below 10,000 units, as only 5,465 two-door sedans and 9,561 convertibles were built. Standard equipment included 88 series items plus front and rear carpeting, foam rubber seat cushions and courtesy lights. Upholstery choices included pattern cloth-and-leather in a variety of colors and combinations. Standard tire size was 7.60 x 15 inches.

The Olds 98 lineup for 1956 was comprised of the four-door sedan, two- and four-door Holiday hardtops and the Starfire convertible. Prices ran from $2,969 to $3,380. The rarest model was the Starfire convertible, of which Oldsmobile built 8,581. Total series output was 90,439.

The lower-horsepower Rocket 8 got a pretty significant boost in energy this year. While it remained at 324 cubic inches of displacement with the same two-barrel carburetor, it got a compression-ratio boost to 9.25:1. This brought horsepower up to 230 at 44 rpm, versus 185 at 4000 the previous year. Torque increased from 320 foot-pounds at 2000 rpm in 1955 to 340 in 1956. The more powerful four-barrel V-8 used in the 1956 Super 88 and 98 also went to 9.25:1 compression, but it gained 38 hp instead of 45 hp. It was rated for 240 hp at 4400 rpm and 350 foot-pounds of torque at 2800 rpm. The 1955 figures were 202 hp at 4000 rpm and 332 foot-pounds at 2400 rpm.

Factory introduction of the 1956 Oldsmobiles was carried out on Oct. 25, 1955. The dealer introductions took place on November 3. Model-year assemblies for all series came to 485,459 units, equaling 7.7 percent of all United States car output. Calendar-year totals were 432,903 vehicles, including 17,795 convertibles; 121,304 two-door hardtops; 128,640 four-door hardtops and 689 early-production 1957 station wagons.

Leather trim was available in the Olds 98 Starfire convertible, 98 Deluxe Holiday Sedan, 98 Deluxe Holiday Coupe, Super 88 convertible, Super 88 Holiday Sedan and Super 88 Holiday coupe.

Even with 38 extra horses, the 1956 Olds Super 88 four-door hardtop was slower than the 1955 four-door sedan. It needed an extra 20 seconds for both 0-to-60 mph and the quarter-mile, due to its extra 107 pounds of weight.

Olds took only one big NASCAR race in 1956, although Lee Petty was able to establish a new Flying-Mile record of 144 mph with an Oldsmobile at Daytona Beach, Fla.

1957 *Oldsmobile*

The 1957 Oldsmobile Super 88 Fiesta wagon offered sporty hardtop styling.

Little League Baseball was catching on across America in the late 1950s. Carl Stotz, of Williamsport, Pa., had founded the Little League in 1939, when a $30 donation bought uniforms for the first three local teams. By 1957, Little League teams existed in all 48 states, including Texas, where young George W. Bush played his third year as a catcher for the Cubs team, in the Central Little League of Midland, Texas. It was also the first year that a non-U.S. team won the Little League World Series. Angel Macias, of Monterrey, Mexico, pitched the first perfect game in a Little League championship final.

Oldsmobile paid homage to youth baseball in an advertisement for its Golden Rocket 88 Holiday Sedan. The illustration of the yellow-and-white four-door hardtop at a sandlot challenge promised Olds buyers "extra innings of fun" and stated "from hooded headlamps to swept-back rear deck, the Golden Rocket is strictly 'big league.'"

New lower and longer Oldsmobile bodies were highlighted by a new, deep-recessed grille with circular parking lights. New "side-notched" headlight hoods were seen and chrome rocket ornaments sat above the single, round headlights.

An "Accent Stripe," exclusive to Oldsmobile, highlighted the rear body side moldings. A higher, wider Span-A-Ramic windshield gave drivers a new slant on style and visibility and the rear window now had divider bars. Also new were the body side trim, a redesigned rear deck, new rear fenders and a new rear bumper.

Oldsmobile's Wide-Stance chassis gave it better cornering ability and sure-footed stability and a new Pivot-Poise suspension system with Counter-Dive provided smooth, level stops. Other new technical features included an L-Bow propeller shaft for a lower center of gravity and new Hi-Lo bumpers. Inside, Oldsmobile buyers found new Tech-Style interiors, a new Strut-Mounted instrument panel (good for easier accessibility and visibility) and a new Dual-Range Power Heater that warmed the car quicker. Station wagons were re-introduced for the first time since 1950 and all were called Fiestas, although sedan and hardtop styles were offered. A new 371-cid Rocket T-400 V-8 (400 foot pounds of torque) was used in all 1957 Oldsmobile models. It had a 9.5:1 compression ratio and a Quadri-Jet carburetor to help it develop 277 hp at 4400 rpm.

To honor GM's upcoming 50th anniversary, Olds named its entry series the Golden Rocket 88 line. No series nameplates or rocker panel moldings were used on these cars. The curved side-accent moldings started near the center of the front door on two-door models and at the front edge of the rear door on four-door models. With two four-door Fiesta station wagons (sedan style and hardtop style) and a convertible added to this line, the model count stood at seven.

Standard equipment included armrests, bumper guards, turn signals, rubber floor mats and sun visors. Upholstery choices included a variety of colors and fabrics. Standard tire size was 8.50 x 14 inches. Prices for the seven models started at $2,478 and ran as high as $3,017. With the United States in an economic recession, production of the low-priced Olds dropped to 172,659 cars, despite the fact that the product had some great improvements. All three new models had production under 10,000 units — 6,423 ragtops, 5,052 regular Fiesta wagons and 5,767 Fiesta Holiday wagons.

The middle Oldsmobile series was the popular Super 88. Wheelbase and body shells were shared with the Golden Rocket 88s. Six body styles were offered including the Fiesta Holiday station wagon (the sedan-style Fiesta was not offered in this series, but all other 88 bodies were). Super 88 prices began at $2,687 and topped out at $3,220.

Standard equipment included all items from the Golden Rocket 88, plus front fender model nameplates, exposed chrome roof bows and side interior courtesy lights. The side window trim was bright metal on hardtops and painted on sedans. A variety of colored cloth-and-leather upholstery combinations could be ordered. Standard tire size was 8.50 x 14 inches. A total of 132,105 Super 88s were built. The lowest body-style production totals were 2,983 for the two-door sedan, 7,128 for the convertible and 8,981 for the Fiesta.

The top-of-the-line Oldsmobile was renamed the Starfire. The same four models were offered in this series. These cars had "Ninety-Eight" nameplates on the front fenders and rear deck lid and bright metal rocker panel moldings. Both hardtops and the four-door sedan had bright metal trim around the side windows and on the center window pillars. Prices started at $3,396 and went to $3,649. Only the convertible — 8,278 built — was somewhat low in production. Standard equipment included all items standard on the Super 88, plus electric windows, power steering, power brakes and Jetaway Hydra-Matic Drive. Upholstery choices included a variety of cloth, moroceen and leather.

As in 1956, both Olds 88s were on a 122-inch wheelbase and 98s had a 126-inch stance. Overall lengths were 208.2 and 216.7 inches, in the same respective order. Tread width was 59 inches up front and 58 inches in the rear. A special J-2 induction system with (300 hp) with three two-barrel carburetors was offered in two versions. The 300-hp version ($83 extra) was for street use. A 312-hp J-2 setup was not recommended for street use. This $395 option was offered only to drag racers and stock car racers for off-road use.

The 1957 Oldsmobiles were introduced Nov. 9, 1956. Model-year production was 384,390 units and calendar-year sales were 390,091 cars. This made Oldsmobile the fifth best-selling American automaker with a 6.2 percent share of market. J.F. Wolfram was the chief executive officer of the division.

The Oldsmobile Mona Lisa show car toured the auto show circuit during 1957 and future racing legend Richard Petty drove Oldsmobiles in NASCAR stock car races. Petty joined the Olds team with his father Lee Petty. Their aim was to win races with Oldsmobile's hot J-2 engine option. However, NASCAR ultimately banned multi-carbureted engines and Olds wound up with only five Grand National wins, before pulling out of factory-backed racing efforts.

1958 *Oldsmobile*

The Dynamic 88 sedan was the low-priced Oldsmobile offering in 1958.

The attention of many Americans was focused on outer space in 1958. The first American satellite, called Explorer I, went into space and the National Aeronautics and Space Administration (NASA) was set up. America satellites detected the Van Allen Radiation Belt. The Space Race even affected the entertainment world, as a song called "The Purple People Eater" raced to the top of the charts in June and July. It told of the "…one-eyed, one-horned flying purple people eater…" who came down from space to "knock 'em dead" on a TV show.

The "Purple People Eater" and the "Witch Doctor" (the subject of another popular tune which reached Number 2 on the charts) sort of summed up 1958. So did the flat-finned, chrome-laden, and all-new '58 Oldsmobile. It was a weird and wonderful year!

Factory announcements of the new cars took place on Oct. 30, 1957 and the 1958 models were introduced in Oldsmobile showrooms on Nov. 8, 1957. This was the era in which the concept of planned obsolescence was at its peak and General Motors carried it to the hilt with totally-new 1958 cars that would last just one model year and would be replaced by totally-new 1959 cars.

Just think how much was spent, heavily retooling factory production lines three years in a row. But when new-car intros rolled around in the fall, it was dramatic and exciting to see news photos of a pretty model undraping a car cover from a completely different looking new car.

In addition to a totally redesigned body, the '58 Oldsmobiles had a new grille with vertical dividers between the horizontal louvers, a medallion in the center and rectangular parking lamps encased in the bumper. Dual headlights (called Four-Beam Headlamps) were introduced. A new arrangement of side trim created reverse "bullet-shaped" accent panels on the front fenders and doors and four-strip moldings on the rear fenders. The rear window dividers used in 1957 were gone.

In 1958, the entry series designation became the Dynamic 88. It offered the same seven models as the 1957 Golden Rocket 88 line. These cars had "Dynamic 88" front fender nameplates and two moldings extending back from the headlights to form the bullet-shaped accent panels on the doors. There were no rocker panel moldings, no medallions at the forward end of the rear fender trim and no "Oldsmobile" lettering on the rear deck lid. There was a white lens in the vertical area below the oval-shaped taillights. Oldsmobile returned to using a less-powerful two-barrel V-8 in its base series.

This was the first year that window stickers were required on domestic automobiles and the Dynamic 88 sticker prices were between $2,772 and $3,395. Seventeen standard colors were available, along with five extra-cost metallic colors. Upholstery choices spanned a variety of colored moroceen-and-cloth combinations. Standard equipment included an oil filter, turn signals, a printed-circuit instrument cluster and an aluminum anodized grille. The 88 wheelbase went up to 122.5 inches and overall length was 208.2 inches. Standard tire size was 8.50 x 14 inches. Production was a strong-for-a-recession-year 146,567 units including just 4,456 convertibles, 3,249 Fiesta sedan-style wagons and 3,323 Fiesta Holiday wagons.

The middle Oldsmobile series again was the Super 88 line. It dropped down to five body styles, with the disappearance of the two-door sedan. Sticker prices went from $3,112 to $3,623. There were "Super 88" nameplates on the front fenders. Placed in the middle of the bullet-shaped accent panel on the front fenders and doors was a wider, spear-shaped molding. There was a crest medallion on the forward end of the four-strip rear body side moldings. Bright rocker panel moldings were used on Super 88s, which also had "Oldsmobile" lettering on the rear deck lid. There were red lenses in the vertical section of each taillight assembly.

The Super 88 shared its wheelbase with the Dynamic 88 and its more powerful V-8 engine with the 98. Upholstery choices included various combinations of leather, cloth and morocceen.

Standard equipment included all Dynamic 88 items plus a padded dash, foam-rubber padded seat cushions, courtesy lights, a parking brake light, special side moldings and chrome rocker panel moldings. Standard tire size was 8.50 x 14 inches.

The 98 series had its own exclusive wheelbase of 126.5 inches, while sharing a more powerful Rocket 8 with Super 88s. Body trim was very similar to that of the Super 88, but the wheelbase was longer and the front fenders had "Ninety-Eight" identification. The same four body styles were carried over at prices between $3,824 and $4,300. Standard series equipment included all items standard on the two 88 series plus Hydra-Matic transmission, power steering and brakes, dual exhaust, electric clock, color-accented wheel discs and chrome wheel frames. Interiors could be ordered in a variety of colored leathers, cloth and morocceen. Standard tires were 8.50 x 14 inches.

The Olds V-8 that came as standard equipment in Dynamic 88s had a 4 x 3-11/16-inch bore and stroke and displaced 371 cubic inches. The hydraulic-lifter engine used a new 10.0:1 compression ratio and an "Economy" type two-barrel carburetor. It produced 265 hp at 4400 rpm and 390 foot-pounds of torque at 2400 rpm. The Super 88/98 engine used a Quadri-Jet four-barrel carburetor and produced 305 hp at 4600 rpm. It produced 410 foot-pounds of torque at 2800 rpm.

The Super 88/98 engine was optional in Dynamic 88 models. In addition. the triple-carbureted J-2 engine option could be ordered for any 1958 Olds. It boosted power to 312 hp. Other engine options included a heavy-duty air cleaner and a heavy-duty crankcase ventilation system. A three-speed manual transmission was standard on cars in the 88 and Super 88 series. The Jetaway Hydra-Matic was standard in all 98s and optional in other models

Model-year production totaled 296,374 units for a seven percent market share. Calendar-year sales of 310,795 cars were recorded, for a fourth place in the sales race.

J.F. Wolfram was the chief executive officer of the division and had Oldsmobile solidly established as a sales leader in the medium-price class of the U.S. automobile market.

1959 *Oldsmobile*

The 1959 Oldsmobile 98 Holiday two-door hardtop was called the "ScenicCoupe."

The famous Daytona 500 stock car race was born in 1959, amidst the first of many controversies that would mark the contest's history. Racing without open factory support, Lee Petty drove a 1959 Oldsmobile two-door hardtop to a photo finish with Johnny Beauchamp's Thunderbird. The sole contenders for victory, Petty and Beauchamp exchanged the lead in the waning laps of the race, while Joe Weatherly, whose '59 Chevy was two laps down, was able to latch on to the leaders' draft.

On the final lap, Petty was leading and they were running three wide coming off Turn 4. The finish was neck-and-neck with the Chevy high, the Olds in the middle and the T-Bird at the bottom.

Beauchamp celebrated the victory, but Petty was declared the winner the following Wednesday when newsreel footage proved he edged Beauchamp at the finish line. Petty collected $19,050 of the $67,760 prize money. Beauchamp earned $7,650. Weatherly came in fifth. Petty's victory may have inspired the slogan "Make a date with the leader" in some '59 Oldsmobile advertisements.

Oldsmobile had entirely new styling for 1959. It was promoted as the "Linear Look" in one advertisement that focused on the airiness and roominess of the new design.

"Here you see the start of a new styling cycle! Sweeping expanses of glass enhances Oldsmobile's new inner spaciousness," the copy pointed out. Also stressed was added luggage space, new Rocket V-8s, Magic-Mirror acrylic finish and new safety-cooled "Air Scoop" brakes. Every line was completely different than in 1958. The windshields swept back into the roof line. A new anodized aluminum grille had the parking lights set between each pair of dual headlights. A new wraparound rear window was seen on four-door hardtops.

The look of the '59 Olds always reminds the author of the folded-paper airplanes we used to make in grade school. There was a lot less unnecessary chrome. The 88 models were on a 123-inch wheelbase and 218.4 inches long. The 98s had a 3.3-inch-longer wheelbase and measured 223 inches long.

The entry-level Dynamic Eight-Eight series offered six body styles: two- and four-door sedans (the four-door was called a "Celebrity" sedan), two- and four-door Holiday Hardtops, a convertible and the sedan-style four-door Fiesta station wagon. Prices on these cars started at $2,837 and went to $3,365. Most models weighed just a bit over 4,200 pounds, but the wagon was about 400 pounds heavier. Olds built 194,102 Dynamic 88s in the model year and the only model with relatively low production was the convertible, of which 8,491 were made.

Cars in the low series had an "88" emblem at the center of the hood, "Oldsmobile" lettered across the radiator grille, front fender top rocket ornaments, a "Dynamic 88" front fender script and a chrome mid-body-side molding running from the headlights to the front door, at a height just above the front wheel opening. There was very little additional trim. There were no front fender chevrons, no wheel lip moldings, no rocker panel moldings and no taillight grilles. On the rear of the car, the word Oldsmobile was centered in the concave panel, extending just a little wider than the license plate. Standard equipment included an oil filter, turn signals and a "Safety Spectrum" speedometer. Upholstery was available in a variety of cloth and morocceen combinations. Standard tire size was 8.50 x 14 inches. The re-tuned version of the 371-cid V-8 used in all 1957 and 1958 Oldsmobiles was standard in the low-rung line in '59. A larger V-8 was standard in Super 88s and 98s.

Super 88 was again the middle series Olds. This line offered all 88 body styles except the two-door sedan. Prices for the five models ranged from $3,178 to $3,669. Series production was 107,660 cars, including just 4,895 ragtops and 7,015 wagons.

There was a "Super 88" script on the front fenders and three vertical "chevrons" intersecting the body side molding just behind the headlights. At the center of the hood, a teardrop-shaped Olds badge replaced the "88" emblem at the center of the hood. Bright metal trim decorated the rear edge of the front wheel openings and rocker panels. There was no bright trim on the rear wheel lip or taillights.

An extra body side molding, mounted lower than the front one, extended forward from the rear bumper towards the rear wheel opening. The Oldsmobile name on the rear of the car was of the slightly-wider-than-the-license-plate 88 style. Standard equipment included all items from the Dynamic 88 series plus a parking brake light, a sponge-vinyl headliner and deep twist carpeting. Upholstery came in a variety of colored leather, morocceen or cloth. Standard tire size was 9.00 x 14 inches.

There were four models in the 98 series: Celebrity Sedan, Holiday Coupe, Holiday Sedan and convertible (the only one without a name). They were priced from $3,890 to $4,163. All items standard on the Super 88 were found on the 98 as well as special emblems and moldings, an electric clock, rear wheel trim moldings, taillight grilles, power steering, power brakes and Jetaway Hydra-Matic Drive. Interiors were selected from leather, morocceen or cloth in different colors.

The "Ninety-Eight" name in chrome script appeared above the lower rear body molding. The Oldsmobile name on the rear beauty panel stretched full-width across the car and the taillights had a double-oval decorative grille. The standard tire size was 9.00 x 14 inches.

The 1959 version of the 371-cid V-8 blended a 9.75:1 compression ratio and a Rochester 2GC "Econ-o-way" two-barrel carburetor to come up with 270 hp at 4600 rpm and 390 foot-pounds of torque at 2400 rpm. A 1/8-inch-larger cylinder bore was featured in the Super 88 and 98 engine, which had 4-1/8 x 3-11/16 measurements and displaced 394 cubic inches. This motor had the same compression ratio, but used a Quadri-Jet carburetor which helped it produce 315 hp at 4600 rpm and 435 foot-pounds of torque at 2800 rpm.

The 1959 Oldsmobiles were introduced on Oct. 3, 1958. Model-year production totaled 382,865 units or a 6.9 percent market share. Calendar-year production totaled 366,305 cars.

The longer Oldsmobile for 1959 was emphasized by that year's Super 88 Fiesta wagon.

Packards
of the Fifties

1950 *Packard*

Note the massive hood ornament on this 1950 Packard sedan.

It was postwar America and life in the United States was in a state of flux. Public tastes were changing. New things were coming into favor. Buried in the year's statistics was the fact that American ownership of television sets had hit the million-households mark. Meanwhile, some of the traditional trappings of the "good life" saw their popularity wane. The Packard motor car was one of them.

Packard's postwar history is a sad one. The company was one of America's oldest carmakers and continued building outstanding versions, but they failed to generate appeal with a new breed of buyers who wanted radically modern cars. Packard's philosophy had been that buyers of high-priced cars did not want annual model-year changes. Company directors felt such customers preferred a quality product that could retain its style value one season after the next. Unfortunately, after 1949, most car buyers were driven by a "latest-and-greatest" type of thinking.

Also contributing to Packard's demise between 1950 and 1958 was the company's role as an independent automaker. Without full-range market coverage and the resources of a giant corporation to back it up, Packard could not adjust rapidly to postwar trends. Even when management realized things had changed, there was no feasible way to react. Packard simply could not afford to create all-new styling year after year.

Not all of this was clear on Oct. 1, 1949, when the one-year-old "Golden Anniversary" Packards began being registered as 1950 models. About the only major change in the cars was Ultramatic Drive. It was made an option for the low-priced Eights. Otherwise, even retail prices and weights stayed the same. A Carter WGD two-barrel carburetor did replace the WDO type as standard equipment and several new options became running additions to the accessories list. Quick identification of Packard's lowest-priced cars was possible by spotting the "Goddess of Speed" ornament on the hood.

The Standard Eight line contained a four-door sedan, a two-door Club Sedan, and the four-door Station Sedan priced from $2,224 and $3,449. The Station Sedan was similar to a station wagon, but a bit more streamlined and access to the rear cargo area was via a side-opening rear door, rather than a tailgate-and-lift-gate arrangement. All models but the Station Sedan were also available as Deluxe Eights for $134 extra. Deluxe Eights were distinguished by three-inch-larger hubcaps than Standard Eights used, but also had other decorative and upholstery upgrades. A total of 40,359 cars of all body types were made in both Packard Eight lines.

The Standard/Deluxe Eights rode a 120-inch wheelbase and measured just a bit more than 204 inches overall. The five-main-bearings flathead engine had a 3-1/2 x 3-3/4-inch bore and stroke and displaced 288 cubic inches. With a 7.0:1 compression ratio and Carter WGD two-barrel carburetor, the horsepower rating was 135 at 3600 rpm. Features of all Packard power plants included full-pressure lubrication, downdraft carburetors, oil control rings, aluminum alloy pistons and "Newtrapoised" engine mountings. A three-speed manual transmission was standard equipment. Overdrive was optional, as was an Electromatic clutch.

Packard Super Eights could be identified by their "Goddess of Speed" hood ornament, a window molding that stopped at the center of the rear fender, and a sweep spear molding that ran from just ahead of the front wheel opening to the taillight housing. Deluxe Super Eights also had a pelican hood ornament, an egg-crate grille, a matching rear beauty panel, and chrome wheel rims.

The Standard Super Eight line offered a 3,800-pound Club Sedan for $3,800 and a 3,870-pound four-door sedan for $2,633. Both styles also came in Deluxe trim versions for an additional $286. Deluxe features added 55 pounds. Two long-wheelbase models, a seven-passenger sedan and a limousine with a partition came on the Super chassis at $3,950 and $4,100, respectively. Also offered was the $3,350 Victoria Convertible. Packard built 4,722 Super Eights, including only 614 open cars.

Super Eights had the same type of engine as the Standard and Deluxe Eight models, but with a longer (4-1/4-inches) piston stroke. This increased displacement to 327 cubic inches. A 7.0:1 compression ratio was combined with a Carter Type WDO two-barrel carburetor to create 150 hp at 3600 rpm. Most Super Eights were on a 127-inch wheelbase and 211-11/16 inches long, but the seven-passenger models had a 141-inch wheelbase and a 225-5/8-inch overall length..

The Packard Custom Eight was the flagship of the fleet. All Custom Eights had the egg-crate grille and matching rear beauty panel, a pelican hood ornament, extra-rich Bedford-cloth-and-leather interior trim and extended-type upper belt moldings that looped around the deck lid. This line included a 4,310-pound four-door sedan at $3,975 and a 4,539-pound convertible for $4,295.

Both prices rose $225 from 1949 to cover the inclusion of Ultramatic transmission being standard equipment. Production of Custom Eights came to just 955 cars of which 85 were ragtops. A 356-cid flathead straight eight with a 3-1/2 x 4-5/8-inch bore and stroke was found in the Custom Eight chassis. Using the same compression and carburetor as the Super Eight engine, the big one produced 165 hp at 3600 rpm. These cars used the same wheelbase as comparable Super models, but measured 213-1/4 inches long.

Packard's model-year production peaked at 106,040 cars. Calendar-year production was 72,138 units, giving Packard the 16th industry ranking. Packard obtained several choice military contracts on the verge of war's outbreak in Korea.

Packard was often promoted for commercial use. One advertisement in the May 8, 1950 issue of Time magazine, included interviews with three businessmen who used Packards.

"Driving 800-1,000 miles a week in my business, I average better than 17 miles per gallon with my 150-HP Packard Super," said salesman Howard F. Barton of Hartford, Connecticut.

"As for upkeep . . . during the war I drove a Packard 181,000 miles at a total expense for repairs, including a paint job, of $306."

Packard driver and commercial fisherman N.R. Steelman, of Oyster, Virginia, said he drove "340,000 miles in commercial service, hauling up to 1,000 pounds of clams to a load" in his '37 Packard. That convinced him to purchase a 1950 Custom Eight for his wife.

S. Robert Johnsom, a Hackensack, New Jersey, public relations counselor, said he had recently done a 11,561-mile trip out West in his Packard. It got 19.7 miles per gallon and repairs cost 50 cents!

1951 *Packard*

In 1951, Packard introduced a new design led by this Patrician 400 convertible.

The music of 1951 was totally in tune with Packard's sophisticated new looks, as Nat King Cole ("Too Young"), Perry Como ("If"), Tony Bennett ("Because of You"), and Mario Lanza ("Be My Love") dominated the Top 10 charts. In fact, Cole's 12 weeks in the number one slot was an all-time record. But rock-and-roll was just around the corner.

Packard wasn't ready for the revolution of youth and new ideas that would accompany it. Nevertheless, Packard was ready to have one of its last flings, as it became one of a few automakers — and the only independent car company — to turn out more cars in 1951 (76,075) than it built in 1950, when 72,089 were made.

Bowing early, on Aug. 24, 1950, the all-new 24th Series Packard had styling more contemporary to the 1950s, designed by John Reinhart.

"Packards for 1951 are only 5-foot 2-1/2 inches high, for in-the-groove roadability with 'hats on' headroom in front and back," said the factory sales literature. "New low bonnets (hoods) and high crown fenders give the outlook of a sports car."

Cars in the base Packard 200 line were identified by a single strip of chrome across the front fenders and door and a "toothless" grille. A low, single-fin hood mascot was seen. Standard equipment on all Packards included twin horns, two sun visors, two variable-speed windshield wipers, a horn-blow ring, front and rear bumper guards, a jack, and tools.

Priced from $2,302 to $2,469, the lowest-rung models were the Business Coupe, Club Sedan, and four-door sedan in the 200 Standard lineup. These cars weighed roughly 3,600 pounds and accounted for 24,310 model-year deliveries. The 200 Deluxe models were further distinguished by chrome wheel rings and turn indicators. The two-door Club Sedan listed for $2,563 and the four-door sedan was $2,616. Production of both models added up to 47,052 cars.

These cars rode a longer 122-inch wheelbase and measured 209-3/8 inches bumper-to-bumper. They used the 288-cid 135-hp "small" Packard eight. A Packard 200 touring sedan exhibited average fuel consumption of 22.023 mpg while participating in the

1951 Mobilgas Economy Run. This was better than 12 other entries in the same class.

The Packard 250 was on the same wheelbase platform as more modestly-priced models, but almost three inches longer. It utilized the 327-cid 150-hp straight eight. Packard's only convertible was included, along with an all-new two-door hardtop. This added midyear hardtop acquired the name Mayfair after its release. Trim identification was provided by chrome moldings across the front fender and door. A toothy-looking grille insert and pelican hood mascot were seen. Three distinctive chrome ornaments decorated the rear fender. Especially colorful and rich upholstery was used for both these sporty cars. Fender skirts were standard. The 3,820-pound hardtop was priced at $3,234. The convertible added 220 pounds and $157. Packard made 4,640 units in this two-car series.

The Packard 300 sedan somewhat took the place of the long-wheelbase production Super Eights as a car for business use. It had a 127-inch wheelbase and 217-3/4-inch length. Salesmen, hotels, funeral parlors, taxi owners, and other professionals loved this model, as did large families. Its trim included a straight chrome molding running across the rear doors, rear fenders, and taillights in a horizontal plane.

Standard equipment included all Packard 200 features plus an oil-bath air cleaner, a tilt-type glare proof rearview mirror, chrome-plated wheel discs, a trunk compartment light, and a robe rail. Double lens taillights were used. A wide variety of interior trims was offered. This 3,875-pound car sold for $3,034 and 15,309 were made. It also employed the 327-cid 150-hp straight eight.

The Packard Patrician 400 was the replacement for the fancy Custom Eight. This Packard was identified by wide, vertically-ribbed, chrome gravel shields on the lower front region of the rear fender bulge, three "jet louvers" on the middle of the rear fenders, a chrome spear high on the front fenders and doors, a second chrome spear running from the gravel shield to the extreme rear of car, chrome-finned moldings atop the rear fenders, and double-lens horizontal taillights.

A unique wraparound-style backlight (rear window) gave the Packard Patrician 400 a hardtop roof look. The grille insert had vertical "teeth" and the tip of the hood had a cormorant. Luxurious "fashion forum" interiors were featured with special carpeting and a chrome-plated steering column. All features of the Packard 300 were incorporated, plus cloisonné wheel cover center medallions. This was the model for buyers seeking an elite machine. The 4,115-pound luxury car listed for $3,662 and 9,001 were made. The Patrician 400 used the 327-cid V-8, but with a 7.8:1 compression-ratio cylinder head. This upped output to 155 hp at 3600 rpm.

Packard tried its best to promote the totally-redesigned cars to a public hungry for new styling and new ideas. Introductions of 1951 Packards began in August 1950 and the Packard 250 line. The all-new hardtop and the convertible were added in March 1951.

On Oct. 12, 1950, the Society of Motion Picture Art Directors proclaimed the 24th Series Packard as "The most beautiful car of the year." A Packard advertisement heralded the "World Premiere of a Daring New Concept in Motor Cars." It highlighted such selling features as "Low-to-the-Road" styling, "Guide-Line" fenders, a "New Horizon-View" one-piece windshield, "Fashion Forum" interiors, "Thunderbolt" engines, Ultramatic Drive, "Hush-Toned" soundproofing, "Load-Ease" steering, "Broad-Beam" suspension, "Limousine Ride," "Armor-Rib body construction," "Tele-Glance" instrument panels, and "Safti-Set" brakes.

A total of 100,132 Packards were supplied to buyers during the 1951 model run. Calendar-year totals were counted at 76,075 cars, good for 16th position on industry sales charts.

An experimental Phantom II sports car was constructed for Packard design chief Ed Macauley. This one-of-a-kind car was based on a highly-modified Club Sedan. It featured a long, wide hood scoop, wide-ribbed bright metal underscores, matching fender skirts, custom concentric circle wheel discs, hardtop coupe styling, and two-place seating.

1952 *Packard*

The new 1952 Packard Patrician 400 sedan wore the famed cormorant hood ornament.

According to Vance Packard's *The Waste Makers*, it was in the 1930s that a General Electric engineer suggested the company could increase sales of flashlight lamps by making them more efficient, but shortening their life. They would last through only one battery, instead of three. Packard (an appropriate name) also noted in his book, a 1934 incident when speakers at an SAE meeting proposed limiting the life of automobiles. The term "planned obsolescence" was coined but Packard (the car company) resisted the trend for as long as possible.

By 1952, Packard Motor Car Company was forced to change its traditional thinking and adopt the annual model-year change system used by its competitors.

Until that point in time, Packards were produced according to series that didn't conform to certain calendar or model years. For instance, the 21st Series entered production in April 1946, and lasted until the summer of 1947. In August 1947, the 22nd Series models started leaving the assembly line. The 23rd Series cars bowed after May 1949 as 1949-1950 models. The 24th Series bowed in August 1950 and cars were marketed as 1951 models.

In late 1951, Packard management decided the company had to bring out a new line every fall, as other automakers did. The 25th Series 1952 models were introduced on Nov. 14, 1951 (my fourth birthday) on a nationwide television comedy show hosted by Red Skelton. After that, a new series was introduced every year.

General styling was modestly changed for 1952. Packard block lettering, seen along the lower edge of the 1951 hood, was removed this year. A medallion bearing the company crest was set into the middle of the upper grille surround. Base level Packard 200s were identified by single chrome spears across the front fender and door, single-fin "jet plane" hood ornaments, hood edge lettering, and exclusive use of the same "toothless" grille seen last season. Upholstery trims were done in plain-looking quality cloth.

Standard equipment included twin horns, two sun visors, two variable-speed vacuum windshield wipers, a horn-blow ring, front and rear bumper guards, front door courtesy lights, and front seat armrests. The Standard line included a Club Coupe priced at $2,475 and a four-door sedan listing for $2,528.

The Packard 200 Deluxe was provided with the toothy-type grille, three jet louvers on the rear quarter of the body and chrome wheel trim rings. It had all Packard 200 features plus foam-rubber front seat cushions, turn indicators, a glove box lamp, and an electric clock. The base level 200 business coupe was dropped. The same body styles were offered for $147-$157 additional.

A total of 46,720 Packard 200s were made and about 7,000 had the Deluxe package. The 288-cid 135-hp straight eight was used in all Packard 200s. Horsepower increased to 138 when the optional Ultramatic transmission was added. All Packard 200s shared a 122-inch wheelbase and 212-3/4-inch overall length.

The Packard 250 was again built on the same platform as the more modestly-priced models, but used the five-main-bearings 327-cid straight eight. Trim and ornamentation features included a new pelican hood ornament (with lower wings), chrome wheel discs, rear fender shields, single spear moldings on the front fenders and doors, and an unlettered lower hood edge. Standard equipment included all 200 Deluxe items, plus hydraulic valve lifters, an oil filter, an oil bath air cleaner, a trunk compartment lamp, a tilt-type rearview mirror, and rear seat armrests.

The $3,293 Mayfair hardtop was provided with six interior upholstery combinations of ribbed nylon and leather materials, while the $3,450 convertible had seats covered with a combination of genuine top grain leather and washable woven leather-like plastic. A total of 5,201 Packard 250s were built, with no body style breakout available.

The $3,094 Packard 300 sedan was on the 127-inch wheelbase again. It could be identified by the straight chrome spear running across the rear doors and fenders, in addition to a spear on the front doors and fenders. The toothy grille, non-lettered hood, low-wing pelican, chrome wheel discs, rear fender shields and wraparound backlight were among other visual distinctions.

Standard equipment included all 200 Deluxe items plus glare-proof inside rearview mirror, robe rail, and rear seat foam-rubber cushions. The number "300," in chrome, appeared at the base of the rear roof pillar. Packard assembled just 6,705 of these cars. Packard called the $3,797 Patrician 400 the "Most Luxurious Motor Car in the World." The 4,100-pound luxury car was like a Packard 300 with appearance and performance improvements. Identification could be made through the rear fender trim.

A strip of chrome molding traced the upper contour of the gravel deflector to the door line break where it met a straight extension molding that swept along the top of the fender shield to the back bumper. Also, on the upper rear fender tip there was a blade of fin-like chrome that dropped down to the horizontal taillight. The section of this molding directly above the red lens was embellished with short, horizontal ribbing. At the base of the wrap over roof pillar there was "400" numbering. Cloisonné-type wheel hub shell covers were used.

Standard equipment included all other Packard 300 styling, trim and equipment features plus hassock foot rests, chrome exhaust extensions, the nine-main-bearing engine, Ultramatic Drive, and four jet louvers. Interior appointments included a special steering wheel, Wilton carpeting, and color-keyed two-tone Bedford cord upholstery with a pattern of alternating pleated and plain sections. Production came to 3,975 units.

Model-year production was 69,921 cars. Calendar-year production was 69,988 cars. Packard was the 16th ranked automaker.

1953 Packard

The low price Packard leader was the '53 Clipper sedan which was listed at $2,588.

Ella Geisman, Byron Barr, Issur Danielovitch, Reginald Truscott-Jones, and Vera Jane Palmer were hot film stars in 1953. Oh, excuse me . . . make that June Allyson, Gig Young, Kirk Douglas, Ray Milland, and Jane Mansfield.

Many Hollywood types changed their names. Statuesque Joan Weldon had screen tests that led to a Warner Brothers contract, but she looked for a new screen name to help her career. Armour Star meats came up with a "Star-Naming Contest" that offered a two-week trip to Hollywood (or $7,500 in cash), plus a brand new Packard Caribbean convertible.

Such contests were popular in the early 1950s and gave Packard Motor Car Company a great way to promote its most exciting 1953 model. Weldon appeared as Dr. Patricia Medford in the '50s sci-fi classic "Them!" and turned up in 1950s television shows. She did survive longer than the Packard Caribbean.

The 1953 Packards were introduced on Nov. 21, 1952, but the Caribbean wasn't the only new model. The classic Clipper name was brought back to identify Packard's entry-level series. The new Clipper grille used a curved, full-width center bar, a new hood ornament and a wraparound back window.

Of all 1953 Packard offerings, the Clipper Special looked most like the 1952 models. It had plain, rounded rear fenders. A straight chrome molding with a barbed tip sat high on the front fenders and doors. A second straight molding was set lower on the rear fenders and back door of the touring sedan. A jet plane hood ornament appeared and plain cloth interiors were used. Standard Packard equipment included twin horns, twin sun visors, twin windshield wipers, a horn ring, front and back bumper guards, a jack, and tools. The Clipper Special added turn signals, a glove box light and a clock.

The $2,534 Clipper Special Club Sedan was the lowest-priced model. It weighed 3,685 pounds and 6,370 were made. The two-door Speedster was a $2,795 car, weighing the same. The Sportster used the two-door Club Sedan body with Mayfair trim features, including chrome interior roof bows, extra-heavy side window

moldings and staggered-type side trim for a hardtop look. "Packard Clipper" was lettered above the body side moldings on the upper rear quarters and a "fishtail" type rear fender treatment was seen.

There were 3,671 Speedsters produced. A $2,588 four-door sedan weighed 3,715 pounds and with 23,126 assemblies, it was one of the most popular Packards. Clipper Specials used the 288-cid Packard in-line eight with a 7.7:1 compression ratio and a Carter two-barrel carburetor that produced 150 hp at 4000 rpm.

A Clipper Deluxe line used front and rear body side moldings that seemed to link via a staggered chrome plate. It actually was part of one long, continuous arrangement of chrome strips.

The Deluxe had all the same features found on Clipper Specials, plus chrome wheel trim rings and fin-shaped chrome blades Packard called "fishtails." They topped the rear fenders. The $2,681 Clipper Deluxe Club Sedan weighed 3,685 pounds and 4,678 were made. There was a $2,735 four-door sedan that had 26,037 assemblies, making it the best-selling '53 model. Clipper Deluxe Eights used the 327-cid flathead engine with 8.0:1 compression and the same two-barrel Carter carburetor, which put out 160 hp at 3600 rpm.

A new Packard Cavalier series included a sedan, a hardtop and two convertibles. The sedan was comparable to the former Packard 300. The Mayfair hardtop and the Caribbean convertible were inspired by the 1952 Packard Pan American show car. All were grouped in the Packard 2631 Series. Cavaliers used a 180-hp version of the 327-cid straight eight with 8.0:1 compression and a Carter WCFB four-barrel carburetor. The Cavalier engine came only with hydraulic valve lifters.

The Cavalier four-door sedan had horizontal taillights, "fishtail" rear fender treatments and Packard lettering on the rear fender. This model was priced at $3,234 and weighed 3,975 pounds. A total of 10,799 were made. The Cavalier's side moldings resembled a lightning bolt with a short upper slash on the front fenders and a long lower slash running from behind the front wheel well to the rear of the car.

The Mayfair two-door hardtop was trimmed like Clipper Deluxes on the outside, but came with richer interior fabrics inside. It had the fishtail-style rear end treatment with "Packard" lettering on the rear fender sides. It listed for $3,278, weighed 3,905 pounds and had a production run of 5,150 units.

The regular convertible also had the Clipper Deluxe (staggered) type molding treatment, but with three jet louvers added under the rear fender spear. The Cavalier convertible began at $3,234 and weighed 3,960 pounds. Only 1,518 left the factory.

Even rarer was the Caribbean ragtop, a show car brought to life via body modifications done by Mitchell-Bentley Corp., of Ionia, Michigan. Its standard features included a full-leather interior.

A Packard script nameplate appeared on the rear-mounted spare tire, which was encased in a metal cover. It had a center cutout to show off a wire wheel with a Packard center wheel disc. Priced at $5,210, only 750 Caribbeans were built.

Identification features of 1953 Packard Patricians included the manufacturer's name in script on the rear upper portion of the back fenders, a pelican (actually cormorant) hood ornament, and horizontal taillights. Packard built 7,456 of the Patrician sedans at $3,735 each and 25 six-passenger formal sedans with Derham coachwork. The latter carried a $6,531 base price.

Long-wheelbase models reappeared in the Packard catalog and were called the Executive Sedan ($6,900) and the Corporate Limousine ($7,100). The 100 sedans and 50 limos were actually built by Henney Motor Company.

These eight-passenger models used the lightning bolt-style moldings, with the rear streak extending toward the back of the car. Derham, a custom body firm, also created a limited number of 1953 Custom Formal Sedans. These cars carried Patrician-style trim. The engine used in Patrician, Corporate Sedan, and Executive Limousine models had the Cavalier engine specifications with a nine main bearing crankshaft.

The 1953 Packards were introduced Nov. 28, 1952 with a model run of 89,730 cars. Calendar-year output reached 81,341 vehicles. Packard ranked 14th among automakers in industry sales. A Packard Balboa show car was constructed this year and put on exhibit on Aug. 31, 1953. Based on the Caribbean body, it had a reverse sloping fiberglass roof and roll-down rear window.

Air conditioning, not offered since 1942, was released as a $625 option (for four models) on July 1, 1953. The first two air-conditioners were installed in two White House fleet cars.

1954 *Packard*

The 1954 Packard Clipper two-door Club Sedan was the entry level model at $2,645.

Airplanes were making news in 1954. Lockheed's F-104 Starfighter fighter jet wowed the public. Equally exciting, even if not as fast, was the Boeing 707. The world's first commercially successful jet was unveiled on July 15. The YC-130 "Hercules" could haul 90 troops over 2,000 miles and land or launch from short-runway airfields.

While the year's "Packard" models retained a heavy dose of traditional, boxy styling and old-fashioned bird-shaped hood ornaments, the modern new Clipper had more of the aircraft-design motifs that other automakers were "taking to the bank." From its airplane-shaped hood mascot to its long, flowing rear fenders with "beacon-style" taillights. The junior Packard was a luxurious "Pan Am Clipper" for America's highways.

The '54 Packards arrived Jan. 15, 1954. The Clipper Special styling changes included new molding treatments, redesigned rear fenders, and new taillights in the fender tips. The Clipper Special had two separate sweep spears. A "Clipper Special" nameplate was on the trunk. Sales fell to 912 of the $2,544 Club Sedans and 970 of the $2,594 four-door sedans.

Deluxe and Super Clippers were on the same 122-inch wheelbase as Clipper Specials, but had the larger 165-hp engine. The Deluxe had a high, continuous sweep spear from behind the headlights to the bottom of the taillights. "Clipper Deluxe" lettering appeared on the trunk lid. Model offerings started with the $2,645 two-door Club Sedan (1,470 built) and the $2,695 four-door sedan (7,610 built).

A third entry was the Sportster, a $2,830 pillared Club Coupe with wide exterior window frame moldings that gave it a hardtop appearance. These cars also had a sporty interior and chrome headliner bows. Only 1,336 were made.

All-new was the Super Clipper, which was identified with model name lettering on the trunk and added a glove box light to the features list. The Sportster wasn't offered in this series, but the two-door Club Sedan ($2,765 and 887 built) and the four-door sedan ($2,815 and 62,70 built) were. A Panama sub-series included a sporty business coupe with two separate sweep spears.

This model had a "Panama" script under the forward section of the rear fender spear. It was trimmed about the same as the Deluxe Sportster. The next step up was the Panama Sports Coupe (two-door hardtop) in the Super Clipper line. It used the same roof line as the Packard Pacific and was otherwise similar to Deluxe/Super Clippers outside. Inside, rich appointments were used. The Panama Sport Coupe listed for $3,125 and 3,618 were made.

The Cavalier was the lowest-priced true Packard — the only one using the five-main-bearings engine. Packard styling included new "horned" headlight rims, curvier rear fender "fishtails," and new side spear treatments. The Cavalier's front spear sat high on the body and ran from behind the headlights to a point just below the rear ventipanes. A lower rear spear traveled from the forward edge of the rear fender to near the rear of the car, passing just above the fender skirts. The area between where the two moldings passed each other was decorated with three short, parallel strips of chrome.

A Packard medallion was placed on the base of the rear roof pillar. A Packard script appeared on the rear fender sides. The Packard center horizontal grille bar had vertical fluting on both sides of the center vertical grille post. The taillight clusters were placed halfway up the rear fenders.

Standard Cavalier extras included directional signals, a tilt-type rearview mirror, chrome-plated wheel discs, a trunk compartment light, and a robe rail. The only model was a $3,344 four-door sedan on a 127-inch wheelbase. Only 2,580 were made.

The sportiest Packards were provided with the nine-main-bearings straight eight, called the "Packard Line." Included were the convertible ($3,935), the Pacific hardtop ($3,827), and Caribbean convertible ($6,100).

The new names stressed a luxury tie-in, but still gave each of these attention-getting models a distinct identity. James Nance felt that if all models had their own names they would not be forgotten or confused. The 359-cid eight had 3-9/16 x 4-1/2-inch bore and stroke measurements With an 8.7:1 compression ratio and Carter WCFB four-barrel carburetor, this motor made 212 hp at 4000 rpm.

The conventional convertible had the same type of side trim featured on the Cavalier, except that the Packard script was moved from the rear fenders to the deck lid. Standard equipment also included a pelican-style hood mascot and rear fender shield. The Pacific looked much like the ragtop, without the folding roof.

The 1954 Caribbean had the new headlight rims, lower rear-wheel cutouts, and a "Caribbean" script on the sides of the front fenders. Standard equipment included power steering, power brakes, windshield washers, white sidewall tires, power windows, a three-way radio with electric antenna, a continental spare tire, chromed wire wheels, and wide-chrome wheel housing surrounds.

A staggered (or step-down) type sweep spear molding, connected by ribbed diagonal chrome ornaments, was used on Patrician models and the Henney-built eight-passenger sedans and limousines. The $3,890 Packard Patrician had round medallions on the rear roof pillar and many rich appointments, but only 2,760 were made. Even rarer were the 65 Executive Sedans and 35 limousines made in the Henney Custom line.

Packard's model-year production was 30,965 cars and calendar-year sales reached 27,593. Packard was America's 16th ranked maker again.

The Panther-Daytona (or Grey Wolf II) experimental Packard sports car was driven by Dick Rathmann at Daytona SpeedWeeks this year. It hit 110.9 mph (officially) and clocked 131 mph (unofficially) later.

1955 *Packard*

Like other automakers, Packard adapted the names of warm, sunny vacation spots to identify some of its sporty postwar hardtops. While GM ("Bel Air" and "Catalina") and Chrysler ("Newport") stuck close to home, Packard went to Latin America. The choice was the "Panama" hardtop that arrived with the Clipper series of cars in 1954.

For the struggling Packard, the timing was not fortuitous. In strife-torn Panama, National Police Commander José Antonio Remón was a controversial figure. On Jan. 2, 1955—15 days before the release of an all-new Packard Panama hardtop—Remón was assassinated at a racetrack. And just 7,016 Clipper Panamas were built.

For Clipper fans, everything seemed new in 1955. Straight eight engines gave way to V-8s. Massive new bumpers had bullet-shaped guards. Clippers had full-width grilles with bowed upper bars and "ship's wheel" center medallions. Fine, vertical blades filled the grille cavity. The front fenders hooded the headlights. Sweep-around windshields appeared. At the rear, the 1954 look was retained. On the rear deck was another "ship's wheel" medallion with model identification scripts on either side.

The left-hand script read Clipper, the right-hand one read either Deluxe or Super. Side moldings curved down and back from the front ventipane to the rear edge of front doors, then ran straight to the taillights. With "integrated two-toning," everything above and behind this molding was painted one color, everything else was done in another color. Clipper script decorated the hood and the fender area above the front bumper's wraparound edges. The only Packard identification was a small script on the right corner of the trunk.

Deluxes had small hubcaps and lacked rocker panel moldings. Supers had chrome wheel discs and bright metal steps on the rockers, along with upgraded nylon and vinyl interiors. A four-door sedan was priced at $2,586 with Deluxe trim or $100 more with Super trim. The Panama hardtop was $2,776. Production included 8,309 Deluxe sedans, 7,979 Super sedans.

Chrome wheel discs, rocker panel moldings and fender skirts were standard on Clipper Customs, except the $3,076 Constellation two-door hardtop, which had no skirts and featured wheel opening moldings. A Custom script was placed on the right-hand side of the trunk. Interior options included genuine leather. Two-tone Constellation hardtops came standard

Now a series of its own is the 1955 Clipper by Packard, like this Panama Super hardtop.

with a side molding treatment that gave a double color sweep effect. This was done by extending the lower front spear downward, across the door, to the rocker molding. The area below this molding was colored to match the roof and the panels above the upper rear side spear. This novel treatment could be ordered, as an option, on the $2,926 Clipper Custom touring sedan. A total of 8,708 sedans and 6,672 Constellations were built.

Senior Packards had grilles shaped as Clippers, but used a grid-type insert. New features included wraparound parking lamps, sweep-around windshields, Packard rear fender scripts and a redesigned hood ornament. All-new rear fenders, with "cathedral"-shaped taillights and the flat, rounded tail fin look were used. At the leading edge were vertical, simulated vent panels finished in chrome. Trim and decoration varied between models.

The $4,080 Four-Hundred was a hardtop. It had Packard block letters on the hood, gold trunk ornaments, gold Packard script on the rear fenders, a modified pelican hood ornament, roof medallions, and a "Four Hundred" signature on the deck lid. A straight spear of chrome ran from the corner of the upper grille bar, over the wheel opening, then across the door to the vertical vent. A second spear ran from the back bumper, over the fender skirt, straight to the front wheel. A gold-finished script on the aluminum beauty panel read "The Four Hundred."

The $5,932 Caribbean convertible had a twin-scoop hood with no ornamentation, except on the front edge of the scoops. An overlapping, fender-within-fender treatment was seen at the rear. The shorter fender was banded with a thin molding that dropped to gas-filler-door level, then ran straight to the headlights. The long fender dropped to the bumper exhaust pod, at which level another horizontal spear ran forward to the front wheel opening. To achieve three-tone finish, everything above the upper molding was one color, everything between the moldings (plus the fender extension area) was a second color and all panels below the lower molding were a third color.

A gold "Caribbean" script also appeared between the two

moldings and a gold "Packard" scripts decorated the upper portion of the rear fenders. Except for air conditioning, every choice option, including dual outside mirrors and rear antennae, was standard.

In comparison, the $4,040 Patrician four-door sedan looked elegantly simple. It had one straight molding on the rear fender and a separate front molding that ran straight from the upper grille bar to the rear of the front door. A split-fin hood ornament was seen and two-toning meant a different color for the roof. However, optional trim was offered to make the Patrician look more like the 400.

All senior Packards came with rocker moldings, fender skirts, chrome wheel discs and Ultramatic Drive. All Patricians had "tinfoil" side trim. Production totals show that 7,206 Packard Four Hundreds, 500 Caribbeans and 9,127 Patricians were built.

Deluxe and Super Clipper models were powered by a 320-cid overhead-valve V-8 with a 3-13/16 x 3-1/2-inch bore and stroke. The hydraulic-lifter engine had an 8.5:1 compression ratio and a Carter WCFB four-barrel carburetor. It made 225 hp at 4600 rpm. Clipper Customs and Packards moved up to a 352-cid V-8 with a Rochester 4GC four-barrel carburetor and 245 hp at 4600 rpm. The Caribbean used twin 4GCs that helped produce 275 hp at 4800 rpm.

Clippers had a 122-inch wheelbase, while Packard's had a 127-inch stance. Overall lengths were 214.8 inches and 218.5 inches, respectively. Torsion-Level suspension was standard on Clipper Custom and Packard models and not available on other models. A 12-volt positive ground electrical system was new. Power brakes were standard on the Caribbean Custom convertible.

Model-year output was 55,247 cars. Calendar-year production was 69,667 units. Packard was America's 14th ranked automaker.

1956 *Packard*

The Custom Constellation two-door hardtop was part of the separate Clipper line again offered by Packard in 1956.

It was advertised as "The Greatest Packard of Them All." To some collectors, it was the last "real" Packard. On July 27, 1956, Studebaker-Packard Corporation entered a joint management agreement with Curtiss-Wright Corporation. Shortly after, James Nance resigned as chief executive officer of SPC.

On Aug. 15, 1956, Packard's Detroit operations ground to a halt. In 1957-1958, a limited range of Packards would be built on the Studebaker platform at Studebaker's South Bend, Indiana, plant. The '57s were called Clippers and the '58s were Packards.

The 1956 Clipper grille had fine horizontal blades. A mesh-type insert filled the front bumper "air scoop" opening. The hood and deck lid were redesigned and wraparound parking lamps were seen. Bumper guards were moved further outward, below the headlights. New chrome trims and horizontal two-toning were adopted. Identifying the Deluxe sedan was a Deluxe script on front fenders and separate side spears, front and rear. The front spear ran straight from the upper grille molding to the rear edges of front doors. The second molding was positioned higher on the rear body, running from under the back ventipane to the taillight cluster. The Clipper Deluxe four-door sedan sold for $2,731 and weighed 3,955 pounds. Only 5,715 were built.

Clipper Supers had front-fender model scripts, but no rocker panel moldings. Two full-length rub rail moldings were used on the body sides. The first ran straight from mid-headlight level to the rear of the body. The second ran from the upper grille bar edge straight to the middle of the front door, then curved to the top of the rear wheel housing.

On all Clippers the rear fenders were redone and ended in a V-shaped notch (referred to as a reverse vertical sweep) that housed "boomerang-shaped'" cathedral taillights. A more massive rear bumper was seen. The Clipper Super four-door sedan sold for $2,866, weighed 4,010 pounds and had a production run of 5,173 units. The Clipper Super Panama two-door hardtop cost $50 more, weighed 25 pounds additional and contributed 3,999 units to the count. Deluxe and Super models shared the same 352-cid 240-hp V-8. It had a 9.5:1 compression ratio and a Carter Type WGD two-barrel carburetor.

A "Custom" front fender script and chrome rocker-panel moldings identified Clipper Customs. Other trim was similar to that used on Clipper Supers, including twin rub rails with the curved lower molding. Interior appointments were the richest for

Clippers. The Constellation hardtop had standard chrome roof bows and available leather trim. The Clipper Custom four-door sedan sold for $3,069, weighed 4,070 pounds, and had a production run of 2,129 units. The Clipper Custom Constellation hardtop sold for $3,164, weighed the same, and had a production run of just 1,466. The engine was the 352 with a four-barrel carburetor and 275 hp at 4600 rpm.

Packard's new Executive was introduced Apr. 9, 1956, as a replacement for the Clipper Custom. This series was designed to fill a gap between the lowest-priced Packard and the Clipper Deluxe. The Executive had a Packard grille and Packard-inspired side body trim, but was more closely related to Clippers. The 352-cid Clipper V-8 was used for power and the body was the Clipper-type with reverse vertical-sweep fenders and taillights. Body ornamentation had a Packard look.

The Executive was trimmed with two straight horizontal rub rails running from behind the headlights to ahead of the taillights. In two-tone color schemes, the area between the parallel moldings was painted to match the roof. There was no vertical simulated vent strip on the rear quarter of this car. Rocker panel moldings were used between the wheel openings only. Packard built only 1,784 of the $3,465 sedan and a mere 1,031 of the $3,560 two-door hardtops.

Changes in the Packard body for 1956 included a redesigned grille with a mesh-type insert with a grid work of vertical and horizontal chrome bars against it. Both the mesh and the grille could also be seen in the air scoop bumper opening. The wraparound parking lamps now had rounded rear edges. The headlight hoods were one inch lower. The front fenders were extended. Packard hood letters were replaced by a centrally-mounted crest. The guards were spaced wider apart, placing them directly under the headlights. Included in this series were the $4,160 Patrician sedan and the $4,190 Four-Hundred hardtop coupe.

Both Packards had vertical rear fender vents and the same arrangement of side trim. This consisted of a wide, chrome-ribbed band extending the length of the car between two horizontal rub rails. Both moldings intersected the vent ornament and outside door courtesy/safety lamps were placed at this spot. A model identification script was set into the contrast panel behind the front wheel housing. Both models were highlighted by bright-metal body underscores that continued across the fender skirts and lower rear panels. The Ultramatic transmission used an electronic push-button selector mounted on the steering column. Series production was 6,999 cars, of which 3,224 were the hardtop model. All Packards utilized a 374-cid V-8 with a 10.0:1 compression ratio and a four-barrel Rochester carburetor.

The Caribbean was now a separate Packard sub-series having two models with special styling and engineering. New three-tone color combinations were offered, such as maroon, light blue, and ivory white. A hardtop priced at $5,495 was a new addition. Its roof had a pair of lengthwise ribs, one on each side. The convert-

ible cost $500 additional. Use of a dual four-barrel induction system was continued with the 374-cid 310-hp Caribbean V-8. Caribbeans had reversible seat cushions.. Only 539 cars were built in this series, of which 276 were ragtops.

Factory introductions were held on Nov. 3, 1955, for Clippers and Packards and on Apr. 9, 1956, for Executives. The total model run of Packards was a mere 28,835 cars. Calendar-year sales dropped to 13,432. Packard slid to the 15th industry ranking. Studebaker ranked 13th. A show car called the "Predictor" was constructed this year.

1957 *Packard*

This photo of a 1957 Packard Clipper Town Sedan reveals its Studebaker-based body.

In 1957, "launching" became the "in" term for getting things underway. The race to outer space had begun and the so-called *Superpowers* were poised to launch rockets into the Stratosphere. Not every early blast off was successful, but the Soviet Union jumped into the lead with a winner. Its launch of Sputnik I, the first artificial satellite, worked out well. About a month later, a dog named Laika successfully rode Sputnik 2 into the heavens. Here in the United States, things didn't go as well, as the first domestic satellite blew up on the launch pad.

The same could be said, more or less, of Studebaker-Packard Corporation's efforts to launch a "modern" Packard that was based largely on the Studebaker President. The 1957 Packard Clippers did get off the ground — but they failed to "fly into orbit." Only 3,940 Town Sedans and 869 Country Sedan station wagons were built. A hardtop was added in 1958, but sales fell nearly 50 percent and a legendary marque crashed to earth. Many folks say that the 1957-1958 models weren't really Packards at all, but they were very interesting — and rare — motor cars.

There's no arguing with the reality that the 1957 Packard

Clipper was a badge-engineered automobile built on the Studebaker President chassis and using the basic Studebaker body. Packard modifications included finned rear fenders, a special rear wheel panel treatment and more elaborate trim. New rectangular grille inserts appeared both above and below the main horizontal bar. The Packard name appeared in individual block letters on the front of the hood. A Clipper script was placed on the rear fenders.

Packard and Clipper scripts were also affixed to the deck lid or station wagon tailgate. The traditional Clipper "ship's wheel" medallion decorated the grille and the rear of the cars. Side trim distinctive to the Packard Clipper consisted of a wide, grooved bright metal band extending the full length of the car.

Standard equipment on both the $3,212 four-door sedan and the $3,384 four-door station wagon included modified 1956 Clipper chrome wheel discs, chrome drip moldings, two-speed electric windshield wipers, back-up lights, front bumper guards, a padded dashboard, a deep-dish steering wheel, an electric clock, a glove box lamp, front and rear carpeting and foam-rubber seat cushions. The Town Sedan also had a rear seat center armrest.

The Packards were powered by a Studebaker overhead-valve V-8 fitted with a McCulloch Model VS-57S supercharger designed to cut in at 3000 rpm. While often identified as a Paxton supercharger, it was not until March 1962 that McCulloch became the Paxton Products Division of Studebaker-Packard Corporation. The cast-iron block engine had a 3-9/16 x 3-5/8-inch bore and stroke and displaced 289 cubic inches. With a 7.8:1 compression ratio and Stromberg WW two-barrel carburetor, it produced 275 hp at 4800 rpm.

The Town Sedan had a 120.5-inch wheelbase and the Country Sedan had a 116.5-inch wheelbase. Overall lengths were 211.8 inches for the Town Sedan and 204.8 inches for the Country Sedan. Tread widths were 56-11/16 inches up front and 55-11/16 inches at the rear. Size 7.60 x 15 tires were standard equipment.

Packard selling features for 1958 included a five-main-bearings crankshaft, dual exhausts, a 12-volt electrical system, a weather-proof ignition, Fast-Action variable-ratio steering, and Self-Centering brakes with weather-sealed drums.

An optional Twin-Traction rear axle was an aid in mud or snow, as it automatically adjusted to the loss of traction at either wheel, helping drivers maintain control and roadability.

Available options included tinted glass for $32, white sidewall tires for $28, power steering for $98, power brakes for $38, power windows for $103, a power seat for $45, front seat belts for $25 and a Country Sedan luggage carrier for $60. Air conditioning was offered in the Town Sedan only for $325. Flight-O-Matic transmission was standard equipment. A limited-slip differential was optional at extra cost. Both models used a conventional suspension, with helper springs on the station wagon.

Dual rear antennas were available, electric for the sedan and manual for the station wagon.

The Studebaker-based Packard Clipper was introduced on Jan. 31, 1957. H.D. Churchill was president of Studebaker-Packard in 1957, which must have been a tough job, as the corporation bled red ink and lost $95 million.

Studebaker-Packard Corporation claimed four main achievements: 1.) A strengthened dealer organization designed to gain increases in profits and working capital. 2) The inauguration (not "launch?") of dealer and field-force training programs. 3.) A summer sales spurt. 4.) The establishment of a marketing network for Mercedes-Benz sales and service.

By the end of 1957, about 300 Studebaker-Packard dealers had been accepted as outlets for Mercedes-Benz automobiles.

An interesting fact is while the Packard automobile was beginning to "drop out of orbit" in 1957, two other entities using "Packard" in their names were launching themselves into American history.

Vance Packard's 1957 book *The Hidden Persuaders* drew critical acclaim and launched his full-time career as a social critic, lecturer, and author.

At the same time, an American electronics manufacturer named Hewlett-Packard went public, launching itself into the financial world as a soon-to-be hot stock to own. In keeping with Bill Hewlett and Dave Packard's respect their workers, H-P took an unusual step in this era and gave stock grants to employees. Possibly, Studebaker-Packard Corporation could have learned something from Hewlett-Packard, but the automaker's Packard brand was so steeped in tradition that change did not come easily or fast enough to save the marque.

1958 *Packard*

The 1958 Packard Hawk added a fiberglass nose to the Studebaker version of the Hawk.

Death is an inevitable part of life. No one likes to dwell on the fact, but each year people—and things—that we love pass into history. In 1958, the obituary pages were filled with a number of notable names including those of Gladys Presley (Elvis' mom), actor Tyrone Power, Pope Pius XII, director Michael Todd (Liz Taylor's husband, who perished in a plane crash), and blues composer W.C. Handy. One name that didn't appear in any "obit" left an empty feeling in the hearts of many auto buffs. That name was Packard. The last car with a legitimate link to the Packard Motor Car Company of Detroit was built on July 13, 1958 in South Bend, Indiana. After that, the active history of the classic Packard automobile we knew and cherished was closed. The name Studebaker-Packard soldiered on until 1962, but the legendary Packard was dead.

To some, it was amazing that Packard returned to the marketplace in 1958 in any form..The new cars didn't appear until January 1958, so you can see they had a very short life. The Clipper designation was dropped. Four models were available. A hardtop was added to the Studebaker President-based "Packard" car-line and there was a separate, one-model, Packard Hawk series that offered a sporty two-door hardtop.

General changes from 1957 included new bodies. The Packard models had low, wide air-intake type grilles with an egg-crate-style insert that showed above and below a slightly "veed" horizontal center bar that wrapped around the body corners. Rectangular twin-slot parking lights were tucked into each end of the grille, above the center bar. Bomb-shaped bumper guards protruded from the center bar, on either side, below the headlights. There were now two round headlights on either side, housed in rather large pods with fine-rimed trim plates surrounding the headlight lenses. The Packard name was block-lettered across the center of the hood and above it was an air scoop with a cross-hatched grille at its front end. Small chrome fins sat above the headlights.

Radical pointed tailfins took the fender-within-fender theme of earlier Caribbeans to the extreme. There were now fins on top of fins, with the top one curving sharply upward. The lower fin turned into a sweep spear contrast panel that tapered as it ran the full length of the body from above the rear bumper to just below the front fender tip. A Packard script was affixed to the fins and rear deck lid.

The four-door returned from 1957, no longer using the Town Sedan name. It carried a base price of $3,212 and tipped the scales at 3,505 pounds. An even 1,200 copies of this model were turned out. The four-door station wagon was carried over, too.

Packard charged a minimum of $3,384 for its 3,555-pound version. Only 159 of the '58 wagons left the factory. New to the Packard line was the two-door hardtop, priced at $3,262.

The $3,995 Packard Hawk had a fiberglass, bolt-on air-intake grille. It was bolted onto the Studebaker Hawk sports car body, a sleek two-door hardtop coupe. The Hawk had an integrated hood scoop, Mylar sweep panel inserts, a wide chrome "halo" roof band, a tachometer, a vacuum gauge, and the 275-hp supercharged engine. A total of 588 of the Packard Hawks were made.

This year's standard Packard engine was the 289-cid V-8 with an 8.3:1 compression ratio, solid lifters, and a Carter four-barrel carburetor. It generated 225 hp at 4500 rpm. A low-compression version with 7.0:1 cylinder heads was optional. The Packard Hawk used the same "mill" with a 7.8:1 compression ratio, a Stromberg WWG-122A two-barrel carburetor and a McCulloch Model VS-57S supercharger. The supercharged 289 produced 275 hp.

The Hawk and Packard sedan shared the 120.5-inch wheelbase. The Packard hardtop and station wagon rode the 116.5-inch chassis. Overall lengths were 205.1 (Hawk), 213.2 inches (sedan), 209.2 inches (hardtop), and 206.2 inches (wagon).

In one black-and-white ad the copywriter wrote: "Wherever you go, people know Packard. In any elegant setting, elegance is immediately apparent... But the most striking feature of the new Packard styling is its originality. A long, forward-sloping hood sweeps down to a simple, tastefully proportioned grille that is unmistakably identifiable. In fact, Packard cars are the most original on the American road. Flatter yourself . . . with this distinction. Guest-drive a 1958 Packard today!"

We'll not comment. A friend departed deserves to leave on a high note.

The 1958 Packard two-door hardtop had a pod-mounted quad headlight arrangement.

Plymouths
of the Fifties

1950 *Plymouth*

Plymouth was well known for its all-steel station wagon, like this 1950 Special Suburban.

The fabulous '50s would become the era known for rock and roll. The latter hadn't quite made the scene in 1950, but it was definitely a year of silly pop tunes like "Rag Mop," "Bibbidi Bobbidi Boo," "I'd Have Baked A Cake," and "Chattanooga Shoe Shine Boy."

Life in America wasn't quite all fun and games and the conservative box-on-box Plymouth was there to prove it. It was a machine for getting to work and going to the market. A few buyers sprung for a top-down version, but even it wasn't quite what you'd call a "sports car."

Styling changes for 1950 Plymouths were mainly of the bolt-on type. In addition to trim variations, they included new peaked rear fenders on most models. This revision was easy to do on a Plymouth. The company advertised its rear fenders were attached with bolts and were replaceable in case of collision damage.

Grille appearances were changed by reducing the number of horizontal blades. The two thick lower bars remained, but thin moldings were gone and a bowed upper bar was used. It had a trim molding right above it, with short extensions onto the fender edges. Plymouth lettering, a small nose emblem and a ship-shaped "Mayflower" hood ornament were seen up front.

The triple-fluted 1949 bumpers were replaced by smoother, plainer ones, but ribbed rocker panel moldings were retained. There was no lack of bright metal trim. Horizontal spears decorated all fenders. Chrome headlight rings and vertical bumper guards were used. The front fender sides carried the model identification. At the rear, smaller trunk ornaments and taillights were featured. The 1950 rear window was slightly larger to increase rear vision.

The lowest-priced 1950 Plymouths were P-19s, which had a short 111-inch wheelbase and Deluxe trim. Three two-door models were offered, a three-passenger coupe, a two-door six-passenger sedan, and a two-door wagon called the Suburban. Prices began at $1,371 and peaked at $1,840. This series contributed 118,902 units to production.

Standard features included a "Deluxe" front fender script, black rubber windshield and rear window moldings, a painted dashboard and garnish moldings and plainer upholstery fabrics. Unlike many other makers, Plymouth didn't use black rubber stone guards on its cheap models. The rear fender gravel shields were simply omitted, but chrome shields were an option. Small hubcaps were standard equipment on Plymouth Deluxe automobiles.

In September 1950, a fancier Suburban with Plymouth's Special Deluxe trim level was added to the model lineup, priced at $1,946. The Special Deluxe weighed about 40 pounds more than the Deluxe Suburban. Both cars were essentially the same and their production was totaled together.

In between the base series and the top-of-the-line models, Plymouth offered two P-20 Deluxe Six models. These cars had a 118-1/2-inch wheelbase and the same level of trim as the small P-19s. Many parts were larger, though shaped the same as P-19 parts. Standard equipment was the same as the P-19 models. This series offered buyers a 3,040-pound Club Coupe for $1,519 and a 3,068-pound four-door sedan for $1,551. Production came to 141,731 and nearly 88,000 were sedans.

The Special Deluxe P-20 series was Plymouth's high-dollar range. Standard equipment included bright metal windshield and rear window frames, richer interior fabric choices, wood grain finish on metal interior panels and "Special Deluxe" front fender scripts. The convertible (officially described as a Convertible Club Coupe) used leather upholstery and a power top-riser mechanism. It came with a simulated leather snap-on top boot. The station wagon had 1949-style rear fenders and taillights.

Factory photographs indicate Special Deluxes came with larger hubcaps, but not full wheel covers. Trim rings are seen on most of these cars. As in 1949, the large cars had slightly bigger tires. Other Special Deluxe model standard equipment included front-door armrests, a cigar lighter and a clock.

Prices for the four models started at $1,603 for the Club Coupe. The four-door sedan cost only $26 more. It was nearly $2,000 for the convertible (12,697 built) and nearly $2,400 for the Special Deluxe station wagon, a real woodie with a small 2,057-unit production run. Despite containing some of the rarer models, this series was the volume leader with total production of 350,490 cars thanks to the sale of some 234,000 sedans and nearly 100,000 Club Coupes.

All 1950 Plymouths use the same 217.8-cid flathead straight six. It had a modest 7.0:1 compression ratio and a one-barrel carburetor. The horsepower rating was only 97 at 3600 rpm. It was sturdy, adequate and reliable. In this era, many motorists did their own mechanical work and the Plymouth power plant was simple and just right for do-it-yourselfers. Features of the counter-balanced Plymouth Six included a high-capacity fuel pump, a Micronic oil filter, a floating oil intake, aluminum pistons, valve inserts, an Oilite fuel filter, and automatic manifold control.

Other outstanding 1950 Plymouth features included Air Pillow Ride, which was described as "an engineered combination of many comfort features from Super-Cushion tires to soft, resilient seat cushions." Airplane-type shock absorbers with large fluid capacity canceled out the hardest bumps. An extra-large Wide-Angle windshield gave a good view of the road ahead. An electrically-controlled automatic choke provided more efficient starting. Other selling points were the chair-high seats, ignition-key starting, Dual-Action brakes, Easy-Press clutch, and synchronized gears. Automatic transmission was not available.

The 1950 Plymouths were introduced on Jan. 12, 1950. Model-year production peaked at 590,000 units. Calendar-year sales totaled 573,166 cars. D.S. Eddins was the chief executive officer of the company and Plymouth was America's third largest automaker with a 15.9 percent market share. Plymouth sales grew less than half a percent as the postwar boom in demand for autos subsided.

1951-1952 *Plymouth*

Practical was the word for the 1951 Plymouth Cranbrook two-door sedan.

As the '50s rolled on, airplanes, cars and dance steps all got faster and faster, but the Plymouth kept moving along at its own steady pace, racking up strong sales — and even racing wins. Plymouths managed to take a few checkered flags in NASCAR stock car races, but not because they were speedy.

The bigger cars would run out of fuel, while the Plymouths sailed across the finish line with enough gas left to drive to the supermarket. While the 1951-1952 hit tune "Slow Poke" might have brought Plymouth-type acceleration to mind, the company set an all-time production record in 1951, the only auto manufacturer to do so that season.

As with most Chrysler products, the 1951 and 1952 Plymouths were considered part of the same series. With the Korean War grinding on, Chrysler built as many cars as the government allowed it to, making running alterations, but avoiding annual model-year changes. The sheet metal was nicely reworked to create a more modern look without major retooling. Styling revisions looked more drastic then they actually were.

The hood contour was smoother, and broader. The front fenders sloped downward. The grille had a full-width, bow-shaped upper bar and a slightly-bowed horizontal center blade. A trio of vertical elements looked more like misplaced bumper guards. Horizontal parking lights were set into vertical extensions. The full wraparound bumper was of more massive design and had two vertical guards. A plate, stamped with the word Plymouth, stretched above the grille. Mayflower emblems and hood mascots appeared.

The new Concord P-22 series played the same role as the P-19. Concord trim included front and rear fender moldings, rocker sill strips, a black rubber windshield frame, hubcaps, upper beltline trim, and a "Concord" fender script.

The Concord Suburban was a two-seat economy station wagon, with the spare tire carried inside. The Concord Savoy replaced the

Special Deluxe Suburban and came with large hubcaps, chrome gravel guards, bright metal window frames, extra trim moldings, and special two-tone luxury upholstery. Standard equipment for the Concord Savoy included front and rear armrests, rear passenger assist straps, rear seat side storage compartments, and sliding central windows. Savoy nameplates were seen on the front fenders. This was now the company's fanciest station wagon-type vehicle.

For 1952, the emblem on the nose of the cars was slightly redesigned. At the rear, the manufacturer's nameplate was repositioned from above the trunk emblem to a relief cut into the top of the emblem. Overdrive transmission became available. Model arrangements were identical both years. The coupe, two-door sedan and two-door Suburban came with Deluxe trim and the Suburban also came with Special Savoy trim. Prices ranged from $1,537 to $2,182. They rose about $100 in 1952. Production for both years included 14,255 coupes, 49,139 two-door sedans and 76,520 of both Suburbans.

The new Cambridge model played the same role in the Plymouth lineup as the former standard-wheelbase Deluxe. Comparable styles were available, too. The word Cambridge appeared on sides of the fenders, above the horizontal trim spear. All 1951 Plymouths came with interior colors selected to match the exterior finish. A completely new dash panel harmonized with other appointments and housed conveniently positioned controls.

Outstanding new features included electric windshield wipers, chair-high seats, a downdraft carburetor, Synchro-Silent gears, a higher compression six-cylinder engine and Safety-Flow Ride. This latter enhancement claimed to utilize hydraulics to create "cushions of oil" to give a smooth ride on rough roads. The 1952 Cambridge was mildly face-lifted. The only variations between both years were number codes, prices and redesigned nameplates, plus new hood and trunk emblems. The 1951 Club Coupe sold for $1,703 and the sedan was priced at $1,739. Both numbers rose about $80 in 1952. Production for both years came to 101,784 coupes and 179,417 sedans.

The Cranbrook replaced the former Special Deluxe and embodied similar attributes. Block letters (script in 1952) spelled out the model designation at the upper, trailing front fender area. The new Belvedere two-door convertible hardtop was added in this line. It featured a smoothly wrapped-around three-piece backlight, wedge-shaped rear side windows, cloth-and-simulated-leather upholstery, and special Belvedere front fender nameplates.

A convertible was another exclusive offering in Cranbrook level trim, but the station wagon was gone. Pricing started with the $1,796 Club Coupe. The sedan was $1,826, the Belvedere was $2,114 and the convertible cost a minimum of $2,222.

In 1952, the same models were offered, and three had the same minor trim changes seen on other '52 Plymouths. The Belvedere received some extra attention. Its identification badge was repositioned to the rear roof pillar and a different type of two-tone finish was employed. The top color with this paint scheme extended onto the rear quarter sheet metal.

While the front and sides of the body were done in one tone, the roof, rear deck lid and deck lid surrounding area were painted a second shade that contrasted with the main color. Prices increased roughly $90, except on the Belvedere, which rose slightly more than $100. Over the two-year span 126,725 Club Coupes, 388,735 sedans, 51,266 hardtops and 15,650 ragtops were produced.

Plymouth engine specifications and body dimensions changed little, if at all, from 1950. A new Lustre-Tone instrument panel was introduced for the 1952 models. This reflection-proof dash board featured easy-to-read dials and more convenient controls. The graceful shape of the lower part of the panel offered increased legroom.

Silent-Synchromesh three-speed manual transmission was standard for both years. Overdrive was made available in 1951 as a $102 option.

The 1951 Plymouths were introduced Jan. 12, 1951, and the Belvedere hardtop appeared in dealer showrooms March 31. Model-year production peaked at 576,000 units and calendar-year sales of 620,870 cars were recorded. Plymouth's business climbed 8.2 percent in 1951, despite an overall decline in auto sales throughout the industry.

The 1952 models came out on Jan. 4, 1952. Sales dropped 23.74 percent, largely due to the outbreak of fighting in Korea. Model-year production peaked at 368,000 units and the calendar-year total was 474,836 cars.

D.S. Eddins was the chief executive officer of the company both years. The Ghia-built Plymouth XX-500 dream car was made in Italy during 1952. It had futuristic features including slab sides, a one-piece curved windshield and a fastback roof. It went on the auto show circuit in the mid-'50s.

1953 *Plymouth*

The hit songs of 1953 included "You're Cheatin' Heart," "Have You Heard," and "Don't Let the Stars Get in Your Eyes." For Plymouth owners, the stars were shining bright as the company celebrated its 25th anniversary this season. Plymouth introduced all-new styling. Annual production totals marked a new, all-time high for Plymouth Division. In addition to new body work and the adoption of a one-piece windshield, the Hy-Drive semi-automatic transmission was first introduced in March. By July, 25 percent of all Plymouths leaving the assembly line were being ordered with Hy-Drive.

All Plymouths rode on a 114-inch wheelbase and measured 189-1/8 inches end-to-end. The modern-looking new body was a bit more rounded than before. Detachable rear fenders were abandoned, with stamped flairs decorating the front and rear quarter panels. The one-piece windshield had a new, more uniform curvature to reduce distortion and give the driver a clearer view of the road ahead. Solex tinted glass was available, as an option, to reduce the heat of the sun. A newly-designed hood ornament represented the Mayflower ship. A new hood emblem had the "Plymouth" name incorporated into its design.

The Cambridge line was the base offering. Cambridge identification features included black rubber windshield frames, "Cambridge" front fender scripts on passenger cars, and "Suburban" front fender scripts on station wagons. These cars had no side spears, no gravel shields, no tail ornaments and stationary rear vent windows. Small hubcaps were standard equipment. A

Plymouth sold more than 298,000 Cranbrook sedans like this one to buyers in 1953.

new feature was a "one-third/two-third" type front seat, which was used in all two-door models. With this seat, the front seat passenger could slide over, next to the driver, to allow passengers in the rear of the car to enter or exit. New equipment features included splay-mounted rear leaf springs, Oriflow shock absorbers, cycle bond brake linings, and a "floating" engine oil intake.

There were five models priced from $1,745 to $2,044 and weighing between 2,888 and 3,129 pounds. Production by model was 56,800 for the two-door sedan, 1,050 for the Club Coupe, 6,975 for the three-passenger Business Coupe, 93,585 for the bread-and-butter four-door sedan and 43,545 for the two-door Suburban wagon.

Cranbrooks shared all 1953 styling changes, such as the new sheet metal and grille design, but had a higher level of trim and appointments. Identification points included chrome windshield moldings, chrome sweep spears on front and rear fenders, chrome gravel shields, chrome 'fishtail' ornaments, operable vent wings in all doors, and special front fender nameplates. The signature script on passenger cars read "Cranbrook" or "Belvedere," while those on the Suburban station wagon read "Savoy."

The $2,044 Belvedere was marketed as a luxury level, two-door pillar less hardtop. Its special features included a band of chrome and medallions on the rear roof pillar plus higher grade interior trim. The $2,187 Savoy Suburban also had special upholstery and interior appointments to set it apart from the basic Suburban. The convertible, as usual, had leather-grained trim, a power top riser, special door panels, and a new, zip-out pliable plastic rear window.

Also offered in the Cranbrook series were a Club Coupe and a four-door sedan. Overall prices ran from a low of $1,823 for the Club Coupe to $2,200 for the ragtop. Production by model was 92,102 for the Club, 298,976 for the four-door sedan, 12,089 for the Savoy and 35,185 for the Belvedere. The convertible had 6,301 assemblies, making it the rarest body style in this series.

Plymouth continued to use a 217.8-cid flathead in-line six. Like most cars of this era, the four-main-bearings engine had a cast iron engine block and cylinder head. It used a 7.1:1 compression ratio and a Carter Type BB one-barrel carburetor. The engine's output was rated as 100 hp at 3,600 rpm. A three-speed manual transmission was standard, Automatic Overdrive was optional and after March, Hy-Drive could be added, too.

Advertised Plymouth selling features included Shock-Proof steering, splay-mounted rear springs, front coil springs, a sway eliminator, Oriflow shock absorbers, rubber body mountings, Hotchkiss Drive, Safeguard hydraulic brakes with Cyclebond linings and safety-rim wheels. Plymouth spoke of a "truly balanced ride" giving the '53 models "…the softest, smoothest, steadiest ride ever known." The balanced design was said to control against roll, pitch and jounce.

Popular Plymouth options offered in 1953 included the MoPar heater, a radio, white sidewall tires, spotlights, a windshield washer system, directional signals, a back-up light and a locking fuel cap,

The 1953 Plymouths were introduced on November 20, and sales increased 39.5 percent over 1952—making Plymouth's 25th Anniversary year a big success. The eight-millionth Plymouth was made in September 1953. Model-year production peaked at 636,000 units. Calendar-year production of 662,515 cars was recorded. J.P. Mansfield was the chief executive officer of the company this year. Plymouth's "home" factory in Detroit accounted for 70 percent of its total production.

1954 *Plymouth*

It was 1954 and rock-and-roll was starting to happen ("Shake, Rattle and Roll"). But pop tunes like "Three Coins in a Fountain," "This Old House," "Sh-boom, Sh-boom," and "Mr. Sandman" were the types of songs that weremore likely to be heard emanating from the radios in Plymouths owned by hard-working, blue-collar types.

Despite the creation of specialty machines like the Ghia Explorer show car and a Belvedere hardtop with a gas turbine engine, the typical Plymouth of this era was a "grocery-getter" for thousands of American families. Through 1953, this role in the market had been sufficient to keep Plymouth third in production, but things changed in 1954.

Women were buying and driving more cars in 1954, like Plymouth's Belvedere hardtop.

In a hot blast of modern "Motorama" styling and V-8 exhaust, the rocking-and-rolling Buicks and Oldsmobiles suddenly found more buyers than six-cylinder Plymouths. It was growing obvious that Chrysler's entry-level car was in need of some modernizing.

Plymouth advertisements of the day stressed there was solid value below the Plymouth's outer beauty. "Take a close look at the Beauty and a long view of the Value," said one banner headline. Another ad stated, "You see at once the longer, lower-sweeping lines, highlighted by the gleam of sculptured chrome. And when you open the door of the new 1954 Plymouth, you step into luxury never before attained in a low-price car. Under all of this beauty are enduring value features. They explain why, of all cars used as taxicabs, there are more Plymouths than other makes combined."

Annual styling revisions amounted to a minor facelift, but the model offerings substantially shuffled. "Plymouth" appeared at the center of the main horizontal grille bar, with wraparound chrome moldings on each side. The headlights were given a recessed look by widening the chrome-plated surrounds. Circular front parking lamps were used and mounted at the outboard ends of the lower horizontal grille bar.

The Plaza line was the base Plymouth series for 1954. Plaza models used black rubber gravel shields and had Plaza front fender script. Power steering was introduced as a new option. On Feb. 26, 1954, fully-automatic PowerFlite transmission was added to the optional equipment list. Plymouth buyers could then order cars with three-speed manual, automatic overdrive, semi-automatic or automatic transmission. A total of about 75,000 of all 1954 Plymouths came with PowerFlite. The Plaza four-door sedan had stationary rear ventipanes. Two-door styles featured a one-third/two-third front seat.

The Plaza series offered a three-passenger Business Coupe, two versions of the Club Coupe, a four-door sedan and a two-door Suburban at prices between $1,598 and $1,745. Plymouth produced 113,266 Plazas, including one chassis used for some obscure purpose. One of the Club Coupes was rare, with just 1,275 built and only 5,000 Business Coupes were made. The other body styles had larger production runs.

The Savoy name was used on an entire series of cars in 1954.

This new middle-rung line included the same body styles offered in the Plaza line. Identification features of the Savoy included full-length side body moldings, newly-designed chrome gravel shields and Savoy signatures placed on the cowl side area of the front fenders. Bright metal windshield frames replaced the black rubber-type used with Plazas.

The Savoy interior was a bit fancier, too. A surprise was the Suburbans weren't normally provided with Savoy level trim, even though the name had been taken from the fancy all-steel station wagon model. However, the Chrysler Historical Archives indicate that 450 Savoy Suburbans were manufactured. The four models ranged in price from $1,815 to $1,853. Production was 199,517 for the entire series.

The Belvedere nameplate no longer identified only the two-door pillarless hardtop. This designation was now used to label a four-model lineup that included this style, a sedan, a convertible and a fancy all-steel Suburban station wagon. Identification points included all extras found on Savoys, plus full wheel discs, chrome "fishtail" fender fins, full-length rocker sill moldings, and "Belvedere" front fender script. The hardtop and sedan also featured roof pillar medallions. The convertible had similar medallions behind the gravel shields and the station wagon (Suburban) had fin-less rear fenders.

Dressier interior furnishings were used on all Belvederes. They included richer combinations of fabrics, extra armrests, special dashboard trim, a Deluxe steering wheel, a clock, and fancier garnish moldings. In the spring, a special trim option was released for Belvedere hardtops and convertibles. It added a narrow, fin-shaped chrome molding below the side window openings, with the area above finished in contrasting color. When the production of 1954 Plymouths ended, on August 20, 1954, the Hy-Drive semi-automatic transmission was dropped.

The lowest-priced 1954 Belvedere was the four-door sedan, which listed for $2,125 and had a production run of 106,601 units. Next in price came the Belvedere two-door hardtop, which sold for as little as $2,125. Plymouth built 25,592 of them. The two-door Suburban, priced at $2,268, had a run of 9,241 units. The priciest model, at $2,281, was the convertible. A total of 6.900 open-air Plymouths were made.

The 217.8-cid 100-hp six remained standard equipment under the Plymouth's hood in 1954. A "high-head" version a larger 230.2-cid six with a 7.25:1 compression ratio was a new option late in the year. It put out 110 hp at 3600 rpm. Three-speed manual transmission was standard. The Hy-Drive semi-automatic transmission cost $145.80 and the PowerFlite fully automatic transmission was $189. Overdrive transmission was also an available option for a price tag of $99.95. Available rear axle gear ratios included the standard 3.73:1 gearing, 4.10:1 with overdrive and 3.73:1 with Hy-Drive.

Introduction date for the 1954 Plymouth was Oct. 15, 1953. Model-year production peaked at 433,000 units. Calendar-year production was 399,900 cars. J. P. Mansfield was the chief executive officer of the company and Robert Anderson, who later became Chrysler Division head officer, was Plymouth's chief engineer. Assemblies of 1954 models stopped on Aug. 13, 1954.

1955 *Plymouth*

Top-of-the-line 1955 Plymouth Belvedere convertible wears optional wire wheels.

It was 1955 and rock-and-roll was here to stay. The Top 10 record charts reflected the change. "Tweedle Dee" was a big hit during the early part of the year. "Rock Around the Clock" arrived in July. "I Hear You Knocking" wound out a year bee-bopping back beats when it rose to number five on the charts in December. Like America's musical tastes, the Plymouth got faster and louder in 1955 with an optional V-8 and all-new body styling. It was enough for Plymouth to regain a notch on the popularity charts, out-producing Oldsmobile. Buick held tightly on to third place — one ahead of Plymouth.

The 1955 Plymouths were completely restyled with new longer, lower bodies. All sheet metal was new and more modern. The upper body edge ran in a straight line from front to rear. A sweeping roofline was supported by Full-View wraparound glass at both ends. The side panels were slab shaped. Both the hood and rear deck lid were flatter. The front fenders hooded single headlights. The grille cavity was highlighted by two wing-shaped, horizontal blades that were joined at the center by a ribbed horizontal tie-bar. The Society of Illustrators gave the 1955 Plymouth an award for being the "Most Beautiful Car of the Year."

The Plaza came with a six or a V-8. No extraneous trim was used. Chrome ornamentation was limited to a large chrome script ahead of the front wheel opening. A fin-shaped hood ornament was used. Windshield framing was in black rubber. Cars with V-8 engines had V-shaped emblems on the hood and trunk. A Plymouth badge graced the hood. The vertical taillights were set into backwards-pointing fender tips.

Features included many new items such as tubeless tires, a follow-through starter, push-button door handles, and a dashboard-mounted automatic gear shifter. Plain-looking cloth upholstery was standard in the Plaza, but vinyl combinations were available at slight extra cost.

A business coupe was still provided in this model range. It used the two-door sedan body shell with only a front seat and storage space in the rear compartment. Suspended-type control pedals were another 1955 innovation.

The Business Coupe, which came only as a six, carried a base price of $1,614. It was a 3,025-pound car and just 4,882 were built. Other six-cylinder models were priced from $1,713 to $2,133 and weighed from 3,089 to 3,282 pounds. Installation of the V-8 added $103 to the prices and about 86 pounds. Plymouth made 53,610 Club Coupes, 84,156 four-door sedans, 31,788 two-door Suburbans (wagons), and 15,442 four-door Suburbans.

The Savoy was Plymouth's mid-priced model range in 1955. Standard equipment included slightly dressier interiors, chrome windshield frames, bright metal roof gutter rail, chrome trim on the rear deck overhang, horizontal sweep spear molding high on front fenders and doors, and "Savoy" front fender signature scripts. A Sport Tone trim option was available on the Savoy (after midyear) at slight extra cost. Only two models made up this series, the $1,812 Club Sedan and the $1,855 four-door sedan. These weighed about 100 pounds more than comparable Plaza models and the V-8 could be added for $103. Plymouth made 74,880 two-doors and 162,741 of the four-doors.

The Belvedere was the high-priced Plymouth line. It had the same general styling features described for other models, with richer interior and exterior finish. All body styles had "Belvedere" front fender script, chrome windshield and rear window moldings, chrome trim on the rear deck lid overhang, chrome trim inside the headlight hoods, moldings decorating the taillights and bright metal highlights on the rear roof pillar. There were four six-cylinder models: two-door Club Sedan ($1,911), four-door sedan ($1,954), two-door hardtop ($2,088) and four-door Suburban ($2,297). They weighed between 3,129 pounds and

3,330 pounds. All were $103 additional with the V-8. The $2,326 convertible came only with the V-8 and weighed 3,409 pounds. Plymouth built 41,645 Club Sedans, 160,984 four-door sedans, 47,375 two-door hardtops, 8,473 ragtops, and 18,488 wagons.

The base engine in all Plymouth models except the Belvedere convertible remained an in-line flathead six. It was the larger 230-cid job with a higher 7.4:1 compression ratio. This gave it a rating of 117 hp at 3600 rpm.

Next came the smaller "My-Fire" overhead-valve V-8. This modern engine had a cast-iron block and head and five main bearings. It had a 3.44 x 3.25-inch bore and stroke, giving it a displacement of 241 cubic inches. With a 7.6:1 compression ratio and a Carter two-barrel carburetor, it generated 157 hp at 4400 rpm.

Two additional options based on a larger V-8 were offered. This motor had 3.563 x 3.25-inch measurements and 259.2 cubic inches. Compression was 7.6:1. The two-barrel version of this engine was good for 167 hp at 4400 rpm. A "Power Pak" version with a four-barrel carburetor had 10 extra horsepower. This made it "the most powerful V-8 in the lowest-price field."

Three-speed manual transmission was standard. Overdrive transmission was a $100 option. Automatic transmission cost $165. Available rear axle gear ratios included the standard 3.73:1, the 3.54:1 axle used with automatic transmission and the 4.00:1 axle used with overdrive. All Plymouth models had a 115-inch wheelbase and 203.8-inch over all length. Tread widths were 58-13/32 inches in front and 58-1/2 inches at the rear. And all models came with 6.70 x 15 tires.

The 1955 Plymouths were introduced on Nov. 17, 1954 and the Suburban appeared in dealer showrooms Dec. 22, 1954. Model-year producton for the Plymouth Division of Chrysler Corporation peaked at 672,100 units. Calendar-year sales of 742,991 cars were recorded.

One fact of note was the production lines at the Detroit factory were made 67 feet longer because the 1955 models were larger than past Plymouth products.

The 157-hp V-8 was dropped (except for Canadian and export models) by the end of calendar-year 1954 so Plymouth could advertise that it had the highest standard horsepower V-8 (167) in the low-priced field. Chevy and Ford both offered 162-hp V-8s.

1956 *Plymouth*

Plymouths grew fins in 1956 like this two-tone Belvedere convertible.

In 1956, the popularity of Elvis Presley helped turn rock-and-roll into a national phenomenon. Hit songs of the year included "Don't Be Cruel," "Blue Suede Shoes," and "Hound Dog." But there was another side to America's musical tastes that was fulfilled by tunes like "I Could Have Danced All Night" and "On the Street Where You Live," which also made the Top 10 charts.

In a similar manner, Plymouth was in the enviable position of playing to both the future-thinking rock-and-roll set and conservative middle America. With new finned "Flight-Sweep" styling and new models like the Fury, Plymouth found itself reaching the evolving youth market, but many car buyers on the other side of the spectrum bought the economical Plaza and Savoy models that were well-suited for running chores.

Plymouth's face lifted body, introduced the previous season, was certainly on target. Styling changes were dominated by the new fin-type rear fenders. In one advertisement, Plymouth published positive views on the new Flight-Sweep Belvedere from a boat

designer, an aircraft engineer, and a fashion designer. "The Flight-Sweep looks like motion," said fashion artist Anne Fogarty. "It's eager, vital, with a feeling of the future."

The new Plymouth grille featured a grid pattern center piece, which was decorated with a gold V-shaped emblem if the optional V-8 engine was ordered. Vertical taillights extended from the tip of the rear fins to the back-up lamp housing. "Plymouth" block lettering stretched across the upper lip of the hood. A wide jet airplane-type hood mascot was used. The arrangement of side trim varied according to series.

The Plaza range included the economy offerings. Identification features included rubber windshield and rear window gaskets, painted taillight trim, "Plaza" rear fender scripts, painted back-up light housings, small hubcaps, single horizontal front fender spears, and painted roof gutter rails.

The Deluxe Suburban was one of four models trimmed like a Plaza. The others included a Business Coupe, a Club Coupe and a four-door sedan. Prices for sixes ran from $1,726 to $2,138. A V-8 was $103 extra. Plymouth made 130,813 Plazas. The Business Coupe was rare, with just 3,728 assemblies, although low production in itself doesn't make a collector car.

The second step up the Plymouth ladder was represented by the Savoy and Custom Suburban models. Standard equipment on these cars included front fender horizontal sweep spear moldings, chrome taillight moldings, chrome headlight trim, painted back-up lamp housing, bright metal windshield and rear window frames, small hubcaps, and "Savoy" rear fender scripts. The Custom Suburban came in two- and four-door models. As usual, the interiors on the mid-priced Plymouths earned a few extra rich appointments. Buyers could also dress-up the exterior of Savoys and Plazas with optional Belvedere-style "Sport Tone" moldings.

The Savoy series did not have a Business Coupe, but added a Sport Coupe (two-door hardtop) and the two-door Custom Suburban station wagon. With standard six-cylinder engine prices on the five models went from $1,924 to $2,255 and the V-8 engine was $103 extra. Savoys and Custom Suburbans were popular cars and 168,984 were made. The low-production model was the two-door Custom Suburban (9,489 built), but the 16,473 Savoy two-door hardtops made are probably more collectible.

The Belvedere was again Plymouth's high-trim-level car. The four-door Sport Wagon, in the Suburban series, also had Belvedere features. A new body style was the four-door hardtop or Sport Sedan. Belvederes had "Belvedere" front door model nameplates, chrome back-up lamp housings, rocket-shaped rear fender "Forward Look" medallions, interior armrests, a clock, a deluxe steering wheel and dressier interior trim. Bright metal moldings highlighted the windshield, rear window, headlights and taillights, rear deck lid overhang, and front edge of the hood. Belvederes and Sport Suburbans came standard with Sport Tone side trim arranged in a distinctive, angled-back pattern.

The Sport Suburban also had Forward Look medallions on the rear fenders and tweed pattern seat cushions and backs, plus a rooftop luggage carrier. Added body styles in this six-car series were the Sport Sedan and convertible. Prices ranged from $2,008 to $2,425 for sixes a V-8 added $103. The convertible came only as a V-8-powered car priced at $2,478.

Introduced as a midyear model, the $2,807 Plymouth Fury high-performance sport coupe was actually part of the Belvedere V-8 series. Its custom features included: off-white exterior finish, tapering gold anodized aluminum side trim, a gold-finished aluminum grille, directional signals, back-up lights, variable-speed windshield wipers, a dual exhaust system with chrome deflectors, windshield washers, dual outside rearview mirrors, a prismatic inside rearview mirror, special tires, gold anodized spoke-style wheel covers, and a special 240-hp V-8.

There was also Fury rear fender script. On Jan. 10, 1956, a Plymouth Fury ran the Flying Mile at Daytona Beach, Florida and hit a speed of 124.01 mph. The high-performance hardtop could do 0-to-60 mph in 9.6 seconds and the quarter mile in 17 seconds. Plymouth made just 4,485 of these cars.

Plymouth's base engine was a 230.2-cid, 125-hp flathead in-line six with a one-barrel carburetor. A two-barrel version with 131 hp was optional. The optional V-8 had a 3.63 x 3.256 inch bore and stroke and 268.8 cubic inches. With an 8.0:1 compression ratio and two-barrel carburetor it delivered 180 hp at 4400 rpm. An optional 277-cid V-8 with a four-barrel "Power Pack" and solid valve lifters produced 187 hp. The Fury used a 303-cid solid-lifter V-8 with 9.25:1 compression and a Carter four-barrel that cranked out 240 at 4800 rpm.

All 1956 Plymouths retained the 115-inch wheelbase and measured 204.8 inches long. Tread widths were 58-13/32 inches front and 58-1/2 inches rear (except Fury). On most models 6.70 x 15 tires were standard, but the Fury used 7.10 x 15 size. Three-speed manual transmission was standard, overdrive was $108 extra and automatic transmission was $184. New technical features for 1956 included a 12-volt electrical system, independent safety handbrake, and push-button automatic transmission controls.

The 1956 Plymouths were introduced Oct. 21, 1955, and the Fury sport coupe appeared in dealer showrooms on Jan. 7, 1956. Model-year production peaked at 521,000 units. Calendar-year sales of 452,958 cars were recorded. The Plainsman station wagon, a futuristic show car powered by a Plymouth engine and riding on a Plymouth chassis, appeared at the Chicago Auto Show. An experimental turbine-powered Fury sport coupe was also constructed.

1957 *Plymouth*

"Suddenly it's 1960" was the slogan for 1957 Plymouths like the Belvedere Club Sedan.

It was 1957 and more than ever before the hit songs of the year reflected the American culture's swing towards being young or "young at heart." Among the leaders on the charts were "Young Love," "Wake Up Little Susie," and "That'll Be the Day." Although the brand was nearing age 30, Plymouths seemed to be getting "younger." Plymouth used the slogan "Suddenly, It's 1960" to get this concept across.

According to the copywriter, the '57 Plymouth was: "...the only car that dares to break the time barrier...the car you might have expected in 1960."

The updated Flight-Sweep (that meant "tail-finned") styling was supported by a number of technical innovations from a revolutionary Torsion-Aire suspension, to a Fury "301" V-8 and new Total Contact brakes. Traditional Plymouth buyers weren't neglected and other ads stressed low price and value.

Styling on all 1957 models was completely redone. New touches included a wraparound aluminum grid-style grille with a vertical air slot bumper, tower-type tail fin rear fenders, a dart-shaped body profile, and parking lamps set alongside the headlights.

The Plaza/Deluxe Suburban models featured front fender model nameplates, untrimmed body sides, small hubcaps, painted roof gutter rails, and V-shaped front fender tip emblems on V-8 models. Tapered "Sport Tone" side moldings were available at extra cost. Standard equipment and body style offerings were the same as in 1956. Prices for sixes were $1,874 to $2,174. The base V-8 was $100 extra. Series production jumped to 142,370. The rarest model was again the Business Coupe, which dropped slightly to 2,874 assemblies. A Taxi Special version was offered to fleet buyers at $2,174 and could also be ordered with the V-8. The economical 230-cid 132-hp flathead, with its one-barrel carburetor, did have some advantages to offer cabbies.

Savoys and Custom Suburbans shared the same general level of trim and appointments, which was much the same as in 1956.

The Suburbans had slightly different rear fenders than other models. Dual, tapering "Sport Tone" molding treatments were an option available at extra cost. This series grew with the addition of a midyear Savoy Sport Sedan (four-door hardtop) that came out in March 1957. Available in the Savoy series were a two-door Club Sedan ($2,122), four-door sedan ($2,169), two-door Sport Coupe ($2,204), four-door Sport Sedan ($2,292), two-door Custom Suburban ($2,415), six-passenger four-door Custom Suburban ($2,469), and the latter with nine-passenger seating ($2,624). Series production was 208,439 units.

The Belvedere/Sport Suburban group was as good as it got. Belvederes had single side moldings as standard equipment and tapering dual side moldings, with "Sport Tone" contrast panels were an option. Belvedere block letters were positioned at the middle sides of the rear tail fins, just above the moldings. Standard equipment included full wheel covers, rear quarter stone shields, an electric clock, and a locking glove box. The Sport Suburban had a special thick pillar roof treatment. Model offerings were mostly the same as in the Savoy lineup. A convertible replaced the two-door station wagon. Prices for sixes were $2,239 to $2,752.

The convertible again came only with the V-8 and had a $2,613 list price. Plymouth built 204,016 Belvederes, not counting Fury versions. The Sport Suburban, with 7,988 assemblies, was rarest, followed by the convertible, of which 9,866 were built.

The Fury was re-introduced in January 1957 as a midyear high-performance model. With the 318-cid/290-hp engine, it could do 0-to-60 mph in 8.6 seconds and cover the quarter-mile in 16.5 seconds. The Fury had many standard extras. It came only as a two-door hardtop with "Fury" rear fender nameplates. Standard features included Sand Dune White finish with gold anodized aluminum Sport Tone trim inserts and a 290-hp V-8. The Fury hardtop listed for $2,900 and 7,438 were assembled.

A 197-hp version of the 277-cid engine was Plymouth's base V-8. The heavy Deluxe Suburban used the Fury "301" engine (actually a 299.6-cid V-8) as standard equipment. The standard version of this motor had an 8.5:1 compression ratio and a Carter two-barrel carburetor. It produced 215 hp at 4700 rpm. A "Super-Pak" version with a four-barrel carburetor was optional.

A new three-speed TorqueFlite automatic transmission was used the Belvedere and Fury V-8 lines. Other transmission options included three-speed manual, manual with overdrive and PowerFlite two-speed automatic.

Plymouth's new-for-1957 "Safety Power" passenger-car frame had a 118-inch wheelbase (Suburbans 122 inches) and overall length was 206.1 inches for the Fury, 204.6 inches for other passenger cars and 208.6 inches for Suburbans.

Plymouth's Torsionaire front suspension combined the use of front torsion bars with Oriflow shock absorbers. At the rear were "outrigger" mounted rear springs.

"One of the great thrills in driving your new Plymouth is discovering you're the master of where it's going . . . not the road!" said an advertisement promoting the 1957 model's smoother, more level ride and improved handling.

The majority of 1957 Plymouths were introduced Oct. 25, 1956. The Fury appeared in dealer showrooms just a little later on Dec. 18, 1956 and the Savoy Sport Sedan was added in the spring. Model-year production peaked at 762,231 units. Calendar-year output of 655,526 cars was recorded. Plymouth retained third rank in American auto sales.

During 1957, Plymouth sponsored the "laugh and love" television hit of the year—"Date With The Angels" (starring Betty White)—as well as Lawrence Welk's "Top Tunes and New Talent" and "The Ray Anthony Show" with former Notre Dame coach Frank Leahy.

1958 *Plymouth*

Plymouth refined the previous year's styling with the even prettier 1958 Fury hardtop.

The American economy might have been a little sluggish in 1958, but it was a great season for Broadway hits. Some of the best included "The Music Man," "The World of Suzie Wong," "Flower Drum Song," "Gypsy," "Destry Rides Again," "A Raisin in the Sun," and "Redhead." A Plymouth ad of the year played on the popularity of such productions. It depicted a White Belvedere two-door hardtop parked outside the old Mark Hellinger Theatre at 1655 Broadway, in New York City. Theatre posters for "My Fair Lady," then in the third year of its nine-year run, can be seen in the ad. "Only From Plymouth:" says the headline. "The Broadway Look at a Main Street Price."

No one could argue that the '58 Plymouths had a rich "Broadway" look, but the low prices for many models were equally attractive to the average new-car buyer.

"We're not the richest people in town . . . but we're the proudest!" says a family gathered around a blue Plymouth in another ad.

A third shows two identical, bronze-and-white Belvedere hardtops parked across the street from each other. The car in the foreground belongs to "Mr. Average American," the one in the background has a chauffeur behind the wheel and a doorman helping the owner get in. "It's a rich man's kind of car . . . but my kind of price," says the first fellow.

Styling revisions for 1958 Plymouths weren't dramatic. They included a new, horizontal-bar grille below the front bumper, fin-type front fender top ornaments on Belvederes and Savoys, new taillights, redesigned side-trim treatments and four-beam headlights on all models. Hockey-stick-shaped anodized aluminum "Sport Tone" moldings and inserts were now optional on Belvederes and Sport Suburbans.

The Plymouth Plaza/Deluxe Suburban series was home to the lowest-priced '58 Plymouths. Normal side trim consisted of a straight sweep spear molding extending from the rear bumper to nearly across the front door. A molding arrangement forming a bullet-shaped side body cove with contrasting finish was optional.

Deluxe Suburbans had the same features as Plaza models, except for different rear fender side nameplates. Gold V-shaped emblems at the center of the grille were used to identify models with V-8 power. There were again the same five models priced between $1,993 and $2,451 this year. The price for the base V-8 crept up to $108. Series production was 125,888.

Savoys and Custom Suburbans had such extras as foam seats, a horn ring, and fancier upholstery. Standard body side trim was a full-length, single horizontal molding running from headlights to taillights. Finger-shaped Sport Tone treatments were a $20 option on passenger cars and $24 extra on wagons. The molding ran from the rear bumper to nearly the front edge of the front door, then looped back, along the doors and quarters, dropping down to the rocker sill just ahead of the rear wheel opening.

The area within the moldings was painted a contrasting color, which usually matched the roof. In the spring, a special Silver Savoy Special was marketed. It was a club sedan with special Sport Toning, front door and fender spears, a Metallic Silver roof and wheels, turn signals, electric wipers and washers, and a price tag that matched the model year. It sold for $1,958. Otherwise the same seven models offered in '57 re-appeared with prices from $2,219 to $2,712 (or $108 higher with a V-8). Series production was 171,907 cars. The two-door and nine-passenger wagons were rarest.

At the top of the Plymouth lineup was the Belvedere/Sport Suburban series, which technically included the Fury sub-series. Nameplates on the rear fender identified each particular car. The standard Belvedere side trim was a single, full-length horizontal molding of slightly distinctive design. Running with a slight downward slant, it moved from headlight to rear fender. About a foot ahead of the taillights, the molding angled up towards the top of the fin. When optional Sport Tone finish was added, a lower molding was added. It ran from above the back bumper and tapered towards the upper molding at the front fender tip. The area inside the moldings was then finished with contrasting colors, usually matching the roof.

Extra equipment features included full wheel covers, rear fender stone shields, an electric clock, and front fender top ornaments. Belvedere prices ran from $2,354 to $2,865 and the Fury sold for $3,032. Production included 5,303 Furys, 116,531 Belvederes, and 23,170 Sport Suburbans.

The Fury was a limited-edition Buckskin beige two-door hardtop with Fury rear fender nameplates, Sport Tone moldings (with special Gold anodized aluminum inserts), bumper wing guards, a padded interior, front and rear foam seats, back-up lights, dual outside rearview mirrors, and special Dual Fury or Golden Commando V-8 engines. Furys equipped with the wedge head 350 cid/305 hp big-block V-8 were capable of 0-to-60 mph in 7.7 seconds and could run the quarter-mile in 16.1 seconds.

The same 230-cid 132-hp six remained Plymouth's base engine, but the base V-8 was now the 318-cid job with a two-barrel carburetor and 225 hp. A 250-hp "V-800 Fury Super-Pak" edition

was also offered as an option in cars other than Furys. The base Fury engine was called the "V-800 Dual Fury" V-8. It was the 318 with 9.25:1 compression, dual four-barrel carburetors and 290-hp at 5400 rpm.

Two "Golden Commander" V-8s were marketed as well. These were on a new 350-cid block and had a 10.0:1 compression ratio. The first ran dual four-barrel Carter carbs and generated 305 hp at 5000 rpm. The second was fitted with a Bendix-built electronic fuel-injection system. A very limited number of EFI-equipped Golden Commando V-8s were made before this option was recalled. Then, the cars so-equipped were retro-fitted with two four-barrel carburetors.

The 1958 Plymouths were introduced October 16, 1957 and the Fury appeared in dealer showrooms at the same time. Model-year production for Plymouth peaked at 443,799 units. Calendar-year production of 367,296 cars was recorded. Plymouth retained its number three sales rank for the industry as a whole, with a 30.6 percent market share.

1959 *Plymouth*

Plymouth Sport Suburban wagons came in six- and nine-passengers versions in 1959.

Television sports programming was having a strong run in 1959, with everything from baseball and football games to the Daytona 500 showing up. Thoroughbred horse racing was another TV hit and millions of Americans watched three different horses win the Triple Crown events. It was Tomy Lee in the Kentucky Derby, Royal Orbit in the Preakness, and Sword Dancer in the Belmont Stakes. Plymouth was quick to pick up on this audience with an ad showing the first Fury convertible leaving a starting gate surrounded by ponies and jockeys.

"Full of Fury and Eager to Run," said the headline. "They're off! And this sleek, sure-footed Plymouth Sport Fury steps ahead and stays ahead. With its New Golden Commando 395, biggest V-8 in the low-price field, it gives you instant response without the least bit of strain – all the 'horses' you could want for modern driving… learn why the smart money's riding on Plymouth for '59."

In 1959, the Plaza became the Savoy, the Savoy became the Belvedere, and the Belvedere became the Fury. The special high-performance range, formerly known as the Fury, was now called the Sport Fury. General styling features included a twin-section anodized aluminum egg-crate grille, new "double-barrel" front

fenders, longer outward-canted tail fins, oval-shaped horizontal taillights and flatter, more sweeping rear deck contours.

Savoy identification features included rear fender nameplates, single side spears running from the front wheel opening to the back of the car, and small hubcaps. The Deluxe Suburbans (now available in two- or four-door styles) were station wagon counterparts of the Savoy. The two-door station wagons had thin, straight roof pillars, while the four-door models had a thicker "C" pillar and a flat-top roof.

Dual side trim moldings were optional on the low-priced Plymouths. Passenger models were down to the two-door Business Coupe (only 1,051 made), the two-door Club Sedan and the four-door sedan. Prices for all five six-cylinder models ranged from $2,143 to $2,574. A V-8 was $119 additional, but the Business Coupe didn't come with a V-8. Series production came to 182,464 units.

Belvederes and Custom Suburbans were now middle-rung Plymouths. The side moldings on these cars began behind the front wheel opening, flaring into a fin-shaped, tapering dual molding. This ran from just ahead of the front door, to the rear of the body. "Belvedere" or "Custom Suburban" nameplates appeared near the top of the fins. A special silver anodized insert could be ordered for $18.60 to fill the area between the body side moldings. The convertible was a V-8-only car.

Many new options appeared, such as swivel-type front seats and a deck lid spare tire impressions. Due to growth of the station wagon market, Plymouth offered three Custom Suburbans. Six-passenger editions came in two- and four-door styles, while the latter model could also be had with a rear-facing third seat. The nine-passenger Custom Suburban and two-door Custom Suburban also came only with V-8 power. The five six-cylinder models ranged from $2,389 to $2,762 in price. The V-8 was $119 extra in these cars. The V-8 only models cost $2,814 for the convertible, $2,814 for the two-door wagon and $2,991 for the nine-passenger wagon. Series production amounted to 108,728 cars.

Furys and Sport Suburbans were marketed as higher-level offerings and now came only with a V-8. A Fury signature script was positioned high on the tail fins. Dual molding side chrome began as a single spear behind the headlights, flared into a double level arrangement behind the front wheel opening and tapered to a point in front of the taillight wraparounds. A single molding continued around the rear body corner and across the rear deck lid overhang. A chrome Plymouth signature was placed at the left corner of the deck lid.

The rear bumper ran straight across the car and wrapped around the body corners, with a center depression below the license plate holder. V-shaped V-8 emblems (also used on other Plymouths with V-8s) were placed near the Plymouth signature on the rear deck lid. This series offered a four-door sedan ($2,691), two- and four-door hardtops ($2,714 and $2,771), the six-passenger Suburban ($3,021) and the nine-passenger Suburban ($3,131). A total of 82,030 Furys were made.

Alphabetical suffixes appearing in Plymouth codes were: L for low-priced, M for mid-priced, H for high-priced and P for premium-priced. This year the "P" cars were called Sport Furys. Two body styles, sport coupe and convertible, were marketed only with V-8s. The upper branch of the dual side spears curved upward on the rear fenders, repeating the general fin contour. The lower branch wrapped around the rear body corners and ran across the deck lid overhang.

A silver anodized aluminum insert panel was standard and a "Fury" signature script was placed inside the dual moldings at the rear. Positioned directly behind the moldings were large, colorful "Forward Look" medallions. Standard equipment for these cars included swivel front seats, a Sport deck lid tire cover stamping and a custom padded steering wheel. The hardtop sold for $2,927 and had 17,867 assembles. The new ragtop was $3,125 and 5,990 were built.

Plymouth engines went up in power. The base 318-cid two-barrel V-8 was rated at 230 hp. The base Sport Fury V-8 added four-barrels with 260 hp. The only option was a 361-cid V-8 called the "Golden Commando 395" based on its torque rating. It ran a 10.0:1 compression ratio and carried a single Carter AFB four-barrel carburetor. The engine generated 305 hp at 4600 rpm.

The 1959 Plymouths retained a 118-inch wheelbase for passenger models and the 122-inch station wagon stance. Overall lengths were 210 inches and 214.5 inches, respectively. All models used 7.50 x 14 tires except the nine-passenger Suburban, which used 8.00 x 14 size tires. A three-speed manual transmission was standard, PowerFlite automatic transmission was optional with all but Golden Commando V-8s for $189. Overdrive cost $84. TorqueFlite automatic transmission was used with the big engine and cost $227.

The 1959 Plymouths were introduced in October 1958. Plymouth sales leaped 11.6 percent. Model-year production peaked at 458,261 units. Calendar-year production of 413,204 cars was recorded. Plymouth was again third, but its market share declined to 13.19 percent. General Manager Harry E. Cheesbrough marked the production of the company's 11-millionth vehicle in 1959, Plymouth's 30th anniversary.

A Fury four-door hardtop was converted into a Chrysler turbine-engined car and made a 576-mile "cross-country" reliability run. It didn't cross the country, but Chrysler's promotional copywriters still used the term.

The Sport Fury, like this hardtop, was Plymouth's most luxurious series in 1959.

Pontiacs
of the Fifties

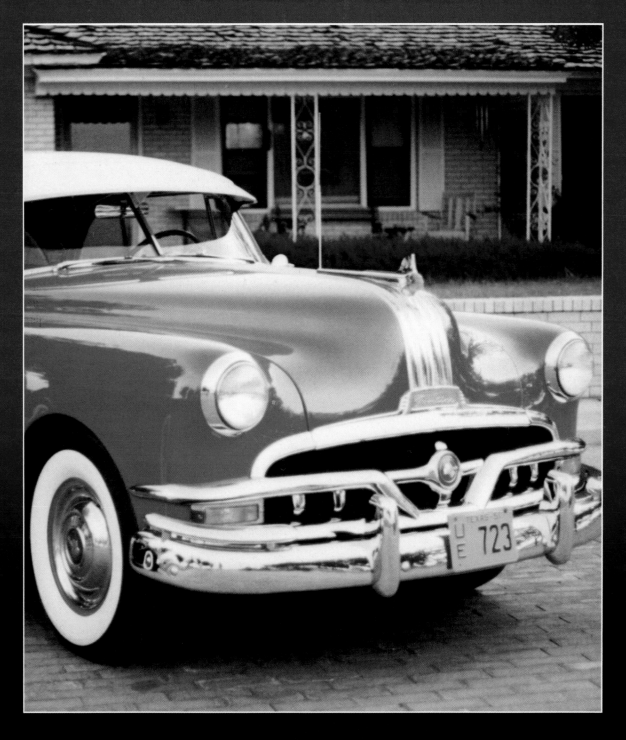

1950 *Pontiac*

The 1950 Pontiac Chieftain Deluxe convertible has the Silver Streak straight-8 symbol.

The war had ended. After several years of adjusting back to "normal" life, Americans were looking forward to an exciting new era that would bring them increased prosperity and more leisure time. Television, though growing in popularity, hadn't yet eroded the enchantment of Hollywood and theatregoers were flocking to local movie houses to see a variety of films ranging from "Rio Grande" (starring John Wayne) to "Harvey" (starring Jimmy Stewart).

In the automotive world modern innovations like overhead-valve V-8 engines were also finding more buyers each year, but the durability of a time-tested flathead engine continued to entice many visitors to Pontiac showrooms.

Known as the conservative automaker that dominated the lower-mid-priced class (where it outsold both De Soto and Mercury), Pontiac did make at least one concession to modernity in 1950, by releasing the first Catalina two-door hardtop.

Optional Hydra-Matic Drive, introduced in 1948, also continued to help Pontiac salesmen achieve their goals. By the end of 1950, business was running very strong with 446,426 cars built during the model year and 467,555 assemblies counted for the calendar-year.

Pontiac factories began cranking out the 1950 models on Nov. 10, 1949. The cars used the envelope body that had been all-new in 1949 with some modest, but well-conceived updates to trim and appointments. The chrome bar that ran horizontally across the center of the grille opening now wrapped around the corners of the body. It had five chrome uprights spaced across it with the center one bearing a round insert showing the Pontiac Indian head symbol. The lip of the hood was trimmed with a curved chrome bar with shorter curved extensions onto the fenders. Above the center of the grille was a winged Pontiac nameplate. The hood and nose of the car were decorated with five chrome bands ("Silver Streaks") that "waterfalled" down towards the grille. The hood mascot was an Indian head.

Although often referred to as "Silver Streak" Pontiacs, the cars were actually Chieftains and Streamliners. These terms referred to the design of the body, rather than the level of trim and both Chieftains and Streamliners came in standard and Deluxe versions.

Chieftains were "bustleback" models with a protruding trunk. In the standard Chieftain lineup there were four standard-trim cars (Business Coupe, Coupe-Sedan, two-door sedan and four-door sedan). The Chieftain Deluxe line had three of the same models (no Business Coupe), plus three additional styles — the Catalina, the Catalina Super, and the convertible.

Streamliners were fastback a two-door Coupe-Sedan, a four-door sedan (both with the trunk lid blended into the roofline) plus, for some strange reason, a metal station wagon. Also a little strange was the fact that the standard Streamliner wagon came with eight-passenger seating, while the Streamliner Deluxe wagon came with six-passenger seating.

Standard models — whether Chieftains or Streamliners — had no chrome body strip, no chrome wheel rings and painted headlight rims. Deluxe models had a chrome body strip, chrome wheel rings, chrome headlight rings and stainless steel gravel guards. Sixes had a chrome "Silver Streak" script on their fenders and Eights had "Silver 8 Streak," plus "8" emblems on the hood and rear deck lid.

The six-cylinder engine was an in-line L-head (flathead) with a cast iron block and large, "flat" cast-iron cylinder head. With a 3-9/16 x 4-inch bore and stroke, it displaced 239.2 cubic inches. A 6.5:1 compression ration was standard, but a 7.5:1 "high head" was optional and mandatory with Hydra-Matic Drive. The standard horsepower rating was 90 at 3400 rpm (93 at 3400 rpm with the high head). The straight six had four main bearings, solid valve lifters and a Carter WA1-719-S one-barrel carburetor.

The Pontiac six was not a very exciting engine, but it was reliable and also nearly as fast as the eight. However, the bigger engine sold better. This was because Pontiac could honestly advertise that it had "the lowest-priced eight in the industry." Priced at $68-$69 more than the six, the Pontiac straight eight was similar in overall design. It had 3-3/8 x 3-3/4 bore and stroke measurements and a displacement of 268.2 cubic inches. It also had five main bearings and a Carter WCD-719-S two-barrel carburetor. The horsepower ratings were: (standard) 108 at 3600 rpm and (optional) 113 at 3600 rpm.

Chieftains were built off General Motors' postwar A-body shell. The four standard Chieftain sixes were priced between $1,571 and

$1,745. They weighed 3,209 to 3,299 pounds. Eights cost about $70 additional and weighed an extra 80 pounds or so. Like all Pontiacs, the Chieftains rode on a 120-inch wheelbase and measured 202-1/2 inches from bumper to bumper.

Chieftain Deluxe six-cylinder models ranged in price from $1,789 to $2,122, with Catalinas and convertibles in the over-$2,000 bracket. The eight-cylinder versions were, of course, about $70 more and about 80 pounds heavier. The new Catalina hardtop made headlines and proved so distinctive that, until 1959, the terms "hardtop" and "Catalina" would be interchangeable in Pontiac nomenclature. The Super Deluxe Catalina came only in San Pedro Ivory, Sierra Rust or two-tone combinations of those colors and its genuine leather was done in color-coordinated rust-and-ivory combinations.

Streamliner sixes were priced from $1,673 to $2,264, with the station wagon being the priciest. The wagon could be ordered with simulated wood-grain exterior paneling, but not with real wood. With the straight eight, the price and weight went up the same as in the Chieftain lines.

Most Pontiacs made, especially in the Deluxe series, came with the larger engine and Hydra-Matic. In fact, other options and accessories from wheel trim rings to sun visors and spotlights were quite common on Pontiacs, as the typical buyers in this market niche was upwardly-mobile middle class people such as professionals and small businessmen. They may not have reached the Cadillac class yet, but they wanted their Pontiac to look like one!

Unfortunately for historians and car collectors, Pontiac records of body style production prior to 1955 were either not kept or have been lost over the years. Production break outs by engine and transmission show the assembly of 115,542 Streamliner and Chieftain sixes (24,930 with Hydra-Matic and 90,612 with synchromesh) and a total of 330,887 Streamliner and Chieftain eights (263,188 with Hydra-Matic and 67,699 with synchromesh).

1951 Pontiac

The 1951 Pontiac Streamliner Eight Deluxe station wagon used wood-like inserts.

It was a year of classic American films in 1951, with John Wayne starring in "Flying Leathernecks" and Bogart and Hepburn riding the "African Queen." Whether it was an "American in Paris" or a "Streetcar Named Desire," film history was being made. So was automotive history. At Pontiac, the company celebrated its Silver Anniversary and marked the milestone by adding gold highlights to the round medallion in the center of the new "gull wing-styled" grille.

Production of the 25th Anniversary 1951 Pontiacs started up Nov. 27, 1950. They were introduced a few weeks later on December 11 and commemorated the company's 25th anniversary year. The Silver Streak theme continued, but these words no longer appeared on the cars themselves. The Pontiac nameplate on the hood lost its wings and took a new shape. The cars were the same size as in 1950 and had the same engine choices with a bit more power.

Pontiac Chieftains had GM's bustle-back A-body shell. The Deluxe models had chrome mid-body-side moldings, bright gravel guards and headlight rings. The new mid-body moldings used on Deluxe models had the shape of a spear tip on the front fender with "Pontiac" or "Pontiac Eight" in script right behind it. The tip was embossed with three stars, a hint that the Star Chief model was coming in a few years. Belt line moldings on all Deluxe passenger cars, except station wagons, had a dip behind the doors. Standard belt moldings were straight.

The Chieftain Business Coupe came only in the standard line. The Coupe-Sedan, two-door sedan and four-door sedan came with both types of decorations and trim. Convertibles came with Chieftain Deluxe features only. Chieftain Catalina hardtops came with a choice of Deluxe or Super Deluxe trim. The Chieftain Deluxe Catalina had an interior similar to other Chieftain Deluxe models. Chieftain Deluxe Catalina Super models offered a choice of exclusive blue-and-ivory leather-and-cloth trim or optional all-leather trim in the same colors.

The four standard Chieftain Sixes ranged in price from $1,713 for the Business Coupe to $1,903 for the four-door sedan. The same cars were available with a straight eight at prices between $1,787 and $1,977. The eights were about 80 pounds heavier. Chieftain Deluxe six-cylinder models — the Coupe-Sedan, two- and four-door sedan, Deluxe and Super Deluxe Catalina and convertible — had prices between $2,026 and $2,388, with the eights having the normal additions to price and weight.

Streamliners again used the fastback GM B-body shell, which was actually losing popularity in this era. The public thought fastbacks had a prewar look, so Pontiac began phasing the Streamliner out this year. The four-door sedan was dropped. Ads for the year often showed the Streamliner wagon, but rarely depicted fastbacks. Only the Coupe-Sedan and the metal station wagon were offered, but in four variations—Streamliner Six, Streamliner Deluxe Six, Streamliner Eight, and Streamliner Deluxe Eight. Prices ranged between $1,824 and $2,629.

New carburetors and minor revisions upped horsepower to 96 on the standard six and 100 on the "high-horsepower" job. The eight increased to 116 and 120 hp, respectively. Pontiac pushed the eight-cylinder engine as a motor "built to last 100,000 miles," although I will guarantee that you can blow one up before that odometer reading if you really try. I've done it!

The 100,000-mile promotional theme was very much aimed at Pontiac's formidable competitor, De Soto, which built many taxicabs that saw hundreds of thousands of miles of rugged use. Pontiac advertised the 1951 Chieftain Deluxe Eight four-door sedan as "Spectacular . . . The First Mile or the First Hundred Thousand!" Two other sales slogans that Pontiac employed repeatedly were "Dollar for Dollar you can't beat a Pontiac" and "The Most Beautiful Thing on Wheels."

Selling features for 1951 Pontiacs included rugged all-steel Fisher bodies, harmonized interior colors, Deep-Rest seats, Long-Flex springs, Sweepstream fenders, a wide curved windshield, wide Easy-Access doors, a Handi-Grip parking brake, Finger-Tip starting, a Twin-Duct heating system, quality floor coverings, the use of regular gas (a shot at the new V-8s that required premium-grade fuel), and "Silver Streak performance." The year's new instrument panel featured a soft, rich two-tone finish with brilliant chrome-and-black control buttons, and back-lighted instruments.

As we said above, Pontiac buyers liked the extras that made the cars look more expensive then they were and Pontiac Motor Division obliged them with a long list of options and accessories that, in addition to sprucing up the cars, added to dealer profits.

Popular items included the Chieftain radio seven-tube radio with mast antenna, No-Blo wind deflectors, car cushions, a Venti-Seat under seat heater, chrome Venti-Shades for the window frames, a windshield sun visor (which required the use of a prismatic traffic light viewer), a Polaroid visor (for the fold-down inside visors), rear fender panels (the "fender skirts" which almost all Pontiacs had), chrome license frames, an illuminated Indian head hood ornament (yes, they really did cost extra), wheel trim rings, steel wheel discs, white sidewall discs, a Deluxe steering wheel, and even a Remington Auto-Home shaver. Even directional signals were an add-on in 1951.

A column-shifted three-speed manual transmission with synchromesh on all gears was standard on all models. The four-speed Hydra-Matic Drive automatic transmission was available for $159 additional Pontiacs came with a standard 4.1:1 rear axle ratio. There was a 3.9:1 economy option, a 4.3:1 mountain-driving option and a 3.63:1 rear axle to use in cars with Hydra-Matic Drive.

Pontiac made 343,795 cars during the calendar-year. Model-year production came to 343,795 units. This included a total of 53,748 Streamliner and Chieftain sixes (10,195 with Hydra-Matic and 43,553 with synchromesh) and a total of 316,411 Streamliner and Chieftain eights (251,987 with Hydra-Matic and 64,424 with synchromesh).

On an industry-wide basis, for the calendar-year, Pontiac built 6.7 percent of America's convertibles; 9.6 percent of domestic hardtops; and 4.7 percent of domestic station wagons. In the final count, car output was down 26 percent from 1950, but was still the second-best production total in Pontiac history.

1952 Pontiac

This 1952 Pontiac Chieftain Deluxe convertible seems to enjoy basking in the sun.

"Limelight," "High Noon," and "The Greatest Show on Earth" thrilled American moviegoers in 1952. By comparison, the year's Pontiac offered few thrills to buyers. The car was essentially the same one introduced in 1949, with the mandatory new-grille/new-side-trim/new-taillights treatment at the start of the new model year.

In fact, the grille wasn't much different at all. It had four black, oblong indentations below the slightly-redesigned Pontiac nameplate. The spear tip on the front fender of Deluxe Chieftains became a scallop and a second molding was added. It ran straight back, above the first one, to a point on the rear half of the front door. With the minor nature of the 1952 updates, it's quite likely the taillights were totally unchanged. Perhaps only the *Pontiac Master Parts Catalog* and Kurt Kelsey know for sure!

Even Pontiac general manager, Arnold Lenz, realized his division needed youthful thinking to offset its declining sales numbers. Model-year production had dropped by 76,270 cars from 1950 to 1951 and was sliding towards another 99,786-unit decline for 1952. With the Korean War in full swing, there were some government restrictions on output, but they didn't explain away the entire problem. In Pontiac's "secret" engineering labs, technicians were already changing the Pontiac chassis with the goal of installing a V-8 for 1953. As things turned out, the Pontiac V-8 didn't arrive until 1955.

Streamliner fastbacks—a visual throwback to prewar days—were an easier problem to deal with. Lenz dropped them from the plan for 1952. Pontiac station wagons then joined the Chieftain line — the only series left. Standard Chieftain models had no chrome body side moldings, rubber gravel shields, no chrome wheel rings, Dark Gray check pattern cloth door trim, and solid Gray wool cloth seats. Six-cylinder models had "Pontiac" on the glove compartment door and interior door name plates, while Eights said "Pontiac Eight."

Chrome body side moldings, stainless steel gravel guards, and chrome wheel and headlight rings characterized Chieftain Deluxe models. The new double moldings on the front fenders and doors were promoted as "Dual-Sweep bright-metal spears."

Most of these cars were trimmed in rich wool diamond-pattern cloth with a button-back look. Chieftain Deluxe convertibles and Catalina hardtops had leather-and-cloth trims. Chieftain Super Deluxe Catalinas had two-tone Green top-grain cowhide seats. Leather-and-cloth trim was still optional on these flagship models. Standard station wagons featured seats in rust-colored imitation leather. Deluxe station wagons offered a choice of Gray Bedford cord cloth with genuine leather in tan, red, green, blue, or black.

Entry-level buyers could still get a Chieftain Six two-door sedan for under $2,000. The highest-priced model was the Chieftain Eight Deluxe Station Wagon with a suggested retail price of $2,772. Pontiac's sportiest models were the Super Deluxe Eight Catalina hardtop at $2,446 and the Chieftain Deluxe Eight convertible, which cost $2,518. Compared to some other American cars, Pontiac convertibles were not all that exciting for the price, but they were and are handsome cars and you don't see many survivors today.

The Catalina "hardtop convertibles" seem to be easier to come by and nearly as desirable to collectors. The name Catalina seems to have some magic and certainly fits the trend towards more leisure pursuits in the early '50s.

Pontiac's "Silver Streak" trim dated back to the Art Deco era,

when designer Franklin Quick Hershey first applied it to 1935 models. By 1952, it was a sign of the past, rather than the future. Changes in horsepower ratings were another indication of the "Grandpa's car" image the flathead-powered, Silver-Streak Pontiacs were facing in 1952. The company had never before raised carryover engine output two years in a row before, but did so in 1952. This was a case of trying to get everything possible out of a motor that dated back to 1933 and there wasn't that much more to get. Compression ratios on both power plants were pushed to 6.8:1 with manual transmission and 7.7:1 with the new "town-and-country" Dual-Range Hydra-Matic Drive. This added from two to four horsepower, but 122 hp was nothing to brag up with 190-hp V-8s around. *Motor Trend* road tested the 1952 Pontiac Chieftain Deluxe sedan, recording a 21-second quarter mile run and top speed of 95.24 mph. Fuel economy was 16.4 mpg in overall driving.

As it had for a long time, Pontiac again did a pretty good job of selling its "one-step-up" buyers enough extra-cost options to make their neighbors think they were two steps up. Rarely did you see a Pontiac without rear fender skirts, although they were not standard equipment. The same went for bumper guards, back-up lights, and No-Mar fuel door guards. For real luxury, Pontiac also offered the Venti-Seat under seat heater, Polaroid sun visor, illuminated Indian head hood ornament, and a Remington Auto-Home electric shaver.

Production of 1952 Pontiacs registered a 19.4 percent decrease from 1951. This followed general industry trends and was affected by some of the Korean War restrictions. For instance, Sedan Delivery truck production was held down under National Production Agency guidelines that favored production of heavy-duty trucks. Only 984 were made.

Pontiac escaped a complete shutdown during a steel shortage in 1952, although production hit rock bottom in July. The division quickly got up steam after the strike ended, and achieved full utilization of resources in October, when 32,843 cars were built. Model-year assemblies came to 271,373 units. Model-year production included a total of 19,809 Series 25 Chieftain sixes (15,582 with Hydra-Matic and 4227 with synchromesh) and a total of 251,564 Series 27 Chieftain eights (218,602 with Hydra-Matic and 32,962 with synchromesh). Production was 277,156 cars for the calendar-year, giving Pontiac fifth rank in the American auto industry.

Pontiac history came to a dramatic new juncture on July 13, 1952, when Arnold Lenz and his wife were killed when their car struck a train at a grade crossing near Lapeer, Michigan. This put a hold on the idea of introducing a V-8 in 1953 and ultimately led to a string of management changes that would affect the brand's destiny and give it an entirely new image.

1953 *Pontiac*

The top films of 1953 had a lasting, enduring quality. I can still remember going to the drive-in theatre in dad's De Soto to see Victor Mature in "The Robe." I'm sure we also saw "Julius Caesar" (dad loved those Roman epics). "From Here to Eternity" was not a film for the kids–not back in those days.

Like these classic motion pictures, the '53 Pontiac also has a lasting and enduring quality—at least around my house. I've

owned and driven one of these cars for the past 32 years. My first one, purchased for $175 in 1972, was a Spruce Green Metallic four-door sedan that traveled with me from New York to Wisconsin. My current '53 is a Deluxe Catalina hardtop.

By Pontiac's conservative standards, the 1953 model had "...magnificent new beauty, with its increased size and its long list of engineering advances." According to one advertisement, the

The 1953 Pontiac Chieftain Custom Catalina hardtop has a very memorable profile.

annual new-product revisions included "completely new" Dual-Streak styling, a new longer wheelbase, longer and lovelier and roomier bodies, a new one-piece Panoramic windshield and rear window, optional new power steering, and "spectacular new overall" performance.

Other changes included new Indian hood ornaments, ignition-key starting, stepped-up rear fenders, more massive chrome headlight doors, a new grille that encircled the front parking lamps, and a "Panorama View" instrument panel that attracted many appreciative looks in the supermarket parking lot (and still does at car shows today). New "Tru-Arc" safety steering and a "Curve Control" front suspension system were also heavily promoted as improvements. And all this, the same ad pointed out, "still carries last year's price tag!" Not a bad deal.

The standard 1953 Pontiacs were called Specials. Small hubcaps, rubber gravel guards, straight upper belt line trim and short, arrow-shaped side trim characterized these cars. A chrome Indian head mascot was standard and an illuminated version with an orange Lucite plastic face was optional on all models. The wheelbase of all 1953 Pontiacs increased to 122 inches and overall length of the passenger cars grew slightly to 202-11/16 inches. Station wagons, at 205.3 inches long, actually shrunk a tad.

The upholstery used in Specials was of bluish-gray, tri-tone novelty-weave cloth and was smooth to the touch. Its simple lines were relieved by three equally-spaced buttons centered in the seat backs. The upholstery material was carried over the top of the seat back and terminated just below the robe cord. The back and base of the front seat was covered with durable dark gray broadcloth.

Near the floor, the base of the front seat was trimmed with durable gray imitation leather. The door trim was divided into three horizontal panels with dark gray wool in the center and light gray imitation leather borders above and below. There was a two-toned twin-spoke Special steering wheel.

Six models were offered in the Special series. They were a two-door sedan, a four-door sedan and quartet of four-door station wagons. The "painted" wagon and the "wood-grained" station wagon were merchandised as separate models, as were wagons with two seats or three-seats. Each station wagon could also be had as a six-cylinder or eight-cylinder car. Prices for six-cylinder models ranged from $1,956 to $2,585. The eight-cylinder engine was $75 additional. The fancy "wood-grained" station wagons carried simulated wood-grain exterior moldings around the side windows and moldings and panels on the tailgate.

Deluxe Chieftains had long "dual streak" body moldings, stainless steel gravel guards with rear fender extensions, dipping belt moldings, and chrome full wheel discs. Eights had an "8" emblem between twin "Silver Streaks" on the deck lid. Cars finished in Caravan Blue, Spruce Green, Marathon Gray and black had red Pontiac nameplates in front, while those done in other colors had black front nameplates.

The Deluxe sedans had interiors color-coordinated with the exterior body colors. The seat cushions and top of the seatbacks was trimmed in patterned Nylon, the lower seat back and front seat base trim were done in broadcloth and the headlining a door panels were also color-coordinated. Green cars or cars with green in a two-tone combination had a green interior. Blue was used for cars with solid blue finish or blue in a two-tone. Gray was used in all other cars. Deluxe Catalinas had color-harmonized cloth-and-leather trim, convertibles offered a choice of cloth-and-leather or all-leather upholstery and Deluxe wagons used cloth-and-leather in specific color combinations.

The Custom Catalina coupe was a Super Deluxe model with special finish and features. Horizontally-grooved trim plates decorated the bases of the rear roof pillars. Custom Catalinas came only in Laurel Green, Milano Ivory or two-tone combinations of these hues. A Nylon-and-leather interior of harmonizing tones was featured and an all-leather option was available and frequently ordered.

Pontiac's 239.2-cid L-head six packed more horsepower for 1953. With the standard 7.0:1 compression ratio it delivered 115 and with the 7.7:1 "high head" it produced 118 hp. Changes included a new duplex carburetor, slightly higher compression ratios, a new intake manifold, a new camshaft, more compact combustion chambers, and electroplated aluminum pistons.

Pontiac promoted the 1953 straight eight as "the most highly perfected power plant in the industry." That meant it had been around long enough to have many refinements. The compression ratios used in 1953 were 6.8:1 with synchromesh transmission and 7.7:1 with Hydra-Matic Drive. Respective output ratings were 118 hp at 3600 rpm and 122 hp at 3600 rpm. The five-main-bearings eight had solid valve lifters and a Carter WCD two-barrel carburetor.

A three-speed synchromesh gearbox with column-mounted gearshift was standard on all Pontiac models. The Dual-Range four-speed Hydra-Matic was a very common $178 option. Chevrolet's two-speed Powerglide automatic transmission was installed in some Pontiacs built at Pontiac, Michigan, only from Sept. 8, 1953, to Nov. 19, 1953. This was due to an August 12 fire at GM's Livonia, Michigan Hydra-Matic factory.

Robert Critchfield was Pontiac's new general manager. Under his direction, production lines started cranking out 1953 Pontiacs on November 17 of the previous year. The cars were introduced to the public on Dec. 6, 1952. A total of 38,914 Chieftain sixes were built. Of these, 33,705 had synchromesh, 4,507 had Hydra-Matic and 702 had Powerglide. A total of 379,705 Chieftain eights were built. Of these, 68,565 had synchromesh, 293,343 had Hydra-Matic and 17,797 had Powerglide.

Model-year output came to 418,619 units. Calendar-year production was 414,011 cars. Pontiac remained America's fifth best selling brand.

1954 *Pontiac*

Mike Carborella

This graceful 1954 Pontiac Star Chief Deluxe convertible is ready for the open road.

You have to have star quality to succeed in America, whether it's in the movies or on an automobile assembly line. Take 1954's favorite monster, Godzilla, for example. While he hit it big in Japan, no one here had seen the giant lizard's paw prints embossed in the sidewalk outside Grauman's Chinese Theatre. He was just another pretty face as far as American moviegoers were concerned. The "Godzilla" movie was renamed "Godzilla, King of the Monsters" when released in the United States and Perry Mason—excuse me, Raymond Burr— was spliced into the film as a new character named Steve Martin. With help from this budding super star, old Mr. 'Zilla went on to achieve nationwide fame.

The 1954 Pontiacs also had star quality. At least a new, top-priced Star Chief series did. In addition to its twinkly name, this Pontiac luxury-car line also had three chrome stars on the sides of its rear fenders.

New series designations greeted Pontiac buyers, as the company struggled to catch up with modern trends. There was a new grille with a massive horizontal chrome member that divided in its center to form an oval with five vertical dividers. The hood ornaments (standard or illuminated) and the red-white-and-blue hood name ornament were also revised. Also new were the parking lights.

Pontiac offered a total of three series. Chieftain models (sixes and eights) were on a 122-inch wheelbase and had an overall length of 202.7 inches. The new Star Chief Eights were on a 124-inch wheelbase and measured 213.7 inches bumper-to-bumper. Chieftain Six models were priced from $1,788 to $2,286, Chieftain Eights were priced from $1,858 to $2,356. Star Chief Eights sold at $2,097 to $2,403. For Chieftains, Special and Deluxe trim levels were offered. Catalinas could be had with Deluxe or Custom trim.

The new long-wheelbase Star Chief line was actually quite simple to create. A completely new body was not necessary. Pontiac added an 11-inch frame extension towards the rear of the regular GM "A" body. Longer rear sheet metal was then grafted on to the body behind the rear window. Though much longer, Star Chiefs had the same 76.6-inch width as Chieftains.

The economical Chieftain Specials had straight upper belt line moldings, small stainless steel gravel guards, four Silver Streaks on the deck lid, and short front fender spears. This line included the two-door sedan, four-door sedan, two-seat station wagon, and three-seat station wagon. All Pontiac wagons had four doors. Wood-grained Di-Noc exterior paneling was a $140 option.

Chieftain Deluxe models had broad, full-length sweep spears that blended into the gravel guards. In addition, the stainless steel gravel guards had rear fender extensions and the upper belt line trim dipped down. Deluxe Chieftains also had four deck lid streaks. Two- and four-door sedans, as well as a two-seat station wagon, were part of the Deluxe line. Also included was a Deluxe Catalina hardtop and a Custom Catalina hardtop.

The Custom version was outwardly distinguished by decorative edge plates on its roof pillars. Custom Catalina hardtops also had special chrome plated interior roof bows. Interior trims ranged from two-tone pattern cloth-and-Elascofab combinations on standard models to all-leather options on Catalinas, convertibles and Deluxe station wagons.

The Star Chief was advertised as America's lowest-priced *luxury* car. "One look inside a Star Chief Custom Sedan will capture your heart," said an ad in *The Saturday Evening Post*. "Upholstery of lustrous Nylon combined with butter-smooth genuine leather—and every handsome interior detail—is perfectly color-keyed to the exterior colors." The Star Chiefs came only with the straight eight.

Five Silver Streaks on the deck lid identified these cars, along with special taillight doors—that had little chrome visors—and chrome extensions that ran along the taillight bulges. Longer chrome sweep spears brightened the doors of all Star Chiefs and three stylized stars decorated their rear fenders. Deluxe trims were considered regular equipment, but the "Super Deluxe" level Custom Sedan and Custom Catalina were further distinguished by extra rich cloth-and-leather upholstery and distinctive exterior roof trim. Star Chief Custom Catalina hardtops also had special bright metal interior roof bows.

Prices for carry-over Pontiac models increased only a few dollars in 1954. In fact, even the brand new, long-deck Star Chief Custom Catalina was only $111 more than the short-deck eight-cylinder version of 1953.

"Big, beautiful and luxurious as it is, the Pontiac Star Chief is still priced comfortably within the range just above the very lowest," copywriters noted. "Prove to your own beaming satisfaction that luxury and low cost have never been so beautifully combined."

New options for 1954 included the auto industry's first true under-hood air conditioner, power brakes, a 360-position Comfort-Control manually operated front seat, and automatic (electric) front window lifts. A Safety-Cushion padded instrument panel was also available as factory-installed special equipment. Power steering – first introduced in 1953 – was improved by reducing the steering-gear ratio. Deluxe and Custom models with power steering got a special new horn button indicating this extra was installed.

This year the 239-cid in-line flathead six remained the same, offering 115 hp when linked to manual transmission and 118 hp with Hydra-Matic Drive. The: 268.4-cid Pontiac straight eight was basically unchanged. Cars with synchromesh used a 6.8:1 compression ratio, while cars with Hydra-Matic Drive used a 7.7:1 ratio. The stick shift engine was rated for 122 hp at 3800 rpm and the Hydra-Matic made 127 at 3800 rpm. Eights used a Carter WCD 719SA carburetor in early production and later switched to a Carter WCD 720SA (synchromesh) or WCD 2122S (Hydra-Matic).

The 1954 models were introduced Dec. 18, 1953. Model-year production dropped by 130,845 cars, although calendar-year sales fell by 25,364 units. Pontiac slid to sixth on the charts. Some 1954 assemblies took place in a new B-O-P assembly plant in Arlington, Texas. A Catalina hardtop built on June 18, 1954, was the five millionth Pontiac ever produced.

1955 *Pontiac*

Standing parade-ready is the 1955 Pontiac Star Chief convertible with continental kit.

Showmanship was alive in 1955, highlighting productions in both Hollywood and Detroit. Hit films of that year that reflected the showman's touch included "Guys and Dolls," "Oklahoma" and "The Benny Goodman Story." Millions of Americans flocked to see them.

General Motors also had a flair for showing off when it hit important milestones, such as building its 50-millionth car. The company's five-millionth car had been a first-year 1926 Pontiac and, for that reason, the automaker put the 1955 Pontiac front and center in a unique "show" it was planning.

The new 1955 Pontiac was one of the big stars of General Motors "50 million Golden CARnival of Cars" celebration. This event was held in Flint, Michigan on Nov. 23, 1954. Thirteen of the all-new Pontiacs (including a special golden model) were used to showcase the marque's completely new "panoramic" body styling and Strato-Streak V-8 engines. The 13 cars formed an honor guard for two Pontiac floats in the mammoth parade. A 1926 Pontiac coupe (which the company still owns today) was on the first float, while a '55 Pontiac rode the second one.

The '55 Pontiac was the star of the show just about anywhere that it was seen in 1955. The Strato-Streak V-8 and the new bodies headed an impressive list of new Pontiac features. The new cars had an exciting range of modern colors, Vogue two-toning, exquisite interior styling, a new panoramic wraparound windshield, area, a functional jewel-like instrument panel, a powerful 12-volt electrical system, a newly-designed frame, a new vertical-kingpin front suspension system, larger brakes, improved ride and handling, attractive new accessories and dozens of mechanical refinements.

"The Pontiac for 1955 incorporates more engineering innovations than any model since the Pontiac was first produced in

1926," said an official pronouncement. "The new car has 109 outstanding new features."

Twin silver streaks, a popular feature of Pontiac "dream cars" like the Bonneville Special and the Parisienne swept back from the radiator grille of the 1955 Pontiac. They terminated at a cowl-wide passenger compartment air intake. The Silver Streak motif continued with chrome streaks that ran along the crown of each rear fender fin and terminated at the massive taillights.

Pontiac color choices for 1955 reflected the influence of the public's taste for lighter and brighter tones. Vogue two-toning, which brought the color of the top of the car down to the middle of the body, added greatly to the streamlined appearance of the new Pontiacs.

The cars were available in two new series. The Chieftain line continued to use a 122-inch wheelbase and the larger Star Chief models had a 124-inch wheelbase. Coupe and sedan models were 2-3/4 inches lower than in 1954.

A new two-door station wagon was introduced in the fall, and later a two-door hardtop wagon called the Star Chief Custom Safari was added. All Pontiacs had lowered hood lines that exposed both front fenders to the driver's vision. In all, 12 body styles were offered.

The base cars were known as Chieftain 860 models. Chieftain 860s had small hubcaps, painted taillight housings and no upper belt line moldings. This series offered four body styles. This is the first year for which Pontiac model-year production totals by body style are known.

The company built 65,155 four-door sedans, 58,654 two-door sedans, 6,091 four-door eight-passenger wagons and 8,618 two-door six-passenger wagons. Prices for these entry-level models ranged from $2,105 to $2,518.

The one-step-up line included four Chieftain 870 models. Chieftain 870s had full wheel discs, chrome taillight rings and upper beltline trim. The Chieftain 870 body styles were not exactly the same as those offered in Chieftain 860 trim. A Catalina two-door hardtop replaced the two-door "Colony" wagon and there was only one station wagon, a four-door version with six-passenger seating.

The 1955 Chieftain station wagons used Chevrolet station wagon rear fender styling. The Chieftain two-door station wagon was sometimes called the Colony wagon.

Pontiac made 91,187 Chieftain 870 four-door sedans, 28,950 two-door sedans, 72,608 Catalina hardtops and 19,439 four-door six-passenger wagons. Prices for these mid-range models ranged from $2,209 to $2,603.

The production-type Safari was announced on Jan. 31, 1955. The unique station wagon was Pontiac's version of the Chevrolet Nomad, which evolved from a Corvette Motorama "dream car."

This was the only 122-inch-wheelbase Pontiac to carry the Star Chief name.

It had a special hardtop wagon body with slanting roof pillars, a slanting tailgate, vertical tailgate slats, load area rub strips and Star Chief level interior trimmings. It sold for $2,962 and only 3,760 were built. This special hardtop Safari model would only survive for three years, but the Safari name was later used for all Pontiac wagons.

This car should be referred to as the Star Chief Custom Safari to differentiate it from later Safaris.

Other Star Chief models had the new panoramic body styling with an 11-inch rear frame extension. These cars featured tapered slanting vertical slash moldings and three stylized star emblems on the front fenders and doors. The Catalina coupe and the convertible had wide fluted lower rear fender extensions. The Custom four-door sedan had stainless steel moldings encircling the side windows.

Full wheel discs were regular equipment on all Star Chiefs. The series included four non-wagon body styles divided into two trim lines called Star Chief and Custom Star Chief. Prices started at $2,362 and ran to $2,499. Pontiac built 44,800 Star Chief sedans and 35,153 Custom Star Chief sedans. The non-Custom convertible sold 19,762 copies, while the Star Chief Custom Catalina hardtop was the most popular of the large cars with 99,929 assemblies.

Pontiac's single new 1955 engine was a 287.2-cid overhead valve V-8. When linked to a manual transmission, this motor had 7.4:1 compression and 173 brake horsepower. Adding Hydra-Matic Drive upped compression to 8.0:1 and horsepower to 180.

Pontiac engineers Clayton B. Leach and Ed Windeler developed this cast-iron engine with ball-and-stud rocker arms, gusher type cooling, pressure-suction crankcase ventilation and easy-to-cast block construction to keep costs and make it efficient. It had five main bearings, hydraulic valve lifters and a Carter WGD or Rochester 2GC two-barrel carburetor.

It was the first overhead valve V-8 produced by Pontiac but the second in company history. The first V-8 had been used in 1932.

Production of 1955 Pontiacs started Oct. 4, 1954. They were introduced to the public 15 days later and the Star Chief Custom two-door Safari bowed Jan. 31, 1955. Calendar-year production of 581,860 cars made Pontiac America's sixth ranked manufacturer. Model-year production was 554,090 units. An all-time Pontiac record was set in December 1955. On August 11, a Safari produced for Professor A.E. Neyhart—a pioneer in the field of high school driver education—became the 500,000th Pontiac made that year. The production of a half million cars in a single season was a first for Pontiac Motor Division.

1956 *Pontiac*

The social changes taking in place in 1956 were reflected in the films that people went to see that year. Those films were as diverse as "Giant," "Friendly Persuasion," and "The Forbidden Planet." At Pontiac Motor Division, the year's most important change was a new general manager. That change would be reflected in the cars that hit Pontiac showrooms the following year.

Forty-three-year-old "Bunkie" Knudsen was appointed to the company's top post in July of 1956 and within just a few weeks he removed the traditional Silver Streaks (or as he called them, "chrome suspenders") from the front of the 1957 models. It would be the first step in a complete makeover that, within a few years, would make Pontiac America's Number 3 car company for a full decade.

This pink-over-gray combination says 1956 on this Pontiac Chieftain Catalina hardtop.

Of course, Knudsen arrived after Pontiac's 1956 products, which were developed under Robert M. Critchfield, had been updated and he had nothing to do with the year's modest styling changes. They included a combination bumper-grille with enclosed circular parking lights and round, bomb-type bumper guards. The body side moldings slanted the opposite way this year, as compared to 1955. On the smaller, lower-priced Chieftains, the slash accents were of constant width. There were reflectorized oval embossments on the rear fenders, with gull-wing and circle medallions on the deck lid.

"Special" trim level Chieftain 860s lacked upper belt moldings. They wore small hubcaps and had plain taillight rings. New body styles were added to this series, including a Catalina two-door hardtop and a Catalina four-door hardtop. Prices for the six models began at $2,236 and ended at $2,648. Production included 41,908 two-door sedans, 41,967 four-door sedans, 46,335 Catalina coupes, 35,201 Catalina sedans, 6,099 two-door station wagons, and 12,702 four-door nine-passenger station wagons.

Deluxe level Chieftain 870 models (except station wagons), had visored taillight rings, full wheel discs, and upper beltline trim. In some factory literature, Chieftain 870s were called "Super Chiefs," a name that was adopted as a series designation in 1957. Like the base series, the Chieftain 870 line also had a four-door hardtop (a.k.a. Catalina sedan) added. This made a total of four Chieftain 870 body styles, including the four-door sedan and the four-door six-passenger station wagon, with the four priced from $2,409 to $2,744. Series production amounted to 22,082 four-door sedans, 25,372 four-door Catalina hardtops, 24,744 two-door Catalina hardtops, and 21,674 station wagons.

The sporty two-door Custom Safari was continued as unique entry on the Chieftain chassis, but with Star Chief level trim. It now came with the Star Chief's more powerful four-barrel-carburetor engine. Returning as part of the hardtop wagon's image was a sleek ribbed roofline, a slanted tailgate with vertical slats and bright metal load floor strips. The Star Chief two-door Custom Safari listed for $3,124 and only 4,042 were made.

All other Star Chiefs rode the longer 124-inch wheelbase and were distinguished by tapered diagonal accent slash moldings on the front doors and three stylized star emblems on the front fenders and doors. Custom Catalinas (priced at $2,731) and convertibles ($3,917) had wide fluted lower rear fender extensions. The Custom Catalina sedan ($2,731) had stainless steel window sur-

round moldings and all Custom Star Chiefs used hooded taillight rings. The fourth model was the Star Chief four-door sedan ($2,523). Series production totals included 18,346 sedans, 13,510 convertibles, 43,392 Catalina coupes, and 48,035 Catalina sedans.

Pontiac's improved 316.6-cid Chieftain V-8 had a compression ratio of 7.9:1 with synchromesh and 8.9:1 with Hydra-Matic Drive. Horsepower ratings were 192 and 205, respectively. A Rochester 2GC carburetor was used. The Star Chief V-8 was essentially the same, except with a four-barrel carburetor (a Rochester 4GC was most common, but some cars were built with Carter WCFBs). Horsepower in this case was 216 or 227, respectively. The 227 hp 1956 Star Chief four-door sedan was good for 0-to-60 mph in 11.4 seconds and an 18.1 second quarter-mile.

In March 1956, an "extra hp" V-8 was released. It also displaced 317 cubic inches, but came with 10.0:1 compression heads, dual four-barrel Rochester carburetors (part no. 7009820), a special intake manifold, a fuel pump with larger valves, a dual-element Delta-Wing air cleaner, a greater overlap high-output camshaft, revised valve timing, longer-stemmed valves, high-tension valve springs and shields, anti-pump-up hydraulic lifters, and modified electrics.

The output of this so-called "NASCAR" engine was 285 hp at 5100 rpm. It was tested for 0-to-60 mph in 11 seconds flat and 16.2 mpg fuel economy. Pontiac experts estimate that 200 cars were equipped with this motor, which was intended primarily for professional stock cars, but found its way into amateur drag racing cars.

The potential of the 285-hp engine was not lost on 73-year-old speed ace Ab Jenkins. In June 1956, with his son Marvin as his relief driver, Jenkins took a stock Pontiac Chieftain 860 two-door sedan —Pontiac's lightest car—equipped with that engine around the Bonneville Salt Flats circle course at an average speed of 118.375 mph for 24 hours, breaking the old 109 mph record and shattering all existing American unlimited and class C stock-car racing records in the process.

Jenkins drove nearly two-thirds of the 2,841 miles the Pontiac covered. That August, Jenkins went to Wisconsin to drive a pace car in the Road America auto races north of Milwaukee. The evening of August 9 he went to a baseball double-header with Pontiac regional manager George Bourke. While driving to a hotel, Jenkins pointed out a tractor advertisement on a billboard and said, "I took a wild ride on one of those a few years ago."

Then he slumped in his seat and collapsed of a heart attack. He was pronounced dead at a nearby hospital. The limited edition 1957 Pontiac Bonneville convertible was named in honor of Jenkin's 1956 record run.

"It's the talk of the Test Drivers!" boasted one advertisement for the '56 Pontiac. The ad copy said it wasn't easy to impress a test driver, but the new Pontiac was being cheered by such pros. "What's set them buzzing is that big and vital General Motors 'First' combining Pontiac's new big-bore Strato-Streak V-8 with the terrific thrust of 227 horsepower. General Motors' new Strato-Flight Hydra-Matic that gentles this mighty 'go' to smoothness beyond belief."

Production of 1956 models started Oct. 3, 1955. They were introduced October 21. Model-year output was 405,730 cars. Calendar year output was 332,268 cars.. On Aug. 3, 1956, the six-millionth Pontiac—a Star Chief Custom Catalina coupe- was built and photographed with Pontiac employees Frank Bridge, "Bunkie" Knudsen, and Buel E. Starr.

1957 *Pontiac*

The mid-level Pontiac series in 1957 was the Super Chief like this Catalina hardtop.

The stars were out again in 1957 and what a lineup. Rita Hayworth in "Pal Joey," Tyrone Power in "Abandon Ship," Audrey Hepburn in "Funny Face," Cary Grant in "An Affair to Remember," and Burt Lancaster in "Gunfight at the O.K. Corral."

The stars were out at Pontiac, with three stars decorating the sides of the new Super Chief model was aimed at enthusiasts. The Tri-Power Catalina hardtop that *Hot Rod's* Ray Brock tested in June 1957 was a "stock rod." As Brock put it near the end of his article, "...we'd say that the Pontiac is no longer grandma's car, because we don't think that granny could stand the acceleration built into this torpedo without blacking out."

As soon as "Bunkie" Knudsen took over in the summer of 1956, he attacked the late-pre-production '57 model parked in the styling studio. Its side trim and twin Silver Streaks quickly wound up in the trash bin (that's "recycling container" today). The Chieftain 860 became the Chieftain, the Chieftain 870 became the Super Chief, the Star Chief name was retained and in the middle of the year, the limited edition, fuel-injected Custom Star Chief Bonneville blasted onto the scene. The Tri-Power Super Chief may have been faster than the "fuelie."

Knudsen believed an old man would buy a young man's car, but it didn't work the other way. His goal was to sell a car that both would be interested in. So, Pontiac's new "Star Flight" styled bodies had guide-missile-shaped side trim and optional light-up front fender rockets instead of illuminated Indian heads. A more massive bumper grille crossed the '57 Pontiac's front end. The rear fenders were flatter and taller and ended in V-shaped tips above horizontal-oval taillights. The use of 14-inch wheels and tires made the whole car look lower. The basic body was the same used in 1955 and 1956, but the plain, lower hood line produced an entirely new image.

Even the Chieftains in Pontiac's new entry-level series—with prices starting below $2,500—looked cleaner and more modern. This line included six cars with "bottle cap" style hubcaps, three stars on their rear fenders and "Chieftain" front fender scripts. There were six body styles in this series, two- and four-door sedans and hardtops and a pair of station wagons, one with two doors and two seats and one with four doors and three seats. Prices varied from a low of $2,463 to $2,898. Series production totaled 162,575 cars, including just 2,934 of the "Colony" station wagons with two doors.

The new Super Chief line replaced the old Chieftain 870. It was on Pontiac's smaller 122-inch wheelbase, but carried deluxe body trim. There were four 1957 Super Chiefs and they came with full wheel discs, upper belt moldings, three stars on the rear fenders and "Super Chief" front fender scripts.

This series included just four models, which were the four-door sedan, two- and four-door Catalina hardtops and a six-passenger station wagon with four doors. They were priced in the $,2664 to $3,021 range and series output was 64,500 units. This was pretty much evenly distributed among the four body styles, suggesting that Knudsen's plan worked. The Super Chief was the car aimed most directly at the youth market and Pontiac was selling as many "old man" versions (sedans and wagons) as "young man" versions (hardtops). The 1957 Pontiac Super Chief two-door Sedan with the 290-hp V-8 was capable of doing 0-to-60 mph in 8.5 seconds and the quarter-mile in 16.8 seconds.

All 1957 Pontiac station wagons used the name Safari, but the two-door Star Chief Custom Safari was the only one with the special "hardtop" styling. It remained on the smaller chassis, but had upscale upholstery and a V-8 with a four-barrel carburetor. With prices starting at $3,636, this model was the priciest of all 122-inch wheelbase Pontiacs.

A $3,481 companion model with four doors and sedan roof styling came out in January, the same day that the Bonneville arrived. It was dubbed the Custom Safari "Transcontinental." Pontiac built only 1,292 Custom Safaris and 1,894 Transcontinentals.

Star Chiefs other than Safaris had a 124-inch wheelbase. They carried added bright work and equipment such as "Star Chief" front fender scripts, four rear fender stars, chrome semi-cylindrical bulges on the "guided-missile" trim and full wheel discs. The four-door sedan cost a bit under $3,000 and the convertible was a bit above $3,000. There was also a Custom Star Chief line featuring a four-door sedan with special "off-shoulder" interior patterns, a Catalina sedan, a Catalina Sports Coupe and the new Bonneville. Series production (except Bonneville) came to 102,582 cars and the rarest was the four-door sedan, of which only 3,774 were made.

The first news of the $5,782 Star Chief Custom Bonneville convertible was heard on Dec. 2, 1956. General sales manager Frank V. Bridge announced the car in a Jan. 11, 1957 letter. Bonneville's availability was limited to 630 production versions and three prototypes. Two pre-production prototypes were convertibles with four bucket seats and small trim differences. The third was a two-door hardtop with a floor-mounted four-speed gearbox.

The base Pontiac engine was a 347-cid V-8 with 227 hp or 252 hp depending on whether the transmission was a "stick" or automatic. The four-barrel carburetor on the Super Chief-Star Chief version of the engine boosted output to 244 hp and 270 hp, respectively. The fuel-injected Bonneville version was rated 315 hp.

In December 1956, three triple two-barrel engines were released. The first was an option for the standard Hydra-Matic V-8. The others were options for the "extra-horsepower" (NASCAR-certified) V-8s with either synchromesh or Hydra-Matic transmissions. The "standard" Tri-Power engine produced 290 hp. A Super Chief two-door sedan with this engine went 0-to-60 mph in 8.5 seconds and did the quarter-mile in 16.8 seconds. Both extra-horsepower jobs were rated 317 hp. They shared 10.0:1 compression ratios, hydraulic lifters and three Rochester carburetors, but the stick-shift engine had a dual-breaker-point ignition system.

Bunkie Knudsen made some personnel changes after he took over at Pontiac Motor Division. In early September 1956, he convinced body engineer Elliott "Pete" Estes to move from Oldsmobile and replace George Delaney as Pontiac chief engineer. He brought in John Z. DeLorean from Studebaker-Packard as his advanced engineering director.

Production of 1957 Pontiacs started Oct. 17, 1956. They were introduced Nov. 19, 1956. Model-year output was 334,041 cars. Calendar-year output was 343,298 cars. Pontiac was ranked the sixth largest automaker.

1958 *Pontiac*

In 1958, the Bonneville Sport Coupe was one of Pontiac's top choices.

Just before the '50s began, there were in 820 drive-in theatres in the United States. By 1958, the number had grown to 4,063. Some great films like "Vertigo," "The Last Hurrah" and "Witness For the Prosecution" were projected on those outdoor screens. No wonder there were so many '58 Pontiacs at the old drive ins. There was plenty of room in a Star Chief or Bonneville.

The 1958 Pontiac had an aircraft look and all 16 models carried "guided-missile" side trim and "jet-pod" rear fenders. "It's a wholly new car, with nothing left over from '57 except the wheels," said *Motor Trend*. And it was.

The cars were longer and lower looking, with a new honeycomb grille, dual headlights, dual taillights and a new Bonneville series. A stronger tubular X frame allowed lower recessed floors. A new ball-joint suspension was used up front and optional "Ever-Level" rear air suspension was available. A Safe-T-Track no-spin differential added $54 to the Pontiac's price.

Chieftains had model scripts at the front of side coves and three stars on the rear fenders. Small hubcaps were standard. Taillights without trim rings were used on all models except the new Chieftain convertible, which was in a separate series sharing a unique ribbed rear deck lid with the Bonneville convertible.

Princess pattern Lustrex upholstery with Morrokide imitation leather trim was used, but the convertible had special Seville-finish Morrokide (imitation leather) seats in "off shoulder" designs. There were seven 122-inch wheelbase models in this series priced from $2, 573 to $3,019. They included two- and four-door sedans and hardtops, the convertible, a two-door nine-passenger wagon and a four-door six-passenger wagon. A new 370-cid "two-barrel" V-8 generating 240-hp (270-hp with Hydra-Matic) was featured as standard equipment. Series production was 128,819 cars.

The Super Chief name was used on three cars riding a 124-inch wheelbase and having the two-barrel V-8. Identification features included full wheel discs, tail lamps with chrome rings and rear fender coves decorated with Super Chief script and four stars. Deluxe steering wheels were used. The four-door sedan was upholstered in a blend of Palisades pattern Lustrex with Plaza pattern bolsters.

Catalina buyers could choose either all-Morrokide or Morrokide and Lustrex trims at the same price. The $2,834 four-door sedan was the least expensive model and the most popular with 12,006 assemblies. The $2,880 Catalina coupe and the $2,961 Catalina sedan had 7,236 and 7,886 assemblies, in the same respective order.

There were four cars with "Star Chief" front fender scripts. They had four stars within the side coves, taillight trim rings and funnel-shaped decorative scoops with golden rectangular "V" badges and triple wind split moldings at the front of the insert panels. Full wheel discs, a deluxe steering wheel and an electric clock were standard. Upholstery was in tri-dimensional Prado pattern Lustrex in the Catalina sedan and all-leather was optional on both Catalinas. A roof rack, horizontal tailgate moldings and distinct Safari gate scripts identified the Custom Safari. All Star Chiefs boasted "Stardust" carpeting. Jeweltone Lucite acrylic lacquer paint finish was standard.

The Custom Star Chief four-door sedan had a $3,071 window sticker and 10,547 were built. The Star Chief Catalina Coupe, priced at $3,122 had 13,888 assemblies. With 21,455 assemblies, the four-door Catalina, with its $3,210 price tag, was more popular by a long shot. The new four-door Star Chief Custom Safari station wagon sold for $3,350 and 2,905 were built.

The Star Chief V-8 had a four-barrel carburetor that boosted horsepower to 255 with synchromesh and 285 with Hydra-Matic. The synchromesh engine had 8.6:1 compression. It was stamped with an "L" (for low-compression) inside a circle on the engine serial number pad. The Hydra-Matic V-8 had 10.0:1 compression and no "L."

"Bonneville" became a series name in 1958. A convertible and Sport Coupe were offered. Base power plant was the Star Chief V-8. Both models used the shorter Chieftain wheelbase, but with a special longer, ribbed rear deck lid also used on Chieftain convertibles.

There were "Bonneville" fender scripts and hood and deck lettering, four chevrons on the lower front fenders, four stars on the rear fenders and rocket-shaped, ribbed semi-cylindrical moldings on the "guided missiles." Standard equipment included a Deluxe steering wheel, chrome wheel discs and special upholstery. The Bonneville coupe sold for $3,481 and the convertible was $3,586. Pontiac built 9,144 hardtops and 3,096 convertibles.

New options included a deluxe "Electromatic" radio and, for Bonnevilles, bucket seats. Tri-Power carburetion on standard blocks was $84 for Chieftains and Super Chiefs and $93.50 on Star Chiefs and Bonnevilles. The "standard" Tri-Power setup used three two-barrel Rochester carburetors, 10.5:1 cylinder heads, and a high-lift camshaft for 300 hp at 4600 rpm. Rochester fuel-injection was a $500 option on any 1958 Pontiac. This option included 10.5:1 compression ratio cylinder heads and gave 310 hp at 4800 rpm. Pontiac experts believe that 200 Bonnevilles carried this option. A Bonneville hardtop with the 300 hp engine was road tested by a magazine. Zero-to-60 mph took 7.6 seconds and the quarter-mile took 16 seconds.

In March 1958, two NASCAR-certified "extra hp" (Tempest 395-A) V-8s were released. The "PK" option was $254 on Chieftains or Super Chiefs and $233 on Star Chiefs or Bonnevilles. It included a four-barrel carburetor, 10.5:1 cylinder heads, higher-lift camshaft, low-restriction dual exhausts and other special components good for 315 hp. The "PM" option was $331 on lower-priced lines and $320 on upper lines and it combined special high-performance hardware with Tri-Power induction to generate 330 hp.

To celebrate General Motors' 50th anniversary, a special "Golden Jubilee" trim and paint scheme was announced in November. Special Golden Jubilee ornamentation was applied to a limited number of cars, all of which are believed to have been Star Chief Custom four-door sedans. The number made is not known. A Tri-Power Bonneville convertible was picked to be the Official Pace Car for the Indy 500 race in May 1958.

Model-year production was 217,303 units for a 5.1 percent share of market. Calendar-year output was 219,823 cars. To celebrate General Motors' 50th anniversary, a special "Golden Jubilee" trim and paint scheme was announced in November. This color was applied to a limited number of cars, all of which are believed to have been Star Chief Custom four-door sedans.

1959 *Pontiac*

In the movies, it was the year of Haley Mills. The cute British actress had five big hits that year: "Pollyanna," "The Parent Trap," "Summer Magic," "The Moon-Spinners," and "That Darned Cat." The 1959 Pontiac also had five big hits: Wide-Track wheels, Gyro-Level Ride, a distinctive "split" grille, Tempest 420 V-8s, and new flat-roof "Vista styling."

For the third time in three years, Pontiacs were totally new. They were longer, lower, and wider. In fact, when Bunkie Knudsen first saw the wider new bodies on the carryover 1958 chassis he thought it resembled a "linebacker in ballet slippers" and decided to widen the front track nearly 5 inches. "Wide-Track" described the new look perfectly. Veteran Pontiac stylist Joe Schemansky created the new twin-grille theme. Twin-fin rear fenders, a "V" contour hood, and increased glass areas were also new.

The base series was Catalina. Identification features included

Even Pontiac's entry level Catalina series offered a consertible in 1959.

Catalina script on rear fins, plain deck lids and body sides trimmed by Clean-Sweep moldings with undecorated projectile flares. Standard equipment included directional signals, electric wipers, dual sun visors, dome lamps, cigarette lighter, dual headlights, front and rear ashtrays, coat hooks, an instrument panel "Snak Bar," dual horns, tubeless tires, a bumper jack, and a wheel-lug wrench.

There were seven models on the 122-inch-wheelbase Catalina platform, including the two-door Sport Sedan, the four-door sedan, a two-door hardtop, the four-door Vista sedan (a hardtop), the convertible and a pair of four-door wagons, one with two seats and one with three. A total of 231,561 Catalinas were built, including 221,622 with Hydra-Matic Drive. The 280-hp 1959 Catalina two-door hardtop was tested at 8.8 seconds for 0-to-60 mph and 16.9 seconds for the quarter-mile. Star Chiefs combined the larger 124-inch wheelbase with the 280-hp Catalina two-barrel V-8. They had "Star Chief" emblems on the fins, four stylized stars on the projectile flares, sweepspear body side moldings and a narrow deck lid ornament. Regular equipment included all standard Catalina features, plus two-speed electric wipers, a deluxe steering wheel, an electric clock, deluxe chrome wheel covers and loop-pile Lurex-flexed carpeting. The two-door Sports Sedan, four-door sedan and four-door Vista hardtop were priced from $2,934 to $3,188. A total of 68,815 Custom Star Chiefs were built and 68,482 had Hydra-Matic Drive.

Bonneville Customs were the same size as Star Chiefs, but had fancier trim and a four-barrel V-8 as standard equipment. Golden scripts decorated the right-hand grille, rear fins, and deck lid on these models. There were four groups of short, horizontal louvers on the rear fenders and crest medallions on the deck lid and doors. Standard equipment included all Star Chief features, plus a padded dashboard, inside door safety reflectors, rear seat foam cushions, dash courtesy lights, and padded assist rails for passengers.

The model lineup included a two-door hardtop, a four-door Vista sedan, a convertible and a station wagon for prices in the $3,257 to $3,532 range (the wagon being priciest). A total of 4,673 Bonneville Custom Safari station wagons (Series 27) and 78,271 Bonnevilles (Series 28) were built. Only 16 Custom Safaris had synchromesh and 4,657 had Hydra-Matic, while 673 Bonneville Customs had synchromesh and 77,596 came with Hydra-Matic.

All 1959 Pontiacs had 389-cid V-8s, but there were low-horsepower and high-horsepower options. The Catalina-Star Chief two-barrel V-8 came with 8.6:1 compression and 245 hp in synchromesh cars and 10.0:1 compression and 280 hp in cars with optional Hydra-Matic transmission. The Tempest 420E V-8 was a no-cost super-economy engine. It had an especially fuel efficient camshaft, a Rochester two-barrel carburetor, an 8.6:1 compression ratio and 215 hp.

Bonnevilles used a four-barrel V-8 with 260 or 300 hp, depending on transmission. This engine was $20 extra in Catalinas and Star Chiefs. Tri-Power on the standard 10.0:1 Hydra-Matic block produced 315 hp. Extra horsepower options included four-barrel and Tri-Power setups on the special heavy-duty NASCAR-certified block, both with 10.5:1 compression. The output ratings were 330 hp and 345 hp, respectively. Dual exhausts were standard with these engines.

The 122-inch wheelbase Catalinas were 213.7 inches long. The Star Chiefs and Bonnevilles had two extra inches of wheelbase and were 220.7 inches long. However, all Pontiac station wagons were 214.3 inches long. Tread widths of the first Wide-Track models were 63.7 inches in front and 64 inches at the rear. The standard tires were 8.00 x 14, but station wagons and all cars with air conditioning had 8.50 x 14s.

Production started on Sept. 11, 1958 and dealer introductions were made one month later. Model-year output was 383,320 units for a 6.9 percent market share. Calendar-year production included 388,856 cars for fourth place in the industry. *Motor Trend* selected the 1959 Pontiac as its "Car of the Year." *Car Life* named the 1959 Bonneville Custom "Best Buy in the $2,000-$3,000 Class."

Pontiacs won many races in 1959, including the Daytona 500 and Darlington 500. "Wide-Tracks" also captured the National Hot Rod Association's "Top Eliminator" title and earned the checkered flag at Pikes Peak.

Studebakers
of the Fifties

1950 *Studebaker*

A low-priced Studebaker model was the 1950 Champion two-door sedan.

"New" in 1950 meant television. Although the technology dated back several decades, it was only after the war that television sets began showing up in the homes of average Americans. Some classic shows like "Truth or Consequences," "The Burns and Allen Show," and "You Bet Your Life" made their debut this year.

"New" in cars meant Studebaker. The independent automaker from South Bend, Indiana, had bet its life on the belief that styling innovations would help it sell enough postwar cars to keep up with the "Big 3." During the early part of the decade, there were signs the gamble was going to pay off.

For 1950 Studebakers, a "bullet-nose" front end and rear fenders with vertical taillights were ways to refresh what had recently been "dramatically new" styling at a reasonable cost. With its shoestring design budget, Studebaker would become the master of making cars look very different without spending very much money. The central body section was unchanged in 1950, but the car was hard to confuse with the previous model. Studebaker promoted it as "New Look" styling. It was certainly individualistic. A wide windshield contributed to safe all-around vision.

On both Commanders and Champions, a new "Miracle Ride" coil spring and A-arm arrangement replaced the former planar cross-leaf spring independent front-suspension system. The long-travel coil-spring front suspension neutralized rough roads. "Sea-Leg" mounted rear shock absorbers and anti-sway stabilizers assured Studebaker buyers an "even-keel" ride. The cars had a relatively low center of gravity for this era, which reduced roll and side sway. Studebaker's seats-between-the-axles layout was promoted as "Cradled Ride."

The model identification was on the front fenders. Small headlight trim rings were used on Champions. They also had a distinctive-looking straight bumper guard. Starting in midyear, these rings were chrome plated on Champion Deluxe and Regal Deluxe models. A low-priced Champion Custom model was introduced at mid year. A new Automatic Drive was introduced as an option at the same time.

Available body types were the same as 1949. There was no hood ornament on Custom models. Stainless steel rocker panel moldings were standard on Regal Deluxe versions. A growing buyer's market reduced prices from 1949 and during the year they were reduced again.

The Champion came in two- and four-door sedan models, a two-door coupe, a convertible, and a Starlight coupe. The convertible was offered only with Regal Deluxe trim. Other models came as Custom, Deluxe and Regal Deluxe cars. The Starlight coupe had the unique, aircraft-inspired rear window treatment that made Studebakers stand out in this era.

Prices for Champions ranged from a low of $1,419 for the Custom Coupe to a high of $1,981 for the Regal Deluxe convertible. Most models weighed around 2,700 pounds, but with its top-riser hardware, the ragtop was some 200 pounds heavier. A total of 270,604 Champions were built in the model year.

Studebaker's top-of-the-line car was the Commander. It had the same new bullet-nose front and new rear fenders as the Champion, but its front fenders and headlight rims were much larger. Model identification was on the front fenders. There were extra ornaments on the front fenders. The bumper guards were heavier and wider than the Champion style and slightly rounded at the top and bottom. A "Land Cruiser" script was adjacent to the rear deck lid on that model.

Body style and trim offerings in the Commander series were different than for Champions. The Deluxe line included a two-door sedan, four-door sedan, and Starlight coupe. The Regal Deluxe line included all these plus a convertible. The Land Cruiser was a larger four-door sedan on a four-inch-longer wheelbase. Standard chrome headlight trim rings and optional Automatic Drive were introduced as running changes for Commanders. Prices for all models were slightly reduced at midyear.

Most Commanders weighed about 3,200 pounds, with convertibles and Land Cruisers being slightly heavier. Prices for the full range of eight models started at $1,871 and climbed to $2,328 for the convertible. The Land Cruiser was priced at $2,187. Total series production came to 72,560 units and slightly more than one-third were Land Cruisers.

Champions were powered by an in-line six with an L-head valve arrangement. The four-main-bearing engine had a 3 x 4-inch bore and stroke and 169.6 cubic inches of displacement. With a 7.0:1 compression ratio and a Carter WE one-barrel carburetor it made 85 hp at 4000 rpm. The Commander six had a larger 3-5/16 x 4-3/8 inch bore and stroke for 245.6 cubic inches, but was otherwise basically the same.

Some Commanders did use a Stromberg BXOV carburetor in place of the Carter WE. The bigger six was rated 102 hp at 3200 rpm. Both motors had solid valve lifters.

A three-speed manual transmission with column-mounted gearshift was standard on all models. Overdrive was available for $92 extra on Champions and $98 extra on Commanders. Automatic Drive was available for $201 extra and was promoted as: "…the automatic transmission that has everything."

It combined a torque converter and direct mechanical drive, anti-creep control, safety lock-outs for reverse and parking, built-in hill-holding characteristics, outstanding downhill engine braking and independent air cooling. A 7.5:1 compression ratio was optional on both engines.

Studebaker Champions had a 113-inch wheelbase and 197.25-inch overall length. The Land Cruiser rode a 124-inch wheelbase and other Commanders used a 120-inch stance. Overall lengths were 211.9 inches for the Land Cruiser and 207.9 inches for other Commanders. The Champion had a slightly wider (56.4 inches) front tread than the Commander, which measured 55.5 inches. However, both shared the same 54-inch rear tread. Tire sizes were 6.50 x 15 for Champions and 7.60 x 15 for Commanders. The self-adjusting, self-centering hydraulic brakes were designed to automatically adjust for lining wear.

Model year sales of all Studebakers totaled 320,884 units. The company was America's ninth largest automaker, a good showing for an independent company.

1951 *Studebaker*

The bullet-nosed 1951 Studebaker Champion two-door sedan also has an optional sunvisor.

In America in 1951, television was starting to become a much larger factor in the world of sports. In August, a Brooklyn Dodgers' double-header against the Boston Braves was the first baseball game to be broadcast in living color. The following month, a football game between Duke and the University of Pittsburgh became the first live sporting event seen nationwide. By October 3, the World Series was being broadcast coast-to-coast as television became part of American life.

As TV and sports together became a bigger part of life, interest in sporty cars seemed to grow. Studebaker made its 1951 Commander sportier by reducing its size and adding a new engine.

The Champion continued as Studebaker's low-priced series. The outer edge of the "bullet-nose" section was painted body color and the center piece was made of plastic. One-piece curved windshields were a standard of all body styles. The former two-piece rear window on two- and four-door sedans was replaced by a one-piece unit.

Champion and Commander models, except the Land Cruiser sedan, now shared the same wheel base and overall length. All body and fender panels used on comparable models in both car-lines were identical. This must have saved Studebaker a lot of money. Model identification scripts were located on the left front edge of the hood. The Commander Land Cruiser sedan used a new 119-inch wheelbase and measured 201.5 inches long overall.

Champions could easily be identified by the model name in script on the front of the hood. Painted headlight and taillight trim rings were used only on entry-level Custom models. Deluxe models had chrome headlight and taillight trim rings, but lacked the stainless steel rocker panel moldings that were standard on Regal models. The "Deluxe" term was deleted from the top-of-the-line Regal trim name.

The same four body styles offered in 1950 were carried over as Custom and Deluxe Champions in 1951. The fancier Regal line added the convertible as a fifth model. Prices started at $1,471 for the Custom two-door coupe. The $2,034 Regal convertible was the priciest Champion. Most models weighed around 2,600 to 2,700 pounds, with the 2,890-pound ragtop being the heaviest again. All models rode a two-inch longer (115 inches) wheelbase and were 197.5 inches long. Tread widths and tire sizes matched those of 1950 Champions.

New for Commanders in 1951 was the shorter 115-inch wheelbase (except Land Cruiser) and an overhead-valve V-8 engine. The Deluxe trim name was discontinued and the Regal Deluxe became just the Regal. A new State name was used for top-of-the-line models. State models came standard with fender ornaments. Body selections were the same as in 1951, except that the Los Angeles plant produced one Commander business coupe. Styling changes were the same as on Champions.

The grille on both Commanders and Champions was increased in size and moved forward so it was flush with the front sheet metal. The Commander name written in chrome script could readily be seen on the left-hand side of the hood. Both Commanders and Champions had larger taillight lenses than in 1950. The Land Cruiser name remained on the front fenders.

The Regal lineup included two-door sedan, four-door sedan, and Starlight coupe models. These were all offered in the Commander State line, along with a convertible. The Land Cruiser sedan, on the longer wheelbase, was the top Commander offering. Prices for these nine models started at $1,807 and ran as high as $2,244 for the ragtop. Series production was 124,329 units. Of these, 38,055 were Land Cruisers. Only 3,770 Commander convertibles were made.

Champions again used the 169.5-cid 85-hp L-head six. This engine's long suit was economy of operation. The Champion Six beat all other standard-size cars in the 1951 Mobilgas Grand Canyon Economy Run by averaging 28.621 miles per gallon.

The Commander's new five-main-bearings overhead-valve V-8 had a 3-3/8 x 3-1/4-inch bore and stroke. With 232.6 cubic inches, a 7.0:1 compression ratio and a Stromberg two-barrel carburetor it was good for 120 hp at 4000 rpm. The V-8 was said to be of high-efficiency design with "thrilling power and acceleration." It was a responsive engine and had good flexibility in all driving ranges. It ran out smoothly and vibration free on regular gasoline.

A three-speed manual transmission with column-mounted gearshift was standard on all models again. Overdrive was available for $92 extra on Champions and $98 extra on Commanders. Automatic Drive was available for $201 extra on all models. A 7.5:1 compression ratio was optional on the Champion engine only.

Studebaker offered buyers a very long list of optional equipment including Hill Holder, directional signals, a choice of three radios (Stratoline 8-tube push-button, Starline 6-tube push-button or Starline 6-tube manual-tuned), a vacuum-powered front fender radio antenna or reel-type cowl radio antenna, a Climatizer heater-and-defroster, a Strat-O-Vu, Stratoline or Universal exterior rearview mirror, No-blo wind deflectors, Venetian window shields, Select-O-Seat cushion springs, and literally hundreds of other extras that did not have such cute names.

Studebaker's Wide-Leaf rear springs gave a softer ride and more consistent springing action with weather-proof plastic inserts between all leaves. Tubular direct-acting shock absorbers were used on all models with "Sea-Leg" style mounting in the rear.

Other selling features included an automatic choke, automatic ignition timing, automatic manifold heat control, a counter-balanced crankshaft with vibration dampers, insert-type Micro-Babbitt main and connecting rod bearings, full-pressure engine lubrication, a floating oil screen, full-length water jackets, Jumbo steering posts, front suspension stabilizers, a 40-amp generator, a three-spoke steering wheel, foam rubber seat cushions on Regal Champions and all Commanders, Nylon cord upholstery on State Commanders and Land Cruisers, front and rear Select-O-Seat cushion springs, and single-knob light controls. Commanders had Hill Holder and electric windshield wipers. Land Cruisers came with an oil filter, an electric clock, and rear suspension stabilizers.

Model-year sales reached 246,195 units and Studebaker remained ninth on the sales chart.

1952 *Studebaker*

More television history was made in 1952, starting at the beginning of the year, when the "Today Show" made its bow on the NBC network. It was the year the first political ads popularized the Presidential candidates with "The Man from Abilene" touting Dwight Eisenhower and a musical tribute for Adlai Stevenson. Later, when he purchased a half hour of national air time, people were angered that candidate Stevenson delayed the weekly telecast of "I Love Lucy." Cigar-smoking Ernie Kovacs never rivaled Lucille Ball in popularity, but he developed a cult following. My father loved his antics and we liked watching his pretty wife, Edie Adams.

Nineteen fifty-two made history at Studebaker, too. It marked the final year that South Bend used the same body that had shaken up the automotive industry back in 1947. That unforgettable design was promoted as "Jet-Stream" styling in 1952, but a new name did not disguise the reality that it had been used for more than half a decade. Fresh and exciting when it was introduced, the look had now grown old and stale as far as new-car buyers were concerned. (Collectors today love it of course.) It was also the final year Studebaker used "suicide" style front-opening rear doors on four-door sedans.

All 1952 Studebakers had a new sloping hood, a wrap-around grille, four front bumper guards, and hooded headlights and taillights. The "bullet-nose" front end design was dropped and a horizontal grille, somewhat similar to the upcoming 1953 design, was adopted. The grille molding bent down to form a "V" in the center. Six vertical bars sloped back into the grille. Except on the new Starliner hardtop, the center section of the Studebaker body was six years old and the rear fenders were unchanged from the 1950-1951 type. A model identification script fashioned out of chrome-plated metal was located on the left front edge of the hood. Two-tone finish was available on Starliner hardtops.

Studebaker Champions had an oblong emblem above the grille molding. The top one-third of each taillight was hooded. Body style and trim selections were the same as 1951, except the business coupe was discontinued and the new two-door hardtop was added. That left the two- and four-door sedans and a Starlight Coupe in all three lines: Custom, Deluxe, and Regal. The two-

This 1952 Studebaker Commander Starliner was powered by a new V-8 engine.

door hardtop—called the Starliner Coupe—as well as the convertible, were extra body styles available with Regal decorations.

The Starliner hardtop was said to be based on the convertible's styling. Prices for the 11 cars ranged from $1,735 to $2,273. The Custom Starlight Coupe (1,096 built) and the convertible (1,575 built) were low-production models. A few others had less than 10,000 assemblies.

Commander styling changes were essentially the same as those described for the Champion. A two-door hardtop was also added to the Commander State lineup. Commanders had the same basic new grille as Champions, but a V-shaped Studebaker crest was mounted above the grille molding. The instrument panel inside Commanders was different than the one used in Champions.

Since 1950, the Champion's instruments had been housed in a single enclosure, while the Commander's, since 1947, were held in three round dials. Commander model identification was located on the left front edge of the hood and on the deck lid. The Land Cruiser name was moved from the front fender to the rear deck lid. Front fender ornaments were standard on State models.

The two-and four-door sedan and Starlight coupe were found in the Commander Regal and State lines. The State trim level also offered the Starliner two-door hardtop and the convertible. The 119-inch-wheelbase Land Cruiser four-door sedan was in its own series. The Land Cruiser was a stretched version of Studebaker's

"W" body with vent windows in the rear doors. The Land Cruiser featured State trim.

The model count added up to a total of nine cars that were priced from $2,086 to $2,548. The convertible was the most expensive, however, even with just 1,715 assemblies, it was not the rarest Commander. The two-door sedan in the Commander State line (1,529 built) held that distinction. Total series production was 84,850 units.

The Studebaker Champion soldiered on with the L-head type 85-hp straight six. The Commander utilized the 232-cid overhead-valve V-8 with a new Stromberg AAUVB two-barrel carburetor and had 120 hp at 4400 rpm on tap. The cars were dimensionally unchanged from 1951. Overdrive was $105 extra on Champions and $118 extra on Commanders. Automatic Drive was $231 extra on Champions and $243 extra on Commanders. A 7.5:1 compression ratio was optional on both engines.

Model-year sales totaled 167,662 cars. Studebaker maintained a ninth ranking on the industry sales chart. A Studebaker convertible was selected to be the official pace car of the 1952 Indianapolis 500-Mile race.

A 1952 Commander State Starliner hardtop with serial number 7,130,874, was the final car built in Studebaker's first century of operations, which started with wagons and spanned the years 1852 to 1952.

1953 *Studebaker*

Television was becoming a star-studded medium by 1953. Lucy and Desi signed an $8-million contract to continue the "I Love Lucy" show. Even though his boss hated him, freckle-faced Arthur Godfrey was already famous for his "Arthur Godfrey's Talent Scouts" and "Arthur Godfrey and Friends," both in TV's top 10 shows for the year. Meanwhile Steve Allen was making a name for himself on the new "Tonight Show." And when it came to cop shows, Jack Webb (Sgt. Joe Friday of "Dragnet") was king of the airwaves.

Studebaker's 1953 "stars" were two sporty new models: the Starlight Coupe and the Starliner hardtop. The latter car, styled by famed industrial designer Raymond Loewy, was soon honored by the Museum of Modern Art.

Studebaker introduced all-new bodies for 1953. They were restyled to have more aerodynamic lines. The new sedans (not counting the Land Cruiser) were shorter and higher than the sporty Starliner hardtop and the Starlight coupe. The new Starlight Coupe abandoned use of the four-piece wraparound rear window that gave Studebakers the "is-it-coming-or-going?" look that had been such a hit seven years earlier.

The Starliner hardtop featured a new single-piece rear window in place of the three-piece design used in 1952. The convertible, which had dropped dramatically in annual sales, was discontinued all together.

The 1953 grille had two front openings located above the bumper. They ran the full width of the car, with a horizontal fin "floating" in each air-scoop-like opening. Parking lamps and directional signal lights were mounted at each end of the grille.

The Raymond Loewy-designed 1953 Studebaker pictured is the Commander Deluxe Starliner hardtop.

Studebaker's Champion series remained the entry-level line. A "Champion" Model identification script was on the left-hand grille bar. The hood ornament was supplemented by the symbol "S." Champion Custom models continued to be characterized by the use of painted headlight rims, body-color taillight trim rings and black rubber windshield moldings. The one-step-up Champion Deluxe models featured narrow stainless steel windshield moldings and bright rear window moldings.

The top-of-the-line Champion Regals had wide stainless steel windshield moldings and chrome side window moldings. The Champion instrument panel featured three circular instrument clusters covered by a single piece of glass. Plastic taillight lenses replaced the former glass ones.

The Custom line included the two-door sedan for $1,735 and the four-door sedan for $1,767. Both weighed just about 2,700 pounds. Production amounted to 3,983 two-doors and 5,496 four-doors. There were three Champion Deluxe offerings: two-door sedan for $1,831 (7,564 built), four-door sedan for $1,863 (17,180 built), and Starlight Coupe for $1,868 (9,422 built).

Four Regal models made up the top series. They were the $1,917 two-door sedan (2,968 built), the $1,949 four-door sedan (17,897 built), the $1,995 Starlight Coupe (16,066 built), and the $2,116 Starliner hardtop (13,058 built).

Commanders received the same new bodies as Champions in 1953. They had "Studebaker Commander" across the grille and V-8 emblems on the side cowl vents. The State trim level was discontinued and the Deluxe level was brought back again. The Commander Deluxe models featured narrow stainless steel windshield moldings and bright rear window moldings. The top-of-the-line Commander Regals had wide stainless steel windshield moldings and chrome side window moldings. Grille styling was similar to that of the lower-priced series. Commanders also had a hood ornament supplemented by the symbol "8" as one of several V-8 emblems.

At the midyear, the tri-star emblems used on the hood and deck lid of early Commanders and Champions were replaced by large "V" emblems. The new Commander instrument panel featured four hooded instrument pods. Model identification was on the left grille bar and on the deck lid of some, but not all models. Coupes and hardtops had V-8 emblems on the rear quarter panels.

The long-wheelbase sedan had "Studebaker Land Cruiser" spelled out across its grille. It was the sole four-door model with rear vent windows and a folding armrest in the center of the rear seat. It also had chrome side window moldings.

There were three Commander Deluxe offerings: two-door sedan for $2,089 (2,371 built), four-door sedan for $2,121 (10,065 built), and Starlight Coupe for $2,127 (6,106 built). Three Regal models made up the top series. They were the $2,208 four-door sedan (7,454 built), the $2,213 Starlight Coupe (14,752 built), and the very popular $2,374 Starliner hardtop (19,236 built). The Land Cruiser was $2,316 this year and 15,981 were assembled.

Engine choices were identical to 1952 with only slight carburetor differences. All Studebaker sedans, except the Land Cruiser, used a 116.5-inch wheelbase and a 198.6-inch overall length. The Land Cruiser was six inches longer in wheelbase and four inches longer in overall length. All models were 56.5 inches front and 55.5 inches rear. Champions again used 6.40 x 15 tires with 7.10 x 15 rubber on Commanders.

Model year sales reached 151,576 units. Studebaker remained ranked ninth on the industry sales chart. According to Automotive News in 1972, the new Studebaker Starliner hardtop was acclaimed the top car of all time in a poll taken by the *Chicago Daily News* of stylists representing the big four automakers — General Motors, Ford, Chrysler, and American Motors.

1954 *Studebaker*

Comedy was big in television land in 1954 with "The Milton Berle Show," "The Jackie Gleason Show," "The Colgate Comedy Hour," and "The Red Buttons Show" all in the top 20 between October 1953 and April 1954.

Unfortunately, there was nothing funny about the drop off in Studebaker sales this season. Independent automakers were struggling. At the beginning of the year, Hudson merged with Nash-Kelvinator to form American Motors. By June 22, 1954,

New for 1954 was the Studebaker Conestoga two-door station wagon.

Studebaker announced it was merging with Packard to become the Studebaker-Packard Corporation of America. With so much happening on the corporate front, it wasn't a big year for product changes.

The addition of 10 vertical "teeth" in the grille and new flat-faced front bumper guards were the main exterior styling revisions for 1954. The model identification remained on the left horizontal grille bar and for 1954, it was also placed on the rear deck lid handle on all body styles, except the new station wagon. Deluxe models had chrome window trim. Regal models had a rub molding extending from the front door panel to the rear fender. All Regal and Deluxe sedans and station wagons featured an "air scoop" hood ornament as standard equipment.

Except for the addition of a new Conestoga two-door station wagon, the Studebaker Champion body style offerings were the same as in 1953. "Studebaker Champion" was spelled out on the grille and the trunk-lift bar. Regal models had an "S" in a circle just behind the side cowl vent, stainless steel rub-rail moldings along the doors and rear fender, stainless steel moldings on the front quarter posts and cowl, and wide chrome side window moldings.

Station wagons had chrome body belts, instead of side window moldings and "Studebaker" just behind the door. Champion coupes and hardtops had the "S" within a circle emblem on the rear fenders. All new interior fabrics were color-keyed to the exterior paint scheme. Two-tone finishes were available on all Studebaker Champions except Custom line models.

The Custom line included the two-door sedan for $1,758 and the four-door sedan for $1,801. Both weighed a little over 2,700 pounds. Production amounted to 2,653 two-doors and 2,860 four-doors. With the new Conestoga station wagon there were four Champion Deluxe offerings: two-door sedan for $1,875 (4,449 built), four-door sedan for $1,918 (9,668 built), Starlight Coupe for $1,972 (7,042 built), and Conestoga for $2,187 (3,910 built). Five Regal models made up the top series. They were the $1,983 two-door sedan (1,066 built), the $2,026 four-door sedan (7,286 built), the $2,080 Starlight Coupe (5,125 built), the $2,241 Starliner hardtop (4,302 built) and the $2,295 Conestoga (3,074 built).

Commander exterior styling features were the same as those seen on comparable 1954 Champion models. On the inside a single instrument visor replaced the four separate units used in 1953. A Commander Conestoga two-door station wagon was also introduced. Deluxes had "V-8" on the side cowl vents, a trim strip on the rear fender only, narrow stainless steel side window moldings on sedans and no belt molding or side nameplate on station wagons.

Regal models had a stainless steel rub molding extending from the front door panel to the rear fender, V-8 emblems in a circle just behind the side cowl vents, and front quarter post and cowl moldings. Station wagons had chrome body belts instead of side window moldings and a "Studebaker" nameplate just behind the doors. Land Cruisers had a folding rear seat armrest.

There were four Commander Deluxe offerings: two-door sedan for $2,136 (1,086 built), four-door sedan for $2,179 (4,615 built), Starlight Coupe for $2,233 (2,868 built), and Conestoga for $2,448 (1,912 built). Four Regal models made up the middle series. They were the $2,287 four-door sedan (2,571 built), the $2,341 Starlight Coupe (3,151 built), the $2,502 Starliner hardtop (5,040 built), and the $2,556 Conestoga (2,878 built). The Land Cruiser sold for $2,438 this year and 6,383 were assembled.

The 169.6-cid Champion six still carried an 85-hp rating, although it had 7.5:1 compression and a new Carter WE one-barrel carburetor. The Commander's 232-cid overhead-valve V-8 also got a 7.5:1 compression ratio. It now developed 127 hp at 4000 rpm. A three-speed manual transmission with column-mounted gearshift was standard on all models. Overdrive was available for $105 extra on Champions and $118 extra on Commanders. Automatic Drive was available for $216 extra on Champions and $227 extra on Commanders.

Wheelbase remained at 116.5 inches for all models but the Land Cruiser, which had the same 120.5-inch wheelbase used last year. Overall length for all sedans except the Land Cruiser was 198.6 inches. The Land Cruiser was 202.6 inches long, the coupes and hardtops were 202.2 inches long, and the new station wagons were 195.6 inches. Tread widths were unchanged. Tires were 6.70 x 15 for the Champion wagon, 6.40 x 15 for other Champs and 7.10 x 15 for Commanders.

This was the final year that the Land Cruiser name was used. Studebaker slipped to 11th rank on the industry sales chart as model-year sales amounted to only 68,708 units. A $60 ambulance conversion for the station wagon was introduced at midyear. Called the "Ambulet," it was available as a Champion or Commander with Deluxe or Regal trim. Options, including a siren, red beacon light and cot, were available for the Ambulet.

1955 *Studebaker*

There was no shortage of chrome on the front end of the 1955 Studebaker President sedan.

Many new television shows made their debut in 1955. The list included "The Honeymooners," "The Lawrence Welk Show," and "The Mickey Mouse Club." All of these programs proved successful. Not as successful was Studebaker's new-for-1955 President series, which included a limited-production Speedster hardtop introduced in the middle of the year. The revived President line sold under 25,000 cars and just a bit more than 2,000 Speedsters. Studebaker needed all the sales it could get at this time, but numbers like these were not going to save the nameplate from extinction.

Changes from 1954 made 1955 Studebakers a little more glittery. The new top-of-the-line President series actually revived an old name that Studebaker hadn't used in 13 years. A redesigned 1955 bumper-grille seen on all 1955 models had a gold-faced "S" mounted on a wide, flat "V" ornament in the grille opening. The character line of the hood was raised and new side trim treatments were used, varying from model to model. Exterior series identification was placed on the deck lid handle. The Starlight Coupe and Starliner Hardtop model names were dropped. The Conestoga station wagon was still only available in two-door form.

The low-priced Champion series continued with the same models and trim levels offered in 1954,. One model, the Regal two-door sedan, was dropped from production. After Jan. 1, 1955, wraparound windshields were introduced on sedans and station wagons. The low-priced Champion Custom two- and four-door sedans had rubber windshield moldings, rubber rear window moldings, untrimmed side windows, no body side moldings and no built-in sun visors.

The trim on Champion Deluxe models varied according to body style. Two-door sedans had a special wing-shaped stainless steel molding on the rear fenders, plus stainless steel windshield, side window, and rear window moldings. Four-door sedans had stainless steel windshield, side window and rear window moldings, and narrow stainless steel body side moldings. They lacked the built-in sun visors used on some other models. Station wagons did

not have body side moldings and also lacked built-in sun visors. Deluxe hardtops and coupes did not have full-length side moldings or extra-wide windshield moldings.

Champion Regal sedans had full-length side moldings, built-in sun visors over the windshield, stainless steel side window moldings, and bright windshield and rear window moldings. Regal coupes and hardtops had full-length side moldings and an extra-wide stainless steel windshield molding. Regal Conestoga station wagons had built-in windshield sun visors and stainless steel moldings on each side.

There were 10 Champion models in all. The four-door sedan was available in all three series. The two-door sedan was available in the Custom and Deluxe series. The two-door coupe was available in Deluxe and Regal series, as was the Conestoga station wagon. The hardtop came only in the Regal line. Prices for cars in all three lines ranged from $1,741 for the Custom two-door sedan to $2,312 for the Regal Conestoga. Total series production was 50,374 vehicles.

The mid-range Commander series offered the same body styles and trim lines as the 1955 Champions. Both series shared a 116.5-inch wheelbase for sedans and wagons and a 120.5-inch wheelbase for coupes and hardtops. As in the Champion line, Regal and State models had a belt molding, extending from the headlights to the taillights. This molding widened at the edge of the rear door. Series designations were in script on the rear fenders. Exterior model identification was also on the deck lid handle. The 10 models varied in price from $1,873 to $2,445. Total Commander production in all three trim lines combined was 58,788.

Basic styling for the new 120.5-inch-wheelbase President was the same as for 1955 Champions and Commanders. President four-door sedans came in a choice of Deluxe and State trim levels. State models differed from Deluxe models in having wider "butter-knife" style full-length stainless steel side moldings, all stainless steel front window pillars and "fin-type" hood ornaments on top of the front fender. After Jan. 1, 1955, sedans got the new wraparound windshield. Model identification was on the deck lid handle and rear quarter panels.

A three-toned President Speedster hardtop was introduced in January 1955. Instrument panels were shared by all Champions, Commanders, and Presidents, except the Speedster. The Speedster had an engine-turned instrument panel insert. Almost every conceivable option was standard equipment on the Speedster. Speedsters made in the home plant in Indiana said "Speedster" on the rear quarter panels, while those made at Studebaker's Los Angeles factory had "President" and "Speedster" on these panels.

In addition to the Deluxe four-door sedan, there were four President State models: four-door sedan, two-door coupe, two-door hardtop, and Speedster Hardtop. Prices for the five cars ranged from $2,311 for the Deluxe sedan to $3,253 for the Speedster Hardtop. Series production of 24,665 units included 2,215 President State Speedster Hardtops.

There were three new Studebaker engines in 1955. The Champion models still came with an in-line six featuring in-the-block valves. It had a 3 x 4-3/8-inch bore and stroke and 185.6 cubic inches. There were four main bearings and solid valve lifters combined with a 7.5:1 compression ratio and a Carter one-barrel carburetor. This engine was rated for 101 hp at 4000 rpm. Early-production Commanders had a 224-cid overhead-valve V-8 with 7.5:1 compression and a Stromberg two-barrel carburetor. It made 140 hp at 4500 rpm. Late-1955 Commanders got a two-barrel version of the 259.2-cid "President" V-8 It developed 162 at 4500 rpm. The President version of the engine had a Carter WCFB carburetor. Cars built early in the model year had 175 hp. Later cars got 185 hp.

By the time the curtain had closed on model-year 1955, Studebaker model-year production totaled 116,333 automobiles. With this, Studebaker dropped to 13th on the industry sales charts. Adding fancier, pricier models may have appealed to Studebaker's new Packard management team, but the public wasn't buying the cars. In a year during which most automakers set records, Studebaker experienced only a rather modest boost. That was good, of course, but hardly enough to save the company.

1956 *Studebaker*

Hawk models took flight for Studebaker in 1956 including this Sky Hawk V-8 hardtop.

In 1956, the year's top television show was "The $64,000 Question," which began as a summer replacement program and became the first of many high-jackpot quiz shows. Based on a 1940s radio quiz show called "Take It Or Leave It," the show focused on culture and academics with a serious attitude.

In automotive circles, the $64,000 question in this era was whether Studebaker-Packard was going to survive. The cars brought out in 1956 did not provide the answer to the company's problems. However, they were more of a change then had been seen in the past few years.

The front and rear sections of all Studebaker sedans were greatly restyled in 1956. The station wagons, which had front ends like the sedans, were fitted with small fiberglass fins on the rear quarter panels. The coupes and hardtops were named Hawks and featured a square-shaped grille and flat-backed deck lid. Custom sedan models, which included the two-door sedanet, had horizontal side trim along the front two-thirds of the car.

Regular sedans had full-length side trim. The rare Regal model, which was built mainly for sale outside the United States, had dual full-length side moldings. A new "Cyclops Eye" speedometer was introduced on sedans and station wagons. All models were switched from six-volt to 12-volt electrical systems.

The Champion four-door sedan came in Custom, Deluxe, and Regal trim lines. The Deluxe line also offered a two-door sedan and a two-door sedanet. The Flight Hawk coupe and hardtop and the Pelham two-door station wagon were merchandised with Champions. That made a total of eight models priced between $1,717 and $2,232. Total series production was 28,916. With 560 assemblies, the Flight Hawk two-door hardtop was a rare car.

The Commander series offered four-door sedan as a Deluxe or Custom model, a Deluxe two-door sedan and a Deluxe two-door Sedanet. These were marketed alongside the Power Hawk coupe and the Parkview two-door station wagon. Styling changes were the same as those made on the Champions. Exterior trim variations were also the same as on Champions. The model identification was located on the front fenders of sedans and station wagons and all deck lids. These cars were priced between $1,829 and $2,354. The production total for all six models was 30, 649 cars.

The President series was limited to the top-line trim, which featured dual side trim moldings on sedans and station wagons. The President Classic had wide grooved, horizontal moldings just above the rocker panels. The model identification locations were the same as on Commanders and Champions. Except for the Golden Hawk model, the President series continued as Studebaker's top-line offering.

Base President models included the two-door sedan and the four-door sedan. The latter also came in President Classic trim. In the same general price range was the Skyhawk two-door hardtop and the Pinehurst station wagon. These five models had pricing in the $2,188 to $2,529 bracket. Together they accounted for 21,815 assemblies.

The Studebaker Golden Hawk, like the Sky Hawk and Flight Hawk hardtops, were based on the original 1953 Starliner body.

Small upright fiberglass fins on the top of the rear fenders were a Golden Hawk exclusive among the four 1956 Hawk models. Like the President Classic, the Golden Hawk had wide grooved, horizontal moldings just above the rocker panels. It had a base retail price of $3,061. A total of 4,071 Golden Hawks were built.

Champion and Flight Hawk models used a 185.6-cid 101-hp L-head straight six. Commander and Power Hawk models shared the 259-cid V-8 with a two-barrel carburetor and 170 hp at 4500 rpm.

Presidents and Sky Hawks moved up to a 289-cid V-8. Classic and Sky Hawk models used a 210-hp four-barrel version, while other models had a 190-hp two-barrel version. The Golden Hawk used a 352-cid Packard overhead-valve V-8. This engine had a 9.5:1 compression ratio and a four-barrel carburetor. It produced 275 hp at 4600 rpm.

Studebaker's model-year production slumped to 69,593 units. Things got so bad that the California assembly plant was shuttered, leaving production only in South Bend, Indiana, and Hamilton, Ontario, Canada.

1957 *Studebaker*

The 1957 Studebaker President V-8 sedan offers a dignified profile.

Comedy was a big part of television history again in 1957. "The Phil Silvers Show," "Father Knows Best," and "Leave it to Beaver' put smiles on the faces of millions of viewers. Silver's boisterous Sgt. Ernie Bilko and his sidekick Private Duane Doberman were a laugh a minute, while Jim Anderson (Robert Young) and "The Beav" (Jerry Mathers) blended their homespun brand of light-hearted humor with tidbits of family wisdom. Rumor has it the beleaguered Studebaker executives were big fans of such shows—they needed all the comic relief they could get, as sales figures continued to race down the chart.

In the Studebaker product lineup, changes from 1956 models included new canted-fin fenders on Hawks and a new wraparound cellular grille on Champion, Commander, and President models. A new "maximum-economy" model called the Scotsman was released as part of the Champion series. All Studebakers had new side trim treatments.

All Studebaker Champions had six-cylinder engines and the "Champion" name on the front fenders. Scotsman models had no nameplates or side trim. They had the cheap-style black rubber

moldings around the windshield and rear window. Custom-trim Champions had a three-quarter-length body side molding running from the front of the car to a point below the rear side window and black rubber windshield and rear window moldings. Champion Deluxe models were the fanciest version of the six-cylinder Studebaker. They carried full-length body side moldings and had bright metal moldings around the windshield and rear window.

There was a super-economy Scotsman station wagon and a sporty Pelham two-door station wagon in the official model listings for the Champion series. However, a small run of 25 station wagons with Custom-level trim were produced, along with one Deluxe station wagon.

Scotsman, Champion, and Pelham models were all on a 116.5-inch wheelbase and 202.4 inches long. The Champion in-line six-cylinder engine was still the 186-cid flathead type fitted with a Carter one-barrel carburetor. It had a 7.8:1 compression ratio and generated 101 hp at 4000 rpm. The Scotsman, Custom, and Deluxe lines all offered three models: two-door sedan, four-door sedan, and four-door station wagon. The Pelham station wagon added a 10th six-cylinder model and Studebaker also turned out 247 Regal four-door sedans. Prices on all 11 non-Hawk six-cylinder models ranged from $1,776 to $2,382. Total production of the 11 cars was only 29,121 units.

The Silver Hawk was the six-cylinder version of Studebaker's "sports car" using the same basic body that Raymond Loewy designed in 1953 with tail fins grafted on the rear. Hawks rode a longer 120.5-inch wheelbase and measured 204 inches long. At 71.3 inches wide, they were considerably narrower than the sedans and wagons, which were all 75.8 inches wide. Where they really differed from other models was in height. The Hawks were 55 inches high, compared to 59.8 inches for sedans and 61.7 inches for wagons.

Officially, the only Silver Hawk model available was the pillared coupe, which had a $2,142 list price and a production run of 4,163 units. However, factory production records indicate that 120 six-cylinder Silver Hawk hardtops were also made. The six-cylinder engine in these cars was the same one used in Champions.

The main difference between Studebaker Champions and Commanders was under the hood, where the Commander models housed a V-8 engine. Otherwise, styling changes were the same, as were the Custom and Deluxe trim features. There was no Scotsman V-8 and there were no Custom or Deluxe Commander station wagons. Instead, a separate series included the two-door Parkview wagon and the four-door Provincial wagon. Both of these carried Deluxe-level trim features.

Commander sedans, Parkview wagons, and Provincial wagons had the same wheelbase and length as comparable Champion models. The Commander's two-barrel overhead-valve V-8 was the 259 with an 8.3:1 compression ratio and 180 hp at 4500 rpm. Available models included the Custom and Deluxe two- and four-door sedans and the two- and four-door station wagons. Prices ran from $2,124 to $2,561. Production of the six models totaled 18,448 vehicles.

Certain Silver Hawk models were limited to sales outside the United States. For instance, though not listed in all contemporary sources, factory production records show that Studebaker built 1,180 Silver Hawk coupes and 248 Silver Hawk hardtops with the Commander V-8 for the Canadian market. All 1957 Silver Hawk models used the engine-turned instrument panel insert introduced on the 1955 President Speedster.

The 1957 Studebaker President models had "President" nameplates on the front fenders and guided-missile shaped rear side moldings. The Custom, Deluxe, and Regal sedans made in this series rode the smaller wheelbase, but there was a fancier Classic four-door sedan that continued the old Land Cruiser concept. This car used the longer Hawk wheelbase. The Classic sedan had five bright metal chevrons on the rear fenders and a rear vent window. President type moldings were used on the Broadmoor four-door station wagon, along with the President V-8.

Prices for the seven President sedans and three President station wagons were in the $2,358 to $2,666 range. The Custom and Deluxe sedans and wagons in the President series had very low production totals and were probably made only for export sales. The Regal sedans on the 116.5-inch wheelbase, the Classic sedan and the Broadmoor were the cars sold mostly in the United States and had somewhat larger production runs. Nevertheless, factory records show totals for all of 10 of these models came to just 12,586 units.

Two Hawk series models were offered with the President V-8. The Silver Hawk came only as a $2,263 pillared coupe. The $3,182 Golden Hawk came only as a hardtop. Standard on the Golden Hawk engine was a belt-driven supercharger. Factory records show that 9,607 President Silver Hawks and 4,356 Golden Hawks were made.

The President 289-cid V-8 had an 8.3:1 compression ratio and produced 210 hp at 4500 rpm in standard two-barrel form. When used in Classic sedans it got a four-barrel carburetor and 225 hp at 4500 rpm. The supercharged Golden Hawk version ran a 7.8:1 compression ratio and a Stromberg two-barrel carburetor. This boosted output to 275 hp at 4800 rpm.

Studebaker's 1957 model-year sales totaled only 63,101 units. For the third year in a row, Studebaker was ranked 13th on the industry sales chart.

1958 *Studebaker*

The 1958 TV shows "Wagon Train," "The Rifleman," and "Have Gun Will Travel" reflected Americans' growing pride in their nation's exciting Western heritage. Henry and Clem Studebaker had played a major role in settling the West during the latter part of the 19th Century. The brothers opened a blacksmith and wagon making shop, in South Bend, in 1852.

During the Civil War they became the largest manufacturer of horse-drawn vehicles in the world and were awarded lucrative government contracts. They produced in excess of 750,000 wagons over 67 years, many in the post-Civil War period, when Studebaker thrived. The post World War II period unfolded differently. In the decade since that fighting had ended, Studebaker's automobile business lost ground to the "Big Three," who could afford to change their designs more frequently. Studebaker could not and was barely hanging on.

Studebakers for 1958 had some noticeable design changes, including a lowered roof line and new "V" emblems in the grilles of all models except the Hawk sports cars. Dual headlights were standard equipment for President and Commander models. They were also optional for the low-priced Champion. The canted tail fins that were used only on Hawks in 1957 were now added to all models except the low-end Scotsman. The Commander and President series got new two-door hardtop models.

Scotsman models had restyled round taillights, Studebaker lettering on the left rear quarter panel, and a square mesh radiator grille. The Scotsman had no model identification and the Scotsman 116.5-inch-wheelbase models included the $1,795 two-door sedan, the $1,874 four-door sedan, and the $2,055 two-door station wagon. A 121.5-inch-wheelbase Scotsman four-door sedan called the "Econ-O-Miler" was introduced later. This series did fairly well in the marketplace with the four body styles contributing 21,990 production units. The 101-hp Champion six was carried over from 1957 with no big changes.

Champions rode the small wheelbase again and used the same basic flathead six to get to the supermarket. Model identification names were placed on the rear fins. There was a two-door sedan

Studebaker-Packard Museum Archives

The 1958 Studebaker President two-door hardtop was fitted with pod-mounted quad headlights and taller fins..

priced at $2,189 and a four-door sedan priced at $2,253. In addition, 12 Champion Deluxe four-door station wagons left the factory in South Bend. Production was 1,455 and 5,178 units, respectively. In addition, 120 Champion two-door hardtops were built, possibly for export.

A total of 2,442 Silver Hawk coupes were built with the Champion six under the hood. The $2,219 Silver Hawk was again built on the 120.5-inch wheelbase chassis. The sporty Studebaker had a new grille mesh in the side grille openings and small dual fins on the front fender-mounted parking lights. A large round Hawk emblem was placed in the lower center of the grille. A Silver Hawk nameplate decorated the rear deck lid.

Except for the fact that they came standard with dual headlights, Studebaker Commanders were like Champions with a V-8. They used the 259-cid 180-hp two-barrel V-8. Studebaker even made 88 Scotsman models (in all three body styles) with this motor under the hood. The regular Commander models included the $2,493 two-door hardtop, the $2,378 four-door sedan and the $2,644 four-door Provincial station wagon. These cars had 2,555, 6,771 and 2,412 assemblies, in the same respective order. The new two-door "sedan-size hardtop" was called a Starlight in most publicity announcements.

Two versions of the Silver Hawk model were also made with the Commander V-8. The coupe version sold for $2,219 and weighed 2,795 pounds. Only 367 were made for the domestic

market. In addition, factory records show that 56 Silver Hawk 259 hardtops were produced. Most likely, these were export-market cars.

Studebaker Presidents had the same basic styling changes as other models, but more decorative trim. The tinsel included "President" name scripts and five bright metal chevrons inside the guide-missile-shaped body side moldings. Special President-powered Scotsman police cars, called Marshals, were introduced. The Marshal came in two-door sedan, four-door sedan and two-door station wagon models. Only 274 were built in all. Regular President models included the $2,352 four-door sedan (3,570 built) and the $2,695 two-door hardtop (1,171 built). In addition, a single four-door Deluxe station wagon was produced. Presidents, except for the one station wagon made, used a 289-cid 225-hp four-barrel V-8.

The 289-cid engine was also used in the Silver Hawk 289 coupe, which listed for $2,352 and had production of 4,485 units. In this case, the motor carried a two-barrel carburetor and a 210-hp rating. The Golden Hawk two-door hardtop returned in 1958, but only 878 were made. This car employed a supercharged version of the 289-cid V-8 that cranked out 275 hp at 4800 rpm. The Golden had a $3,282 base price.

Model year sales continued to slide with only 44,759 units. The Packard portion of the Studebaker-Packard Corporation ceased production of automobiles this year.

1959 *Studebaker*

Top TV shows of 1959 included some real classics like "Maverick," "Rawhide," "Real McCoys," and "Dennis the Menace." That year, Studebaker brought out a new car called the Lark that looked dramatically different from previous models, even though it incorporated the same main body structure used since 1953. Ads described the Lark as being "Perfectly practical and practically perfect." It would prove successful enough to give Studebaker a new lease on life for the next six years. In addition, in its Daytona form, it became a hot '60s performance machine.

The central body section of the Lark was basically the 1958 Studebaker body, but the front and back sections were drastically shortened with rounded edges. No fins or garish add-ons were attached. Deluxe models had painted headlight moldings, no grille moldings and lacked padded instrument panels. Regal Larks had chrome moldings around the grille and headlights and a padded instrument panel.

On sedans and station wagons the former "Cyclops Eye" speedometer was replaced by a normal speedometer, although the central glove box was retained. All models had only single

John Gunnell

The Studebaker Lark was welcomed by the public in 1959, a much needed sales success story for Studebaker.

headlights. The two-tone paint option was discontinued. An Econ-O-Miler long-wheelbase four-door sedan—also based on the Lark—was made available. The Econ-O-Miler had a stretched Lark body with non-functional rear door vent windows. Most Econ-O-Miler sedans were sold as taxis, although some were sold outside the United States for private use.

Lark sedans and hardtops (except for the Econ-O-Miler version) had a 108.5-inch wheelbase and an overall length of 175 inches. A special Lark two-door sedan without a rear seat was also offered. It was called the Utility Sedan. The cars were 71.38 inches wide and 57.5 inches high. Lark station wagons used a 113-inch wheelbase and were 184.5 inches long. They were the same width as other models, but had a height of 58.75 inches. A kit was sold to convert Lark station wagons to Panel Wagons.

Six-cylinder Larks (and Silver Hawks) used a 90-hp L-head six with an 8.3:1 compression ratio and a one-barrel carburetor. The only V-8 used this year was the 259-cid 180-hp overhead-valve job with an 8.8:1 compression ratio and two-barrel carburetor.

Six-cylinder-powered Larks were called "Lark VI" models. They came in Deluxe and Regal trim lines. Lark VI model identification was placed below the deck lid on sedans and on the tailgate of station wagons. The Deluxe range offered a two-door sedan at $1,925, a four-door sedan at $1,995, and a two-door station wagon at $2,295. The production totals for the three models were 33,259 for the two-door sedan, 26,566 for the four-door sedan, and 13,227 for the wagon. The Lark Regal series offered a two-door hardtop at $2,275, a four-door sedan at $2,175, and a two-door station wagon at $2,455. The production totals for these were 7,075 for the hardtop, 11,898 for the four-door sedan, and 5,685 for the wagon. In addition,

1,033 Econ-O-Miler four-door sedans were assembled.

The Silver Hawk coupe was the only carryover Studebaker model. On this model the parking lights were relocated in the side grilles for 1958. "Silver Hawk" identification was on the rear fins. Selling for $2,360, the Silver Hawk six had just 2,417 assemblies.

Body style offerings and trim differences in the Lark VIII (V-8) line were the same as they were for the Lark six-cylinder models. "Lark VIII" model identifications were also in the same locations. Both Lark VI and VIII models featured a circular emblem with raised hawk wings against a black background, at the right-hand lower corner of the grille and on the tailgate of station wagons.

A total of 2,295 Deluxe models were made, along with 92 long-wheelbase Econ-O-Liner sedans. These cars were limited to special order sales, Marshal sales, fleet sales, and sales outside the United States. The regular-order models were the $2,310 Regal four-door sedan, the $2,410 Regal two-door hardtop and the $2,590 Regal two-door station wagon. Studebaker counted 14,530 sedans, 7,996 hardtops, and 7,419 wagons leaving the factory in South Bend.

The V-8-powered version of the Silver Hawk used the same engine as Lark VIIIs. Like the six-cylinder version, this sporty full-pillared coupe was on a 120.5-inch wheelbase with an even 204 inches of overall length. It was the same width as the Lark (since the main body structure was identical) but two to three inches lower than the Larks at 55.5 inches high.

Studebaker ended the 1950s on a high note, as its model-year sales soared to 126,156 cars. This helped the South Bend automaker rise to 10th position on industry sales chart.

PRICINGS

The prices listed here represent a selected cross-section of American cars of the 1950s, taken from the *2004 Old Cars Price Guide.* If you do not see your car here, check the 2005 edition of the *Old Cars Price Guide,* published by Krause Publications, or contact the club for your car.

Vehicle Condition Scale:

1. Excellent. Restored to current maximum professional standards of quality in every area or perfect original with components operating and appearing as new. A 95-plus point show car that is not driven.
2. Fine. Well-restored or a combination of superior restoration and excellent original parts. An extremely well-maintained original vehicle showing minimal wear.

3. Very good. Completely operable original or older restoration. A good amateur restoration, or a combination of well-done restoration and good operable components or partially restored car with parts necessary to complete and/or valuable NOS parts.
4. Good. A driveable vehicle needed no work or only minor work to be functional. A deteriorated restoration or poor amateur restoration. All components may need restoration to be "excellent" but the car is useable "as is."
5. Restorable. Needs complete restoration of body, chassis, and interior. May or may not be running. Isn't weathered or stripped to the point of being useful only for parts.
6. Parts car. May or may not be running but it weathered, wrecked and/or stripped to the point of being useful primarily for parts.

BUICK

	6	5	4	3	2	1
1950 Special Series 40, 8-cyl., 121-1/2" wb						
2d S'net	920	2,760	4,600	9,200	16,100	23,000
4d S'net	840	2,520	4,200	8,400	14,700	21,000
4d Tr Sed	800	2,400	4,000	8,000	14,000	20,000
1950 Special DeLuxe Series 40, 8-cyl., 121-1/2" wb						
2d S'net	960	2,880	4,800	9,600	16,800	24,000
4d S'net	880	2,640	4,400	8,800	15,400	22,000
4d Tr Sed	840	2,520	4,200	8,400	14,700	21,000
1950 Super Series 50, 8-cyl.						
2d Conv	1,480	4,440	7,400	14,800	25,900	37,000
2d Riv HT	1,080	3,240	5,400	10,800	18,900	27,000
2d S'net	1,000	3,000	5,000	10,000	17,500	25,000
4d Sed	880	2,640	4,400	8,800	15,400	22,000
4d Sta Wag	1,720	5,160	8,600	17,200	30,100	43,000
1950 Roadmaster Series 70, 8-cyl.						
2d Conv	1,880	5,640	9,400	18,800	32,900	47,000
2d Riv HT	1,360	4,080	6,800	13,600	23,800	34,000
2d S'net	1,120	3,360	5,600	11,200	19,600	28,000
4d Sta Wag	1,800	5,400	9,000	18,000	31,500	45,000
4d Riv Sed DeL	960	2,880	4,800	9,600	16,800	24,000
1951-52 Special DeLuxe Series 40, 8-cyl., 121-1/2" wb						
4d Sed	800	2,400	4,000	8,000	14,000	20,000
2d Sed	800	2,400	4,000	8,000	14,000	20,000
2d Riv HT	1,080	3,240	5,400	10,800	18,900	27,000
2d Conv	1,400	4,200	7,000	14,000	24,500	35,000
1951-52 Super Series 50, 8-cyl.						
2d Conv	1,480	4,440	7,400	14,800	25,900	37,000
2d Riv HT	1,200	3,600	6,000	12,000	21,000	30,000
4d Sta Wag	1,720	5,160	8,600	17,200	30,100	43,000
2d S'net (1951 only)	960	2,880	4,800	9,600	16,800	24,000
4d Sed	880	2,640	4,400	8,800	15,400	22,000
1951-52 Roadmaster Series 70, 8-cyl.						
2d Conv	1,600	4,800	8,000	16,000	28,000	40,000
2d Riv HT	1,360	4,080	6,800	13,600	23,800	34,000
4d Sta Wag	1,800	5,400	9,000	18,000	31,500	45,000
4d Riv Sed	960	2,880	4,800	9,600	16,800	24,000
1953 Special Series 40, 8-cyl.						
4d Sed	840	2,520	4,200	8,400	14,700	21,000
2d Sed	860	2,580	4,300	8,600	15,050	21,500
2d Riv HT	1,080	3,240	5,400	10,800	18,900	27,000
2d Conv	1,480	4,440	7,400	14,800	25,900	37,000
1953 Super Series 50, V-8						
2d Riv HT	1,240	3,720	6,200	12,400	21,700	31,000
2d Conv	1,600	4,800	8,000	16,000	28,000	40,000
4d Sta Wag	1,720	5,160	8,600	17,200	30,100	43,000
4d Riv Sed	880	2,640	4,400	8,800	15,400	22,000
1953 Roadmaster Series 70, V-8						
2d Riv HT	1,400	4,200	7,000	14,000	24,500	35,000
2d Skylark	2,800	8,400	14,000	28,000	49,000	70,000
2d Conv	1,720	5,160	8,600	17,200	30,100	43,000
4d DeL Sta Wag	1,800	5,400	9,000	18,000	31,500	45,000
4d Riv Sed	960	2,880	4,800	9,600	16,800	24,000
1954 Special Series 40, V-8						
4d Sed	760	2,280	3,800	7,600	13,300	19,000
2d Sed	760	2,280	3,800	7,600	13,300	19,000
2d Riv HT	1,160	3,480	5,800	11,600	20,300	29,000
2d Conv	1,520	4,560	7,600	15,200	26,600	38,000
4d Sta Wag	1,040	3,120	5,200	10,400	18,200	26,000

	6	5	4	3	2	1
1954 Century Series 60, V-8						
4d DeL	800	2,400	4,000	8,000	14,000	20,000
2d Riv HT	1,280	3,840	6,400	12,800	22,400	32,000
2d Conv	1,840	5,520	9,200	18,400	32,200	46,000
4d Sta Wag	1,080	3,240	5,400	10,800	18,900	27,000
1954 Super Series 50, V-8						
4d Sed	760	2,280	3,800	7,600	13,300	19,000
2d Riv HT	1,200	3,600	6,000	12,000	21,000	30,000
2d Conv	1,640	4,920	8,200	16,400	28,700	41,000
1954 Roadmaster Series 70, V-8						
4d Sed	800	2,400	4,000	8,000	14,000	20,000
2d Riv HT	1,400	4,200	7,000	14,000	24,500	35,000
2d Conv	1,840	5,520	9,200	18,400	32,200	46,000
1954 Skylark Series, V-8						
2d Spt Conv	2,640	7,920	13,200	26,400	46,200	66,000
1955 Special Series 40, V-8						
4d Sed	760	2,280	3,800	7,600	13,300	19,000
4d Riv HT	880	2,640	4,400	8,800	15,400	22,000
2d Sed	760	2,280	3,800	7,600	13,300	19,000
2d Riv HT	1,240	3,720	6,200	12,400	21,700	31,000
2d Conv	1,880	5,640	9,400	18,800	32,900	47,000
4d Sta Wag	960	2,880	4,800	9,600	16,800	24,000
1955 Century Series 60, V-8						
4d Sed	800	2,400	4,000	8,000	14,000	20,000
4d Riv HT	920	2,760	4,600	9,200	16,100	23,000
2d Riv HT	1,320	3,960	6,600	13,200	23,100	33,000
2d Conv	1,960	5,880	9,800	19,600	34,300	49,000
4d Sta Wag	1,000	3,000	5,000	10,000	17,500	25,000
1955 Super Series 50, V-8						
4d Sed	800	2,400	4,000	8,000	14,000	20,000
2d Riv HT	1,280	3,840	6,400	12,800	22,400	32,000
2d Conv	1,880	5,640	9,400	18,800	32,900	47,000
1955 Roadmaster Series 70, V-8						
4d Sed	880	2,640	4,400	8,800	15,400	22,000
2d Riv HT	1,400	4,200	7,000	14,000	24,500	35,000
2d Conv	2,080	6,240	10,400	20,800	36,400	52,000
1956 Special Series 40, V-8						
4d Sed	760	2,280	3,800	7,600	13,300	19,000
4d Riv HT	880	2,640	4,400	8,800	15,400	22,000
2d Sed	760	2,280	3,800	7,600	13,300	19,000
2d Riv HT	1,240	3,720	6,200	12,400	21,700	31,000
2d Conv	1,840	5,520	9,200	18,400	32,200	46,000
4d Sta Wag	920	2,760	4,600	9,200	16,100	23,000
1956 Century Series 60, V-8						
4d Sed	800	2,400	4,000	8,000	14,000	20,000
4d Riv HT	1,000	3,000	5,000	10,000	17,500	25,000
2d Riv HT	1,320	3,960	6,600	13,200	23,100	33,000
2d Conv	1,920	5,760	9,600	19,200	33,600	48,000
4d Sta Wag	960	2,880	4,800	9,600	16,800	24,000
1956 Super Series 50						
4d Sed	800	2,400	4,000	8,000	14,000	20,000
4d Riv HT	1,080	3,240	5,400	10,800	18,900	27,000
2d Riv HT	1,280	3,840	6,400	12,800	22,400	32,000
2d Conv	1,840	5,520	9,200	18,400	32,200	46,000
1956 Roadmaster Series 70, V-8						
4d Sed	840	2,520	4,200	8,400	14,700	21,000
4d Riv HT	1,160	3,480	5,800	11,600	20,300	29,000
2d Riv HT	1,360	4,080	6,800	13,600	23,800	34,000
2d Conv	2,040	6,120	10,200	20,400	35,700	51,000

1957 Special Series 40, V-8

	6	5	4	3	2	1
4d Sed	720	2,160	3,600	7,200	12,600	18,000
4d Riv HT	920	2,760	4,600	9,200	16,100	23,000
2d Sed	720	2,160	3,600	7,200	12,600	18,000
2d Riv HT	1,200	3,600	6,000	12,000	21,000	30,000
2d Conv	1,720	5,160	8,600	17,200	30,100	43,000
4d Sta Wag	960	2,880	4,800	9,600	16,800	24,000
4d HT Wag	1,360	4,080	6,800	13,600	23,800	34,000

1957 Century Series 60, V-8

	6	5	4	3	2	1
4d Sed	760	2,280	3,800	7,600	13,300	19,000
4d Riv HT	960	2,880	4,800	9,600	16,800	24,000
2d Riv HT	1,320	3,960	6,600	13,200	23,100	33,000
2d Conv	1,800	5,400	9,000	18,000	31,500	45,000
4d HT Wag	1,360	4,080	6,800	13,600	23,800	34,000

1957 Super Series 50, V-8

	6	5	4	3	2	1
4d Riv HT	1,000	3,000	5,000	10,000	17,500	25,000
2d Riv HT	1,320	3,960	6,600	13,200	23,100	33,000
2d Conv	1,760	5,280	8,800	17,600	30,800	44,000

1957 Roadmaster Series 70, V-8

	6	5	4	3	2	1
4d Riv HT	1,040	3,120	5,200	10,400	18,200	26,000
2d Riv HT	1,400	4,200	7,000	14,000	24,500	35,000
2d Conv	1,880	5,640	9,400	18,800	32,900	47,000

NOTE: Add 5 percent for 75 Series.

1958 Special Series 40, V-8

	6	5	4	3	2	1
4d Sed	680	2,040	3,400	6,800	11,900	17,000
4d Riv HT	800	2,400	4,000	8,000	14,000	20,000
2d Sed	680	2,040	3,400	6,800	11,900	17,000
2d Riv HT	1,040	3,120	5,200	10,400	18,200	26,000
2d Conv	1,240	3,720	6,200	12,400	21,700	31,000
4d Sta Wag	720	2,160	3,600	7,200	12,600	18,000
4d HT Wag	1,120	3,360	5,600	11,200	19,600	28,000

1958 Century Series 60, V-8

	6	5	4	3	2	1
4d Sed	720	2,160	3,600	7,200	12,600	18,000
4d Riv HT	840	2,520	4,200	8,400	14,700	21,000
2d Riv HT	1,160	3,480	5,800	11,600	20,300	29,000
2d Conv	1,320	3,960	6,600	13,200	23,100	33,000
4d HT Wag	1,200	3,600	6,000	12,000	21,000	30,000

1958 Super Series 50, V-8

	6	5	4	3	2	1
4d Riv HT	880	2,640	4,400	8,800	15,400	22,000
2d Riv HT	1,200	3,600	6,000	12,000	21,000	30,000

1958 Roadmaster Series 75, V-8

	6	5	4	3	2	1
4d Riv HT	920	2,760	4,600	9,200	16,100	23,000
2d Riv HT	1,240	3,720	6,200	12,400	21,700	31,000
2d Conv	1,480	4,440	7,400	14,800	25,900	37,000

1958 Limited Series 700, V-8

	6	5	4	3	2	1
4d Riv HT	1,200	3,600	6,000	12,000	21,000	30,000
2d Riv HT	1,560	4,680	7,800	15,600	27,300	39,000
2d Conv	2,120	6,360	10,600	21,200	37,100	53,000

1959 LeSabre Series 4400, V-8

	6	5	4	3	2	1
4d Sed	680	2,040	3,400	6,800	11,900	17,000
4d HT	760	2,280	3,800	7,600	13,300	19,000
2d Sed	700	2,100	3,500	7,000	12,250	17,500
2d HT	880	2,640	4,400	8,800	15,400	22,000
2d Conv	1,240	3,720	6,200	12,400	21,700	31,000
4d Sta Wag	760	2,280	3,800	7,600	13,300	19,000

1959 Electra Series 4700, V-8

	6	5	4	3	2	1
4d Sed	760	2,280	3,800	7,600	13,300	19,000
4d HT	840	2,520	4,200	8,400	14,700	21,000
2d HT	1,000	3,000	5,000	10,000	17,500	25,000

1959 Electra 225 Series 4800, V-8

	6	5	4	3	2	1
4d Riv HT 6W	800	2,400	4,000	8,000	14,000	20,000
4d HT 4W	840	2,520	4,200	8,400	14,700	21,000
2d Conv	1,480	4,440	7,400	14,800	25,900	37,000

CADILLAC

1950-51 Series 61, V-8

	6	5	4	3	2	1
4d 5P Sed	960	2,880	4,800	9,600	16,800	24,000
2d HT Cpe	1,440	4,320	7,200	14,400	25,200	36,000

1950-51 Series 62, V-8

	6	5	4	3	2	1
4d 5P Sed	1,000	3,000	5,000	10,000	17,500	25,000
2d HT Cpe	1,200	3,600	6,000	12,000	21,000	30,000
2d HT Cpe DeV	1,680	5,040	8,400	16,800	29,400	42,000
2d Conv	1,920	5,760	9,600	19,200	33,600	48,000

1950-51 Series 60S, V-8

	6	5	4	3	2	1
4d Sed	1,200	3,600	6,000	12,000	21,000	30,000

1950-51 Series 75, Fleetwood

	6	5	4	3	2	1
4d 8P Sed	1,240	3,720	6,200	12,400	21,700	31,000

1950-51 Series 75 Fleetwood

	6	5	4	3	2	1
4d 8P Imp	1,320	3,960	6,600	13,200	23,100	33,000

1952 Series 62, V-8

	6	5	4	3	2	1
4d Sed	1,000	3,000	5,000	10,000	17,500	25,000
2d HT	1,160	3,480	5,800	11,600	20,300	29,000
2d HT Cpe DeV	1,680	5,040	8,400	16,800	29,400	42,000
2d Conv	1,960	5,880	9,800	19,600	34,300	49,000

1952 Series 60S, V-8

	6	5	4	3	2	1
4d Sed	1,200	3,600	6,000	12,000	21,000	30,000

1952 Series 75, V-8, Fleetwood

	6	5	4	3	2	1
4d Sed	1,240	3,720	6,200	12,400	21,700	31,000
4d Imp Sed	1,320	3,960	6,600	13,200	23,100	33,000

1953 Series 62, V-8

	6	5	4	3	2	1
4d Sed	960	2,880	4,800	9,600	16,800	24,000
2d HT	1,400	4,200	7,000	14,000	24,500	35,000
2d HT Cpe DeV	1,760	5,280	8,800	17,600	30,800	44,000
2d Conv	2,160	6,480	10,800	21,600	37,800	54,000
2d Eldo Conv	4,440	13,320	22,200	44,400	77,700	111,000

1953 Series 60S, V-8

	6	5	4	3	2	1
4d Sed	1,440	4,320	7,200	14,400	25,200	36,000

1953 Series 75, V-8, Fleetwood

	6	5	4	3	2	1
4d 7P Sed	1,480	4,440	7,400	14,800	25,900	37,000
4d Imp Sed	1,560	4,680	7,800	15,600	27,300	39,000

1954 Series 62, V-8

	6	5	4	3	2	1
4d Sed	960	2,880	4,800	9,600	16,800	24,000
2d HT	1,320	3,960	6,600	13,200	23,100	33,000
2d HT Cpe DeV	1,600	4,800	8,000	16,000	28,000	40,000
2d Conv	2,160	6,480	10,800	21,600	37,800	54,000
2d Eldo Conv	2,560	7,680	12,800	25,600	44,800	64,000

1954 Series 60S, V-8

	6	5	4	3	2	1
4d Sed	1,280	3,840	6,400	12,800	22,400	32,000

1954 Series 75, V-8, Fleetwood

	6	5	4	3	2	1
4d 7P Sed	1,400	4,200	7,000	14,000	24,500	35,000
4d 7P Imp Sed	1,480	4,440	7,400	14,800	25,900	37,000

1955 Series 62, V-8

	6	5	4	3	2	1
4d Sed	960	2,880	4,800	9,600	16,800	24,000
2d HT	1,600	4,800	8,000	16,000	28,000	40,000
2d HT Cpe DeV	1,640	4,920	8,200	16,400	28,700	41,000
2d Conv	2,160	6,480	10,800	21,600	37,800	54,000
2d Eldo Conv	2,560	7,680	12,800	25,600	44,800	64,000

1955 Series 60S, V-8

	6	5	4	3	2	1
4d Sed	1,280	3,840	6,400	12,800	22,400	32,000

1955 Series 75, V-8, Fleetwood

	6	5	4	3	2	1
4d 7P Sed	1,400	4,200	7,000	14,000	24,500	35,000
4d 7P Imp Sed	1,480	4,440	7,400	14,800	25,900	37,000

1956 Series 62, V-8

	6	5	4	3	2	1
4d Sed	960	2,880	4,800	9,600	16,800	24,000
2d HT	1,640	4,920	8,200	16,400	28,700	41,000
4d HT Sed DeV	1,400	4,200	7,000	14,000	24,500	35,000
2d HT Cpe DeV	1,680	5,040	8,400	16,800	29,400	42,000
2d Conv	2,160	6,480	10,800	21,600	37,800	54,000
2d HT Eldo Sev	1,880	5,640	9,400	18,800	32,900	47,000
2d Brtz Eldo Conv	2,560	7,680	12,800	25,600	44,800	64,000

1956 Series 60S, V-8

	6	5	4	3	2	1
4d Sed	1,280	3,840	6,400	12,800	22,400	32,000

1956 Series 75, V-8, Fleetwood

	6	5	4	3	2	1
4d 7P Sed	1,400	4,200	7,000	14,000	24,500	35,000
4d 7P Imp Sed	1,480	4,440	7,400	14,800	25,900	37,000

1957 Series 62, V-8

	6	5	4	3	2	1
4d HT	800	2,400	4,000	8,000	14,000	20,000
2d HT	1,480	4,440	7,400	14,800	25,900	37,000
2d HT Cpe DeV	1,600	4,800	8,000	16,000	28,000	40,000
4d HT Sed DeV	1,400	4,200	7,000	14,000	24,500	35,000
2d Conv	1,880	5,640	9,400	18,800	32,900	47,000

1957 Eldorado, V-8

	6	5	4	3	2	1
2d HT Sev	1,640	4,920	8,200	16,400	28,700	41,000
2d Brtz Conv	2,000	6,000	10,000	20,000	35,000	50,000

1957 Fleetwood 60 Special, V-8

	6	5	4	3	2	1
4d HT	1,040	3,120	5,200	10,400	18,200	26,000

1957 Eldorado Brougham, V-8

	6	5	4	3	2	1
4d HT	1,400	4,200	7,000	14,000	24,500	35,000

1957 Series 75

	6	5	4	3	2	1
4d 8P Sed	1,080	3,240	5,400	10,800	18,900	27,000
4d 8P Imp Sed	1,160	3,480	5,800	11,600	20,300	29,000

1958 Series 62, V-8 & Series 63, V-8

	6	5	4	3	2	1
4d HT Sh Dk	720	2,160	3,600	7,200	12,600	18,000
4d 6W Sed	1,000	3,000	5,000	10,000	17,500	25,000
4d Sed DeV	1,040	3,120	5,200	10,400	18,200	26,000
2d HT	1,320	3,960	6,600	13,200	23,100	33,000
2d HT Cpe DeV	1,400	4,200	7,000	14,000	24,500	35,000
2d Conv	1,800	5,400	9,000	18,000	31,500	45,000

1958 Eldorado, V-8

	6	5	4	3	2	1
2d HT Sev	1,440	4,320	7,200	14,400	25,200	36,000
2d Brtz Conv	1,920	5,760	9,600	19,200	33,600	48,000

1958 Fleetwood 60 Special, V-8

	6	5	4	3	2	1
4d HT	1,200	3,600	6,000	12,000	21,000	30,000

1958 Eldorado Brougham, V-8

	6	5	4	3	2	1
4d HT	1,560	4,680	7,800	15,600	27,300	39,000

1958 Series 75

	6	5	4	3	2	1
4d 8P Sed	1,000	3,000	5,000	10,000	17,500	25,000
4d 8P Imp Sed	1,080	3,240	5,400	10,800	18,900	27,000

1959 Series 62, V-8

	6	5	4	3	2	1
4d 4W HT	1,000	3,000	5,000	10,000	17,500	25,000
4d 6W HT	960	2,880	4,800	9,600	16,800	24,000
2d HT	1,200	3,600	6,000	12,000	21,000	30,000
2d Conv	2,120	6,360	10,600	21,200	37,100	53,000

1959 Series 63 DeVille, V-8

	6	5	4	3	2	1
2d HT Cpe DeV	1,480	4,440	7,400	14,800	25,900	37,000
4d 4W HT	1,080	3,240	5,400	10,800	18,900	27,000
4d 6W HT	1,040	3,120	5,200	10,400	18,200	26,000

1959 Series Eldorado, V-8

	6	5	4	3	2	1
4d HT Brgm	1,480	4,440	7,400	14,800	25,900	37,000
2d HT Sev	1,640	4,920	8,200	16,400	28,700	41,000
2d Brtz Conv	2,800	8,400	14,000	28,000	49,000	70,000

1959 Fleetwood 60 Special, V-8

	6	5	4	3	2	1
4d 6P Sed	1,240	3,720	6,200	12,400	21,700	31,000

1959 Fleetwood Series 75, V-8

	6	5	4	3	2	1
4d 9P Sed	1,320	3,960	6,600	13,200	23,100	33,000
4d Limo	1,400	4,200	7,000	14,000	24,500	35,000

CHEVROLET

1949-50 Styleline DeLuxe, 6-cyl.

	6	5	4	3	2	1
Spt Cpe	800	2,400	4,000	8,000	14,000	20,000
2d Sed	732	2,196	3,660	7,320	12,810	18,300
4d Sed	736	2,208	3,680	7,360	12,880	18,400
2d HT Bel Air (1950 only)	1,020	3,060	5,100	10,200	17,850	25,500
2d Conv	1,520	4,560	7,600	15,200	26,600	38,000
4d Woodie Wag (1949 only)	1,240	3,720	6,200	12,400	21,700	31,000
4d Mtl Sta Wag	920	2,760	4,600	9,200	16,100	23,000

1949-50 Fleetline DeLuxe, 6-cyl.

	6	5	4	3	2	1
2d Sed	776	2,328	3,880	7,760	13,580	19,400
4d Sed	780	2,340	3,900	7,800	13,650	19,500

1951-52 Styleline Special, 6-cyl.

	6	5	4	3	2	1
2d Bus Cpe	780	2,340	3,900	7,800	13,650	19,500
2d Spt Cpe	788	2,364	3,940	7,880	13,790	19,700
2d Sed	732	2,196	3,660	7,320	12,810	18,300
4d Sed	728	2,184	3,640	7,280	12,740	18,200

1951-52 Styleline DeLuxe, 6-cyl.

	6	5	4	3	2	1
2d Spt Cpe	840	2,520	4,200	8,400	14,700	21,000
2d Sed	752	2,256	3,760	7,520	13,160	18,800
4d Sed	752	2,256	3,760	7,520	13,160	18,800
2d HT Bel Air	1,000	3,000	5,000	10,000	17,500	25,000
2d Conv	1,560	4,680	7,800	15,600	27,300	39,000

1951-52 Fleetline Special, 6-cyl.

	6	5	4	3	2	1
2d Sed	696	2,088	3,480	6,960	12,180	17,400
4d Sed (1951 only)	692	2,076	3,460	6,920	12,110	17,300
4d Sta Wag	800	2,400	4,000	8,000	14,000	20,000

1951-52 Fleetline DeLuxe, 6-cyl.

	6	5	4	3	2	1
2d Sed	764	2,292	3,820	7,640	13,370	19,100
4d Sed (1951 only)	760	2,280	3,800	7,600	13,300	19,000

1953 Special 150, 6-cyl.

	6	5	4	3	2	1
2d Bus Cpe	720	2,160	3,600	7,200	12,600	18,000
2d Clb Cpe	732	2,196	3,660	7,320	12,810	18,300
2d Sed	688	2,064	3,440	6,880	12,040	17,200
4d Sed	684	2,052	3,420	6,840	11,970	17,100
4d Sta Wag	800	2,400	4,000	8,000	14,000	20,000

1953 DeLuxe 210, 6-cyl.

	6	5	4	3	2	1
2d Clb Cpe	800	2,400	4,000	8,000	14,000	20,000
2d Sed	740	2,220	3,700	7,400	12,950	18,500
4d Sed	736	2,208	3,680	7,360	12,880	18,400
2d HT	1,040	3,120	5,200	10,400	18,200	26,000
2d Conv	1,600	4,800	8,000	16,000	28,000	40,000
4d Sta Wag	820	2,460	4,100	8,200	14,350	20,500
4d 210 Townsman Sta Wag	840	2,520	4,200	8,400	14,700	21,000

1953 Bel Air

	6	5	4	3	2	1
2d Sed	784	2,352	3,920	7,840	13,720	19,600
4d Sed	780	2,340	3,900	7,800	13,650	19,500
2d HT	1,080	3,240	5,400	10,800	18,900	27,000
2d Conv	1,720	5,160	8,600	17,200	30,100	43,000

1954 Special 150, 6-cyl.

	6	5	4	3	2	1
2d Utl Sed	680	2,040	3,400	6,800	11,900	17,000
2d Sed	688	2,064	3,440	6,880	12,040	17,200
4d Sed	684	2,052	3,420	6,840	11,970	17,100
4d Sta Wag	800	2,400	4,000	8,000	14,000	20,000

1954 Special 210, 6-cyl.

	6	5	4	3	2	1
2d Sed	740	2,220	3,700	7,400	12,950	18,500
2d Sed Delray	800	2,400	4,000	8,000	14,000	20,000
4d Sed	736	2,208	3,680	7,360	12,880	18,400
4d Sta Wag	840	2,520	4,200	8,400	14,700	21,000

1954 Bel Air, 6-cyl.

	6	5	4	3	2	1
2d Sed	788	2,364	3,940	7,880	13,790	19,700
4d Sed	784	2,352	3,920	7,840	13,720	19,600
2d HT	1,080	3,240	5,400	10,800	18,900	27,000
2d Conv	1,760	5,280	8,800	17,600	30,800	44,000
4d Sta Wag	920	2,760	4,600	9,200	16,100	23,000

1955 Model 150, V-8

	6	5	4	3	2	1
2d Utl Sed	720	2,160	3,600	7,200	12,600	18,000
2d Sed	800	2,400	4,000	8,000	14,000	20,000
4d Sed	720	2,160	3,600	7,200	12,600	18,000
4d Sta Wag	760	2,280	3,800	7,600	13,300	19,000

1955 Model 210, V-8

	6	5	4	3	2	1
2d Sed	840	2,520	4,200	8,400	14,700	21,000
2d Sed Delray	880	2,640	4,400	8,800	15,400	22,000
4d Sed	720	2,160	3,600	7,200	12,600	18,000
2d HT	1,280	3,840	6,400	12,800	22,400	32,000
2d Sta Wag	820	2,460	4,100	8,200	14,350	20,500
4d Sta Wag	780	2,340	3,900	7,800	13,650	19,500

1955 Bel Air, V-8

	6	5	4	3	2	1
2d Sed	880	2,640	4,400	8,800	15,400	22,000
4d Sed	800	2,400	4,000	8,000	14,000	20,000
2d HT	1,440	4,320	7,200	14,400	25,200	36,000
2d Conv	2,440	7,320	12,200	24,400	42,700	61,000
2d Nomad	1,280	3,840	6,400	12,800	22,400	32,000
4d Sta Wag	880	2,640	4,400	8,800	15,400	22,000

NOTE: Add 10 percent for A/C; 15 percent for "Power-Pack". Deduct 10 percent for 6-cyl.

1956 Model 150, V-8

	6	5	4	3	2	1
2d Utl Sed	720	2,160	3,600	7,200	12,600	18,000
2d Sed	800	2,400	4,000	8,000	14,000	20,000
4d Sed	720	2,160	3,600	7,200	12,600	18,000
2d Sta Wag	800	2,400	4,000	8,000	14,000	20,000

1956 Model 210, V-8

	6	5	4	3	2	1
2d Sed	840	2,520	4,200	8,400	14,700	21,000
2d Sed Delray	880	2,640	4,400	8,800	15,400	22,000
4d Sed	720	2,160	3,600	7,200	12,600	18,000
4d HT	800	2,400	4,000	8,000	14,000	20,000
2d HT	1,240	3,720	6,200	12,400	21,700	31,000
2d Sta Wag	840	2,520	4,200	8,400	14,700	21,000
4d Sta Wag	760	2,280	3,800	7,600	13,300	19,000
4d 9P Sta Wag	780	2,340	3,900	7,800	13,650	19,500

	6	5	4	3	2	1

1956 Bel Air, V-8

	6	5	4	3	2	1
2d Sed	880	2,640	4,400	8,800	15,400	22,000
4d Sed	800	2,400	4,000	8,000	14,000	20,000
4d HT	840	2,520	4,200	8,400	14,700	21,000
2d HT	1,400	4,200	7,000	14,000	24,500	35,000
2d Conv	2,400	7,200	12,000	24,000	42,000	60,000
2d Nomad	1,240	3,720	6,200	12,400	21,700	31,000

NOTE: Add 10 percent for A/C; 15 percent for "Power-Pack". Deduct 10 percent for 6-cyl. Add 25 percent for dual 4 barrel carbs.

1957 Model 150, V-8

	6	5	4	3	2	1
2d Utl Sed	760	2,280	3,800	7,600	13,300	19,000
2d Sed	840	2,520	4,200	8,400	14,700	21,000
4d Sed	740	2,220	3,700	7,400	12,950	18,500
2d Sta Wag	820	2,460	4,100	8,200	14,350	20,500

1957 Model 210, V-8

	6	5	4	3	2	1
2d Sed	880	2,640	4,400	8,800	15,400	22,000
2d Sed Delray	920	2,760	4,600	9,200	16,100	23,000
4d Sed	820	2,460	4,100	8,200	14,350	20,500
4d HT	1,280	3,840	6,400	12,800	22,400	32,000
2d HT	1,280	3,840	6,400	12,800	22,400	32,000
2d Sta Wag	880	2,640	4,400	8,800	15,400	22,000
4d Sta Wag	800	2,400	4,000	8,000	14,000	20,000
4d 9P Sta Wag	820	2,460	4,100	8,200	14,350	20,500

1957 Bel Air, V-8

	6	5	4	3	2	1
2d Sed	920	2,760	4,600	9,200	16,100	23,000
4d Sed	820	2,460	4,100	8,200	14,350	20,500
4d HT	880	2,640	4,400	8,800	15,400	22,000
2d HT	1,480	4,440	7,400	14,800	25,900	37,000
2d Conv	2,520	7,560	12,600	25,200	44,100	63,000
2d Nomad	1,360	4,080	6,800	13,600	23,800	34,000
4d Sta Wag	920	2,760	4,600	9,200	16,100	23,000

NOTE: Add 10 percent for A/C; 15 percent for "Power-Pack" and 20 percent for F.I. Deduct 10 percent for 6-cyl. Add 25 percent for dual 4 barrel carbs.

1958 Biscayne, V-8

	6	5	4	3	2	1
2d Sed	680	2,040	3,400	6,800	11,900	17,000
4d Sed	664	1,992	3,320	6,640	11,620	16,600

1958 Bel Air, V-8

	6	5	4	3	2	1
2d Sed	760	2,280	3,800	7,600	13,300	19,000
4d Sed	740	2,220	3,700	7,400	12,950	18,500
4d HT	800	2,400	4,000	8,000	14,000	20,000
2d HT	920	2,760	4,600	9,200	16,100	23,000
2d Impala	1,640	4,920	8,200	16,400	28,700	41,000
2d Imp Conv	2,400	7,200	12,000	24,000	42,000	60,000

1959 Biscayne, V-8

	6	5	4	3	2	1
2d Utl Sed	640	1,920	3,200	6,400	11,200	16,000
2d Sed	652	1,956	3,260	6,520	11,410	16,300
4d Sed	648	1,944	3,240	6,480	11,340	16,200

1959 Bel Air, V-8

	6	5	4	3	2	1
2d Sed	672	2,016	3,360	6,720	11,760	16,800
4d Sed	668	2,004	3,340	6,680	11,690	16,700
4d HT	720	2,160	3,600	7,200	12,600	18,000

1959 Impala, V-8

	6	5	4	3	2	1
4d Sed	680	2,040	3,400	6,800	11,900	17,000
4d HT	760	2,280	3,800	7,600	13,300	19,000
2d HT	1,120	3,360	5,600	11,200	19,600	28,000
2d Conv	1,640	4,920	8,200	16,400	28,700	41,000

CHRYSLER

1950 Royal Series, 6-cyl., 125.5" wb

	6	5	4	3	2	1
4d Sed	650	2,000	3,350	6,700	11,800	16,800
2d Clb Cpe	700	2,150	3,600	7,200	12,600	18,000
4d T&C Sta Wag	1,100	3,350	5,600	11,200	19,600	28,000
4d Sta Wag	1,200	3,600	6,000	12,000	21,000	30,000

1950 Royal Series, 6-cyl., 139.5" wb

	6	5	4	3	2	1
4d Sed	700	2,150	3,600	7,200	12,600	18,000

1950 Windsor Series, 6-cyl., 125.5" wb

	6	5	4	3	2	1
2d Conv	1,150	3,500	5,800	11,600	20,300	29,000
2d HT	900	2,750	4,600	9,200	16,100	23,000
2d Clb Cpe	800	2,350	3,900	7,800	13,700	19,500
4d Sed	700	2,050	3,400	6,800	11,900	17,000
4d Trav Sed	700	2,050	3,400	6,850	12,000	17,100

1950 Windsor Series, 6-cyl., 139.5" wb

	6	5	4	3	2	1
4d Sed	750	2,300	3,800	7,600	13,300	19,000
4d Limo	850	2,500	4,200	8,400	14,700	21,000

1950 Saratoga, 8-cyl., 131.5" wb

	6	5	4	3	2	1
2d Clb Cpe	750	2,300	3,800	7,600	13,300	19,000
4d Sed	700	2,050	3,450	6,900	12,000	17,200

1950 New Yorker, 8-cyl., 131.5" wb

	6	5	4	3	2	1
2d Conv	1,300	3,950	6,600	13,200	23,100	33,000
2d HT	1,100	3,250	5,400	10,800	18,900	27,000
2d Clb Cpe	750	2,300	3,800	7,600	13,300	19,000
4d Sed	700	2,150	3,600	7,200	12,600	18,000

1950 Town & Country, 8-cyl., 131.5" wb

	6	5	4	3	2	1
2d HT	2,200	6,600	11,000	22,000	38,500	55,000

1951-52 Windsor Series, 6-cyl., 125.5" wb

	6	5	4	3	2	1
2d Clb Cpe	760	2,280	3,800	7,600	13,300	19,000
4d Sed	660	1,980	3,300	6,600	11,550	16,500
4d T&C Sta Wag	1,120	3,360	5,600	11,200	19,600	28,000

1951-52 Windsor Series, 6-cyl., 139.5" wb

	6	5	4	3	2	1
4d Sed	660	1,980	3,300	6,600	11,550	16,500

1951-52 Windsor DeLuxe, 6-cyl., 125.5" wb

	6	5	4	3	2	1
2d Conv	1,080	3,240	5,400	10,800	18,900	27,000
2d HT	920	2,760	4,600	9,200	16,100	23,000
2d Clb Cpe (1951 only)	760	2,280	3,800	7,600	13,300	19,000
4d Sed	664	1,992	3,320	6,640	11,620	16,600
4d Trav Sed	680	2,040	3,400	6,800	11,900	17,000

1951-52 Windsor DeLuxe, 6-cyl., 139.5" wb

	6	5	4	3	2	1
4d Sed	700	2,100	3,500	7,000	12,250	17,500
4d Limo	720	2,160	3,600	7,200	12,600	18,000

1951-52 Saratoga, V-8, 125.5" wb

	6	5	4	3	2	1
2d Conv (1952 only)	1,080	3,240	5,400	10,800	18,900	27,000
2d HT Nwpt (1952 only)	960	2,880	4,800	9,600	16,800	24,000
2d Clb Cpe (1951 only)	800	2,400	4,000	8,000	14,000	20,000
4d Sed	740	2,220	3,700	7,400	12,950	18,500
4d T&C Sta Wag (1951 only)	1,160	3,480	5,800	11,600	20,300	29,000

1951-52 Windsor or Saratoga, V-8, 125.5" wb

	6	5	4	3	2	1
4d Sed	780	2,340	3,900	7,800	13,650	19,500
2d Clb Cpe (1952 only)	780	2,340	3,900	7,800	13,650	19,500
4d T&C Sta Wag (1952 only)	1,080	3,240	5,400	10,800	18,900	27,000
4d Limo (1951 only)	860	2,580	4,300	8,600	15,050	21,500

1951-52 New Yorker, V-8, 131.5" wb

	6	5	4	3	2	1
2d Conv	1,200	3,600	6,000	12,000	21,000	30,000
2d HT	1,000	3,000	5,000	10,000	17,500	25,000
2d Clb Cpe (1951 only)	860	2,580	4,300	8,600	15,050	21,500
4d Sed	820	2,460	4,100	8,200	14,350	20,500
4d T&C Sta Wag (1951 only)	1,160	3,480	5,800	11,600	20,300	29,000

1953 Windsor Series, 6-cyl., 125.5" wb

	6	5	4	3	2	1
2d Clb Cpe	700	2,150	3,600	7,200	12,600	18,000
4d Sed	700	2,050	3,400	6,800	11,900	17,000
4d T&C Sta Wag	1,100	3,250	5,400	10,800	18,900	27,000

1953 Windsor Series, 6-cyl., 139.5" wb

	6	5	4	3	2	1
4d Sed	700	2,050	3,400	6,850	12,000	17,100

1953 Windsor DeLuxe Series, 6-cyl., 125.5" wb

	6	5	4	3	2	1
2d Conv	950	2,900	4,800	9,600	16,800	24,000
2d HT	900	2,650	4,400	8,800	15,400	22,000
4d Sed	700	2,100	3,450	6,900	12,100	17,300

1953 New Yorker, V-8, 125.5" wb

	6	5	4	3	2	1
2d Clb Cpe	800	2,350	3,900	7,800	13,700	19,500
2d HT	950	2,900	4,800	9,600	16,800	24,000
4d Sed	700	2,150	3,550	7,100	12,500	17,800
4d T&C Sta Wag	1,100	3,350	5,600	11,200	19,600	28,000
4d Sed	750	2,200	3,650	7,300	12,800	18,300

1953 New Yorker Deluxe, V-8, 125.5" wb

	6	5	4	3	2	1
2d Conv	1,150	3,500	5,800	11,600	20,300	29,000
2d HT	1,000	3,000	5,000	10,000	17,500	25,000
2d Clb Cpe	800	2,400	4,000	8,000	14,000	20,000
4d Sed	700	2,150	3,600	7,250	12,700	18,100

1953 Custom Imperial Series, V-8, 133.5" wb

	6	5	4	3	2	1
4d Sed	800	2,400	4,000	8,000	14,000	20,000
4d Twn Limo	900	2,650	4,400	8,800	15,400	22,000

1954 Windsor DeLuxe Series, 6-cyl., 125.5" wb

	6	5	4	3	2	1
2d Conv	1,150	3,500	5,800	11,600	20,300	29,000
2d HT	1,000	3,000	5,000	10,000	17,500	25,000
2d Clb Cpe	750	2,200	3,700	7,400	13,000	18,500
4d Sed	700	2,050	3,400	6,800	11,900	17,000
4d T&C Sta Wag	1,000	3,000	5,000	10,000	17,500	25,000

	6	5	4	3	2	1

1954 Windsor DeLuxe Series, 6-cyl., 139.5" wb

4d Sed	750	2,200	3,700	7,400	13,000	18,500

1954 New Yorker Series, V-8, 125.5" wb

2d HT	1,100	3,250	5,400	10,800	18,900	27,000
2d Clb Cpe	800	2,400	4,000	8,000	14,000	20,000
4d Sed	750	2,200	3,700	7,400	13,000	18,500
4d T&C Sta Wag	1,050	3,100	5,200	10,400	18,200	26,000

1954 New Yorker Series, V-8, 139.5" wb

4d Sed	750	2,300	3,800	7,600	13,300	19,000

1954 New Yorker DeLuxe Series, V-8, 125.5" wb

2d Conv	1,400	4,200	7,000	14,000	24,500	35,000
2d HT	1,100	3,350	5,600	11,200	19,600	28,000
2d Clb Cpe	750	2,300	3,800	7,600	13,300	19,000
4d Sed	800	2,350	3,900	7,800	13,700	19,500

1955 Windsor DeLuxe Series, V-8, 126" wb

2d Conv	1,300	3,950	6,600	13,200	23,100	33,000
2d HT Newport	1,050	3,100	5,200	10,400	18,200	26,000
2d HT Nassau	1,000	3,000	5,000	10,000	17,500	25,000
4d Sed	700	2,150	3,600	7,200	12,600	18,000
4d T&C Sta Wag	900	2,750	4,600	9,200	16,100	23,000

1955 New Yorker Deluxe Series, V-8, 126" wb

2d Conv	1,450	4,300	7,200	14,400	25,200	36,000
2d HT St. Regis	1,100	3,250	5,400	10,800	18,900	27,000
2d HT Newport	1,050	3,100	5,200	10,400	18,200	26,000
4d Sed	750	2,300	3,800	7,600	13,300	19,000
4d T&C Sta Wag	1,000	3,000	5,000	10,000	17,500	25,000

1955 300 Series, V-8, 126" wb

2d Spt Cpe	1,650	4,900	8,200	16,400	28,700	41,000

1956 Windsor Series, V-8

2d Conv	1,300	3,850	6,400	12,800	22,400	32,000
2d HT Newport	1,100	3,250	5,400	10,800	18,900	27,000
2d HT Nassau	1,050	3,100	5,200	10,400	18,200	26,000
4d HT	800	2,400	4,000	8,000	14,000	20,000
4d Sed	700	2,150	3,600	7,200	12,600	18,000
4d T&C Sta Wag	950	2,900	4,800	9,600	16,800	24,000

1956 New Yorker Series, V-8

2d Conv	1,400	4,200	7,000	14,000	24,500	35,000
2d HT St. Regis	1,150	3,500	5,800	11,600	20,300	29,000
2d HT Newport	1,100	3,350	5,600	11,200	19,600	28,000
4d HT	900	2,750	4,600	9,200	16,100	23,000
4d Sed	750	2,300	3,800	7,600	13,300	19,000
4d T&C Sta Wag	1,000	3,000	5,000	10,000	17,500	25,000

1956 300 Letter Series "B", V-8

2d HT	1,650	4,900	8,200	16,400	28,700	41,000

1957 Windsor Series, V-8

2d HT	1,000	3,000	5,000	10,000	17,500	25,000
4d HT	800	2,400	4,000	8,000	14,000	20,000
4d Sed	700	2,050	3,400	6,800	11,900	17,000
4d T&C Sta Wag	750	2,300	3,800	7,600	13,300	19,000

1957 Saratoga Series, V-8

2d HT	1,100	3,250	5,400	10,800	18,900	27,000
4d HT	900	2,650	4,400	8,800	15,400	22,000
4d Sed	700	2,100	3,500	7,000	12,300	17,500

1957 New Yorker Series, V-8

2d Conv	1,400	4,200	7,000	14,000	24,500	35,000
2d HT	1,200	3,600	6,000	12,000	21,000	30,000
4d HT	900	2,750	4,600	9,200	16,100	23,000
4d Sed	700	2,150	3,600	7,200	12,600	18,000
4d T&C Sta Wag	800	2,400	4,000	8,000	14,000	20,000

1957 300 Letter Series "C", V-8

2d Conv	2,200	6,600	11,000	22,000	38,500	55,000
2d HT	1,750	5,300	8,800	17,600	30,800	44,000

1958 Windsor Series, V-8

2d HT	950	2,900	4,800	9,600	16,800	24,000
4d HT	750	2,300	3,800	7,600	13,300	19,000
4d Sed	700	2,050	3,400	6,800	11,900	17,000
4d T&C Sta Wag	800	2,350	3,900	7,800	13,700	19,500

1958 Saratoga Series, V-8

2d HT	1,000	3,000	5,000	10,000	17,500	25,000
4d HT	800	2,400	4,000	8,000	14,000	20,000
4d Sed	700	2,150	3,600	7,200	12,600	18,000

	6	5	4	3	2	1

1958 New Yorker Series, V-8

2d Conv	1,500	4,450	7,400	14,800	25,900	37,000
2d HT	1,100	3,250	5,400	10,800	18,900	27,000
4d HT	850	2,500	4,200	8,400	14,700	21,000
4d Sed	750	2,300	3,800	7,600	13,300	19,000
4d 6P T&C Sta Wag	800	2,350	3,900	7,800	13,700	19,500
4d 9P T&C Sta Wag	800	2,350	3,950	7,900	13,800	19,700

1958 300 Letter Series "D"

2d Conv	2,150	6,500	10,800	21,600	37,800	54,000
2d HT	1,720	5,160	8,600	17,200	30,100	43,000

NOTE: Add 40 percent for EFI.

1959 Windsor Series, V-8

2d Conv	1,100	3,250	5,400	10,800	18,900	27,000
2d HT	900	2,650	4,400	8,800	15,400	22,000
4d HT	700	2,150	3,600	7,200	12,600	18,000
4d Sed	650	1,900	3,200	6,400	11,200	16,000

1959 Town & Country Series, V-8

4d 6P Sta Wag	700	2,100	3,500	7,000	12,300	17,500
4d 9P Sta Wag	650	2,000	3,350	6,700	11,700	16,700

1959 Saratoga Series, V-8

4d Sed	650	1,900	3,200	6,400	11,200	16,000
4d HT	750	2,300	3,800	7,600	13,300	19,000
2d HT	900	2,750	4,600	9,200	16,100	23,000

1959 New Yorker Series, V-8

2d Conv	1,400	4,200	7,000	14,000	24,500	35,000
2d HT	1,000	3,000	5,000	10,000	17,500	25,000
4d HT	800	2,400	4,000	8,000	14,000	20,000
4d Sed	650	2,000	3,300	6,600	11,600	16,500

1959 Town & Country, V-8

4d 6P Sta Wag	750	2,300	3,800	7,600	13,300	19,000
4d 9P Sta Wag	750	2,300	3,850	7,700	13,400	19,200

1959 300 Letter Series "E", V-8

2d Conv	2,050	6,100	10,200	20,400	35,700	51,000
2d HT	1,640	4,920	8,200	16,400	28,700	41,000

CORVETTE

1953

6-cyl. Conv	4,480	13,440	22,400	44,800	78,400	112,000

1954

6-cyl. Conv	2,800	8,400	14,000	28,000	49,000	70,000

NOTE: Add $1,800 & up for access. hardtop.

1955

6-cyl. Conv	2,880	8,640	14,400	28,800	50,400	72,000
8-cyl. Conv	3,000	9,000	15,000	30,000	52,500	75,000

NOTE: Add $1,800 & up for access. hardtop.

1956

Conv	2,840	8,520	14,200	28,400	49,700	71,000

NOTE: All post-1955 Corvettes are V-8 powered. Add $1,800 & up for removable hardtop. Add 20 percent for two 4 barrel carbs.

1957

Conv	2,880	8,640	14,400	28,800	50,400	72,000

NOTE: Add $1,800 for hardtop. Add 50 percent for F.I., 250 hp. Add 75 percent for F.I., 283 hp. Add 25 percent for two 4 barrel carbs, 245 hp. Add 35 percent for two 4 barrel carbs, 270 hp. Add 15 per

1958

Conv	2,440	7,320	12,200	24,400	42,700	61,000

NOTE: Add $1,800 for hardtop. Add 25 percent for two 4 barrel carbs, 245 hp. Add 35 percent for two 4 barrel carbs, 270 hp. Add 40 percent for F.I., 250 hp. Add 60 percent for F.I., 290 hp.

1959

Conv	2,080	6,240	10,400	20,800	36,400	52,000

NOTE: Add $1,800 for hardtop. Add 40 percent for F.I., 250 hp. Add 60 percent for F.I., 290 hp. Add 25 percent for two 4 barrel carbs, 245 hp. Add 35 percent for two 4 barrel carbs, 270 hp.

DESOTO

	6	5	4	3	2	1
1950 S-14 DeLuxe, 6-cyl.						
2d Clb Cpe	700	2,100	3,500	7,000	12,300	17,500
4d Sed	650	2,000	3,300	6,600	11,600	16,500
4d C-A Sed	650	2,000	3,350	6,700	11,700	16,700
1950 S-14 Custom, 6-cyl.						
2d Conv	1,100	3,350	5,600	11,200	19,600	28,000
2d HT Sptman	900	2,650	4,400	8,800	15,400	22,000
2d Clb Cpe	700	2,150	3,600	7,200	12,600	18,000
4d Sed	700	2,050	3,400	6,800	11,900	17,000
1951-52 DeLuxe, 6-cyl., 125.5" wb						
4d Sed	652	1,956	3,260	6,520	11,410	16,300
2d Clb Cpe	700	2,100	3,500	7,000	12,250	17,500
4d C-A Sed	652	1,956	3,260	6,520	11,410	16,300
1951-52 Custom, 6-cyl., 125.5" wb						
4d Sed	660	1,980	3,300	6,600	11,550	16,500
2d Clb Cpe	720	2,160	3,600	7,200	12,600	18,000
2d HT Sptman	960	2,880	4,800	9,600	16,800	24,000
2d Conv	1,120	3,360	5,600	11,200	19,600	28,000
1951-52 Firedome, V-8, 125.5" wb (1952 only)						
4d Sed	680	2,040	3,400	6,800	11,900	17,000
2d Clb Cpe	800	2,400	4,000	8,000	14,000	20,000
2d HT Sptman	1,000	3,000	5,000	10,000	17,500	25,000
2d Conv	1,240	3,720	6,200	12,400	21,700	31,000
1953-54 Firedome, V-8, 125.5" wb						
4d Sed	664	1,992	3,320	6,640	11,620	16,600
2d Clb Cpe	700	2,100	3,500	7,000	12,250	17,500
2d HT Sptman	1,000	3,000	5,000	10,000	17,500	25,000
2d Conv	1,240	3,720	6,200	12,400	21,700	31,000
1955 Firedome, V-8						
4d Sed	650	1,950	3,250	6,500	11,400	16,300
2d HT	900	2,750	4,600	9,200	16,100	23,000
2d HT Sptman	1,100	3,250	5,400	10,800	18,900	27,000
2d Conv	1,250	3,700	6,200	12,400	21,700	31,000
1955 Fireflite, V-8						
4d Sed	650	2,000	3,350	6,700	11,800	16,800
2d HT Sptman	1,100	3,350	5,600	11,200	19,600	28,000
2d Conv	1,300	3,850	6,400	12,800	22,400	32,000
1956 Firedome, V-8						
4d HT Sptman	850	2,500	4,200	8,400	14,700	21,000
2d HT Sev	1,000	3,000	5,000	10,000	17,500	25,000
2d HT Sptman	1,100	3,250	5,400	10,800	18,900	27,000
2d Conv	1,300	3,850	6,400	12,800	22,400	32,000
1956 Fireflite, V-8						
4d Sed	650	1,900	3,200	6,400	11,200	16,000
4d HT Sptman	850	2,500	4,200	8,400	14,700	21,000
2d HT Sptman	1,100	3,350	5,600	11,200	19,600	28,000
2d Conv	1,300	3,950	6,600	13,200	23,100	33,000
2d Conv IPC	1,600	4,800	8,000	16,000	28,000	40,000
1956 Adventurer						
2d HT	1,150	3,500	5,800	11,600	20,300	29,000
1957 Firesweep, V-8, 122" wb						
4d Sed	600	1,800	3,000	6,000	10,500	15,000
4d HT Sptman	700	2,150	3,600	7,200	12,600	18,000
2d HT Sptman	950	2,900	4,800	9,600	16,800	24,000
1957 Firedome, V-8, 126" wb						
4d Sed	550	1,700	2,800	5,600	9,800	14,000
4d HT Sptman	750	2,300	3,800	7,600	13,300	19,000
2d HT Sptman	1,000	3,000	5,000	10,000	17,500	25,000
2d Conv	1,300	3,950	6,600	13,200	23,100	33,000
1957 Fireflite, V-8, 126" wb						
4d Sed	600	1,750	2,900	5,800	10,200	14,500
4d HT Sptman	800	2,400	4,000	8,000	14,000	20,000
2d HT Sptman	1,050	3,100	5,200	10,400	18,200	26,000
2d Conv	1,550	4,700	7,800	15,600	27,300	39,000
1957 Fireflite Adventurer, 126" wb						
2d HT	1,440	4,320	7,200	14,400	25,200	36,000
2d Conv	2,000	6,000	10,000	20,000	35,000	50,000
1958 Firesweep, V-8						
4d Sed	600	1,800	3,000	6,000	10,500	15,000
4d HT Sptman	700	2,150	3,600	7,200	12,600	18,000
2d HT Sptman	850	2,500	4,200	8,400	14,700	21,000
2d Conv	1,360	4,080	6,800	13,600	23,800	34,000

	6	5	4	3	2	1
1958 Firedome, V-8						
4d Sed	600	1,800	3,050	6,100	10,600	15,200
4d HT Sptman	800	2,400	4,000	8,000	14,000	20,000
2d HT Sptman	900	2,650	4,400	8,800	15,400	22,000
2d Conv	1,400	4,200	7,000	14,000	24,500	35,000
1958 Fireflite, V-8						
4d Sed	600	1,850	3,100	6,200	10,900	15,500
4d HT Sptman	850	2,500	4,200	8,400	14,700	21,000
2d HT Sptman	950	2,900	4,800	9,600	16,800	24,000
2d Conv	1,550	4,700	7,800	15,600	27,300	39,000
1958 Adventurer, V-8						
2d HT	1,320	3,960	6,600	13,200	23,100	33,000
2d Conv	1,920	5,760	9,600	19,200	33,600	48,000
1959 Firesweep, V-8						
4d Sed	550	1,700	2,800	5,600	9,800	14,000
4d HT Sptman	700	2,150	3,600	7,200	12,600	18,000
2d HT Sptman	800	2,400	4,000	8,000	14,000	20,000
2d Conv	1,200	3,600	6,000	12,000	21,000	30,000
1959 Firedome, V-8						
4d Sed	600	1,750	2,900	5,800	10,200	14,500
4d HT Sptman	750	2,300	3,800	7,600	13,300	19,000
2d HT Sptman	850	2,500	4,200	8,400	14,700	21,000
2d Conv	1,240	3,720	6,200	12,400	21,700	31,000
1959 Fireflite, V-8						
4d Sed	600	1,800	3,000	6,000	10,500	15,000
4d HT Sptman	800	2,400	4,000	8,000	14,000	20,000
2d HT Sptman	900	2,650	4,400	8,800	15,400	22,000
2d Conv	1,360	4,080	6,800	13,600	23,800	34,000
1959 Adventurer, V-8						
2d HT	1,000	3,000	5,000	10,000	17,500	25,000
2d Conv	1,600	4,800	8,000	16,000	28,000	40,000

DODGE

	6	5	4	3	2	1
1950 Series D33 Wayfarer, 6-cyl., 115" wb						
2d Rds	1,200	3,600	6,000	12,000	21,000	30,000
2d Cpe	650	1,900	3,200	6,400	11,200	16,000
2d Sed	600	1,800	3,050	6,100	10,600	15,200
1950 Series D34 Meadowbrook, 6-cyl., 123.5" wb						
4d Sed	600	1,800	3,000	6,000	10,500	15,000
1950 Series D34 Coronet, 123.5" wb - 137.5" wb, (*)						
2d Conv	1,200	3,600	6,000	12,000	21,000	30,000
2d Clb Cpe	650	1,900	3,200	6,400	11,200	16,000
2d HT Dipl	800	2,400	4,000	8,000	14,000	20,000
4d Sed	600	1,800	3,050	6,100	10,600	15,200
1951-52 Wayfarer Series D41, 6-cyl., 115" wb						
2d Rds (1951 only)	1,120	3,360	5,600	11,200	19,600	28,000
2d Sed	560	1,680	2,800	5,600	9,800	14,000
2d Cpe	600	1,800	3,000	6,000	10,500	15,000
1951-52 Meadowbrook Series D42, 6-cyl., 123.5" wb						
4d Sed	580	1,740	2,900	5,800	10,150	14,500
1951-52 Coronet Series D42, 6-cyl., 123.5" wb						
4d Sed	588	1,764	2,940	5,880	10,290	14,700
2d Clb Cpe	624	1,872	3,120	6,240	10,920	15,600
2d HT Dipl	880	2,640	4,400	8,800	15,400	22,000
1953 Series D46 Meadowbrook, 6-cyl., 119" wb						
4d Sed	600	1,850	3,100	6,200	10,900	15,500
2d Clb Cpe	600	1,850	3,100	6,250	10,900	15,600
2d Sub	600	1,850	3,100	6,200	10,900	15,500
1953 Coronet, 6-cyl., 119" wb						
4d Sed	650	1,900	3,150	6,300	11,000	15,700
2d Clb Cpe	650	1,900	3,150	6,300	11,100	15,800
1953 Series D44 Coronet, V-8, 119" wb						
4d Sed	650	1,900	3,200	6,400	11,200	16,000
2d Clb Cpe	650	1,950	3,200	6,450	11,300	16,100
1953 Series D48 Coronet, V-8, 119" wb - 114" wb, (*)						
2d HT Dipl	850	2,500	4,200	8,400	14,700	21,000
2d Conv	1,100	3,350	5,600	11,200	19,600	28,000
2d Sta Wag (*)	700	2,050	3,400	6,800	11,900	17,000

	6	5	4	3	2	1

1954 Series D51-1 Meadowbrook, 6-cyl., 119" wb

	6	5	4	3	2	1
4d Sed	650	1,900	3,150	6,300	11,100	15,800
2d Clb Cpe	650	1,900	3,150	6,300	11,100	15,800

1954 Series D51-2 Coronet, 6-cyl., 119" wb

	6	5	4	3	2	1
4d Sed	650	1,900	3,200	6,350	11,100	15,900
2d Clb Cpe	650	1,900	3,200	6,400	11,200	16,000

1954 Series D52 Coronet, 6-cyl., 114" wb

	6	5	4	3	2	1
2d Sub	650	2,000	3,300	6,600	11,600	16,500
4d 6P Sta Wag	700	2,150	3,600	7,200	12,600	18,000
4d 8P Sta Wag	750	2,300	3,800	7,600	13,300	19,000

1954 Series D50-1 Meadowbrook, V-8, 119" wb

	6	5	4	3	2	1
4d Sed	650	1,900	3,150	6,300	11,100	15,800
2d Clb Cpe	650	1,900	3,200	6,400	11,200	16,000

1954 Series D50-2 Coronet, V-8, 119" wb

	6	5	4	3	2	1
4d Sed	650	1,950	3,250	6,500	11,400	16,300
2d Clb Cpe	650	2,000	3,300	6,600	11,600	16,500

1954 Series D53-2 Coronet, V-8, 114" wb

	6	5	4	3	2	1
2d Sub	650	1,950	3,250	6,500	11,400	16,300
4d 2S Sta Wag	750	2,200	3,700	7,400	13,000	18,500
4d 3S Sta Wag	800	2,350	3,900	7,800	13,700	19,500

1954 Series D50-3 Royal, V-8, 119" wb

	6	5	4	3	2	1
4d Sed	700	2,150	3,600	7,200	12,600	18,000
2d Clb Cpe	700	2,150	3,600	7,200	12,600	18,000

1954 Series D53-3 Royal, V-8, 114" wb

	6	5	4	3	2	1
2d HT	950	2,900	4,800	9,600	16,800	24,000
2d Conv	1,150	3,500	5,800	11,600	20,300	29,000
2d Pace Car Replica Conv	1,300	3,850	6,400	12,800	22,400	32,000

1955 Coronet, V-8, 120" wb

	6	5	4	3	2	1
4d Sed	650	1,900	3,150	6,300	11,100	15,800
2d Sed	650	1,900	3,150	6,300	11,000	15,700
2d HT	950	2,900	4,800	9,600	16,800	24,000

1955 Royal, V-8, 120" wb

	6	5	4	3	2	1
4d Sed	650	1,900	3,150	6,300	11,100	15,800
2d HT	1,000	3,000	5,000	10,000	17,500	25,000

1955 Custom Royal, V-8, 120" wb

	6	5	4	3	2	1
4d Sed	700	2,050	3,400	6,800	11,900	17,000
4d Lancer	800	2,400	4,000	8,000	14,000	20,000
2d HT	1,050	3,100	5,200	10,400	18,200	26,000
2d Conv	1,200	3,600	6,000	12,000	21,000	30,000

NOTE: Deduct 5 percent for 6-cyl. models. Add 10 percent for La-Femme.

1956 Coronet, V-8, 120" wb

	6	5	4	3	2	1
4d Sed	600	1,850	3,100	6,200	10,900	15,500
4d HT	700	2,050	3,400	6,800	11,900	17,000
2d Clb Sed	650	1,900	3,200	6,400	11,200	16,000
2d HT	900	2,750	4,600	9,200	16,100	23,000
2d Conv	1,300	3,850	6,400	12,800	22,400	32,000
2d Sub Sta Wag	700	2,050	3,400	6,800	11,900	17,000
4d 6P Sta Wag	700	2,050	3,450	6,900	12,000	17,200
4d 8P Sta Wag	700	2,100	3,500	7,000	12,300	17,500

NOTE: Deduct 5 percent for 6-cyl. models.

1956 Royal, V-8, 120" wb

	6	5	4	3	2	1
4d Sed	650	2,000	3,300	6,650	11,600	16,600
4d HT	700	2,150	3,600	7,200	12,600	18,000
2d HT	1,000	3,000	5,000	10,000	17,500	25,000
2d Sub Sta Wag	700	2,100	3,500	7,000	12,300	17,500
4d 6P Sta Wag	700	2,100	3,550	7,100	12,400	17,700
4d 8P Sta Wag	700	2,150	3,600	7,150	12,500	17,900

1956 Custom Royal, V-8, 120" wb

	6	5	4	3	2	1
4d Sed	650	2,000	3,350	6,700	11,700	16,700
4d HT	800	2,400	4,000	8,000	14,000	20,000
2d HT	1,100	3,250	5,400	10,800	18,900	27,000
2d Conv	1,400	4,200	7,000	14,000	24,500	35,000

NOTE: Add 30 percent for D500 option. Add 10 percent for Golden Lancer. Add 10 percent for La-Femme or Texan options.

1957 Coronet, V-8, 122" wb

	6	5	4	3	2	1
4d Sed	650	1,900	3,150	6,300	11,000	15,700
4d HT	650	2,000	3,300	6,600	11,600	16,500
2d Sed	650	1,900	3,150	6,300	11,100	15,800
2d HT	900	2,750	4,600	9,200	16,100	23,000

NOTE: Deduct 5 percent for 6-cyl. models.

1957 Coronet Lancer

	6	5	4	3	2	1
2d Conv	1,350	4,100	6,800	13,600	23,800	34,000

1957 Royal, V-8, 122" wb

	6	5	4	3	2	1
4d Sed	650	1,900	3,200	6,350	11,100	15,900
4d HT	700	2,100	3,500	7,000	12,300	17,500
2d HT	1,150	3,500	5,800	11,600	20,300	29,000

1957 Royal Lancer

	6	5	4	3	2	1
2d Conv	1,500	4,550	7,600	15,200	26,600	38,000

1957 Custom Royal, V-8, 122" wb

	6	5	4	3	2	1
4d Sed	650	1,900	3,200	6,400	11,200	16,000
4d HT	650	2,000	3,300	6,600	11,600	16,500
2d HT	1,200	3,600	6,000	12,000	21,000	30,000
4d 6P Sta Wag	650	1,900	3,200	6,400	11,200	16,000
4d 9P Sta Wag	650	1,950	3,250	6,500	11,300	16,200
2d Sub Sta Wag	650	2,000	3,300	6,600	11,600	16,500

1957 Custom Royal Lancer

	6	5	4	3	2	1
2d Conv	1,650	4,900	8,200	16,400	28,700	41,000

NOTE: Add 30 percent for D500 option.

1958 Coronet, V-8, 122" wb

	6	5	4	3	2	1
4d Sed	550	1,700	2,800	5,600	9,800	14,000
4d HT	600	1,800	3,050	6,100	10,600	15,200
2d Sed	550	1,700	2,800	5,650	9,850	14,100
2d HT	900	2,650	4,400	8,800	15,400	22,000
2d Conv	1,300	3,850	6,400	12,800	22,400	32,000

NOTE: Deduct 5 percent for 6-cyl. models.

1958 Royal

	6	5	4	3	2	1
4d Sed	600	1,750	2,900	5,800	10,200	14,500
4d HT	600	1,850	3,100	6,200	10,900	15,500
2d HT	1,000	3,000	5,000	10,000	17,500	25,000

1958 Custom Royal

	6	5	4	3	2	1
4d Sed	600	1,800	3,000	6,000	10,500	15,000
4d HT	650	1,900	3,200	6,400	11,200	16,000
2d HT	1,000	3,000	5,000	10,000	17,500	25,000
2d Conv	1,550	4,700	7,800	15,600	27,300	39,000

1959 Coronet

Eight cylinder models

	6	5	4	3	2	1
4d Sed	550	1,700	2,850	5,700	9,950	14,200
4d HT	650	1,900	3,150	6,300	11,000	15,700
2d Sed	550	1,700	2,850	5,700	10,000	14,300
2d HT	850	2,500	4,200	8,400	14,700	21,000
2d Conv	1,300	3,850	6,400	12,800	22,400	32,000

NOTE: Deduct 10 percent for 6-cyl. models.

1959 Royal

	6	5	4	3	2	1
4d Sed	550	1,700	2,800	5,650	9,850	14,100
4d HT	600	1,800	3,000	6,050	10,600	15,100
2d HT	900	2,650	4,400	8,800	15,400	22,000

1959 Custom Royal

	6	5	4	3	2	1
4d Sed	600	1,750	2,900	5,800	10,200	14,500
4d HT	600	1,850	3,100	6,200	10,900	15,500
2d HT	900	2,750	4,600	9,200	16,100	23,000
2d Conv	1,500	4,450	7,400	14,800	25,900	37,000

EDSEL

1958 Ranger Series, V-8, 118" wb

	6	5	4	3	2	1
2d Sed	550	1,700	2,800	5,650	9,850	14,100
4d Sed	550	1,700	2,800	5,600	9,800	14,000
4d HT	600	1,800	3,000	6,000	10,500	15,000
2d HT	700	2,100	3,500	7,000	12,300	17,500

1958 Pacer Series, V-8, 118" wb

	6	5	4	3	2	1
4d Sed	600	1,750	2,900	5,800	10,200	14,500
4d HT	600	1,850	3,100	6,200	10,900	15,500
2d HT	750	2,200	3,700	7,400	13,000	18,500
2d Conv	1,200	3,650	6,100	12,200	21,400	30,500

1958 Corsair Series, V-8, 124" wb

	6	5	4	3	2	1
4d HT	650	2,000	3,300	6,600	11,600	16,500
2d HT	800	2,350	3,900	7,800	13,700	19,500

1958 Citation Series, V-8, 124" wb

	6	5	4	3	2	1
4d HT	750	2,200	3,700	7,400	13,000	18,500
2d HT	850	2,600	4,300	8,600	15,000	21,500
2d Conv	1,400	4,250	7,100	14,200	24,900	35,500

NOTE: Deduct 5 percent for 6-cyl.

	6	5	4	3	2	1

1959 Ranger Series, V-8, 120" wb

	6	5	4	3	2	1
2d Sed	550	1,650	2,750	5,500	9,600	13,700
4d Sed	550	1,650	2,700	5,450	9,500	13,600
4d HT	600	1,800	3,000	6,000	10,500	15,000
2d HT	700	2,100	3,500	7,000	12,300	17,500

1959 Corsair Series, V-8, 120" wb

	6	5	4	3	2	1
4d Sed	550	1,700	2,800	5,600	9,800	14,000
4d HT	600	1,850	3,100	6,200	10,900	15,500
2d HT	750	2,200	3,700	7,400	13,000	18,500
2d Conv	1,200	3,550	5,900	11,800	20,700	29,500

1960 Ranger Series, V-8, 120" wb

	6	5	4	3	2	1
2d Sed	550	1,650	2,750	5,500	9,600	13,700
4d Sed	550	1,650	2,700	5,450	9,500	13,600
4d HT	600	1,800	3,000	6,000	10,500	15,000
2d HT	950	2,800	4,700	9,400	16,500	23,500
2d Conv	1,350	4,000	6,700	13,400	23,500	33,500

1960 Station Wagons, V-8, 120" wb

	6	5	4	3	2	1
4d 9P Vill	600	1,850	3,100	6,200	10,900	15,500
4d 6P Vill	650	1,900	3,200	6,400	11,200	16,000

NOTE: Deduct 5 percent for 6-cyl.

FORD

1949-50 DeLuxe, V-8, 114" wb

	6	5	4	3	2	1
2d Bus Cpe	800	2,400	4,000	8,000	14,000	20,000
2d Sed	720	2,160	3,600	7,200	12,600	18,000
4d Sed	720	2,160	3,600	7,200	12,600	18,000

1949-50 Custom DeLuxe, V-8, 114" wb

	6	5	4	3	2	1
2d Clb Cpe	840	2,520	4,200	8,400	14,700	21,000
2d Sed	780	2,340	3,900	7,800	13,650	19,500
4d Sed	780	2,340	3,900	7,800	13,650	19,500
2d Crest (1950 only)	880	2,640	4,400	8,800	15,400	22,000
2d Conv	1,280	3,840	6,400	12,800	22,400	32,000
2d Sta Wag	1,600	4,800	8,000	16,000	28,000	40,000

NOTE: Deduct 5 percent average for 6-cyl.

1951 DeLuxe, V-8, 114" wb

	6	5	4	3	2	1
2d Bus Cpe	800	2,400	4,000	8,000	14,000	20,000
2d Sed	750	2,300	3,800	7,600	13,300	19,000
4d Sed	750	2,300	3,800	7,600	13,300	19,000

1951 Custom DeLuxe, V-8, 114" wb

	6	5	4	3	2	1
2d Clb Cpe	900	2,650	4,400	8,800	15,400	22,000
2d Sed	850	2,500	4,200	8,400	14,700	21,000
4d Sed	850	2,500	4,200	8,400	14,700	21,000
2d Crest	900	2,750	4,600	9,200	16,100	23,000
2d HT	950	2,900	4,800	9,600	16,800	24,000
2d Conv	1,300	3,950	6,600	13,200	23,100	33,000
2d Sta Wag	1,600	4,850	8,100	16,200	28,400	40,500

NOTE: Deduct 5 percent average for 6-cyl.

1952-53 Customline, V-8, 115" wb

	6	5	4	3	2	1
2d Clb Cpe	800	2,400	4,000	8,000	14,000	20,000
2d Sed	740	2,220	3,700	7,400	12,950	18,500
4d Sed	736	2,208	3,680	7,360	12,880	18,400
4d Sta Wag	800	2,400	4,000	8,000	14,000	20,000

1952-53 Crestline, 8-cyl., 115" wb

	6	5	4	3	2	1
2d HT	940	2,820	4,700	9,400	16,450	23,500
2d Conv	1,160	3,480	5,800	11,600	20,300	29,000
4d Sta Wag	820	2,460	4,100	8,200	14,350	20,500

NOTE: Deduct 5 percent average for 6-cyl. Add 50 percent for 1953 Indy Pace Car replica convertible.

1954 Customline, V-8, 115.5" wb

	6	5	4	3	2	1
2d Clb Cpe	800	2,450	4,100	8,200	14,300	20,500
2d Sed	800	2,350	3,900	7,800	13,700	19,500
4d Sed	800	2,350	3,900	7,750	13,600	19,400
2/4d Sta Wag	850	2,500	4,200	8,400	14,700	21,000

1954 Crestline, V-8, 115.5" wb

	6	5	4	3	2	1
4d Sed	800	2,350	3,900	7,800	13,700	19,500
2d HT	1,000	3,000	5,000	10,000	17,500	25,000
2d Sky Cpe	1,250	3,700	6,200	12,400	21,700	31,000
2d Conv	1,300	3,950	6,600	13,200	23,100	33,000
4d Sta Wag	900	2,650	4,400	8,800	15,400	22,000

NOTE: Deduct 5 percent average for 6-cyl.

1955 Customline, V-8, 115.5" wb

	6	5	4	3	2	1
2d Sed	650	1,950	3,250	6,500	11,400	16,300
4d Sed	650	1,950	3,300	6,550	11,500	16,400

1955 Fairlane, V-8, 115.5" wb

	6	5	4	3	2	1
2d Sed	700	2,100	3,550	7,100	12,400	17,700
4d Sed	700	2,150	3,550	7,100	12,500	17,800
2d HT Vic	960	2,880	4,800	9,600	16,800	24,000
2d Crn Vic	1,300	3,950	6,600	13,200	23,100	33,000
2d Crn Vic Plexi-top	1,450	4,300	7,200	14,400	25,200	36,000
2d Conv	1,650	4,900	8,200	16,400	28,700	41,000

1955 Station Wagon, V-8, 115.5" wb

	6	5	4	3	2	1
2d Custom Ran Wag	750	2,300	3,800	7,600	13,300	19,000
2d Ran Wag	750	2,200	3,700	7,400	13,000	18,500
4d Ctry Sed Customline	750	2,300	3,800	7,600	13,300	19,000
4d Ctry Sed Fairlane	800	2,400	4,000	8,000	14,000	20,000
4d Ctry Sq	850	2,500	4,200	8,400	14,700	21,000

NOTE: Deduct 5 percent average for 6-cyl.

1956 Customline, V-8, 115.5" wb

	6	5	4	3	2	1
2d Sed	650	2,000	3,300	6,600	11,600	16,500
4d Sed	650	1,950	3,300	6,550	11,500	16,400
2d HT Vic	900	2,650	4,400	8,800	15,400	22,000

1956 Fairlane, V-8, 115.5" wb

	6	5	4	3	2	1
2d Sed	700	2,150	3,550	7,100	12,500	17,800
4d Sed	700	2,150	3,550	7,100	12,400	17,700
4d HT Vic	950	2,900	4,800	9,600	16,800	24,000
2d HT Vic	1,150	3,500	5,800	11,600	20,300	29,000
2d Crn Vic	1,300	3,850	6,400	12,800	22,400	32,000
2d Crn Vic Plexi-top	1,450	4,300	7,200	14,400	25,200	36,000
2d Conv	1,750	5,300	8,800	17,600	30,800	44,000

1956 Station Wagons, V-8, 115.5" wb

	6	5	4	3	2	1
2d Ran Wag	700	2,150	3,600	7,200	12,600	18,000
2d Parklane	900	2,750	4,600	9,200	16,100	23,000
4d Ctry Sed Customline	750	2,300	3,800	7,600	13,300	19,000
4d Ctry Sed Fairlane	800	2,400	4,000	8,000	14,000	20,000
4d Ctry Sq	850	2,500	4,200	8,400	14,700	21,000

NOTE: Deduct 5 percent average for 6-cyl. Add 10 percent for "T-Bird Special" V-8.

1957 Custom, V-8, 116" wb

	6	5	4	3	2	1
2d Bus Cpe	500	1,450	2,400	4,850	8,450	12,100
2d Sed	500	1,500	2,500	4,950	8,700	12,400
4d Sed	500	1,500	2,450	4,900	8,600	12,300

1957 Custom 300, V-8, 116" wb

	6	5	4	3	2	1
2d Sed	600	1,800	3,000	6,000	10,500	15,000
4d Sed	500	1,500	2,500	5,050	8,800	12,600

1957 Fairlane, V-8, 118" wb

	6	5	4	3	2	1
2d Sed	600	1,800	3,000	6,050	10,600	15,100
4d Sed	600	1,800	3,000	6,000	10,500	15,000
4d HT Vic	850	2,500	4,200	8,400	14,700	21,000
2d Vic HT	900	2,750	4,600	9,200	16,100	23,000

1957 Fairlane 500, V-8, 118" wb

	6	5	4	3	2	1
2d Sed	600	1,850	3,050	6,100	10,700	15,300
4d Sed	600	1,800	3,050	6,100	10,600	15,200
4d HT Vic	850	2,500	4,200	8,400	14,700	21,000
2d HT Vic	1,000	3,000	5,000	10,000	17,500	25,000
2d Conv	1,500	4,450	7,400	14,800	25,900	37,000
2d Sky HT Conv	1,650	4,900	8,200	16,400	28,700	41,000

1957 Station Wagons, 8-cyl., 116" wb

	6	5	4	3	2	1
2d Ran Wag	650	1,900	3,200	6,400	11,200	16,000
2d DeL Rio Ran	650	2,000	3,300	6,600	11,600	16,500
4d Ctry Sed	750	2,300	3,800	7,600	13,300	19,000
4d Ctry Sq	700	2,150	3,600	7,200	12,600	18,000

NOTE: Deduct 5 percent average for 6-cyl. Add 20 percent for "T-Bird Special" V-8 (Code E). Add 30 percent for Supercharged V-8 (Code F).

1958 Fairlane, V-8, 116.03" wb

	6	5	4	3	2	1
2d Sed	450	1,400	2,300	4,600	8,050	11,500
4d Sed	450	1,350	2,300	4,550	8,000	11,400
4d HT	750	2,300	3,800	7,600	13,300	19,000
2d HT	800	2,400	4,000	8,000	14,000	20,000

1958 Fairlane 500, V-8, 118.04" wb

	6	5	4	3	2	1
2d Sed	500	1,500	2,450	4,900	8,600	12,300
4d Sed	500	1,450	2,450	4,900	8,550	12,200
4d HT	800	2,400	4,000	8,000	14,000	20,000
2d HT	900	2,650	4,400	8,800	15,400	22,000
2d Conv	1,150	3,500	5,800	11,600	20,300	29,000
2d Sky HT Conv	1,400	4,200	7,000	14,000	24,500	35,000

1958 Station Wagons, V-8, 116.03" wb

	6	5	4	3	2	1
2d Ran	650	1,900	3,150	6,300	11,000	15,700
4d Ran	600	1,850	3,100	6,200	10,900	15,500
4d Ctry Sed	650	2,000	3,300	6,600	11,600	16,500
2d DeL Rio Ran	700	2,050	3,400	6,800	11,900	17,000
4d Ctry Sq	700	2,100	3,500	7,000	12,300	17,500

NOTE: Deduct 5 percent average for 6-cyl.

	6	5	4	3	2	1

1959 Fairlane, V-8, 118" wb

	6	5	4	3	2	1
2d Sed	350	1,050	1,800	3,550	6,250	8,900
4d Sed	350	1,050	1,750	3,500	6,150	8,800

1959 Fairlane 500, V-8, 118" wb

	6	5	4	3	2	1
2d Sed	450	1,350	2,200	4,450	7,750	11,100
4d Sed	450	1,300	2,200	4,400	7,700	11,000
4d HT	750	2,200	3,700	7,400	13,000	18,500
2d HT	850	2,600	4,300	8,600	15,000	21,500
2d Sun Conv	1,300	3,950	6,600	13,200	23,100	33,000
2d Sky HT Conv	1,700	5,150	8,600	17,200	30,100	43,000

1959 Galaxie, V-8, 118" wb

	6	5	4	3	2	1
2d Sed	450	1,350	2,250	4,500	7,900	11,300
4d Sed	450	1,350	2,250	4,500	7,850	11,200
4d HT	800	2,350	3,900	7,800	13,700	19,500
2d HT	900	2,700	4,500	9,000	15,700	22,500
2d Sun Conv	1,300	3,950	6,600	13,200	23,100	33,000
2d Sky HT Conv	1,650	4,900	8,200	16,400	28,700	41,000

1959 Station Wagons, V-8, 118" wb

	6	5	4	3	2	1
2d Ran	500	1,500	2,500	5,000	8,750	12,500
4d Ran	650	1,900	3,200	6,400	11,200	16,000
2d Ctry Sed	700	2,050	3,400	6,800	11,900	17,000
4d Ctry Sed	650	2,000	3,300	6,600	11,600	16,500
4d Ctry Sq	700	2,050	3,400	6,800	11,900	17,000

NOTE: Deduct 5 percent average for 6-cyl.

HUDSON

1950 Commodore Series 504, 8-cyl., 124" wb

	6	5	4	3	2	1
2d Clb Cpe	840	2,520	4,200	8,400	14,700	21,000
2d Conv	1,760	5,280	8,800	17,600	30,800	44,000
4d Sed	720	2,160	3,600	7,200	12,600	18,000

1951 Commodore Custom Series 6A, 6-cyl., 124" wb

	6	5	4	3	2	1
2d Clb Cpe	820	2,460	4,100	8,200	14,350	20,500
2d Hlywd HT	960	2,880	4,800	9,600	16,800	24,000
2d Conv	1,640	4,920	8,200	16,400	28,700	41,000
4d Sed	784	2,352	3,920	7,840	13,720	19,600

1951 Hornet Series 7A, 6-cyl., 124" wb

	6	5	4	3	2	1
2d Clb Cpe	840	2,520	4,200	8,400	14,700	21,000
2d Hlywd HT	1,000	3,000	5,000	10,000	17,500	25,000
2d Conv	1,720	5,160	8,600	17,200	30,100	43,000
4d Sed	804	2,412	4,020	8,040	14,070	20,100

1951 Commodore Custom Series 8A, 8-cyl., 124" wb

	6	5	4	3	2	1
2d Clb Cpe	860	2,580	4,300	8,600	15,050	21,500
2d Hlywd HT	1,040	3,120	5,200	10,400	18,200	26,000
2d Conv	1,760	5,280	8,800	17,600	30,800	44,000
4d Sed	824	2,472	4,120	8,240	14,420	20,600

1952 Commodore Series 6B, 6-cyl., 124" wb

	6	5	4	3	2	1
2d Clb Cpe	764	2,292	3,820	7,640	13,370	19,100
2d Hlywd HT	880	2,640	4,400	8,800	15,400	22,000
2d Conv	1,600	4,800	8,000	16,000	28,000	40,000
4d Sed	720	2,160	3,600	7,200	12,600	18,000

1952 Hornet Series 7B, 6-cyl., 124" wb

	6	5	4	3	2	1
2d Clb Cpe	772	2,316	3,860	7,720	13,510	19,300
2d Hlywd HT	920	2,760	4,600	9,200	16,100	23,000
2d Conv	1,640	4,920	8,200	16,400	28,700	41,000
4d Sed	724	2,172	3,620	7,240	12,670	18,100

1952 Commodore Series 8B, 8-cyl., 124" wb

	6	5	4	3	2	1
2d Clb Cpe	776	2,328	3,880	7,760	13,580	19,400
2d Hlywd HT	960	2,880	4,800	9,600	16,800	24,000
2d Conv	1,680	5,040	8,400	16,800	29,400	42,000
4d Sed	724	2,172	3,620	7,240	12,670	18,100

1953 Super Jet Series 2C, 6-cyl., 105" wb

	6	5	4	3	2	1
2d Clb Sed	660	1,980	3,300	6,600	11,550	16,500
4d Sed	664	1,992	3,320	6,640	11,620	16,600

1953 Wasp Series 4C, 6-cyl., 119" wb

	6	5	4	3	2	1
2d Clb Cpe	712	2,136	3,560	7,120	12,460	17,800
2d Sed	660	1,980	3,300	6,600	11,550	16,500
4d Sed	664	1,992	3,320	6,640	11,620	16,600

1953 Super Wasp Series 5C, 6-cyl., 119" wb

	6	5	4	3	2	1
2d Clb Cpe	720	2,160	3,600	7,200	12,600	18,000
2d Hlywd HT	840	2,520	4,200	8,400	14,700	21,000
2d Conv	1,560	4,680	7,800	15,600	27,300	39,000
2d Sed	664	1,992	3,320	6,640	11,620	16,600
4d Sed	668	2,004	3,340	6,680	11,690	16,700

1953 Hornet Series 7C, 6-cyl., 124" wb

	6	5	4	3	2	1
2d Clb Cpe	760	2,280	3,800	7,600	13,300	19,000
2d Hlywd HT	904	2,712	4,520	9,040	15,820	22,600
2d Conv	1,680	5,040	8,400	16,800	29,400	42,000
4d Sed	720	2,160	3,600	7,200	12,600	18,000

1954 Jet Series 1D, 6-cyl., 105" wb

	6	5	4	3	2	1
2d Utl Sed	640	1,920	3,200	6,400	11,200	16,000
2d Clb Sed	660	1,980	3,300	6,600	11,550	16,500
4d Sed	656	1,968	3,280	6,560	11,480	16,400

1954 Super Jet Series 2D, 6-cyl., 105" wb

	6	5	4	3	2	1
2d Clb Sed	680	2,040	3,400	6,800	11,900	17,000
4d Sed	676	2,028	3,380	6,760	11,830	16,900

1954 Jet Liner Series 3D, 6-cyl., 105" wb

	6	5	4	3	2	1
2d Clb Sed	688	2,064	3,440	6,880	12,040	17,200
4d Sed	684	2,052	3,420	6,840	11,970	17,100

1954 Wasp Series 4D, 6-cyl., 119" wb

	6	5	4	3	2	1
2d Clb Cpe	700	2,100	3,500	7,000	12,250	17,500
2d Clb Sed	652	1,956	3,260	6,520	11,410	16,300
4d Sed	656	1,968	3,280	6,560	11,480	16,400

1954 Super Wasp Series 5D, 6-cyl., 119" wb

	6	5	4	3	2	1
2d Clb Cpe	708	2,124	3,540	7,080	12,390	17,700
2d Hlywd HT	800	2,400	4,000	8,000	14,000	20,000
2d Conv	1,600	4,800	8,000	16,000	28,000	40,000
2d Clb Sed	664	1,992	3,320	6,640	11,620	16,600
4d Sed	660	1,980	3,300	6,600	11,550	16,500

1954 Hornet Special Series 6D, 6-cyl., 124" wb

	6	5	4	3	2	1
2d Clb Cpe	760	2,280	3,800	7,600	13,300	19,000
2d Clb Sed	684	2,052	3,420	6,840	11,970	17,100
4d Sed	696	2,088	3,480	6,960	12,180	17,400

1954 Hornet Series 7D, 6-cyl., 124" wb

	6	5	4	3	2	1
2d Clb Cpe	800	2,400	4,000	8,000	14,000	20,000
2d Hlywd HT	880	2,640	4,400	8,800	15,400	22,000
2d Brgm Conv	1,720	5,160	8,600	17,200	30,100	43,000
4d Sed	704	2,112	3,520	7,040	12,320	17,600

1954 Italia, 6-cyl.

	6	5	4	3	2	1
2d Cpe	1,440	4,320	7,200	14,400	25,200	36,000

1955 Super Wasp, 6-cyl., 114" wb

	6	5	4	3	2	1
4d Sed	620	1,860	3,100	6,200	10,850	15,500

1955 Custom Wasp, 6-cyl., 114" wb

	6	5	4	3	2	1
2d Hlywd HT	800	2,400	4,000	8,000	14,000	20,000
4d Sed	624	1,872	3,120	6,240	10,920	15,600

1955 Hornet Super, 6-cyl., 121" wb

	6	5	4	3	2	1
4d Sed	640	1,920	3,200	6,400	11,200	16,000

1955 Hornet Custom, 6-cyl., 121" wb

	6	5	4	3	2	1
2d Hlywd HT	840	2,520	4,200	8,400	14,700	21,000
4d Sed	660	1,980	3,300	6,600	11,550	16,500

1955 Italia, 6-cyl.

	6	5	4	3	2	1
2d Cpe	1,440	4,320	7,200	14,400	25,200	36,000

NOTE: Add 5 percent for V-8. For Hudson Rambler prices see Nash section same year.

1956 Super Wasp, 6-cyl., 114" wb

	6	5	4	3	2	1
4d Sed	600	1,800	3,000	6,000	10,500	15,000

1956 Super Hornet, 6-cyl., 121" wb

	6	5	4	3	2	1
4d Sed	640	1,920	3,200	6,400	11,200	16,000

1956 Custom Hornet, 6-cyl., 121" wb

	6	5	4	3	2	1
2d Hlywd HT	880	2,640	4,400	8,800	15,400	22,000
4d Sed	680	2,040	3,400	6,800	11,900	17,000

1956 Hornet Super Special, 8-cyl., 114" wb

	6	5	4	3	2	1
2d Hlywd HT	920	2,760	4,600	9,200	16,100	23,000
4d Sed	688	2,064	3,440	6,880	12,040	17,200

1956 Hornet Custom, 8-cyl., 121" wb

	6	5	4	3	2	1
2d Hlywd HT	960	2,880	4,800	9,600	16,800	24,000
4d Sed	700	2,100	3,500	7,000	12,250	17,500

NOTE: For Hudson Rambler prices see Nash section same year.

1957 Hornet Super, 8-cyl., 121" wb

	6	5	4	3	2	1
2d Hlywd HT	920	2,760	4,600	9,200	16,100	23,000
4d Sed	740	2,220	3,700	7,400	12,950	18,500

	6	5	4	3	2	1

1957 Hornet Custom, 8-cyl., 121" wb

	6	5	4	3	2	1
2d Hlywd HT	960	2,880	4,800	9,600	16,800	24,000
4d Sed	780	2,340	3,900	7,800	13,650	19,500

NOTE: For Hudson Rambler prices see Nash section same year.

KAISER

1949-50 DeLuxe, 6-cyl.

4d Sed	812	2,436	4,060	8,120	14,210	20,300
4d Conv Sed	1,800	5,400	9,000	18,000	31,500	45,000

1949-50 Vagabond, 6-cyl.

4d Sed	960	2,880	4,800	9,600	16,800	24,000

1949-50 Virginian, 6-cyl.

4d Sed HT	1,280	3,840	6,400	12,800	22,400	32,000

1951 Special, 6-cyl.

4d Sed	800	2,400	4,000	8,000	14,000	20,000
4d Trav Sed	812	2,436	4,060	8,120	14,210	20,300
2d Sed	804	2,412	4,020	8,040	14,070	20,100
2d Trav Sed	820	2,460	4,100	8,200	14,350	20,500
2d Bus Cpe	880	2,640	4,400	8,800	15,400	22,000

1951 DeLuxe

4d Sed	816	2,448	4,080	8,160	14,280	20,400
4d Trav Sed	824	2,472	4,120	8,240	14,420	20,600
2d Sed	820	2,460	4,100	8,200	14,350	20,500
2d Trav Sed	828	2,484	4,140	8,280	14,490	20,700
2d Clb Cpe	960	2,880	4,800	9,600	16,800	24,000

1952 Kaiser DeLuxe, 6-cyl.

4d Sed	800	2,400	4,000	8,000	14,000	20,000
Ta Sed	820	2,460	4,100	8,200	14,350	20,500
2d Sed	800	2,400	4,000	8,000	14,000	20,000
2d Trav	840	2,520	4,200	8,400	14,700	21,000
2d Bus Cpe	940	2,820	4,700	9,400	16,450	23,500

1952 Kaiser Manhattan, 6-cyl.

4d Sed	860	2,580	4,300	8,600	15,050	21,500
2d Sed	880	2,640	4,400	8,800	15,400	22,000
2d Clb Cpe	960	2,880	4,800	9,600	16,800	24,000

1952 Virginian, 6-cyl.

4d Sed	820	2,460	4,100	8,200	14,350	20,500
2d Sed	824	2,472	4,120	8,240	14,420	20,600
2d Clb Cpe	920	2,760	4,600	9,200	16,100	23,000

1953 Carolina, 6-cyl.

2d Sed	812	2,436	4,060	8,120	14,210	20,300
4d Sed	808	2,424	4,040	8,080	14,140	20,200

1953 Deluxe

2d Clb Sed	820	2,460	4,100	8,200	14,350	20,500
4d Trav Sed	824	2,472	4,120	8,240	14,420	20,600
4d Sed	816	2,448	4,080	8,160	14,280	20,400

1953 Manhattan, 6-cyl.

2d Clb Sed	868	2,604	4,340	8,680	15,190	21,700
4d Sed	864	2,592	4,320	8,640	15,120	21,600

1953 Dragon 4d Sed, 6-cyl.

4d Sed	1,040	3,120	5,200	10,400	18,200	26,000

1954 Early Special, 6-cyl.

4d Sed	864	2,592	4,320	8,640	15,120	21,600
2d Clb Sed	868	2,604	4,340	8,680	15,190	21,700

1954 Late Special, 6-cyl.

4d Sed	860	2,580	4,300	8,600	15,050	21,500
2d Clb Sed	864	2,592	4,320	8,640	15,120	21,600

1954 Manhattan, 6-cyl.

4d Sed	880	2,640	4,400	8,800	15,400	22,000
2d Clb Sed	888	2,664	4,440	8,880	15,540	22,200

1954 Kaiser Darrin Spts Car, 6-cyl.

2d Spt Car	1,680	5,040	8,400	16,800	29,400	42,000

1955 Manhattan, 6-cyl.

4d Sed	900	2,700	4,500	9,000	15,750	22,500
2d Clb Sed	904	2,712	4,520	9,040	15,820	22,600

LINCOLN

	6	5	4	3	2	1

1949-50 Cosmopolitan, V-8, 125" wb

	6	5	4	3	2	1
4d Town Sed (1949 only)	960	2,880	4,800	9,600	16,800	24,000
4d Spt Sed	980	2,940	4,900	9,800	17,150	24,500
2d Cpe	1,080	3,240	5,400	10,800	18,900	27,000
2d Capri (1950 only)	1,240	3,720	6,200	12,400	21,700	31,000
2d Conv	1,440	4,320	7,200	14,400	25,200	36,000

1951 Cosmopolitan, V-8, 125" wb

4d Spt Sed	1,000	3,000	5,000	10,000	17,500	25,000
2d Cpe	1,100	3,250	5,400	10,800	18,900	27,000
2d Capri	1,200	3,600	6,000	12,000	21,000	30,000
2d Conv	1,500	4,450	7,400	14,800	25,900	37,000

1952-53 Cosmopolitan Model BH, V-8, 123" wb

4d Sed	920	2,760	4,600	9,200	16,100	23,000
2d HT	1,120	3,360	5,600	11,200	19,600	28,000

1952-53 Capri, V-8, 123" wb

4d Sed	960	2,880	4,800	9,600	16,800	24,000
2d HT	1,160	3,480	5,800	11,600	20,300	29,000
2d Conv	1,480	4,440	7,400	14,800	25,900	37,000

1954 V-8, 123" wb

4d Sed	900	2,750	4,600	9,200	16,100	23,000
2d HT	1,150	3,500	5,800	11,600	20,300	29,000

1954 Capri, V-8, 123" wb

4d Sed	900	2,750	4,600	9,200	16,100	23,000
2d HT	1,250	3,700	6,200	12,400	21,700	31,000
2d Conv	1,500	4,550	7,600	15,200	26,600	38,000

1955 V-8, 123" wb

4d Sed	900	2,750	4,600	9,200	16,100	23,000
2d HT	1,100	3,350	5,600	11,200	19,600	28,000

1955 Capri, V-8, 123" wb

4d Sed	950	2,800	4,700	9,400	16,500	23,500
2d HT	1,200	3,600	6,000	12,000	21,000	30,000
2d Conv	1,650	4,900	8,200	16,400	28,700	41,000

1956 Capri, V-8, 126" wb

4d Sed	950	2,800	4,700	9,400	16,500	23,500
2d HT	1,300	3,950	6,600	13,200	23,100	33,000

1956 Premiere, V-8, 126" wb

4d Sed	950	2,900	4,800	9,600	16,800	24,000
2d HT	1,500	4,550	7,600	15,200	26,600	38,000
2d Conv	1,900	5,750	9,600	19,200	33,600	48,000

1956 Continental Mk II, V-8, 126" wb

2d HT	1,950	5,900	9,800	19,600	34,300	49,000

1957 Capri, V-8, 126" wb

4d Sed	800	2,400	4,000	8,000	14,000	20,000
4d HT	900	2,650	4,400	8,800	15,400	22,000
2d HT	1,200	3,600	6,000	12,000	21,000	30,000

1957 Premiere, V-8, 126" wb

4d Sed	850	2,500	4,200	8,400	14,700	21,000
4d HT	900	2,750	4,600	9,200	16,100	23,000
2d HT	1,300	3,850	6,400	12,800	22,400	32,000
2d Conv	1,850	5,500	9,200	18,400	32,200	46,000

1957 Continental Mk II, V-8, 126" wb

2d HT	1,950	5,900	9,800	19,600	34,300	49,000

1958-59 Capri, V-8, 131" wb

4d Sed	680	2,040	3,400	6,800	11,900	17,000
4d HT	760	2,280	3,800	7,600	13,300	19,000
2d HT	880	2,640	4,400	8,800	15,400	22,000

1958-59 Premiere, V-8, 131" wb

4d Sed	720	2,160	3,600	7,200	12,600	18,000
4d HT	800	2,400	4,000	8,000	14,000	20,000
2d HT	920	2,760	4,600	9,200	16,100	23,000

1958-59 Continental Mk III and IV, V-8, 131" wb

4d Sed	800	2,400	4,000	8,000	14,000	20,000
4d HT	880	2,640	4,400	8,800	15,400	22,000
2d HT	1,000	3,000	5,000	10,000	17,500	25,000
2d Conv	1,280	3,840	6,400	12,800	22,400	32,000
4d Town Car (1959 only)	1,000	3,000	5,000	10,000	17,500	25,000
4d Limo (1959 only)	1,040	3,120	5,200	10,400	18,200	26,000

MERCURY

1949-50 Series OCM, V-8, 118" wb

	6	5	4	3	2	1
2d Conv	1,520	4,560	7,600	15,200	26,600	38,000
2d Cpe	1,160	3,480	5,800	11,600	20,300	29,000
2d Clb Cpe	1,200	3,600	6,000	12,000	21,000	30,000
2d Mon Cpe (1950 only)	1,240	3,720	6,200	12,400	21,700	31,000
4d Sed	800	2,400	4,000	8,000	14,000	20,000
2d Sta Wag	1,400	4,200	7,000	14,000	24,500	35,000

1951 Mercury, V-8, 118" wb

	6	5	4	3	2	1
4d Sed	800	2,450	4,100	8,200	14,300	20,500
2d Cpe	1,200	3,600	6,000	12,000	21,000	30,000
2d Conv	1,500	4,450	7,400	14,800	25,900	37,000
2d Sta Wag	1,420	4,260	7,100	14,200	24,850	35,500

1951 Monterey, V-8, 118" wb

	6	5	4	3	2	1
2d Clth Cpe	1,300	3,850	6,400	12,800	22,400	32,000
2d Lthr Cpe	1,300	3,950	6,600	13,200	23,100	33,000

1952-53 Mercury Custom, V-8, 118" wb

	6	5	4	3	2	1
4d Sta Wag (1952 only)	960	2,880	4,800	9,600	16,800	24,000
4d Sed	700	2,100	3,500	7,000	12,250	17,500
2d Sed	704	2,112	3,520	7,040	12,320	17,600
2d HT	1,040	3,120	5,200	10,400	18,200	26,000

1952-53 Monterey Special Custom, V-8, 118" wb

	6	5	4	3	2	1
4d Sed	692	2,076	3,460	6,920	12,110	17,300
2d HT	1,080	3,240	5,400	10,800	18,900	27,000
2d Conv	1,280	3,840	6,400	12,800	22,400	32,000
4d Sta Wag (1953 only)	1,040	3,120	5,200	10,400	18,200	26,000

1954 Mercury Custom, V-8, 118" wb

	6	5	4	3	2	1
4d Sed	750	2,200	3,700	7,400	13,000	18,500
2d Sed	750	2,250	3,700	7,450	13,000	18,600
2d HT	1,050	3,100	5,200	10,400	18,200	26,000

1954 Monterey Special Custom, V-8, 118" wb

	6	5	4	3	2	1
4d Sed	750	2,250	3,750	7,500	13,200	18,800
2d HT SV	1,400	4,200	7,000	14,000	24,500	35,000
2d HT	1,100	3,250	5,400	10,800	18,900	27,000
2d Conv	1,350	4,100	6,800	13,600	23,800	34,000
4d Sta Wag	960	2,880	4,800	9,600	16,800	24,000

1955 Custom Series, V-8, 119" wb

	6	5	4	3	2	1
4d Sed	700	2,100	3,500	6,950	12,200	17,400
2d Sed	700	2,100	3,500	7,000	12,300	17,500
2d HT	900	2,750	4,600	9,200	16,100	23,000
4d Sta Wag	700	2,150	3,600	7,200	12,600	18,000

1955 Monterey Series, V-8, 119" wb

	6	5	4	3	2	1
4d Sed	700	2,150	3,600	7,200	12,600	18,000
2d HT	950	2,900	4,800	9,600	16,800	24,000
4d Sta Wag	850	2,500	4,200	8,400	14,700	21,000

1955 Montclair Series, V-8, 119" wb

	6	5	4	3	2	1
4d Sed	750	2,200	3,700	7,400	13,000	18,500
2d HT	1,050	3,100	5,200	10,400	18,200	26,000
2d HT SV	1,400	4,200	7,000	14,000	24,500	35,000
2d Conv	1,400	4,200	7,000	14,000	24,500	35,000

1956 Custom Series, V-8, 119" wb

	6	5	4	3	2	1
4d Sed	700	2,050	3,400	6,800	11,900	17,000
2d Sed	700	2,050	3,450	6,900	12,000	17,200
2d HT	900	2,650	4,400	8,800	15,400	22,000
4d Phae HT	800	2,400	4,000	8,000	14,000	20,000
2d Conv	1,300	3,950	6,600	13,200	23,100	33,000
4d Sta Wag 8P	780	2,340	3,900	7,800	13,650	19,500
4d Sta Wag 9P	800	2,400	4,000	8,000	14,000	20,000

1956 Monterey Series, V-8, 119" wb

	6	5	4	3	2	1
4d Sed	700	2,100	3,500	7,000	12,300	17,500
4d Spt Sed	700	2,150	3,600	7,200	12,600	18,000
2d HT	950	2,900	4,800	9,600	16,800	24,000
4d Phae HT	820	2,460	4,100	8,200	14,350	20,500
4d Sta Wag	800	2,450	4,100	8,200	14,300	20,500

1956 Montclair Series, V-8, 119" wb

	6	5	4	3	2	1
4d Spt Sed	750	2,200	3,700	7,400	13,000	18,500
2d HT	1,050	3,100	5,200	10,400	18,200	26,000
4d Phae HT	900	2,750	4,600	9,200	16,100	23,000
2d Conv	1,450	4,300	7,200	14,400	25,200	36,000

1957 Monterey Series, V-8, 122" wb

	6	5	4	3	2	1
4d Sed	650	1,950	3,300	6,550	11,500	16,400
2d Sed	650	2,000	3,300	6,600	11,600	16,500
4d HT	800	2,400	4,000	8,000	14,000	20,000
2d HT	900	2,750	4,600	9,200	16,100	23,000
2d Conv	1,050	3,100	5,200	10,400	18,200	26,000

1957 Montclair Series, V-8, 122" wb

	6	5	4	3	2	1
4d Sed	700	2,050	3,400	6,800	11,900	17,000
4d HT	850	2,500	4,200	8,400	14,700	21,000
2d HT	950	2,900	4,800	9,600	16,800	24,000
2d Conv	1,200	3,600	6,000	12,000	21,000	30,000

1957 Turnpike Cruiser, V-8, 122" wb

	6	5	4	3	2	1
4d HT	1,100	3,250	5,400	10,800	18,900	27,000
2d HT	1,200	3,600	6,000	12,000	21,000	30,000
2d Conv	1,450	4,300	7,200	14,400	25,200	36,000

NOTE: Add 10 percent for pace car edition.

1958 Mercury, V-8, 122" wb

	6	5	4	3	2	1
4d Sed	600	1,800	3,000	6,000	10,500	15,000
2d Sed	600	1,800	3,050	6,100	10,600	15,200

1958 Monterey, V-8, 122" wb

	6	5	4	3	2	1
4d Sed	600	1,800	3,050	6,100	10,600	15,200
2d Sed	600	1,850	3,050	6,100	10,700	15,300
4d HT	700	2,050	3,400	6,800	11,900	17,000
2d HT	750	2,300	3,800	7,600	13,300	19,000
2d Conv	1,050	3,100	5,200	10,400	18,200	26,000

1958 Montclair, V-8, 122" wb

	6	5	4	3	2	1
4d Sed	600	1,800	3,000	6,000	10,500	15,000
4d HT	800	2,400	4,000	8,000	14,000	20,000
2d HT	950	2,900	4,800	9,600	16,800	24,000
2d Conv	1,100	3,350	5,600	11,200	19,600	28,000

1958 Turnpike Cruiser, V-8, 122" wb

	6	5	4	3	2	1
4d HT	900	2,750	4,600	9,200	16,100	23,000
2d HT	1,100	3,250	5,400	10,800	18,900	27,000

1958 Park Lane, V-8, 125" wb

	6	5	4	3	2	1
4d HT	850	2,500	4,200	8,400	14,700	21,000
2d HT	1,000	3,000	5,000	10,000	17,500	25,000
2d Conv	1,400	4,200	7,000	14,000	24,500	35,000

1959 Monterey, V-8, 126" wb

	6	5	4	3	2	1
4d Sed	600	1,750	2,900	5,800	10,200	14,500
2d Sed	600	1,750	2,900	5,850	10,200	14,600
4d HT	650	1,900	3,200	6,400	11,200	16,000
2d HT	750	2,300	3,800	7,600	13,300	19,000
2d Conv	1,100	3,250	5,400	10,800	18,900	27,000

1959 Montclair, V-8, 126" wb

	6	5	4	3	2	1
4d Sed	600	1,800	3,000	6,000	10,500	15,000
4d HT	700	2,050	3,400	6,800	11,900	17,000
2d HT	850	2,500	4,200	8,400	14,700	21,000

1959 Park Lane, V-8, 128" wb

	6	5	4	3	2	1
4d HT	700	2,150	3,600	7,200	12,600	18,000
2d HT	900	2,650	4,400	8,800	15,400	22,000
2d Conv	1,100	3,350	5,600	11,200	19,600	28,000

NASH

1950 Nash Super Statesman, 6-cyl.

	6	5	4	3	2	1
2d DeL Cpe	650	1,950	3,250	6,500	11,400	16,300
4d Sed	650	1,950	3,200	6,450	11,300	16,100
2d Sed	650	1,950	3,250	6,500	11,300	16,200
2d Clb Cpe	650	1,950	3,250	6,500	11,400	16,300

1950 Nash Custom Statesman, 6-cyl.

	6	5	4	3	2	1
4d Sed	650	1,950	3,300	6,550	11,500	16,400
2d Sed	650	2,000	3,300	6,600	11,600	16,500
2d Clb Cpe	650	2,000	3,300	6,650	11,600	16,600

1950 Ambassador, 6-cyl.

	6	5	4	3	2	1
4d Sed	700	2,050	3,400	6,800	11,900	17,000
2d Sed	700	2,050	3,450	6,900	12,000	17,200
2d Clb Cpe	700	2,100	3,450	6,900	12,100	17,300

1950 Ambassador Custom, 6-cyl.

	6	5	4	3	2	1
4d Sed	700	2,100	3,500	6,950	12,200	17,400
2d Sed	700	2,100	3,500	7,000	12,300	17,500
2d Clb Cpe	700	2,100	3,500	7,050	12,300	17,600

1951 Rambler, 6-cyl.

	6	5	4	3	2	1
2d Utl Wag	650	2,000	3,300	6,600	11,600	16,500
2d Sta Wag	650	2,000	3,350	6,700	11,700	16,700
2d Cus Clb Sed	650	1,950	3,300	6,550	11,500	16,400
2d Cus Conv	800	2,400	4,000	8,000	14,000	20,000
2d Ctry Clb HT	700	2,150	3,600	7,200	12,600	18,000
2d Cus Sta Wag	700	2,050	3,400	6,800	11,900	17,000

1951 Nash Statesman, 6-cyl.

	6	5	4	3	2	1
2d DeL Bus Cpe	650	2,000	3,300	6,600	11,600	16,500
4d Sup Sed	650	1,950	3,250	6,500	11,400	16,300
2d Sup	650	1,950	3,250	6,500	11,300	16,200
2d Sup Cpe	650	2,000	3,300	6,600	11,600	16,500
2d Cus Cpe	650	2,000	3,300	6,650	11,600	16,600
2d Cus	650	2,000	3,300	6,600	11,600	16,500

1951 Ambassador, 6-cyl.

	6	5	4	3	2	1
4d Sup Sed	700	2,050	3,450	6,900	12,000	17,200
2d Sup	700	2,050	3,400	6,850	12,000	17,100
2d Sup Cpe	700	2,100	3,450	6,900	12,100	17,300
4d Cus Sed	700	2,100	3,500	6,950	12,200	17,400
2d Cus	700	2,050	3,450	6,900	12,000	17,200
2d Cus Cpe	700	2,100	3,450	6,900	12,100	17,300

1951 Nash-Healey

	6	5	4	3	2	1
Spt Rds	1,480	4,440	7,400	14,800	25,900	37,000

1952-53 Rambler, 6-cyl.

	6	5	4	3	2	1
2d Utl Wag	660	1,980	3,300	6,600	11,550	16,500
2d Sta Wag	668	2,004	3,340	6,680	11,690	16,700
2d Cus Clb Sed	660	1,980	3,300	6,600	11,550	16,500
2d Cus Conv	800	2,400	4,000	8,000	14,000	20,000
2d Cus Ctry Clb HT	720	2,160	3,600	7,200	12,600	18,000
2d Cus Sta Wag	680	2,040	3,400	6,800	11,900	17,000

1952-53 Nash Statesman, 6-cyl.

	6	5	4	3	2	1
2d Sed	668	2,004	3,340	6,680	11,690	16,700
4d Sed	664	1,992	3,320	6,640	11,620	16,600
2d Cus Ctry Clb	760	2,280	3,800	7,600	13,300	19,000

NOTE: Add 10 percent for Custom.

1952-53 Ambassador, 6-cyl.

	6	5	4	3	2	1
2d Sed	680	2,040	3,400	6,800	11,900	17,000
4d Sed	680	2,040	3,400	6,800	11,900	17,000
2d Cus Ctry Clb	800	2,400	4,000	8,000	14,000	20,000

NOTE: Add 10 percent for Custom.

1952-53 Nash-Healey

	6	5	4	3	2	1
2d Cpe (1953 only)	1,640	4,920	8,200	16,400	28,700	41,000
2d Spt Rds	1,800	5,400	9,000	18,000	31,500	45,000

1954 Rambler, 6-cyl.

	6	5	4	3	2	1
2d DeL Clb Sed	650	2,000	3,300	6,600	11,600	16,500
2d Sup Clb Sed	650	2,000	3,300	6,650	11,600	16,600
2d Sup Ctry Clb HT	700	2,100	3,500	7,000	12,300	17,500
2d Sup Suburban Sta Wag	650	2,000	3,350	6,700	11,800	16,800
2d Cus Ctry Clb HT	750	2,200	3,700	7,400	13,000	18,500
2d Cus Conv	850	2,500	4,200	8,400	14,700	21,000
2d Cus Sta Wag	700	2,100	3,500	7,000	12,300	17,500

1954 Nash Statesman, 6-cyl.

	6	5	4	3	2	1
4d Sup Sed	650	1,900	3,200	6,400	11,200	16,000
2d Sup Sed	650	1,950	3,200	6,450	11,300	16,100
4d Cus Sed	650	1,950	3,250	6,500	11,300	16,200
2d Cus Ctry Clb HT	800	2,400	4,000	8,000	14,000	20,000

1954 Nash Ambassador, 6-cyl.

	6	5	4	3	2	1
4d Sup Sed	700	2,050	3,450	6,900	12,000	17,200
2d Sup Sed	700	2,100	3,450	6,900	12,100	17,300
4d Cus Sed	700	2,100	3,500	7,000	12,300	17,500
2d Cus Ctry Clb HT	800	2,400	4,000	8,000	14,000	20,000

NOTE: Add 5 percent for LeMans option.

1954 Nash-Healey

	6	5	4	3	2	1
2d Cpe	1,700	5,100	8,500	17,000	29,750	42,500

1955 Rambler, 6-cyl.

	6	5	4	3	2	1
2d DeL Clb Sed	650	2,000	3,300	6,600	11,600	16,500
2d DeL Bus Sed	650	1,950	3,300	6,550	11,500	16,400
2d Sup Clb Sed	650	2,000	3,300	6,650	11,600	16,600
2d Sup Sta Wag	650	1,950	3,300	6,550	11,500	16,400
2d Cus Ctry Clb HT	750	2,300	3,800	7,600	13,300	19,000

1955 Nash Statesman, 6-cyl.

	6	5	4	3	2	1
4d Sup Sed	650	2,000	3,300	6,600	11,600	16,500
4d Cus Sed	650	2,000	3,300	6,650	11,600	16,600
2d Cus Ctry Clb	800	2,350	3,900	7,800	13,700	19,500

1955 Nash Ambassador, 6-cyl.

	6	5	4	3	2	1
4d Sup Sed	700	2,100	3,500	7,050	12,300	17,600
4d Cus Sed	700	2,100	3,550	7,100	12,400	17,700
2d Cus Ctry Clb	850	2,500	4,200	8,400	14,700	21,000

1955 Nash Ambassador, 8-cyl.

	6	5	4	3	2	1
4d Sup Sed	700	2,100	3,550	7,100	12,400	17,700
4d Cus Sed	750	2,250	3,750	7,500	13,100	18,700
2d Cus Ctry Clb	850	2,500	4,200	8,400	14,700	21,000

1956 Rambler, 6-cyl.

	6	5	4	3	2	1
4d DeL Sed	600	1,800	3,050	6,100	10,600	15,200
4d Sup Sed	600	1,850	3,050	6,100	10,700	15,300
4d Sup Crs Ctry	650	1,900	3,200	6,450	11,300	16,100
4d Cus Sed	650	1,950	3,250	6,500	11,300	16,200
4d Cus HT	700	2,050	3,400	6,800	11,900	17,000
4d Cus Crs Ctry	650	2,000	3,300	6,650	11,600	16,600
4d HT Wag	700	2,050	3,400	6,800	11,900	17,000

1956 Nash Statesman, 6-cyl.

	6	5	4	3	2	1
4d Sup Sed	650	2,000	3,300	6,600	11,600	16,500

1956 Nash Ambassador, 6-cyl.

	6	5	4	3	2	1
4d Sup Sed	700	2,050	3,400	6,800	11,900	17,000

1956 Nash Ambassador, 8-cyl.

	6	5	4	3	2	1
4d Sup Sed	700	2,050	3,450	6,900	12,000	17,200
4d Cus Sed	700	2,100	3,500	7,000	12,300	17,500
2d Cus HT	900	2,650	4,400	8,800	15,400	22,000

1957 Rambler, 6-cyl.

	6	5	4	3	2	1
4d DeL Sed	550	1,700	2,850	5,700	10,000	14,300
4d Sup Sed	600	1,750	2,900	5,800	10,200	14,500
4d Sup HT	600	1,800	3,000	6,000	10,500	15,000
4d Sup Crs Ctry	600	1,800	3,050	6,100	10,600	15,200
4d Cus Sed	600	1,750	2,900	5,750	10,100	14,400
4d Cus Crs Ctry	600	1,800	3,050	6,100	10,600	15,200

1957 Rambler, 8-cyl.

	6	5	4	3	2	1
4d Sup Sed	600	1,750	2,900	5,800	10,200	14,500
4d Sup Crs Ctry Wag	600	1,800	3,050	6,100	10,600	15,200
4d Cus Sed	600	1,750	2,900	5,850	10,200	14,600
4d Cus HT	600	1,850	3,050	6,100	10,700	15,300
4d Cus Crs Ctry Wag	600	1,850	3,100	6,150	10,800	15,400
4d Cus HT Crs Ctry	650	1,900	3,200	6,400	11,200	16,000

1957 Rebel, 8-cyl.

	6	5	4	3	2	1
4d HT	800	2,400	4,000	8,000	14,000	20,000

1957 Nash Ambassador, 8-cyl.

	6	5	4	3	2	1
4d Sup Sed	650	2,000	3,350	6,700	11,700	16,700
2d Sup HT	850	2,500	4,200	8,400	14,700	21,000
4d Cus Sed	700	2,050	3,400	6,800	11,900	17,000
2d Cus HT	900	2,650	4,400	8,800	15,400	22,000

AMC

1958-59 American DeLuxe, 6-cyl.

	6	5	4	3	2	1
2d Sed	308	924	1,540	3,080	5,390	7,700
2d Sta Wag (1959 only)	312	936	1,560	3,120	5,460	7,800

1958-59 American Super, 6-cyl.

	6	5	4	3	2	1
2d Sed	312	936	1,560	3,120	5,460	7,800
2d Sta Wag (1959 only)	316	948	1,580	3,160	5,530	7,900

1958-59 Rambler DeLuxe, 6-cyl.

	6	5	4	3	2	1
4d Sed	308	924	1,540	3,080	5,390	7,700
4d Sta Wag	312	936	1,560	3,120	5,460	7,800

1958-59 Rambler Super, 6-cyl.

	6	5	4	3	2	1
4d Sed	312	936	1,560	3,120	5,460	7,800
4d HT	320	960	1,600	3,200	5,600	8,000
4d Sta Wag	316	948	1,580	3,160	5,530	7,900

1958-59 Rambler Custom, 6-cyl.

	6	5	4	3	2	1
4d Sed	328	984	1,640	3,280	5,740	8,200
4d HT	336	1,008	1,680	3,360	5,880	8,400
4d Sta Wag	320	960	1,600	3,200	5,600	8,000

1958-59 Rebel Super V-8

	6	5	4	3	2	1
4d Sed DeL (1958 only)	408	1,224	2,040	4,080	7,140	10,200
4d Sed	412	1,236	2,060	4,120	7,210	10,300
4d Sta Wag	416	1,248	2,080	4,160	7,280	10,400

1958-59 Rebel Custom, V-8

	6	5	4	3	2	1
4d Sed	416	1,248	2,080	4,160	7,280	10,400
4d HT	420	1,260	2,100	4,200	7,350	10,500
4d Sta Wag	420	1,260	2,100	4,200	7,350	10,500

1958-59 Ambassador Super, V-8

	6	5	4	3	2	1
4d Sed	448	1,344	2,240	4,480	7,840	11,200
4d Sta Wag	452	1,356	2,260	4,520	7,910	11,300

1958-59 Ambassador Custom, V-8

	6	5	4	3	2	1
4d Sed	452	1,356	2,260	4,520	7,910	11,300
4d HT	456	1,368	2,280	4,560	7,980	11,400
4d Sta Wag	456	1,368	2,280	4,560	7,980	11,400
4d HT Sta Wag	544	1,632	2,720	5,440	9,520	13,600

OLDSMOBILE

	6	5	4	3	2	1
1950 Futuramic 88, V-8, 119.5" wb						
2d Conv	1,900	5,650	9,400	18,800	32,900	47,000
2d DeL Holiday HT	1,350	4,100	6,800	13,600	23,800	34,000
2d DeL Clb Cpe	1,100	3,250	5,400	10,800	18,900	27,000
2d DeL	1,000	3,000	5,000	10,000	17,500	25,000
2d DeL Clb Sed	950	2,900	4,800	9,600	16,800	24,000
4d DeL Sed	900	2,750	4,600	9,200	16,100	23,000
4d DeL Sta Wag	1,300	3,850	6,400	12,800	22,400	32,000
1950 Futuramic 98, V-8, 122" wb						
2d DeL Conv	1,700	5,050	8,400	16,800	29,400	42,000
2d DeL Holiday HT	1,200	3,600	6,000	12,000	21,000	30,000
2d Holiday HT	1,150	3,500	5,800	11,600	20,300	29,000
2d DeL Clb Sed	900	2,700	4,500	9,000	15,700	22,500
2d DeL FBk	900	2,650	4,450	8,900	15,500	22,200
4d DeL FBk	900	2,650	4,400	8,850	15,500	22,100
4d DeL Sed	850	2,600	4,300	8,650	15,100	21,600
4d DeL Twn Sed	900	2,750	4,600	9,200	16,100	23,000

NOTE: Deduct 10 percent for 6-cyl.

	6	5	4	3	2	1
1951-52 Super 88, V-8, 120" wb						
2d Conv	1,280	3,840	6,400	12,800	22,400	32,000
2d Holiday HT	1,080	3,240	5,400	10,800	18,900	27,000
2d Clb Cpe	920	2,760	4,600	9,200	16,100	23,000
2d Sed	832	2,496	4,160	8,320	14,560	20,800
4d Sed	828	2,484	4,140	8,280	14,490	20,700
1951-52 Series 98, V-8, 122" wb						
2d Conv	1,360	4,080	6,800	13,600	23,800	34,000
2d DeL Holiday HT ('51)	1,160	3,480	5,800	11,600	20,300	29,000
2d Holiday HT	1,120	3,360	5,600	11,200	19,600	28,000
4d Sed	840	2,520	4,200	8,400	14,700	21,000
1953 Series Super 88, V-8, 120" wb						
2d Conv	1,400	4,200	7,000	14,000	24,500	35,000
2d Holiday HT	1,150	3,500	5,800	11,600	20,300	29,000
2d Sed	750	2,300	3,850	7,700	13,400	19,200
4d Sed	750	2,300	3,800	7,650	13,400	19,100
1953 Classic 98, V-8, 124" wb						
2d Conv	1,550	4,700	7,800	15,600	27,300	39,000
2d Holiday HT	1,250	3,700	6,200	12,400	21,700	31,000
4d Sed	800	2,450	4,100	8,200	14,300	20,500
1953 Fiesta 98, V-8, 124" wb						
2d Conv	3,900	11,800	19,600	39,200	68,500	98,000
1954 Series Super 88, V-8, 122" wb						
2d Conv	1,500	4,450	7,400	14,800	25,900	37,000
2d Holiday HT	1,200	3,600	6,000	12,000	21,000	30,000
2d Sed	750	2,300	3,850	7,700	13,400	19,200
4d Sed	750	2,300	3,800	7,600	13,300	19,000
1954 Classic 98, V-8, 126" wb						
2d Starfire Conv	1,750	5,300	8,800	17,600	30,800	44,000
2d DeL Holiday HT	1,350	4,100	6,800	13,600	23,800	34,000
2d Holiday HT	1,300	3,950	6,600	13,200	23,100	33,000
4d Sed	850	2,500	4,200	8,400	14,700	21,000
1955 Series Super 88, V-8, 122" wb						
2d Conv	1,450	4,300	7,200	14,400	25,200	36,000
2d DeL Holiday HT	1,100	3,350	5,600	11,200	19,600	28,000
4d Holiday HT	900	2,650	4,400	8,800	15,400	22,000
2d Sed	750	2,300	3,800	7,650	13,400	19,100
4d Sed	750	2,300	3,800	7,600	13,300	19,000
1955 Classic 98, V-8, 126" wb						
2d Starfire Conv	1,700	5,050	8,400	16,800	29,400	42,000
2d DeL Holiday HT	1,300	3,850	6,400	12,800	22,400	32,000
4d DeL Holiday HT	950	2,900	4,800	9,600	16,800	24,000
4d Sed	850	2,500	4,200	8,400	14,700	21,000
1956 Series Super 88, V-8, 122" wb						
2d Conv	1,450	4,300	7,200	14,400	25,200	36,000
2d Holiday HT	1,200	3,600	6,000	12,000	21,000	30,000
4d Holiday HT	1,050	3,100	5,200	10,400	18,200	26,000
2d Sed	900	2,650	4,400	8,800	15,400	22,000
4d Sed	850	2,600	4,300	8,600	15,000	21,500
1956 Series 98, V-8, 126" wb						
2d Starfire Conv	1,700	5,150	8,600	17,200	30,100	43,000
2d DeL Holiday HT	1,250	3,700	6,200	12,400	21,700	31,000
4d DeL Holiday HT	1,100	3,250	5,400	10,800	18,900	27,000
4d Sed	900	2,750	4,600	9,200	16,100	23,000

	6	5	4	3	2	1
1957 Series Super 88, V-8, 122" wb						
2d Conv	1,700	5,050	8,400	16,800	29,400	42,000
2d Holiday HT	1,200	3,600	6,000	12,000	21,000	30,000
4d Holiday HT	1,000	3,000	5,000	10,000	17,500	25,000
2d Sed	800	2,450	4,100	8,250	14,400	20,600
4d Sed	800	2,450	4,100	8,200	14,300	20,500
4d HT Sta Wag	1,200	3,600	6,000	12,000	21,000	30,000
1957 Series 98, V-8, 126" wb						
2d Starfire Conv	1,800	5,400	9,000	18,000	31,500	45,000
2d Holiday HT	1,250	3,700	6,200	12,400	21,700	31,000
4d Holiday HT	1,000	3,000	5,000	10,000	17,500	25,000
4d Sed	850	2,600	4,300	8,600	15,000	21,500
1958 Series Super 88, V-8, 122.5" wb						
2d Conv	1,300	3,950	6,600	13,200	23,100	33,000
2d Holiday HT	1,200	3,600	6,000	12,000	21,000	30,000
4d Holiday HT	950	2,900	4,800	9,600	16,800	24,000
4d Sed	750	2,300	3,800	7,600	13,300	19,000
4d HT Sta Wag	1,100	3,250	5,400	10,800	18,900	27,000
1958 Series 98, V-8, 126.5" wb						
2d Conv	1,500	4,550	7,600	15,200	26,600	38,000
2d Holiday HT	1,150	3,500	5,800	11,600	20,300	29,000
4d Holiday HT	1,050	3,100	5,200	10,400	18,200	26,000
4d Sed	800	2,400	4,000	8,000	14,000	20,000
1959 Series Super 88, V-8, 123" wb						
2d Conv	1,350	4,100	6,800	13,600	23,800	34,000
2d Holiday HT	1,100	3,250	5,400	10,800	18,900	27,000
4d Holiday HT	950	2,900	4,800	9,600	16,800	24,000
4d Sed	700	2,100	3,500	7,000	12,300	17,500
4d Sta Wag	700	2,150	3,600	7,200	12,600	18,000
1959 Series 98, V-8, 126.3" wb						
2d Conv	1,500	4,550	7,600	15,200	26,600	38,000
2d Holiday HT	1,150	3,500	5,800	11,600	20,300	29,000
4d Holiday HT	1,050	3,100	5,200	10,400	18,200	26,000
4d Sed	700	2,150	3,600	7,200	12,600	18,000

PACKARD

	6	5	4	3	2	1
1949-50 23rd Series Custom 8, 127" wb, 2306						
Sed	1,040	3,120	5,200	10,400	18,200	26,000
1949-50 23rd Series Custom 8, 127" wb, 2333						
Conv	1,760	5,280	8,800	17,600	30,800	44,000
1951 24th Series 200, Standard, 122" wb, 2401						
Bus Cpe	680	2,040	3,400	6,800	11,900	17,000
2d Sed	680	2,040	3,400	6,800	11,900	17,000
Sed	680	2,040	3,400	6,800	11,900	17,000
1951 24th Series 122" wb, 2402						
M.F HT	840	2,520	4,200	8,400	14,700	21,000
Conv	1,200	3,600	6,000	12,000	21,000	30,000
1952 25th Series 122" wb, 2531						
Conv	1,200	3,600	6,000	12,000	21,000	30,000
M.F HT	880	2,640	4,400	8,800	15,400	22,000
1952 25th Series Patrician, 400, 127" wb, 2506						
Sed	840	2,520	4,200	8,400	14,700	21,000
Der Cus Sed	880	2,640	4,400	8,800	15,400	22,000
1953 26th Series Clipper, 122" wb, 2601						
2d HT	840	2,520	4,200	8,400	14,700	21,000
2d Sed	720	2,160	3,600	7,200	12,600	18,000
Sed	720	2,160	3,600	7,200	12,600	18,000
1953 26th Series Packard 8, 122" wb, 2631						
Conv	1,280	3,840	6,400	12,800	22,400	32,000
Carr Conv	1,760	5,280	8,800	17,600	30,800	44,000
M.F HT	880	2,640	4,400	8,800	15,400	22,000
1954 54th Series Packard 8, 122" wb, 5431						
Pac HT	920	2,760	4,600	9,200	16,100	23,000
Conv	1,280	3,840	6,400	12,800	22,400	32,000
Carr Conv	1,760	5,280	8,800	17,600	30,800	44,000
1954 54th Series Patrician, 127" wb, 5406						
Sed	840	2,520	4,200	8,400	14,700	21,000
Der Cus Sed	920	2,760	4,600	9,200	16,100	23,000

1955 55th Series Packard, 400, 127" wb, 5580

	6	5	4	3	2	1
"400" HT	1,160	3,480	5,800	11,600	20,300	29,000

1955 55th Series Caribbean 5580

	6	5	4	3	2	1
Conv	1,920	5,760	9,600	19,200	33,600	48,000

1955 55th Series Patrician 5580

	6	5	4	3	2	1
Sed	920	2,760	4,600	9,200	16,100	23,000

1956 56th Series Packard, 400, 127" wb, 5680

	6	5	4	3	2	1
"400" HT	1,200	3,600	6,000	12,000	21,000	30,000

1956 56th Series Caribbean, 5688

	6	5	4	3	2	1
Conv	1,960	5,880	9,800	19,600	34,300	49,000
HT	1,320	3,960	6,600	13,200	23,100	33,000

1957 57th L Series Clipper

	6	5	4	3	2	1
Sed	640	1,920	3,200	6,400	11,200	16,000
Sta Wag	680	2,040	3,400	6,800	11,900	17,000

1958 58th L Series Clipper

	6	5	4	3	2	1
HT	760	2,280	3,800	7,600	13,300	19,000
Sed	560	1,680	2,800	5,600	9,800	14,000
Sta Wag	640	1,920	3,200	6,400	11,200	16,000
Hawk	1,120	3,360	5,600	11,200	19,600	28,000

PLYMOUTH

1950 Special DeLuxe, 6-cyl., 118.5" wb

	6	5	4	3	2	1
2d Conv	950	2,900	4,800	9,600	16,800	24,000
2d Clb Cpe	600	1,750	2,950	5,900	10,300	14,700
4d Sed	600	1,750	2,900	5,800	10,200	14,500
4d Sta Wag	1,000	3,000	5,000	10,000	17,500	25,000

1951-52 P23 Cranbrook, 6-cyl., 118.5" wb

	6	5	4	3	2	1
4d Sed	456	1,368	2,280	4,560	7,980	11,400
2d Clb Cpe	580	1,740	2,900	5,800	10,150	14,500
2d HT	760	2,280	3,800	7,600	13,300	19,000
2d Conv	960	2,880	4,800	9,600	16,800	24,000

1953 P24-2 Cranbrook, 6-cyl., 114" wb

	6	5	4	3	2	1
4d Sed	450	1,300	2,200	4,400	7,700	11,000
2d Clb Cpe	450	1,400	2,300	4,600	8,050	11,500
2d HT	800	2,400	4,000	8,000	14,000	20,000
2d Sta Wag	600	1,800	3,000	6,000	10,500	15,000
2d Conv	1,050	3,100	5,200	10,400	18,200	26,000

1954 P25-2 Savoy, 6-cyl., 114" wb

	6	5	4	3	2	1
4d Sed	550	1,700	2,800	5,600	9,800	14,000
2d Sed	550	1,700	2,800	5,650	9,850	14,100
2d Clb Cpe	600	1,750	2,900	5,800	10,200	14,500
2d Sta Wag	600	1,800	3,000	6,000	10,500	15,000

1954 P25-3 Belvedere, 6-cyl., 114" wb

	6	5	4	3	2	1
4d Sed	600	1,750	2,900	5,800	10,200	14,500
2d HT	900	2,650	4,400	8,800	15,400	22,000
2d Conv	1,100	3,250	5,400	10,800	18,900	27,000
2d Sta Wag	650	1,900	3,200	6,400	11,200	16,000

1955 Belvedere, V-8, 115" wb

	6	5	4	3	2	1
4d Sed	600	1,750	2,900	5,750	10,100	14,400
2d Sed	600	1,750	2,900	5,800	10,200	14,500
2d HT	950	2,900	4,800	9,600	16,800	24,000
2d Conv	1,200	3,600	6,000	12,000	21,000	30,000
4d Sta Wag	650	1,900	3,200	6,400	11,200	16,000

NOTE: Deduct 10 percent for 6-cyl. models.

1956 Belvedere, V-8, 115" wb

	6	5	4	3	2	1
4d Sed	550	1,700	2,800	5,600	9,800	14,000
4d HT	650	1,900	3,200	6,400	11,200	16,000
2d Sed	550	1,700	2,800	5,650	9,850	14,100
2d HT	1,100	3,250	5,400	10,800	18,900	27,000

1956 Belvedere, V-8, 115" wb (conv. avail. as<par>8-cyl. only)

	6	5	4	3	2	1
2d Conv	1,300	3,850	6,400	12,800	22,400	32,000

1956 Fury, V-8, (avail. as V-8 only)

	6	5	4	3	2	1
2d HT	1,200	3,600	6,000	12,000	21,000	30,000

1957-58 Belvedere, V-8, 118" wb

	6	5	4	3	2	1
4d Sed	440	1,320	2,200	4,400	7,700	11,000
4d Spt HT	620	1,860	3,100	6,200	10,850	15,500
2d Sed	444	1,332	2,220	4,440	7,770	11,100
2d HT	1,160	3,480	5,800	11,600	20,300	29,000

1957-58 Belvedere, V-8, 118" wb (conv. avail. as 8-cyl. only)

	6	5	4	3	2	1
2d Conv	1,400	4,200	7,000	14,000	24,500	35,000

1957-58 Fury, V-8, 118" wb

	6	5	4	3	2	1
2d HT	1,240	3,720	6,200	12,400	21,700	31000

Add 20 percent for 318 cid/290 hp V-8 (except Fury) or 350 cid/305 hp V-8 (1958).

1959 Belvedere, V-8, 118" wb

	6	5	4	3	2	1
4d Sed	400	1,200	2,000	4,050	7,050	10,100
4d HT	450	1,400	2,300	4,600	8,050	11,500
2d Sed	400	1,200	2,050	4,100	7,150	10,200
2d HT	850	2,500	4,200	8,400	14,700	21,000
2d Conv	1,250	3,700	6,200	12,400	21,700	31,000

1959 Fury, V-8, 118" wb

	6	5	4	3	2	1
4d Sed	400	1,200	2,000	4,000	7,000	10,000
4d HT	550	1,700	2,800	5,600	9,800	14,000
2d HT	900	2,650	4,400	8,800	15,400	22,000

1959 Sport Fury, V-8, 118" wb (260 hp, V-8 offered)

	6	5	4	3	2	1
2d HT	900	2,750	4,600	9,200	16,100	23,000
2d Conv	1,300	3,950	6,600	13,200	23,100	33,000

PONTIAC

1949-50 Chieftain DeLuxe, 8-cyl.

	6	5	4	3	2	1
4d Sed	612	1,836	3,060	6,120	10,710	15,300
2d Sed	620	1,860	3,100	6,200	10,850	15,500
2d Bus Cpe (1949 only)	700	2,100	3,500	7,000	12,250	17,500
2d HT (1950 only)	820	2,460	4,100	8,200	14,350	20,500
2d Cpe Sed	628	1,884	3,140	6,280	10,990	15,700
2d Sup HT (1950 only)	880	2,640	4,400	8,800	15,400	22,000
2d Conv	1,220	3,660	6,100	12,200	21,350	30,500

1951-52 Chieftain DeLuxe, 8-cyl.

	6	5	4	3	2	1
4d Sed	620	1,860	3,100	6,200	10,850	15,500
2d Sed	624	1,872	3,120	6,240	10,920	15,600
2d Cpe Sed	640	1,920	3,200	6,400	11,200	16,000
2d HT	900	2,700	4,500	9,000	15,750	22,500
2d HT Sup	940	2,820	4,700	9,400	16,450	23,500
2d Conv	1,240	3,720	6,200	12,400	21,700	31,000

1953 Chieftain DeLuxe, 8-cyl.

	6	5	4	3	2	1
4d Sed	600	1,850	3,100	6,250	10,900	15,600
2d Sed	650	1,900	3,150	6,300	11,000	15,700
2d HT	900	2,650	4,400	8,800	15,400	22,000
2d Conv	1,200	3,600	6,000	12,000	21,000	30,000
4d Mtl Sta Wag	650	1,900	3,200	6,400	11,200	16,000
4d Sim W Sta Wag	700	2,050	3,400	6,800	11,900	17,000

1953 Custom Catalina, 8-cyl.

	6	5	4	3	2	1
2d HT	900	2,700	4,500	9,000	15,700	22,500

NOTE: Deduct 5 percent for 6-cyl. models.

1954 Custom Catalina, 8-cyl.

	6	5	4	3	2	1
2d HT	950	2,900	4,800	9,600	16,800	24,000

1954 Star Chief DeLuxe, 8-cyl.

	6	5	4	3	2	1
4d Sed	700	2,050	3,400	6,800	11,900	17,000
2d Conv	1,200	3,650	6,100	12,200	21,400	30,500

1954 Star Custom Chief, 8-cyl.

	6	5	4	3	2	1
4d Sed	700	2,150	3,600	7,200	12,600	18,000

1954 Star Chief Custom Catalina

	6	5	4	3	2	1
2d HT	1,000	3,000	5,000	10,000	17,500	25,000

NOTE: Deduct 5 percent for 6-cyl. models.

1955 Star Chief Custom Safari, 122" wb

	6	5	4	3	2	1
2d Sta Wag	1,050	3,100	5,200	10,400	18,200	26,000

1955 Star Chief, V-8, 124" wb

	6	5	4	3	2	1
4d Sed	650	2,000	3,300	6,600	11,600	16,500
2d Conv	1,500	4,450	7,400	14,800	25,900	37,000

1955 Star Chief Custom, V-8, 124" wb

	6	5	4	3	2	1
4d Sed	700	2,100	3,500	7,000	12,300	17,500

1955 Custom Catalina

	6	5	4	3	2	1
2d HT	1,100	3,350	5,600	11,200	19,600	28,000

1956 Star Chief Custom Safari, V-8, 122" wb

	6	5	4	3	2	1
2d Sta Wag	1,100	3,250	5,400	10,800	18,900	27,000

1956 Star Chief, V-8, 124" wb

	6	5	4	3	2	1
4d Sed	650	1,900	3,200	6,400	11,200	16,000
2d Conv	1,600	4,800	8,000	16,000	28,000	40,000

1956 Star Chief Custom Catalina, V-8, 124" wb

	6	5	4	3	2	1
4d HT	750	2,300	3,800	7,600	13,300	19,000
2d HT	1,160	3,480	5,800	11,600	20,300	29,000

1957 Super Chief, V-8, 122" wb

	6	5	4	3	2	1
4d Sed	650	1,900	3,200	6,400	11,200	16,000
4d HT	700	2,150	3,600	7,200	12,600	18,000
2d HT	1,120	3,360	5,600	11,200	19,600	28,000
4d Sta Wag	750	2,300	3,800	7,600	13,300	19,000

1957 Star Chief, V-8, 124" wb

	6	5	4	3	2	1
4d Sed	700	2,050	3,400	6,800	11,900	17,000
2d Conv	1,500	4,550	7,600	15,200	26,600	38,000
2d Bonneville Conv	3,200	9,600	16,000	32,000	56,000	80,000

1957 Star Chief Custom, V-8, 124" wb

	6	5	4	3	2	1
4d Sed	700	2,100	3,500	7,000	12,300	17,500
4d HT	850	2,500	4,200	8,400	14,700	21,000
2d HT	1,200	3,600	6,000	12,000	21,000	30,000

1958 Star Chief, V-8, 124" wb

	6	5	4	3	2	1
4d Cus Sed	550	1,700	2,800	5,600	9,800	14,000
4d HT	700	2,150	3,600	7,200	12,600	18,000
2d HT	950	2,900	4,800	9,600	16,800	24,000
4d Cus Safari	750	2,300	3,800	7,600	13,300	19,000

1958 Bonneville, V-8, 122" wb

	6	5	4	3	2	1
2d HT	1,400	4,200	7,000	14,000	24,500	35,000
2d Conv	2,200	6,600	11,000	22,000	38,500	55,000

1959 Catalina, V-8, 122" wb

	6	5	4	3	2	1
4d Sed	320	960	1,600	3,200	5,600	8,000
4d HT	550	1,700	2,800	5,600	9,800	14,000
2d Sed	350	1,000	1,700	3,400	5,950	8,500
2d HT	750	2,300	3,800	7,600	13,300	19,000
2d Conv	1,100	3,250	5,400	10,800	18,900	27,000

1959 Star Chief, V-8, 124" wb

	6	5	4	3	2	1
4d Sed	550	1,700	2,800	5,600	9,800	14,000
4d HT	650	1,900	3,200	6,400	11,200	16,000
2d Sed	600	1,750	2,900	5,800	10,200	14,500

1959 Bonneville, V-8, 124" wb

	6	5	4	3	2	1
4d HT	700	2,050	3,400	6,800	11,900	17,000
2d HT	900	2,650	4,400	8,800	15,400	22,000
2d Conv	1,300	3,950	6,600	13,200	23,100	33,000

STUDEBAKER

1950 Commander, 6-cyl., 120" - 124" wb

	6	5	4	3	2	1
2d 5P Cpe Starlight	880	2,640	4,400	8,800	15,400	22,000
2d Sed	740	2,220	3,700	7,400	12,950	18,500
4d Sed	740	2,220	3,700	7,400	12,950	18,500
2d Conv	1,120	3,360	5,600	11,200	19,600	28,000

1950 Land Cruiser, 6-cyl., 124" wb

	6	5	4	3	2	1
4d Ld Crs Sed	760	2,280	3,800	7,600	13,300	19,000

1951 Commander Regal, V-8, 115" wb

	6	5	4	3	2	1
4d Sed	720	2,160	3,600	7,200	12,600	18,000
2d Sed	720	2,160	3,600	7,200	12,600	18,000
2d 5P Cpe Starlight	840	2,520	4,200	8,400	14,700	21,000

1951 Commander State, V-8, 115" wb

	6	5	4	3	2	1
4d Sed	740	2,220	3,700	7,400	12,950	18,500
2d Sed	740	2,220	3,700	7,400	12,950	18,500
2d 5P Cpe Starlight	880	2,640	4,400	8,800	15,400	22,000
2d Conv	1,200	3,600	6,000	12,000	21,000	30,000

1951 Land Cruiser, V-8, 119" wb

	6	5	4	3	2	1
4d Sed	760	2,280	3,800	7,600	13,300	19,000

1952 Commander Regal, V-8, 115" wb

	6	5	4	3	2	1
4d Sed	720	2,160	3,600	7,200	12,600	18,000
2d Sed	720	2,160	3,600	7,200	12,600	18,000
2d 5P Cpe Starlight	880	2,640	4,400	8,800	15,400	22,000

1952 Commander State, V-8, 115" wb

	6	5	4	3	2	1
4d Sed	740	2,220	3,700	7,400	12,950	18,500
2d Sed	740	2,220	3,700	7,400	12,950	18,500
2d Cpe Starlight	920	2,760	4,600	9,200	16,100	23,000
2d Star HT	1,040	3,120	5,200	10,400	18,200	26,000
2d Conv	1,160	3,480	5,800	11,600	20,300	29,000

1952 Land Cruiser, V-8, 119" wb

	6	5	4	3	2	1
4d Sed	760	2,280	3,800	7,600	13,300	19,000

1953-54 Commander DeLuxe, V-8, 116.5" - 120.5" wb

	6	5	4	3	2	1
4d Sed	720	2,160	3,600	7,200	12,600	18,000
2d Sed	724	2,172	3,620	7,240	12,670	18,100
2d Cpe	920	2,760	4,600	9,200	16,100	23,000
Sta Wag (1954 only)	800	2,400	4,000	8,000	14,000	20,000

1953-54 Commander Regal, V-8, 116.5" - 120.5" wb

	6	5	4	3	2	1
4d Sed	740	2,220	3,700	7,400	12,950	18,500
2d Cpe	940	2,820	4,700	9,400	16,450	23,500
2d HT	1,040	3,120	5,200	10,400	18,200	26,000
2d Sta Wag (1954 only)	820	2,460	4,100	8,200	14,350	20,500

1955 Commander Regal, V-8, 116.5" - 120.5" wb

	6	5	4	3	2	1
4d Sed	760	2,280	3,800	7,600	13,300	19,000
2d Cpe	1,140	3,420	5,700	11,400	19,950	28,500
2d HT	1,180	3,540	5,900	11,800	20,650	29,500
2d Sta Wag	880	2,640	4,400	8,800	15,400	22,000

1955 President DeLuxe, V-8, 120.5" wb

	6	5	4	3	2	1
4d Sed	780	2,340	3,900	7,800	13,650	19,500

1955 President State, V-8, 120.5" wb

	6	5	4	3	2	1
4d Sed	800	2,400	4,000	8,000	14,000	20,000
2d Cpe	1,160	3,480	5,800	11,600	20,300	29,000
2d HT	1,200	3,600	6,000	12,000	21,000	30,000
2d Spds HT	1,240	3,720	6,200	12,400	21,700	31,000

1956 President, V-8, 116.5" wb

	6	5	4	3	2	1
4d Sed	860	2,580	4,300	8,600	15,050	21,500
4d Classic	880	2,640	4,400	8,800	15,400	22,000
2d Sed	864	2,592	4,320	8,640	15,120	21,600

1956 Golden Hawk, V-8, 120.5" wb

	6	5	4	3	2	1
2d HT	1,160	3,480	5,800	11,600	20,300	29,000

1957 President, V-8, 116.5" wb

	6	5	4	3	2	1
4d Sed	680	2,040	3,400	6,800	11,900	17,000
4d Classic	700	2,100	3,500	7,000	12,250	17,500
2d Clb Sed	684	2,052	3,420	6,840	11,970	17,100

1957 Golden Hawk, V-8, 120.5" wb

	6	5	4	3	2	1
2d Spt HT	1,120	3,360	5,600	11,200	19,600	28,000

1958 Champion, 6-cyl., 116.5" wb

	6	5	4	3	2	1
4d Sed	392	1,176	1,960	3,920	6,860	9,800
2d Sed	388	1,164	1,940	3,880	6,790	9,700

1958 Silver Hawk, 6-cyl., 120.5" wb

	6	5	4	3	2	1
2d Cpe	800	2,400	4,000	8,000	14,000	20,000

1958 Commander, V-8, 116.5" wb

	6	5	4	3	2	1
4d Sed	520	1,560	2,600	5,200	9,100	13,000
2d HT	580	1,740	2,900	5,800	10,150	14,500
4d Sta Wag	540	1,620	2,700	5,400	9,450	13,500

1958 President, V-8, 120.5" & 116.5" wb

	6	5	4	3	2	1
4d Sed	528	1,584	2,640	5,280	9,240	13,200
2d HT	588	1,764	2,940	5,880	10,290	14,700

1958 Golden Hawk, V-8, 120.5" wb

	6	5	4	3	2	1
2d Spt HT	1,080	3,240	5,400	10,800	18,900	27,000

1959-60 Lark DeLuxe, V-8, 108.5" wb

	6	5	4	3	2	1
4d Sed	400	1,200	2,000	4,000	7,000	10,000
2d Sed	400	1,200	2,000	4,000	7,000	10,000
4d Sta Wag (1960 only)	412	1,236	2,060	4,120	7,210	10,300
2d Sta Wag	416	1,248	2,080	4,160	7,280	10,400

1959-60 Lark Regal, V-8, 108.5" wb

	6	5	4	3	2	1
4d Sed	420	1,260	2,100	4,200	7,350	10,500
2d HT	580	1,740	2,900	5,800	10,150	14,500
2d Conv (1960 only)	780	2,340	3,900	7,800	13,650	19,500
4d Sta Wag	420	1,260	2,100	4,200	7,350	10,500